Making It Perfectly Clear

Making It Perfectly Clear

HERBERT G. KLEIN

DOUBLEDAY & COMPANY, INC.
GARDEN CITY, NEW YORK
1980

ISBN: 0-385-14047-9
Library of Congress Catalog Card Number 79-6166
Copyright © 1980 by Herbert G. Klein
Printed in the United States of America
First Edition

Campaigning and serving in the White House are not easy, but neither is newspapering. All are inspiring and rewarding. This is dedicated to those who sacrificed and helped most through it all, my family—Marge, Joanne, and Patty.

Preface

THIS IS A BOOK recounting my personal experiences with those who have made the news and those who have chronicled the newsmakers and events of the last thirty years.

In looking behind the scenes in five presidential campaigns and in the White House, it is hoped that the reader will gain new insight into many national personalities and their policies and the coverage of them by the media.

Even in this complex age of the eighties, we cling to the belief that each President is a leader who singly shapes his own destiny and that of the nation. To some degree he does. But we are in an era where the press has more influence on public perception of the President than ever before.

The writing of this book has provoked many memories and anecdotes for me, but the authorship also has been difficult because I have attempted to analyze in depth events and people who were important in my professional life, many of whom have influenced world opinion. Judgments involving personal relationships do not come easy, yet I have tried to make them with a critical sense of fairness and balance. These are by nature subjective judgments, and such views are likely to be disputed by some critics, but within my own mind the concepts explored here are based on fact and direct personal observation.

Shortly after leaving the White House in the summer of 1973, my work started on this book with the research assistance of Tom Searson. After struggling for several months, during which President Nixon was drawn under an increasingly foreboding Watergate cloud, it was apparent to me that I was not yet ready to assess fully my experiences. My writing ground to a halt. I realized that to express, in depth, my viewpoint of the press and the government, I needed to examine some of the more traumatic experiences and even the many exhilarating moments of the Nixon White House.

While I have had an unusual variety of experiences in the White House and in journalism, experiences I felt I should record, at moments I have wondered if the pain from parts of this history, such as Watergate, which later engulfed some of my colleagues, had blocked my newsman's mind to a point where the writing was too difficult a form of expression. Still I felt compelled to write because of the unique opportunity which had been given to me to view history as a newsman serving in government.

All through this post-1973 White House period, I have had a driven feeling, centered upon the desire to discuss the ever-changing relationship between the government and the media, a relationship which, one way or another, affects most decisions by the President and the evaluation of those decisions by the public. Some understanding of the personalities who are a part of this daily experience is important to an evaluation of the process which results from the relationship.

By recounting a variety of personal experiences and reporting the background of some historic events, this book seeks to give new insight into the government and the press on a national level.

There is no set career pattern for one to get into journalism or politics. My own role stems from a journalistic, not a political, background. I came into the newspaper and communications business by early choice, a decision made when I became sports editor of the Roosevelt High School *Rough Rider*, a multiethnic school in East Los Angeles. Even though I successfully managed a candidate for sophomore president (Tom Gabbert) in college, sports writing, not politics, consumed my interest at the University of Southern California. Contrary to my intended goal, I have been a newspaper correspondent, reporter, and editor, a television executive and consultant, and a press secretary and communications director, but (sometimes to my dismay) never a sports writer.

For me, politics has been a fascinating sideline, but journalism a fascinating career. My closest professional colleagues have been newspapermen who have provided guidelines I have sought to apply in my forays into politics. Newsmen have been my conscience.

While my communications interest came by choice, my personal interest in politics came by chance, occasioned when I covered for the Alhambra, California, *Post-Advocate* some of the debates between Richard Nixon and Congressman Jerry Voorhis in Nixon's successful race for Congress in 1946. At that point I was a political independent whose only vote for President had been cast for Franklin D. Roosevelt. Nixon and I were fresh out of the Navy, and reporting on him as a candidate and later as an energetic, hardworking congressman stimulated me to take a major interest in the politics and government of the postwar era.

Nixon struck me as a young, new leader whose desire to lessen the bureaucracy of government intrigued me. This was a time when the nation was moving slowly from wartime controls and returning veterans were having difficulty with everything from housing to postal service to finding jobs. My interest was stimulated to a point where I led an Alhambra Junior Chamber of Commerce drive to gain support for the governmental reforms drafted by the Hoover Commission during the Truman administration. Nixon's early excursion into foreign policy with the Herter committee, and eventually his support of the Marshall Plan, interested me even more as the young congressman related details of his experiences in these fields to me. Nixon and I have had a personal bond since 1946, although at times we have disagreed on policy and more times on the media and campaign tactics. He has disappointed me on occasions, and he has let me down. But he also has provided the opportunity for irreplaceable, memorable moments for me.

The basic opportunity for me to serve in a unique political-journalism role was provided because of the personal interest in both fields of my friend and publisher, James S. Copley and our mutual early mentor, Bill Shea, then the San Diego *Union-Tribune*'s general manager, and his successor, Alex De Bakcsy. My Navy captain, E. Robert Anderson, gave me unusual journalism opportunities as I served under him during the war.

The files used as background for this volume go back as far as 1946 and move forward to the present. Over a period of years I have been fortunate in receiving the assistance of capable and dedicated assistants such as Virginia English, Mary Werner, Tina Bucheit Diver, Jeni Brown Norris, and Maria Searson Karno. They have lived through these episodes and personally experienced many of them. Everyone in my business needs a few "hair shirts" among his close friends. Mine have been headed by Peter Kaye but have included Alfred JaCoby, Lewis Scarr, Tom Pownall, Fred Kinne, Ed Thomas, Neil Morgan, Richard Bean, Margita White, Stan Scott, and always Bob Finch, Don Hughes, and Rose Woods. All have been unspoken participants in the development of this book.

Many of the key records quoted in this volume are due to research and files originally brought together by Margita and Stuart White, Wanda Phelan, Susan Low Elliott, Agnes Waldron, Donna Kingwell, Ed Blecksmith, Mary Ann Snow, Charlotte Porte, Beth Mohr, Alice Dykeman, Bianca Doeschur Cowan, Carlos Conde, Ron Baukol, Doris Jones Forward, C. J. Bjorseth, Dorothy Thomas, and Nan Hogan.

I was the beneficiary of sound informal advice from many, but particularly James Michener, Theodore White, Allen Drury, Herman Wouk, Otto Silha, John Cowles, Jr., Jack Kemp, Pete Wilson, James Shea, James Bowling, John Hubbard, J. Robert Fluor, Joe Mansi, Ross Barrett, Tom Nickell, Earl Harris, and journalists such as Irv Kupcinet, Bob Weidrich, Muriel Dobbin, Ed Nichol, Creed Black, Gene Patterson, E. L. McNeely, and Hugh Sidey.

In the final stages, most particular credit is due to Tom Searson, my research director, and to my producer for this book, Maria Searson Karno, and to those professionals who put the project together, Owen Laster and Lisa Drew.

HERBERT G. KLEIN

Introduction

SKILLFULLY, thoughtfully, as has been his manner for all seasons, Herb Klein probes the vexing problem of pervasive, insistent media and its dramatic impact on politics and the exercise of power. He was, in his way, a midwife to this age. Rooted and matured in the ancient and honorable fraternity of shoe-leather print reporters, he carried a deep respect for those rituals and values into the operative political world. His fascination with and attachment to Richard Nixon for the past thirty-five years is one of those mysterious dimensions of the human spirit that must be left to the men themselves. But there is no mystery about Herb Klein's valiant effort through these years to stand as mediator between the colliding world of a brilliant, often unscrupulous, stunningly successful, and, finally, disgraced and tragic leader and the exploding, sometimes superficial, enlightening, reckless, passionate collections of informers and entertainers called media.

His narrative is about the Nixon political caravan, with which he rode a fascinating but rugged journey. His cry is for more understanding by the political advocates, for more reason and caution by the media, for less arrogance by the power brokers, for the admission of vincibility by the folk heroes of the press and prime time.

He has no illusions that our system can or should reach a permanent accommodation between the watchdogs of the public process and the public servants themselves. Contention is the life of our system. Doubt and debate, challenge and reform, will always be a field of friendly battle in a functioning democracy. But less destructive, maybe? Or less personal and

petty? Perhaps fairer and even mindful of the public and government interests in times of stress and cruel deadlines.

Few people can now deny the question which shadows the media in a
nervous and dangerous world. No corner of the globe is immune from the
intrepid camera crews. No government secret is beyond the reach of determined and well-financed, highly mechanized investigative journalists. The
media boom of the past twenty years has astonished its creators as well as
the public. Almost unwittingly, its stars have become in many instances
more influential than elected politicians. Its determined reporters have
found themselves conducting diplomacy, participating in staged White
House dramas, the involuntary choreographers of street demonstrations
and violence. With the too-frequent failure of political leadership, media
spokesmen have become keepers of the national conscience, the extrapola-
tors of national purpose, and, in the extreme, the high priests of a new national theology of total revelation. All of us—people, politicians, and media
—have rushed pell-mell into the 1980s pursuing our interests with the consuming intensity that survival demands. None has fully reckoned with the
new shape of a babbling world in which a whisper in China can produce,
seconds later, a tremor in London.

Herb Klein, maybe more than any other figure of our time, sensed the
approaching collision and attempted to mute its impact. His journalistic
bearings never faltered through the difficult Nixon epoch, nor did his sin-
gular loyalty to that unusual man, though Nixon himself at times lashed
out at his own friend and supporter. Herb Klein in the end may be one of
the few truly "public" servants, a person who holds the nation's interest
above all others', even his own.

Herb Klein and I had our first serious encounter in Alaska in 1958 as
participants in a dog-sled race that deposited one or the other or both of us
in the snow, memory now fading and good brandy enlarging our imagina-
tions. We were both on the hapless voyage of Vice-President Nixon,
sailing as chief political protagonist for off-year Republicans. Most of them
lost, but Nixon perfected techniques and polished friendships that would
serve him later. From that time forward through Nixon's anger and defeat,
times of spectacle and success, Herb Klein was a steady hand and voice,
striving more than we realized to meet the clamorous demands of the
press, tempering, more than the Nixon strong men ever understood, the
hostility of the journalists.

I remember in 1972 standing in the Kremlin at the close of the first
summit meeting between the President and Leonid Brezhnev. It had been
a triumph and the iron men around Nixon were gathering more power in
its wake, preparing to use the earlier opening to China and the new over-
tures to the Soviets as centerpieces in the coming campaign. Men like
Herb Klein were already being elbowed aside. But on that day he was still

with Nixon, though, as he explained later, he could sense a gathering storm. We few Americans and the leaders of Soviet power stood in long rows as Nixon and Brezhnev walked to the front of the hall, a Russian band playing "The Washington Post March." My eye landed on Herb standing across the hall. He was tired, rumpled, but a smile ready for those he knew. I recall thinking then how good it was to have him there. I never knew how right I was until he was gone.

HUGH SIDEY
Time magazine

Contents

1

Inaugural Day Mind-Sets

THE SECOND HAD COME: with a few words Richard Nixon would be President.

I sat fifteen feet away on a long wooden bench with the others who would be part of the team.

For everyone on the small inaugural platform that frosty cold morning, there was a different emotion, a different thought. Emotions ran high. Each guest had a picture of the future, some optimistic, some pessimistic, but none envisioned a Watergate, a threat of impeachment, or a President eventually forced from office.

Hubert Humphrey's feelings were, as always, transparent. This was his last moment as Vice-President of the United States, and but for .7 percent of the vote, he would have been holding his hand high to be sworn in as the next President. The Vice-President's feeling of disappointment and bitterness was apparent on his face. His glibness was gone and he was naked in his understandable silent grief. He had been on that platform before. But this was the lowest moment.

Chief Justice Earl Warren was there to administer the oath of office. He had known Nixon longer than anyone present on the platform except me. He told me later that he could not help thinking, even in those moments of 1968, that but for Nixon he might have won a compromise nomination for President himself in 1952. Dwight Eisenhower had won and Nixon became his running mate—a surprise pick from a list of ten.

The Nixon whom he thought of as he swore in the President was a vision of the "old Nixon," a tough campaigner whom the Chief Justice never trusted, a man he felt had double-crossed him in 1952, when he worked actively for Eisenhower instead of Warren, California's favorite son.

Out of the early days of California Republican politics, Warren and Nixon had emerged the strongest, outdistancing Senator Bill Knowland and Governor Goodwin Knight, both of whom also had dreams of the presidency. In 1956 Governor Knight temporarily played with Harold Stassen in an abortive effort to unseat Vice-President Nixon.

Swearing in Nixon to the only office Warren had found unattainable provided no happy moments for the Chief Justice.

Lyndon Johnson had told me his thoughts when I, at his invitation, sat with him and his assistant, Tom Johnson, in the White House the day before. And later he autographed a picture of the two of us.

He wrote:

"To Herb Klein, With my hope that the end will be as pleasant as the beginning. . . ."

In his own full term of office, the beginning, following his landslide triumph of 1964, had been life's sweetest moment. All that sweet feeling was gone as he left office. The end was unpleasant and bitter.

Part of his concern was for his own future. He did not relish the sidelines. The power would be gone in a few seconds. The change of office comes abruptly for the man leaving the White House. "I found it important to keep President Eisenhower fully briefed," he had told me. "He came back to me with helpful ideas."

President Johnson knew he could not tolerate being idle and this was his way of saying that even in the background at his ranch in Texas, he wanted to remain a part of things, to be informed. His point was well taken.

He had other deep concerns. As for the new President and the nation, Johnson worried over foreign policy, Vietnam in particular. Would the new President be resolute in the war or would he be "bullied by that God-damned New York *Times?*" I had assured him there was no chance of that!

The two majority leaders, Senator Mike Mansfield and Representative John McCormack, were stone-faced. Occasionally they grunted a "yep" or a "nope" as conversation shifted across the platform. Their concern at the final moment was the inaugural address. They had heard the rumor the President would call for new legislation immediately. What was the legislation?

What Pat Nixon thought at the moment, I do not know. She is not one to confide her innermost thoughts, even to family. But, looking at her, I knew her feelings were solemn, not joyous. She had been the "loyal soldier" who honestly did not enjoy campaigning for public office. She had traveled more campaign miles than any wife in history—64,000 miles and 188 cities just in the general election in 1960, for example. The White House was not her idea of happiness ever after.

She was going to six inaugural balls that night, but she had not danced with her husband in perhaps twenty years.

Pat Nixon has a distinct voice, which the public was soon to recognize, but the closest she had come to campaign oratory dated back to a luncheon in 1956 in Oklahoma City. The Nixons were carrying the campaign load for Eisenhower and, on the evening before, the Vice-President had been stricken with a fever, a strep infection, and laryngitis. I worked hard to persuade Mrs. Nixon to speak in his place in Oklahoma and to let the candidate look silently on.

At the last moment Nixon turned a scheduled thirty-second greeting into a fifteen-minute speech. Pat Nixon watched the Oklahoma audience as her husband talked and then spoke two minutes instead of the planned fifteen. That ended her campaign oratory. It also illustrated her desire to avoid the spotlight.

Pat Nixon is a very private person. She kept her children away from the public until they became young adults. When they campaigned in 1968 and 1972, it was their own choice.

Under stress, Mrs. Nixon enjoyed smoking a cigarette, but never in public. She would relax with one cigarette late on a campaign night, in one of the family rooms of the White House. But she cherished respect for public morals, the role of a respected leader, the role of a faultless mother. On the campaign platform, she was silent, but in a crowded airport or hotel lobby she was a great Nixon asset as she spoke with feeling to individuals. No one could chat more meaningfully on a one-to-one basis to children or adults, but publicly she was a study in silence—as she has been since leaving the White House.

As the Vice-President-elect, Spiro Agnew sat nervously awaiting the start of the ceremony; he admittd to me that he was even then among the most surprised to find himself in this position.

He was from the small state of Maryland. Originally he had been a leading supporter of Nelson Rockefeller. When he had decided prior to the convention to back Nixon, it was decided to hold back the announcement until it would have more impact. There was no talk of the vice-presidency at that time. I had arranged for him to arrive at the airport for the National Convention in Miami in time for his first big splash in the news. The timing was such that it was covered live by television in the midst of network evening news of the convention.

Now an election victor, the Vice-President still felt deeply the wounds inflicted on him by the press—unfairly, we both thought, because of stories reporting his "fat Jap" remark and offhand comments which made him sound like a bumbling bigot. In a few moments, he, too, would be sworn in, and he hoped for a role which would vindicate all of this.

In football, the sports page discusses the depth of a team's bench—a measurement of strength.

On the inaugural platform most sit on benches—the cabinet, the leading senators, the senior elected representatives, and the new White House staff.

As I looked across the benches, it was apparent to me that even the experienced congressional leaders Mike Mansfield and John McCormack were men without the power in Congress of earlier leaders, such as a Johnson or a Sam Rayburn. The change of power in the Congress from leadership by strong individuals to leadership by committees had a bearing on the grab for power later in the White House. There was a vacuum in the balance of government power which allowed the strength to tilt to the presidency.

Among the presidential appointees, a few knew what to expect—Bryce Harlow did, Mel Laird, Pat Moynihan, and Arthur Burns did—and that was about it.

Bob Finch, John Mitchell, Maurice Stans, William Rogers, Rose Mary Woods, Henry Kissinger, and I had been around government considerably, and all of us but Mitchell had been a part of it. Still, for this incoming administration it was basically a new world.

Curiously, among those most in view on this day of gaiety and enthusiasm, the only optimist prominently in view of the cameras was the incoming President. For all the others, except possibly Spiro Agnew, gloom or concern outweighed the festiveness of the occasion Lyndon Johnson had described to me as a "pleasant beginning." None of us would admit that we were uncertain then. Perhaps, few would today. However, the unsure feeling was there.

In the early days of the White House, the people most challenging and interesting to me were not the Ehrlichmans or the Haldemans. They were Moynihan, Burns, Harlow, Finch, and Peter Flanigan. And Rose Woods was the stalwart who knew how best to understand the Nixon moods.

A good White House team needs a variety of backgrounds, a variety of flavors. We had that among those who sat on the inaugural back bench. People have talked about the Kennedy Irish Mafia, the Nixon California Mafia, and the Nixon German invasion. But whatever the name tag, the men came from different worlds and had background differences, more so than is apparent among President Carter's Georgians.

Of the senior group assembled in 1969, Pat Moynihan was the most liberal. He was a stranger to most of us, but he was brilliant, academic, humorous, persuasive, disorganized—an Irish pixie.

His opposite, Arthur Burns, reminded me of an old-fashioned college president. His wisdom enthralled me. He was a veteran from the Eisenhower days, when he and Nixon had developed a close friendship. For all of his economic heaviness and conservatism, he loved to dance and his wife loved poetry.

Peter Flanigan grew up in the New York and international worlds of finance and politics. His banker father, Hap Flanigan, had been one of those closest to Eisenhower. Peter joined Bob Finch and me in 1960 and organized Citizens for Nixon, and he had assisted Nixon in his comeback after the 1962 governor's race. He was dedicated.

It seemed to me that no one knew more about government than Bryce Harlow, another veteran of the Eisenhower White House. Bryce could play the role of an Oklahoma farmer or that of a sophisticate. He was direct in his dealings and would be the person all of us would lean on to find our way through the Capitol in those early days.

No one on the staff was closer to me or, at that time, to Nixon than was Bob Finch. In many ways we had grown up together in politics since 1950. To our amazement, people frequently confused us, calling him Herb or me Bob. Our wives were good friends, but neither had great enthusiasm for either politics or the candidate. Bob knew the pragmatics of politics better than most, but he still retained strong academic quality.

When the television camera focuses on the inaugural platform, the appearance is that of men and women with only one thought: the ceremony and, eventually, the President's acceptance speech. The camera can deceive. The fact is, concentration is difficult; everyone's thoughts wander. Mine did.

I heard the President voice his inaugural hopes for achieving the role of peacemaker. I listened intently as he came to the lines "Let all nations know that during this administration, our lines of communication will be open." None of the pundits recognized this as a signal for negotiation with the Soviet Union and the People's Republic of China. I knew that was a hope, but it seemed far off to me also. I picked up the terms "open" and "communication."

In my new role as Director of Communications, even my close friends and colleagues were wondering whether my communications role would signal more openness or, as many cartoonists depicted it, a reign as a czar dedicated to bottling up free access between press and public officials.

In a statement I later came to regret, I had when I was appointed told the press, "Truth will be the hallmark of the Nixon administration." On that inaugural day, I was confident it would be. Because of my news and political background, more than anyone else sitting on that long, cold platform bench, I knew that truth had to be the "hallmark" if we were to succeed. I have not changed my mind on that point.

One cartoonist, Basset of Scripps-Howard, had summed up the situation with a drawing which had Nixon on one edge of a cliff and a reporter looking skeptically across a chasm at the President-elect. Between the two cliffs he had me floating—suspended—not quite touching either edge. The caption was, "This will eliminate any possibility of a credibility gap."

A cartoon by Chuck Haynie of the Louisville *Courier-Journal* showed a complicated ticker-tape machine with the tape emerging from Nixon's head, which was on the top of the device. The machinery was labeled the "New Nixon Magic Module News Machine." Alongside it was a tool kit with my name, and the ticker tape was being examined by a reporter. The caption said, "Believe me, Herb—for everyone's sake—I hope this thing works." Bob Finch quipped, "With Herb's mechanical ability, he can barely run a typewriter, let alone a machine like that."

I was confident that my concept would work. The cartoons, some commentary, and even some criticism from within the new Nixon staff put me on a spot—and in the spotlight. If I failed, it would be known quickly. But if my approach was correct and properly executed, the spotlight also would highlight this fact and thus make far more rapid progress in decreasing the credibility gap and in modernizing government communications.

On my first appearance on "Meet the Press," December 8, 1968, Larry Spivak asked:

"I believe you said that truth will be the hallmark of the Nixon administration. Do you think it is going to be possible always to tell the truth about a situation, or even to know the truth?"

My answer was:

"I certainly do believe so. I think knowing the truth is perhaps the more difficult of the situations we talked about, but I said that to contrast directly to the other theory, which I think has too big a place in government, and that is, a government has a right to lie. I think government's having the right to lie undermines the people's faith in government. One of the main reasons for Mr. Nixon's interest in this particular job is that we feel that one of the first things that is necessary is to regain faith in the American government, both from our own people and from abroad. You can only do this if they believe that they are finding the truth as it comes out."

A credibility gap was not a new problem in government. But the issue had been accentuated during the latter phases of the Johnson administration.

At the time of the "pleasant beginning," we did begin to restore public confidence in the presidency. The opportunity was there.

Going back to the inaugural ceremony, even in this somber, historic atmosphere on the platform, before the eyes of millions, my mind wandered to other inaugurals in which I had participated.

Until the inaugural, my role had been in assisting the Vice-President or, as in 1960, the defeated candidate. The path to the presidency, to the White House, had not been easy for Richard Nixon, for me, or for most of the other senior colleagues in the hopeful administration class of '69.

I found my mind focusing briefly on the Eisenhower-Nixon inaugural in 1957. I had been asked to work with the press in assisting the Vice-President. On the day before the ceremony, a reporter called and asked which Bible or Bibles the Vice-President would use for his oath. This was new territory for me. I found that Nixon planned to use three family Bibles. I called James Hagerty, the President's press secretary, to inquire about the Eisenhower plans. The President was to use three Bibles. Out of protocol, we dropped the Nixon number to two Bibles.

The reporter also had asked, "What chapter and verse would be open?" No one knew. I called Father John Cronin, a learned priest who was a confidant of the Vice-President, and he recommended the verse in Psalms referring to turning swords into plowshares.

At the ceremony I was witnessing, I wondered which verse was open. I did not know because Ron Ziegler had checked it this time.

Few, if any, events are covered more thoroughly by the news media than an inaugural; this was no exception. There were reporters inside the Capitol and outside, anchormen and cameramen in the high booths facing the platform, reporters along the parade route and in the boxes opposite the enclosed presidential area at the end of the parade route in front of the White House on Pennsylvania Avenue.

The press looked at those of us on the inaugural platform with much the same curiosity that we had as we stared back at the long rows of tables strewn with typewriters and carbon paper.

Most of the White House press regulars had spent little time covering the 1968 presidential candidates. They had been assigned to stay with President Johnson as he concluded his term of office. Many of the news outlets change White House correspondents with a change in office-holders, acting on the theory that the reporter who has been on the campaign trail will have more insight into the thinking of the new President and will have built contacts with many on the candidate's campaign staff.

But in the crowd covering the inaugural, I recognized many of the regulars who stayed on regardless of the President, regulars who by experience became the "experts" on the presidency. These were the pundits other reporters listened to and followed. The veterans included John Osborne of *New Republic,* the late Peter Lisagor of the Chicago *Daily News,* the late Merriman Smith of United Press International, Frank Cormier of AP and his colleague, Marvin Arrowsmith, now Associated Press Washington bureau chief, James Reston of the New York *Times,* Bill Anderson of the

Chicago *Tribune,* and Chuck Bailey of the Minneapolis *Tribune,* Hugh
Sidey of *Time,* and Helen Thomas and Frances Lewine, who had accompanied us to Moscow for the wire services.

For the reporters, I was the only known press quality on the platform.
They were genuinely curious about my title of Director of Communications, but we had traveled thousands of miles together. We were
comfortable together.

Not even the most senior of the veteran reporters really understood
Nixon, although he had been on the public scene more than two decades.
Nixon would not admit it, but he also did not understand the newsmen.
All this complicated the situation for Ziegler and for me.

The newsmen had no great admiration for Nixon and wondered how
he would perform as President and how he would work with the press. As
they waited for the ceremony to begin, the reporters also speculated over
Ziegler. Was he tough enough to last, or just a good-looking "college kid"?
He was tough, they would learn.

In preparing for this 1969 inauguration, Mr. Nixon had spent more
time than he would admit studying the Kennedy 1961 ceremony and the
brilliant Kennedy inaugural speech. At times, President Kennedy obsessed
the President-elect. I think he secretly envied the Kennedy style, and the
later fascination over what Kennedy had the power to keep secret was part
of the psychology which led to the Watergate cover-up.

The Kennedy inaugural was part of my wandering thoughts that day
also. On the eve of the 1961 inaugural, Bob Finch and I and our secretaries, Mary Werner and Doris Jones, and other Nixon assistants, such as
Charlie McWhorter and Loie Gaunt, had worked against a midnight
deadline to clear the Vice-President's office in the Senate Office Building,
packing papers that we and Nixon would need for future files.

As we worked into the night, record drifts of snow accumulated outside.
We could hear sirens blaring as police fought to get celebrities to the Kennedy inaugural eve gala. Inwardly, I suspect we were glad for the near-dis-
astrous dilemma outside. Losing the election closely had not been easy, and
we still harbored some traces of bitterness.

As we left the office after midnight and started home, we found the
streets jammed with deserted cars, stuck in the snow. I drove along Constitution Avenue toward the Lincoln Monument, dodging deserted vehicles
like a broken-field runner. I was exhausted and depressed and had to
struggle mentally not to consider the obstacles as ones personally planted
to make my task more difficult.

Inexplicably, at that hour and in those heavy snow conditions, I could
not drive by the Lincoln Monument without stopping. It represented solemn solace and, strangely, gave me mental peace.

Miracles frequently are talked of in Washington, but they occur rarely.

One occurred that night. It seemed to me to be part of Kennedy Camelot magic. The combined armed forces had been called up, with every possible working vehicle clearing the streets. Officers as well as enlisted men were driving Jeep snowplows. The only other time I know of streets being cleared that rapidly for a President was eleven years later. In that case the city was Peking, the street sweepers used brooms, and the ceremonial occasion was in honor of Richard Nixon, President of the United States.

I was on the inaugural platform briefly on that morning of January 20, 1961. I met the outgoing Vice-President at his home in Northwest Washington, and as the moments he would still be in office fleeted by, we sipped coffee with ten reporters—all veterans of the campaign, like Bill Theis and Carroll Kilpatrick—who had been assigned to cover these final hours.

I took the reporters to the Capitol, where we followed the Vice-President to the minority leader's office. While we were awaiting a signal to go to the platform, I went into the Capitol rotunda to visit with the press. Nancy Dickerson, then with CBS, beckoned me over for an interview, which ended suddenly as the incoming President, John Kennedy, arrived and came over to greet both of us. The President-elect was calmly awaiting the signal to walk onto that platform for his moment of great triumph.

I returned to escort Vice-President Nixon and watched him walk down the steps to sit in the seat now, in 1969, occupied by Vice-President Hubert Humphrey.

My job done, I went to Senator Dirksen's office, sipped a brandy, and headed home to gather my family for our trip back to California the next day. We had no plans to return to Washington for another inaugural.

But here I was, sitting on a cold bench between Moynihan and Flanigan, and Nixon was starting his inaugural address.

I knew that those who shared the bench for the Nixon staff had sober, high hopes for a "pleasant ending" to this "pleasant beginning."

2

Omens

IF I BELIEVED IN OMENS, I probably would have resigned from the Nixon staff sometime during my first days in the 1968 campaign.

I arrived on June 1 in the midst of a severe storm, which isolated some of the staff from the candidate. I finally left the White House in 1973 after more of a spiritual storm isolated me and others from the President.

As the presidential campaign took shape in the latter part of 1967 and the spring of 1968, I had been in close telephone and personal touch with Nixon and his staff, principally Rose Woods and Bob Haldeman.

At one time in 1967, Nixon had interrupted a New York meeting with his campaign executive committee to telephone me in California asking that I recruit Dr. Gaylord Parkinson, a San Diegan, who developed the so-called eleventh commandment (Thou shalt not speak critically of other Republican candidates). He had been the California State Republican Chairman. Within a few hours I had Parkinson on a plane to New York, where he accepted a $75,000-a-year offer to head the campaign committee.

His stay as campaign manager was short-lived, and he eventually was replaced by Robert Ellsworth and then by a man I knew little about, John Mitchell. Even in the early days of the campaign there was a struggle for power behind the scenes, a struggle which was to become bitter in the White House after 1970.

As the triumphant Nixon primary campaign moved forward in the spring of 1968 through New Hampshire, Wisconsin, Indiana, and other states, I quietly debated in my own mind whether I would accept the call for one more campaign, if asked. After the 1962 governor's race, I had told myself that was the end of campaigning for me.

In late April 1968, Haldeman asked me to meet him at the Los Angeles International Airport for lunch. After having been recruited five times before to come into major Nixon campaigns, usually following a telephone call or a lunch, I knew what to expect. But I did not know my answer and told Haldeman I was not yet ready to commit to a campaign. His plan was to revamp the press operation, which functioned well but was disorganized during the early 1968 primaries, and to professionalize the media staff prior to the Republican convention. He suggested that we also bring in Ron Ziegler, who had gone to work for Haldeman at the J. Walter Thompson agency after assisting me with the press in the 1962 gubernatorial campaign, and at that time was still in Los Angeles as an executive with the advertising agency.

My publisher and friend at the San Diego *Union*, James Copley, was battling cancer, but he invited me to come to his home to discuss the situation. The decision was important to both of us. Throughout lengthy conversations, neither he nor his wife, Helen (who sat in on each meeting), attempted to direct me, but they helped me focus on the problems a leave of absence would cause at the newspaper and on the challenge of the presidential campaign.

I suspected that my wife reluctantly felt I would join "one more campaign," but she too left the decision to me.

After agonizing, I accepted the Nixon-Haldeman invitation and gave my newspaper staff the long-standing instructions that the only way to get into trouble with me during the campaign was to favor the Republicans or the Nixon campaign on the *Union* news pages. As I had in other campaigns, I took a leave of absence from the newspaper. But this time, I dropped the strong hint to my managing editors, Ed Thomas and Fred Kinne, that I might resign early on if I thought there was a possible conflict of interest.

All this emotional decision-making was running through my mind as I flew across the country on the first Saturday in June to join the campaign forces during a weekend retreat at Key Biscayne, Florida. I could not forget that while politics intrigued me immensely, I loved editing the San Diego *Union*.

While we spanned the country, I reviewed the 1960 campaign and looked critically at past mistakes in the press operation, planning a new structure for the 1968 effort.

Since 1962, I had had a mental block on every rereading of the text that had become known as Nixon's final press conference—the public session where Nixon interrupted me to tell the startled newsmen they wouldn't "have Dick Nixon to kick around anymore."

As I read and reread the text to prepare for obvious questions which would come to me upon my arrival in Florida, I found that six years had partially mellowed the impact upon me. The full text did not sound quite as bad as it had on that seemingly fatal morning in 1962—the morning which had led to the bitter Howard K. Smith program on ABC Television proclaiming the political obituary of Richard Nixon.

But nonetheless, the Nixon text was bad, and it complicated my new assignment. Some said the television tapes of the confrontation would be replayed. I doubted that. But it was a threat.

The first bad omen of the campaign was the swirling tropical rainstorm which bounced and covered the airplane as we made a rough landing in Miami. It was almost as if I were not supposed to land and join the campaign.

I drove through flooded streets to the Key Biscayne resort hotel where the campaign party was staying and found it virtually deserted.

Most of the press corps had gone out earlier by boat to a small offshore island, Walker's Cay, owned by Nixon's close friend Bob Abplanalp. Nixon had planned to fly later that day to the cay with me and hold an informal press conference. The tropical storm Abby moved in with hurricanelike winds and isolated the press from the candidate, forcing the cancellation of the news conference, where, among other things, my appointment was to have been announced.

Amid the rain, I gained my first impressions of John Mitchell during a long evening of discussion with him and Bob Haldeman in one of the Key Biscayne villas. Mitchell had no previous experience in a national campaign and in my mind I wondered what his real role would be in this race. Would he be the campaign manager in more than just title?

In the 1960 presidential effort there had been in reality three campaign managers. Nixon himself attempted to manage the campaign even as he flitted through campaign appearances in all fifty states. He called too many of the shots, and that turned out to be a major weakness. Strangely, many years before, he had pointed out to me in strong terms the folly of a candidate's attempting to manage his own campaign.

The other two managers were the veteran Leonard Hall and the younger strategist Bob Finch. Hall had the title of campaign manager and Finch was titled campaign director. The result was constant overlap and confusion compounded often by the candidate frequently sending out duplicate instructions. As President, Nixon overdelegated power. As Vice-President he underdelegated and thus in the 1960 campaign he managed strategy poorly, and he lost despite strong professional efforts by Finch and Hall.

When I talked to Mitchell and Haldeman on that first campaign night in 1968, I suspected initially that the real manager would be Haldeman, who had directed the 1962 gubernatorial effort. I also felt certain that despite what he was saying to the contrary, Nixon would again insert himself into a managerial role.

As the evening progressed, to my dismay as the new campaign press manager, I discovered that neither Mitchell nor Haldeman seemed worried about the fact that part of the press corps and staff was marooned on an island offshore, although I tried to explain the complications of separating the newsmen from a candidate. In a presidential campaign, newsmen rightfully feel that they should never be far from the candidate, and I knew even a freak of weather would irritate them.

As we talked, I soon found that Mitchell was stronger and understood more of the realities of national politics than I had anticipated. Mitchell puffed his pipe and Haldeman sipped a beer as they discussed the success of a meeting held earlier in the week with Southern Republican leaders. The meeting in Atlanta had followed the Nixon triumph in the Oregon primary. The Oregon victory was looked at as effectively blocking late efforts to renew the Rockefeller presidential campaign. In Atlanta, Nixon won major support from conservatives, including Senator Strom Thurmond of South Carolina. That was looked upon as a key thrust that could prevent the successful blooming· of the growing Reagan flower—even though Reagan was assured of victory in the California primary the following Tuesday. Nixon had left the field in California open to the governor, who was theoretically campaigning as a "favorite son."

At about midnight on that first evening I answered the telephone, which was ringing in another room of the Mitchell Key Biscayne villa. A woman was calling—screaming into the phone demanding to speak to John Mitchell. The tone was so high and the words so distorted that I was embarrassed to have answered the phone. I merely told the hysterical caller that Mitchell had stepped out for a few minutes and suggested that she call back. That was my midnight introduction to Martha Mitchell. And it was my only conversation with her during the campaign. I never mentioned it to her or anyone else. We later became friends in Washington and discussed many of her problems. No Martha Mitchell conversation with me in the next few years ever was like the first, although I listened to her often—occasionally hearing good ideas but, more often, emotional tirades or eccentric schemes.

My first inquiry concerning the campaign came from the press early the next morning. A reporter from United Press had picked up a story that Nixon planned to appeal to young voters by campaigning in a Nehru jacket, a popular costume for some of the youths. Nixon in a Nehru jacket? A man who usually shunned a sports shirt in public in a "mod" costume? It was an unbelievable start to a campaign where I would answer hundreds of press questions, but never one so absurd as this. The reporter did not really believe the story either, so he was checking. That was easy to deny even though I had not seen the candidate since arriving in Florida the afternoon before.

During the weekend, I learned that the press operation was being supervised by Leonard Garment, who was one of Nixon's law partners and who later became a sensitive, bright White House counsel and the administration's civil rights adviser. Arch McKinley, who had won public attention earlier by creating the brilliant idea of a nationally televised safety test for drivers, was in charge of press operation before I arrived. He became my New York deputy in the new arrangement.

Earlier I had agreed that on Tuesday, the night of the California primary election, I would comment on the results of the vote in an interview with veteran reporter Peter Hackes on NBC Television. Garment and McKinley were aghast at the idea of someone just three days into the campaign going on television. They invited me to cocktails at the University Club in New York to see if I could answer their questions. With some amusement, I passed my Garment-McKinley test and went late in the evening to NBC for the TV interview with Hackes.

It went well.

Haldeman had rented apartments and rooms in the small but old and comfortable Wyndham Hotel in Manhattan for some of us who were senior in the campaign. After finishing the Hackes interview, I returned to the hotel to watch the television election coverage from California.

Ronald Reagan made his Republican victory statement on television, and then I watched Robert Kennedy speaking from the familiar Ambassador Hotel in Los Angeles. The Ambassador Hotel had been our headquarters many times, including the election night of 1960. Kennedy left his victory rally and disappeared toward the hotel kitchen door, which Nixon and I had used frequently as a point of quick departure from a meeting or rally.

Then came the news that Kennedy had been shot.

I watched, almost unbelieving, as the story unfolded tragically. Perhaps because of my optimistic nature, I chose at first to believe the most favorable reports that the candidate was alive and thus the wounds might not be critical. Death seemed inconceivable.

As I saw the tragedy grow and heard Kennedy's press secretary, Frank Mankiewicz, answer questions, I debated whether or not to awaken Nixon and advise him of what was happening. I decided there was nothing he could do and whatever the fate of Kennedy would be, it would put added pressure on Nixon the next day. About 3 A.M. I called Haldeman in the hotel suite below mine and told him what had happened and of my decision not to awaken Nixon. He agreed and turned on his own television. What we did not know was that Julie Nixon and David Eisenhower were also watching and that they had awakened Nixon, so he too watched in disbelief.

I tried to find the private chief of security for the campaign, James Golden, who earlier had been in the Secret Service detail assigned to Nixon as Vice-President. I never reached him, but during that long horrible night the Secret Service had been alerted, and long before dawn they were on duty, guarding the residence of Nixon and other major candidates.

President Johnson had acted quietly and quickly.

I have had some horrifying moments in politics but none more tragic and depressing than this. I knew John Kennedy better than Robert, but here I was watching a friend, Mankiewicz, nearly in tears as he courageously briefed the nation on a shooting in a hotel almost as familiar to me as my office.

I had a few moments to wonder who would be shot next. What about those standing closest to the candidates in a crowded rally? Me, another aide, a Secret Service agent? In matters such as this, I am a fatalist and I have never worried long—but this brought the cause home.

A hurricane, an assassination—the omens were not good during those first four days. But all that was out of my mind at daylight.

Campaigning has many peculiarities. One of them is that there rarely is time for the luxury of looking back. Something occurs, such as the Robert Kennedy assassination, and even while one mourns, one must concentrate on the immediate—and the future.

As the sun rose and America awakened to the tragedy in Los Angeles, my job was to recommend first how Nixon should react publicly to the event. And what about the California primary, conceded to "favorite son" Reagan? Though of minor consequence to the national public, this was a matter of strong impact on politicians. In addition, the days to the nominating convention were few, and I had little time to reorganize the Nixon press office under me; I had already found it was in bad shape.

Nixon's reaction to the assassination was to declare a moratorium on his personal campaigning and to issue a statement of sorrow over the death of Senator Kennedy. He had liked John Kennedy personally, but the feeling did not extend to Robert. Nonetheless, he was genuinely shocked and depressed because of the death.

At the same time we looked at Reagan's uncontested victory in California in two ways. One was to consider it the likely starting point of a late but expanded and major effort by the governor to seek the presidential nomination. The other was to take it in stride as something we expected.

All of the candidates declared a public moratorium during mourning for Kennedy, but that did not apply to private strategic campaign efforts. I could readily envision telephone calls from Lyn Nofziger of the governor's staff, and others, spreading the word of Reagan strength proved in California.

We also had to begin new studies on the effect the Kennedy death would have on the Democratic nomination battle. Where would the senator's strength transfer? Would the assassination unite' the badly split Democratic Party or would it accentuate the battle? Would President Johnson now change his mind about not running, entering as a candidate to pull the party out of the ashes of tragedy and shattered emotions?

Basically the question was, Who would be the Democratic nominee and how should we begin planning for him? In this situation we thought Eugene McCarthy would be the opponent we would like most to face. We thought he would split the Democratic Party and would be easy to beat; however, Hubert Humphrey was the most likely opponent because he had the organization and experience needed at that moment.

He was an experienced, well-balanced opponent. He would be tough. No question.

Then, there was the third candidate, George Wallace. He added an element which was difficult to calculate. We believed he could not win. But he drew from the South in states where we could dominate against the liberals, McCarthy and Humphrey. He would draw from the Democratic candidate in larger states by attracting blue-collar voters who traditionally voted a solid Democratic ticket but who now were upset by a number of things, including the inroads of blacks into their home areas and into their unions.

The Nixon campaign of 1968 borrowed strategy on timing from the Kennedy effort of 1960, but we then added other communications techniques which were ahead of their time and provided a modern example for varied campaigns of the seventies. It also indicated to the astute observer the way Nixon would later operate from the White House.

Nixon always has considered himself to be a politician who takes the offensive—tough ball control, he would say, using a common term from football. But in 1960, because of a knee injury which hospitalized him and threw him off pace and because he was ahead early in the race, he played more of a defensive game until the last three weeks before election, to protect his position and, of necessity, to defend the Eisenhower positions he had shared. Thus he was vulnerable to attacks on issues where he should have been strong, such as the so-called missile gap and Cuba.

Kennedy sensed that his first effort had to be to solidify the Democratic Party, which was and is in the majority. He started fast in 1960 with a freewheeling attack and then held on by his fingertips in the last few days when the Nixon offensive finally started to take hold with the swing voters. To use the candidate's football terminology again, we had a "two-minute drill" in the last few days before election, but time ran out before we reached the goal.

In 1968, Nixon decided to start early and to hit hard, taking advantage of the confusion in the Democratic ranks following the riot-torn Democratic convention.

He had been prepared to be on the offensive even during the Democratic convention and had sent a team to stay in the heart of Democratic headquarters in the Conrad Hilton Hotel in Chicago to counter opposition statements from the convention hall—a so-called truth squad.

The staff for the Chicago counterattack included Bill Safire and Pat Buchanan, later White House speech writers, and Bill Timmons, who eventually directed White House liaison with Congress. Spokesmen were to be the implacable Governor John Love, of Colorado, and Don Rumsfeld, then a rising young Illinois congressman.

On instructions from Nixon, the offensive never was really mounted. The campaign leadership felt that the Democrats at the convention were effectively destroying themselves without Republican statements.

One of the incidents left untouched by the Nixon staff in Chicago was the effort by a television team from NBC to electronically bug a caucus at the Democratic convention, the first known use of electronics to gather domestic political intelligence. The media covered the story—but sparingly.

As the conventions were concluded, the 1968 Nixon campaign structure included four coordinated divisions. One was the financial staff, headed by Maurice Stans, a veteran campaigner, with offices separate from any other part of the campaign structure so as not to be caught up in the day-by-day hurdles and demands of the election drive. It was organized with the mandate to raise millions, which it did at record pace, both in dollar amounts and in numbers of contributors, large and small.

The lack of space in the original campaign building put John Mitchell and those who would worry about the physical and strategic direction of the staff in another building across Park Avenue. They worked with state chairmen and, for example, developed a strategy of key battleground states where the campaign emphasis was to be placed. California and Texas were two naturals from the West. The emphasis also was on thirteen large Eastern and Middle Western states, such as New York, Pennsylvania, Ohio, and Illinois, plus border and changing Southern states such as Florida, Tennessee, the Carolinas, and Virginia.

This did not exclude an interest in other states, but basically, those states not in the fundamental battle plan were looked at as almost certain to be locked in for one of the three candidates regardless of campaign efforts. Alabama thus would be considered for Wallace, Massachusetts for Humphrey or McCarthy, and Arizona for Nixon.

Polling was an extensive part of the strategy directed by Mitchell.

There were the routine demographic samples, but the most interesting poll was directed by an Indiana University political science dean, David Derge, who arranged regular checks with a given set of voters from the key battle areas. He found that during the campaign voters might well change their choice three or four times before deciding on a candidate to vote for on election day. A Democrat, for example, sometimes would defect from Humphrey, his party's nominee, to switch to Wallace. He then might be convinced that such a vote would be wasted and would switch to Nixon. The vacillation worked both ways.

All these factors were studied by Mitchell's strategic division.

Across from the Mitchell headquarters on the west side of Park Avenue was the creative staff, dealing more with the public. This group varied from my own communications staff to the speech writers and researchers, to the mail room, and to the public reception headquarters. We were housed in an old Bible Institute building at 450 Park Avenue, which was scheduled to be torn down and replaced with a skyscraper after the election. Mixed with our political posters were Bible quotations carved in the ancient building walls. Nixon originally had planned to work from this building, but his visits there were rare. He preferred his apartment.

The building was so confused that it was hard to find anything or anyone in it. I once was directed by my campaign secretary (and later White House assistant), Tina Bucheit (now Mrs. Neil Diver), to meet a prominent official for a quick courtesy drink at 6:30 P.M. This was a request from a state chairman and, fifteen minutes later, I strode swiftly into the scattered lobby area to meet the man. I saw only one person waiting and introduced myself, inviting him to step around the corner to Fifty-sixth Street for a quick drink. He seemed delighted. In conversation a few minutes later, it dawned on me that I must have the wrong visiting dignitary. He confirmed this but thanked me for the hospitality.

Embarrassed, I whisked him back and found the man I was to meet. He had been patiently waiting for me. We returned to the same bartender, who by now was so confused he could only stutter.

The fourth segment of the campaign staff was the traveling group headed by Haldeman. John Ehrlichman was called tour director, and Ron Ziegler was my representative as traveling press aide. Speech writers alternated stints on the aircraft.

Despite the strength of the three campaign segments in New York, the traveling group, following the old adage of those closest to the candidate gain his confidence, became the dominant element of the campaign, and Haldeman worked out a close-knit, close-to-the-vest operation which later served as the modus operandi at the White House. Mitchell particularly contested Haldeman, but these were the beginnings of eventual tight White House control by Haldeman.

A President running for reelection has many advantages because of communications equipment set up routinely by the Army Signal Corps. Telephones are in every key staff room, switchboards are ready at each stop, and dozens of lines of communication are open on Air Force One.

Haldeman brought an innovation into campaigning by a nonpresidential incumbent and equipped the privately chartered staff aircraft with expensive electronic vehicles almost equal to Air Force One. It included six ground-to-ground press phones when the plane was at an airport, plus four for the staff, two ground-to-air telephones, a teletype which could receive or send messages in air or on ground, varied walkie-talkie devices, including those which would reach ground staff personnel when we were over the airport, and a machine I did not understand but which I used frequently, a radio-receiving Xerox. I dubbed it a "magic carpet" and used it to receive and send full messages, clippings, and other materials essential to keep minute-by-minute contact between Ziegler and myself. I also had one of the first telephones in a briefcase. It was more effective for publicity than for actual operations.

The campaign newsmen rarely see the backstage effort which is necessary to organize a full-scale press media communications effort for a modern campaign. Once a man is in office, as was true in 1972 for President Nixon, the task is comparatively easy because most of the candidate's staff is in place and the campaign organization need only concern itself with strategy and with organizing the various state campaigns. The ease of the task before the Nixon Committee to Re-elect the President in 1972 was such as to make the events of Watergate even more politically inexplicable.

As I had looked earlier at the campaign communications apparatus in New York, in June of 1968, I found that Haldeman and Garment had started work on the production units that would show the candidate on paid programs on television. Joe McGinnis later tried to describe this aspect in his quickie campaign book *The Selling of the President,* but his view was so limited that he had no accurate idea of how it worked. McGinnis said, for example, that those selected to appear on a series of half-hour shows, where they informally questioned the President, were supposed to be friendly to Nixon. Many were. But Nixon reacts better to tough questions than easy ones, and some of the panelists who were either neutral or against the candidate asked the best questions and provoked the best answers. Martin Castillo, a Mexican-American leader from Los Angeles, was an example of an uncommitted panelist.

The basic television concept, developed by producer Harry Treleaven, was to present the candidate in informal television, such as in question-and-answer sessions. We wanted to avoid the old, more formal statements which when presented on television bored all but the most loyal, faithful supporters.

Many of these ideas have since been refined in an era of media-oriented campaigns, but this was a start of using television advertising which would be interesting to the casual viewer as well as to the campaign worker. Long speeches were avoided on TV, although some were taped for radio to emphasize the major importance we placed on some position papers.

The basic principle, however, was that the former Vice-President could come across on television far better than most of the newsmen realized. They remembered only the first debate with Kennedy and the 1962 "last press conference." They had forgotten that the 1952 "Checkers Speech" drew more response than any political statement in history. It now was popular to disparage the Checkers Speech. Out of mind was the Nixon success in the television version of the Kitchen Debate with Khrushchev and the 1966 Nixon response on television to President Johnson.

Newsmen's surprise at Nixon's strong television performance in 1968 led to a favorable press. The surprise as well as the substance was a major factor in the Nixon comeback.

Another part of the 1968 communications operation had to be the routine campaign literature, bumper stickers, buttons, and the like. This had been organized by Clint Wheeler around the theme "Nixon's the One."

I found the rest of the Nixon press operation in a state of confusion. The media campaign staff lacked the confidence of the candidate; it was staffed with young and eager personnel, but included no one with campaign or extensive press experience except McKinley. Effort had been concentrated on preparing campaign-issue books with good writing and graphics. They were well done but for internal consumption—not the press.

There was one experienced politician, a nervous former Rockefeller man. He was writing, editing, and printing a house organ directed at key workers. I first looked at the paper in horror. The headlines were jammed and sensationalized. The makeup violated all of my more pure newspaper concepts. But before I objected, I checked with some of the campaign workers and found that the big capitalized headlines excited them. The house organ was in exactly the form to intrigue Nixon campaigners into reading it.

The reporter, editor, printer, was Frank Leonard, a veteran of not just Rockefeller but other nonpresidential campaigns. I soon found that he coupled this experience with excellent judgment even in critical moments. Leonard could be trusted not to create political problems, and he could help build enthusiasm.

I found in the inherited staff no lack of enthusiasm or loyalty to Nixon, just confusion created by inexperience and some resentment of me, a new man coming in to run the operation.

One of the young staff thought that the way to demonstrate the first-class nature of the press operation was to deliver the releases to newspapers and the wire services in a Cadillac-chauffeured limousine. Fortunately, I spotted that before the newsmen did.

The easiest part of a press operation is to have the candidate make an advance statement and then be sure it is covered by the media and that copies of what he says are widely circulated.

But a successful operation depends upon many other things. The press secretary, or "manager of communications," as I was called in 1968, first must be a part of all key strategy and should have a voice in issue decisions. His staff must be in liaison with all parts of the campaign from the state organizations to the variety of committees which are recruited, such as Attorneys for Nixon, Farmers for Nixon, the Hispanic Committee, Black Leadership, and so on. Crisp press releases for each are necessary.

There must be liaison with columnists, reporters, editors, broadcasters, and commentators across the nation. We worked hard on winning newspaper endorsements and that often meant having the candidate, me, or another senior staff member meet with editorial boards.

In 1960 I had discovered that the press aide with the candidate should know the demographics, the candidates, the issues, and the characteristics of each city and state before the press plane lands. Background is essential for reporters and accurate information for them was important to us. I persuaded Mrs. Margita White, who had been in the 1960 campaign with me and in the 1964 Goldwater campaign, to research and prepare such a formal notebook. She was out of active campaigning because she was expecting a second child (a son, Stuart, Jr.). The book she produced was so valuable that I limited it to five copies to prevent the opposition from turning up with one. Mrs. White eventually became my administrative assistant and later was President Ford's communications director; she became an effective FCC commissioner.

We had another innovation—an organized surrogate campaign. The campaign organization recruited Republican leaders to speak nationally and scheduled them just as it did Nixon. The job of my office was to work with the speech writers and develop news themes several times a week so that in each geographic area of the country they would hear basically the same "party line" expressed simultaneously by a different speaker. Surrogates working in this manner, rather than with haphazard speeches developed on the fly, made news and gave the campaign a feeling of unity. Several regional stories in a day can have the impact of a national news story. Each day the surrogates received detailed news summaries by teletype, and an issues office in Washington, headed by Senator John Tower and his assistant Jerry Friedheim, developed additional information for them. All this gave meaning to an expanded news scope in the campaign.

Ziegler and I worked frantically together to recruit additional experienced personnel for the campaign staff and for his traveling staff. It was up to Ron, also, to placate some of the interoffice resentment stemming from our invasion into the staff ranks. He was my emissary to smooth relations with those who had been a part of the early staff.

Ziegler found two young but effective assistants for his traveling team, Allen Woods of Missouri and Bruce Whelihan, then working in New York. They were inexperienced but energetic and they fitted well with him. At this campaign stage there are many small but important details to work out, such as a team to transcribe accurately each speech or press conference.

For the New York campaign staff, I leaned first on old friends, Mrs. Virginia Savell, who had grown up in California campaigns, and Alex Troffey, a college classmate, who was a professional with the media and had assisted me in 1960. They handled the surrogate campaign. Over a drink at the O'Hare Inn in Chicago, I talked with Gerhard D. Bleicken, chairman of John Hancock insurance, and discovered he had an experienced newsman on his staff, Paul Costello, who could take leave and join the campaign. He moved swiftly from Boston to shore up our press relations.

A good communications office needs someone who can handle the multiple telephones, deal with two hundred or more calls a day, and be charming, yet careful, as to the answers even to routine questions. Peter Flanigan suggested Mary Ann Snow, who had sung professionally, including a key role in the traveling *Hello, Dolly!* company that had performed in Moscow. She filled that coordinating role capably both in New York and later in my White House office.

The best new find was the first—Tina Bucheit—my executive secretary and assistant, a journalism graduate of Northwestern University, who originally had worked with Ray Price and the speech writers but who was best fitted to assist me in all the details of working with the press.

Before the convention in August, we had an adaptable working team which meshed with the more capable of the personnel recruited early by Arch McKenzie. They included Susie Low, a brilliant young researcher, Tom Sedlar, who had worked with the press in the final Nixon primary campaigns, Jo Guthrie, Copp Collins, Ann Duggan, Mike Monroe, Buffie Parker, Steve Moynahan, and Aimie Merriam.

During the interval after the assassination of Robert Kennedy, our campaign executive group decided on a strategy of cool confidence, but confidence couched in terms which would avoid an appearance of overconfidence regarding the nomination. We deliberately avoided the phrase used so much in the Goldwater nomination campaign—"locked up." Reporters would ask if we had enough votes to have the convention "locked up." The strategic answer was that we were pleased to be far ahead, but Nixon did not think we had all the necessary votes, and he insisted it would be an open convention with no pressure on anyone. We added that we expected to win on "an early ballot," again avoiding predictions of a first-ballot victory which might come back to haunt us. It is a political mistake to be quoted overconfidently. The fact was that we believed we would win on the first ballot but we did not have the necessary votes assured until we began our private counts at the convention. Even then, it was close.

Nixon's early strategy in 1968 was to enter the early primaries and to use those to dispel the argument that his losses in the 1960 presidential race and the 1962 California gubernatorial race proved that he was a "loser"—a loyal party man "who can't win."

The Oregon primary had provided the final stroke in connoting an image of a winning new approach to the name Richard Nixon.

As the Oregon primary approached, Nixon had commented:

"I believe the primaries have a special additional role to play in this watershed year of 1968. Primaries give a chance to meet many thousands of Americans and to speak to hundreds of thousands more.

"The choices facing Americans this year are too many and too fundamental to be presented to the people in a single either/or, take-it-or-leave-it package in November. They need to be developed and debated, step by step."

The statement had the dual purpose of focusing on the Nixon winning streak and at indirectly brushing off the late-moving Rockefeller candidacy, which had not been based on primaries but concentrated on the argument that only Rockefeller could win.

In a later press release I pointed out that in ten primaries Nixon had gained 1,590,025 votes to 105,057 for Rockefeller. Nixon's totals in the ten states had exceeded Republican winners in 1964 in all but two states: Wisconsin, where the Republican favorite son in 1964 had been unopposed and won 99.7 percent of the vote, and Massachusetts, where Henry Cabot Lodge had won easily in 1964 and where Rockefeller had received 5,000 more votes than Nixon in a contest where the names of both men were written in. Rockefeller, of course, was a "noncandidate" during most of this time and so the comparison was not entirely valid, but it had favorable political effect.

With victory seemingly close at hand, the strategy moved from aggressiveness to one which football players would call a "prevent defense," based on moving the candidate around enough to keep everyone happy but to avoid mistakes which might be capitalized upon by Ronald Reagan or Rockefeller during the last two months before the convention.

Part of the game was to play to all sides within the party.

On one of the few occasions I ever heard Nixon admit that he had made an error, he told Washington congressional supporters that he had been wrong in vowing to campaign in all fifty states in 1960 (thus flying to Alaska and back on the Sunday before the election), and he promised to concentrate heavily on the large states and big cities if he were nominated.

Still he went west to Nevada, Montana, and Idaho to confer with the Republican governors and "learn firsthand" about the current problems of the West. Reporters also noted the more important fact—all three states were uncommitted at that point.

With all of these precautions, it still was not possible to avoid small errors which could be magnified and exploited by bored newsmen and the opposition. In a campaign, a seemingly minor incident suddenly can loom on the scene and for a short time take on more political importance than the public gives to stands on big issues in areas of foreign or domestic policy.

In early July, for example, two of Nixon's law partners who lived in New Jersey helped arrange for him to give a private cocktail party for that state's forty convention delegates and their wives. The New Jersey contingent was uncommitted and was being heavily wooed by Rockefeller supporters and by us.

The party was at the Baltusrol Country Club in Springfield, New Jersey, about fifteen miles from Nixon's Manhattan apartment, a club the former Vice-President had joined several years earlier, strictly to play golf. Baltusrol had been the site of three national open golf tournaments, including one in 1967, and about the only controversy it had stirred was among golfers and sports writers over the putting speed on the greens.

The club bylaws had no exclusion provisions but the fact was that it had no members who were either black or Jewish. Nearby there were other private clubs which had no gentile members, but that was not part of the issue.

As we drove into the club I saw a few youthful pickets with antiwar signs, but my only concern was placating the feelings of the press, which was excluded from the private delegate reception. To compensate for that, we had an informal press conference in another room in the clubhouse, and it was there that the restrictive membership of the club was broached by the reporters.

That issue made the lead on the story nationally. The Chicago *Sun-Times,* for example, carried the headline "Nixon Defends Membership in 'Lily White' Country Club." At the press conference, Nixon said:

"I do not approve of these restrictions," and he went on to say he had not had time to play golf there for "a couple of years."

When asked why he joined the club or why he did not resign, Nixon said:

"It has never been my practice to resign from such clubs but rather to work from within to change the policy." Democrats jumped to denounce Nixon, and the American Civil Liberties Union accused the candidate of "participating actively in discrimination against Negroes and Jews . . . what had he done 'from within' to stop discrimination at Baltusrol up to now?" it asked. Rockefeller had an issue going for him, an issue which caused tremors within the ranks of our sensitive staff. He raised questions, but let others carry the battle for him. It was easy.

Nixon held firm rather than back down under pressure. Later, when the incident was long past, he resigned from the club. At the national convention, most of the New Jersey delegates finally supported Nixon, but they wavered right up to the time for the first ballot.

The incident was not unlike that raised in 1956 and 1960 when the Democrats accused Nixon of having signed a deed on his house in Northwest Washington which had a restrictive convenant against selling to blacks. The covenant had long before been declared unconstitutional, and similar deeds had been signed by Democrats and other Republicans who lived in the area. But an issue is an issue in a campaign.

In 1968 when some of the Nixon strategists had tried to raise the covenant issue against Hubert Humphrey, I blocked the effort, pointing out that Nixon was not blameless.

In another incident during this time of political caution, Howard "Bo" Calloway, our newly appointed Southern regional campaign director, suddenly became a national figure.

Calloway, an attractive young textile manufacturer, had exemplified to us the new spirit of Republicanism in the South as a congressman. Only two years earlier he had come close to winning the governorship of solidly Democratic Georgia. Later, as Secretary of the Army, he again gained national attention because of his efforts with the U. S. Forest Service to enlarge a Utah ski resort he owned in part. The conflict-of-interest charge appeared political again.

I first heard of a speech Calloway had made in Jackson, Mississippi, when Governor Rockefeller picked up on it in an address to the National Press Club in Washington. In this and in subsequent speeches, in the Northeast, Rockefeller called upon Nixon to repudiate Calloway and his Jackson statement. Rockefeller hit hard.

As best we could determine, Calloway had said, "Perhaps we can get George Wallace on our side. That's where he belongs."

Rockefeller pointed out that Southern senators Strom Thurmond and

John Tower were already avowed Nixon supporters, and he indicated that the Calloway statement had racist overtones because it implied that there was little difference between the views of Nixon and Wallace.

I knew we had a problem because to denounce Calloway could open the door to an erosion of conservative Southern delegates, possibly to Ronald Reagan. And yet to be tied to anything racist would endanger Nixon's position in the big states of the Northeast and probably Illinois.

I did not believe Calloway was racist, and I do not in any way believe that now. It was a case of a political misstatement by one not schooled in national politics. We quickly got Calloway off the speaking circuit, and Nixon refused to denounce him—thus refusing to bow to Rockefeller.

The problem caused us to speed up anti-Wallace strategy already in the making.

In Lansing, Nixon said he had been "in politics for twenty-two years and never had a racist in my organization, and I don't have any now."

He went on to say that the Wallace appeal was "in the direction of the racist element . . . such an appeal wouldn't be made by either of the two national parties. We will be able to present the American people a choice, but we will not divide the country on a race basis."

We went on to quickly implement three parts of our strategy.

1. Nixon said he would campaign heavily in the big cities; and in Philadelphia, with basketball superstar Wilt Chamberlain at his side, he met with black leaders.

2. We emphasized what we believed Calloway really meant and certainly what we believed: Wallace eventually would lose votes he now commanded because Nixon would emphasize emphatically that a vote for the Alabama Governor would be wasted and might help a liberal Democratic candidate win.

3. In Philadelphia, Nixon also announced that if the election were deadlocked and moved to the House of Representatives for a decision on who would be President, he would rule out any deal with the third-party candidate.

As the convention drew nearer, editorials and comments by columnists became more and more a matter of concern.

There were favorable columns by David Lawrence, Jack Kirkpatrick, John Chamberlain, and others. Because we anticipated them, they bolstered spirits, but we expected those supportive comments. In the same way we paid little attention to Max Lerner's description of Nixon as "an iceberg in seventh incarnation." A column by George Packard III, Washington chief for the Philadelphia *Bulletin,* made a case that the Nixon camp contained few intellectuals. He cited examples of intellectuals as Henry Kissinger, then assisting Rockefeller, and Dr. Zbigniew K. Brzezinski, assisting Humphrey. That shook up few in the inner circle.

There was more concern over a July 19 column by Rowland Evans and Robert Novak where they claimed that Republicans were worried that Nixon was reverting to shooting from the hip again. They cited two incidents as a "miniaturized version of killing bloopers of the past, containing seeds of potential trouble in the immediate future."

The statements they labeled as "bloopers" concerned an airplane seized by the Soviets and a Supreme Court appointment.

First, Nixon had toughly branded the seizure of an American aircraft a "flying *Pueblo*" incident. As events turned out, the Soviets quickly released the American airplane, making the Nixon comment sound petulant, according to Evans and Novak.

Then, Earl Warren announced that he would step down as Chief Justice of the Supreme Court, and President Johnson said he would appoint the Warren successor. Nixon strongly opposed this proposal by Johnson, which would have major effect on the philosophy of the court. Nixon said the appointment should wait for the next President, and privately he looked upon the timing of the move by Warren as being vindictive because of the Chief Justice's known dislike for him.

Johnson announced that his choice to succeed Earl Warren as Chief Justice was Associate Justice Abe Fortas, who is Jewish. The religious aspect made this Nixon comment politically sensitive, particularly when coupled wtih the Baltusrol incident. This became a nonissue when Fortas resigned in face of charges of conflict of interest. Earl Warren stayed on and eventually was succeeded by Nixon appointee Warren Burger.

Evans and Novak were looked upon by the campaign staff as independents who could start a negative snowball rolling. At this critical point and brief as the incidents were in the news, they created fear within our staff.

What really angered Nixon and his staff was an editorial in the New York *Times* on June 19. The *Times* obviously was strongly for Rockefeller and against Nixon, but it was unlikely that the *Times* had the power to change the mind of any of the pro-Nixon delegates, most of whom disliked the paper's editorials almost as much as did Nixon. The only power the *Times* had in this Republican fight was to influence others who wrote editorials elsewhere or who commented on the news for the networks. That power, of course, is considerable.

The June 19 editorial was headed "The Negative Campaigners." The article had one paragraph rapping Humphrey for "a silence not of words but fresh ideas," and it praised Gene McCarthy.

Richard Nixon, it said, is "standing four-square for silence."

"If the former Vice President sticks to this policy of no confrontation with his chief rival from June into August's convention, the real meaning will be no confrontation with the American people—who will have the final say in November.

"A candidate who goes into dead storage nearly two months before the delegates convene is downrating both the interest and intelligence of the electorate. He is relying on the weighted opinions of a few thousand polled persons and the stampeding effect that these secret surveys will have upon the professional politicians."

This editorial and others hardened the Nixon view against the *Times* to such an extent that neither when he was a candidate nor when he was President was I ever able to get him to meet with the editorial board of the newspaper. Later when pressmen briefly struck the *Times* to protest an anti-Vietnam editorial, Nixon was personally elated and sent Chuck Colson to New York to congratulate the strikers.

The reaction to the editorial which surprised me most came from Ray Price, a mild-mannered and highly sophisticated former New York *Herald Tribune* editorial writer and editor, who was one of our principal speech writers.

Within hours after he saw the editorial, Price wrote a semiprivate letter to John B. Oakes, *Times* editorial-page editor. He opened with "There's no softer way to say it: I've frankly been appalled lately at the *Times* editorial comments on the Presidential campaign. It seems to me they've crossed the bounds of editorial license, and entered the realm of a revisionist rewriting of recent history."

On the issue of "weighted opinions," Price said:

"For Heaven's sweet sake! Who's playing to the polls? Who's let it be known that his [Rockefeller's] whole strategy is to appeal to the 'weighted opinions' of a few thousand polled persons in an effort to overrule the overwhelming verdict of the primaries? . . .

"Dead storage . . . silence . . . Where the hell do you get this? For four solid months while Rockefeller sat like the silent sphinx of the Palisades, Nixon held press conferences, answered questions from college audiences, submitted himself to Q and A before the nation's editorialists, went on interview shows, did a live telethon, made speeches, and covered virtually every issue before the American people in greater depth than any candidate of either party."

We knew, of course, that the aim of the *Times* and of the Rockefeller strategists was to engage Nixon in some type of debate which would put the New York governor on equal campaign footing with the former Vice-President.

Nixon resisted the temptation to debate.

We had two other major concerns during that low-key period of campaigning.

The veterans of the Nixon campaign understood that despite the physical stamina and discipline which the candidate showed outwardly, he eventually would become exhausted and prone to error. At that point his television appearance would become poor and his speeches pallid. The ultimate example of an exhausted Nixon was in his appearance for the "last press conference" following his loss in the 1962 governor's race.

Haldeman did a thorough job in reserving some time for Nixon's privacy during the primary campaign swings, but the fact was that Nixon had been on the political trail constantly since early January when he announced his candidacy in a letter to the voters of New Hampshire. With the trials of a convention and, hopefully, a full race for the presidency facing us, it was important to give Nixon some measure of rest and a slower pace, particularly during July.

Our other concern was the growing Reagan effort.

Most of the Eastern press was acutely aware of the Rockefeller campaign which was heavily financed and included major full-page newspaper ads and frequent television spots. They wrote about it in great volume.

Perhaps more dangerous to us was the Reagan campaign, which, while undeclared, nonetheless was being waged with full fervor. Both Rockefeller and Reagan hoped to gain enough delegates to run the convention into several ballots when some of the formal commitments to Nixon would expire and the race could become wide open.

Many of the Southern and Western delegates committed to Nixon felt more comfortable with the Reagan philosophy, but Reagan had moved late. Still, Reagan was a growing factor in the race.

Our strongest weapon during the final month before the convention was a highly systematized program of keeping close touch with every delegate and alternate. The method used had been developed highly successfully by the Eisenhower forces in their convention battle with Senator Robert Taft, and it had been employed less thoroughly in the Nixon convention effort in 1960 and in the Goldwater convention landslide in 1964.

The Nixon file system on delegates, set up under John Mitchell in 1968, was the most thorough I had seen. It was organized by Richard Kleindienst, assisted by Murray Chotiner, young Robert C. Odle, and others.

The effort was aimed at taking a constant political pulse on the feelings of each delegate: Who needed to be talked to more, and by whom? Who were the friends most likely to influence the delegate? What was known of the philosophy of the delegate, and what had been his past political activities and affiliations?

The elaborate charts and files for these activities were moved to Miami on the eve of the convention, and charts for daily reports on each delegate were organized in a renovated solarium at the top of the headquarters Hilton Hotel in Miami Beach. The solarium was guarded with security precautions rivaling those around the situation room in the White House basement. We tried to think of everything.

As a precaution to prevent any possible break in staff or delegate communications, I purchased daily time on a closed-circuit television system which was aired into most rooms of the Miami Beach hotels. We instructed delegates to watch the channel periodically, and occasionally we featured interviews with a cross section of delegates. But in an emergency, we could have used the cable to communicate directly to delegates.

Months and years of campaigning had brought Nixon to the point where, at the start of the convention, we felt we had a few votes in excess of the 670 necessary for nomination on the first ballot.

Early press policies helped him reach this point. During the first six months of 1968, he was informal and he was more available to the press than he normally was. He had long conversations with Theodore White, the author; he talked with columnists and reporters even in small communities; he gave in-depth interviews to John McDermott of the Miami *Herald* and to *U.S. News & World Report*. He dropped that ready and successful availability as the convention approached and in the general election.

In the final days before the convention, Nixon moved to the quiet of Montauk on the eastern tip of Long Island and began preparation of the acceptance speech he would make before what would be his largest television audience to date.

It was up to his staff to retain the convention lead he had built, holding off the frantic late efforts of both the Rockefeller and Reagan forces.

In my view, the two most important factors in retaining that lead and thus gaining a first-ballot victory were (1) a Gallup Poll issued a week before the convention and (2) the thoroughly organized Kleindienst group, which never lost touch with key delegates.

Rockefeller's hope was that he could convince the delegates that only he could win in November. The convention eve Gallup Poll showed that Nixon, after trailing for months, finally had emerged as doing better than Rockefeller against either Humphrey or McCarthy. I moved quickly.

My early press operation at the convention thoroughly exploited this break and thus blunted the main Rockefeller argument at that critical time. A Harris Poll favorable to Rockefeller came out a few days later and the governor countered with it. But it was too late to gain the same attention and, at best, the delegates only accepted the fact that the polls were uncertain.

The Mitchell-Kleindienst delegate operation found erosion here and there, but it was able to convince other noncommitted delegates that Nixon would win on the first ballot, and they could join now and be a part of that winning effort. As in sports or debates, people usually remember only who won or who lost. But the margin was to be close in 1968, and we knew it.

Nixon gained 692 votes on the first ballot, 22 more than the necessary 670. We had been tipped earlier that there was some sort of a secret agreement between Rockefeller and Reagan. We learned later that they had agreed neither would withdraw early. Rockefeller won 277 votes on the first ballot and Reagan 182.

There were large "favorite son" votes for Rhodes of Ohio (55), Romney of Michigan (50), Case of New Jersey (22), and Carlson of Kansas (20).

What would have happened with them in later ballots and what would have happened to the committed Nixon votes can only be speculated upon.

But the fact is that had Nixon not won on the first ballot, he might not have been the Republican nominee and thus, eventually, the President of the United States.

3

Director of What?

I CAME VERY CLOSE to not being on the platform for the inaugural of 1969.

There was no question whether I could have a job in the new administration, but there was a real question during the period between the election and the inauguration whether the job offered me would be one I would accept. The President-elect's concept of press organization was different from what I had anticipated.

I had been a friend and a working colleague of the President-elect since 1946 when he first ran for Congress, a matter of political seniority equaled only by Murray Chotiner, who also had worked in every Nixon campaign but was not as prominent in 1968. I expected to be one of the first named to the White House staff. But that was not the case.

During the campaign of 1968, Haldeman, Ziegler, and I sometimes would walk back late from the Park Avenue headquarters to our apartments at the Wyndham Hotel and would stop off occasionally for a beer or a late dinner at the old Reuben's Restaurant on Fifty-eighth Street.

We argued over the candidate's relations with the press and the lack of contact with some of the political leaders who would call me. It seemed to me that too many of the decisions we were debating were being made by Haldeman. I said so. I did not have the ready access to the former Vice-President I needed or had been accustomed to. He was too isolated.

The situation varied by the day, but it was a harbinger of what was to come.

I sometimes found Haldeman checking telephone calls to the candidate and questioning me as to why I had tried to phone Nixon directly, not through him. He felt that was how the system should work—through him. We were friends and respected each other but we disagreed on this all-important point of procedure.

I was one of the primary points of contact for those who had been the President's friends and supporters for years past, but the tendency in the new-era campaign of 1968 was to diminish contact with them and give priority to newcomers on the scene, many of whom also were talented and eager but often politically unknowledgeable.

As we neared the election, I found that Haldeman and John Ehrlich-man were reading books on theories of White House staff organization. And as I looked around, I found that the only four senior advisers who understood the White House staff structure thoroughly were Bryce Harlow, Bob Finch, Rose Mary Woods, and me. We were being consulted little. Additional help and advice were soon to be coming from Bob Gray, who had served on the Eisenhower staff but was not fully active during the campaign.

Despite his Washington experience, it appeared that Nixon had not carefully studied the staff system.

In today's government, most public attention is given to the selection of cabinet members, but with the possible exceptions of the Attorney General and the Secretaries of State, Defense, Treasury, and HEW, the senior staff is far more important to the efficient and imaginative operation of the presidency. This was to become even more apparent later in the Carter White House. And in some cases even the above-named cabinet positions do not figure that strongly in policy decisions.

Nixon's key concept of the White House staff seemed to be that he wanted a strong National Security Council adviser and that he did not want a Sherman Adams or a Jim Hagerty—referring to the Eisenhower strong chief of staff and strong press secretary. He liked those men personally—but he wanted a weaker staff. He was vague about how that would relate to the cabinet and the presidency.

The transition of power between President Johnson and the Nixon crew during the period between the election and the inauguration was hailed by us and by the press as the smoothest in history. Lyndon Johnson did his best to make it that way, but even so, the confusion within the ranks of the incoming administration was greater than was realized publicly.

With much fanfare we announced that the President-elect was seeking the best talent in the country to fill key posts in the new administration. State and county political leaders throughout the nation were urged to send in their recommendations. Heads of various Nixon committees, past government officials, newspaper editors, and even the public were solicited. The names were to be placed in a computer which would analyze qualifications and give those making the key decisions ready access to the names of qualified candidates. The job data bank was headed by Harry Flemming, a young businessman whose father, Arthur Flemming, had been Secretary of HEW in the Eisenhower administration and who later became a White House adviser on the aged.

We soon discovered several problems. The number of appointments the President could make in the gigantic bureaucracy was limited, realistically, to only about two thousand. We were not prepared to fully utilize the computer, and the result was that thousands of the recommendations which poured in were never scrutinized, and few of those who sent them in were thanked for their trouble. In the long run, the plan to make more leaders across the country feel they had a voice in the formation of a new administration backfired, and it created far more embarrassed and angry citizens than pleased friends. This was a disaster.

One heavily sought after position was Secretary of the Navy, a position now subcabinet in level. I personally had friends of three well-qualified candidates from San Diego urging appointment of their men, but that was only a small part of the pressure from all over the country. The eventual appointee was John Chaffee, an able Republican who had been governor of a largely Democratic state, Rhode Island.

Johnson provided temporary office space for the transition team only a block from the White House and made his staff available for consultation. He remembered vividly the bitterness in the transfer of power from President Truman to President Eisenhower and, in turn, from Eisenhower to President Kennedy. Truman and Eisenhower barely spoke even when they met at the West Door of the White House for the long ride up Constitution Avenue to Capitol Hill for the inaugural ceremonies. Johnson set high new standards.

Nixon accepted the space provided by Johnson in the new Executive Office Building on Seventeenth Street in Washington, but he chose to make his personal headquarters in New York's Pierre Hotel, a few short blocks from his apartment. Vice-President Agnew and I commuted to the Transition Office, as did Harry Flemming.

It was quickly apparent to me that an inner clique had been formed on the Nixon staff, dominated heavily by Haldeman, Ehrlichman, and the traveling staff. From the campaign headquarters staff only John Mitchell had a key role in selecting members of the new administration, although some recognition was given to the views of Leonard Garment and Peter Flanigan. While the traveling staff and Mitchell, augmented by Bryce Harlow and Bob Finch, were in Key Biscayne immediately after the election pondering the problems of organization, I helped set up the quarters at the Pierre, including the press offices and briefing rooms. I was not a part of the key staffing discussions.

When it came to announcements and briefings at the Pierre head-quarters, it was Ziegler who was running them while I shuttled between Washington and New York making arrangements with the Johnson staff and the outgoing government departments for the transfer of power—particularly where it applied to the press staffs in the executive departments.

After much study, I decided we should revamp all of the government press offices except three. I urged retention of Bob McClosky, an extremely able State Department spokesman, who then served with Secretaries of State Rogers and Kissinger and eventually was appointed an ambassador.

The incoming Secretary of Defense, Mel Laird, had an intense interest in news relations and at first planned to appoint as his press assistant either Jerry Friedheim, an assistant to Senator Tower, or Richard Capen, a Copley News Service executive. I convinced him that both men could be groomed for key roles, but, capable as they were, it was a mistake to toss them to the Pentagon lions too soon. We agreed on the retention of Daniel Z. Henkin, a Johnson administration veteran, and Friedheim and Capen were brought aboard and groomed to eventually take over the press operation and congressional relations, respectively. Friedheim now is president of the American Newspaper Publishers Association, and Capen is a senior vice-president of the Knight Newspapers.

The third man I retained was Joe Laitin. Every administration needs someone whose seniority goes beyond any one President. It seemed to me that Laitin, once a Hollywood press agent, had been in Washington forever, sometimes in other parts of the executive branch. He knew the bureaucracy, and I kept him with the President's economic advisers and the Management and Budget Office. The old pro kept a low profile and was invaluable. He wound up in the Carter administration having served five Presidents, most of whom did not know him personally.

Cliff Miller, a longtime Los Angeles public relations executive, was brought into New York several times, mainly to consult with Ziegler. He was a capable outside counselor and continued to serve in that role later in the White House, but in this period he often was caught in a cross fire between Haldeman and me.

Bob Finch and I conferred frequently, analyzing what was happening. He is unique among all the politicians I have known. He has great political intuition, or "gut reactions," about feelings of people and issues. He is so highly principled that he turned down the Vice-Presidency because he thought he was too close a friend of Nixon. Most of all, he is loyal regardless of any pressure. At times in campaigns and in the White House when I was fighting the battle for cooperation with the press, he was my most vocal and effective supporter.

During the campaign and the transition, Finch was Nixon's political philosopher; he was not a part of the power struggle and could look at the problems from the President's point of view with no personal motives. At this point he was the Lieutenant Governor of California. He had won election two years earlier with 100,000 more votes than the candidate for governor, Ronald Reagan, received. Reagan never fully accepted that.

In 1960, Finch and I had developed a system for election night where each of us had input from his own constituencies that enabled us to examine accurately the potential outcome of the election in states which were likely to be close and which were large enough to determine the election.

Finch would be in contact with a few frank political leaders of the key states. He was aided by Murray Chotiner, who had his own very reliable political contacts. I would check with editors in key cities such as Chicago or Columbus, Ohio, to see where the early returns were coming from and assess what areas of strength or weakness were yet to report publicly; election-night decisions and comments require all the sophisticated information one can make available.

Television and the wire services have developed finely their program of early computerized reactions from key precincts which project accurately to their viewers the results in most states. In states which will be close, their early precinct checks sometimes become meaningless, and they are dependent on actual detailed results which can come in late. The Finch-Klein personal projection system enabled us to know the exact moment when we had lost in 1960 (Minnesota went for Kennedy) and the exact time when we were assured of the 1968 victory (a combination of a few late states, including California).

On every election night that I have been with Nixon, he has preferred to sit in isolation, sometimes watching television, making his own calculations on the election results. He occasionally chatted with his family, but basically Pat Nixon and their daughters visited with a few friends and dropped in on the candidate only occasionally, leaving him to his inner thoughts.

Finch, Chotiner, and I (and in 1968 Haldeman and Ehrlichman) would visit with him mainly to give him our projections and to listen to whatever thoughts he wanted to relay. The parties went on in the hotel, but for us it was a tough, solemn, solitary night each time.

On election night in 1968, Ziegler and others on my staff coordinated with the press in the ballroom of the Waldorf-Astoria while a few of us worked on the results from upper stories of the Waldorf Towers. Ziegler was my liaison with the networks, and periodically throughout the night, under his guidance, I would drop into the network booths or to the main press room to give our impression as to what was happening in a very close election. We even had dozens of foreign reporters and I had Pier and Tania Talenti, friends who spoke eleven languages, to handle their queries. I was candid about trends as I saw them, and I never lost confidence, despite network projections which forecast a Humphrey victory early in the evening.

My wife, Marge, ran a hospitality suite on the sixth floor where many of our friends from San Diego and other political and press associates dropped by during the long evening. I was there only long enough to say hello a couple of times and to take a quick half-hour nap at about 3 A.M. before going on TV again, this time in the early hours with John Hart of CBS.

Among those who were back and forth between the VIP reception area and our suite were Mr. and Mrs. C. Arnholt Smith, major contributors. My old newspaper, the San Diego *Union,* later reported in its social column that the Smiths spent part of the evening with the Nixons. But to the best of my knowledge, the closest they came was our suite.

Where they were that evening became politically important later when Smith's impressive financial empire in San Diego collapsed, and he became the target of varied federal criminal and civil indictments and civil lawsuits. Most of the news stories described him as one of Nixon's closest friends, who had spent election night in the candidate's suite. The truth was that both were friends of Nixon, but Smith's wife, Helen, was the closer friend and she had raised major money for Nixon in 1962 and in 1968. Smith himself was a more casual Nixon associate and fund raiser who was politically active in San Diego—not an intimate who spent the evening watching election results with him.

When the long night of the 1968 election was over, Nixon went to the stage of the Waldorf ballroom and made his acceptance comments. There were two sentimental highlights. One came when he displayed a crewel-work presidential seal given to him that night by daughter Julie. The other came from an idea of Bill Safire's. Dick Moore, a veteran of television management at KTTV in Los Angeles, had joined the campaign to spot color items. In Deshler, Ohio, during a train whistle-stop he had noted a teen-age girl carrying a sign which said, "Bring us together." As we flew from Los Angeles to New York on election day, Safire discussed several ideas with me and then on his own initiative drafted comments, first to be made if the election were lost and then others to be made if we won. "Bring us together" was his winning theme, and he gave it to me to be sure the candidate had it as he composed what he might say.

The comment provided an inspirational early tone for the victorious Nixon. But the theme of togetherness fell apart later as Vietnam and Watergate tore the nation apart.

When Nixon had completed his early morning statement, he invited all of us to his suite for a champagne victory brunch. He was tired but relaxed and more gracious than I had seen him in years. He finally had it made. The word was passed that he and the traveling staff would depart early and fly to Key Biscayne. Arrangements for a plane had been made with President Johnson, although the aircraft turned out to be the one part of the White House fleet of Air Force jets which had no windows. We later called the converted jet tanker "Air Force Five."

As Nixon started to depart, he stepped over to me and said, "Pat and the girls have been telling me how terrific you have been on television. I want you to do all of the television you can for us. This will be a major part of your assignment."

I knew he also had seen me on television, but in his unfathomable way, he wanted to put the assessment on the part of his family.

While Bob Finch was with the President in Key Biscayne and I was in New York, we talked daily, and it was apparent to me that there was confusion about the cabinet, the future staff, and particularly arrangements regarding the press.

He told me of the Nixon decision to have only a low-key press operation in the White House. When Haldeman discussed it with me later, he said that Ziegler was young, and he planned to pay him only eighteen thousand annually as a press aide, not a press secretary. I was disappointed in the concept and in my own role. I had envisioned coming in as a strong press secretary.

What Haldeman outlined was part of the scenario to avoid a Jim Hagerty image and play down the press role. Either Haldeman was downplaying the point to me or he had no idea of the major role that salary levels and job status and authority had in determining the respect one would receive from the press working in the White House hall of mirrors. I told him that was a ridiculous idea and later repeated the conversation to an amazed Ziegler. Together we went to bat for Ziegler, and a few weeks later, he was given the upgraded title of press secretary with the appropriate salary. Still the job was downgraded in the Haldeman-Nixon mental concept. They wanted someone they could control.

Many of the reporters who were to cover Nixon and Ziegler had remained in Washington during most of the campaign. They were the White House regulars who had continued to report on President Johnson, and thus they speculated that Ziegler, a former advertising man, would last only sixty or ninety days. They underestimated his staying power and failed to recognize that Haldeman and Nixon originally pictured a press secretary in a weaker press aide role than had been the White House custom.

Haldeman knew he could control Ziegler at that point, but I was his puzzle. It was clear that he and the President wanted me to direct some government or political press operations, but they were uncertain as to what the role would be and how it would operate. To them I must have resembled a loose cannon on their ship's deck, someone they could not control but who was unquestionably loyal and outspoken. I was the only person they had who had wide political and news experience and who was trusted by newsmen and politicians at all levels.

One suggestion was that I organize an operation working from a base as one of the two top people in the Republican National Committee. I rejected that as too partisan.

Quietly I discussed the government press operations with several of my friends who had served previous Presidents as press secretaries—Hagerty, Pierre Salinger, George Christian, George Reedy, and later Tom Johnson. They pointed to a basic need to coordinate all of the government's widespread press activities, something which never had been done. That fitted my idea of what I wanted to do in part.

As speculation grew regarding my plans, I also began to receive inquiries from some media organizations and other corporations as to whether I was interested in discussing working with them instead of government.

From Key Biscayne, Finch advised me that there was still confusion about staff organization. The first appointment had been announced for Rose Mary Woods, who had been Nixon's personal and executive secretary since 1951, when he was a senator. No one was more capable or more deserving.

I told Finch that I thought I could best bring the indecision on my role to a head either way by making my own power play on television. He concurred.

Following the Nixon instructions to appear more on television, I had accepted an invitation to appear on the nationwide broadcast of the CBS news show "Face the Nation" on November 16, 1968. Finch alerted the President-elect and the staff at Key Biscayne to watch the show. I knew that if I handled the show well, I would be in the driver's seat to dictate my own terms. If I did not do well—we would see.

I planned carefully what points I wanted to make and prepared for the adversary questions of the news panel.

The late Merriman Smith, United Press's all-time star reporter, summarized this part of the show with this story:

"Richard M. Nixon will exercise 'a very personalized leadership' as President in an effort to win the nation's confidence, according to a top aide and confidant.

"Herbert G. Klein, who directed communications for the Nixon campaign, said that Nixon, like any new Chief Executive, must give top priority to establishing individual trust and support among the people.

" 'I think he has to do this through a very personalized leadership,' Klein said in a television interview."

As the interview moved forward, I was inwardly pleased to find that the questions seemed wide-ranging. This gave me the opportunity to win or lose my point with the President by displaying my style and my perception of issues ranging from congressional politics to future relations between Nixon and the black community. I had not consulted with anyone in Key Biscayne as to how I would answer whatever questions were thrown at me, but I was highly conscious of the fact that besides the normal broad "Face the Nation" audience, I had a special jury which was auditing me. No one else from the new administration had ventured on national television since the election.

In answer to questions on the show, I pointed out that the image the Democrats had painted of Nixon during the Eisenhower years as "a man who uses subterfuge and stratagems" had not been a problem during the 1968 campaign. "There was very little emotional opposition to Mr. Nixon. The emotionalism was mostly in terms of issues—Vietnam and other things." I wanted to start early destroying any image that "Tricky Dick" was in the White House. I added that Nixon had conducted his campaign "at a very high level."

It was generally agreed that Nixon had received few black votes and yet his theme now was to bring the country back together. I was asked how Nixon expected to win support from blacks and other minorities. I had expected the question and answered: "You don't win the confidence by motorcades through the areas, but you win it by concrete programs. The way you get at them is to prove yourself through practical programs. Probably the most dynamic program proposed during the campaign was the program for black capitalism." I added that there was a need to implement the programs and to work with responsible black leaders. This followed the campaign thesis that the blacks no longer felt they could trust campaign rhetoric.

I felt I would be asked to analyze critical moments in the election and the future of Nixon legislative proposals with a heavily Democratic Congress.

The analytical question centered around the effect of President Johnson's dramatic halt in the bombing of North Vietnam five days before the election. This was a delicate area because we did not want to offend the President at this time, and I did not want to leave an opening for a discussion of whether or not Anna Chennault, a major Nixon supporter with influential connections in Asia, had privately exerted any influence on South Vietnam to reject the bombing halt. I was reasonably sure that Mrs.

Chennault had at least attempted to urge the South Vietnamese to ignore the Johnson move, but I was not certain of the answer.

Basically, I said that had the bombing halt "come forty-eight hours later it might have made a greater impact." The immediate political impact was to give "a major shot in the arm to Mr. Humphrey and Democratic workers," I opined. I then expressed the belief that the South Vietnamese rejection of the plan had nullified the effect and made it appear that Johnson's decision was unilateral and political and thus the election trend "started swinging back to us." There fortunately was no Anna Chennault question.

I predicted a solid future working relationship with the Congress because of Nixon's old alliances on Capitol Hill and because the presidential race indicated the voters wanted "conservative, middle-of-the-road politics."

After the first few questions, I felt relaxed and confident that I was giving solid answers both from the viewpoint of making news for "Face the Nation" and from the viewpoint of those watching in Key Biscayne.

I watched the monitor clock in the studio carefully and when we reached the final two minutes, I decided to drop my message to Key Biscayne. I quickly answered a question on Vietnam and then turned to a brief discussion of my own plans. The Associated Press led the story this way:

"Herbert G. Klein, a top campaign aide of President-elect Richard M. Nixon, said today he has been offered a 'policy role' in the new administration but is not sure whether he will take it.

"Klein was Nixon's Manager of Communications during the campaign, a job which included dealing with newsmen. There had been speculation that he would be named presidential press secretary, but Nixon has now indicated there will be no press secretary as such.

"In a radio-TV interview (CBS, Face the Nation) Klein said he and Nixon have been friends and associates since 'we got out of the Navy' and that he would like to 'have a role with him if it were structured right.'

" 'Otherwise, I would have to go back into private enterprise,' Klein said.

"He did not specify just what he meant by the term 'structured right.' "

A few minutes after we went off the air, the White House operator called with a connection to Key Biscayne. It was Haldeman, who was bubbling with enthusiasm as he congratulated me on the program. Then he said the President-elect does not want you to make any move until we get back in midweek and can sit down and talk to you.

Ziegler called a few minutes later, cautioning me as a friend not to make any rash statements or accept any offers. He said the press suddenly was asking what I had meant. In Key Biscayne the President-elect had heard my message loud and clear.

In the next few days, I put together my thoughts on how my role could be "structured right."

Basically, I would report directly to the President. I would direct government press operations other than Ziegler's office. I would supervise television appearances for the executive branch and would be the overall television spokesman. I would be a part of all cabinet meetings, and I would develop a new kind of liaison between the White House and the newspapers and broadcast stations in the country.

I discussed this extensively with Finch and Haldeman; we then arranged a Saturday afternoon meeting with Nixon at the Pierre Hotel.

Finch, Haldeman, Ehrlichman, Bryce Harlow, and Ziegler joined Nixon and me for the discussion. In one part of the room television was on with the sound turned down as Army and Navy went into the last quarter of their game in Philadelphia.

Nixon listened carefully to my plan and appeared enthusiastic about it. He was particularly interested in the television aspect and asked that I put emphasis on it.

I watched the time carefully because I knew that the traditional game between the University of Southern California and UCLA would be next on television. I also knew that Nixon would be anxious to get home to watch the game with David Eisenhower and Julie, and my wife and I had invited Haldeman, Finch, and the other senior staff members who were alumni of the two schools to watch the game at our Wyndham Hotel apartment suite.

We had covered the ground of job description I wanted, and Nixon looked up and said, "What should your title be?"

I had not thought about this a lot. I had picked the title of manager of communications for the campaign job, but I felt that the word "manager" would not fit a White House position. Government already was accused of seeking to manage the news.

With game time only about ten minutes off, I paused briefly and then answered, "Director of communications."

Nixon agreed readily, and we broke up the meeting to make it to the television sets in time for the kickoff.

USC, my alma mater, also won.

To my later amazement, "director of communications," the term I had quickly improvised for the job, became a common title in state governments and corporations within a short time.

My appointment was announced a few days later by Ziegler. During the press conference which followed, I explained my desire to develop an open administration and to provide the kind of access which would help restore credibility to government. In the process, I made a statement which I then believed but which I later had reason to regret.

"Truth will be the hallmark of the Nixon administration," I said.

That was correct for the first years, and although most of the press now has forgotten the sentence, I have not.

Anything new in the media area puzzles the newsmen and brings out speculation. A "director of communications" brought press questions and speculations. Headlines heralded me as the new press czar. Was there something diabolic in playing down the role of the press secretary and then announcing someone who would supervise all government information policy?

The reporters and editorial cartoonists wondered and speculated on what my power would be. They raised legitimate questions, but they also used this as a way to play down Ziegler and speculate on the President-elect's novel idea that he would not have a press secretary in the traditional sense.

The speculation was good, I reasoned, because the press legitimately should be the watchguard against any superpower within the government. The result was that I was more acutely sensitive to any violation of traditional freedom of the press, and I also gained additional public attention, which made it easier for me to be accepted as the spokesman for the United States Government.

One highlight came in December when two columnists for Knight News, Vera Glaser and Verna Stephenson, gave a party in my honor and presented me with an oversized poster with my picture under the title "Official U.S. Blabbermouth." Among those who autographed the proclamation were: Jerry and Betty Ford (Ford signed as Republican leader), Senator Mike Gravel of Alaska, Representative Margaret Heckler of Massachusetts, Senator Bob Griffin of Michigan, Vice-President Hubert Humphrey, Senator Vance Hartke of Indiana, Perle Mesta, and a variety of correspondents including Richard Wilson and Clark Mollenhoff of Cowles, Pat Hefferman of Reuters, Paul Martin of U.S. News, and Julius Frandsen of UPI.

I had one embarrassment in regard to the party. I was to meet my wife and daughter, Joanne Mayne (whose husband, Bob, was in Vietnam), in a car below the transition office and rush to the party. I changed from a brown suit to a tuxedo in my office and then discovered that I had forgotten to bring from home a change of shoes. Mine were brown.

As I waited for an elevator in the Executive Office Building, an attorney and old friend, Roemer McPhee from the Eisenhower administration, strolled into the lobby. I looked at his feet and saw black shoes about my size, explained the dilemma, and on the spot we sat down and traded shoes.

In keeping with my pledge for an open administration, I set up Wash-

ington press conferences for each of the new cabinet and key departmental appointees as they were announced in New York.

Only William Rogers, Secretary of State, and Melvin Laird, Secretary
of Defense, were excluded. Their posts were held too sensitive for such
early exposure.

The conferences provided a launching pad to make the appointees better known, and they allowed an avenue for supervised interviews rather
than catch-as-catch-can, which normally is the case.

Walter Hickel, who had left his construction business and the governorship of Alaska to become Secretary of the Interior, had the most
difficult time during the series of introductory press conferences. He had
some press experience at the nominating convention and in Alaska—but
the experience was limited. Two or three reporters in Alaska don't compare to the punch of a hundred Washington newsmen who, in this case,
believed that Hickel as a builder and developer would be a strong foe of
environmentalists. The reporters also had not been reluctant to create this
impression with the news stories. During the stormy news confrontation,
Hickel never got around to explaining what he meant when he said early
in the session that he did not believe in "conservation for conservation's
sake"; thus the statement gained him not only negative press but delayed
his Senate confirmation. When he much later explained and demonstrated
his views on "conservation for conservation's sake," he became a friend of
the environmentalists, and he became even more a hero when he was fired
after a blunt letter to the President on Vietnam.

The most humorous moment was when General George "Abe" Lincoln
arrived as the new head of the Office of Emergency Protection. He had
been a distinguished professor at West Point. He had only a uniform, no
suit, with him, and on one hour's notice he and his wife had to scramble
for new clothes to present him best on television.

We had one scare.

David Kennedy, a veteran Chicago banker, had been appointed Secretary of the Treasury. He was frank and easygoing. When someone asked
him about the gold standard, he answered honestly, saying he thought
change away from the gold standard should be considered. There was silence in the press corps. A second startled reporter followed up to be sure
he had heard right. Kennedy was equally firm.

The future Secretary learned about the problems he could create with
casual speculation as he saw the gold market and the stock market react
strongly to his remarks the next day. But at that point he was an "innocent abroad" with the press.

During that period of transition, there were four appointments which
were to have the most effect on the future of the administration.

Two of the appointees were expected: Arthur Burns, long a Nixon confidant and former chairman of Eisenhower's Council of Economic Advisers, and Bryce Harlow, knowledgeable veteran who also had served on the Eisenhower staff. Burns was named Counselor to the President, cabinet rank. Harlow became the senior congressional liaison officer.

There were two surprises to all of us. Both came from Harvard, a school Nixon professed to despise.

One was Daniel Patrick Moynihan, a liberal Democrat, who had also served as an informal adviser to Presidents Kennedy and Johnson. He was to direct domestic programs.

The second was Henry Kissinger, who also had been a Nixon critic and had worked closely with Nelson Rockefeller for years. Before and during the campaign, Nixon had read some of Kissinger's articles and books on foreign policy and had admired him even while he worked for an early opponent—an opponent who at the right time strongly recommended Kissinger to Nixon.

None of the four ever lost his individuality, and each in his own field of competence contributed greatly to making the first two years of the Nixon administration successful. Of the four, only Harlow understood the indepth intricacies of politics. But each of the four supplied checks and balances in the administration, and they added creativity, which decreased noticeably when Moynihan returned to the Harvard faculty and Burns was appointed chairman of the Federal Reserve Board.

They, along with Finch, provided the soul for the new administration.

Soon after Burns and Moynihan left, the White House changed distinctly and became an organization where hardball replaced political philosophy as the major consideration.

4

The "Last Press Conference"

IN A STRANGE WAY, the defeat of Richard Nixon in the race for governor of California in 1962 eventually became a factor which helped him win the Republican nomination for President in 1968.

A victory over incumbent governor Pat Brown in 1962 would have propelled Nixon into an all-out bid for the presidency in 1964, a year when Lyndon Johnson was unbeatable and Republicans were enamored of Barry Goldwater. Nixon ran for governor with the idea that it would keep him alive politically on the national scene and that it would be a stepping-stone for another run for the presidency. The governorship did not interest him that much. Local issues did not challenge him. This fact was an issue in both the primary and the general elections. He denied such presidential ambitions, as do most candidates. But fact is fact. He had the presidential bug.

The early sixties were years of resurgence for conservatism in the Republican Party, years when the John Birch Society thrived. The hard-line conservative activists looked upon Nixon, a moderate conservative, as a liberal who had no right to contest the new move behind Goldwater. Nixon learned of the full impact of this early in the California primary when he found himself in a bruising battle with a lesser-known conservative legislator, Joe Shell, who refused to back out of the race for the gubernatorial nomination. Shell gained about one third of the votes in the primary—a large number against a man who had carried California when he sought the presidency—and the primary battle wounds never were healed.

Had Nixon won the governorship in 1962, inevitably he would have charged into battle with Senator Barry Goldwater, where, win or lose, the bloodletting was much more likely to lead to political death than anything which happened in 1962.

Nevertheless, Howard K. Smith went on the air after the 1962 election with "The Obituary of Richard Nixon," featuring among others Alger Hiss and Nixon's loyal friend, Murray Chotiner. Equally devastating was print commentary. Richard Starnes's column was headlined "Nixon's Political Suicide" and Max Freedman wrote a column in the Los Angeles *Times*, headlined, "Nixon's Rise, Fall, Warning for Americans."

Every campaign has a formal launching ceremony, but in reality, each starts with a variety of quiet decisions.

The ill-fated Nixon bid for governor started seriously in January 1962 with a long afternoon brainstorming session at the beach home of a prominent California Republican, Margaret Brock. Ten of us were called to the beautiful residence on Trancas Beach, near Malibu, overlooking the Pacific.

There were divergent opinions expressed by Rose Mary Woods, Bob Finch, Earl Mazo, Jack Drown, Ray Arbuthnot, me, and the others.

But as we debated the merits of a Nixon campaign in California, I became convinced that it did not really matter whether I and others came down on one side of the issue or the other. Nixon already had made up his mind. And as he guided the conversations, I could see that his decision was reluctant but, nevertheless, firm. He would run.

The Nixon I have known has always been a "loner." Many in political life are, but I believe the emotional scars of the battle to stay on the ticket in 1952, after the Nixon fund story, had an impact on him which made him feel that he could listen to advice, but basically he had to depend upon his own wits.

The Malibu discussion on the governorship ended as the sun was sinking into the Pacific and darkness was setting in.

Nixon said he would run for governor.

His only hedge was that he wanted to talk with his family on the matter. But in fact he was already discussing the date for a formal announcement and how it would be handled.

We drove down the beach for dinner at a gourmet seafood restaurant, and later I flew back to my home in La Jolla still wondering about the merit of the decision. I had opposed Nixon's running so soon again. I thought he had a national forum anytime. As the nominee of 1960, he was the titular head of the party. But as Nixon turned the conversation toward running, I finally muted my arguments.

Today it is difficult to determine who was for Nixon's running and who was opposed to it. There were others Nixon consulted extensively, including the late Thomas Dewey, Herbert Brownell, Eisenhower's first Attorney General, William Rogers, Nixon's close friend, and two veterans of the Nixon and Eisenhower campaigns, Leonard Hall, his 1960 manager, and J. Clifford Folger, the 1960 finance chairman. Most were from New York, in touch with major party financial powers, and most urged Nixon to run.

Ten months later the campaign ended in defeat on November 6, 1962, and the postmortem came a day later: Nixon's "last press conference."

I have been through election days with candidates and all are painful, win or lose. But this was the first one where I felt certain of defeat, days before the election.

Campaign experience had taught me to accept information I did not want to believe, if it was properly documented. In this case, the polls, the press, and my gut feeling all said the same thing. We would lose.

With all that, there was nothing in Nixon's behavior which prepared me for his confrontation with the press the next morning. On the day of election Nixon was unusually quiet.

Perhaps it would have been better if he had made one of his more usual election excursions. He might have been more relaxed and philosophic on election night and postelection morning.

"Election excursions" can mean a variety of things. For a few candidates the outlet may be a female companion. In the opposite way, for some others, it is a day with the children, trying to alleviate the guilty feeling of having been away on the campaign.

Win or lose, election nights are rarely exuberant occasions for an experienced campaigner. More likely, they provide hours of sober, weary reflections.

For any candidate, election day brings a feeling of uselessness. No more can be done by him or by his equally lonely immediate staff. The voters and the political organizations are now in control.

There is some routine to election day for a major candidate. Inevitably he goes out to the polls early so that his photograph will be flashed across the country as a final reminder to his supporters that their effort in getting out the vote is essential.

The candidate's picture is as routine as the early votes in tiny precincts in New Hampshire, just minutes after midnight. Both are media exercises.

For Nixon, an election excursion usually meant some unpredictable event which took his mind off the voters and relaxed him mentally as he prepared to handle the tension of election night and the morning after.

I first learned of Nixon's election-excursion pattern, and of the loneliness of election day in 1952, when he voted and then disappeared while the nation was determining whether or not he would become Vice-President.

Neither Jim Bassett, then Nixon's press secretary, nor I had the vaguest idea what had happened to him and his friend Bill Rogers after they jumped into a car driven by a Los Angeles policeman. They simply evaporated into the suburbs of Whittier, where he had voted moments before. Even Pat Nixon did not know what had happened to Dick, except she knew he wanted to get away from the press.

After an anxious day of wondering where the missing candidate was, a relaxed Nixon returned to our headquarters at the Ambassador Hotel at six o'clock.

Nixon and Rogers had driven to nearby Laguna Beach, where they purchased swimming trunks and a football. Their election day excursion had been spent swimming and playing touch football with a half dozen Marines from Camp Pendleton. I often wondered what these Marines thought when they turned on television that night or the next day and realized that the dark-haired man ("Dick") they had been knocking down was Vice-President-elect of the United States. Perhaps later they recognized Rogers when he became a member of both the Eisenhower and the Nixon cabinets.

In 1956, there was no problem between Nixon and the press on election day. The candidate for reelection was in Washington.

Our challenge that year revolved around making the most out of Nixon's voting by absentee ballot. I decided that the ideal thing was to vote on Saturday to make the Sunday newspapers, which would be announcing their final election endorsements.

We were on a railroad whistle-stop tour that weekend, traveling through Ohio and Indiana. The nostalgia of whistle-stopping attracts more reporters to a campaign than anything else. Thus the situation was ideal as we approached the small town of Valparaiso, which had the added attraction of being the town where Nixon's father, Frank, had grown up. Two thousand people greeted us at the tiny rail station—including scores who claimed to be Nixon relatives.

As we stopped, I spotted a small old-fashioned depot, ideal for a picture of the Nixons posting their ballots. I asked my assistants Dick Bean and Pete Kaye to look after the press while I personally scouted for this pictorial coup. The station was ideal! Old. Potbellied stove. What better?

No mailbox!

The stationmaster said the only mailbox was at the post office, several blocks away. I dropped that bad, but tempting, idea.

Little things like this become major in a moment of a campaign, and thus the absentee-ballot caper became a drama, even involving the photographers who were eager to make Sunday deadlines.

Columbus, Ohio, had to be the place for the mailing. As we pulled into the railroad complex in Columbus, I had Jack Drown and Ray Arbuthnot, both over six feet tall, posted high on the train steps to spot the first mailbox. They made a sighting, and I stopped the train. The Vice-President made a lackluster platform speech and then I led him through the crowd to the site of the real drama.

He voted in time to make the Eastern Sunday editions.

Three days later, election night, 1956, we had headquarters on one floor of a Sheraton Park Hotel wing in Washington. President Eisenhower and the cabinet occupied the next floor.

About 9 P.M., I accompanied Nixon to the Eisenhower floor to check with the presidential press secretary as to what the plans were to be for an appearance at a rally below. I was surprised to find little buoyance in the crowd. They had expected victory and were waiting for the formalities.

President Eisenhower seemed tired from the day-long wait. He was impatient to get his speech of acceptance and thanks over with and return to the White House. Each return posted on television indicated an Eisenhower landslide.

Jim Hagerty and I conferred with John Eisenhower in a small bedroom away from the crowd and watched television as we talked. The screen flashed to Chicago, but there was no sign of Adlai Stevenson.

Finally, the President strode into the room and asked what we knew about a Stevenson concession. We had no knowledge of it.

Looking at his son, the President said, "John, I am not going to stand here and wait for that fellow. Get the cars organized, and we'll go down as soon as you're ready."

At that moment the television cameras picked up Governor Stevenson entering the massive hall where he was headquartered in Chicago.

"Mr. President," I said, "there's Stevenson now. If you stay, you can watch his remarks while we get ready for your appearance."

Eisenhower looked me in the eye and paused a moment. He turned to leave the room and said, "I haven't watched that fellow during the campaign. I don't see why I should start now." And he didn't.

Television was a major factor in the elections of 1952 and 1956, but with the debates and more sophisticated news coverage, TV really came into its own in the 1960 election. As I awakened after little more than two hours' sleep on the morning of the 1960 election, I looked at the day forebodingly. I was exhausted from our final desperate efforts in the campaign, and yet I knew I had to "psych" myself up for a strong appearance as our spokesman on television that night. I would be interviewed starting with the early return from the East, and the public psychology created by the Nixon team might have a bearing on the votes in California during the final hours of polling. We knew California would be close. My voice was hoarse and as the morning progressed it seemed to be getting worse. I wondered if that was psychological or physical. I feared the loss of the election, but managed to hold strong hope.

In a frantic and almost successful effort to close the gap between Nixon and Kennedy, we had, between Sunday afternoon and 2 A.M. Tuesday election morning, campaigned from Los Angeles to Anchorage, Alaska, to Madison, Wisconsin, to Detroit for a rally and four-hour television show; to Chicago for a live television finale, to Ontario, California (near Los Angeles), for a postmidnight rally—all on one much criticized but desperate swing.

We were up at 6 A.M. election day to be in Whittier again for the pictures of Pat and Dick casting their votes.

There is a touch of democracy in the voting process even for a presidential candidate.

Nixon's polling place was in a small garage. The election officials insisted that the Nixons individually identify themselves by full name and address. And then the candidate and his wife waited and eventually were admitted to voting booths while cameras photographed the entire scene for national television.

As we left the polls, Mrs. Nixon climbed into one car and the Vice-President into another. Immediately I envisioned another election day excursion. Relaxation was fine, but not for a candidate for President, I thought.

Nixon was frank enough with me. "I'm going to try to get away from you and the damn press," he said. "I want to be away from everything today. Understand!"

I protested that it was unfair to the press, which had covered him in all fifty states. What if anything happens? What the hell is he up to now? I asked myself. Almost any answers I had would not measure up to what happened.

He was in no mood to listen. It was election day. "Do what you must," he said, "but I'm going to damn well lose you and the press." He did.

I put the press in a variety of cars and took a pool of key newsmen with me to follow the candidate. I knew I was right and the candidate was wrong. But my driver was no match for the Secret Service driver as we sped through Orange County in an absurd game of chase.

The Vice-President outran us and disappeared. I finally stopped my car at Knott's Berry Farm and sought to placate the angry reporters with a relaxed breakfast. I tried to hide the fact that I was as angry as they were —perhaps angrier.

Back at the Ambassador Hotel in early afternoon I received a call from Don Hughes, the military aide, which explained the 1960 election day caper.

"You'll never guess where we are," he said.

"Try me," I said coldly.

Hughes replied, "We're in Tijuana at the Old Heidelberg Inn having lunch with the mayor of Tijuana." Hughes explained, "We started driving down the coast in silence. The Vice-President was tired, but he seemed elated to lose the press. Then the Vice-President said, 'Let's have lunch in Tijuana. I love Mexican food.'" From a filling station along the way, the Secret Service cleared the trip and had the mayor of Tijuana notified.

I took the number of the phone where Hughes said he was calling, but I really couldn't believe it all. As a San Diego editor I thought I knew Tijuana. Was this one of the good restaurants or one of the places where the girls hang out? I wondered. Or was this all a gag? I found myself sweating. I did not know the Old Heidelberg. And the Tijuana mayor was not the man who was in office when I left in 1959. He was new.

I nervously called my newspaper, the San Diego *Union,* and found that Hughes had given me the mayor's correct name and there was a good clean restaurant by the name Old Heidelberg or something close to that. I tipped off the newspaper and confirmed this again with Hughes. A reporter and photographer from the *Union* reached the restaurant in time to record a toast to Mexican-American friendship. At least I had a reporter there. That was my revenge.

On election day in 1962, the day when the voters of California appeared to have cut off the political life-support system from Richard Nixon, we again tried to appear confident. But the process was difficult. And there was no excursion. Nixon was too tired and tense.

The most accurate and interesting chronicle of the day when the death knell struck comes from the candidate himself.

On a ruled yellow pad, he kept a careful diary of some of his thoughts and his activities.

None of the notes provide a clue as to his final statement to the press. Why? Did he anticipate it? I think it was pure Nixon spontaneity.

At that time I believed Nixon knew the odds against his winning were tremendous. We needed a miracle. But an analysis of his notes indicates to me that I was wrong. He thought he had a chance. The realism that was typical of other election days was not there in 1962.

Nixon started out his diary for the day by noting, perhaps for historians, that he had had dinner the night before with screen stars Dick Powell and June Allyson. They had been with him at the studio of KTTV for an emotional televised election eve appeal to the voters. Nixon wrote that his early breakfast included oatmeal and orange juice. He was up at six-thirty so he and Pat could vote early.

The Nixons then were living in Trousdale Estates, an exclusive Los Angeles area adjacent to Beverly Hills. Their polls were in the garage of a magnificent home. After they had voted and posed for pictures, the lady of the house invited them and a few of us into her home for coffee. She insisted. The coffee turned out to be a full spread of lox and bagels, coffee cake, sweet rolls, and other breakfast delicacies. There were a few guests and the man of the house turned up in a bathrobe, as if he were surprised at the commotion.

Nixon was nervous, ill at ease. Trapped on election day. And so he started off the breakfast with a few of his homespun piano renditions. He relaxed a little and then escaped home. Reporters made notes on the "event" until we all finally worked our way out of the early morning social.

In Nixon's notes on election day, he records the fact that he went to his office about noon and "spent time calling friends."

"Had Chinese food this afternoon—sent by friend David Chow," he noted in methodical fashion.

His first comment on the election was this:

"No prediction—however we won't wait as long as in '60 absentee already being counted."

He was referring to the fact that absentee ballots had given him a 35,000 margin of victory in California in 1960, but the count on them wasn't near completion until late on the day after election. On the morning after the election, as I announced the Nixon concession to Kennedy, I had also predicted that we would carry California because historically absentee votes had gone strongly Republican.

In his 1962 notes, Nixon next observed:

"Maybe won't know result until tomorrow if it stays in this neighborhood."

He still held hope.

"Will not make statement until results are known," he wrote on his yellow pad.

"Only God & people know who is winning."

He showed a little humor as he noted:

"This race will be 50½–49½ somebody will win by a noze [he spelled it that way presumably to amuse himself]—only hope my noze is longer."

Curiously he interrupted the election comments to note, "was going to house but called and found family had already eaten." Earlier he had recorded his dinner—pineapple milk shake and coffee.

"Last results showed we are 10,000 votes ahead," he wrote. "No trend as yet however."

Then came the finale. He recorded in one word what he thought was the political end of the trail line for him:

"Never."

Bob Finch and I had again organized our informal system of analyzing election results as they came in after the polls had closed. Finch checked with politicians he respected in key counties, and I called editors. Murray Chotiner augmented this with his own information.

Finch and I reported to the candidate periodically through the evening. He was immobile and almost silent as he sat mainly by himself, alone with his thoughts.

I had a difficult time with the press.

My young assistants, Ron Ziegler and Sandy Quinn, were no match for the impatient veterans who had the taste of blood on that night and about the best they could do to help me was to join my veteran San Francisco assistant, Jan McCoy, in reporting on queries or comments they heard. It was almost as if the press sensed a kill and was anxious to get at it. Defeat was a bigger story than victory in this case.

I made periodic press conference appearances to give our views on the election. But this time the heat was on full blast and it was difficult to show any optimism. The press diagnosed this as a Brown victory but, recalling 1960, was reluctant to call it clearly. In the Nixon headquarters in the Beverly Hilton Hotel, entertainers such as Johnny Grant sought to keep up crowd spirits. But most eventually sensed defeat. Early evening enthusiasm disappeared rapidly.

In the midst of the hassles with the press, which demanded an audience with the candidate or at least a statement of concession in time to make various national deadlines, I even gave a wrong steer on a camera location to Herb Kaplow, a good personal friend, then of NBC and now with ABC. He was angry, with good cause, and that only added to my personal anguish of the evening. The error was inadvertent.

I last saw Nixon that night about midnight.

He had decided to concede. He even had written out a telegram to Governor Pat Brown.

There still were heavily conservative areas, particularly in Orange and San Diego counties, where the vote was uncounted at that hour. By the time Finch and I reanalyzed the situation and discussed it more with Nixon, I knew the crowd below was small and most of the deadlines of newsmen were past. I put the Nixon concession telegram in my pocket and said, "Why read it now when there's still a slight chance?"

With that we urged the glum and exhausted Nixon to bed and went off to tell the press there would be no announcement from the candidate until morning. I said we would hold a press conference at 10 A.M.

Finch and I found our wives in one of the suites and explained the situation as we each took a stiff drink. Bob joined Ziegler and Quinn and helped us with the last of the angry press. I finally got to bed about 4 A.M. for three hours of sleep. Looking back at the events of postelection day, a little rest was my best decision of the evening.

Shortly after 7 A.M. Bob Finch, Bob Haldeman, and I met over coffee to analyze for the last time the election results. Brown had led through most of the night, but the margin had remained reasonably close. Now it appeared certain that with a voter turnout exceeding 81 percent and with more than 5.5 million votes cast, Brown had been reelected by about 300,000 votes.

The three of us knew Nixon's moods and reactions better than most close friends, and we knew he was exhausted mentally and physically. We had no report on how much he had slept during the night.

We determined to follow the 1960 plan. I would face the press and read the telegrams of concession to the governor and of appreciation to the campaign workers. We discussed our views on the reasons for the Nixon defeat, with the thought that I would give the press this background, as I had in 1960. It also would give us a chance to congratulate Senator Thomas Kuchel, who had bucked the trend and won election by more than 100,000 votes. Interestingly in that election Kuchel, a liberal Republican, won at the same time that Dr. Max Rafferty, a strong conservative, won elections as state superintendent of schools. Rafferty later was to defeat Kuchel in the Republican primary of 1968 and then lose to Alan Cranston.

When we had our plan worked out we found that Nixon was stirring around and looking for coffee. Finch, Haldeman, and I went into his suite to confront him. He knew by then that the results were decisive.

His first words were, "Herb, don't try to talk me into going down and facing the press. Damn it, I am not going to do it."

I assured Nixon that I agreed with him, and I explained what the three of us had decided for the morning. He, meanwhile, was to go home.

We discussed a telegram of thanks to the campaign chairman and to the workers and another telegram to Governor Brown congratulating him and conceding the election.

My notes, scribbled on a Beverly Hilton pad, said:

"Congratulations on your reelection as Governor. I wish you the best in your leadership of the first state in the nation." I later embellished that a little so the final message read:

"Congratulations on your reelection as Governor. I wish you the best in your great honor and opportunity which you now have to lead the first state in the nation."

Nixon was haggard, with the lack of sleep showing particularly in his eyes. He looked bad. But his spirits did not seem as low as I had anticipated. We talked for some time about the campaign, where it had gone well and where it had gone badly. He was philosophical about it. He felt —with some justification, I thought—that he might have won if it had not been for the Cuban missile crisis, which had taken attention away from

the election at a time when he hoped a late sprint would influence undecided voters and allow him to catch up with and perhaps pass Brown.

Our final agreement was that Nixon would leave during the press conference and go home, where his family was waiting. We worked out such
details as having tall assistants at one end of the hall to screen out
onlookers or cameras. Pete Wilson found a back entrance from the Ambassador, where he could be met with a car and then driven home. Not the
best farewell, but we felt he was in no shape to do anything else.

The next time I saw Nixon was minutes later, at my press conference!

After leaving Nixon, Finch, Haldeman, and I discussed in more detail
the strategy for the press conference, and the telegrams were prepared for
Governor Brown and for the workers.

I went down to one of the ballrooms for the 10 A.M. news conference,
where I read the telegrams and had them distributed. I announced that
Nixon was exhausted and would not make an appearance that day. I then
went into the painful discussion of strategy and the election loss and
prepared for questions.

Unknown to me, Finch, or Haldeman, Nixon wandered out of his suite
to thank members of the staff individually. It was an emotional scene with
many of the office girls crying. Nixon then was embraced by an emotional
Italian staff television producer, who also broke into sobs.

Almost simultaneously, Ray Arbuthnot and Jack Drown, two of Nixon's
oldest friends, arrived and learned of our plan for his departure. They
were indignant. One led off by telling the now emotionally upset Nixon,
"You can't let the press chase you out the back door. You ought to face
them or at least go out in your own style!"

That was enough. With that, Nixon headed for the elevator and said
he was going down to make a statement to the press. Finch and Haldeman
were told of the decision, but it was too late.

Haldeman somehow ran down the hotel stairs and got ahead of Nixon
and his entourage. He rushed to the side of the platform where I was
answering press questions. He waved at me frantically, and I took that to
mean that all was clear, that Nixon had departed for home.

I announced that Nixon had left the hotel, but within seconds I heard
scattered applause from the adjacent lobby of the hotel.

No one was as surprised as was I when Nixon stalked onto the platform
and told me he had a comment to make.

"Now that Mr. Klein has made a statement, now that all the members
of the press I know are so delighted that I lost, I would just like to make
one myself," Nixon started.

I looked at Nixon and listened to those rambling first words, and I
knew we were in trouble. I wanted somehow to hide, but there was no

place to go. I knew that the cameras would also catch my expressions, and I tried to mask them, but to little avail.

I tried to think of something I could do as I stood there hopelessly listening to the meandering fifteen-minute tirade, during which Nixon discussed Kennedy foreign and domestic policy, Cuba, little-boylike reflections on his patriotism, newspapers, and television.

In a prizefight ring one can stop the bout by throwing in the towel. Onstage there is the old-fashioned hook to drag off a performer. But at a televised press conference, there is nothing one can do.

I looked out at the reporters and Carl Greenberg, a veteran of California political wars, was easily the most embarrassed. He had been singled out by Nixon as the only reporter on the Los Angeles Times who "wrote it fairly, wrote it objectively."

Several times Nixon said he had "one last thing" to say, and I hoped that was true, but it wasn't.

Finally, he said the ill-tempered words most remembered:

"As I leave you now, I want you to know, just think how much you're going to be missing. You won't have Nixon to kick around anymore because, gentlemen, this is my last press conference. . . ."

I moved to get Nixon offstage quickly.

This time we headed for the front door, where the car now awaited. We were silent until we reached the door. Nixon turned to me and said:

"Damn it, I know you didn't want me to do that. But I had to say it. I had to say it."

I put him in the car and found an old friend, Reavis Winckler, standing a few feet away. He guided me away from the reporters and out a side door onto Wilshire Boulevard, where we walked in silence as I tried to compose myself.

I thought it was the end of Nixon. Strangely, the two public figures who said it was not the end were former President Truman and Governor Brown.

The press reaction came in many forms—all bitter. Even close friends were shocked. An opponent, Mary McGrory of the Washington Star, described it as "exit snarling."

The Los Angeles Times was resentful because it had supported Nixon in every race he had entered. Besides being critical of Times reporters, except Greenberg, Nixon had said the newspaper had reported a flub he had made ("running for governor of the United States") and had left out a last-minute Brown flub ("vote a solid Democratic ticket including Tom Kuchel"). Nixon was accurate there.

My own publisher, James Copley, was angry because Nixon had cited only Greenberg as a fair reporter and he correctly felt that his and many other newspapers had covered the campaign thoroughly and fairly.

Copley joined most of the newspaper publishers who had endorsed Nixon in feeling bitterly resentful over the candidate's references to television as the medium which had kept the record straight.

I too was puzzled by this, because although Nixon believed that television was the strongest medium for a direct candidate appeal, I had listened for hours to him in both 1960 and 1962 as he complained privately over the unfairness of television news reporting.

The next day I tried to smooth the waters by drafting the following statement for Nixon:

"On the morning after the election, I made a concluding statement which has been interpreted by some as a general attack on the press. This was not my intent.

"My irritation has been with some specific reporting but certainly not with the press as a whole. Obviously, in the stress of the hour, I did not make this as clear as I intended to.

"Over the years I have built many friendships with members of the press, and I treasure these greatly. I also would like to reiterate my comment that many of the newspapers have done an outstanding job of reporting.

"In any event, I have concluded after reflection that these remarks were inappropriate and ungraceful, and I desire to withdraw them. At some future time I may perhaps set forth with deliberate care my observations on the role of the press corps in political campaigns."

The statement was never issued by Nixon and I am not sure he ever read it through. For the next three or four days after the election, he was in a daze, sometimes just wandering off in his car for hours. Then, as now, he found it extremely difficult to admit he was just plain wrong.

As I looked back later, I personally forgave Nixon. I thought ironically that his worst outburst was a show of human, spontaneous anger which was contrary to the image of him as a mechanical political figure.

But in many ways, the public statement illustrates clearly the continued feeling of Nixon toward a critical press. He could contain this feeling when he needed to, but later, after his first two years in the White House, he felt no great need to disguise his contempt for the working press, and thus he would issue a variety of outlandish orders which further strained the relationship.

Was the press unfair in 1962? On some occasions, yes, but basically the answer is no.

There were some outstanding veteran reporters covering the California election, some from the Eastern press as well as those from California. Most particularly, it is difficult to fault many individuals in the California press—the press which could have influenced the 1962 vote between Nixon and Brown.

Jack McDowell, then of the San Francisco *Call-Bulletin*, Squire Behrens, dean of the press corps and political reporter for the San Francisco *Chronicle*, and Don Thomas of the Oakland *Tribune* certainly were fair. At one point, I had even tried to hire McDowell away from his newspaper; President Nixon later presented a Freedom Medal to Behrens. No one could accuse Harry Farrell of the San Jose *Mercury News* or Jim Anderson of United Press International of anti-Nixon bias. Maurie Lansberg, then Sacramento bureau chief of Associated Press, and Syd Kossen of the San Francisco *Examiner* showed emotion occasionally, but they were strong, honest newsmen. It would be hard for Nixon to fault the writing of Henry Love of the San Diego *Union* or Ralph Bennett of the San Diego *Evening Tribune*. If in doubt, Love, like McDowell, Behrens, or Farrell, would have favored Nixon.

There were agitators occasionally in the traveling press crew, such as Mark Harris (*Life*), who later wrote *Mark the Glove Boy*. We felt there was some biased reporting in the Sacramento *Bee*, but we considered that expected opposition from a strong Democratic newspaper. Reporters from the national press were divided, but basically they were there to interpret rather than report daily speeches and news happenings, and their columns, while sometimes published locally, were not daily features in California. Many were negative to Nixon, but not all. The candidate, who had grown up politically with the national press, put too much personal emphasis on the Easterners and failed to recognize that while these reporters might influence Western reporters, they had relatively little impact on California voters. Still, negative national interpretative reporting and columns, particularly in the last campaign weeks, irked Nixon beyond reason.

The reporter who bothered Nixon most was Richard Bergholz of the Los Angeles *Times*, and he, more than anyone else, explains the press-conference references to Greenberg and the *Times*. Bergholz is intelligent and experienced. He can be charming at a party but he also can rub like a rough file, and it was the latter aspect which stuck in the mind of the candidate. Greenberg rarely inserted an opinion in his stories. The Bergholz style included some negative personal observations, few of which Nixon agreed with or liked. He felt this reflected bias in the state's largest newspaper. Bergholz also pressed questions on the sensitive Hughes loan to Nixon's brother, Don.

A few days before the election, one of the Nixon staff members overheard a motel switchboard operator placing a call from Bergholz to Brown's press secretary. The reporter may have been arranging to cover Brown's campaign a day or so later, but with emotions running high, the suspicion that Bergholz was reporting to Brown on Nixon campaign activity ran through the staff and eventually seeped to the candidate despite my efforts to avoid this. I felt a rumor like this would only agitate Nixon at a bad time. But he heard it.

When one looks back, there is quite a contrast between running for President one year and two years later running for governor, even in a state as large as California.

The press corps which follows the statewide candidates regularly is small, sometimes down to four or five and rarely above ten. National campaigns attract a hundred or more reporters regularly. Because of the national attention given to the comeback effort of the former Vice-President, there occasionally would be more reporters from Washington than from California.

In a state campaign, television is more difficult to work with than is the written press. Stations did not want to send out crews for any length of time, and there would be no TV if we went into the far northern portions of the state, the areas with only small towns. I devised a system for making film clips of the candidate and sending them by plane to stations in key population centers. That was helpful, but it still left a void.

In presidential campaigns, we were used to a statement by the candidate on any subject getting major play, usually on page one. In a state campaign it did not work that way.

While Nixon lost in 1962, Nelson Rockefeller, George Romney, and William Scranton became potential presidential candidates by scoring major victories, winning the governorship of the large states of New York, Michigan, and Pennsylvania, respectively. They, not Nixon, became the threats to the nomination of Barry Goldwater.

Rockefeller had been followed by the national press corps briefly in 1959, but basically the three winners were acclimated only to a small press corps and to local and state issues.

The personal lack of understanding of how a large national press corps functions damaged the chances of all three men in later presidential races, but for the moment, their provincialism helped them as much as a lack of a local feeling hurt Nixon.

In an editorial printed after the 1962 press statement, the Miami *Herald* said: "Of course, a part of the press has always had the needle out for Dick Nixon." That was true.

But Nixon liked to say he was insensitive to barbs from the press. That was not true.

Even little things sometimes bothered him. When I finally agreed to join the 1962 campaign in early September, one of Nixon's comments to me related to a courtesy his press assistant Sandy Quinn was extending to Eastern reporters.

"He even sends fruit to their hotel room," Nixon said with disdain. "Being nice doesn't make a damn bit of difference."

Looking at Nixon's press conference statement about TV, it should be noted that a candidate's impressions of television come more from what he is told about it than from what he actually sees. Campaign schedules permit little time for television viewing.

Despite the Nixon statement about television keeping the newspapers honest, the TV coverage of both Brown and Nixon was spotty to say the least. California stations covered the candidates mainly when they were in their own local areas. When there was a traveling television crew, it was usually from one of the networks which was curious about the race involving a former presidential nominee. Television reporters, like newspaper reporters, frequently asked touchy and irritating questions. Bill Stout, a veteran Los Angeles TV newsman, asked about the Hughes loan to Nixon's brother Don as frequently as did Bergholz of the *Times*.

Probably the best explanation of Nixon's feeling for television at that time comes from his use of paid television programs, in a pattern similar to his direct television reports later from the Oval Office. He felt that if the public heard his own words directly, the chances of effective distortion by newsmen diminished.

The centerpiece of the 1962 Nixon television advertising program was a series of eight telethons, each broadcast on a local regional basis in cities from Salinas to Los Angeles and San Diego.

The telethons, produced theatrically by Jack Rourke, averaged about three hours in length and were patterned after the four-hour Nixon national telethon from Detroit that we believed had had dramatic influence on the voters in the waning hours of the 1960 presidential race. One estimate was that the 1960 telethon had changed up to 4 percent of the vote.

The California telethon formula, which was also adopted by Nelson Rockefeller in his race for governor in New York, basically had the candidate answering questions telephoned in by viewers. Pretty volunteers were seen answering telephones, and the questions were screened by the staff. The press was allowed to examine some of the questions to see if they thought the screening was fair. Interspersed with the questions were celebrity appearances, which inevitably led to on-the-air endorsements. It was "show biz" with a town hall flavor. President Carter's radio question-and-answer program was a later modification of this.

The campaign audiences were large, but somehow the Nixon 1962 California telethons did not have the impact that was evident in 1960. One of the reasons was that Nixon said little that was dramatic regarding local or state issues where the viewer had his most direct interest. The Nixon answers on national and international issues were in greater depth, and while they were more interesting, they had less voter appeal. When he touched on local issues, he usually spoke of law and order and the death penalty or disorder and communism at the University of California. Brown hit more on "gut" issues.

There were two other major Nixon television appearances in the final days of the lagging campaign, one regarding the Cuban missile crisis, the other aimed at "campaign smears."

We were at a motel in Oakland when we heard of the Cuban missile crisis. It came as a shock. We had been gloomy before, but this cast a real pall over all of us, nationally and politically.

As Nixon analyzed the situation, he was afraid that President Kennedy might give up some missile sites in Europe near the Communist-bloc nations in exchange for removal of the base in Cuba. He booked precious television time to urge united support behind a strong Kennedy stand against the Soviet Union. More to the point, Nixon felt he had to act quickly to remind California voters that their candidate for governor was a major figure with national impact, or he would drop in the dust.

The telecast gained attention, but it came at a time when elections were far from the minds of the voters. The political effect was nil, a failure.

On election eve Nixon made his final desperate television appeal, joining Dick Powell on a statewide broadcast originating at station KTTV in Los Angeles. The time was booked, he said, to allow him an opportunity for direct answers to the voters on any last-minute charges from newsmen or from Brown.

There were no last-minute smears, but the campaign had ended in a blitzkrieg of charges and countercharges by both sides during the last ten days. It was dirty. There were suits and countersuits, but all were political. A week before the election, Nixon predicted that his opposition would "launch the most massive campaign of fear and smear in the history of California elections." The press reported the statement, but the fear was unfounded. This was a tactical statement, not one based on fact.

At one point Murray Chotiner had printed a small brochure which showed Governor Brown on a surfboard off Waikiki. It was humorous but a childish and unfair distortion. It featured photographs of the overweight governor wavering from side to side on the board and then falling off. Chotiner's theory was that it illustrated what a bumbler the governor was. But Chotiner had never tried to conquer a surfboard. I had. I saw to it that the pamphlet had little circulation.

The last outcry from the "fears and smears" of the final days of the 1962 campaign surfaced strangely in 1972, referring to a questionnaire printed in 1962.

The questionnaire was similar to ones used even today by candidates wherein they pretend to be taking a poll of public feelings on issues. Questions are worded to lead to a preconceived conclusion. In this case the questions were written by Leone Baxter, noted California publicist, and were sent out in a mailing to Democrats under a front name of a nominal Democratic chairman. It was a thinly disguised pro-Nixon ploy. The purpose was to lead those who answered the questions into a thought process which would make the governor seem soft on communism on the University of California campus. It was a psychological approach which went unreported in the press.

In 1972, long after I had forgotten the questionnaire, I had a call from Mrs. Baxter just prior to a White House press briefing. She told me about a news story that a San Francisco judge had settled a suit regarding the brochure and had reprimanded Nixon, Chotiner, and the 1962 campaign manager, Bob Haldeman.

The more I look back at 1962, the more clear it is that, regardless of what Nixon said in his "last press conference" or how fair the press was or was not, the election was not decided by press coverage. The press mainly reported what was said by the two candidates—and, with exception, little more.

One of Nixon's greatest breaks came in a debate before the press at a state convention of editors of newspapers subscribing to United Press International. After the 1960 Kennedy-Nixon confrontation, this 1962 debate was widely covered, although it occurred during the morning, not on prime time. Questions for the televised debate were to come from editors and publishers in the audience.

The questions we felt were most sensitive were over the Hughes loan, an issue which first surfaced in the 1960 campaign and was being raised again in 1962. It involved a loan made by the Hughes Tool Company to the candidate's brother, Don Nixon, against a collateral of Whittier family property which was developed as a lease site for a gasoline filling station. Don Nixon needed the money for financing an ill-fated restaurant location. Opponents claimed that the loan was made by Hughes in an effort to seek help with government contracts. I do not believe Dick Nixon knew of the loan until after the fact. Nixon claimed the loan was sound, and Hughes made money from it. The case was never proved, but it made an interesting issue. I never saw any evidence of Hughes's seeking a favor or getting one from the Vice-President. Interestingly, though, a large Hughes campaign contribution to Bebe Rebozo became a point of controversy in 1973.

As I negotiated conditions for the 1962 debate with Brown, I was highly sensitive, aware of the prior impact of the Kennedy debate. One of the conditions I imposed was that the debate would be on issues and would include no questions of a personal nature.

About midway in the UPI debate, Tom Braden—later a national columnist and author of *Eight Is Enough,* but then a California publisher and a Brown appointee as chairman of the California Board of Education—stood up and asked a question regarding the Hughes loan. The impeccable moderator, Theron Little, publisher of the Salt Lake City *Deseret News*, declared the question out of order because of the rules on personal questions.

This was the moment I had hoped most for—a Hughes question coming from a Brown appointee. Nixon looked properly pained but jumped up and said he would like to overrule the moderator and answer the question once and for all. The tactic and the answer won the debate and won the applause of the California publishers and editors.

The only unanswered question concerning 1962 is how much of the vote was for Brown and how much was against Nixon. Or one could reverse the question.

Whatever the answer, the fact is Brown made a comeback equal to that of Harry Truman.

Just two years earlier, in 1960, after he had given a reprieve from a death sentence to the sensational murderer Caryl Chessman, Brown's popularity was so low that he received the most intense booing I have ever heard.

The occasion was the official opening of the new Candlestick Park Stadium in San Francisco. Brown was introduced as the governor and was booed so vehemently he appeared too stunned to leave the pitcher's mound. I felt so bad I went out and helped him to the sidelines. Nixon was introduced and received a tremendous standing ovation. Yet two years later Brown defeated Nixon.

The Cuban missile crisis was a factor in evaporating all possibility for a traditional last-minute effort by the Republican candidate in California to attract the large independent vote. People simply did not pay enough attention to the election during that crisis to change their mind either way.

But the more basic factor was that Brown was cool and ran a locally flavored, grass-roots campaign appealing to his area of strength, the dominant Democratic registration in California.

Even when Nixon ran for the U. S. Senate in 1950 against Helen Gahagan Douglas, he campaigned more on national than on state issues. This time the voters were more interested in California issues. And while Nixon made efforts to be local, with media events ranging from a 4 A.M. appearance at the Los Angeles produce market to an afternoon at a peach festival in Chico, California, he never appeared to be the man interested in peaches or produce.

While the bitter postelection press statement seemed aimed at the California newsmen, it was in reality the unleashing of fifteen years of bitterness Nixon felt toward the national press, which had brought him to peaks and depths so many times.

5

Opportunities Lost:
The Press—the Ever-new Nixon

SHORTLY BEFORE NOON on January 27, 1969, I walked out of the East
Ballroom of the White House in the company of the scores of journalists
who had just completed the first press conference of President Nixon.

There could not have been a greater contrast than that between this
performance by the new President of the United States and the "last press
conference" of the defeated, heavily bearded, weary gubernatorial candidate on that unhappy morning in 1962. The comeback was complete. At
the moment, even the relationship with the press was full circle. The contrast between the confident statesmanlike President dealing with the news
media and the exhausted, bitter enemy of the press, in what he then
thought was his last public moment, vividly illustrates the inner conflict
that went on within the man during most of his public career.

On many occasions during the twenty-two years of his public life between the time when he emerged from a Navy uniform and ran for
Congress in 1946 and when he was elected President in 1968, he had been
castigated and mistreated by an unfair press, and yet on more occasions he
had risen, aided considerably by objective news coverage. He accepted this
unappreciatively. Here was his opportunity, in 1969, to open a new vintage Nixon, one who dealt effectively with the communications media and
one who could build an honored place in history if the press viewed him
as a statesman.

In this televised conference, seven days after the 1969 inaugural, fifteen
questions were asked. By common consent of the news representatives, the
senior White House correspondent from the wire services—in this case

Helen Thomas of United Press International—had concluded the session by standing and saying the traditional "Thank you, Mr. President."

The President had been in good form. He was relaxed, and he had handled a range of questions varying from Miss Thomas's request that he reveal his so-called secret plan to end the war in Vietnam, to queries on arms limitation, inflation, crime in Washington, D.C., and nominations for posts in the Justice Department.

Interestingly, the question which received the headlines was asked by the veteran broadcaster Edward P. Morgan, once an outspoken critic of Nixon on his shows sponsored by organized labor. The President spotted Morgan four rows back on the left side. Morgan searched for the President's views on what he thought constituted adequate strategic arms levels to prevent war between the United States and the Soviet Union. He asked: "Mr. President, back to nuclear weapons. Both you and Secretary Laird have stressed, quite hard, the need for superiority over the Soviet Union."

His key point was, "What is the real meaning of that [arms superiority], in view of the fact that both sides have more than enough already to destroy each other, and how do you distinguish between the validity of that stance and the argument of Dr. Kissinger calling for 'sufficiency'?"

(I checked a short time later, and Kissinger told me that "sufficiency" was not his word. "I have never used it," he said.)

But the President liked the word.

"Here, again, I think the semantics may offer an inappropriate approach to the problem," he replied to Morgan. "I would say, with regard to Dr. Kissinger's suggestion of sufficiency, that that would meet, certainly, my guideline and, I think, Secretary Laird's guideline with regard to superiority.

"Let me put it this way: When we talk about parity, I think we should recognize that wars occur, usually, when each side believes it has a chance to win. Therefore, parity does not necessarily assure that a war may not occur. By the same token, when we talk about superiority, that may have a detrimental effect on the other side in putting it in an inferior position and, therefore, giving great impetus to its own arms race. . . .

"I think 'sufficiency' is a better term, actually, than either 'superiority' or 'parity.' "

The headlines which followed quoted the President as launching a policy of "sufficiency."

This added to the appeal of the press conference. But the fact was that "sufficiency" was a policy born from a word in Ed Morgan's question, not a term resulting from a secret White House discussion on semantics and policies of military balance of power.

Thus a reporter became author of policy—or at least the description of a policy, a description still under much discussion.

In the next question, Paul Healy, another veteran political reporter, from the New York *Daily News*, followed up on strong statements which had been made by the President late in the campaign regarding the crime rate in Washington, D.C.

We had released the crime statement for Sunday newspapers. It pointed out that Washington, D.C., is the one city in the country "where the federal government is the agency responsible for law enforcement. It is the one city in America where the crime statistics give a precise reading of a national administration's concern over the national crime crisis.

"Today, felonies are being committed at an annual rate of 50,000 in that city of only 800,000 people. Scrip is being used on the buses as though Washington were some occupied city. . . .

"Since Dwight Eisenhower left office in 1961, crime in Washington has risen 175 percent. Before we put any stock in Mr. Humphrey's promise to make it a model city, he should tell every American why he allowed it to become a national disgrace."

The campaign statement of the problem was correct, but the Humphrey reference was unfair as he had not the slightest control over the machinery of justice. But it was a political season.

And now Healy wanted to know what we were going to do. Nixon could do something. The basic plan was to strengthen the hand of the District police force with more men, more money, and more outside help.

Crime was very much on the minds of all of us from the President on down. Crime in the nation's capital had been developed as a major thesis in the campaign. In a final attack, the "white paper" Healy referred to was issued ten days before the election. Nixon had made headlines by stressing the disgrace of a capital where it was not safe to walk on the streets.

Ten days after the inaugural I learned about street violence firsthand.

Shortly after midnight on January 31, I started for the door of the exclusive Sulgrave Club, which is off Dupont Circle only blocks from the White House. We had been attending a Perle Mesta party honoring Washington social columnist Betty Beale and her husband, George Graber.

As I approached the street I heard shots. Senators Howard Baker, Mark Hatfield, and Hugh Scott rushed outside to join me.

We found a wounded man lying on the grass. I went back in without disturbing the party and telephoned police. Another party guest, Representative Tim Lee Carter, of Kentucky, administered first aid, using his medical training. The victim told us his name was Thomas Donleavey, a trainee treasury agent. He had been accosted by a man demanding his wallet. He wrestled with the man and was shot in the leg in the process. The story for the Washington *Post* was written by a young police reporter: Carl Bernstein.

When the President received Paul Healy's press conference question on crime in the District of Columbia, it was like receiving a pitch ready to be hit out of the stadium as a home run.

The President acknowledged the seriousness of the crime problem and illustrated it with a notation that a young woman on his staff had her purse snatched just outside the White House gate.

He said he had been warned personally regarding the crime problem when he had told the Secret Service he would like to take a walk in the district the day before.

"I had read Mary McGrory's column and wanted to try her cheesecake. But I find, of course, that taking a walk here in the District of Columbia, and particularly in the evening hours, is now a very serious problem, as it is in some other major cities."

The fact that he had quoted the Mary McGrory column in the Washington *Star* intrigued me. And it surprised me. The day before, McGrory's column had been a letter to the President, referring to the problem of crime in the District. She mentioned that policemen from Precinct 8, after investigating four robberies at her residence, had sat down to enjoy cheesecake she had personally prepared for them.

But I remember Mary in 1956 when I first met her. She was a new columnist, who had been a librarian on the staff of the Washington *Star*. She had a great talent for words, but also an outspoken liberal political prejudice. Still, no one worked harder on news stories than Mary McGrory. I noticed her first on the press bus. We were in a motorcade where the crowds were enthusiastic, waving Eisenhower-Nixon signs at the press. Mary couldn't hold herself in. She periodically shouted back at them cries of "Yea, Stevenson." She was young and enthralled with Stevenson. And, more so, with Jack Kennedy in 1960. In 1968 my feeling was that she had little emotional feeling about the campaign. Throughout it all she wrote brilliantly, even when I did not like it. Her colleagues worshiped her Irish humor and admired her style. And she was an interesting critic, who was hated by the Johnson White House and later the Nixon White House. Finch and I were notable exceptions.

When I found Mary in the main portico of the White House leaving the first Nixon presidential press conference, I was anxious to know how she evaluated the session. Her view was important. I respected it.

I found her enthusiastic!

"Your man was great," she said. "He handled everything well, and I was encouraged by what he said about Vietnam and arms limitation—'sufficiency.'"

"Maybe he is different now that he is President."

We had a staff follow-up session after the press conference. It was the only one we ever had to critique a news session, at least the only one I was invited to. The session included Ron Ziegler, Bob Finch, John Ehrlichman, Bryce Harlow, James Keough, Patrick Buchanan, Ray Price, Bill Safire, and Bob Haldeman who not only presided but took notes for the President, who was not present.

We critiqued the President's performance. All of us were enthusiastic, but we honestly tried to point out areas where there could be improvement. I reported the reaction of McGrory and other key reporters I had talked with.

Someone mentioned that this was a "new Nixon," one who would do well with the press. I always shuddered at the term "new Nixon". When one looks at the history of Nixon and his relations with the press, "new Nixon" comes out almost like code words. I lived through "new Nixon" after "new Nixon". A "new Nixon" was an invention of the press.

The fact was, however, that the press concept of a new Nixon was helpful. It was an easy way for the newsmen to change their view of the candidate without admitting they may have been wrong before. The result each time was a better relationship between Nixon and the press—and, importantly, far better stories.

Had the President, and more of those close around him in the tense moments, accepted the press evaluation that there was a "new Nixon" and followed through in kind after that first press conference, many of the later troubles, including Watergate and the excessive harassment of the President's press secretary, Ron Ziegler, might never have happened. A more open, give-and-take relationship with the media would have made the White House more sensitive to public perceptions.

The White House did not accept the concept of openness and gradually we drifted from an atmosphere of mutual working arrangements to an unproductive bully attitude toward the news media. The problem stemmed not from a lack of attention to the media, but more from obsession with it.

It seemed to me that half of the President's staff considered themselves experts on press and public relations. The President himself spent a disproportionate part of his time complaining about the press and our dealings with it.

This was evidenced by a constant flow of memorandums from my earliest to my final days.

Typical are these memorandums of March 20, 1969, June 22, 1970, June 17, and June 12, 1972:

THE WHITE HOUSE
WASHINGTON

March 20, 1969

MEMORANDUM FOR: MR. KLEIN

The President is concerned that we are still relying too much on what he does and not putting enough emphasis on thinking of what others can do to supplement the President's activities.

He is especially anxious that you build a stable of television personalities from within the Administration who will look good, and can handle the situation on TV, and then get them on as much as we can.

He believes that he can only carry the load about once every two weeks and then in the interim period it is imperative that other members of the Administration are on on a reasonably regular basis.

H. R. HALDEMAN

THE WHITE HOUSE
WASHINGTON

CONFIDENTIAL

June 22, 1970

MEMORANDUM FOR: MR. KLEIN

Would you please forward to me your analysis of the strengths and weaknesses surrounding our whole approach and relationship with the press and media. In this analysis please address yourself specifically to the topics of:

1) The balance of our use of TV vs. printed media.

2) Our relationship with TV, radio and press.

3) Any recommendations you have as to what we should be doing, what we are currently doing that is a waste of time, and what we are currently doing that is really good.

Your analysis should include ideas for better uses of time for some of our other key staff members in relation to the press. In order for this to be useful, I will need your thoughts submitted to my office no later than 5:00 p.m., June 24.

H. R. HALDEMAN

THE WHITE HOUSE
WASHINGTON

June 12, 1972

EYES ONLY

MEMORANDUM FOR: HERB KLEIN

FROM: H. R. HALDEMAN

It has been requested that you summarize your views and analysis on the following points:

1. What should the President's posture be between the Conventions?

2. What should the President's posture be from the Republican Convention to the election? When should he start campaigning? How much travel should he do, where should he go, what type of activities should he engage in?

3. Any general thoughts you have as to strategy for the campaign on issues, timing, points of attack, etc.

4. Your thoughts as to what the opposition strategy will be and how we should meet it.

Please let me have your memorandum by 5:00 p.m. Friday, June 16.

THE WHITE HOUSE
WASHINGTON

June 17, 1972

CONFIDENTIAL—EYES ONLY

MEMORANDUM FOR: H. R. HALDEMAN

FROM: HERBERT G. KLEIN

RE: *Campaign 1972*

Between Conventions

1. Between Conventions I would suggest that the President concentrate on domestic duties in Washington. Congress will be in frenzied session, and this will be the time to build on issues concerning congressional failures. It also will be the time to build the case between the Democratic platform and the Democratic performance in Congress.

I would suggest one excursion out of town. This would be an ideal time to emphasize the President's concern for the environment and to point up his legacy of parks program while people vacation. The trip should include a stop in perhaps two national parks to check facilities and to inspect two or three of the new "legacy" parks closer to cities, such as in California and Texas. In the national parks, we should stress pool press coverage of some events where he and Mrs. Nixon and Julie could check trailer facilities, see some animals, etc.

Post Convention

2. After the convention and into the fall the President should continue to stress the duties of office, particularly on foreign policy, but I believe he must campaign visibly so as not to give the impression of over-confidence which might be conveyed to workers and contributors. He should maintain a high level posture, but it must also be a fighting pose. Both can be done with the battle emphasis on rallies and quiet talk on television.

I would use the week after the convention for meetings with party and campaign leaders, ala Mission Bay. This could be done at San Clemente or Washington. This would give the feeling of gearing up and would show strong Presidential interest. I believe the President should launch his campaign efforts with a week of major activity in key states during the first week in September. This would knock down the idea of apathy. During the remainder of September, I would suggest that he work in Washington, invite in key groups here, and travel on long weekends only. We also have the fund raiser on September 26.

In early October I would step up the President's campaign activities to travel one or two days during the week and then again on Friday and Saturday with Sundays off. I think this should lead up to intensive travel and campaigning in the last two weeks. If he plans to campaign intensively prior to the election, the idea should be dropped to many of the newsmen much in advance so it won't appear to be last minute panic.

Travel should emphasize the key states, of course, but particularly in September, it should emphasize places which will bring good visibility with minimum trouble. Saturdays, for example, he could touch some states close by such as Pennsylvania, Connecticut, New Jersey, Tennessee, Ohio and upstate New York. He should mix this with some time in California, Texas and Illinois.

Some of the first week of September activities should be rallies to tie down the Nixon supporters early since the President will be leading in the polls. We have the early majority, as in 1968. The President might tie some events to tours of facilities such as high trade manufacturing plants (computers, etc.). Republicans haven't done this. He should have one or more events each emphasizing Black, Mexican American and, perhaps in some way youth. Early contact with these voting segments would avoid the idea we are not seeking their votes. Throughout the campaign, I would look for special ethnic opportunities, particularly if Muskie is not on the ticket. The Vice President should work these areas hard, also.

General Thoughts

3. I would hope that the President personally would use informal television considerably, interspersed with short, direct television talks to the public. I would avoid most rally television even on a state basis. If the President is to answer questions on television, either regionally by community leaders or by newsmen, he should emphasize more press conferences this summer to avoid the charge that he will not answer newsmen but will handle the other programs.

I would prefer to see more 5 to 10 minute addresses by the President and few of 30 minutes duration. The addresses should be of high tone—the Presidency and the record. A contrast should be built between professionalism, calm competence and achievement as opposed to radicalism, uncertainty, confusion, and inexperience at a time when the world can't afford to experiment. I'd take some examples from the Roosevelt campaign in 1944 when you didn't want to change horses in the middle of the stream. A key point should be the high cost of McGovern.

4. The opposition (presuming McGovern) will hammer on the economy, Vietnam in one way or the other, food prices, taxes and, believe it or not, law enforcement (why haven't we done more?). They will stress the honest George theme, frank new face which is credible. They will try to focus on distrust and credibility and relate it to the President.

One part of our strategy should be humor. At the leadership meeting, for example, two jokes came up on whether the nation is McGovernable. A Chicago item columnist tried an idea I had: After this was printed without attribution, several people mentioned it to me in Chicago. All this has to be subtle and by word of mouth, of course.

In a more major way, I believe the President should spend most of his time emphasizing the positive. He is the leader and has a great record. If he meets the attack by staying above it, I think we gain. There must be hard punches taken at McGovern, of course, and occasionally, particularly if Q and A television is used, the President could do this to give emphasis in the public mind. Most of the counter battle should be carried in organized drum beat fashion by the Vice President, surrogates and congressional candidates. Regional drum beats carry nationally if they are organized.

My recent soundings, documented in another memo, indicate to me that at this moment, the people are interested more in the big issues than the dissatisfaction supposedly shown in the McGovern-Wallace vote. Much of the dissatisfaction of Wisconsin may have been with other Democratic candidates (particularly Wallace votes). I get fewer questions on personal problems (social security, veterans benefits, etc.) and more on foreign policy and the economy than I did even three months ago.

From the start, the press had a major role in the career of Richard Nixon. When he ran for Congress in 1946, the press was generally supportive of him, and he worked to develop a close relationship with each of the publishers and editors in his district.

Two of his earliest "big-league" political confidants were newspapermen, Kyle Palmer of the Los Angeles *Times* and Bert Andrews, prizewinning Washington bureau chief for the old New York *Herald Tribune*. They were major power brokers long before the Washington *Post*'s Bob Woodward and Carl Bernstein were born.

Actually, Nixon has always understood the importance of the writing press, although since midway in the fifties, he has considered television the most important medium. His first instructions to me on the morning after the 1968 election were, "I want you to do a lot more television."

Nixon understood the mechanical problems facing reporters—deadlines, need for filing time, the importance of facilities for filing stories. He knew how both newspapers and the broadcast media operated far better than most professionals.

Despite his understanding of the vital importance of the media and of their operations, Nixon too often allowed the personalities of some of the newsmen and his resentment of the liberal philosophic inclinations of reporters in general to cloud his view and his working relationship with the press. This took different forms. Don Irwin of the Los Angeles *Times* and Aldo Beckman of the Chicago *Tribune* were thought of highly. He liked and trusted Robert Semple of the New York *Times* but he hated his newspaper. Still he read it. He disliked syndicated columnists Rowland Evans and Robert Novak, but he recognized their power and influence. Columnist Nick Thimmesch appeared in fewer newspapers than Evans and Novak, but Nixon was inclined to favor him. Sunday night supper at the home of Tom and Joan Braden or Max Frankel of the New York *Times* was considered fraternizing with the enemy. Kissinger and I were among those who "fraternized" most frequently.

The fact is the press and the broadcast media helped bring Nixon to the heights, and they helped bring him to the depths—they had a role in most of the happiest and the saddest moments of his life. The Nixon press relationship was both a hate and a love affair during the almost thirty years of his public career. Few men have had more myths or more facts written about them.

Some of the myths which now reflect public thinking regarding Nixon's first campaign for Congress against a strongly entrenched incumbent, H. Jerry Voorhis, range from small things, such as the story that he entered the race after hearing about it in a newspaper classified ad, to the more serious charge that Nixon spent most of the campaign building the innuendo that Voorhis was a Communist or a red sympathizer.

Actually, Nixon learned of the possibility of running against Voorhis while he still was in the Navy and in Washington. The invitation came in a letter from an old family friend from Whittier, Hubert L. Perry. Nixon flew to California, appeared before a Republican screening committee of one hundred, and won its support and eventually the Republican nomination. (Later when he became President, it seemed to me that a thousand persons claimed to have been among the original hundred endorsers. When he resigned, the number shrank drastically.)

In that initial race, Nixon received the enthusiastic editorial support of most of the newspapers of the old Twelfth Congressional District (a suburban area east of Los Angeles) and, most important, he had the strong support of the Los Angeles *Times,* which then wielded powerful impact in each Southern California congressional district. The *Times* political editor, Kyle Palmer, was a realistic kingmaker.

It was during that race that I first met Nixon as I covered one of his four decisive debates with Voorhis. I then was news editor of the Alhambra *Post-Advocate,* one of the dailies in the district, and as news editor of a small daily one reports as well as edits. It was not until after the election that we got to know each other well on a personal basis.

Newspaper files confirm that communism was not the major issue of the 1946 campaign. The issues related more to veterans' problems, housing, mail, jobs, etc., and to other bread-and-butter issues such as prices and inflation and the general public's attitude that it was fed up with the bureaucracy and incumbents who had imposed wartime rationing and regulation on the voters. It was "time for a change."

There were allegations of a whispered telephone campaign against Voorhis on the Communist issue and of the negative impact of an endorsement of the incumbent by a Communist-sympathizing Seaman's Union. But those factors received little attention in the media, and if there were such phone calls made, I do not believe they were authorized by Nixon or extensive in number. It should be said, however, that Voorhis feels these unfair charges were his undoing. Nixon was convinced that he won the election when Voorhis agreed to the series of public debates.

For Nixon, his most serious early scars from the press came as a result of his role in the Alger Hiss case and his later tough campaign for the United States Senate against Helen Gahagan Douglas. His negative feelings toward the press became even deeper seated during what I consider to be the excessive press blowup of the so-called Nixon fund, in 1952, and the innuendo that he and Murray Chotiner were unethical, junior-grade McCarthys in their attacks on Democrats in the 1954 congressional campaign. One of those who resented the tough Nixon campaign was Harry Truman, who never really forgave the then Vice-President for what he considered to be an insinuation that he was a traitor. Nixon insisted that he was referring to treason toward Democratic Party principles. Truman chose to interpret the remark in its broadest national context. The closest the two men ever came to making up was when Nixon as President flew to Independence to present Truman with his favorite piano from the White House.

The Nixon tactics in the Alger Hiss case have been a matter of dispute since the investigation in 1948. At one time, the press criticism became so intense that Nixon speculated in a conversation with me that he thought it would be best if he left both the House Un-American Activities Committee and the Labor Committee. He briefly, and probably not seriously, considered leaving Congress. I am convinced that Nixon pursued the investigation in a thorough, legalistic fashion.

The merits of the case—in which Hiss, an attractive high-ranking State Department official, was eventually convicted of perjury regarding his testimony as to whether he had ever known an admitted Communist agent, Whittaker Chambers—were disputed in the late forties and the early fifties and even now are being argued as historians review new files released under the Freedom of Information Act. But two facts are clear relative to Nixon:

The young congressman gained major national publicity from the case, partly guided by his close friend and confidant from the New York *Herald Tribune*, Bert Andrews. In his book *Six Crises*, Nixon refers to the Hiss case as his first crisis and quotes a friend who told him that if it had not been for the investigation, he would have won the presidency in 1960. He quotes another as saying that, if it had not been for the publicity of the case, he never would have become a candidate for Vice-President or for President. His conclusion is that "both of my friends may have been right."

The second fact is that Nixon earned the enmity of many in the press corps who had been cultivated by the charming Hiss as close personal friends and who never believed that the State Department official was guilty. They felt that Nixon had "jobbed" Hiss, and this personal feeling of the newsmen could be seen in the bias in some of the stories about Nixon in the period between 1949 and 1954 or longer. The split between this part of the press corps and Nixon caused him to believe early on that many of the newsmen were enemies and to feel that he should play to others in the news corps, to a few friends, such as Walter Trohan of the Chicago *Tribune*, and Andrews, Palmer, and Robert Richards of the Copley News Service. The case had a long-range effect on Nixon's estimate of the news corps and his emotional distrust of reporters. On the other side, the Hiss case brought reactions from many reporters who considered the man they dealt with to be "a ruthless, opportunistic Nixon."

California has had many hard-fought campaigns but none more rugged than the Nixon-Douglas fight. Communism was an issue in the 1950 Senate race. Both Nixon and Douglas were relatively junior members of the House of Representatives when they decided to seek the seat being vacated by retiring Democratic Senator Sheridan Downey. Nixon had a relatively easy primary battle for the nomination, but the Democratic primary was bloody. Mrs. Douglas won over a mixed field of candidates, which included Manchester Boddy, publisher of the now defunct Los Angeles *Daily News*. Boddy made a variety of attacks on Douglas, including a comparison of her vote on international issues with Vito Marcantonio, a Communist-sympathizing congressman from New York.

In the general election, Nixon, with Chotiner as his manager, built a young political organization statewide, including many men I recruited from the Junior Chamber of Commerce. The issues were varied, with a clear-cut liberal or conservative approach to government at stake. Both candidates were reckless in their charges. The document, however, which most antagonized the Douglas supporters and built long-range press criticism of Nixon was a so-called pink sheet. The simple flyer was printed on long and narrow pink paper. It listed varied issues regarding national defense and international programs such as Greco-Turkey aid and used Boddy's research to compare the votes of Douglas and Marcantonio. The implication was that they voted similarly on these issues, which affected then heated U.S.-Soviet relationships, and the unspoken rub-off was that Mrs. Douglas also must be a "pinko." The pink sheet was widely discussed by the press in California and nationally, and Nixon was severely criticized by many in the media for using what they considered an unfair tactic. In the history of the campaign, most of the other severe charges and countercharges of the race have been forgotten, as have the clear-cut differences on other policies which, more realistically, probably determined the winner of the election.

Nixon felt then, and does now, that the pink sheet was just one of a number of dirt-slinging charges which came from both sides. He felt that in the Senate, which deals with international issues, a discussion of his record and that of his opponent on their voting record on matters affecting the Soviet Union was of legitimate concern to the voters. There is much to be said for this point, most of which was overlooked by the press.

But the comparison of Mrs. Douglas to Marcantonio was unfair, whether it was the Boddy charge or the Nixon charge. I was glad I had no part in the idea and was in Washington as a newsman during the worst of the battle. The pink sheet left the wrong impression that the two (Douglas and Marcantonio) had voted in alliance. Douglas was in no way closely associated with the New York congressman and voted independently. The pink sheet was a smearing distortion.

On one occasion during the campaign, Nixon and Marcantonio were stranded on one of the small traffic islands which separate the Capitol from the House Office Building. After looking around to be sure no one would hear him, Marcantonio whispered to Nixon, "I hope you beat that bitch out there in California."

Interestingly, President Truman—who was supported by Nixon on many of the international issues where Douglas opposed the President, but who was strongly supported by Douglas on domestic issues—went out of his way to endorse the Democratic congresswoman.

At a press conference just prior to the 1950 election (the first presidential press conference I ever covered), Truman jumped from a question regarding housing to an ardent statement of support for Douglas and criticism of Nixon.

Nixon won the Senate seat; however, in the process, his campaign further alienated the national press.

But in 1956, when Nixon was to be the lead campaigner because of Eisenhower's fragile health, I thought all these things were past. There was a new effort by the Vice-President to deal with the press more directly and to have numerous press conferences. He handled them well. There was no mudslinging. It was then that I first heard the press refer to the Vice-President as a "new Nixon."

As we were signing reporters aboard for the first campaign swing, one who checked in was Earl Mazo, national political editor of the late New York *Herald Tribune*. I had read many of his Nixon stories and considered him overly critical of the Vice-President but a man who was important not only for what he wrote but for what he said to other reporters. He was a leader in the press corps.

With my encouragement, Mazo set out to know Nixon honestly. I gave him some opportunities to talk individually with the Vice-President. He reported fairly and later wrote two important books on Nixon, one coauthored by Stephen Hess.

As we began to move around the country in 1956, my problems in dealing with the press diminished by the degree to which the Vice-President would hold press conferences, talk to columnists, and, in general, keep the tone of the campaign positive. This, they said, was a "new Nixon."

Perhaps it was, in their eyes.

But I remembered an earlier Nixon who, as a congressman, thrived on dealing with the press. And I remembered a Nixon who at other times, particularly in 1952 and 1954, had sometimes let his contempt for the working press show on his sleeve. There is no consistent pattern in the Nixon press relations.

The most tense moment in the 1956 campaign came at the least ex-

pected time, and it came from an encounter, not with the press professionals but with college editors from all parts of the country.

Early in the 1956 campaign, I worked with leaders of the Young Presidents Club, a bipartisan organization of youthful company chief executives, to organize a televised intercollegiate press conference with the Vice-
President of the United States. The Young Presidents Club was the host
and the sponsor.

We invited the editors of leading college newspapers from throughout
the United States for a day at Cornell University. The program included
attendance at an airport conference between the Vice-President and the
traveling campaign press and lectures by distinguished scholars of the
presidency, including Dr. Clinton Rossiter. It was a fully educational day.

At the time the idea was developed, it appeared that Adlai Stevenson,
again the Democratic nominee, might give the Eisenhower-Nixon ticket a
close race. I envisioned the televised intercollegiate press conference as an
event which would attract a larger audience than most political broadcasts,
appeal to young people, and provide the Vice-President a platform where
he would demonstrate his knowledge and skill in handling questions.

All of those things worked out as I had hoped. But the event also came
at a time when President Eisenhower was so far ahead of Stevenson that
no dramatic new appeals were needed. Stevenson's only chance was a
major misstep on the Republican side, particularly by the Vice-President,
who was the major target of the Democrats. President Eisenhower always
was difficult to attack.

I was elated when the event at Cornell was completed. The young editors had been coached, in many cases, by their professors, and they not
only covered the general range of domestic and foreign policy questions,
but they bore in with venom on more touchy issues such as Joe McCarthy,
the Checkers Speech, campaign tactics, and the Hughes loan. Nixon
never was shaken publicly. He was calm and patient.

With the event over, I took Nixon to an adjoining hall, where he
briefly addressed Cornell students before motoring to the airport. At the
airfield, he hung back as we loaded the plane with reporters and staff, and
then suddenly he walked into the dark by himself. When I caught up
with him, I realized he was sick to his stomach. He was more tense than
he allowed to show.

The plane ride that night was a disaster—almost literally.

The flight was bumpy as we headed toward Boston. The candidate
called each of us to sit beside him and proceeded to dress us down for putting him in such a spot. He resented the student questions. He resented the press. He resented his staff. He was angry! After talking to
him so were all of us, to a point where four key people—Bassett, Rose

Mary Woods, her assistant, Marje Peterson (now Acker), and I—refused to speak any more with the candidate.

On the ground, the fog moved in and suddenly Logan Airport was closed down. We had an alternate airport, Worcester, nearby, but as we approached it the pilot got off course and only avoided slamming into a hangar by a quick maneuver which tossed coats and typewriters around the cabin. We were so close I could see inside the hangar doors. It was frightening. Sensing some panic, I picked up Pat Nixon's hat and donned it, parading up and down the aisle clowning until calm was restored. At least the press laughed at me, and tension decreased.

We ended up the night with a long motorcade and an early morning arrival in Providence, Rhode Island. The candidate and the staff still were locked in virtual silence. Ray Arbuthnot, a longtime friend and volunteer assistant, told Nixon he would have to make the first break.

The tenseness between the tired staff and the tired candidate continued until later the next day when we arrived in New Haven for a rally on the green. There was no time for temperament there. A band of Young Democrats from Yale was lined up on one side of the platform with Stevenson posters and water bags to be thrown on signal. This was to be revenge for disturbances caused by Young Republicans from Yale at an earlier Stevenson rally.

Jack Drown, a personal friend of Nixon, and I went out into the crowd to stand by the students with the water bags.

We had made Nixon aware of the problem and as Senator Prescott Bush went into a long introduction, Nixon finally pulled on Bush's coattails as a signal to stop.

Stepping briskly to the podium, Nixon looked directly at the students with the Stevenson placards and said:

"I know some of the Young Republicans harassed Mr. Stevenson when he was here, and I regret that. It was wrong.

"I would ask you today, however, for the opportunity to speak because free discussion and the right to express oneself is an essential part of our American heritage, your heritage. You will disagree with me on some things. I hope you will agree with me on others, but hear me out."

He addressed the student protesters a few more minutes and then turned to the main topics of his speech. The students gradually dropped the water bags, and there was no incident.

The press was never aware of the staff tenseness nor of the full story of the Yale incident, so the illusion of a new Nixon carried on for a few more days. But from the evening of the Cornell intercollegiate press conference until the end of the campaign, Nixon somehow shied away from the press again, and I was confronted more and more with problems of reporters seeking to reach the candidate. The vision of a "new Nixon" vanished.

Typically, the idea that there was a new Nixon seemed to crop up at the start of each campaign and to disappear about midway. There were many reasons for this, but most important was the fact that the candidate would allow himself to become more accessible to the press early on and then would feel that he was being mistreated and react by withdrawing from the press.

My argument was that if he thought the press hated him or was out to get him, as it sometimes was, he played into the hands of the newsmen by withdrawing and leaving them to their own devices.

Typically in 1958 again, when the Vice-President was campaigning to help candidates for Congress and the Senate, we started out with almost daily press conferences and ended with none.

In the congressional campaigns of 1954 and 1958 and in the races with Eisenhower in 1952 and 1956, Nixon attracted more reporters than normally follow a Vice-President or a candidate for that office. We worked to gain maximum coverage. A campaign swing on a train, for example, was bound to increase the number of reporters covering the candidate because even the most senior of the news veterans were somehow hypnotized by the romance of the old-fashioned back-platform speeches. In today's world, there is no other good reason for a campaign train. Reporters also followed Nixon in large numbers because he inevitably became a part of the controversy of each campaign and because President Eisenhower left the lead campaign role to Nixon after 1952. Nixon made campaign news.

In 1958 the role of the Vice-President was to generate additional coverage for key candidates for both Senate and House by appearing with them and by highlighting issues of national importance. The Nixon reference to local issues would normally be minimal.

In a campaign such as 1958, euphoria builds around the chief party spokesman. He is in demand to help. Local leaders tell him only the good news. What the spokesman sees in the press is the big regional headline of the moment. What the spokesman lacks is a realistic way to assess his effect on the campaign.

For Nixon, 1958 had critical importance as a buildup for his race for the presidency in 1960. If he impressed local leaders or left them with a sense of obligation, they were more likely to support Nixon at the 1960 convention. "Due bills" were carefully filed for later reference. A campaign performance rated mediocre in the press could be a major setback, but campaigning leading to Republican gains could be a big plus.

We traveled the country mainly with chartered DC-6 aircraft that year. The press was on the same airplane as the candidate. The planes were arranged to ensure that all of the seats were "first class," and the press was charged the equivalent of first-class fare. In the early stages of the campaign, the "new Nixon," 1958 vintage, not only held frequent press conferences but occasionally would stroll through the plane just prior to landing and talk with the reporters informally. For me that kind of conduct was a delight.

In the last month of the campaign, talk of a "new Nixon" gradually dwindled as the candidate had fewer press conferences and informal discussions and as both the candidate and the press began to show signs of exhaustion from the continual travel.

About three weeks before election day, Nixon began to realize that the GOP campaign was in trouble. His predictions of off-year gains for the Republicans had been overly optimistic. Newsmen began to sound out local reporters and politicians privately during campaign stops, and the stories emphasized more and more the likelihood of small Republican gains and some key losses.

Nixon began to brood privately and the press was the closest target. It was not enough that most of the candidates we campaigned for were endorsed by their local newspapers. It was the reporters who counted, he reasoned, and they now were the critics of what was emerging as the "old Nixon." Antagonism again was building.

Nixon knew that many of the Republican candidates were not up to standard. Once in Idaho he was pressed as to what he could say favorably about a candidate for Senate reelection. He settled for praising him lightly and urging that he be sent back to Washington because the candidate's daughter was "the best baby-sitter in the capital."

When a campaign begins to run sour, there is no stopping the process.

We received an emergency call from Alaska, which was having its first elections as a new state. Two Senate seats, one House seat, and the governorship were at stake. Equally important was the fact that the new governor could set up the political machinery that could give the winning party an advantage for several years in a new state.

Nixon called his friend Congressman Bob Wilson and asked him to rush to Alaska and try to salvage the organization. I spent almost one full night in Fairbanks conducting candidate instruction classes on practical elections, and we developed much publicity for our candidates.

But it was too late. And despite the press coverage we stimulated and the spark Wilson implanted as an organizer, the election was lost.

In retrospect, however, the quick visit may have helped Nixon carry Alaska in 1960 against Jack Kennedy. Before the 1960 election, the forecast was that the Democrat would carry Alaska and the Republican nominee would win in Hawaii. The opposite occurred.

On the Saturday before the 1958 elections, the Gallup Poll to be printed Sunday reached us. It showed heavy Democratic strength and predicted that the Democrats would continue to dominate the Congress. Even then, Nixon found the poll difficult to believe. However, the Democrats did well; the press had been right. Nixon resented it.

In 1960, there were two separate but related reasons for the break between Nixon and the press. Each case provides a classic study of the delicate relationship between the media and the candidate and the power each has over the other. Emotions on both sides played a large role in this.

Since the early days of the Roosevelt presidency, there never has been a love affair between the press and the candidate that in any way approaches the way Kennedy captured the hearts and minds of the traveling newsmen in 1960. Many of the reporters who were caught up in the wave of personal feeling have long since realized what happened and have discussed it openly with me. Emotions affected their stories.

The second factor in the break in Nixon press relationships in 1960 was the candidate's own fault. He allowed himself to be needled by reporters and lost his perspective.

The combination of the two things—obvious Nixon enmity toward the press and Kennedy cultivation of the press—had an effect on campaign reporting and on public reaction, and thus it affected the results of a close election. I now believe that, in this critical presidential year of 1960, emotion-tainted news reports provided more of the difference between victory and defeat than did Mayor Daley of Chicago.

One would have to conclude that Kennedy played the situation well. Neither Nixon nor the press handled the situation as they should have—to understate the case. Nixon must share the blame fully.

Jim Hagerty once said to me, "Never lose an election closely because everyone second-guesses a close election; no one does when an election is won or lost big." His comment, made in 1959, certainly applied to 1960.

After the Kennedy victory, everyone who had made a suggestion on campaign strategy informed me that we needed only to follow their idea and we would have won. Perhaps so.

The consensus was that the basic mistake was the Nixon agreement to debate Kennedy. In my own view, the first debate hurt Nixon badly. But the key to victory and the key to recovery after the first debate revolved around the relationship between the candidates and the press. The press is that powerful. Reporting affects election results. Every major candidate realizes that. But few major candidates equate recognition of the problem with proper handling of it, with realization that a press problem in this case also is a communications opportunity.

Working conditions are important to good reporting. I met early in 1960 with Bob Haldeman, who was to head the advance men, the men who make all arrangements ranging from who will sit on the platform to what kind of food will be available quickly for the press and the staff at a campaign stop.

I dubbed Haldeman the chief "frogman" who would have advance people leaping out ahead to make the arrangements. He brought in John Ehrlichman, a UCLA friend, as his key assistant.

The best of the frogmen, from my view, was Thomas G. Pownall, who had taken two months off from his job as an executive of what was then the Convair Corporation. He later became president of the Martin-Marietta Corporation. When there was a problem with press or politicians, he could solve it smoothly. He was the best, but he also was typical of the caliber of men who took the tough campaign assignments voluntarily and applied their intelligence and poise skillfully.

The press traveling with us found the physical arrangements unexcelled —from working time to Western Union filing of news copy, to room assignments, to care on the airplanes, to the timing of news breaks.

Strangely, this was an area of weakness in the Kennedy organization. Pierre Salinger, Kennedy's genial press secretary, had little experience and was temperamental. Arrangements often were bungled. Food often was cold or nonexistent. Press-room arrangements were difficult. But somehow the press did not resent this, as it definitely would have had the situation been reversed. The difference in attitude centered around the candidates.

Senator Kennedy, aided by Salinger, took the time to romance the press. The newsmen could be irked or even angry at the lack of proper accommodations, but the most important thing in their lives was the news and the background. A smile from Kennedy and a few words of background on the campaign would make up for scores of technical mistakes.

While Kennedy was wooing the press, Nixon was openly showing his contempt for it. It is extremely doubtful that Nixon could have approached Kennedy's charisma with the press, but a difference in approach easily would have narrowed the gap, lessened the emotional barrier, and changed the coverage—decreasing the bias.

The 1960 version of a "new Nixon" ended early in September.

The normal pattern for reporters, even in press conferences, is to compete hard with each other with questions designed to create headlines. But once in a while an informal consortium is formed. Over a few drinks, a few reporters decided Nixon was avoiding them; he was twisting their questions; he was unfairly attacking Kennedy; he was "getting away with murder on the U-2 incident."

And thus early in the 1960 campaign, the American spy plane—the U-2 —became the focal point of dispute between Nixon and the press, with Khrushchev an important side issue.

On May 1, 1960, I was riding with Nixon from the Capitol to Constitution Hall, when we first heard that an American U-2 spy plane had been shot down by the Soviet Union near Sverdlovsk, which, ironically, was one of the areas on the Siberian border we had visited after the 1959 Kitchen Debate.

Over the radio-telephone in the limousine, I received an urgent message from the Eisenhower press secretary, Jim Hagerty, asking me to go immediately to a "land line" (pay telephone) before we met the press awaiting the Vice-President's speech at Constitution Hall. We found a telephone booth and the Vice-President waited in the car while I called.

In quick fashion, Hagerty told me that a U-2 had been shot down, and he warned against any comment by me or the Vice-President. "We are in deep trouble on this, and the cover story we use may not last," Hagerty said. Hagerty rarely missed a political beat even in an international crisis.

The cover story issued by the State Department said that a plane had wandered off normal air patterns in an unauthorized flight direction and had been shot down over the Soviet Union. At that point, we did not know fully the fate of either the plane or the pilot. Later, the Russians announced that they had captured the pilot, Francis Gary Powers. Eisenhower soon felt forced to admit that the State Department story was false and that the U-2 was a high-altitude plane used to photograph military installations and movements in the Soviet Union.

The incident occurred almost on the eve of a scheduled conference between President Eisenhower and Premier Khrushchev. The Soviet leader used the untimely incident to denounce the United States and Eisenhower personally. He then broke off the conference.

Nixon's personal feeling was that it was a mistake to fly the mission just prior to the conference, but the military had gone ahead on a routine basis because it was believed the Russians had no weapons which could approach the height flown by the U-2. Nixon also believed strongly that Khrushchev did not want the summit and used the U-2 as a propaganda excuse to force cancellation.

The pattern of U-2 and Kennedy-related campaign questions began to emerge in the first week of Nixon's return to the campaign trail after a brief hospitalization because of a serious knee infection. In Minneapolis on September 17, 1960, one of the veteran reporters asked:

"Mr. Vice-President, as you go around the country you say well-intentioned people were wrong in advocating that President Eisenhower express regrets to Khrushchev at the time of the U-2 incident. You have indicated that one of those persons is Senator Kennedy. Who do you think the others are? Would you identify them, sir?"

Nixon answered: "Yes, I think that the same view was expressed by certain observers in the press, certain observers in radio, whose names I don't think it would be particularly constructive to mention, but this was not a view espoused only by Senator Kennedy. There were others who felt that the President might have been able to have saved the conference by acceding to Mr. Khrushchev's request that he express regrets for the U-2 flights, and I want to make clear that he was not the only one who held that view."

Question: "Mr. Vice-President, does the speech tonight mark a turning point? Are you going to comment directly on the statements by Senator Kennedy during the campaign? I mean, you are attacking a statement tonight that he made this week. Are you going to continue to do that?"

The Vice-President: "I think it is the responsibility of both Senator Kennedy and myself to take notice of any statements which raise a major issue and in which the statement made is in disagreement with what we believe. The reason I selected this particular statement of Senator Kennedy was that I thought it was an unfortunate statement, and I did not think that it should go without reply. . . ."

"Mr. Vice-President, Senator Kennedy says you misquoted—in effect, distorted—some Labor Day remarks of his in which you quoted him as saying, 'What the American prolabor movement wants for America and what the American labor movement opposes, I oppose.' Is that a direct quote from his or a paraphrase?"

The Vice-President: "Did Senator Kennedy raise this point?"

"Yes."

Nixon repeated the question and said he was quoting a newspaper column.

"The column from which I read was Mr. Roscoe Drummond's report in the New York *Herald Tribune* and the Washington *Post*. The same quote was used in *Life* magazine, and apparently this was generally the impression of those who covered Senator Kennedy that this is what he had said."

Nixon finished his answer by saying:

"If Senator Kennedy feels that he was misquoted he should indicate, first, where he does disagree with the position of labor leaders, particularly the CIO-AFL, who have endorsed him. I stand on what I said because I would only rely on the reports of what I considered to be responsible newsmen covering him, and the words I read were an exact quote."

With this last turn back to the quotes from newsmen, Nixon began the battle with reporters, who soon felt they had been made part of the issue. They were emotionally eager to join battle.

Before the conference concluded, there were nine questions relating to Kennedy statements, ranging from further discussion of Khrushchev, to religion, to the accusation by Kennedy that the Republican farm plan was really a "Benson-Nixon plan." Two more questions related to Lyndon Johnson's comments on religion.

Three days later, as we started the second leg of the intensive campaign swing, a press conference was scheduled for the ancient Hotel Casey in Scranton, Pennsylvania.

When this conference was concluded, Nixon was convinced that there was a conspiracy involving William Lawrence, then of the New York *Times* and later with ABC; Sander Vanocur, at that time of NBC, Phil Potter, a tough veteran of the Baltimore *Sun,* and others including Arthur Sylvester of the Newark *News,* later a Kennedy appointee as assistant secretary of defense. (It was Sylvester who, in 1962, said a President had a right to lie and brought great press wrath on himself.)

Lawrence opened the conference by referring to a "Meet the Press" program in which Ernest Lindley had asked the Nixon vice-presidential nominee, Henry Cabot Lodge, whether, in view of the U-2 incident and the breakup of the Eisenhower-Khrushchev summit meeting, he thought "we have as much prestige and as much influence in the world as we had eight years ago?"

Lawrence quoted Lodge as saying, "Let me just point to the U-2 case. You might say if ever there was a case we didn't have the law on our side, it was the U-2 case and yet when the Soviet Union proceeded against us in the Security Council on the U-2 case, they got the most dreadful defeat. Now, does that show the Soviet Union has got more prestige than we have, when they had a case where, you might say, they had us in the wrong? To me, that answers your question in a convincing way."

Lawrence then asked: "Do you agree with Ambassador Lodge?"

Nixon: "From a technical standpoint, Ambassador Lodge is correct. In peacetime, the gathering of intelligence information, while there is, of course, no body of international law which makes it illegal, is considered to be beyond the usual activities to be engaged in by countries that are supposed to be on peaceful terms. On the other hand, I think it should be pointed out that the kind of peace that we live in today is such that the United States and our allies have no other choice but to gather intelligence information in whatever way we can, not because we desire to do so but because the aggressive actions of the Soviet Union and other Communist countries require us to do so; and I think that was the reason why the United Nations and the other nations, all of whom perhaps would prefer that the world were such that it was not necessary for either the United States or its other allies to engage in intelligence activities of this type, did support us because they recognized the practical situation, and they recognized that if it were not for the aggressive activities of the Soviet Union— their threat to the peace of the world, the fact that they threatened surprise attack with their power—the United States would not have had these flights. So, technically, the ambassador was correct. From a practical standpoint, the United States had the body of world opinion on its side."

The next question seemed to Nixon to be one previously planned as a follow-up to create division between him and his running mate, Lodge, or to defeat the Nixon argument with Kennedy over the value of apologizing to the Soviet Union for the U-2 overflight.

"Mr. Vice-President, following Mr. Lawrence's question, if we were in the wrong on this from a nontechnical point of view, then do you think that you could criticize Senator Kennedy for offering the possibility of expressing regrets to Soviet Premier Khrushchev about this? If we are wrong from a moral point of view, I think your answer seems to imply, if not from a technical point of view, does the United States never express regrets on an occasion like this?"

In a long answer, Nixon handled the question by saying he was "implying the opposite. I don't think the United States was wrong from a moral point of view. The United States was wrong only from the standpoint of a purely technical point of view."

The Vice-President went on to the Kennedy portion of the question by saying that Kennedy had not raised a point of morality in suggesting that the United States apologize or express regret. He said the senator's comment was directed at a tactic which might have saved the summit conference. "My point is, this was a very naïve attitude with regard to Mr. Khrushchev. . . . For the President to have apologized or to express regrets, as Senator Kennedy suggested, under those circumstances, would have been a mistake of the greatest magnitude. . . ."

Nixon began to show his exasperation as virtually every other question in the conference in Scranton seemed to touch on his informal debate with Kennedy regarding the treatment of Khrushchev and the handling of the U-2 question.

Typical was this exchange with Phil Potter: "Mr. Vice-President, now I would like to go back to your answer on the U-2 flight. Why weren't people told that and why did the President waste his time in going there if that were the case?"

Glaring back at Potter, Nixon opened his reply, saying: "I think you know very well the reason for that, Mr. Potter, because you're somewhat of an expert in this field. The reason that the people were not told that is that the indications in these fields are from intelligence sources, as well as from Mr. Khrushchev's public actions. . . ."

Two more questions followed regarding Nixon's comments on the summit breakup and its relation to the U-2 incident. Two local reporters finally broke in with questions on crowd reactions in Pennsylvania and a decline in stock market prices.

On that note, I was able to logically break off the half-hour conference and leave both the candidate and the press to their own thoughts on the encounter. Nixon had masked the depth of his anger while he stood before the reporters; but at the first moment where we had privacy, he snapped out orders to cancel all further press conferences. I told him that we already had passed out to the media schedules that listed a press conference in Springfield, Missouri, two days later, on September 21.

"Cancel that one too," he ordered.

I said nothing to the press, and at the end of the day I convinced the candidate that canceling a conference already scheduled would only provoke a negative story.

"That's the last one, then," he finally conceded.

I agreed to that because I thought I later could change Nixon's mind on the subject. I underestimated his anger.

Springfield brought the kind of day where everything seemed to go wrong. A small motorcade had been arranged to drive through the crowds assembled on the few blocks of Springfield's main street. An advance rally man had arranged for the crowd to shower the Nixons with confetti. As the Nixons drove through the procession, they suddenly found that the confetti had a sting to it. It was hard and sharp, not soft. Finally to avoid being injured by the confetti, the Nixons turned to face the rear of the open convertible in which they were riding. And thus they rode through the crowds of Springfield facing backward to avoid being cut by our own flying confetti. I thought at first that this might be a trick by Dick Tuck, who was following us to file intelligence reports for the Kennedy camp. Tuck was justly famous for such pranks. But the fault was in the Nixon camp. A young advance man had bought defective confetti at bargain prices, not knowing the effect of dampened and wadded paper chips. He was demoted.

We arrived at Springfield's Kentwood Hotel, where I found that segregation still existed. But we had a black reporter with us. I found the manager quickly and told him that all of our party would stay there, or none would. The manager capitulated and the black reporter was registered without ever knowing there had been a segregation problem. I made no announcement of the breaking of the race barrier. What I had done routinely, I thought, would look like grandstanding if I commented on it.

The September 21 Springfield press conference, almost seven weeks before the election, evolved into Nixon's last public confrontation with the media during the 1960 campaign. The conference started easily with a local question pertaining to the Senate race which was developing rapidly following the unexpected death of Democratic Senator Tom Hennings. The veterans of the traveling press started to move in with the second question:

"In clarification of the statement you have made for tonight, do you believe that foreign policy is a proper subject for discussion in this campaign?"

"Yes, I certainly do."

"Mr. Vice-President, I wonder if you could clarify this line in your speech in the excerpts Mr. Klein has given us: 'If Senator Kennedy intends to continue to address himself to Khrushchev and the Communist leaders, I say the American people will hold him accountable for his words.' The only speech I can recollect that he has done this in was the speech in Baltimore Friday night, in which he said to Mr. Khrushchev, 'Don't try and divide us.' Is that the speech you are referring to?"

"That one and the one he made last night in Washington, in which he followed the same line."

"Did you personally, sir, find these words objectionable?"

"No, not at all. I think he has a perfect right to address himself to Mr. Khrushchev, just as I have, but I disagree with what he is saying to him. I certainly disagree with him as I indicate very strongly in my speech tonight."

Two of the local reporters innocently interrupted the sparring with their questions and then Nixon went back to the veterans, recognizing Bill Lawrence.

The New York *Times* reporter returned to the Khrushchev-Kennedy subject again, this time asking if a moratorium on criticism of the United States policies did not give Khrushchev "some unusual power to control debate in an American election."

Nixon answered, as he had before, saying that the Kennedy emphasis "has been primarily and sometimes almost exclusively on the weaknesses," with no mention of American strengths.

Phil Potter was waiting next:

"Mr. Vice-President, in the speeches at Fort Wayne and Louisville today, you alluded to the fact that Senator Kennedy had in May suggested an expression of regrets from the President might have saved the summit conference. You said that to offer such a concession without a concession in return was working toward the cause of surrender. At Louisville you said it was the road to surrender or even to war. Do you mean to imply and indicate or infer that Mr. Kennedy is espousing a surrender policy toward the Soviet Union?"

I could see Nixon tightening up again. He knew that Potter, who had followed every detail of the Joe McCarthy case and trapped McCarthy in excesses and lies again and again, was looking for Nixon to say something impugning the Kennedy patriotism or perhaps indicating that the Democratic nominee was "soft on communism," buzz words in 1960.

Directing himself to the Potter question of whether he had implied that Kennedy espoused a surrender policy, Nixon replied:

"Absolutely not. Mr. Kennedy didn't know what he was espousing. That was the trouble. I've indicated time and again that Mr. Kennedy is a man that is just as strong against communism as I am, and as most Americans are, but I indicated that in this view, because of perhaps lack of understanding and experience, he was naïve in making a suggestion that I think would have led to exactly the thing he would have been just as strongly against as I am."

A local reporter changed the line of questioning to Cuba, but eventually the veterans returned to the forefront to continue debate over what Nixon and Kennedy were saying regarding Khrushchev.

A question regarding a Kennedy statement that the Russian economy was growing faster than the American economy was followed by another question on the "soft on communism" reference.

"Mr. Vice-President, some of us in the back of the room didn't get your complete answer to Mr. Potter's question. You said you thought that Mr. Kennedy didn't know what he was espousing and what was—would you mind repeating the rest of your answer, sir?"

"Well, as I recall Mr. Potter's question was: Was I indicating that Mr. Kennedy favored surrender to the Soviet Union, that he was espousing a policy of surrender when he suggested that President Eisenhower should have expressed regrets to Mr. Khrushchev?

"And my answer was: Absolutely not; that I had said that Mr. Kennedy really didn't know, in my opinion, what he was saying and the implications of what he was suggesting, and I suggested that the reason he, therefore, had made that statement was that he had a lack of understanding of what it would lead to. I went on and further said that Mr. Kennedy was just as strong against communism as I was; he would oppose surrender just as strong as I would. The question is the particular procedure that he recommended here, the advisability of it. In my opinion, it was a procedure that if followed would have ended up in a result that he would have opposed as much as I do."

The last question of the conference was again a local one: "How's the old knee? How's it coming along?"

Nixon replied that the knee injury was not a problem.

"It's in good shape."

He answered that with a smile, but inwardly he was seething from the earlier line of questioning and determined to break off further press conferences.

Indeed that marked the end of any formal conferences between Nixon and the media during the 1960 campaign. Even within the staff there was running debate in the weeks that followed over whether or not the candidate was right in breaking off the relationship. We all thought the questioning had been contrived.

The intense dislike of the press shared by Nixon and some of the hard-liners on the staff was equaled by emotions apparent to me within the press corps. As reporters switched between following Kennedy and Nixon, they seemed to build up an emotional bond to Kennedy and a growing hatred of Nixon. I tried to stem the tide by arranging a press party in the Petroleum Club of the Great Northern Hotel in Billings, Montana, where we spent a Sunday off duty on October 9.

We had flown in from Milwaukee, where Nixon further agitated the writing press by appearing on a local television question and answer. The local program was good for the campaign in Wisconsin, but it was damaging to the ego and morale of the national newsmen, who had no access to him. Nixon chortled in delight at the press's discomfort.

Early in the morning on the Sunday we were to take a holiday, Nixon awakened at dawn and decided to take a walk by himself. He was followed at a distance by two Secret Service men as he wandered aimlessly over the hilly streets of Billings.

Had he followed the Truman system of walks and even allowed a few reporters to accompany him, the dialogue would have been healthy. But the Vice-President felt a need to hold his own counsel that morning.

The day provided another insight into Nixon.

Willard Edwards, a respected veteran of the Chicago *Tribune*'s Washington bureau, later looked up his notes and recounted his experiences with Nixon on that October 9 in this way:

"The 70 newspaper reporters, radio and television observers following Nixon found the Sunday stopover in Billings a source of levity. Nixon had stated he needed these weekly stops for relaxation and thought. After a survey of the town, the press corps agreed there could be no more relaxing place in the United States than Billings on a rainy Sunday afternoon. There was little to do but relax.

"Nixon, of course, was not relaxing. He was up shortly after sunrise and, ordering the Secret Service to stay clear, he strode through the streets of the mountain city, an icy rain beating down on his uncovered head. He was unrecognized with the Secret Service observing from a distance until he stopped at the Squire Restaurant and ordered hot cakes, country sausage, milk and coffee. One couple from Great Falls recognized him and struck up a conversation. No one else paid much attention. He had to borrow $2.50 from a local policeman to pay for his breakfast.

"Walking on, Nixon came to the First Methodist Church, which was conducting early morning services, and slipped into a rear pew. The pastor, Dr. Vern L. Klingman, however, recognized the visitor and preached on peace, referring to the Vice President's world travels in its behalf.

"After this absence of three hours, Nixon returned to the Northern Hotel, where he was quartered, and disappeared from public view. He was working on speeches to be delivered later that week, it was announced. He would 'relax' by watching a World Series game on TV part of the time.

"The boredom of the day was delightfully dissolved in my case by a call from Herb Klein. Slip away quietly, I was instructed, and come to the small corner suite on the hotel's 10th floor where Nixon was installed.

"Only Nixon and Klein were present when I arrived. The candidate was in a mood for talking. He lifted his feet to a chair, leaned back in a cushioned chair, and rambled for an hour.

"Nixon discussed the vagaries of Presidential politics, the moments of triumph and the assaults of doubt which alternate in Presidential campaigns. He spoke of the small worries, the frustrations, the occasional resentments stirred up by his opponent's methods. He became specific:

"Kennedy, he said, was pounding away at what he called the Eisenhower-Nixon failure to take some strong action to control Castro in Cuba. The Central Intelligence Agency at that very moment, he confided, was training a band of Cubans for invasion of Cuba in Central America. Kennedy knew this, he insisted, he was being 'briefed' on all foreign policy developments, but, knowing Nixon was bound by security injunctions not to discuss this top-secret project, kept hammering away on the subject.

"He was in a position, he noted, to reduce Kennedy to an abject discomfiture by revealing that the Eisenhower administration was planning an action more bold against Castro than any Kennedy had suggested. He simply could not do so.

"The gag was the more infuriating because Nixon was becoming increasingly angry over Kennedy's refusal to attribute to his Republican opponent the same good motives Nixon freely accorded to his rival. Nixon had accused Kennedy of naivety, recklessness, gullibility and extreme bad judgment but always interpolated in his speeches a reminder that he thought Kennedy's goals the same as his—for a better, stronger and more prosperous America.

"But Kennedy, beginning with his acceptance of the nomination in Los Angeles, in which he assailed Nixon as a man with 'malice for all, charity for none,' had never once conceded that Nixon's motives might be good.

"The frustrations of campaigning were never more vividly outlined. I went back to my hotel room, aware that I had a sensational story if I wanted to break Nixon's confidence. The off-the-record nature of the CIA plan was implicit. If Nixon couldn't talk about it, neither could I. I had plenty to write about anyway (it was a remarkable interview in other respects), but I couldn't resist a guarded paragraph:

"Nixon's position as Vice President and member of the National Security Council has both advantages and disadvantages. In the field of foreign policy, he is privy to certain government operations which he may not discuss when Kennedy attacks the administration for inaction. He accepts this frustration as a penalty of his office."

The story of the CIA trainees was eventually broken after the election.

Inherited by Kennedy, the project was to become a disaster for him, due, some believe, to stupendous bungling on his part. If firmly conducted and backed by air power, as originally planned, it might have toppled Castro.

"The question entered my mind then and later: Was I the beneficiary of a 'leak' which, when published, would have accomplished what Nixon could not openly accomplish? I deemed the answer negative but some years later, when I saw Nixon on one of his trips to Washington in the 60's, I asked him directly if a 'leak' had been his intention. His answer was firm and immediate—no. After a moment, he added with a grin: 'In light of hindsight, I perhaps would not have been unhappy if you had published it.'

"In that Billings, Montana, interview, approximately one month before the election, I heard more about Nixon's political sagacity. Nixon outlined with sensitive perception the strengths and weaknesses of both Kennedy and himself. He saw the two of them running neck and neck right down to the deciding day. The result could be so close, he speculated, that Hawaii's three electoral votes might decide the final result hours after the count had been completed in the other 49 states.

"He thought at the time that he would win Illinois, a belief endorsed by most political experts. But on October 30 in Chicago, he startled even some of his own intimates by listing Illinois as 'up for grabs.' He proved correct, even in a cynical sense of the phrase. He thought he had a good chance of capturing Texas, which was wrong. He was sure of California and he was right."

There was more to the Billings stopover.

An evening cocktail party I had arranged for the press at the Billings Petroleum Club started off perfectly. Service, food, and drinks were good and the party gave the reporters a chance to mingle with the campaign staff and with the crew from the American Airlines plane which we had chartered.

After persuading the staff to attend, I finally had convinced the candidate to join the press party for a few minutes.

Nixon came in a little late and started mingling with the reporters. But some of the more eager newsmen began trying to turn the event into an informal press conference, violating the rules. When I tried to break this off, Nixon, looking for social conversation, tried to make a joke, referring to the stewardesses as "bar girls." The two senior stewardesses, Dee Holton and Phyllis Stockhausen, were campaign veterans and Nixon admirers. They thought it was funny. Most of the airline crew had traveled with us in several campaigns, so they understood the attempt at humor. A few in the press chose not to and began agitating about Nixon "taste." What was to be a reconciliation of press and Nixon turned into another disaster of press relations.

I could not help but think that the same type of remark made by Kennedy would have brought laughter. In the emotional ranks of the 1960 press corps, the Nixon comment added fuel to the fires of bitterness.

On the evening of October 27, we ended a day of back-platform rallies along the rail lines of Ohio and Michigan with an evening meeting outdoors in Muskegon. The crowd was large and it was demonstrating enthusiasm as the reporters slowly moved into seats in the front rows. Most of the newsmen were exhausted and some dozed through the preliminaries. Others read newspapers. Most of them had filed their stories and were at the rally to monitor any changes in the excerpts or the basic speech. I noticed that in the back of the crowd there were pickets gathering in larger numbers than usual. As Nixon began to speak, he politely asked the pickets to pull their signs down so those behind them could see. The comment only served to stir the pickets into shouts and hoots of derision.

Nixon broke from his planned remarks again and said:

"Now, incidentally here, just so we can keep the record straight, I appreciate the fact that some of our friends here support my opponent, and I just want them to know that I expect them to give me the same attention that my people give him when he comes to this town, and I know that they will.

"And I would also suggest, while I am talking about manners, incidentally, that I have been heckled by experts. So, don't try something on me or we'll take care of you. All you do is to show your own bad manners when you do that."

About that time, Nixon was greeted by a barrage of eggs and tomatoes, which fell harmlessly on the platform.

The Vice-President paused and controlled his anger, then said to the hecklers: "Now, boys, go on around. I didn't hire you, so stay right out of here. Okay?"

The incident was over and Nixon moved ahead with his remarks. The reporters were suddenly alert again, telephoning or writing new leads about the eggs, tomatoes, and hecklers. I wondered if they had heard fully the Nixon comment "we'll take care of you" and, if so, how they would interpret it. Fortunately, that comment was generally lost.

We returned to the train which was scheduled to continue from Michigan to Illinois. We did not know who had organized the pickets, but we jumped to the conclusion that it must have been the United Auto Workers since we were in their territory. I was instructed by Nixon to take Bill Rogers with me back into the train's press car and make a statement attacking "Walter Reuther's hired goons." He saw a political advantage here.

Some in the press corps accepted that as fair comment on the incident. A few of the reporters passed the word that the pickets may have been hired by the Nixon camp to stir resentment against Kennedy's labor support.

The incident ended with some humor late the next afternoon when Merriman Smith, the veteran United Press White House reporter, appeared with campaign buttons he had somehow had made between train stops. The buttons read:

"Klein's goon squad."

The incident broke some of the tension between the press and the candidate. But it had no effect on the pro-Kennedy emotion that continued to run high within the hearts of the reporters.

The less tense atmosphere of the moment also helped me convince Nixon to hold one more meeting with the press. Late on Saturday night, October 29, the newsmen gathered in a CBS studio in Chicago, first listening to a televised speech by the Vice-President and then preparing for what I called a background briefing by the candidate. The ground rules for the session were that the press would attribute the information it received to sources close to the Vice-President or the press would use the phrase "the Vice-President is known to believe."

The session with the press was peaceful and largely devoted to evaluations of political strategy. The resultant stories, printed the following Monday, were excellent for us, in my opinion. The meeting proved to me again that we had made a serious blunder in breaking off direct relations with the media, a blunder that, as I have said, changed the margin from election victory to defeat.

In the midst of the tense campaign, occasionally there was some staff retaliation. An exhausted Rose Mary Woods overheard a remark by reporter Bill Lawrence which she thought was unfair to Nixon. She angrily poured a drink over Lawrence's head. The remarks stopped.

Another incident which illustrated the tense nerves of the Nixon staff and of the press occurred during the final week of the campaign. Nixon had vowed to speak in all fifty states, and one of those still untouched was Wyoming. We flew from the heat of Fort Worth, Texas, into a snowstorm in Cheyenne, Wyoming. The weather was closing in as we approached in the chartered American Airlines plane. The pilot made one attempt to land and then aborted it as weather decreased visibility below minimums. We circled once more and missed again. The passengers, press and staff, were by now nervous. On the third try, we landed and skidded to a stop amid the ice on the snow-covered field.

Before we left the plane, the senior stewardess, Dee Holton, rushed up to me and said the reporters were talking about the Vice-President's forcing the pilot to make an unsafe landing so he could say he had been in Wyoming. I checked and found a mild rebellion growing in the press corps. Some claimed that our military aide, Air Force colonel Don Hughes, had, on instructions from Nixon, told the pilot he had to land. Nothing was further from the truth. I had been sitting with Hughes and he had not left his seat, but the emotional mood of the exhausted reporters was such that when they were frightened, they were willing to believe almost anything.

I rushed back to the plane from town and talked to the American Airlines captain, a very senior flyer, who was indignant to hear the rumors. As soon as the press corps was back from Cheyenne, we poured cocktails and the pilot came on the plane intercom.

"I understand some of you think I was forced to make an unsafe landing," he said. "I want you to know I value my life. I have eight children and they depend only on me. No one asked me to do anything, but if that had happened, I can assure you that I rely only on my own judgment developed in years of flying.

"Now I will be back with you before takeoff if there are any questions."

The captain wandered through the plane but all was quiet.

The incident was mentioned in just two stories, and then only briefly. Without the captain's comment, it could have been distorted into a major incident.

In all my election and news experience, no other year was quite like 1960. The campaign is remembered by most as exemplified by the dramatic televised debates; the issues, foreign and domestic; and the vigor of two bright young candidates for President. Even debate over Khrushchev figured into it. But I also remember it as a period when the nation's top political reporters and a very good Nixon staff found themselves locked in emotional hand-to-hand combat as the Republican candidate covered the country seeking votes.

Another highly unusual aspect of the 1960 elections was the fact that Nixon atypically made snap decisions with no staff consultation on some of the developments that had critical impact on his election fate and on the Republican Party platform. The decisions all occurred while Robert Finch, Leonard Hall, and I were in Chicago, in July, for the preliminaries of the convention. Bill Casey, later Reagan's manager, joined us.

The four of us, and some of the campaign staff, had moved our headquarters to the Blackstone Hotel in Chicago (a week in advance of the convention) to be on hand for the platform hearings and to direct the general Nixon strategy with both the delegates and the press. Throughout the week, all seemed to be moving smoothly. There still was a threat to the nomination from Nelson Rockefeller, but we did not consider it to be a major danger. Charles Percy was chairman of the platform committee, and he conferred regularly with Finch, James Shepley, and those most concerned with issues. The thunder from the right wing of the party had been mounting under the growing strength of Senator Barry Goldwater and others. There was more liberal pressure from the Rockefeller forces, but the platform which was emerging was moderate and consistent with the Eisenhower administration's policies. Nixon was in Washington during this time and President Eisenhower was vacationing at the naval base in Rhode Island.

On the Friday before the convention, Rockefeller let forth his initial blast against the form the platform was taking. He was critical of its "strength and specifics." In Chicago, we had the votes and did not take the criticism seriously. But in Washington, Nixon did. He was more fearful of a party split than of losing the nomination because of the Rockefeller statement.

On his own, Nixon suddenly placed a call late that Friday afternoon to Herbert Brownell, Eisenhower's former Attorney General and a close friend of both Nixon and Eisenhower. He suggested a secret meeting between himself and the New York governor at Brownell's home in New York. That would be neutral area. Brownell relayed the offer to Rockefeller and then awaited an answer. I later learned that the Rockefeller staff had convinced the governor to "hang tough," and after lengthy conversations between New York and Chicago, Rockefeller said he would meet Nixon—but only at his apartment in New York. It then was Nixon's turn to call Rockefeller, and the Vice-President acceded to the demand and agreed he would be there for dinner that evening.

With just that much notice, the Vice-President told his military aide, Don Hughes, to get them on a commercial flight to New York. The first plane to the New York area was one that shuttled between National Airport and Newark, and Nixon, Hughes, and the Secret Service men were shortly aboard. The notice to the Secret Service in New York was so short that the agents there could only find two of their men to help. They had just confiscated a counterfeiter's car, and they used that vehicle to meet the Vice-President and drive him to the sumptuous Rockefeller apartment on Fifth Avenue.

In Chicago, none of us on the Nixon staff was aware of any of the developments, nor were Percy and the platform committee. Evelyn Nelson, the hotel public relations director, told me something was stirring in the Rockefeller camp, but that did not then mean much. Bob Finch received the first clue when Don Hughes telephoned him about 9 P.M. and said that he should know Nixon and "the old man" were in the Rockefeller apartment in New York and his instructions were that absolutely nothing was to be said about it. Finch discussed this with me, but we followed instructions and said nothing as we anxiously paced awaiting the outcome of whatever was going on.

My next clue came from James "Scotty" Reston of the New York *Times*, who confronted me with a rumor of the meeting, which had been leaked to him from the Rockefeller headquarters. I was embarrassed and almost tongue-tied, but I managed to say I could not confirm such a meeting. I felt I had not handled the situation well and instructed Mary Werner, my secretary, to keep the reporters away from me while we tried to learn what was going on.

We got our first real information at about 3 A.M. when Hughes telephoned from the airport to say the meeting was over and the party was going back to Washington. Finch was told that some agreements had been reached on platform content and that Rockefeller and his staff would issue the written communiqué on the meeting in Albany, Chicago, and Washington. We did not know any details. I decided that regardless of the content of the communiqué, the worst thing that could happen from my point of credibility was for the reporters to learn of the meeting from the Rockefeller people, not us. Finch called Leonard Hall and gave him his sketchy information, and then he and his secretary, Doris Jones, and my secretary, Mary Werner, and I systematically started awakening reporters in Chicago hotels to tell them there had been such a meeting. I called Travis Cross, press secretary to Mark Hatfield, then Oregon's governor, who was assisting me at the convention, and in the dawn hours he was our roving emissary to the press. Within a short time the Rockefeller communiqué on what came to be known as the fourteen-point "Compact of Fifth Avenue" had been mimeographed and released.

The agreement covered controversial issues ranging from defense spending to the touchy and more meaningful platform stand on civil rights. President Eisenhower angrily considered it critical of his policies, particularly on national defense, and the party conservatives and Southerners were offended by the more liberal stand proposed on civil rights.

Thus a spur-of-the-moment Nixon decision to make a telephone call and a trip to Rockefeller's apartment burst like a bomb on a quiet convention, which earlier had appeared to be more of a coronation than a battlefield. Hall, Finch, Charlie McWhorter, Lee Potter, Murray Chotiner, Colgate Prentice, Travis Cross, Peter Kaye, and everyone else we could muster suddenly found ourselves overwhelmed with the task of trying to reshape the thinking of a platform committee that had met and debated the issues for weeks and months. Separately, we also had to deal with angry and rebellious delegates and other party people who found it difficult to accept a series of fourteen points that had been agreed upon in the dead of night. Eisenhower remained unsold and unhappy with the "compact" to the point where Nixon's first stop after the nominating convention had to be at the Newport, Rhode Island, military base where he and the President reached some compromise on strategic views.

Goldwater characterized the Rockefeller-Nixon agreement as "surrender" and "the Munich of the Republican Party." I talked to him and finally Nixon did, in a secret meeting in the Blackstone, to convince him to be supportive enough to speak on Nixon's behalf at the convention. He did so out of party loyalty. During the scramble, the newsman who seemed to be picking up the most accurate tidbits on what was happening was the Chicago *Sun-Times*'s most read columnist, Irv Kupcinet.

Some degree of unity finally was restored, but the resentment against Nixon and Rockefeller among party regulars helped build the strength of Barry Goldwater for his run at the presidency four years later. The other long-range factor of most significance was the more liberal civil rights stand, which later was expertly but quietly exploited by Lyndon Johnson with Southern politicians as he helped John Kennedy in many states that earlier had looked as if they would go toward Nixon.

Despite the weekend party uproar over platform, Nixon arrived in Chicago serenely, on the Monday the convention opened, to accept the fanfare of a wild and gigantic welcome from the public as he toured the old downtown loop at noon and finally arrived amid the hotels in the central convention area. As our motorcade neared the Blackstone on the well-planned route from the then primitive air facilities at O'Hare, the mob was so jammed that the Nixons left their car and walked the last block to the hotel. I was so concerned for their safety that I stepped hard on the foot of someone who was grabbing them by the arm. To my embarrassment, it turned out later that this was John Nidecker, a new advance man, and I had broken his foot.

Nixon was not in Chicago long before he dropped his second bombshell —again completely to the surprise of all of us close to him. In Washington meetings with the Vice-President, we had discussed the possibility of televised debates with the Democratic nominee. We had agreed that we would tepidly support the effort by the networks to suspend Article 315, which demanded equal air time for all recognized candidates. There were about fourteen such candidates, other than Nixon and Kennedy, including Lar Daly of the Tax Cut Party, Symon Gould of the American Vegetarian Party, J. Bracken Lee of the Conservative Party of New Jersey, Orval Faubus of the National States Rights Party, and so on.

With the suspension of Article 315 for the one year, there could be debate between the two principal candidates without the necessity of cluttering the air with a proliferation of all.

While we gave lip service to the change in law, we had met with Nixon on it, and he had been an outspoken, strong advocate of avoiding a debate on the principle that a President or Vice-President is in a position where he cannot answer all the questions fully because of his knowledge of security information. This actually did become a factor in the fourth of the Nixon-Kennedy debates, where Nixon had to advocate a policy regarding Cuba which was contrary to his views. To approach the problem differently would have violated security regarding the training of forces for the eventual ill-fated attempt to land on Castro's shores. He also felt Kennedy was dangerously using knowledge that the United States was secretly training troops to overthrow Castro.

During a Blackstone Hotel press conference following nomination at the Chicago convention, Nixon again startled all of us, including Ted Rogers, his television adviser, by reversing all the views he previously had expressed regarding televised debates with Kennedy. He announced that he was accepting the networks' invitation and would debate John Kennedy. I was standing a few feet away from him during the conference and almost fell over as I heard this. Len Hall was to hear it from a reporter and Bob Finch from me. Nixon avoided all discussion with us as to why he had changed his mind or at exactly what moment he had made the decision. I could attribute the reversal only to the fact that he did not want his manhood sullied by appearing as if he were afraid to debate his opponent face-to-face, and he was confident that he could win such an encounter. On the other hand, he rightfully believed that a refusal to debate would be used by Kennedy as an issue and would be heavily emphasized by network newsmen, who, along with the executives of their companies, were pressing hard for the history-making debates.

Once that decision was made, it was up to network representatives to gain agreement on ground rules and dates for the meetings. Kennedy's forces were headed by Leonard Reinsch, an astute and experienced broadcaster from the Cox Broadcasting Company in Atlanta, Bill Wilson, a younger TV producer, and Pierre Salinger. Our team included Ted Rogers, Caroll Newton, an imaginative and creative advertising executive who was assisting us in the campaign, me, and, occasionally, Bill Rogers. Basically, Kennedy wanted as many debates as possible to gain the television exposure, and we wanted as few debates as possible, perhaps only one. We compromised on four debates, although in the last weeks of the campaign there was an effort to schedule one more confrontation. We said we would consider it but made certain that the conditions and schedules we imposed would make such a debate impossible. We believed that Kennedy approached the proposal in about the same way. We insisted that there be no live audience for the debates, because we feared a "Kennedy clique" would have emotional impact. Even the press was kept in a separate room, although I escorted pool reporters in and out of the studio at the start and at the conclusion. Otherwise, the stories were written by reporters watching television monitors, not the actual physical debate.

Nixon felt that he would do best if the first debate was on domestic policy and the final one was limited to foreign policy. He wrongly reasoned that interest in the debates would grow as they went along and that the fourth debate, in the area where he felt strongest (foreign policy), would fit his sense of tempo, as he planned to peak his election effort during the last three weeks of the campaign.

The first debate, of course, we later found, had the greatest impact, and while the fourth debate attracted almost as large an audience as the first, it lacked the impact. Polls varied on audience reaction to each of the debates, but all agreed that Kennedy clearly influenced the viewers most during the first debate and as a result climbed ahead of Nixon in the popularity polls. Interestingly, while the polls of television viewers showed Kennedy winning, those of radio listeners, for whom appearance could not be a factor, showed Nixon winning. But the TV audience was gigantic and the radio audience small. There was a difference also in the polls regarding who won the subsequent debates, but our surveys showed the second and third encounters about even, although Nixon seemed to gain strength in the third debate, where he was in a Los Angeles ABC studio and Kennedy was in New York. We believed that Nixon won the fourth debate, and we were told that Kennedy left the stage so angry that he slammed his fist into the wall of the temporary huts which had been provided to act as dressing rooms for the occasion.

The Committee on Commerce of the Senate published three volumes on the Nixon and Kennedy general election efforts and in them it refers to the debates as the "joint appearances of Sen. John F. Kennedy and Vice President Richard M. Nixon." History always will remember the classic Lincoln-Douglas debates, but the debate which reached the largest percentage of the American population and which had the most dramatic impact was the first "joint appearance" of Nixon and Kennedy. Other debates, such as those between Jerry Ford and Jimmy Carter in 1976, have had important political impact; however, the 1960 debate not only had an effect on the election, but it was a major factor in bringing television to the forefront in news and documentary reporting. Significantly, while newspaper and magazine journalists participated in the questioning, which marked the second and third debates, the first and last featured only broadcast newsmen. For the first debate, Howard K. Smith was the moderator and the reporters' panel included Sander Vanocur of NBC, Charles Warren of Mutual, Stuart Novins of CBS, and Bob Fleming of ABC. Fleming had the first question.

With this importance given to the event, it is surprising not only how the Nixon decision was made to participate but also the lack of recognition given to the importance of details which led to the Nixon defeat. It is fair to say that Nixon and his staff, in the effort to stump the country with routine campaign appearances, contributed to the Vice-President's own embarrassment before the national television audience by not forcing him to rest and prepare better for the TV battle. We knew the importance of talking to the TV audience at home, but he acted more as a debater, face to face with his opponent, Kennedy.

During a trip to the Carolinas, shortly after the Chicago convention, Nixon had bumped his knee and bruised it severely. By August 29, this developed into a severe hemolytic staphylococcus infection which had the Vice-President hospitalized and canceling schedules until September 9. I found myself issuing medical bulletins instead of political comments. When he left the hospital, we launched the campaign amid a severe tropical storm which had swept heavy rain into our point of departure, Baltimore. President Eisenhower was on hand to wish his Vice-President well. In the frantic scramble to make up lost campaign time, we covered the country, sometimes hitting two or three states a day but, in the process, wearing down Nixon's vitality, which already had been sapped by the illness. We saw him so much that it was difficult to recognize how haggard he looked. He had lost so much weight that even his shirts no longer fit him, but no one replaced them.

The weekend before the first debate was action-filled, with little time for rest and little attention given to preparation for the confrontation. On the morning of the debate, Nixon made a dreary and futile appearance before a Chicago convention of the Carpenters and Joiners Union. During this period, there was no discussion between him and his TV expert, Rogers, and while Jim Shepley prepared a book of questions and answers to consider for the debate, the volume went largely unopened.

Nixon worked in isolation on his opening statement, and generally he accepted counsel from Henry Cabot Lodge (by phone) and a few others to be the "nice guy." The result was that he was apologetic and defensive from the opening second of the debate and not only disappointed his own followers but lost vast numbers of undecided voters who had expected to see a strong, statesmanlike, tough leader.

During the primary elections, Kennedy had debated Humphrey in Wisconsin and one of the issues was the fact that Humphrey wore pancake makeup—standard television procedure. But somehow the Kennedy camp made it appear that Humphrey was putting on a false face. Nixon wanted to avoid such an image and informed me and Rogers before the debate that he would wear no makeup. It turned out that Kennedy took a similar stand, but he needed none because he was rested and had made sure that he was tanned. Nixon was pale gray from his illness.

About an hour before the debate, Nixon and I left his suite in the Pick-Congress Hotel in Chicago and proceeded to the CBS studios. I thought he looked bad wearing a shirt which was too large, but it seemed like no time to disturb the candidate with such impressions. He was tense and silent. I briefed him on the procedures which would follow our arrival at the studio, and left him to his own thoughts.

Guided by Ted Rogers, he inspected the studio and allowed the technicians to test his voice and picture. The producer was Don Hewitt, who, among other things, later went on to produce "Sixty Minutes" for CBS.

Hewitt later told me and Frank Stanton, the CBS president, that he was worried about Nixon's appearance. The backdrop for the studio setting had been repainted several times, and the lights in front of Nixon were lowered to better penetrate his deep-set eyes, but it never was clear who set the final color for the backdrop. The fact was, however, that Nixon's ill-fitted light gray suit looked dull against the backdrop and Kennedy's darker suit looked far more dramatic. Kennedy had concentrated on his appearance to a point where he changed from a white to a blue shirt even at the studio. Nixon and our staff had not concentrated on this.

Everett Hart, whom we had borrowed from the BBD&O advertising agency for television assistance during the campaign, applied a light "Lazy Shave" powder makeup to Nixon's dark beard. It reminded me of the quick makeup I had asked John Daly to apply to Nixon in Moscow at the time he was to address the Soviet people on television. On the day after the debate, while we were in Boston for a fund-raising dinner, reporters approached me with the rumor that Kennedy had slipped a makeup man into our quarters and this led to Nixon's bad physical appearance. Obviously, I denied it. There were other rumors, all untrue, regarding sabotage as the loyal Nixon followers could not believe he had lost the debate in the eyes of the voting public.

As I watched the debate from the studio, appearances did not strike me personally as did contrast in style. I was more worried about the fact that the Vice-President was defensive and the initiative in the debate had been with Senator Kennedy.

When the program was over, I accompanied Nixon back to the Pick-Congress in virtual silence. He was clearly exhausted. At the hotel he quickly went to bed and then called several of us in individually to discuss the event. I think he felt he had done well, and none of us disillusioned him that evening. When I departed from his suite, I left with Peter Kaye and Travis Cross to find as many reporters as we could. I thought it was highly important to put on a confident front and to find out what they really thought as we sipped a drink in the bar of two or three hotels. Most of them had concentrated so much on the content of the debate that they offered few opinions on the outcome, and the initial stories generally treated the "joint appearance" with balance. It was only later when the public opinion favoring Kennedy started seeping in that the press began its interpretation of the debate's negative consequences on Richard Nixon's campaign for the presidency.

Belatedly, Nixon accepted the help of professional studio makeup men and women prior to each of the last three debates. But it was too late. The damage was done.

6

"PR" Experts

During 1969, Nixon's first year as President, he enjoyed a traditional, but not wholly expected, honeymoon with the media, particularly with newspapers. There was controversy between the White House and the networks over television's critical instant commentary, which followed most of his major televised reports and addresses, but the overall coverage was better balanced than we had anticipated.

The breach between reporters and the administration began to widen in 1970. There were many factors: a growing lack of presidential press conferences, a revival of bias by some reporters who had strong emotions over the Vietnam situation and the handling of youthful protesters, the start of the attacks on the media by Vice-President Agnew, and a frustrated feeling by reporters that they were not privy enough to the unexpressed thoughts and motives of the President. The gap between press and President was growing.

A key factor in enlarging the breach was a love-hate obsession with the press, which grew in the White House. Any praise of the President was eaten up like a gourmet dessert and any criticism was greeted by the staff with anguish and anger.

From the President on down, an amazingly excessive amount of time was spent worrying about plans to conjure up better and more favorable coverage. In striving for coups with the news media, many self-designated White House experts forgot the simple fact that direct and honest dealings with the press work best, as was evident in the initial months of the Nixon administration.

When one looks at the memos written, the hours in meetings, and the long informal discussions, one might think that the White House staff was made up basically of top PR men from New York, with the help of a few other PR experts from perhaps Washington, Chicago, and Los Angeles. The fact is that with few exceptions, none of those who were dreaming up new press-relations ideas had any experience in the field and most of them had never met a leading newsman before receiving a presidential appointment.

The tempo for such interest in a particular field stems from the top, and in this case it was the President and his chief of staff, Bob Haldeman. With their interest apparent, the PR effort soon covered both first- and second-rank men (and sometimes the younger third echelon) in every area of the White House. On too many occasions, interest in promotion of a program exceeded interest in details of substance.

Some genuine understanding of the problems was evident from James Keogh, who capably headed the speech-writing team, and by his three experienced top assistants, Bill Safire, Pat Buchanan, and Ray Price. Each of the four men had a long background with the President and understood him. They combined this with imagination and a strong media background. And they worked well with experienced professionals on my staff and Ziegler's such as Devan Shumway, Paul Costello, Stan Scott, Al Snyder, and Jerry Warren.

Each speechwriter had a different approach and provided professional background. Buchanan is more the fire-eater and advocated conservative toughness. Keogh and Price were more evenhanded and tended toward milder, less emotional approaches. Safire was the most imaginative. Dick Moore later added another factor by supplying color and humor, but when humor was needed for a major appearance, such as the gridiron, Paul Keyes—a leading TV gag writer and producer—regularly came to the rescue.

More often than not, ideas and demands regarding public relations and the press came from the President or from lesser aides whose thoughts were funneled to me and/or Ron Ziegler through memorandums signed by Haldeman.

Typical of those which started coming through in early 1970 was this Haldeman memo of February 4, 1970:

WASHINGTON

February 4, 1970

MEMORANDUM FOR: MR. KLEIN

The story we were to get out and run somewhere about how the President has overcome the great handicaps under which he came into office— specifically, the hostile press epitomized by the NEW YORK TIMES, WASHINGTON POST, TIME, NEWSWEEK, etc., the hostile network commentators, the generally hostile White House press corps, the hostile Congress, etc. This is the whole pitch that we talked about sometime ago. The story has not been gotten through. If we can't get someone to take this and write the story along the lines we've been talking about, let's at least get Ralph de Toledano in, put the thing squarely to him, and get him to write it. Do it on the basis that it's a test case, or something, so that there's some heat on it; but some way or other, let's get it out. Everybody's failed so far. & the heat is building [This last handwritten.]

H. R. HALDEMAN

cc: Mr. Magruder
    Mr. Ziegler

The theme of the President overcoming "great handicaps" ran through many of the public relations theses. In the February 4 context, the reference was to the fact that the President had continued to climb in the polls and to develop accepted programs domestically and internationally despite the handicaps of an opposition Congress and "three networks which continually opposed him."

The most frantic example of this concern over whether or not the press would cover a story came immediately after news of the Kennedy Chappaquiddick accident was flashed on the wires. John Ehrlichman excitedly asked me to come to his office to discuss how the press would play this. Would they bury it? He wanted me to call some of the major newspapers and subtly urge them to cover the tragic story. I told him I would not call any newspaper regarding this. They would cover it. A call on such a thing would be in our own worst interest. With that I walked out.

Ehrlichman soon rushed Jack Caulfield, a White House aide and former New York policeman, to Martha's Vineyard to investigate. He found little, if anything, new.

Even on routine questions, no matter what the origin of the idea, once a PR program or project was endorsed with a Haldeman memo, it was difficult to get rid of it without taking some kind of action.

The memo would be accompanied by a cover sheet signed by the White House staff secretary. The sheet included a logged reference number, a due date for a reply, a brief summary of the memo requested, and a form to be checked illustrating the action desired. The form's action options included: for necessary action; prepare agenda and brief; for your comments; for your recommendations; draft reply and/or draft remarks.

The answer to the memo included again the log number for reference. The log number was the key. If the deadline for action was missed, a telephone call would come from the staff secretary. The calls and follow-up memos would continue until the log number could be checked off. Sometimes this would go on for days, while I was avoiding doing anything, if I disagreed with the proposed action. When I left town on one of my frequent business trips, I learned to take the unwanted or dangerous memos with me to avoid the possibility that my deputy, Jeb Magruder, might react to the staff secretary's heavy prod and implement the suggested program just to end the telephone calls, and to please Haldeman, who was not always aware of the harassment.

At one time I wrote a hot memo to Haldeman protesting the heavy volume of paper work created by this system of memorandums and required answers to memorandums. Here we were trying to reform the bureaucracy and we were outdoing it in volumes of paper work. My argument to Haldeman was that if he believed he had a competent senior staff, he should just assume that the action was taken unless there was a good reason for nonaction. If he was alert, he would know through results if people were performing.

Haldeman agreed that there was excessive paper work, but said that much of what he wanted done might be shoved aside unless there was his staff secretary's tickler system ready to follow up and report results in each case. The false assumption was that each memo was important. In fairness, Haldeman also was under pressure from the PR-minded President for constant reports. The President also was unaware of the mountains of paper work created.

Under the White House system of do-it-yourself public relations, the written game plan became an essential feature. It worked well when there was a major program to be launched, but like everything else the idea was overdone.

I wrote much of our original major game plan designed to gain understanding, among the public, press, and Congress, for the President's early proposal to depoliticize the Post Office Department—a program most thought was impossible to pass in Congress. The core of this idea for postal reform was to provide for well-organized regional briefings by all of the key postal officials from the Postmaster General on down. On the day of the announcement, James Holland, the public affairs assistant to Winton "Red" Blount, Postmaster General, had spokesmen in ten cities across the country ready with simultaneous press conferences and media and public briefings.

The difficulty with excessive plans for minor ideas was that they brought forth no creative ideas and resulted in wasted action which undermined more important work. They were repetitive, but they were grist for the paper-work mill.

Typical, in 1970, was a memo I received on August 4 requesting quick effort to gain added attention for a favorable Gallup Poll.

WASHINGTON

August 4, 1970

MEMORANDUM FOR: MR. KLEIN

It is crucial that we get the mailing piece on the Gallup Poll out quickly. I have therefore asked Lyn Nofziger to have the original Buchanan column placed in the Congressional Record and appropriate reprints made. He indicates that this will be completed by Wednesday, August 5.

Rather than mailing out the Dallas Times Herald editorial and the William S. White column, both of which were favorable, but not really that good, we should just mail the poll, the Congressional Record reprints, and a cover letter from you or the appropriate official.

As you know, the President wants the widest possible circulation to take place on this item.

H. R. HALDEMAN

The memo prompted this game plan drawn up by Jeb Magruder and his assistant on my staff, Gordon Strachan, an ambitious but inexperienced young lawyer.

GALLUP POLL GAME PLAN

DESCRIPTION: President's popularity increases 12% over last poll.

OBJECTIVE: To disseminate widely and tie in with President's Vietnam policy.

PRESIDENT: No action.

PRESS COVERAGE: No White House coverage. If brought up in press briefing, Ziegler should indicate direct tie with poll and President's Vietnam policy, including moratorium.

FOLLOW-UP:

Immediate:

1. Heavy comment on Hill—insert in Record—Nofziger
2. Circulate poll on Hill—Nofziger
3. Circulate poll to all staff and Administration personnel with instructions to disseminate this poll wherever appropriate, i.e., speeches, interviews, word of mouth, etc.—Klein
4. Send poll with note to all editors, selected columnists, and radio and TV commentators. Indicate the relationship of surge in popularity to the President's Vietnam policy and approach to the moratorium. Indicate President's ability to rally nation behind him may be worthy of further comment—Klein
5. Send poll to Executive Directors of every business group or association in Washington with a note that association members might be interested. Note should also tie new figures to Vietnam —Colson
6. Have Morton issue statement regarding poll—Dent
7. RNC [Republican National Committee] should mention in *MONDAY* (—Klein) and notify State Chairmen and other spokesmen—Dent
8. Notify GOP Governors of poll and reasons for popularity increase. Urge Governors to discuss it publicly—Dent
9. Vice President should be urged to include poll in all speeches—Klein
10. Ask Douglas Committee to tie this in with their program—Colson
11. Ask Perot to tie in with his program—Butterfield
12. Paris negotiators should be told to push this as a sign of unity—Kissinger
13. South Vietnam Government should be asked to push this as a sign that Americans back Nixon policy—Kissinger

The obsession with public relations fed on two themes within the White House. One was that the President was not getting enough recognition from the press for his accomplishments. The second theme was that through game plans the means could be devised to go beyond the Washington press and gain more favorable grass-roots attention. In fairness, it should be said that most administrations, including President Carter's, constantly seek new and dramatic ways to affect public opinion.

Throughout the first two years of the administration, Henry Kissinger and the President worked incessantly on ideas for bringing the Vietnam War to an "honorable conclusion." Kissinger would return from his Paris negotiating sessions with Le Duc Tho of North Vietnam, sometimes highly optimistic and on other occasions badly depressed. It would seem as if we were within inches of a solution and then suddenly the North Vietnamese would again pull the bottom out. Peace seemed to be "at hand" many times.

At home, during this same time, the protests mounted and demonstrations increased in intensity and in numbers, and this was perceived within the administration as having influence on North Vietnamese attitudes.

There were important efforts made to maintain public support, which was deemed essential in convincing the North Vietnamese that the President would not cave in because of public outcry. There were presidential reports, Kissinger briefings, speeches by me and all of the cabinet officers and by many in Congress, and meetings with key American leaders.

But along with these professional efforts came some of the inevitable amateur public relations. One of these ideas was that we could rally support within the Republican Party by printing a special issue of *Monday*, the weekly publication of the National Committee.

The idea for self-glorification was discussed in an after-the-fact memo to Magruder from Haldeman's young assistant Larry Higby.

THE WHITE HOUSE
WASHINGTON

CONFIDENTIAL

October 16, 1970

MEMORANDUM FOR: MR. MAGRUDER

FROM: L. HIGBY

I've just gone through a session with Bob on the Special Report. He made the following observations:

First of all, the important thing is not the fact that we have a Special Report, but the "World-Wide Acclaim for Nixon's Peace Initiative". Special Report should have been in very small letters at the top with "WORLD-WIDE ACCLAIM FOR NIXON'S PEACE INITIATIVES" in bold lettering. This is something we completely over looked and, in fact, I'll assume blame for it since I did see the layout. Beyond that, it simply takes the format of another Monday with Special Report instead of Monday across the top. We're getting there but we still have a ways to go.

Incidentally, I think you'll recall that when we started this and when we talked to your RNC man on Friday afternoon we agreed that the "World Wide Acclaim for Nixon's Peace Initiatives" was supposed to be across the top.

Earlier, someone had the public relations notion that what we needed was a series of documentaries, telling the administration side of what was happening in Vietnam and Cambodia:

THE WHITE HOUSE
WASHINGTON

May 19, 1970

CONFIDENTIAL

MEMORANDUM FOR: MR. KLEIN

You will recall a couple of the very well executed documentaries which were done after the Cuban Invasion. Some of these, I am sure, were Kennedy inspired. We need to launch a couple of producers on the documentation of our side of the Cambodian decision, the aftermath, and the results.

Perhaps one of the more friendly broadcasting organizations (undoubtedly an independent) will undertake this project. It could be used on their stations or perhaps some supporters can eventually get some network air time for it.

Please let me have your thoughts on this.

H. R. HALDEMAN

I explained the impracticality of the idea of government-sponsored documentaries, which in effect would be looked upon as propaganda. But the staff secretary system came forth again with a second memorandum in August:

THE WHITE HOUSE

WASHINGTON

August 7, 1970

MEMORANDUM FOR: MR. KLEIN

Regarding my memorandum to you on May 19th, we still need to launch a couple of producers on documentation on our side of the Cambodian decision, the aftermath and results. Your July 13th memorandum to me was true enough of the immediate aftermath of the Cambodian action. However, all those efforts that we made at that time including the President's network interview are going to leave the public's mind.

What we need is a documentary which comes out sometime in the next couple of months that further substantiates the President's Cambodian action and the courage that he illustrated by his moves.

This is one of those watershed decisions that we cannot afford to let anyone forget.

Please let me know what producers you are able to line up to work on this documentary.

H. R. HALDEMAN

I made a few perfunctory efforts with possible producers so I would have an honest answer to the memo, and eventually I was able to stall the project enough to allow it to die an anguished death. I felt my stubbornness had been more beneficial than the President recalled.

Throughout this sensitive period, I found it necessary to take extra precautions to protect the credibility of my office of communications, and on this basis I ruled out participation in most of the amateur public relations schemes. Mrs. Margita White, a remarkably skilled political scientist, was my administrative assistant and the watchdog of the office, reviewing anything that was to go out publicly and protecting me from some of the illogical pressure wrought by the PR onslaughts.

Minor game plans did not interest me. I left those to Magruder and Strachan, and I took an interest in them only if the PR proposal might violate the ethical guidelines of fact, not opinion, that I held for my office. This often meant killing portions of the programs to the chagrin of these young assistants. Because of this need for credibility in my and Ziegler's offices, Haldeman sometimes would use others on the staff to carry out a plan. He was under pressure to execute at least perfunctorily.

Because the President felt that television was the most important medium, the public relations amateurs concentrated on it and frequently came up with ideas ranging from an effort to intimidate broadcasters to seeking novel means of getting White House programs on the air.

Some of the plans involved the Tell-It-to-Hanoi Committee, a front committee organized by Chuck Colson to raise money and sponsor advertising that either attacked Vietnam protesters or supported the administration's war effort. This in itself was looked upon as a public relations effort and it was supported by many sincere, patriotically minded citizens.

During the late spring of 1970, some of the Vietnam opponents bought time on television to air their views, and they paid for this with money raised through an appeal at the end of the program. This led to a variety of schemes, developed in hours of discussion, to counteract the impact. Even Senator Ed Gurney, Florida Republican, came up with his own plan, which was eventually aborted.

THE WHITE HOUSE
WASHINGTON

June 10, 1970

CONFIDENTIAL

MEMORANDUM FOR: MR. HALDEMAN

FROM: JEB S. MAGRUDER

RE: TV Special to Counteract Democratic Senators on War

One idea that was brought up after Senators McGovern, Goodell, etc., had a paid TV show was to counteract with our own show. Senator Gurney, on his own, began to develop this idea and approached us through his Administrative Assistant, Robert Ryan, to fund it and help produce it. After a number of false starts we were able to gain financing through the Tell-It-To-Hanoi Committee on the condition that it would be a plus for the President. We were also able to engage Roger Ailes to assist in the production. The line up was scheduled to be Gurney, Dole, Dominick, McClellan, and Stennis.

After Roger Ailes and his crew were involved in this and had talked to all of the Senators, it was their considered opinion that the show would not be successful and would be a minus for the President. Based on that opinion the Tell-It-To-Hanoi Committee felt it would be a mistake to continue and I agreed. This morning I talked with Bill Timmons and Lyn Nofziger relative to the problem that might develop, particularly with Senator Gurney, and they agreed that if the show would not be successful it should be cancelled.

This afternoon the Tell-It-To-Hanoi Committee called Ryan in Senator Gurney's office and cancelled the show. Although no indication was given of White House involvement, naturally Senator Gurney is very upset because he feels he was let down by us. Lyn Nofziger and Ken BeLieu have covered the subject with Senator Gurney and any further information regarding the Senator's reaction should be discussed with them.

cc: Mr. Klein

Lyn Nofziger skillfully played a difficult and unique role during this period.

Nofziger is a veteran California newspaperman who had worked with me, and for me, during a 20-year span with the Copley News Service. He was one of the few conservatives who were popular at the Press Club because of his strong sense of humor and notorious puns. Most of his professional career had been spent writing politics from Washington for the Copley News Service.

In 1966, Nofziger had left his newspaper job to become press secretary to Ronald Reagan as candidate and as governor and, except for his stint in the White House, he had a key role with Reagan until the summer of 1979.

One of the public relations functions which the President felt was neglected was in providing speech material for his supporters in Congress. He wanted a more vigorous attack-and-counterattack program and felt it would not be forthcoming from the Hill without direct White House support and prodding. Attack, attack, attack.

Nofziger was the choice of Bryce Harlow and myself for the position. Operating as a one-man show, which he preferred, he would write one-page remarks, to be used by a variety of senators and congressmen in comments on the floor of Congress, and speeches. The plan worked ideally in its early stages. Nofziger was tough and knew how to make news. Congressmen liked and trusted him. He could attack, but within bounds of reason. He was content to stay completely in the background.

More and more, however, as the year developed, Colson sought to use Nofziger's skills for his own purposes. Nofziger paid lip service to Colson but managed to avoid his more unsavory schemes. As long as he remained rough and tough in his own way, Colson found it difficult to attack him.

During the same period, Colson began to expand his empire to delve into public relations.

I paid fairly little attention to Colson when he joined the staff in late 1969 at Harlow's request. Colson was a former assistant to Senator Leverett Saltonstall of Massachusetts and a veteran of political wars against the Kennedys. He joined the White House staff to develop closer liaison for the President with outside groups such as veterans and labor, and he was skillful in this field.

We worked together with Red Blount on early postal union disputes. On another occasion, I flew with Colson to the home of Henry Cabot Lodge to gain his support for a White House project regarding Vietnam. My relationship with Lodge was close, but there were some earlier campaign scars between him and Saltonstall's staff. Pulling me aside, Lodge asked if he could trust Colson. I assured him he could in this project. Fortunately, I said "this project."

My first insight into the one-minded ruthlessness of Colson came in mid-1970, however, when Jeb Magruder asked for help to protect him from a Colson onslaught over who would operate a special mailing office which dealt with opinion makers. Earlier it had been decided that responsibility for the small office would be divided since it was used by both of us for mailings to our own clientele. The mailing operation had been started by my assistants, who built up sizable lists of addresses.

I called Colson and Magruder into my office to lay out a plan for the operation and, to my surprise, Colson was immovable.

We met the next day at lunch at the Sans Souci restaurant, with Magruder and Bart Porter joining Colson and myself.

At this point, Colson was not only unbending, refusing any compromise, but he launched into a demeaning attack on Magruder. It was the most unpleasant lunch I ever had at the Sans Souci.

I believe that luncheon had a psychological effect on Magruder, leaving him in fear of Colson, even though he openly hated him. That psychology of fear is cited by Magruder as one of the reasons he felt pressured particularly by Colson to come up with a supercampaign-intelligence scheme in 1972 (eventually Watergate)!

In a memo to Nofziger regarding mailings, Colson concluded, "You know I am meaner than anyone else."

Colson was particularly skillful in working with blue-collar groups, which basically had many conservative instincts but traditionally had been more closely allied with the Democratic Party. He built close ties with veterans, many union leaders, and some professional groups. But as one of our amateur public relations experts, he was hammer-handed, never subtle.

When he was about to bring the hardhats from the construction unions into the cabinet room, we had a debate over whether they should wear the hats while at the meeting table. I opted against that; I also opposed the idea of asking the President to put one of the hats on. I had seen a variety of bonnets presented to candidates, including Nixon, ranging from cowboy hats to Indian headdresses, and inevitably they were too large and presented a ridiculous picture of a man drowning in his headgear.

Colson won the hard-hat debate—and he had a hat which fit the President.

Colson's attack mood would result sometimes in a memo such as this to Paul Costello, one of my press assistants:

THE WHITE HOUSE
WASHINGTON

November 21, 1970

CONFIDENTIAL

MEMORANDUM FOR PAUL COSTELLO

We have a very juicy little story about Congressman Ottinger—a release which he put out three days before the election commenting on the President's peace initiative in language in large part identical to what the North Vietnamese had said about it.

I would like to find a very friendly columnist who would help us do a hatchet job which could be used in the future if Ottinger ever again rears his ugly head.

CHARLES W. COLSON

Costello showed the memo to me. We did nothing but file it.

Colson and his staff also loved game plans. Typical was a five-page plan produced on July 17, 1970, to devise a program to fight "McGovern-Hatfield Projects." This was in reference to an amendment sponsored by the two senators to force the withdrawal of American troops from Vietnam within a preannounced timetable.

The Colson plan included formation of an attack group in Congress to be headed by Senator Robert Dole, and it included not only press conferences in Washington, but in New York, where the sponsor would be the Tell-It-to-Hanoi Committee. Colson suggested describing the McGovern-Hatfield amendment as a "declaration of defeat" or the "surrender amendment."

"McGovern-Hatfield sponsors are really trying to steal a political issue away from the President; the President has a withdrawal plan which is working and the McGovern-Hatfield backers are trying to capture credit for the success of our Vietnamization program by making it appear that they, not the President, are bringing it about," Colson wrote.

"The idea that this would be the first defeat in American Army history —defeated not by an enemy in the field but by irresponsible, demagogic politicians at home is also a powerful argument," he added.

A major game plan such as this included not only points of argument, but documentation of varied activities to fulfill the project's objective.

In this case, Tell-It-to-Hanoi would be the focal point for organized public activities with an outside public relations man, Gene Bradley, serving as the organizer. It included help which could be obtained from veterans' groups and conservative youth organizations.

It concluded with the suggestion of programming administration speakers including possibly the President but concentrating on the Vice-President, cabinet secretaries George Romney and John Volpe, "because they have some national visibility and because they are hard-hitting speakers and, eventually the plan should include every administration spokesman."

The public relations phenomenon was not a Nixon White House invention. It has been a part of all recent administrations. For some, such as President Kennedy and President Eisenhower in the early months of their administrations, warm press relations made the task easy. The Nixon plans were more frantic and hard-line because of the strong White House belief that there were no friends in the press. The public was getting a fairly presented look at the real Nixon.

Occasionally I would receive an anonymous third-person look at what the President himself thought his public image should be. Sometimes this would be in the form of two or three paragraphs with a cover memo from Haldeman, Higby, or presidential deputy assistant Alex Butterfield (who later revealed the existence of the Nixon tapes). These were never attributed directly to the President but the source was obvious. On September 16, 1970, I received a lengthy third-person presidential assessment—the President's perception of his own image. Accompanying it was a simple transmission note from Higby:

THE WHITE HOUSE
WASHINGTON

September 16, 1970

MEMORANDUM FOR: MR. KLEIN

FROM: L. HIGBY

Mr. Haldeman asked that I forward the attached to you. It is his feeling that many of the points made in this document are things our people should be promoting.

Attachment

PR POINTS TO BE MADE

To the extent that the President had *any* public support during the Cambodian venture, this was a devastating indication of the lack of credibility of the national media—especially *Time* and *Newsweek*, the Washington *Post*, the New York *Times*, and the three networks. All of them have opposed RN violently on this issue.

This is not something new. RN is the first President in this century who came into the Presidency with the opposition of all of these major communication powers. Since he has been in office, with only very few exceptions, he has been heavily opposed—not just editorially by these publications and networks—but primarily by the slant of the news coverage due to the attitude of reporters.

The fact that he now survives this with 55–60% approval by the people indicates not so much something about RN as it does something about the news media. This support percentage, incidentally, is a rather remarkable figure in view of the fact that it is in a period of economic slow-down. Eisenhower, in the whole year of 1958, when he had Lebanon and other foreign policy successes, had a Gallup rating which dropped into the 50's.

In other words this is a time for soul-searching on the part of the press as to whether it is they who are out of tune with the people rather than the President.

The President has taken all this with good grace. He has never during

his period of office, called a publisher, commentator, editor, etc., for
purposes of criticizing him.

The real meaning of this is that the President himself has finally
reached the conclusion which should be one which should cause the
media some concern. He now realizes he does not have to have their support. He realizes they are going to write from a biased viewpoint and he
just doesn't pay any attention to their views—although he of course, reads
many of the columns. In other words, the news media are losing their
most important listener and viewer—the President of the United States—
not because he personally objects to what they say about him (because
he doesn't) but because they have consistently opposed everything he
stands for, regardless of the merits, with an occasional exception like
the postal strike where nobody could be on the other side. The reason
they've lost him is because he knows that their influence in the country
is not what the people in Washington think it is. Obviously the President
wouldn't be where he was if he had to depend upon national news
media and the pollsters. He got where he was in spite of what they did
and said rather than because of them.

Along these lines also, no one has been written off more frequently or
completely than RN. In the Hiss case, the '52 fund, several times during
the Vice Presidency, in 1962, and of course before the convention in
1968. Obviously RN is resilient and seems to do best when the going is
roughest.

RN's effectiveness in using the television medium is remarkable. This
is due, of course, to the tremendous amount of preparation that he takes
before making a TV appearance. With the exception of TR, Wilson
and Hoover, RN is probably the only President in this century who still
sits down from time to time and completely writes a major speech himself. This makes it possible for him to use the television medium much
more effectively than anyone had before him.

The President does an enormous amount of communicating to and
with people throughout the nation—the letters that he writes and the
calls that he makes to candidates, sports figures and others who lose as
well as win—calls during the Christmas season to parents of men killed
in Vietnam and to old friends across the country who are sick. His
solicitude for the widows of Senators and Congressmen like Mrs. Dirksen
and Mrs. Lipscomb and of course his treatment of Johnson and
Humphrey which has been 180 degrees different than the way he was
treated while he was out of office. In eight years he was never invited to
a lunch or dinner at the White House while we had Humphrey to the
Astronauts' Dinner and the Johnsons on numerous occasions.

Also, we have had a practice of inviting the families of all former Presidents to the White House at some time while President Nixon is in

office including the Cleveland sisters, John Coolidge, etc. Another similar point is the invitation to Charles Lindberg [sic]. These acts of civility are another hallmark of this President.

In 23 years of press conferences, hundreds of them in the United States and around the world, RN has never had a question planted. Also the stand-up television press conference which the White House correspondents seem to have "discovered" has been standard operating procedures for RN throughout his public life. He has no planted questions, he does not recognize favorite reporters—he takes them as they come— prefers the tough questions rather than the easy ones and he has always used the single mike technique. The reaction to the coup at the Gridiron is interesting. Everytime Kennedy appeared before the Gridiron, there were reams of columns with regard to the effectiveness of the appearance, although on several of them he dropped a real bomb. It's interesting that in spite of the 100% agreement by everyone there that the RN-Agnew appearance was an all time high, very little press reflected this afterwards. There is very little realization of the enormous effect RN has in his unpublicized appearances—such as the dinner for the AP editors— the Cabinet and sub-Cabinet meeting at Christmastime—the NATO luncheon—the Armed Forces breakfast—Cabinet Meetings—meetings with Labor Leaders, etc.

Re: the opposition to RN by the establishment and the press. The most dramatic example, perhaps, was where the cover stories on *Time* and *Newsweek,* as well as editorial comments by Sevareid and all of the pundits on television, wrote off RN during late September and most of October before his November 3rd speech. When he made the speech regarding Vietnam he went exactly the opposite way. He had been urged by this group to declare a cease-fire and a massive withdrawal of troops. Instead he stood firm. These people subsequently never gave him credit for the turn-around, but obviously it nevertheless occurred.

Re: Press Conferences. He also never uses notes or opens with a fili-bustering statement at a Press Conference and he never issues a correction afterwards. Some of his critics complain that he doesn't have enough press conferences, but when he has one and does well, they complain because they weren't able to knock him out of the box—in other words, he can't win.

When this Administration came into office a year ago there was a credibility gap as far as the Presidency was concerned. Now, ironically, there is a credibility gap as far as the press is concerned.

The key to all this, of course, is that RN, very consciously, has taken an entirely different tact [sic] from LBJs and a different tact than was urged upon him by some of his friends. Instead of trying to win the press, to cater to them, to have backgrounders with them, RN has ignored them and has talked directly to the country by TV whenever possible. He has used the press and not let the press use him. He has particularly not allowed the press, whenever he could avoid it, to filter his ideas to the public. This is a remarkable achievement.

Again, the press was the major subject of the President.

While game plans such as that developed by Colson for the McGovern-Hatfield amendment were basically attack documents, most of the public relations proposals, especially those of the professionals, were positive in nature. We launched the administration's plan for welfare reform with a multifaceted project that included everything from speech materials to briefings across the country and appearances on all possible television shows. We worked against the Howard Hughes effort to stop underground nuclear testing near Las Vegas, and we developed support programs for the SST.

The fight against drug abuse received major attention from the President. My staff, led by Magruder, capably developed a conference of national leaders with Art Linkletter and Richard Nixon as the costars. It featured a well-attended briefing and exhibitions on the White House grounds with trained dogs sniffing for narcotics in postal packages. We worked with television producers, assisting with materials and research for episodes in police dramas, which would be educational as well as entertaining. It was a sound program well supported by television. Among other strong supporters was David Hartman, now of ABC.

In my view, the most fruitful public relations evaluations came from an informal group I chaired called the Saturday Morning Planning Committee. Participants included Dwight Chapin, presidential appointments secretary; Richard Moore, a creative general-utility assistant to the President; Safire, Price, Keogh, Magruder, Nofziger; and Rob Odle and Ed Blecksmith, bright young assistants on my staff. Ziegler was invited but showed strange disdain for these meetings. Late in 1970, Colson attended once or twice and then in typical fashion tried to break up the committee with meetings of his own.

The Saturday morning sessions provided an example of freewheeling discussion and debate, which was lacking in too many areas of the White House. While we had a small agenda, anyone was free to bring up other topics during the two-hour brainstorming session. Frequently other members of the White House staff would provide a memo or appear before the group to try out a new idea.

Topics ranged from an insignificant discussion of neckties—which looked best on the President—to school integration problems; from the problems created by a man who vowed to fast until death across from the White House in Lafayette Park, to press protests of difficulty in covering Vietnam and Cambodia.

There were serious, but unheeded, recommendations, illustrated by the summary from a discussion on May 25, 1970, which said: "Regardless of whether or not the Vice-President's Friday speech [a major media attack] was thought beneficial, it was felt [by the committee] that he should now find a new target to attack, other than the media and student unrest. Because of the problem of his weak staff, Buchanan might be the person to suggest a new target."

More amusing was this notation:

"Dick Moore discussed the problem of the *Women's Wear Daily* report on the Attorney General's comments at a cocktail party Thursday. The group suggests taking a low profile, saying the Attorney General was badly misquoted out of context at a cocktail party by a second-rate gossip columnist.

"The group feels that the Attorney General should not immediately go on the Frost show as he had planned; Safire will give the Vice-President an answer to this controversy if he's asked about it on the Frost show which is taped tonight."

Much ado about little.

Out of these committee sessions came ideas passed along to writers for potential books, ranging from the factual *Setting the Course,* by Richard Wilson, to *Courage and Hesitation,* a book of independent observations of the White House written by author Allen Drury, with photographs by Fred Maroon, a top free-lance photographer.

John Ehrlichman once suggested to the group that the Republican chairman, Rogers Morton, walk into the Democratic chairman's office with a tall stack of legislation which the President had proposed. The Democratic chairwoman, Mary Lou Burg, had accused the President of a do-nothing approach to domestic legislation. The committee killed the Ehrlichman gimmick.

Late in 1970, we developed the idea for a televised conversation between the President and British Prime Minister Heath, who was due to visit Washington early in 1971. The program would be made available for network coverage in the United States and would be sent by satellite to Europe. This would have been the first program of its kind and the idea was greeted with enthusiasm, particularly by CBS in private conversations I had with CBS president Frank Stanton to test the waters. The proposal died when Nixon ruled against it on the grounds it might look artificial.

Another constructive idea to restructure cabinet meetings was outlined to the Saturday morning group in this fashion:

1. *The President's Accessibility.* Obviously, with Hickel's letter as a peg, the "isolation of the President" will become a major theme, as the Janssen piece in the *Wall Street Journal* presaged.

A strong point to counter this is the system of breaking the Cabinet meetings up into *working sessions of groups within the Cabinet,* which meet at length with the President. As an example, the Cabinet Committee on Economic Policy, which includes six Cabinet members, meet with him at length about every six weeks. In this, the President's most frequent question is "You don't agree with that, do you?" That is, he seeks out the conflicts of opinion that always exist among strong men. After one of these three-hour sessions, a Cabinet member leaves with the knowledge that he had his chance to present his views personally and forcibly, no holds barred—as, for example, Shultz did on tight money last fall and Romney did on jawboning this spring.

Basic point: *There has never before been this kind of regular forum for Cabinet members to make their points on overall policy.* In addition, a Cabinet member can do what Secretary Kennedy chose to do on one portion of the tax reform debate—to "go into the silences," as he put it [an old Mormon phrase], and to give his opinion to the President privately and personally later.

I believe this idea still has much merit for the current President, but it was never tried during the Nixon administration.

7

Nixon, the Inscrutable Man

THE DIRECT QUESTION most asked is, What makes Richard Nixon tick; what goes on deep inside of him?

There is no simple answer. He is a complex man—extremely complex, a man of many contrasts. I've yet to find a simple sentence or paragraph to describe him for the press.

Richard Nixon is a man with great drive who also is deeply embroiled in his own ego and pride. He possesses or is possessed by overwhelming ambition; a sense of and a desire for accomplishment in a historic sense, yet a deep-seated insecurity and fear of failure. Despite these things, he often has been willing to take a courageous gamble. I believe a combination of these elements frequently has brought conflict within the man, causing him to strike out at others, motivated by anxiety.

He is inhibited and keeps thoughts, feelings, and problems to himself for the most part. His silences can be deafening to a close colleague or family member sensitive to his many moods and volatile nature.

He has tremendous power of concentration when probing into a major problem. This gives him the ability to absorb and understand facts quickly. He is a student of history.

He can become as angry as any man I have ever seen. He can be ruthless, and he has been. He can be compassionate, and he has been. He is a man of contrasts. He can be most thoughtful, generous, solicitous, or kind. He is very analytic. It is difficult to measure happiness within him.

He used to scoff at intellectuals, but he longed to be recognized as one. He is a scholar and yet a pragmatist. He is gifted with high intelligence,

and amazing memory for detail. He has extraordinary perception and intuition.

After meeting Nixon individually or in a small group, people usually
would say that they had a new and warm feeling for him. "Isn't it too
bad he doesn't come across that warmly in an auditorium or on television,"
they would say.

I have seen him stand in long reception lines by the hour and remember
by name, or at least city, more than half of the thousands he would see.
He has great powers of memory.

In a small reception line before a state dinner in the White House
he would be more stilted. On at least fifty occasions he warmly greeted
my wife by her first name, Marge, and then spoiled the effect with the
same line: "What a pretty dress. How can Herb afford it?" It didn't matter
what the dress was, the line was inevitable.

Those of us close to him learned to read his anger or impatience by
a change in his voice tone, and the structure of his sentences. As anger
or resentment built, the words came quicker and were clipped.

The first time I saw the full display of his quick anger was on the
Friday night before the presidential election of 1952.

As the vice-presidential nominee, Nixon had been assigned campaign
responsibility for carrying his own state, California. This was the first of
my five presidential campaigns and, at his request, I had been granted
leave from my job as editorial-page editor of the San Diego *Union* to
handle press relations for the state and to help plan and execute the
strategy.

Following the instructions of Murray Chotiner, a climactic campaign
rally had been planned by Bernard Brennan, Charles Ducommun (Nixon
state and county chairmen), and me. While Nixon was the speaker, the
rally at the Hollywood Legion Stadium, a boxing arena, included ten of
the top Hollywood stars, ranging from Jane Russell to John Wayne.

The crowd was enthusiastic. The stars played their roles well. But the
stadium was only three fourths full. The empty seats stood out in Nixon's
eyes, and mine, much more than did the full ones.

In a political campaign, a small crowd is usually interpreted as meaning poor organization or a candidate who is failing to build an enthusiastic
following—or both.

In this case, neither answer was correct.

It was Halloween night, the toughest night to gather a crowd in a political campaign. The younger people we had thought would be developing
into an overflow crowd, listening to speakers we had installed outside as
well as in, were simply with their children playing games of trick or treat.

This was not a game to the vice-presidential nominee. We knew he
was angry. He left the stadium hurriedly, almost losing the press. Peter

Kaye, my young assistant, had to scramble to herd newsmen into a bus.

Once inside his suite at the Ambassador Hotel, Nixon exploded. How could he have entrusted the California campaign to such nincompoops? We would probably lose California and the election. No one, and I mean no one, is to take any time off in the next four days, he shouted. He went on and on. Finally he looked at Chotiner and me and ordered us to reorganize the campaign immediately. He would campaign as scheduled elsewhere in the country, but we were to stay there and make up for all the "dumb things" we had done.

Chotiner was not as surprised at the anger as was I. He had seen the temper displayed on the plane after the Checkers Speech and on one or two other occasions.

We sat on the hotel hall steps pulling ourselves together and devising new strategy. We sent telegrams to every committee chairman in the state, ordering an all-out effort even through the weekend.

What the effect was, I don't know. I did see my friend Representative Clinton McKinnon, the Stevenson state chairman, complacently going home to San Diego and taking the weekend off.

The Eisenhower-Nixon ticket carried California by 700,000 votes.

In March of 1959, Nixon was appointed chairman of a cabinet committee on price stability and economic growth. Arthur Burns, then chairman of the President's economic council, recommended Dr. Allen Wallis, young dean of the Graduate School of Business at the University of Chicago, as the ideal person to be executive vice-chairman and the staff person who would direct the committee activities. There were two advantages. A Wallis appointment would give the committee added stature in the economic community and the association would help Nixon gain better coloration in the academic halls. Early on, Nixon, an economic conservative, recognized that he was not expert in this field but that what happened to the country economically affected every other issue. Wallis was not political, but he was open-minded. He was outspoken on behalf of things he believed in. The dean accepted the appointment and also became a special assistant to the President.

Later that year, Wallis, on behalf of the University of Chicago, invited the Vice-President to speak at the dedication of a new law school. Prior to the dinner and formal session, there was a private reception and question-and-answer session with members of the University of Chicago faculty.

The faculty meeting went well and had great favorable impact. Nixon had been well briefed by Wallis on the way in from the airport, and he was able to recall personal notes about individuals as he met them in the receiving line. One professor had objected strongly to the treatment of the Rosenbergs, who had been convicted of conspiracy. Nixon remembered the briefing and the man, as he greeted him and brought up the sensitive subject for discussion. The professor was amazed and impressed.

The first question in the more formal session with the faculty came from Professor Richard Stern, who has since become a novelist. He asked Nixon what reading he had done during his youth.

Nixon first tossed it off lightly by saying he was "flattered you think a Republican reads."

He then said he did not feel he had read sufficiently before he had entered college, but his freshman English professor had had great impact upon him, and he became thoroughly engrossed in reading. When he asked the professor for suggestions on summer reading, he had suggested Tolstoy. That summer he read most of the weighty works of the Russian author. Later he read Voltaire, and he suggested "maybe this was where I got my radical ideas." The faculty laughed with him.

At Duke University, where he studied law and worked as an assistant to Dr. Lon Fuller, the latter suggested that he read Austrian law during one summer. He cited the value of this in gaining the basis of comparison with American law.

Another Chicago professor followed up to probe the reality and depth of the Nixon statement by asking which books of Tolstoy were the best, in his opinion. Nixon said that he had a divided opinion between *Anna Karenina* and *War and Peace*. He thought least of some of Tolstoy's writing when he was bordering on spiritualism.

As the later questions covered foreign and domestic policy, it was obvious that the faculty was taking a new look at Nixon.

When Nixon left to go to the Quadrangle Club about a dozen student pickets appeared nearby, protesting Nixon's appearance on campus.

We avoided them and went upstairs to a suite of rooms for "staff time."

Pickets were not a common collegiate commodity at that time. We were concerned that all of the good from the trip would be erased if the one picture which emerged was Nixon and the pickets. We inquired but there was no way to remove them without causing a worse incident and headline, even though the Vice-President was a guest of the university, there upon its invitation.

Colonel James Donald Hughes, the Vice-President's military aide, and I went in to see Nixon in his suite to work out the timing and logistics for the dinner. The Secret Service was devising a route to avoid confrontation with the pickets.

Nixon was so upset by the pickets that he was overcome with his black Irish anger. He could barely speak, but what he did say was that he would not go to the dinner. Why had we allowed this to happen? Did we realize how bad this was?

He was so angry he was shouting.

Hughes and I left the room in quick retreat, suggesting that he turn on the World Series.

We huddled for about ten minutes and decided we had to face him again and insist that he make his speech. We could avoid meeting the pickets where a picture would be taken.

While we were trying to stem the storm, Wallis and Dr. Sheldon Tefft, a law professor, waited below to escort the Vice-President. We sent down word that the Vice-President was still working on his speech and watching the World Series. He would be late and suggested that they go ahead since he rarely ate dinner before he spoke.

Tefft insisted he must wait. Finally he was convinced that he need not worry about protocol, we would be there.

We rejoined Nixon. He had cooled off and was working on his speech. We arrived late, avoided the pickets, and his address was hailed as a well-delivered academic success. His is a temper which flares hotly and can disappear quickly.

Most other recent Presidents have also displayed their tempers—Harry Truman, Dwight Eisenhower, John Kennedy, and Lyndon Johnson, even Jerry Ford and certainly Jimmy Carter. Each had another bond in common: temper was put aside and they were more cool in a crisis. Quick outbursts seem to help even Presidents relieve the tension. But anger was the furthest thing away from President Truman's mind when he ordered the atomic bomb dropped, from President Eisenhower's when he sent the Marines into Lebanon, from President Kennedy's during the missile crisis, or from President Johnson's during the most tense moments in Vietnam.

The most tense moment in Nixon's vice-presidential career came when a mob attempted to kill him in Caracas. He was cool in the crisis although openly angry after the ordeal when he finally reached the American Embassy.

Strong resentment was apparent, but unreasoned anger was not a factor as the student mobs surrounded the White House when he was President. Patience was a key ingredient as he worked for the first SALT agreement with the Soviet Union, and as he masterminded the strategy which led to the opening of the door to the People's Republic of China.

Interestingly, Henry Kissinger also can be quick in anger but always outwardly cool in negotiations. I saw him in one of his most angry moods one evening in the spring of 1973, when we were in Peking just after having spent five days in Hanoi negotiating postwar relationships between the United States and North Vietnam. Kissinger, who by this time had developed a warm personal as well as professional relationship with Chou En-lai and his subordinates, was tired after seemingly nonstop negotiations in Thailand, Laos, North Vietnam, and now the PRC—all during this one trip. He felt disappointed and frustrated that he had not up to this moment been able to arrange a personal meeting with Mao Tse-tung. He returned from a long meeting at the Great Hall of the People to the government guesthouse where we were staying. At about 10:30 P.M., I found him pacing one of the halls of the guesthouse letting off steam by swearing and denouncing the Chinese bureaucracy for failing to arrange a meeting with Mao. I paced with him for about five minutes, and suddenly we were interrupted by the announcement that Chou En-lai had arrived unexpectedly. It was almost as if the Chinese had listened to the Kissinger angry outburst and responded. Chou said that Mao wanted to see Kissinger and his brilliant young aide Winston Lord. Kissinger's mood changed instantly to one of geniality as he went off to a midnight meeting with the leader of the People's Republic of China.

In trying to analyze Richard Nixon long after I left the administration, I more fully realized that one consistent characteristic of the former President is that a great number of loyal people rose quickly in his favor and fell out of favor just as rapidly. But in the aftermath, most remained loyal to him. He ran through a great number and a great variety of people who served on his staff during the years of his public service. Most survived, at best, a few years and then disappeared. There was no one reason apparent for the constant change in Nixon's regard for people. Some of the personnel failed to live up to his needs or expectations. They were poor selections in the first place, too weak for him. Others displeased him because they disagreed too often or because they developed strong personality conflicts. Rarely were there open conflicts. It was almost like the case of a young suitor who frequently would become enamored of one date and then become disappointed or tired and switch to another. Yet Nixon retained an affection for the individual, and it was returned almost without exception.

Bill Arnold was first in and first out. A Californian and the son of the political editor of the Los Angeles *Herald-Express,* Arnold became administrative assistant to Congressman Nixon after he was elected in 1946. He lost his key role in 1950, when Nixon was elected to the Senate.

Bob King arrived, highly heralded from the public relations and advertising field, working for Southern Comfort Distillers. After his tenure, he remained a friend and eventually, with Nixon's sponsorship, was appointed to organize part of the 1960 Winter Olympics at Squaw Valley.

James Bassett joined Nixon hours after he was nominated to be Vice-President in 1952. Bassett, later an associate editor of the Los Angeles *Times,* had impressive credentials as a political correspondent and eventually as an author of the book and movie *In Harm's Way.*

Bassett was the first Nixon press secretary, and a highly capable one. He was witty; he was intelligent. He kept things together in the critical days of the Nixon fund dilemma, and after the election he loyally stayed on in Washington another two years to represent the Vice-President and to guide press and public relations for the Republican National Committee in 1953 and 1954.

In 1956 Bassett, like myself, took leave from his newspaper to be the traveling campaign chief of staff, although his title was press secretary. I was his assistant and working press secretary. Bassett was effective as a leader.

But by 1960, he too had been ground up in the mill and he had a lesser position than he deserved, serving in the Washington headquarters as the chief assistant to Leonard Hall, the campaign manager.

Murray Chotiner was Nixon's top political adviser and strategist from 1950 to 1954. Rough, pragmatic, brilliant, but always controversial, he devised the strategy for the Senate race against Helen Gahagan Douglas in 1950, and he later helped Senator Nixon gain the national attention which led to his nomination as Vice-President. Long before anyone had given serious thought to Nixon as a vice-presidential possibility on an Eisenhower ticket Chotiner had discussed the question with Governor Thomas Dewey and Herbert Brownell, two of the key men in the "Ike" movement.

Chotiner and William Rogers, who later became Attorney General and Secretary of State, helped Nixon most as he fought to stay on the presidential ticket when the story of a so-called secret fund broke late in the 1952 campaign. Chotiner argued for toughness and a strong emotional appeal in what became the Checkers Speech.

Typical of his professional pragmatism was Chotiner's answer to a leaked story saying that Eisenhower might ask Nixon to get off the ticket.

"Why do the Republicans have to play right into the hands of the enemy? How stupid can they be? If those damned amateurs around Eisenhower just had the sense they were born with they would recognize that this is a purely political attack, and they wouldn't pop off like this."

Just before the Checkers Speech in Los Angeles Chotiner lectured Nixon to remember, "This is politics. The prize is the White House. The Democrats have attacked you because they are afraid to take on Eisenhower. You are the lightning rod."

When the broadcast speech was over, I met Chotiner and Nixon in a suite at the Ambassador Hotel. We waited tensely for reaction. It came in a telephone call I took from a man in Florida who said the Western Union lines were so jammed he couldn't get through so he had called the hotel to urge Nixon to stay on the ticket. Then the deluge of calls and telegrams followed.

With the battle won, it was Chotiner who refused a telephone call from Fred Seaton on the Eisenhower train, arguing, "Let the bastards wait for us this time."

In later years, Chotiner was mired under by a congressional investigation into whether he had illegally sought favors for "unsavory" clients (nothing was proved, but his name was hurt badly), he continued to play a role in each campaign through 1972, but not in the same position. Only his political quickness and tough persistence kept him on the staff. His was a background role, hidden almost as if he were operating from a closet. Each year a new story would appear discovering Chotiner. Typical was a column by Rowland Evans and Robert Novak which appeared on October 13, 1968, headlined "Out of the Past, Former Aide Chotiner Reappears."

Chotiner developed the Nixon political intelligence operation for the 1960 and 1968 campaigns.

The code words for the operation were "Chapman's friend."

Chapman's friend was not one person but several persons who filled this political intelligence role. The job of the agent was to observe as much as possible on a firsthand basis in the opponent's camp and then to telephone Chotiner daily with a report. This was a legal approach to the intelligence problem and was routine for most candidates, Democratic or Republican, in those days. It is in contrast to the illegal and immoral intelligence and harassment later developed by Jeb Magruder, Gordon Liddy, and others.

Chotiner was intrigued by the need for intelligence, and some of his tactics, such as using part-time newsmen for part of the operation, bothered me, just as did similar CIA activities. But I rarely knew who "Chapman's friend" was, and I was used to being followed by the other side.

Looking back, I believe I made a mistake in telling Magruder too many stories about humorous incidents involving both "Chapman's friend" and Dick Tuck, the perpetual Democratic and Kennedy spy, who seemed to follow Nixon and me everywhere we campaigned. Tuck followed us so much that we became personal friends. I believe that the Tuck and Chapman stories had perhaps a subconscious effect on Magruder, making him under pressure more eager to come up with a scheme which would please John Mitchell and Bob Haldeman, a scheme he hoped would be recognized as more efficient than the old Chotiner or Kennedy staff systems.

I rarely saw anything in the reports from "Chapman's friend" which justified the money and effort put into them. Richard Nixon rarely saw the reports, but the fact that they were there satisfied "the old man's" intensely competitive feeling in this intelligence field.

Typical of the intelligence reports were these filed on September 13 and 19 and on October 29, 1968.

MEMORANDUM

TO: Bob Haldeman

FROM: Murray Chotiner

DATE: September 13, 1968

12:30 a.m. (that's ½ hour after midnight Sept. 12!!) Chapman's friend reports:

There was almost a press meeting on the subject of going back to Washington from Seagirt for a few hours and then taking off again for Pittsburgh.

At first they said those who wanted to return with Humphrey could ride back to Washington and the plane would pick up the rest in Lakehurst. It was then decided that everyone would stay in New Jersey and leave at 7:00 p.m. for Pittsburgh from Lakehurst.

HHH will be at Pittsburgh Friday night, September 13, for a meeting with Democratic "wheels." Saturday, he meets with women in Pittsburgh. The times of the meetings have not been given to the press.

He returns Saturday night to Washington and remains there Sunday and Monday. It is understood that LBJ and HHH will meet this weekend.

The following schedule (which I gave to our scheduling department) has been received:

Tuesday—Buffalo and Rochester, New York

Tuesday night and Wednesday—Washington (subject to change)

Thursday—Boston and Sioux Falls, South Dakota

Hours of the meetings are not given to the press, and they have been running 2 to 3 hours behind what they understand to be arrival times.

Chapman's friend thought at first the reason the schedule was so sketchy in details was that they were being terribly smart in not giving it out for "security." He is convinced that is not the reason, and it is only because of lack of planning and organization.

Thursday night—travel from Sioux Falls to Springfield, Illinois, to remain overnight.

Friday—Louisville; Saturday—Columbus, Ohio; Sunday—Cleveland; Monday—Toledo; and then home to Waverly.

Added comments from Chapman's friend about Flint. There were a lot of anti-war people. Some people fainted, and HHH was afraid they would fall into the glass windows in the crush that followed.

One press man asked if HHH got rid of his advance man.

A set expression has come over HHH's face that looks as though he has congealed.

Bob Young of the *Chicago Tribune* and the press man from the *Washington Post* are expected to write Sunday feature stories.

I will try to get the papers.

cc: John Mitchell
     Pete Flanigan
     Herb Klein
     Sherm Unger
     Pat Hillings

MEMORANDUM

TO: Bob Haldeman

FROM: Murray Chotiner

DATE: September 19, 1968

Chapman's friend reports from Boston Rally:

The noisiest and biggest reception so far, probably 10,000 or more gathered on four corners of downtown Boston and spreading outward from there.

The protesters were facing four directions, too, and shouted "boos" throughout the rally. They even booed Ted Kennedy, who responded by saying, "We'll get nowhere by shouting and screaming."

Kennedy introduced HHH to the crowd as "your next President," which was met with intensive booing that lasted for a full three minutes, along with chants of "No, no, no!" The band attempted to cover up the heckling, and as a result, nothing could be heard.

HHH's voice cracked several times, and he appeared rather shaken by the disturbance. But he told the crowd: "This is hardly disturbing; frankly it is ridiculous."

He went on to address the protesters, saying, "If you want to demonstrate for peace, ask your Senators to ratify the Non-Proliferation Treaty."

Then HHH spoke directly to Nixon: "The people in America have a right to know where you stand—on gun control, on the Treaty, on order in the streets . . ."

He then pledged "in the presence of a great friend, a great Senator" to bring the war to an end, if elected.

As the protest groups moved closer to the podium, he said: "Your actions here are disgusting the American people and will injure the cause of peace." "I will stand by what I believe; I will not be shouted down."

Kenny O'Donnell and Eddie McCormack were on podium but did not speak.

HHH berated Nixon by saying that he says one thing to Northerners and takes a different attitude when in the South.

There were McCarthy banners, SDS banners and Nixon banners. Some read "Sieg Heil!", "Dump the Hump," etc.

After Ted Kennedy opened with pleasantries, he said HHH has been in the forefront of every domestic issue and "I have no hesitancy in urging you to support HHH." This was met with strong boos and only a smattering of applause. He continued, "The alternative is a Republican candidate who would hold up ratification of the Non-Proliferation Treaty, which Robert Kennedy said is the most vital issue of the day."

Most of the press were stranded in a bus quite a way from the scene of the speech, as the police had blocked entry to the downtown area. Chapman's friend jumped onto a TV truck and arrived in time for all the activities.

Muriel Humphrey is there, and following the rally, the Humphreys, Joan and Ted Kennedy, and Boston Mayor Kevin White and wife drove away together.

cc: John Mitchell
     Pete Flanigan
     Herb Klein
     Sherm Unger
     Pat Hillings

MEMORANDUM

TO: Bob Haldeman   cc: Bob Ellsworth

   Truth Squad (c/o Harry Flemming, RNC)

FROM: Murray Chotiner

DATE: October 29, 1968—1:30 a.m.

Chapman's friend reports:
   The Humphrey people are expecting the McCarthy endorsement
on Tuesday, October 29. Mayor Stokes of Cleveland will be campaigning
in San Francisco this weekend. Stokes predicts that HHH will carry
Cleveland by 150,000 votes.
   HHH will concentrate the balance of the campaign in the 8 key
states.
   Peter O'Grady of Cleveland said that a secret Republican poll showed
Nixon is leading Humphrey by only one percent in Ohio.
   Humphrey took issue with the Cleveland *Plain Dealer*, which
shows RN running ahead.
   More detail on the HHH schedule:
   Friday, November 1, HHH will be in Peoria, Rock Island and Chi-
cago, Illinois and then on to Youngstown, Ohio.

cc: John Mitchell
      Pete Flanigan
      Herb Klein
      Pat Hillings
      Sherm Unger
      Fred LaRue

Dick Tuck was the most colorful and most publicly known of the intelligence sources of this time. He was Pat Brown's press secretary in 1958, and he worked for candidate Kennedy in 1960, for Governor Brown in 1962, and for Hubert Humphrey in 1968. He was a pixie and a prankster in perpetual motion. He was humorous and thrived on tricks. How effective he was is open to question in my mind.

When he first appeared as a "spy" in 1960, I spotted him quickly. I had known him well when he was Pat Brown's press secretary and later director of the California Department of Motor Vehicles.

Early in the 1960 campaign we were in Memphis, Tennessee. Tuck was there in the crowd. We later crossed the river into West Memphis, Arkansas, as part of the strategy for the candidate to say he had carried the campaign to all fifty states. In West Memphis, I asked Tuck how he happened to be there. He told me there was a transportation meeting in the area. The next day we were in Garden City on Long Island. So was Tuck.

He then admitted that he was working for Senator John Kennedy. I was secretly delighted to know who the political intelligence agent was and quietly gave him at least part of the schedule. We had fun needling each other, and occasionally I poured him a drink. Tuck became famous for a variety of tricks, mostly harmless, but some would be called "dirty tricks" under later terminology. When he went to a telephone booth to report his observations, I usually had someone in the next booth to listen. That was political intelligence—and counterintelligence—legitimate intelligence.

There are varying degrees of loyalty among Nixon supporters. None is more loyal than Rose Mary Woods.

When Nixon felt badly hurt, Rose Mary Woods felt hurt. When Nixon disliked a reporter, Rose Mary Woods expressed it by pouring a drink on his head or speaking her piece.

Rose joined Nixon in 1950, and she worked for him even after he left the presidency. Neither her hours nor her life have been her own during most of this time. But her mind is her own, and, unlike many who joined the White House staff, Rose would express her opinion directly when she thought "the boss" or those around him were wrong. Over the years, only a handful of those closest would argue with "the boss" or later with Bob Haldeman.

I would argue. Bob Finch would. Earlier Leonard Hall, Jim Bassett, and Chotiner would. Occasionally, military aide Don Hughes would.

Rose Woods's knowledge and loyalty were such that she could not be ground up in the Nixon machine. However, in the 1968 campaign she played an important but lesser role than before. While she was the first appointee to the Nixon White House staff, she soon found Haldeman moving her office from the customary personal secretary's place next to the

Oval Office, and she was effectively excluded from most meetings where she might argue.

I was in Saigon, gathering a report for the President on the Cambodia intrusion, when I learned that Bob Finch had been caught in the grinder. Haldeman called me about midnight Vietnamese time to inform me that my closest friend on the White House team was resigning as Secretary of Health, Education, and Welfare.

Halfway around the world there was nothing I could do to carry Finch's case back to the President. I wondered about the timing. Haldeman's explanation to me was that Finch was physically exhausted by trying to handle the bureaucratic pressures of the Department of Health, Education, and Welfare while serving additionally as a political counselor to the President.

Bob could be of more help to the President by retaining cabinet rank and serving like Arthur Burns and Bryce Harlow as a counselor to the President, Haldeman said. I didn't think of it then, but it also meant a pay cut of about $20,000 for Finch. In the circumstances, that was not most important. I was exhausted from trips to and from the battlefields in Vietnam and Cambodia, and this added blow to my friend distressed and depressed me. I was damned angry.

When the cabinet selection process had started in 1968, Bob Finch, then the popular lieutenant governor of California, had been offered a choice of several posts, including Attorney General and Housing and Urban Development. He knew that the toughest job was HEW, and no one had been able to conquer the bureaucracy there. That is still the case. But he selected HEW because he was interested in its program, and he felt he could make his greatest contribution there.

Finch had found himself in a cross fire. The more he attempted to reorganize HEW, the more the opposition from the bureaucracy. When he defended some of the social policies of the agency, he ran into a buzz saw of the conservatives in the administration. All this left him vulnerable to attack by the more hard-line elements—Mitchell, Haldeman, Colson, Ehrlichman, and some of the President's personal friends outside government. In the long run, I had to admit to myself that the President had supported Finch in many early White House battles but in the final crunch, he had not stood up firmly enough for a man he looked at almost as a son.

In his own mind, the President may have honestly felt that Bob Finch would be better off away from the HEW and in the White House, but the fact is that his act in permitting the Finch demise inflicted permanent damage on the effectiveness and the political future of a loyal friend.

Others rose quickly to stardom and dropped more rapidly.

In 1968, the President's close friend Don Kendall, chairman of Pepsi-Cola, was given a memo outlining a foreign-policy position developed by

Dr. Glenn Olds, then president of Springfield College in Massachusetts. Its theme was negotiation by indirection. Kendall was intrigued and gave the memo to Nixon, who also appreciated it.

On a Saturday night, Olds received a call from Leonard Garment, then a staff strategist and law partner of Nixon. Olds was asked to fly to Cheyenne, Wyoming, to meet with Nixon and discuss the position he had outlined in the memorandum.

Nixon liked the idea and the man and invited Olds to join the staff to head a project on manpower development for the future administration. He was to lay out a transition plan to attract the best people in the country to join the Nixon team after the election. He was instructed to stay nonpolitical.

Olds accepted the challenge, but rarely got through to Nixon again. He developed charts and interviewed hundreds, but about the only person he could get to listen to him was me. I did not attempt to judge the merits of the whole plan, but some parts appeared naïve. Olds's star had dropped from sight. Eventually he was appointed ambassador to the United Nations for the Economic and Social Council. Later he became president of Kent State University, an irony in itself.

The opposite side of Nixon is his loyalty and support for those close to him during a crisis. The stars who rose and fell in the eyes of Nixon lost ground and support during a noncrisis period. This crisis loyalty led the President to cling to Haldeman and John Ehrlichman as long as possible while Watergate was unfolding in 1973. Even as he announced their resignations he described them in warm terms.

"Today, in one of the most difficult decisions of my presidency, I accepted the resignations of two of my closest associates in the White House —Bob Haldeman, John Ehrlichman—two of the finest public servants it has been my privilege to know."

That was on April 30, 1973.

When the reluctant President asked for their resignations in a final meeting at Camp David, Haldeman was more understanding of the decision than was Ehrlichman. "Haldeman took it more like a man," Rose Woods said later.

The relationship between the President and John Mitchell was different from that between Nixon and anyone else I have known. He respected Mitchell as an attorney, as a friend, and as a man of judgment. His loyalty during crisis prompted him to be protective of Mitchell too long. He seemingly could not face up to abandoning the Attorney General even if he was involved in approval of the Watergate break-in. And that two-way loyalty in part led to the cover-up. Eventually Mitchell was asked to resign from the chairmanship of the Committee to Re-elect the President, a position he had moved to after leaving Justice. Even in the aftermath of Mitchell's term in prison and Nixon's pardon by President Ford, the two men remained close, and in September 1979 the Nixons invited Mitchell to San Clemente, where they honored him with a party including many campaign friends. Superficially, the party was like a happy but strange event marking a personal end to one part of a tragic episode in the lives of both men—and the country.

Jeb Magruder remained active in the full 1972 campaign and later in the inaugural, but that was not because of the same presidential loyalty. Magruder was never close to the President; the Nixon concern, in this case, centered more on what the young assistant might do or say if exposed. In the same way John Dean was never in the inner circle and would have been dumped by the President without a qualm—except for what he might say, and as it turned out, what he did say. His prominence came from Watergate, not White House achievement.

Two small incidents again illustrate another facet of Nixon.

One of the most senior political correspondents in California was Henry Love, of the San Diego *Union*. He had covered Nixon since he ran for Senate in 1950. In the mid-sixties, Love asked me as *Union* editor if he could be assigned to cover an American Legion convention in Miami and then to return home via a stopover in New York. I was amazed to find that, as much as he had traveled, he had not been in New York.

Love covered the convention and then flew to New York, where he was stricken with a heart attack and died within hours. In assisting his family with arrangements for bringing Love's body home for services, I discovered that release of the body was complicated by a New York law which required personal identification. Adding to the problem was the fact that a Jewish holiday was to start in hours and that would further slow down release. I called Nixon, then practicing law: he could personally identify Love, and within a few minutes the former Vice-President surprised all at the morgue by appearing to identify Love's body and gain his release.

A short time before I left the White House in 1973, our youngest daughter and her husband and son visited Washington. Her husband was fresh from naval service in Vietnam, and I wanted them to see Washington before we left the city. I mentioned this casually to the President, hoping a few minutes could be set aside for him to greet them.

When we arrived for an appointment in the Oval Office, the President was relaxed and took time to explain the details of the room to the visitors with special attention to my then five-year-old grandson, Tommy. For a few moments he seemingly dropped all thoughts of the growing pressures of Watergate and the other critical world situations. He called in a White House photographer and told Tommy, "I am going to make you President for a moment." He had the youngster sit in his chair (something I would never dare do) and said, "Now the rest of us will be your staff." He carefully arranged the picture as to where he would stand next to the "acting President" and where the rest of us would be for the picture.

It was a moment of interesting human insight.

When he was out of office in the sixties, Nixon would frequently telephone Finch, me, and others for Sunday afternoon chats, exchanging information on what we saw happening politically and in world affairs. During these relaxed fifteen or twenty-minute conversations, he would inquire about newsmen he knew best as well as about the California view we might have on world affairs. He rarely discussed any personal ambitions, although he asked our opinions about the role he would take in the 1964 and 1966 elections. These were all private conversations, not related to anything for the press, but in some ways they gave us a healthy commonality of approach when we were asked by politicians or, in my case, newsmen, about our views in world affairs, and it provided all of us additional insight.

On election night, 1966, when Nixon felt the exhilaration of political victory for the first time since 1956, the former Vice-President called me at the newspaper office to get my rundown on what was happening in the congressional races in California and to give me his estimate of the surprising gains the Republicans were making nationwide that night, after a campaign in which the congressional campaign chairman, Representative Bob Wilson of San Diego, had made Nixon the leading GOP figure. As Nixon talked on the telephone from his headquarters in New York, it was almost as if he felt rebirth at that moment. I never heard him sound happier. He had led a campaign and the party had won. He never mentioned it, but it was clear that he knew he now had a launching pad for another try at the presidency.

These informal telephone calls found Nixon at what I considered his best in the ability to communicate and to listen and understand our frankly stated views. He was open with his opinions.

The other side of Nixon is that this relaxed type of discussion was rarely repeated when he was under the stress of the 1968 presidential campaign and the presidency. Cross-fertilization of ideas was an unfortunate rarity.

Nixon is a man who worked hard at everything he approached in life. Work was a common ingredient in his life as his mother and father struggled for a living and to provide a wholesome, productive atmosphere for their family. His mother was his inspiration. In college at Whittier and Duke, Nixon studied hard and worked hard to support himself. Even football and acting—he once had amateur stage ambitions—did not come easily. As a public-office holder he allowed himself relatively few leisure moments, and when he found himself with leisure time for golf and recreation while practicing law privately, he quickly became bored with it.

He worked hard at the presidency and at campaigning. And yet Haldeman recognized validly, when he organized the 1968 campaign and eventually the White House operation, that Nixon has a highly sensitive energy tolerance point, and exhaustion can make a major difference in his performance and personality.

Those who have probed the Nixon character have raised questions regarding various aspects of his integrity. In the latter months of his presidency and after his resignation, it was determined that he had taken tax credits beyond what he was entitled to. My view relating to this aspect of his character is that he paid too little personal attention to these matters and accepted the advice of lawyers and aides who were overly anxious to please. He was not a man who understood his personal financial situation well. The money manager for his home was his more frugal wife, Pat. Nixon often would walk out of his office or home with no money in his pocket. He had a great desire to succeed financially, having been born of a relatively poor family, but money was not his prime concern. Fiscal integrity, personally and in government, was important to him. For advice on personal investments when out of office, he was more likely to take the advice of personal friends such as Bebe Rebozo and Bob Abplanalp or business friends than to rely on his own judgment. It was not until he moved to law offices on Broad Street in New York that he even began to pay attention to the stock market.

His weakness was not financial honesty, but it was in the area of the use of power and the misuse of it.

Throughout his career, the nature of Nixon was such that he attracted many strong and unforgiving enemies, but he also attracted undying loyalties. During Labor Day weekend of 1979, for example, the San Clemente party given by the Nixons honoring John Mitchell included many others from the White House staff, some of whom had flown across the country to attend, and others, such as Dwight Chapin and Herbert Kalmbach, who had served prison sentences as a result of acts they believed were helping the President. The "clan" regathered in the warm afternoon sunshine almost as if nothing had happened.

In Washington and Los Angeles, smaller groups of former Nixon staffers still gather for lunch or cocktails periodically to renew acquaintances and catch up on news of "the old man."

In the spring of 1974 I was on a trip which took me to Montreal and several Eastern and Midwestern cities. Before leaving I received a tip from the White House that an effort was about to be made to convince me I must return to the staff to assist on Watergate.

Calls from the White House appointments secretary began following me from city to city, but I delayed answering them. I wanted to think about the problem and to build up personal resistance to the pressure I knew I would receive.

Finally, I called the White House and we arranged that I would fly from St. Louis to Key Biscayne in time for dinner with General Al Haig. I would confer with the President aboard Air Force One, arrive in Washington in time to helicopter from Andrews Air Force Base to Dulles, where I would catch a late plane for Los Angeles.

During dinner with Haig and his wife we discussed the status of the Watergate hearings and the Middle East, but there was no direct comment on the reason for the urgent Air Force One meeting.

Once we were airborne, the atmosphere changed. Ron Ziegler broached the subject first.

"Watergate and continued conferences with the President are taking so much of my time that I have no time for my regular press secretary activities," Ziegler began. "You can't believe the hours I spend in the President's office, sometimes just talking with him. Besides that I am reading transcripts, trying to map strategy with our attorneys, Len Garment and Jim St. Clair, spending all my time on that damn thing," he continued.

"Herb, my reputation is hurt. I have got to get out of handling Watergate."

I knew what was coming.

"Herb, the President needs you as never before. You have got to come back, if even for six months."

Haig joined in the emotional pitch. It became clear to me that both men considered the President to be in a more desperate situation than I had believed. They knew more than they were willing to admit at that moment. They were not trying to trap me, they were just in over their heads and were reaching out for help.

"Herb, you can't turn down the President," Haig said. "He needs you. Your country needs you right now. No job is more important than that."

Ziegler chimed in. "If you will do this, the President will call Mr. Kluge [chairman and president of Metromedia], and ask him to loan you to us for six months."

At that point the intense conversation slowed down enough to allow me to respond.

"You know, I have never turned the President down," I said. "Sometimes I have not carried out his directions because I have felt that was in his best interest not to. I have argued with him, but I have not said I would not serve.

"This time I may have to do so. I have job responsibilities with a publicly owned company. I have my family to think of. I can't just skip in and out of politics anymore. Watergate may be so far along no one can save the situation," I said.

"I want to talk to the President, and I want to help, but you should know that whatever he asks of me now will take a lot of thought on my part. I don't want anyone talking to Mr. Kluge to put pressure on him."

I put emphasis on the last point because I was not sure how any business executive who had not worked in the White House would respond to direct presidential pressure. The decision had to be mine alone and then the details could be handled later.

Haig, Ziegler, and I talked back and forth for another half hour before I went in to join the President.

I found the President in a relaxed frame of mind. He was in the separate office–sleeping compartment of the presidential 707. Typically on Air Force One he was wearing a blue smoking jacket.

We chatted about the Congress and the Middle East situation. He always enjoyed briefing me and other visitors on foreign policy particularly.

Haig joined us and outlined for the President our earlier conversation.

"I told Herb, Mr. President, that you need someone who can devote full time to the Watergate situation and direct not only public statements but take full charge of our strategy," Haig said.

I noticed that the President seemed reticent to get into the subject.

"Herb, I would appreciate it if you could see your way clear to do this," he said. "But I also realize you have not been with Metromedia long and that you may find it difficult to get away from your duties there."

Inwardly, I felt sudden relief. The President would not pressure me. He wanted my help, but he did not want to jeopardize my future.

The President went on in low-key fashion.

"The job has gotten just too much for Ron, and the lawyers don't understand political strategy.

"If you would like me to, I will call John Kluge for you. But if you and Kluge feel you should not take off the six months this may require, I will understand."

I told the President, as I had told Haig and Ziegler, that I would have to think the matter over and there was no need to call Kluge at this time. I explained to him the intricacies of a public company, particularly one in the broadcast business.

Almost as if he were relieved to be past the subject, the President offered me a drink or coffee and then began reminiscing with me over early campaign experiences, even recalling details of a Junior Chamber reception I had arranged for him in 1950.

Haig and Ziegler renewed the pressure campaign when I left the President's compartment.

But I was struck more by the President's consideration in refusing to "twist my arm."

I called Haig a few days later and told him I regretted to say I could not help full time but, as always, I was available to consult with anyone in the White House.

I then called John Kluge and reviewed with him what I had done.

In some ways I felt I had let down the President of the United States when he needed me. But in retrospect, the request for this type of help came two years too late. The presidency was already gone, as were the Nixon dreams of greatness. Nothing I could have done would have changed all that. The deed was done.

8

The Discombobulating Agnew

BETWEEN 1968 AND 1974, Spiro T. Agnew advertently and inadvertently placed me on the spot more times than I care to count. Basically, I still liked him personally until the day in 1973 when he lied to me about his involvement in the Maryland scandals, which eventually brought about his resignation.

As a Vice-President he was many things: a student who did his homework, intelligent and hardworking, prim and proper, a little vain, loyal to colleagues, thoughtful of most people, appreciative of help, heavy-handed with an inexplicable instinct for blunders; a man who reveled politically in going for the jugular when he thought it would give him the attention he sought. It is hard to name many great Vice-Presidents in history, but even without the scandal he was not one of them. And yet he came close to being President of the United States, and for a time his popularity with Republicans was high. He was considered a prime prospect for the nomination in 1976.

The early press problems Agnew created ranged from his blundering campaign-plane remark about a "fat Jap" to the pressure he exerted after the election for a new press staff.

But the roundhouse left hook he delivered to the press with a Des Moines speech attacking the television industry came as a surprise to me, although I later learned the President was aware of it beforehand in general terms. That date I now remember vividly, November 13, 1969. The speech led to open warfare between the Nixon administration and the media.

Surprises seemed to be a part of the Agnew syndrome from the moment I met him.

If a newsman had asked me to comment on Spiro T. Agnew, even a few weeks before the 1968 Republican convention, I would have "toe-danced"—which in press secretary terminology means dodging the question.

I knew that the Maryland governor had been a leading supporter of Nelson Rockefeller, going so far as to organize an ill-fated draft-Rockefeller move. I was vaguely aware of the fact that he had become dis-illusioned with the New York governor when, to Agnew's surprise, Rocke-feller announced on March 21, 1969, that he was not available as a candi-date. I learned later from him that he felt betrayed when the New Yorker withdrew from the race without tipping off any of his supporters, includ-ing Agnew.

When Rockefeller changed his mind and reentered the race on April 30, it was too late as far as Agnew was concerned. Nixon and others had worked on the Maryland governor, and while Agnew played his cards coolly by not announcing a change of mind, the decision to support Nixon was made by him well before the convention.

Looking back, these episodes revealed several things about Agnew, fac-tors which influenced his conduct as Vice-President.

Agnew appears tough outside, but inside he is sensitive. He is thin-skinned and quick to take offense when he feels he is slighted. He believed heavily in loyalty (in this case loyalty to Rockefeller), but he was unforgiving of anyone he felt had wronged him, anyone who betrayed his loyalty.

Agnew had political principle, but he was very much an astute prag-matist, not an idealist. He flowed with the power, and thus it was easy for him to move to Nixon from Rockefeller or from the point of being a Rockefeller leader to later a Vice-President who attracted many of Barry Goldwater's strongest supporters, even to a place where they were ready to back him for President.

When Rockefeller decided in March that he would not be a candidate, Agnew was so confident that the announcement would be the opposite that he invited staff and some press to his office to watch the Rockefeller press conference on television.

Yet a bitter and disappointed Agnew had the political instincts to cover his embarrassment and eventually parlay his open Rockefeller support to a public position of being uncommitted and controlling eighteen Maryland votes, to a position where he was asked to be the principal nominator of Nixon on national television before the Republican convention. That speech was an important factor in the later selection of Agnew for the vice-presidential nomination. Had he not impressed Nixon with that speech he would never have been selected. Nixon did not make the final decision to select Agnew until a short time before the announcement of it.

My strategy at the 1968 convention was to dominate the news and build a bandwagon psychology against Reagan and Rockefeller challenges by introducing a key figure at each of two daily press conferences, each formally announcing for the first time that he or his delegation would support Nixon. In this strategy announcements by governors from even small states, such as Alaska (Walter Hickel), Massachusetts (a larger state, of course, and headed by John Volpe), New Mexico (with the elusive Governor David Cargo), and, of course, Maryland (with Agnew) could gain national attention and created a constant feeling of movement toward the Nixon nomination.

Agnew's early support for Rockefeller and then his reversal of position made him a key figure in the strategy of spotlighting leaders and delegations announcing firm support for Nixon.

Many factors were involved in Nixon's holding on to his early lead as delegates arriving prior to the convention in Miami also found themselves under pressure to switch to Rockefeller or Governor Ronald Reagan, both of whom had well-organized and effective teams working in their behalf. I decided that one of the keys to countering the late Reagan and Rockefeller efforts would be to start press conferences in Miami a week before the convention, seeking to develop a bandwagon psychology through announcements which in turn gave Agnew and others a national forum they normally would not receive.

Nixon, who went to a Long Island hideaway at Montauk Point, remained theoretically aloof from the preconvention scramble and never acknowledged even personally to me appreciation for the strategy, but the value of it was seen quickly by John Mitchell and Dick Kleindienst, who headed the complex effort to ride herd on the delegates—keeping track of every individual who would vote.

In Agnew's case, our buildup was massive.

David Broder, the astute Washington reporter and columnist who is now with the Washington *Post,* had heard Nixon once mention the Maryland governor's name as a possible vice-presidential nominee. During an NBC broadcast in June, Broder had asked Agnew if he would like to be Vice-President. Agnew replied, "I am not sure. Sometimes I find it very difficult just to be governor. I would have to think about that."

Early on, Agnew sought an alliance with Governor James Rhodes of Ohio and Governor George Romney of Michigan, seeking a three-state coalition controlling 132 nominating votes, possibly the determining factor in the convention. The effort broke down when Rhodes announced he would continue to be a favorite son candidate, holding out with Ohio's 58 votes.

Unknown to most, Agnew had decided before reaching Miami that he would drop his own favorite son role, and late in July, he accepted a personal invitation from Nixon to deliver the nominating address.

Agnew and his party arrived in Miami on August 2, three days before the convention, and they were besieged at the airport by youth groups for Nixon and for Rockefeller.

Thus began the buildup which gave disproportionate attention to the Maryland votes pledged to Agnew.

I made arrangements with Herb Thompson and others on the Agnew staff for the governor to convene the Maryland delegation in late afternoon on August 5, just prior to the convention. On schedule, with the networks alerted for an announcement to come, early in the live evening news broadcast time, Agnew stepped out of the caucus and went before the cameras to say he had reached a decision after "months of soul-searching. . . . Richard Nixon has the courage to make hard decisions, to take positions that may be temporarily unpopular but will be proven right. Richard Nixon has forsworn promises he knows cannot be fulfilled and denounced policies built on expedience, instant answers, or the easy way out."

As Agnew's announcement was being made at the Eden Roc Hotel, Nixon's chartered plane landed at the Miami Airport and pulled up before a giant rally crowd with banners waving. The door of the plane opened once and then was closed. The timing was off. Then at 6:24 P.M., again before live network cameras, the Nixon family stepped from the aircraft into the waiting arms of supporters, among them professional basketball star Wilt Chamberlain, who towers over all.

The Nixon staff had television experts work out the timing with network producers who were searching for live news breaks during their news shows from Miami.

The bandwagon was moving.

Later that night, John Mitchell met secretly with Agnew and said that now that he had announced his decision, he wanted to know what Agnew's reaction would be if he were suggested for Vice-President. The rest of us were not aware of this. A decision between Agnew and other candidates was not made, however, until three days later.

Had Agnew not been highlighted nationally with his firm public commitment to Nixon, and had he been wooed back by Rockefeller, his small bloc of eighteen votes (out of twenty-five Maryland votes) could well have had a reverse influence on wavering delegates in states such as Pennsylvania and New Jersey and possibly denied Nixon a first-ballot victory.

Ironically, Governor Rockefeller eventually became Vice-President after the resignations first of Agnew and then of Nixon.

Actually during the convention, the governor from a small state I tried most to convert was David Cargo, a young Mexican-American liberal who was governor of New Mexico. Cargo and his attractive Spanish-speaking wife appealed to me as leaders who could have immense effect in the general election with Hispanic voters. I also thought of Cargo as one who eventually would join the administration and give major representation to his Spanish-speaking constituents. He appeared bright and personable to me. His wife was a political rebel, but that added to the appeal of the twosome.

One could say that an Agnew on the team would bring in Greek votes and—later—as we debated the vice-presidency, Governor John Volpe of Massachusetts marshaled figures to prove the power of an Italian on the ticket.

But to me the largest bloc of votes which had not been dedicated to any one party or person since the death of John Kennedy and Robert Kennedy was the Spanish-speaking vote, which had a major base in such key states as California, Texas, Illinois, New York, and Florida.

Cargo lacked the experience to envision the role of leadership he might have taken.

No promise of future opportunity was even suggested to him. But the young governor from a small state lacked the experience in national politics to understand that the attention given to him by me and other senior Nixon campaigners even at a time when Nixon was well ahead in every delegate count meant that he could have been launched into the national spotlight as even a seconder of the nomination in a way which could have made him a major figure very quickly—possibly a cabinet officer.

Cargo became a tortured man. He was involved deeply in a fight in his own state party. He had run against the organization and won. And neither side had made peace in the aftermath. At one time I had his promise to appear at a 10 A.M. press conference and announce his support for Nixon. He had talked to his wife, convinced her on Nixon, and he was enthusiastic at the moment about his opportunity. But when I later found him at five minutes before the press conference hour, he was again struggling undecidedly, asking us to enter into an interparty fight in New Mexico; he was so torn inside that he postponed his announcement.

I scrambled quickly and found Governor Walter Hickel of Alaska, who was ready to announce at any time, and I ushered him to my podium on two minutes' notice. His support surprised no one, but he kept my news conference going.

Cargo ended up indecisive to a point of self-disaster politically.

He changed his mind several times even up to the convention roll call, and the New Mexico delegation had to be polled. His personal vote was lost in the confusion, as far as the public was concerned. He was subsequently defeated and moved from New Mexico to Oregon. With a little more decisiveness, he could have become a meaningful political leader.

Cargo was never considered for Vice-President, but Agnew, the other governor we wooed from a small state, seemed to surface more and more in Nixon's mind until when Bob Finch turned down the nomination, he suddenly emerged as the candidate for Vice-President in the final hours of decision.

When Agnew was nominated, there was no real thought as to what his relationship would be with the press or what appeal he might have to Greeks. In the long elimination process, he simply emerged as the available candidate who Nixon thought would have a unifying effect on the party and who impressed Nixon as a man who would be a vice-presidential campaigner more in a Nixon-type tough mold than had been the two previous nominees, Henry Cabot Lodge (1960) and Bill Miller (1964). The additional factor favoring Agnew was that he was looked at as a candidate who could be effective in the border states and some Southern states, thus fitting into Nixon's campaign strategy.

My first full relationship between Agnew and the press came about an hour after he had been notified that he would be Nixon's choice as nominee for Vice-President.

After Agnew had been informed by Rogers Morton of his selection, he was rushed from the Eden Roc Hotel to the Presidential Suite at the Hilton, where he conferred briefly with Nixon and his new campaign colleagues. I then had about ten minutes to brief him on what he would face in a full-fledged press conference, which would be televised live nationally.

My first mistake was to introduce him before this audience of television viewers and reporters by mispronouncing his first name, saying "Spy-ro" instead of "Spero." Agnew countered well by saying he realized his name Spiro was not a household word. It was a good quip.

But from that point on, the press problems I encountered through Agnew only multiplied.

In the week immediately after the nominating convention, it became apparent that it is difficult for someone to suddenly shift gears from local to national campaigning. With some irritation, but not a lot, I told a reporter that the problem in planning the Agnew campaign was that previously his biggest trips with the press were between Annapolis and Baltimore.

We sent him speech writers, schedulers, and some press help to remedy the situation.

In respect to press problems, he was not unique. In the period from 1952 through 1976 the Republicans had only one candidate for Vice-President who did not run into trouble with the media.

Richard Nixon had his crises with the press over the "fund" in 1952 and over McCarthyism and hard-line anticommunism in 1956.

On most occasions, however, the troubles between the press and the various Republican candidates for Vice-President stemmed from offhand remarks or an overly casual attitude with the reporters.

Henry Cabot Lodge in 1960 proved to be a disappointment even as a seasoned candidate: he had little instinct as to what the national impact would be from his campaign statements.

Lodge found himself written up by a bored press corps as a candidate who required a nap each afternoon.

The description was accurate.

In the 1960 campaign, Lodge casually approved a speech for delivery in the Hispanic part of Harlem which declared that the Nixon cabinet would include a black. Not only did he drop the statement in the wrong part of Harlem (with no prior consultation with the candidate for President), but he did it on the eve of appearances in the South. He was bewildered by the press pickup of the statement, and by the questions with which he was bombarded as he stepped off the airplane a few hours later in the Carolinas. He was an outstanding and popular public servant, but not a strong candidate for Vice-President.

Bill Miller, the Goldwater running mate in 1964, was the exception. Early on he accepted the fact that he was engaged in a losing campaign, and he was far from despondent because he had planned to retire from Congress long before he suddenly found himself swept up in the Goldwater campaign.

Miller's attitude toward the press was casual. And the attitude of the press toward Miller was casual. Both press and candidate felt they were a part of a losing campaign.

Instead of debates and strategy, the major confrontations aboard the Miller campaign plane were games of bridge which included the candidate as well as the reporters.

Senator Robert Dole, Jerry Ford's running mate in 1976, was casual and had a good sense of humor which was appreciated by the newsmen, but as he became more strident in the campaign, attitudes changed from friendly to adversary.

In Spiro Agnew's second campaign for Vice-President in 1972, he was the target. He had chosen his ground in his battering-ram approach to both the press and liberals during his first term of office. His situation was not unlike that of Nixon in 1956. The press was eager to retaliate but in the process it also gave him more news space.

The battle between the press and Agnew in 1968 impacted that campaign and had a lasting effect on his attitudes as he served as a constant campaigner and Vice-President in the 1969–72 period. Unlike 1972,

Agnew in 1968 was a random target of opportunity—and the newsmen struck home.

Interesting to a student of press-government relations, the stories of a "bumbling, insensitive" vice-presidential candidate in 1968 were not dissimilar to the stories which plagued President Ford unfairly in the 1976 election.

Agnew's troubles with the newsmen in 1968 illustrate fully the many small things which develop into factors of major impact in long-range relations between government officials and the news media. An offhand statement can become a major point of controversy during a campaign.

Later Earl Butz, Secretary of Agriculture, was to learn this when he was forced to resign as a result of an off-color comment to a seatmate on a commercial flight with John Dean turning up as an eavesdropper and reporter.

There was no question but that Agnew was badly hurt personally and politically by an offhand comment about a reporter he referred to face to face as the "fat Jap." Publicly I passed it off casually but privately I was astounded and angry over the blunder.

The incident occurred on a Western campaign swing by the vice-presidential candidate on September 19, early in the 1968 campaign. Agnew had made a speech in Las Vegas and then flown to Carson City, Nevada's capital, with the then governor, Paul Laxalt.

As the aircraft left Reno, the candidate wandered through the airplane to greet those who had stayed in Las Vegas.

Agnew paused at the seat of his longtime friend, Gene Oishi, a reporter from the Baltimore *Sun*.

Oishi was dozing, as were many of the Las Vegas entourage.

"What's the matter with the fat Jap—too much Las Vegas?" Agnew mused.

According to Herb Thompson, "Gene opened his eyes and smiled. I don't think he was really insulted—not until it became a big public incident and he was a *cause célèbre*; then he was hurt, angry, and embarrassed."

Thompson, who had been Agnew's press secretary as governor, says Oishi frequently was referred to as the "fat Jap" and the term in the Maryland statehouse was one of affection, not insult.

Regardless of the lack of merit of the comment, the most interesting factor is the press handling of the matter.

No one wrote of the comment until three days later, when Agnew landed in Hawaii, a state with heavy Japanese population.

Thompson recalls that Dick Homan, of the Washington *Post*, filed the comment along with his more major story to his newspaper. Homan told Thompson he included it because he had learned that the comment had been relayed to *Time* magazine and wanted to protect himself.

Time did not use it.

The Washington *Post* did.

Representative Sparky Matsunaga, an astute Democratic Congressman from Hawaii who is of Japanese ancestry, picked up the comment quickly and attacked the vice-presidential candidate as if he were anti-Japanese.

Agnew, ever oversensitive, reacted with countercomment in Hawaii. At a luncheon speech in Maui, Agnew apologized for the remark, but most in the audience had not even heard of the incident. But Matsunaga and now Agnew received heavy press coverage.

And thus an offhand comment in an airplane became a major campaign issue which gave the implication that Agnew, himself of minority Greek ancestry, was one given to deprecatory comments regarding minorities. The Washington *Post* timing on the story had every implication of bias, and it gave Agnew an image which was inaccurate.

That evening the Agnew staff had a long and informal session with the press, seeking to repair the damage. Interestingly, Homer Bigart of the New York *Times* was most critical of Agnew and Bob Clark of ABC defended the nominee.

The overall effect was that Agnew became bitter toward the press and communicated less with the newsmen traveling with him.

Agnew made other blunders that were enlarged upon by the media. In Chicago he made an unfortunate reference to Poles which created a two-day furor.

Then there was his comment, "If you've seen one slum, you've seen 'em all."

Uniquely, Agnew thought the only fair treatment he received on the "slum" comment was written by a black reporter for the "hated" New York *Times,* Thomas Johnson.

Johnson reported the comment but went on to explain that the candidate was responding to a question as to whether he would campaign in the ghetto areas. Agnew replied that he noted many blacks attending his general rallies and he did not need the educational experience of being in the slums and ghettos since as governor he had spent much time in the areas— "and, if you've seen one slum, you've seen 'em all."

Even aside from the incidents with the press, it was generally judged that the Democratic nominee, Edmund Muskie, had been a more effective vice-presidential campaigner than Agnew. But the difference was at least partially the press. Both candidates for Vice-President worked hard and were willing to face "gut issues." But Muskie received an unusual amount of press adulation, perhaps the most since John Kennedy. And directly opposite, Agnew was hit by a hostile press, perhaps partly striking at him because he was running with a Richard Nixon who was more difficult to attack in 1968 than he had been in earlier years.

Muskie could coast at a low key, with Humphrey taking the hard line. Nixon, who was trying to avoid baiting from Humphrey and keep on the high road so as not to allow himself to be depicted again as "Tricky Dick," assigned the tough slugging to Agnew, much as Eisenhower had done with Nixon years earlier.

Agnew seemed to like the role but he lacked finesse and sounded querulous and shrill. That coupled with the blunders rendered him ineffective in the broad national scene, easily a loser by comparison to Muskie.

But in an area more difficult to calculate, he won votes for the ticket in key border and Southern states, and thus, like Lyndon Johnson in 1960, he had more influence in the electoral count than first was understood by the pundits of the press—probably more influence on the election outcome than Muskie.

In 1960, Henry Cabot Lodge was a subject of controversy in internal debates within the Nixon staff—and Agnew was likewise. But then so was Nixon when he ran with Eisenhower.

One of those who saw the scene on the Agnew campaign plane *Tricia* most closely was the young former editorial writer and later speech writer, Patrick Buchanan, who volunteered to help for a brief time in mid-campaign.

In his book *The Making of the President—1968* the well-informed Theodore White described Buchanan as leaving the Agnew campaign plane and returning to the Nixon entourage dolefully. Buchanan, according to White, said that Agnew eventually might be trained to become a "reliable Vice President," but for the moment he thought it best "to ice Agnew and keep him under wraps."

After previewing the White book in 1969, Buchanan wrote one of his usual candid memos to the Vice-President in which he analyzed the Agnew campaign.

The Vice-President, sensitive to anything White wrote, immediately had Thompson bring to my attention the Buchanan report:

THE WHITE HOUSE
WASHINGTON

July 1, 1969

MEMORANDUM TO THE VICE PRESIDENT

FROM: PATRICK J. BUCHANAN

I have just had a look at an advance copy of *The Making of the President*, 1968, by Theodore H. White. In it, on page 371, there is a paragraph purporting to describe a "doleful and candid report" which I gave the President on returning from traveling with "the Agnew party."

According to White, ". . . the best Buchanan could report to Nixon was that Agnew might, with some training and some hard seat-of-the-pants application, eventually turn out to be a reliable Vice President, but for the moment it was best to ice Agnew and keep him under wraps."

This is wholly inaccurate.

When I came aboard the Agnew campaign plane, it was not at Mr. Nixon's initiative, but at my own. On the Tricia, by early October we had settled down into a routine, with some six writers turning out the regular copy. The Agnew plane was "where the action was," as I told the President when I asked for "leave." When I left your tour, it was not at my request, but rather at the President's who wanted me, not to report on a damn thing, but to help him with the fifteen radio speeches to which he had committed himself.

The thrust of my comments to the President on my return were the same that I gave to the national press and to my colleagues on the Nixon Staff; that our swing through North Carolina, Florida, Tennessee and Virginia had been a great success, that the national press was not reflecting at all what was being accomplished, that our local press and local and regional TV were winning us votes in the border states by the carload and that the more often we sent you through the upper South and Florida, the better our chances of pulling these states out of the Wallace column.

My call to both George White and you in the immediate wake of that campaign reflected my judgement then as it does now. Had it not been for your efforts in these states, the upper South would have gone to George Wallace and we would have been in the House of Representatives.

I can still recall hanging outside the door of the President's suite when Bob Haldeman came out and leaked the fact to me that you were going to be the V.P. choice. I was delighted with the news then—and your performance during that campaign and subsequent to it confirmed both my own feeling and the wisdom of the President's judgment. I can't apologize for what Mr. White has written, because what he wrote is not my doing. But I do hope you will feel at liberty to convey these thoughts to Mrs. Agnew and to George White and Charlie Bresler, who will find this paragraph as perplexing as I did.

PAT BUCHANAN

When the election was only a few weeks past, and we were in the middle of the transition process, I asked to meet at the Pierre Hotel with Agnew and John Mitchell. After the usual pleasantries, Agnew and Mitchell went directly to the point of the meeting: find a press secretary for the Vice-President who would build a new image for him. It was as if they believed someone could wave a magic wand and presto there would be a new public view of Agnew. Politicians frequently get an idea like that. Somehow, Mitchell and Agnew had the idea that I had been full-time press secretary for Nixon when he was Vice-President and they wanted someone with the same background.

I explained that I could not have worked full time for the Vice-President and built the professional experience I had in the newspaper field.

It became clear that they had no understanding of the problems which had led to Agnew's poor relationship with the press during the campaign. Without saying so, they put the major blame on the Agnew press secretary, Herb Thompson, an Associated Press veteran reporter from Annapolis who had been recruited by Agnew when he was governor of Maryland.

Thompson is a thoroughly honest, likable newsman and press assistant. He was completely loyal to Agnew. His wife, Ann, a newspaperwoman, assisted Agnew's wife, Judy, as a press assistant and friend. Thompson lacked experience in national politics, as did Agnew and all his staff, and thus found it difficult to relate on an equal basis with the pundit leaders of the national press corps. But so would almost anyone else brought into the office.

The simple fact was that Agnew was under heavy early pressure from the Nixon political staff to cleanse himself of errors with the press by accepting a scapegoat dictated by Mitchell and Haldeman—neither of whom even knew the scapegoat, Thompson.

I did not think this was the time to get to the central point of the issue regarding Agnew's growing bitterness toward the press nor Mitchell and Haldeman's lack of understanding of it.

I pointed out that Nixon had not had a full-time press secretary at any time in his career except during campaigns. The best answer, I said, would be to assign Thompson to my office with responsibilities to coordinate the press activities of the Vice-President and to accept additional duties within my own office. In turn, I would oversee generally the Vice-President's press relationships.

My understanding of this was applied well in the early days of the administration, when I worked with Thompson in recommending to the Vice-President important television shows and interviews to accept. In early 1969, my clout would make it mandatory that Agnew accept these assignments, and he won new respect handling himself well. Meanwhile,

Thompson spent probably two thirds of his time working on Agnew press relations and traveling occasionally with him.

Looking back, the Agnew campaign and the meeting at the Pierre Hotel take on much significance in the whole role of Agnew as Vice-President of the United States.

During the campaign, Agnew felt he was treated unfairly by the news media and his reaction, like Nixon's, was to coil back, to pull away in a sea of bitterness rather than to make an effort to correct the problems realistically. This eventually led to the desire, encouraged by Nixon, to be the spearhead in an attack on the news media.

In the meeting at the Pierre, it was easy for Agnew to bow to the pressure of Mitchell and Haldeman because of his personal feeling about the press, but in failing to defend a member of his staff, he lost ground to Mitchell and Haldeman, ground which he never would regain in a power-prone administration. They had asserted dominancy in a lesser matter which had bearing in the game of one-upmanship.

When one considers Nixon's vice-presidency, President Nixon's relationship with Vice-President Agnew was sometimes easily predictable and at other times it was inconsistent. All in all, it left Agnew insecure and easy prey for administration power brokers.

In 1972, when there were rumors that Agnew would be replaced as the candidate for Vice-President, it was easy for me to refute the comments without seriously consulting Nixon. I knew that one of Nixon's innermost hurts was the thought that he might not have had the opportunity to run for reelection with Eisenhower in 1956. With this background, there was little chance he would be known as a President who dumped his Vice-President, as Harold Stassen had suggested that Eisenhower do—unless there was a political crisis where this would spell the margin of victory. This was not the case in 1972, nor was it the case in 1956.

I wondered how so many newsmen missed this point.

The second factor they missed was that the principal political and news criticism of Agnew was based on the fact that he freely attacked the media and that he played heavily to the conservatives.

Nothing could have fit Nixon's political appetite better.

The more puzzling aspect of the Nixon-Agnew relationship was the failure of the President to assign major responsibilities to the Vice-President. Nixon had thrived and savored every responsibility assigned to him by President Eisenhower. He felt that he had been the first working Vice-President, the first man in his office who exercised real power in government.

In all of our conversations leading to the vice-presidency, Nixon had stressed the importance of having a working Vice-President, one who also would be fully informed if he were to suddenly become President.

What he talked about and what he did about Agnew were two different things.

Agnew was made a part of the key government operations, so he was well informed as to the state of the presidency at any time. He was a member of the National Security Council and the Domestic Council and other key decision-making bodies.

But rarely was his opinion solicited—or heard.

And in the area of active leadership within government, Agnew's most conspicuous effort was in behalf of the successful governmental space programs. He learned to know them and assisted the space scientists politically.

But after a man landed on the moon, this was not a top administration priority. In fact, it fell low on the scale of priorities, a direction which I, like Agnew, also opposed because I thought it shortsighted in point of important research applicable to many other fields.

In a lesser way, the problems which confronted Agnew were similar to President Carter's. They are problems of how to avoid being devoured by the government power structure when your principal experience has been that of governor of a small state coupled with a relatively brief experience as a national campaigner.

Agnew basically had his own "Maryland Mafia" as his staff. They were attuned to things on a less than national basis. They came on the scene when John Ehrlichman and Bob Haldeman were moving in a direction they honestly felt correct: absorb the power around the presidency in close quarters.

Agnew did not fit their picture of governmental power. And he easily allowed himself to be muscled out—as had most of his predecessors in that office.

Within the White House there were several intellectual cultures, some of the highest quality, such as the philosophical theorism of Pat Moynihan, Henry Kissinger, Bob Finch, and Arthur Burns. But alongside this there was a pragmatism reflected from Haldeman and Ehrlichman; they considered that most top officials they had helped select lacked either high intellectual qualities or pragmatic political ability, or both. They were contemptuous of them. Haldeman and Ehrlichman would never allow themselves to think they considered academic intellectualism this important, but in Agnew's case, he was, among other things, a victim of the feeling of the chief Nixon aides, that he lacked the ability intellectually or politically for major responsibility.

In his state of arrogance at that time, the President concurred.

Nixon may even have been right, but the problem was that this was the Vice-President he had personally selected to follow his own image in that

office, to carry out any presidential assignments—any presidential responsibility—including the presidency.

On the national scene, Agnew was Nixon's own creation, even though
he first had asked Bob Finch to be the vice-presidential candidate.

One of the responsibilities assigned to Nixon by President Eisenhower
had been to serve in a liaison capacity between the White House and
Congress, particularly on sensitive issues. The Nixon vice-presidential
offices were in the Senate Office Building, augmented by the ceremonial
office off the Senate floor and a more beautiful "hideaway" office deep in
the Capitol.

Agnew, like Hubert Humphrey, made his principal headquarters in a
series of offices in the Executive Office Building adjacent to the White
House, and, unlike Humphrey, he rarely spent time in his Senate suite. It
was apparent early on that he lacked experience in dealing with Congress
and had no real interest in developing a liaison role.

The Vice-President thus occupied himself with briefings, with a few international missions, and with many campaign appearances. I persuaded
him on several occasions to do national television shows, which he handled quite well.

But none of these activities attracted major public attention. The two
most non-Nixon administration characteristics I noticed were that he
stressed physical fitness with considerable golf and tennis. He coupled this
with a run up three stories of steps to his office each morning, followed by
a panting Secret Service corps. None of us had time for much golf or tennis. The other noticeable factor was that Agnew was easily the best-
dressed man in a White House where Pat Moynihan occasionally startled
everyone with pink or purple shirts. Each time Agnew sat at his desk he
carefully pulled up his pants legs so as not to disturb the crease.

When Agnew made his major attack on the press in 1969, he did so
with the full knowledge of the President and of Haldeman, although Ron
Ziegler, Thompson, and I were not consulted. To put it another way, the
press experts were the most surprised people in the White House when
we discovered what Agnew was launching.

The plan for the Agnew speech against the news media, particularly
television, was concocted by the President's loyal young, conservative
speech writer, Pat Buchanan, himself a former editorial writer for the St.
Louis *Post-Dispatch*. Buchanan gained the approval of Nixon for the
speech and proceeded to work on it with the Vice-President. They built
their thesis on a debate reporters themselves long had been engaged in and
touched a sensitive public nerve.

In the news business of recent years there has been a running debate
over the balance between advocacy reporting, news interpretation, and
straight reporting.

In politics that translates to whether the reporter has a right to indicate his own feelings in the midst of a story (advocacy), to give background interpretation to a story, or to be confined to reporting what is said with little or no challenge to the accuracy of the comments by a politician. In between these positions a case can be made for accurate, helpful interpretation of background on what the speaker said.

In the eyes of many news veterans, advocacy reporting places the newsman in the position of making Godlike judgment calls on the wisdom and veracity of the candidate. In the eyes of many younger reporters, journalism is "where the action is," and they feel they have a duty to judge the story and express their views, sometimes almost to the point where the facts of the story become obscured because of their personal opinions.

The prime case in 1969, which opened the doors for strong public and administration criticism of the media, came ten days before the Agnew speech, when Nixon appeared on television to make a major speech on the situation in Vietnam.

Over much opposition from the President, we had developed a system in which key network newsmen were invited to the Roosevelt Room of the White House to read the basic text of an important televised speech and be briefed by a senior White House official such as Dr. Henry Kissinger if the speech was on foreign policy. This was arranged capably by Ron Ziegler.

When President Nixon made this particular speech on Vietnam on November 3, 1969, the audience was estimated at about 88 million.

At the completion of the address, commentators on all three networks appeared on the screen to "analyze" the presentation. A few years back, this would have meant background on the President's speech based on the experience of the reporters and on the briefing they had received prior to the broadcast.

The analysis of the November 3 speech, however, represented little interpretation but considerable "advocacy," all negative to the President of the United States. Basically, the reporters set themselves up as the outspoken, controversial opposition instead of as pro-and-con discussion leaders who were mainly concerned with giving the public better understanding of the President's remarks so each individual viewer could decide the issues for himself. One network (ABC) included a bitter Vietnam critic from an earlier administration—Ambassador W. Averell Harriman. There was no one to oppose Harriman.

In my office I watched the comments on a three-screen television set (built for Lyndon Johnson for the Oval Office), and I listened with astonishment at the negative emotional quality of the comments. It was almost like a debate between the President of the United States and the assembled network "experts." The debate was heightened by the emotions that surrounded any Vietnam discussion.

We also had a system in the White House in which my office force would call editors and broadcasters in various geographical sections of the country and ask their immediate reaction. It gave us an instant private sampling of important opinion. We included known opponents and more proponents of the Nixon policy and reported them accurately to the President minutes after the speech was completed. Others on the White House staff checked businessmen and politicians in the same way.

In the cross section of opinion leaders after the November 3 Vietnam address, we received little negative comment and an overwhelming margin of support, except for the network broadcasts.

The commentators came on strong, probing weaknesses in the President's comments. In the tense atmosphere of the White House it appeared that television, contrary to other opinion, had set out to knock down every argument that Nixon had made and to challenge his veracity in his report before the television audience gathered to hear the President.

The commentators were not in Vietnam. Nor was the President. But the question was who had the best information. From a journalistic point of view, did the commentators fulfill their duty by becoming advocates? The White House answer came quickly.

Whatever the logic, the after-speech comment sped up the pace of a rapidly fading honeymoon with the media, and it signaled a tense era of battle between the White House and the media.

The President was incensed and thus easily susceptible to a hard-line approach suggested by Buchanan. Agnew, who was still nursing his 1968 wounds, was eager.

With all this background, it was incongruous for the Vice-President of the United States to deliver this major speech before an unheralded regional Republican meeting in Des Moines, Iowa. Why not in a national forum? It was all a matter of timing.

Des Moines became a national forum accidentally. It happened to be the place he was scheduled for when the speech was ready.

After Agnew had departed Washington for the speech in Iowa, I received a copy of his address. I might have routinely put it aside, but for an unknown reason I read it immediately.

As I looked with unbelieving eyes, I was astonished. I was angry at the speech and at what I considered a sneak attack on my authority to determine press policy, particularly regarding the networks.

One of Agnew's key phrases was "instant commentators." It became often repeated, but it was inaccurate. The commentators had read the speech and been briefed by us in advance. Theirs was not instant comment.

Agnew said:

"A small group of men, numbering perhaps no more than a dozen anchormen, commentators, and executive producers, settle upon twenty minutes or so of film and commentary that's to reach the public. . . . We do know that to a man these commentators and producers live and work in the geographical and intellectual confines of Washington, D.C., or New York City. . . . They draw their political and social views from the same sources. Worse, they talk constantly to one another, thereby providing artificial reinforcement to their shared viewpoints."

It was the conspiracy theory.

With some shock I had read news accounts earlier of a speech made by Bob Haldeman at Stanford University, where he gave the indirect impression that the dozen or so men huddled over cocktails and came forth with concerted views as to what the public would be allowed to know and thus then vastly influenced public opinion—a conspiracy. I criticized Haldeman but he passed it off lightly as a jab at Otis Chandler of Stanford and the Los Angeles *Times*.

Agnew was correct in part. New York and Washington have disproportionate influence on the news. And the decision makers who live and work there are few in number and all-powerful in impact.

But the more important fact is that all are highly competitive. In New York, the *Daily News* resembles the New York *Times* in no way in thought, appearance, or philosophy. And with the networks, one point's difference in the ratings can mean millions of dollars. They are deadly competitors. Some competitors are personal friends—until they get on the air.

When I read the Agnew Des Moines speech with some truths and some justified criticism of the networks intermixed with statements so ridiculous they were easily subject to attack, I found there was nothing I could do to change it. Agnew was airborne. The speech was out.

I decided to send copies of it to the twelve largest news bureaus and to each of the network news operations in Washington. My logic in doing this was that I did not want to encourage the idea we were making a sneak attack in Des Moines while hiding it in Washington.

The speech copy caused instant panic with each of the networks. They debated individually whether to televise it. They had no plans for this. None had facilities in Des Moines for such a national broadcast transmission on short notice, but an Iowa public broadcasting station had made arrangements to cover the Vice-President locally.

How much, if any, discussion there was among the networks, I do not know. I suspect there was considerable. ABC finally made the decision to work with the public broadcasting station and go live with the speech. Soon after that announcement CBS and NBC followed. In my view each was afraid to be accused of hiding such an inflammatory speech negative to broadcasting.

Yet, in retrospect, the combination of my decision to send out the speech and the network decision to televise the Vice-President live on prime time for the first time in his career led to the storm of public protest against broadcast news and simultaneously to the start of full-fledged open warfare between the news media and the Nixon administration.

It was like an accidental start to all-out war in an arena where tensions had been smoldering for months or years. Stumbling into war is disastrous. From my viewpoint, this was. I could defend part of the Agnew logic, but I also agreed with his opponents that in effect this was a McCarthy-like speech.

I considered resigning. However, I decided that, in view of my role with both the press and the administration, I could do more good by staying on and fighting the battle within the White House. Resigning would have been a good grandstand trick, but it would not put a restraint on an administration which badly needed someone who understood the real facts of the communications world.

Looking back, I think my assessment was correct, but even a right decision can often make life more difficult.

By a coincidence of timing, I had agreed earlier to do "Face the Nation" on what turned out to be the Sunday following the Des Moines bombshell, and I was to be the principal speaker in New York before the International Radio and Television Society on the following Friday.

In both appearances, I took the moderate approach that Agnew had raised some legitimate considerations as to whether there was maximum fairness and balance in the coverage by the news media. The response of the public to the Agnew speech made it clear that there were thousands of readers and viewers who had long felt they were getting biased coverage.

Under "Face the Nation" questioning in the CBS studio in Washington, I said, "I think there's a legitimate question to be debated within the industry. I would be opposed to government participation in it. But in the industry, whether we're doing a good enough job, whether we're being objective enough, and whether we might not spend more time in self-examination . . .

"I think that any time any industry—if you look at the problems you have today and you fail to continue to examine them, you do invite the government to come in.

"I'd like not to see that happen."

I later added that while Agnew had originally attacked the television networks, the problems were similar in any part of the news media, including newspapers.

A few hours after the "Face the Nation" program, another hard-hitting

CBS program, "Sixty Minutes," placed me in the position of seeking to intimidate radio and television stations by calling some of them and asking whether they intended to editorialize on the President's address. We had openly called stations regularly and asked for a copy of whatever was said, pro, con, or neutral. I looked upon that not as intimidation but as an effort to understand the viewpoint of broadcast stations in the same way we needed to gain the views of newspapers through their printed editorials. I originally proposed the idea of sending commentary texts to us at a meeting of the broadcast editorial writers, and I was applauded for recognizing their power. On one occasion a young assistant of mine had mistakenly asked about editorial content. I reprimanded him.

When, a few days later, I walked into a press conference prior to the New York Television Society luncheon, I was confronted with mass chaos among the reporters. The room was too small and the newsmen thought they could smell blood. They were shouting at each other and pushing and shoving. I finally had to restore order to answer their questions.

One of my major points was that censorship was not an issue. We were talking about balance, which had been lacking in commentary, and about fair reporting. Present at the head table were the presidents of news for all three networks. I praised them.

With emotions running high, I found that my efforts to bring some calm out of the storm succeeded in part. But only temporarily.

A week later before the same television society, Dr. Frank Stanton, president of CBS and a longtime close personal friend of mine, led the public assault by the networks as he lumped me with Agnew, Dean Burch, chairman of the Federal Communications Commission, Clark Mollenhoff, White House special counsel, and someone I had never heard of, Paul O'Neil, a member of the long inactive Subversive Activities Control Board.

O'Neil, who apparently needed something to do, had called television stations in Washington, while his wife had done the same in Florida, requesting logs of news coverage devoted to comment on the administration's Vietnam policy.

Clark Mollenhoff, a firebrand in the White House and an outstanding investigative reporter on leave from the Cowles newspapers, was guilty of voicing the opinion that Agnew reflected "the administration's views," and of supporting the Vice-President.

At the request of Chuck Colson, I had called Dean Burch to ask him if he could get copies of the transcripts of the post-Vietnam speech network commentary. Stanton attacked the Burch phone calls as intimidating. That was the last thing on Burch's mind or mine. I was not aware how unusual it was for the Federal Communications Commission chairman to seek transcripts. I would have thought that the commissioners frequently tried to get the facts when there were complaints against program content and there were plenty in this case. But that was not the case, and it was a mistake—not one aimed at intimidation, however, by either Burch or me. Burch's excellent record in later years bears this out.

Nonetheless, in the context of the times it provided ammunition to the broadcast chiefs, and, after thinking the matter over, Burch made public a letter clearing himself and defending the networks. Actually, I do not think Stanton thought he was being pressured, but he knew a good line of attack when he saw one.

What surprised me most was the attack by Stanton and others on the comment that called for industry self-examination so as not to "invite the government to come in." I had said that as a matter of principle in a "Face the Nation" broadcast even before I took office, and it was a comment made by me and by many colleagues in the newspaper business during speeches at newspaper forums long before I entered government.

The point is valid today. Industry self-criticism is good preventive medicine against unwanted bureaucratic intervention.

Even in their own sheltered world, it is surprising that the broadcasters did not anticipate the depth of the public criticism of them, particularly outside the Eastern seaboard. They were surprised and overwhelmed by the public response that urged the citizenry to let the broadcasters know what its feeling was. They were bewildered and, under siege and led by Stanton, they responded with fierce counterattack. With all of this, my feeling was that enough is too much. And when I received an advance copy of the next Agnew blast at the media, I demanded and received an immediate meeting with Haldeman.

The next Agnew speech, which was to be delivered at Montgomery, Alabama, was even more harsh than his Des Moines address. I convinced Haldeman that the Vice-President had made his point but that continued artillery fire would only have the effect of alienating many in the media who were in support of the Nixon Vietnam policy. The Dallas *Times-Herald* and the Chicago *Tribune* were two excellent examples. They were supportive of Nixon but they rallied to defend the media and criticize Agnew. Haldeman and I gained the endorsement of the President in calling a halt to the proposed Agnew speech text for Montgomery, and I thought the battle was won.

Not until years later did I find that Pat Buchanan had become infuriated when he heard we had killed the speech, and he quietly went back to the President and convinced him that we were making progress with the Agnew antimedia approach. The President was convinced easily since he had not really wanted to change his mind in the first place.

The speech was modified, although the Washington *Post* and the New York *Times*, which received the full fire of the Agnew Montgomery address, would find that hard to believe, even today.

Agnew said the *Times* and the *Post* had grown "fat and irresponsible" because of lack of competition. They have grown fat with advertising, particularly the *Post*, and they do exert influence on opinion makers far in excess of that of any other newspapers. We often felt they were irresponsible, and, of course, we were aware of the fact that their views were liberal, generally pro-Democratic and anti-Vietnam. But all that was their right in a free society.

"The time for blind acceptance of their opinion is past . . . and the time for naïve belief in their neutrality is gone," Agnew said.

Having made these points, Agnew, in typical fashion, went on to blame the problem on growing monopolies in the news business, and he cited specific items to criticize the New York *Times*'s news judgment.

The fact was that, monopolies or not (and most newspapers have a monopoly situation), we were gaining overwhelming editorial support outside of Washington, New York, and a few other cities. And in New York some of the staunchest support for Nixon policies was being voiced by the New York *Daily News* and the *Wall Street Journal*, both of which have circulation in excess of the *Post* or *Times*.

Agnew could well have argued effectively for more balanced coverage in the *Post* and the *Times*, but his method of attack was such that while it gained some public applause, it gave strength to critics of the administration in the media and weakened the ties with supporters.

All in all, the entire 1969 Agnew-press fracas, which continued beyond, amounted to the incongruous situation where the combination of my eagerness to keep everything in the open by rushing out the Des Moines speech to the press, and the network decision to lay the issue in the open by broadcasting Agnew's speech live, brought the opposite result of what any of us wanted: a major series of attacks and counterattacks which in the end were damaging both to the news media and to the presidency. Meanwhile, public confidence in both institutions lagged.

At about the same time, Agnew also was engaged in the administration's most hard-line attack on young demonstrators. In New Orleans he referred to "an effete corps of impudent snobs who characterized themselves as intellectuals" and who have encouraged "a spirit of national masochism." Again, the Agnew attack had merit, but it was how it was said—aided in most cases by White House speech writers. Agnew's own speech writer, Mrs. Cynthia Rosenwald, resigned in protest despite my efforts to convince her to stay.

A story by Boston *Globe* reporter James Doyle (later a member of the Jaworski Watergate staff) quoted an unnamed member of my staff as saying I was playing Agnew down. The Vice-President replied in a note signed personally with his initials, STA, "Frankly, I am disturbed about the non-attributed remarks to this reporter by one of your aides.

"In my judgment, there is too much off-the-record discussion to hostile news people by staff in the Executive branch. I would appreciate your comments." I replied that we didn't judge a reporter's politics or bias before talking to him.

Agnew's personal sensitivity was illustrated vividly in 1971 following a February 2 broadcast on "Sixty Minutes" which the Vice-President felt unfairly attacked his intelligence and his educational background. He had a valid point, but he also was too thin-skinned.

The show opened thus:

Mike Wallace: "Spiro Agnew on his father's knee at ten months (illustrated with snapshots from Agnew). With his dog, Frisky, at ten years. His high school graduation picture. Drafted before Pearl Harbor. Married at twenty-four. Vice-President of the Kiwanis Club in 1959. Vice-President of the United States in 1969."

Agnew: "I don't think that it's fair to say that suddenly a yokel has descended upon the national government."

The quote for the opening of the show was accurate, but it was taken out of context, a fault which hurts media credibility.

Actually the yokel comment came as part of a response to a Wallace query as to whether the Vice-President had the ability to make up for inexperience and "is politically educable fast enough to catch up with the kind of responsibilities we're told he's going to be given."

The interview painted Agnew as a man who had come up the hard way, gone through a number of jobs, turned Democrat to Republican opportunistically, faced serious problems as governor, compiled a good record, and counted himself to be an "average man."

One could take parts out of it and say it was a negative program. On balance, the show ended on a strong pro-Agnew note with an analytical comment by the editor of the Baltimore *Sun*, Brad Jacobs.

The point that irritated Agnew was revealing: There were scattered comments about his grades in school.

"His grades at Forest Park High School were mediocre at best. . . . From high school he entered Johns Hopkins University, where he majored in chemistry. Again, his grades were no source of pride and Spiro Agnew dropped out of college after his second year, when his father just cut off his support. So, to support himself, Agnew found a job paying eleven dollars a week in the file room of an insurance company. . . . Later, he enrolled in night classes at the University of Baltimore Law School, an institution not accredited by the American Bar Association. Here too, he did poorly scholastically. He admits he cut a lot of classes."

These were a few sentences in twenty minutes or more of the program, in which Agnew was described by Mike Wallace generally as a self-made man.

But the education comments cut a deep personal wound within the mind of this seemingly hard-boiled politician. He asked me to discuss his personal feelings with CBS executives.

Three weeks later I was scheduled by Elie Abel, dean of the Columbia School of Journalism, to address his students and I also made an appointment while I was in New York, to see Richard Salant, president of CBS Television News.

As it turned out, the New York day was preceded by the President's announcement the night before that the United States troops were entering Cambodia.

My session with students at Columbia University was emotional and tense, to say the least.

But, unexpectedly, my meeting with Salant was almost as delicate. I discussed a number of subjects with him and then said I thought he should be aware privately of the reaction of the Vice-President to the "Sixty Minutes" program. I confessed I had not seen the show and asked for a transcript so I could understand the problem. He gave me his views and the transcript, and I left believing the Vice-President had been oversensitive. In my later note to Agnew I described Salant's treatment of the discussion as "a mixed bag."

I long had regarded personal discussions such as that with Salant as private and helpful for both sides. They had always been treated as such by broadcast and newspaper executives. But somehow, the Salant discussion was leaked to the media, and I never felt after that I could speak in confidence to Salant—although I regard him as an able news executive, doubtless one of the best.

Agnew was the lead campaigner in the 1970 congressional campaign. He had massive media coverage. He had the assistance of such White House seniors as Bryce Harlow, speech writer Bill Safire, and Pat Buchanan—among others.

Three days before he was to start on his campaign schedule, Haldeman called me frantically and asked who I could find to handle the Vice-President's traveling press activities. He again ruled out Thompson.

I thought of two people. And both responded favorably after much persuasion from me.

I first called Carl DeBloom, conservative editor of the Columbus *Dispatch* and formerly a veteran Washington correspondent. DeBloom was highly respected, and he knew the Washington and campaign scenes thoroughly. His publisher, Preston Wolfe, had long been concerned with both government and politics. He was of the breed of publisher who frequently visited Washington to be sure he understood the issues and voiced his opinion when it counted.

My calls to DeBloom and his publisher were successful: the editor would be given a short leave of absence and thus would see another side of government and campaigning. The situation was similar to my own when Nixon was Vice-President.

My next recollection was that one of the most effective assistant press secretaries for a campaign since 1960 had been Vic Gold, who had worked in 1964 for Paul Wagner, Goldwater's press secretary. They had been through hell in an unpopular campaign, and both Wagner and Gold emerged with excellent personal reputations.

Gold is excitable. He is personable. He is brilliant, and he is not afraid to tackle any job.

On this short notice he gave up most of his public relations business and stepped into the gap with DeBloom.

With Agnew's campaign harshness and his running battle with the press, the combination of the cool, calm DeBloom and the excitable but thorough Gold did much to hold together the fiber of the vice-presidential national off-year election campaign effort in 1970.

There was much debate over whether Agnew had helped more or hurt more in that campaign. He covered every assignment asked of him. And weighed on a scale, I would say he helped more than he hurt. He captured headlines. He raised great amounts of money, and he focused on issues assigned him.

The Republicans lost, but the fault lies more with local committees, candidates, and the issues focused upon by White House strategists who were not in tune with the voters in 1970.

The sensitivity and insecurity of the inner Agnew came out again when he queried me after a story had been written by Frank Cormier, senior White House correspondent for Associated Press, saying, "Members of Nixon's inner circle remain divided on whether Agnew should be nominated for second place on an expected Nixon bid for reelection in 1972." This was at a time when some Republicans already were talking of Agnew as a presidential candidate in 1976.

Bob Finch, Ron Ziegler, and I had covered this potential problem with the President and, anticipating the likelihood that the press would seek a hole in the Nixon armor, had deliberately gone out of our way to praise Agnew for his campaign efforts as we discussed the 1970 election results at a San Clemente press conference the day after the disappointing election. I gave Agnew a transcript to reassure him that we had been appreciative of his efforts.

When the 1972 campaign began, Agnew was easily the most controversial figure in the administration. From the press side, DeBloom had long since returned to his responsibilities as editor of his successful newspaper in Columbus. Vic Gold stayed on loyally, although he frequently was distressed by acts by the Vice-President where he was not consulted or by a lack of communication between him and other members of a growing Agnew staff bureaucracy. We had frequent consultations at the end of some of Gold's long and distressing days, and both jointly and singly met with Agnew to emphasize the need for more consultations regarding media relations, but by this time his feeling toward the press was bitter and contemptuous.

By this time Agnew was looked upon by more and more conservative Republicans as the front-runner to succeed Nixon for the nomination in 1976. Despite the rumors to the contrary, some created by reporters, as I said earlier, he was the sure choice for renomination in 1972, and he accepted eagerly the role of the cutting edge in the campaign.

Interestingly, the 1972 campaign committee (Committee to Re-elect the President, CREEP) never included his name. He was a side issue. Normally the committee would include candidate names, i.e., Eisenhower-Nixon, Carter-Mondale. And while CREEP scheduled the Vice-President, relayed issue messages, and integrated its advance men with those of Agnew, it rarely consulted him on issues. And Agnew rarely discussed strategy with CREEP.

On occasion, he would call me for such a discussion, and he had other meetings with Haldeman and Harlow. Somehow, he felt alien to Finch and Ehrlichman.

Basically, the main task for Agnew in that campaign was to stir working Republicans into action and to avoid the kind of error or controversy which could turn a sure Nixon victory over George McGovern into a defeat.

Agnew did that. He performed well.

After the resignations of Bob Haldeman, John Ehrlichman, and Richard Kleindienst and the firing of John Dean, amid the growing Watergate revelations in the press, in the Congress, and by investigators, Agnew called me to his office several times to tell me of "harassment" he said he was undergoing.

He told me that through some actions he could not understand, the United States attorney's office was harassing him and his friends in Baltimore. He assured me there was nothing to it.

I was busy and concerned much more over Watergate so I took the comment in stride and thought little about it.

Oversensitivity again, I thought.

On the third occasion of this kind in the fall of 1973 after I had left the White House, Agnew told me that his Maryland problem was increasing because the U.S. attorney involved was a Kennedy man who had somehow been appointed by a Nixon Justice Department. He went on to decry the Justice Department and in particular to criticize Elliot Richardson as a "cabinet officer from New England with a particular Kennedy-type bias" long before he became Attorney General. Kennedys were Agnew's scape-goats.

The Agnew denials appeared more serious to me each time I heard them, and I finally decided to discuss them with General Al Haig, who by then had succeeded Haldeman as chief of staff.

"The SOB is lying," Haig said. "I can't tell you more at this time, but don't in any way defend him to the press or anyone else. Your credibility is too valuable and you could lose it by not heeding what I am telling you."

Haig gained my promise to discuss the subject with no one else, informing me that he was receiving damaging information regarding Agnew and would keep me informed at the right time—if that became necessary.

I tried to warn loyal Vic Gold, but it was difficult, and his job was to do what he could for the Vice-President. Even when the story broke, he found himself among the last to believe it because of his deep dedication to a job and a Vice-President.

And yet, strong man that he is, he was among the first to admit that he had been duped by the Vice-President.

As the public reports on Agnew's acceptance of small gifts not only as governor of Maryland but even as Vice-President surfaced publicly, I talked with Agnew once more.

Days before he resigned, he again assured me of his innocence and of his persecution somehow connived by Ted Kennedy and Richardson.

I walked over to see Al Haig once more.

"He will have to resign," Haig said. "There is no choice. We're already up to our ears in congressional committees looking at Watergate and out to get the President. He was such a dumb SOB to get involved in these things, but believe me, there is evidence."

Shortly after, Haig met with the Vice-President and confronted him with evidence gathered by Richardson.

And the Agnew story became one of how he would deal with the Justice Department and a federal judge who eventually agreed to a plea of nolo contendere to one charge of failing to report gifts as taxable income. He was placed on probation and fined ten thousand dollars.

Prior to the brief court appearance, Agnew followed his confrontation with Haig with a personal meeting with the President on October 9 wherein he tendered his resignation.

Agnew was a man of great pride. He was self-made. His wife, Judy, was as hard hit by the abrupt change in events as the Vice-President. Quiet and loyal, she had been an integral part of the Agnew climb from obscurity to the nation's second highest office.

As the President later recounted his personal talk with Agnew with the two men sitting privately before the fireplace in the Oval Office, it was apparent that the Vice-President even then found it almost impossible to accept the circumstances which had forced him from office. He felt victimized by Richardson.

9

"The Ron and Herb Show"

FROM THE OUTSET of the transition period between the 1968 election and the 1969 inaugural, the press found it difficult to understand the dual activities which had been set up in the White House dividing the media activities of Ron Ziegler, the press secretary, and Herb Klein, the director of communications. This was further complicated by my unique relationship with Agnew and with the cabinet.

While the press and the majority of the public most remembers the Nixon administration in this regard for its barefisted battles with the media, many of the operations we organized widened the scope of information available to the newsmen and thus the public. This is not to assert that the Nixon administration, like those which preceded and succeeded it, did not make a major effort to manage the news and that it did not on far too many occasions take oppressive measures. It is simply to say that the negative is far better remembered than the positive.

Ron Ziegler seemed to vary between insecurity and overconfidence on a day-to-day basis as he first moved into the enormous responsibilities attendant to the position of press secretary to the President of the United States. He was intelligent, with an ability to absorb knowledge quickly, and while he had no direct media experience, he had pointedly tried to study the operations of newspapers while working for J. Walter Thompson advertising agency. Usually when he called on a San Diego client, Seaworld, he would come to my office for several hours and watch as the paper was being organized for the next morning's edition. In the political arena, he had worked with the press as a legislative assistant shortly after he left the

University of Southern California, and when I joined the Nixon campaign for governor of California in 1962, he was already there as a hard-working but inexperienced press assistant.

I learned early in the campaign for governor that I rarely had to explain something twice and that he was alert, tough, and at the same time pleasant to newsmen. In 1968, I felt he worked well with me as he traveled on the campaign plane functioning as my senior press aide and meanwhile learning more than the newsmen realized about the operations of the national press corps.

His problems as he moved into the White House were compounded because of his youth—he was twenty-nine—and lack of visible experience. He first had to prove to the White House press corps that he could stand up to them. The newsmen gave him a fair chance to prove his worth, but they were skeptical and it was a tough role for both parties. Meanwhile, as someone who knew neither Washington nor the government, Ziegler had to double his efforts to learn both the operations of the White House and the functions of the office of the press secretary. Most press secretaries, including, more recently, Jody Powell, have had this challenge. In this situation, Ziegler somewhat resented the respect paid me by the press as the senior newsman in government, someone the reporters had known for years; while he realized that I could be his strongest asset, he asked for surprisingly little aid. He was Haldeman's captive, but I doubt Ziegler ever felt I would do other than try to help him succeed.

Given the situation, Ziegler handled himself well, but he also was fortunate that the news corps chose to give him time to settle into the job. Nixon and Haldeman had given him unprecedented opportunity, but in reality they had been unfair. Starting someone off at twenty-nine years of age with less than eight years' business experience puts the person at a tremendous disadvantage when he must move into a role this important in government and must, on an adversary basis, face cynical news veterans, some of whom had been covering the beat since the time of Franklin Roosevelt. Ziegler, the bright rookie, did well in his first year, but the toughness of the competition had a negative personality effect which, along with White House attitudes, never allowed him to develop into a great press secretary. Even without Watergate and the excruciating pain his debates with the reporters in 1974 caused him, he had little chance to reach his full potential as a knowledgeable and able public leader.

Despite my news and political background, I also found my role difficult. I was carving out an operation entirely new to government. And the press, rightfully suspicious of the scope of the assignment and of the Nixon background of antagonism toward the media, speculated in print and broadcast as to whether I would be a help or a hindrance to the information process of the executive branch. "News czar" was a job description attached to me by some of the reporters and cartoonists.

During the transition period, Haldeman had written me a memo saying that the President was anxious to keep my and Ziegler's staffs small. He did not want a gigantic press or public relations operation, at least in numbers. I kept my senior staff small with Paul Costello as press assistant; Alvin Snyder, broadcast; Margita White, administration; Virginia Savell, speakers' bureau; and two loyal principal assistants, Susie Low, research, and Tina Bucheit, personal administrative assistant. What I lacked was a deputy, someone I felt could replace me while I was out of town, or eventually when I would leave the White House staff. I envisioned finding an experienced broadcaster or managing editor of a newspaper who would be challenged by the role, but I made the mistake of being too selective and never recruiting the right man. This left a spot open for a Haldeman man, Jeb Stuart Magruder, who filled a major mechanical need on the staff, but did not fit the concept of the deputy I had sought. Magruder was once told by Haldeman he was on the White House staff to act, not to think. But he became my deputy.

One of Ziegler's best early moves was in his selection of a deputy, Gerald Warren, who had worked for me on the San Diego *Union* from trainee to city editor and eventually assistant managing editor. I was hesitant about recruiting anyone from my newspaper, but Warren was suggested to Ziegler and Haldeman by Clifford Miller, Los Angeles public relations executive, and it was Miller who recruited Warren as Ziegler's strong right arm. Warren brought an aura of newspaperism to the staff of the press secretary, and in his mature, reasoned manner he was the ideal deputy for Ziegler. Despite our close friendship, I made a point of seeing Warren privately only on rare occasions during the early days of the Nixon White House to avoid giving Ziegler any impression that Warren was my agent on his staff. I felt that Ziegler was sensitive to a degree that he might make his and Warren's assignments more difficult if he felt in any way that Warren's first loyalty was not to him. My problem was not one of fact but of perception.

From the start, it was apparent that Ziegler was to be completely dominated by Haldeman. He became the young mouthpiece of Haldeman as much as that of the President. He was under constant Haldeman pressure, although he later fought this. On one side he had to endure the continued needling of Ehrlichman, who delighted in digging into Ziegler and embarrassing him at a 7:30 A.M. senior staff meeting. On the other side, Ziegler seemed to get along well with Kissinger, who briefed him on foreign policy questions due from the press. During the first few weeks in the White House one of the newsmen's questions was, Did Ziegler really talk to the President or just to Haldeman and Kissinger? From the start,

Ziegler bucked through to the President directly but not for the amount of time he deserved to interpret Nixon during the tough early days. Later when Watergate was inundating the President, Ziegler had to virtually give up his role as press spokesman and turn it over to Warren, partly because of press harassment and decreased credibility and mainly because he became a close confidant of the President.

I worried about Ziegler's troubles but concentrated upon my own. My first job was to pick the public affairs assistants to the cabinet, and I found it more difficult than I had expected to locate newsmen who were sympathetic to the Nixon philosophy of government and who had both leadership qualities and experience. At one time I tried to get Bob White, who had been publisher of the New York *Herald Tribune* and now was a prize-winning owner and publisher of his own daily in Mexico, Missouri. He was a registered Democrat, but that meant little to me. He had the depth and reputation to operate in any capacity in the Washington arena, including becoming my successor. I wooed him ardently, but he was unable to leave his job as the operating chief of his newspaper.

My job included placing appropriate administration leaders on national television as well as appearing myself. This part came easy with the experienced help of Alvin Snyder. I ran a quick informal television training course for each man in the cabinet.

Revamping the news departments in the cabinet offices came harder. With Costello directing the program, I set up a *"Wall Street Journal* bureau" system wherein members of my staff were in daily contact with the public affairs officers to discuss what their major news was and then to summarize it in a daily report prepared for my information and guidance. But the departments were creaky and antiquated. They barely recognized broadcasting. They needed much change.

I recalled that as an editorial writer in San Diego, I often had to depend only on sketchy Associated and United Press reports to gain the facts I needed. As a result, the editorials were often too shallow. The wire services were factual, but did not provide enough background sometimes. I instituted a plan to mail fact sheets to newspaper editors and broadcasters across the country, giving them an in-depth report on new administration programs. This was a delicate operation, one where we had to stick to fact and avoid opinion—in other words, avoid the mantle of propaganda. Once or twice material I considered propaganda went out of my office without my approval, such as a Joe Alsop column on Vietnam which was perceptive but argued for the President so strongly that I felt it wrong to go into the mail with a White House return address. It was opinion, not cold fact. That was mailed under my name because Colson bypassed me and pressured Magruder while I was speaking in the Middle West. My name was forged on a cover memo without my knowledge.

One role my office inherited was one I had not expected. Congress had passed the Freedom of Information Act in 1967, and it fell upon me and the new Nixon team to implement it during its early stages. I found great resistance to the Information Act within the administration and in most cabinet departments. The bureaucracy and the politicians both resisted. Inevitably attorneys in these departments would insist that they were the judges of the legitimacy of requests for information, rather than the public affairs appointees; lawyers and newsmen differ more often than not on questions of what information should go to the public.

When they were turned down on a request, newsmen started coming to me for help and in most cases I was able to pry the information loose. Even the attorneys were hesitant about defying a senior White House staffer who was known as a longtime friend of the President. In the early stages of the administration, some of the astute reporters, such as Don Oberdoerfer of the Washington *Post,* found that they could buck their way through bureaucratic red tape simply by threatening to call me into the case.

There were some serious problems with implementation of the act, however. I was interested primarily in helping the newsmen get information I thought was of public news interest. I did not look at the act or my job as designed to answer voluminous requests from special-interest groups, and I was not prepared for the pressure for information that was being developed by Ralph Nader and other consumer-activist leaders. They would send young interns to the departments with such broad requests for information that it appeared to me they were on fishing expeditions. They required such great volumes of information that one would have to hire more workers or transfer others from essential duties just to service the college students Nader had enlisted for summer intern work.

Nader sought to exploit the situation, and at one time I was called on a Saturday afternoon by the Washington *Post* asking my comment on a letter Nader had written to me castigating me for not being of greater assistance. I had never heard of the letter, and I read its text in the Sunday newspapers before actually receiving the letter on the following Monday or Tuesday. Nader obviously wanted a public issue and apparently mailed the letter to me well after leaking copies of it to the press.

I sometimes wonder if any other business in the world could survive the pressure of exposure of internal communication placed today on the United States Government.

Early in 1970, I received, on behalf of my office, a large plaque from the N. W. Ayer company for operating the office which had done the best job of providing public information in the year 1969. The award was presented at the National Press Club with several members of my staff present to share the honors. The main speaker, however, was Ralph

Nader, who followed the presentation with a speech wherein he was highly critical of the whole operation of the director of communications. I was honored one moment and attacked the next, all at the same luncheon.

To add to the irony of the situation, a few years later I placed the plaque on the wall of my family room. Beneath it was a hide-a-bed. Guests were visiting one night and as I was about to go to sleep in the hide-a-bed, the copper plate from the plaque became unglued and fell, hitting me on the head. It was like receiving Nader's last blow.

One of the traditions of the Executive Office Building, where I and my staff were quartered, is that the most prestigious offices are in the four corners of the beautiful old structure. The corner room that went with my suite faced Pennsylvania Avenue and the White House and had a magnificent old porch extending off it. It is said that it was here the Japanese diplomats were waiting for the Secretary of State when he found out that Pearl Harbor was being bombed. On my wall was a gigantic ten-by-twelve-foot colored map of the world, a map I admired until Jim Hagerty walked in one afternoon and pointed out to me that it was out of date. Country names, particularly in Africa, had long since changed and the map still read as if it were colonial times. We replaced the map.

For my own space, I selected a large office adjacent to the corner and installed three LBJ television sets.

The office, like many others, had a beautiful fireplace, and after watching the various fireplaces burning in the White House I inquired about fuel for this one. In typical fashion, the General Services Administration made a survey of chimneys in the entire building and informed me that the fireplaces in the old building could be fixed, but it would take an authorization of at least three or four million dollars. I canceled the plan.

Across Executive Avenue in the White House, Ziegler was told that he had to get the reporters out of the official reception room of the White House's West Wing. There were a few offices for reporters off the reception room, but, in the main, visitors to the executive staff offices would find that they had to climb over reporters and photographers who filled the room as they waited for press briefings. There were not even enough seats for all the White House regulars. Ziegler and Haldeman came up with the idea of building a new press working room in the basement of the Executive Office Building with a tunnel connecting the area to the White House. They soon found there were two faults with the plan. One was cost. Again the tunnel and rebuilding of rooms would cost millions. Second, the press corps opposed even the mention of moving that distance from the President and the press secretary. The compromise answer was to rebuild the White House indoor swimming pool. The indoor pool had been constructed for Franklin Roosevelt, supposedly with the "pennies from children." The pool walls were left intact but the more delicate task was to peel from the walls the Roosevelt murals and to preserve them for historic purposes. This was accomplished and a two-story press room complete with permanent camera platforms, a press lounge, and offices was constructed. It was a good solution, but it eliminated swimming for me and for Moynihan, who used the pool most.

Another of the early crises facing Ziegler was preparation for a trip with the President to Western Europe. This was to be a grand tour, signaling the relationships a new President would have with America's NATO allies. Ziegler had never been on a foreign mission, either official or unofficial, and I tried to help him with arrangements, but he rebuffed me. He did consult with George Christian, Lyndon Johnson's excellent press secretary, and worked closely with an old pro, Bob McCloskey, from the State Department. Tim Elbourne, who had been with Ziegler at USC and at Disneyland, became the press advance man, and together they assembled a somewhat criticized but generally successful press operation, working often with the press secretaries of foreign countries and with United States Information Service officers. Kissinger was launched during the trip as the official briefing officer and did it extremely well. Connie Girard, who served as a secretary for the press office of Presidents Johnson, Nixon, Ford, and Carter, added a needed element of experience, as did the White House military transportation office. Much staff help is available in the White House if used properly by a newcomer.

One of the things which clouded the relationship between Ziegler and the newsmen was his use of advertising terminology. Old-fashioned words from the newsroom such as deadlines and briefings and photo sessions were replaced by such words as photo opportunities, information opportunities, and time frames. "Bottom line" and "stonewall" became great buzz words in this style. A photo opportunity, for example, meant that the photographers would be allowed two or three minutes to photograph the President in one situation or another. Usually the still cameramen would come in for a few minutes and then the television crews. Two or three reporters were admitted to make notes which would be available to the entire news corps. Traditionally, a "news pool" also travels on Air Force One and the five or six reporters included are expected to turn their notes over to the general press corps.

In preparing for his briefings with the news corps once or twice a day, Ziegler was well organized and asked the kind of questions newsmen would have approved. Part of his difficulty was that the President did not always want to give him full answers, and Haldeman reflected this view more strongly. A press secretary needs to have the full story whether he uses it or not. An example of the problem Ziegler faced was in a memo written on June 10, 1969, by Alex Butterfield, who had the job of transcribing notes the President had scrawled by hand alongside items he read in the daily news summary.

"The President read in a recent news summary that many of his critics complain about the Administration's not being 'as open as promised,'" Butterfield said. His only comment addressed to you [John Ehrlichman in this case] appears below:

"'John—tell Herb and Ron to ignore this kind of criticism. The fact of the matter is that we are far too open. If we treat the press with a little more contempt we'll probably get better treatment.'" Ziegler and I were copied in on the memo. I ignored it, as did Ziegler, but I was troubled by this growing antipress attitude even in the first six months of the administration.

Ziegler felt that I was making a mistake by spending very little time socializing with the White House staff and by using most of my spare time in organized fashion lunching or having a late-afternoon drink with the members of the press corps. Some on the White House staff looked at this as fraternizing with the enemy, and noted that Safire, Finch, and Garment also were falling into this "bad habit." Buchanan could fraternize, but he was considered an exception. He was more critical of the news corps and met usually with conservatives. Moynihan and Kissinger socialized with the press at Georgetown parties, but Haldeman and Ehrlichman considered them beyond their scope. Ziegler felt a strong common bond with many of the higher-ranked younger members of the White House staff such as Dwight Chapin, Larry Higby, Kenneth Cole, and Steve Bull. He felt less relaxed with newsmen and wanted time to get away from them. His interest in this area was more internal, mine more external.

Prior to the start of our White House tenure, I invited the heads of the leading journalism societies to dinner in New York to meet with Ziegler and me and freely discuss problems and opportunities they saw in the relation between government and press. This included the heads of such organizations as the White House Correspondents, the Gridiron Club, Broadcast News Directors, the National Press Club, the Congressional Correspondents, the Washington Press Club, Sigma Delta Chi, the National Journalism Society, the Press Photographers, and the Broadcast Correspondents. I also invited Jim Hagerty. To my surprise, I found that Ziegler seemed uncomfortable with the group and unwilling to take a major part in the discussion.

A year later, on December 10, 1969, Ziegler and I hosted a similar group of journalism organization leaders at a dinner in the White House Staff Mess Dining Room. The session, which came at a time when the Vice-President was lambasting the media, drew more open and critical discussion than had our first meeting, and it was noticeable to me that by then Ziegler felt more at ease with the newsmen, participating more fully in the give-and-take. In addition to criticizing Agnew, the news representatives urged more frequent press conferences by the President and by his cabinet. We felt the same way privately. Their cabinet criticism focused on John Mitchell, Bill Rogers, Wally Hickel, and Secretary of Agriculture Cliff Hardin.

Had I spent more time mending fences within the White House instead of concentrating on outside contacts for us, I probably would have been less vulnerable to attack from within. But I think there is a major need for outside contact, even with today's White House. I also felt there was vast overemphasis on memo writing and game plans. They did not fit my style, although strategic plans for major projects had a great deal of merit.

A basic difference was that I felt that although a lunch with a newsman at the Sans Souci Restaurant or the Metropolitan Club would take longer than one in the White House mess, it generally would result in an interesting column or background story. It had the side benefit of allowing me to watch who was talking to whom in the official circles and thus I usually would be able to recognize the source for a leak or a background story or column.

At Key Biscayne on weekends Ziegler relaxed more with reporters, perhaps feeling that the informal atmosphere there put him under less pressure from Haldeman and the President and allowed him time for a tennis game, boat trip, or swim with newsmen. He enhanced his relationship with the reporters at this time. Pierre Salinger used to use weekends away with Kennedy to entertain the reporters with his piano playing in the hotel bar.

There is a definite point at which there is danger in an overly social relationship on the side of either the reporters or the press assistant, but capable professionals handle this. There also is a need to build a relationship between the newsmen and the government official based upon understanding of the individual personalities. It is important, for example, for the press secretary to know that a tough Dan Rather or Ted Knapp can be a vicious tiger in a press conference or news briefing and yet can be charming and interesting in a more informal situation.

Jerry Warren handled the reporter-press office situation differently. He had relatively little time for socializing outside the White House during the week, but he would spend time chatting with reporters in the press lounge or on a trip, and occasionally he and his wife would host a relaxed party at home, bring the newsmen and their wives together informally with a few from the staff. He gained good understanding of individuals and was respected for it.

During presidential press conferences, I stood in the front of the room, just outside camera range but at a place near the podium where I could observe the reporters from the President's vantage point. Ziegler would join me there, and we could get an intimate feeling for the cross currents between the President and the news corps. I kept an informal box score with notes on questions, who asked them, and the flavor of the Nixon answer. On some occasions Nixon would pontificate to a degree that he would take only twelve or fourteen questions during the thirty-minute period. Once, shortly after someone told him Kennedy used to answer far more questions, Nixon in thirty minutes handled thirty-two press queries in excellent form.

Every official has a particular way of closing news conferences. For a President the answer is easy. A televised conference always ends with the senior White House correspondent—for years Merriman Smith and later either Helen Thomas or Frank Cormier, of UPI and AP respectively—saying, "Thank you, Mr. President." Carter adhered to that but then stayed to answer a few more questions informally. That was dangerous and he was burned more than once. During more informal press conferences in the Oval Office or at San Clemente or Key Biscayne, Ziegler would try to break off the questioning when he thought enough time had been allotted or he would signal some newsman to say, "Thank you." It gave the President a chance to appear gracious by brushing off his press secretary and continuing to answer three or four more questions if he chose to.

Ziegler usually followed the presidential technique and waited for someone to say, "Thank you, Mr. Secretary." On a few occasions when I was attending one of his briefings which I thought had gone beyond the time of productivity, Warren or I would signal one of the senior correspondents to bring the meeting to a halt. The reporters usually would respond. He normally gave the press full time for questions even when queries went beyond the bounds of reason and into the arena of bitter harassment. By 1974, with Watergate dominating everything, the White House press corps on occasion dragged the briefing on for an hour and a half with useless, delicate questions, and it was an exercise in frustration.

For me, I found that during nontelevised press conferences, the most professional way to bring a meeting to a halt at what I considered the proper time was to smile and say, "I'll take one more question." Occasionally, I would joke with an audience by saying I had learned that taking one more question could be a mistake because frequently the last question was the zinger, the toughest question. Actually I enjoyed taking one more question because it was usually one which the newsman had taken the time to think out carefully, and thus coming up with a full answer was a greater challenge for me.

I do feel that taking several questions and then "one more question" is far superior to the tendency to take only limited questions, a practice all too often followed by government officials.

I strongly believed that the success of having two press operations in the White House was dependent on having constant coordination between the two offices to avoid overlap and to be certain we were not taking opposite views. That coordination was more difficult than I expected. Until we got to the White House Ziegler and I had communicated well together. Once we were there the communication became far too sporadic. I would have someone from my staff at most of the briefings of the press secretary so we would be informed on both the questions and the answers supplied. To provide background material for my own press conferences and briefings I relied almost entirely on my own staff and on direct contact with cabinet officers, two or three senior White House presidential assistants, and the President himself.

Magruder told me when he left my staff to go to the Committee to Re-elect the President that he had fought serious battles with Ziegler when he was invited to Ziegler's office to listen to him criticize my operation. This was never said to me when it occurred—when it counted—but I did realize that Magruder harbored a bitter feeling toward Ziegler, just as he did toward Colson. But he did not fear Ziegler as he did Colson.

Every few weeks Ziegler and I would meet in private, usually in his office at seven or eight in the evening, and try to work on joint strategy. Over a couple of scotches we would solidify our stand against those on the White House staff who were pushing constantly for more open breaks with newsmen and attacks on the media. We communicated best on those relaxed occasions. But they were too rare. If things were going very well for him, Ziegler would sometimes drop into my office and take time to chat with others on the staff. He was relaxed. If the going were tougher than usual or he felt depressed and perhaps repressed, he would want me to come over to his office, where he would bring out his favorite scotch, Chivas Regal. Occasionally, we would philosophize, but more often we would work on a practical basis to deal with a problem or to find a way to talk the President into more contact with the press. We succeeded too rarely.

The President who was the roughest on press secretaries was Lyndon Johnson. His press secretary as Vice-President was George Reedy, who had worked for him on Capitol Hill and had a background as a news service reporter. In a chance meeting in New Orleans in the spring of 1963, he informally asked if I was interested in heading his press staff. It was not a firm inquiry, and perhaps not even a planned or a serious one, but I said I enjoyed his friendship, but I did not want to return to politics in the immediate future.

When Johnson became President after the John Kennedy assassination,

Pierre Salinger stayed on to run the press office, but he lacked the principal ingredient a press secretary must have: the confidence of the President. Johnson looked at him as part of the Kennedy team, not his.

With the encouragement of Johnson, Salinger resigned in the spring of 1964, just in time to run for Senate in California. He had been in the state so little while working in Washington for John Kennedy that he had difficulty qualifying. He then won the Democratic primary, only to lose in the general election to George Murphy. While Salinger's boss, Kennedy, was helped by debates in defeating Nixon in 1960, Salinger was hurt by his debates with Murphy in California. It wasn't so much a question of who had the better answers as it was of mannerisms, and Salinger looked too tough against a well-liked movie star, George Murphy.

The only time I ever seriously considered running for senator was at the time Salinger announced. I felt that Salinger and I could dominate the primary elections by debating each other as two rivals from 1960. We were close personal friends and shared a mutual respect, but that would not preclude political debate up and down the state. I decided against the race for three reasons: there was too little time to raise the money for a campaign prior to the filing date, I was not sure whether I was considering this because I really wanted elective office or because I like challenges, and I very much knew I liked the idea of being at home with my family and with a job I enjoyed tremendously, editor of the San Diego *Union*.

Salinger's resignation made him first out in the Johnson string of presidential press secretaries. Reedy succeeded him and found himself blamed by Johnson for everything that went wrong with the press (which was often). Reedy, who eventually wrote a thoughtful book on the presidency (*Twilight of the Presidency*) and became dean of the school of journalism at Marquette University, resigned for what was said to be physical reasons. He had a foot problem which required hospitalization, but I always suspected that he wanted out of the arena. Bill Moyers, who succeeded Reedy, was a contrasting personality who was younger, quicker, and a harder target for the Johnson barbs. He was succeeded by George Christian, who won the respect of all as one of the best men to handle that office—in my book second only to Jim Hagerty, among those I have known. And in the last days of the Johnson regime, young Tom Johnson, who had served as an assistant, took over the job capably. President Johnson had five different men handle the press for him. Overall, I believe, he felt he was his own best press secretary and never realized how often he was too heavy-handed and too sensitive in his impulsive dealings with the media.

Ziegler lasted through the entire Nixon administration for many reasons, including a particular capability for handling difficult foreign affairs questions, which Kissinger approved of, but especially because he had the confidence of the President and thoroughly retained it.

At one time in 1973, after my future departure was well known, I was sounded out about staying and replacing Ziegler, but the discussion never became formal, and I firmly discouraged any consideration of it. The press had much more confidence in me than Ziegler, but the President did not, and my role would have been only to mediate with the press, not to change news relations by opening up media access. As the Watergate troubles mounted, Mel Laird and John Connally on separate occasions urged the firing of Ziegler, but I regarded this as both unnecessary and unfair. There also was a negative report from a special committee of the National Press Club which suddenly decided it wanted to investigate and give its opinion on government communications. The makeup of the committee almost predetermined what it would say and the critical report never was accepted by the elected president of the club. But it hurt Ziegler personally more than he let it be known when it said he "misled the public and affronted the professional standards of the Washington press corps." The Press Club serves as a great forum in Washington, but its membership is so divided between Washington newsmen and others in affiliated public relations and lobbying activities that it was hardly the one to determine compliance with the "professional standards of the Washington press corps."

Under pressure and harassment from an increasingly hostile White House news corps, Ziegler made the mistake of referring to Watergate as a "third-rate burglary." He later had the grace to apologize to the Washington *Post* for misstatements he had made about the paper, although when he uttered them he thought the paper was wrong. He was not alone in this early conclusion—in the White House or among the press corps.

In 1973, the word "inoperative" became almost synonymous with the name Ziegler. In many ways that was unfair. It was not his original term. During a stormy briefing with the press on April 17, Ziegler told the newsmen that because of major developments in the Watergate investigation he was issuing for the President a new "operative statement." The veteran political reporter from the New York *Times* R. W. "Johnny" Apple asked Ziegler if that now indicated "the other statement is no longer operative, that it is now inoperative." Ziegler jousted with Apple but finally conceded, "The President refers to the fact that there is new material; therefore, this is the operative statement. The others are inoperative."

Most of the public remembers the word "inoperative" as a Watergate comment coined by Ziegler when, in fact, it was a term he agreed to after a long debate with a rough and ready reporter.

It is difficult to understand how the press operation of any White

House staff works unless one actually has been there. One problem the press officer constantly confronts is that there are many experts or advocates within the government who do not think that what they are doing should be public knowledge unless they agree. And when they decide to make their program public, they expect only favorable comment.

In a general way, it is important for the press secretary to be informed on all major subjects. Thus he must be at cabinet meetings and national security meetings, at project subcommittee meetings and at major discussions with the President. All this is time-consuming and keeps the secretary from the press. In the early stages of the administration, Ziegler forced his way into some meetings he felt obligated to attend, ones which even the President thought were beyond his scope. The strategy was essential to his success and he had the brashness and the guts to push through some of the White House walls that blocked others, sometimes including me.

The modern classic on the need for a press secretary "to know" came to public attention when President Ford's first press secretary, Jerry terHorst, resigned after he was caught by surprise with the decision of his boss to pardon former President Nixon. As Ford has written, he felt the pardon of Nixon was in the best interest of a country already emotionally torn by the Watergate cover-up and its subsequent events including the President's resignation. But Ford erred in not at least consulting terHorst on his views regarding public and press reaction to the decision. I think Ford would have stayed with his conviction that he was right regardless of what terHorst said. But the press secretary cannot serve fully unless he is consulted, and he could have at least prepared the President for the criticism which was sure to come. I also believe that terHorst should have stayed with President Ford through this first big crisis even if he chose to resign later. He let Ford down during a time of crisis. He had the background and potential to become one of the nation's best press secretaries, if he had the toughness for battle. His journalistic ability has been demonstrated in the quality of his syndicated column in recent years.

The constant detailed planning which goes daily into White House press operations is far greater than is generally recognized.

A routine trip for the President requires a telephone switchboard and special telephones for the staff at each stop and more for the news corps. There are dozens of other details from security to housing facilities and intricate scheduling. Little is spontaneous. For the press secretary the operation requires an entirely separate advance corps and on foreign trips the problem is multiplied. Ziegler was excellent in organizing smooth press operations. He was weaker on human relations. In preparing for his own briefings he asked good questions, as he tried to anticipate the queries of fifty correspondents who would be at his daily briefing. Thorough research is essential, and Diane Sawyer and Jerry Warren provided top backup for this.

The planning for events reached a new White House high of detail and numbers of people involved during the Nixon administration. I organized rough plans for the use of an all-out top administration team effort in our attempt to establish such programs as the changeover in the post office and the various phases of our development of an unsuccessful plan for welfare reform.

One of the most complete plans, which eventually covered two years of hard work, was organized by both Ziegler and me to gain passage of approval for an antiballistic missile system. ABM, like Vietnam, was a major emotional controversy which was a carry-over from the Johnson administration. Unlike Vietnam, ABM would have been easy to close off with just one brief presidential statement which depicted it as unnecessary. Demonstrators, particularly in Massachusetts, were railing against ABM development, somewhat in the manner of later demonstrations against nuclear development. Less than two months after he took office, the President announced his decision to go ahead with the antiballistic missile but with modifications of the original Johnson plan. His basic thesis was that while the country was seeking an end to the nuclear arms race with the Soviet Union it could not afford massive new ballistic missile programs, but it should take note that the Soviets were ringing Moscow and key missile sites with antiballistic missile deployments, which theoretically would allow them to fire at the United States while protecting their own key areas. Nixon said that the ABM program of protection would allow the United States to have the threat of retaliation against surprise attack. He also discussed the possibility of an attack from the People's Republic of China, which he said would be developing this capability throughout the 1970s.

The new name to be applied to the Sentinel program put forth by President Johnson in 1967 was the Safeguard system. This was a public relations title which emerged from somewhere in the corps of speech writers. Nixon looked upon this as a crisis of credibility with the Soviets as they evaluated his ability to lead the country, as well as a necessary move both for national defense and for negotiations which eventually were to be called SALT. And for Ziegler and me it was a bath under fire on conditions we were expected to face in working with the press, the cabinet, the Congress, and every possible instrument of public opinion to mount support for a program which originally was assessed as having little chance for passage. The President himself took note of every detail of the operation, ranging from the media to the reactions of labor unions, during what turned out to be a battle extending well into 1970. Kenneth BeLieu, an able deputy to Mel Laird in the Defense Department, was asked to organize all the technical forces and factual ammunition to support the program. I was to head the public side and Bryce Harlow had the customary responsibility for Congress.

On April 11, less than a month after the President had announced his decision on Safeguard, he dictated a memorandum to John Ehrlichman which showed his attention to small detail in this matter:

"On Tuesday of next week or possibly Monday afternoon, I would like to have a hard nosed briefing from BeLieu, Klein and any others who have responsibility for ABM.

"I do not want this to be a bull session. I do not want this to be a session in which they come to me for some kind of statement they want me to make and other functions they want me to appear on.

"What I want to hear from them is what their particular plans are in regards to the individual Senators that are on the fence, in regards to newspapers and columnists who might be swung in our direction, and particularly with regard to what we are going to do on a matter I have messaged Klein on during several occasions—the approximately 10 to 1 ratio [against us] that the networks are following in their news coverage of the ABM debate.

"I particularly want a report from Klein as to what we are possibly doing to force the networks to put some of our pro-ADM people on to respond to the scientists and others that have gone on for the other side."

I immediately made an effort to find how Nixon was getting the wrong idea that network news coverage was running ten to one against us. I knew that while he rarely watched television news, he carefully read the White House news summary prepared by Mort Allen. Those on the news summary staff who monitored the evening news shows were giving him their personal impressions of the television film coverage of those speaking against ABM versus those speaking for it. The news summaries did not include in the assessment the "stand-up" coverage of the television reporters examining the news of the day or commenting on it. The fact was that the news coverage and comment was roughly balanced but that the opponents were gaining more film coverage from the networks and thus more time on the air. They had the more dramatic senators such as Kennedy, while many of our supporters refused to be on television, and they were not willing to attack even their opponents in the Senate. Our best spokesman was Dr. John S. Foster, Jr., director of Defense Research and Engineering.

There was network bias on the issue, but our answer eventually was to augment the nonglamorous allies in the Senate with added pressure on cabinet officers to speak out before the cameras. The imbalance had been in dramatic spokesmen, not news output.

Pushed by this kind of detailed personal interest from the President, we developed what probably was one of the most elaborate organizations the executive branch of government has seen in support of a major issue. And the President was correct in demanding this, because without such a campaign we would have lost a vote count which was to have long-range world implications and which carried the Senate by a margin of only one.

My strong point in a program such as this was in the development of strategy and in articulating it. Magruder, my deputy at that time, was strong in developing game plans on paper and in following up on each individual item. All this he did very well. In the midst of the battle for Phase II of Safeguard in 1970, a typical daily or weekly report from Magruder would take a form like this August 10, 1970, memo to Haldeman.

"The ABM working group consisting of Klein, Magruder, Colson, Nofziger, BeLieu and Jerry Friedheim [of Defense] has met on a weekly basis. Most of our actions have been carried out through the Citizen's Committee to Safeguard America. This committee has been moderately effective. It has been hampered by [Dean] Acheson's ill health, which made him unable to make public appearances. Another factor was [Henry Cabot] Lodge's appointment to the Vatican. Following his appointment he was less willing to make public appearances and to take a hard line. . . ."

Magruder then pointed out that the privately founded Safeguard committee now had completed mailing 250,000 copies of an ABM brochure we had edited. It was aimed specifically at Kansas, New Hampshire, North Dakota, Vermont, Nevada, West Virginia, Ohio, and Utah, states where we thought the votes of undecided senators might make the difference between victory and defeat. The brochure and a copy of an article written by Lodge for *Reader's Digest* had been sent along with the brochure to editorial writers and to 80,000 veterans. A full-page ad from the committee was to appear in the Washington *Star* and in the *Post*.

Magruder then included in his memo an account of the news play given to the formation of the Safeguard committee headed by Senator John Tower and Foy Kohler, former U.S. ambassador to the Soviet Union. "This received limited play in the *Times* and *Post* but ran well in other sections of the country," Magruder observed. That evoked more presidential anger against the two papers.

The memorandum concluded with a summary of five other areas of coverage ranging from the distribution of broadcast tapes from Lodge and Tower in twelve states to lobbying action taking place in the Senate.

When it was assumed that Safeguard was about to squeeze through the Senate, Magruder drew up a "victory statement" plan assigning specific projects to himself, Keogh, Nofziger, Paul Costello, Margita White, Mel Laird, and Senator Gordon Allott with Magruder's assistant Gordon Strachan assigned as project manager.

Even Henry Kissinger took a major role behind the scenes in analyzing what was happening to public opinion as expressed in newspapers and the Senate. In a memo to Ziegler and me, he criticized a story by Joseph C. Harsch of the *Christian Science Monitor* as "blatantly" wrong in its analysis of the rationale for proceeding with Safeguard. He felt similarly negative about a story written by John Finney for the New York *Times.*

"I think it terribly important that we take every opportunity to correct such distortions of the facts," Kissinger said. He then laid out in clear logical quotations proof that the President's views in 1970 followed the pattern of the statement on the entire project made by Nixon when in 1969 he announced his decision to proceed with the ABM.

Kissinger's conclusion was, "I believe it is terribly important that we communicate these ideas clearly during this year's debate, and that we correct any misinterpretation that may arise before they become part of the opposition's dogma."

The four-page Kissinger memo was of major help to Ziegler, me, and our staffs, and it was typical of the fact that Henry was not the type of National Security Council director to launch a project with the President and then sit back and view it in the abstract as it was debated in the public arenas. He was a consistently helpful philosophic leader at a pragmatic level. He enjoyed congressional and press liaison, and behind the scenes he was effective even with opponents in both public areas.

One other observation which we were to make in this early all-out effort was contained in an interesting memo to me from Susie Low, who astutely headed research for me.

"The 'debatable' columnists are difficult to put into a category because one day they will be for a point in the missile debate and the next day be against a point in the debate. Most columnists seem to be hedging a great deal. Where most papers will come out strongly one way or another, the columnist will explain in depth a particular point which might lead one to a conclusion but the next column might lead one to a different conclusion." Susie, together with Wanda Phelan and later Donna Kingwell on my staff, kept us attuned to public opinion across the country as expressed in the press, not only on this issue but on all other major subjects and sometimes their observations regarding editorials or editorial cartoons provided an early warning system regarding changes in public opinion outside the areas we observed most, Washington and New York. We kept close to the grass roots, and this is essential to successful White House news operations.

As Haldeman, through his assistant Higby, pressed us to gain public support of more and more projects, Magruder found it necessary to hire people such as Strachan just to manage the paper work and Bart Porter to schedule the people who could speak on the subjects involved. They were bright but inexperienced and there seemed no limit now to the budget for personnel who could be added to the "paper work" part of the staff.

At the end of July 1970, Rob Odle compiled for Magruder and me a list of projects involving our office. Even we were surprised at the size of the efforts. The project list included Paul Costello and Jim Hogue, a young assistant, working on plans opposing congressional spending bills, Hatfield and McGovern on Vietnam, and in a positive way on programs regarding an expected Gallup Poll, the family assistance plan, the environment, blue-collar workers, briefing teams on school desegregation, a national goals report, the President's trip to Denver to meet with legal assistance officers (a meeting where he caused an uproar when he declared Charles Manson guilty while Manson was facing trial for murder), crime and FBI statistics, postal reform, an Eisenhower-stamp ceremony, and forthcoming briefings in both San Clemente and Washington.

A major project was to develop and execute a plan which included a wide variety of the cabinet and White House staff members in an effort to popularize the idea that countless Americans were part of the "Silent Majority." Originally this was to be called the "Silent American Majority." Part of the response to the plan was organized, part spontaneous, but nothing was left to chance.

As stated in the plan this was to be a program "to have citizens identify with the Silent Majority, and to have the Silent Majority identified with the President. Then, to expand and strengthen this identification."

The objective of the program was "to continue the mobilization of the Silent Majority behind the President in his efforts to bring peace in Asia." The long-range plans were "to orient the Silent Majority toward issues other than foreign policy (e.g.: inflation, crime, law and order, etc.) and then to increase public support for the President's foreign and domestic proposals."

It was suggested that the President "stress in press conferences and speeches his belief that the overwhelming majority of Americans support his efforts in Asia, in combating inflation, etc. Place emphasis on terms such as 'Silent American Majority,' 'Middle America,' etc. By his appearance at and interest in such events as athletic contests, cultural affairs, etc., demonstrate his identification with the Silent Majority."

This was accompanied by plans to include most of the appointees of the executive branch in programs which ranged from wearing American-flag lapel pins to consideration of such ideas as a "Freedom Day Rally," a "Proud American Day," or a "National Unity Week."

This was all part of an effort to let citizens who were not in favor of the objectives of the anti-Vietnam demonstrators know that they were not alone in such "silent" feelings which seldom were depicted on television or in the press.

It was in this atmosphere that the "Ron and Herb Show" was developed on the basis that we would concentrate on two different constituencies although there would be some overlap. Ziegler's concentration was on the White House press corps and upon the President and his immediate senior staff. He or the President made the official major announcements, and if there was to be a televised presidential speech, he and his staff would organize all the briefings connected with it. In preparation for these daily encounters with the press, Diane Sawyer, who had been a popular TV newscaster in Louisville, was his chief assistant and organizer.

Although Vice-President Agnew, with White House encouragement, complained of "instant commentary," Ziegler and his staff offered the television commentators the opportunity to examine presidential speeches in advance of air time and to participate in briefings on them with Kissinger, Ehrlichman, Moynihan, or whoever had most expertise on the subject.

When traveling, domestically in particular, Ziegler on rare occasions would meet with outside editors or reporters and, in the same way, White House correspondents frequently would be in my office seeking additional information to that provided in White House briefings.

I felt strongly that it was important to get the President and his key advisers out of the sophisticated environment of Washington where they could meet in a local atmosphere—away from the umbrella of the awesome White House. We thus organized what I called regional briefings, although some became national in scope. Presidents Ford and Carter later adopted this approach.

Our first effort was our best one, and it was organized jointly by Ziegler and me. We invited about seventy-five of the nation's top news executives to San Clemente for a day of briefing and discussion on foreign policy. The logistics involved were tremendous by themselves, with executives flying in from all parts of the country. Ziegler arranged a helicopter shuttle to transport them from the Los Angeles International Airport to San Clemente. Content of the briefing was my responsibility.

On the day before the briefing I was committed to an Orange County speech arranged by Pat Neiser, some television appearances, and a cocktail meeting with Otis Chandler and his chief news executives of the Los Angeles *Times,* so I was scheduled to drive rather than fly to San Clemente to be the host of the day. I drove from Hollywood with a close friend since college, Reavis G. Winckler, an executive with Metromedia. Winckler, along with another close friend, Albert Harutunian of San Diego, and Mrs. Zan Thompson, press sage of the Republican National Committee, made most of my public arrangements when I was in Southern California. Winckler also assisted frequently, as a volunteer, in special projects using television. As we started out in early morning in what

Winckler, a nervous driver, considered a major mission to be certain that the host for the national meeting was there on time, a red light suddenly started blinking on the dashboard of his Pontiac Firebird. We had a serious question. Should I change cars, get a taxi to the heliport, check on the repair of the red light, or brave it all out on the freeway? We took the latter choice and the car functioned perfectly—better than my friend's nerves.

The San Clemente briefing was a big success and set a pattern for meetings between Presidents and newsmen from around the country, not just in the Washington-New York axis. Henry Kissinger was at his best as he took the news executives on an imaginary global tour, explaining his views on the current situation in areas ranging from Vietnam to the Soviet Union and the SALT negotiations. Joe Sisco, assistant secretary of state for the Middle East, who had a close, personal relationship with Kissinger, covered the Middle East negotiations, which he headed for several years. The President hosted an informal lunch alongside the swimming pool at his San Clemente home and spent time answering questions and meeting each individual. It was an informative day which most who attended still remembered clearly years later, and many executive offices included photos from that day. The group was a blue-ribbon cross section of the news industry, a rare intermix of television, radio, and newspaper executives.

We later had briefings for regional news executives in areas of the country ranging from Hartford, Connecticut, to New Orleans, to Portland, Oregon.

Two had dramatic impact of which the newsmen were not aware. At a briefing in Kansas City the President reviewed abstractly his more conciliatory views toward the People's Republic of China, but his comments also signaled a possible new policy regarding the PRC. As he spoke, Henry Kissinger was on his way to Pakistan and eventually to Peking for a secret meeting with Chou En-lai, a meeting which shortly thereafter led to the China breakthrough. The President's comments to the press in Kansas City were broadcast by the Voice of America and monitored by the Chinese. When Kissinger arrived in Peking, unaware of the President's informal statement in Kansas City, Chou provided him with a well-marked copy of the text, translated into English.

In 1973, we organized a Western news briefing at the Newporter Inn near San Clemente. The briefing came at a time when news stories were breaking on Watergate—almost, it seemed, by the hour. We had a well-planned program, but my speakers from the senior White House staff kept changing or canceling minutes before they were to appear. I suddenly had to call upon Bob Finch and Al Haig to carry the burden. They did it extremely well as I "vamped" in between speakers, all the time wondering what was happening at the Western White House. It turned out, again unknown to the audience and to me, that Ehrlichman and others including Ziegler, had to change schedules to grapple with new and critical Watergate news developments.

My office of communications attempted to bring the government into the modern era of journalism, one which recognized the growing influence of the broadcast media without ignoring the printed press. This was easy in the White House because the President had learned of the power of television and radio during his political campaigns. He was obsessed with television, frequently to the detriment of newspapers, magazines, and radio. And Ziegler's office worked with specialists ranging from Roger Ailes to Bill Carruthers in the production of television appearances for the President. This also became an area of special interest to Dwight Chapin.

In the cabinet departments, the recognition of the importance of radio and television was more difficult to implant. The effectiveness of the public affairs department for a cabinet officer too long had been measured in terms of how many releases were turned out. Quality and program interest were not major considerations in most departments with the exception of State and Defense. The domestic departments were the weakest from the public information point of view. We did several things to change this. We hired new men or women at the top of public affairs in most departments. Regularly scheduled meetings were organized in my office wherein the public affairs officers spoke to each other face to face, an amazing development in the bureaucracy of departmental news offices. We placed new emphasis on television and less on the routine printed releases which were seen by few. In several departments we installed Spotmasters, a device by which a cabinet can record a few moments from a prepared speech and have it available to any radio station in the country which dials the Spotmaster number at the department.

There were a number of "think tank" operations in the White House, but usually they dealt with specific problems of the moment. My favorite, the "Saturday Morning" group, would meet about two hours each Saturday and try to develop ideas on how we could have a more creative public information program. We wrestled unsuccessfully with the question of how we could more constructively use the time of those who stood in line outside the White House fence awaiting a tour of the building. It seemed like a good opportunity to instruct those in line with the history of the White House. I feel that the organization at Williamsburg does an excellent job in this regard. We explored routing the crowd through the Treasury basement, the only facility available, but this involved hazards in crossing the street. President Carter's staff later issued tickets, but this still does not respond to the educational opportunity.

With more success, the Saturday planning group came up with ideas for network interviews with the President and for Christmas programming. I pushed hard for a satellite interview between the President and four newsmen in different parts of the world. He did not accept the idea.

My office worked closely with both local and national television. On one of the most interesting evenings, we provided all the guests for "The Dick Cavett Show." I was co-host as Cavett interviewed John Mitchell, Len Garment, and Bob and Carol Finch. My toughest television appearance was during another Cavett show at a time when emotions were running highest against Vietnam. I was just back from the battle lines of Cambodia, and there were sufficient threats against me that the Secret Service had men both in the audience and backstage during my appearance.

We placed great emphasis on radio talk shows, and on several occasions I was invited to be a guest host for shows of two or three hours' duration during the vacation season. One of my favorite "guest stars" for these shows was David Hartman, then an actor who was helping in our drug abuse program. My longest shows were from 6 A.M. to 10 A.M. "Rambling with John Gambling" on WOR, New York.

One of the nonpolitical things we discovered was that United States ambassadors have difficulty keeping current with presidential policies, particularly those with some political tint. Walter Annenberg, who was always attuned to the news while a popular ambassador at the Court of St. James's, would call frequently for political background. We finally decided to send to key ambassadors the fact sheets we gave to the press or the staff so they could be more knowledgeable on domestic and political affairs when they represented the President in informal conversations.

When newsmen look back at "The Ron and Herb Show," most of the speculation centers around Ziegler. He was controversial. He kept a protective barrier around himself, and few, if any, of the newsmen really understood him. He had an ego which became too big at times, and he could be vindictive or nasty to his disadvantage. Left on his own without the pressures from Haldeman and Ehrlichman and the President, he had the innate ability to perform at a high level whatever assignment was given to him, a fact he later proved in the business world. But under the circumstances in which he served as press secretary, Ziegler zigzagged so much that he badly undercut the credibility of government and the White House. Newsmen kidded about "ziggies," which meant obfuscating answers. They resented "ziggies" even though they understood that they sometimes were necessary.

More press secretaries than not have lacked statesmanship and depth. And Ziegler was among them, even though he was more respected by the press aides in other parts of the world than by his Washington contemporaries. Despite some personal conflicts, we have enjoyed and do enjoy each other as friends.

Probably Zeigler's greatest mistake was that he allowed himself to be duped by those who were covering up the Watergate case. He accepted too many of their answers blindly and thus lost his credibility as the spokesman for the White House. By the time of the cover-up, he had been in office long enough to resist the pressures put upon him more than he did. No one ever seriously accused him of being part of the cover-up, and he had no role in it. Those who were later convicted were afraid to confide in him, and they chose to use him as a tool rather than as a confidant, a cover-up role I do not believe he would have accepted.

But Ziegler's early failure to recognize the duplicity of those who were advising him on answers for the press regarding Watergate, led to the greatest bloodletting the White House has seen between a press secretary and the news corps. Ziegler handled this phase of his career badly, but the press corps with its emotional hang-ups against him was even more disgraceful in its conduct in 1974, before the President left office.

Still it must be said that Ziegler handled a traditional White House office, that of the press secretary, basically in the long established form of the position. He represented the President in a way that Nixon generally approved.

Our personal problems between each other would have been less painful had he accepted more fully the need for both of our offices and functions in the White House.

The function of a communications office now seems firmly established as part of the executive branch of government. When I left the White House at the end of June 1973, Kenneth Clawson, who had been my second deputy, was designated as my successor, but he reported to Ziegler under a reorganization plan which gave the press secretary jurisdiction over all communications functions.

Clawson was a dedicated newsman and a good one who learned the business in the Middle West and eventually became a key reporter for the Washington *Post*. He at one time was accused of the "dirty trick" of writing a letter posted in Florida quoting Senator Edmund Muskie with strongly derogatory comments regarding French Canadians. Bill Loeb, the publisher of the Manchester, New Hampshire, *Union Leader*, not only ran the "canuck" letter but gleefully accompanied it with a front-page editorial denouncing Muskie. Clawson was said by Marilyn Berger, a Washington *Post* reporter who later joined NBC, to have bragged over cocktails that he wrote the letter. Clawson claimed that his statement was that he would like to have written the letter. I believe the latter story because Clawson was with me in New Hampshire at a meeting with Loeb and his staff the day before the letter was printed, and I had no indication that he knew of anything dramatic which was forthcoming, except a snowstorm which forced us to leave the state early. Regardless, Clawson could be tough almost in the Colson fashion. And yet I felt he had judgment, which was lacking in the Colson syndrome. Clawson stayed on in the last desperate moves of the Nixon White House as it started sinking under the weight of Watergate and the concept of the office changed perceptibly.

Later during the Ford administration, the office continued in a role secondary to that of the press secretary with David Gergen, a former speech writer, and my assistant, Margita White, heading it. Mrs. White came closest to restoring the broad scope of the office before leaving to accept an appointment as a commissioner of the Federal Communications Commission. Jody Powell and President Carter's staff made a detailed study of the concept and, with the full cooperation of the President, Powell restored many of the original concepts, including frequent briefings for out-of-town press. Walt Wuerfel and Pat Bario headed the operation, but, like their immediate predecessors, neither had the public visibility important to making full use of the office. Carter later brought in Gerald Rafshoon as his communications assistant in a highly visible role separate from what Powell called the media liaison office. He was effective but weighted toward television and eventually left to accept campaign responsibilities.

In today's world, where the public perception of a President and an administration depends so strongly on mass communications, I believe that there is a role for two strong men or women in the field, one as a press secretary and the other as director of communications. The concept will not work if the participants are receiving on-the-job training, but if both are respected professionals with the confidence and ability to carry out their wide-ranging assignments to the fullest, they can make a major contribution to communication between the President and the press and the public in a way which has a potential not fully reached to date.

With a President who fully understood that he needed to communicate openly, a better-coordinated "Ron and Herb Show" could be a major public asset and could do much to start restoring public confidence in government and the presidency—even now.

10

The Tough Get Tougher

"When the going gets tough, the tough get going," read a sign posted conspicuously in the office of Ken Clawson. He paraphrased the sign with "the tough get tougher."

Clawson at various times attributed the words and the thought to John Mitchell, Dick Kleindienst, Senate Judiciary Committee chairman James Eastland, and more often to Chuck Colson. It was not original with any of them but, each, including Clawson, believed in the phrase, each in a different way ethically and tactically. Clawson had a particular interest in the Justice Department and the Judiciary Committee and thus quoted from his friends there frequently. Clawson was a good newsman and a tough one. He came into my office at a time when Jeb Magruder was leaving to run the Committee to Re-elect the President under John Mitchell's direction. Initially, I was pleased to find him because of his news background and his understanding of Washington. Later, as the going got tougher, I at times had reason to believe he was a loyal deputy but too often I had strong suspicions that he was an unwitting pawn of Colson who reveled in plotting the tough tactics of political "hardball."

The phrase which Clawson picked up on toughness describes in many ways what regularly happens in the White House when the honeymoon with the news media is over—and what happens to the opponent, the newsmen. They both get tougher. And the tougher they get, the more likely it is that they will view each move of the other side as a part of a possible conspiracy.

If the "going gets tougher" early, as it did in the Nixon administration, the more likely it is that the news veterans, particularly the network industry leaders, have some advantage because of experience ranging over a variety of administrations. They are combat veterans. A new White House staff is bound to be accident-prone, and sometimes an innocent White House mistake will be interpreted by the network veterans as an indication of future policy even though it may not be intended as such. They also pick up quickly on deliberate antagonism. I learned that little slips by the newsmen.

In an atmosphere of suspicion, such as existed in most of the Nixon years, misinterpretation of motives becomes common. And the tendency is not limited to the Nixon era alone. President Johnson, for example, went far out of his way to talk personally with news executives and reporters. He had in the Oval Office three large color television sets built by CBS into one beautiful piece of furniture. (I later inherited the three sets for my office.) He constantly watched the Associated Press and United Press news wires to see how they reported the news. He was suspicious of the motives of the reporters, and they developed a personal dislike for him. On both sides it was a matter of suspicion feeding upon suspicion.

I later received a good example of what can happen in a rumor mill which is hyped by suspicion when I addressed the convention of the National Association of Broadcasters in 1970. I did not think this was the time for criticism by me, so in my speech I avoided in-depth discussion of the networks, but I strongly praised local stations for the progress they were making in developing better coverage of the news. In 1970, the networks were competing hard against each other, but they were doing little in an innovative way to improve news content. Local stations had moved rapidly from the era where an anchorman basically stood up and read the news (rip and read), and they were hiring more reporters, covering more events with film, and expanding the time for news coverage. I thought my point praising local news development was well accepted by the broadcasters.

To my surprise, a few days later, I found an item in a television column by Jack Gould of the New York *Times* which said I had met secretly with a Texas broadcaster and encouraged him to drop network news and rely only on his own local coverage. I had no such meeting and would not have taken that view because I believed fully that the networks or a strong independent association are essential to cover national and world events. Local news was highly important, but it could not replace national. Even the independent stations have developed their own "network" to give them competitive film and coverage of world events.

I decided against answering the New York *Times* column, thinking the assertion too absurd to be dignified.

But a short time later I found the news wires covering a speech by Fred

Friendly, veteran and respected broadcast news executive and by then a Ford Foundation executive, in which Friendly denounced me for seeking to undermine the networks by urging local affiliates to drop network news.

An atmosphere that made inaccurate reporting believable, in a period of growing suspicion of White House motives, had created a situation where I was being accused of views I did not hold—in fact, views directly opposite of my own.

From my standpoint, one of the most able broadcast and newspaper executives I have known is Dr. Frank Stanton, who finally left as vice-chairman of CBS in 1973 to become president and chief executive officer of the American Red Cross (a presidential appointment).

I met Stanton by telephone in 1959 in a midnight call I made from Moscow to discuss the decision of CBS to run as a special feature a tape which had been smuggled out of the Soviet Union depicting the so-called Kitchen Debate between Nixon and Khrushchev. For serious reasons of international policy considerations, I wanted to ask him to delay the showing of the secretly smuggled tape, but by the time the Soviet telephone operators allowed us to talk, the program had been aired. I was too late.

Over the years Stanton and I have been close personal friends, despite strong disagreement on some issues, particularly during Agnew's press attacks. I recall that at one time early in the 1960 campaign, he came to my hotel room in San Francisco and soon found himself helping to answer some of my phones while he was simultaneously wearing his hat as CBS president and trying to convince me of the merit of presidential candidate debates. At one time after that election, he offered me a job with what appeared to be a good future with CBS news. I decided to decline and return to the San Diego *Union*. Stanton was chairman of the USIA's prestigious advisory board and I later helped persuade him to remain on the board while I also helped persuade the President to reappoint him when his original term in that office expired. He was appointed originally by President Johnson. When Frank Shakespeare became director of the USIA, his old boss, Stanton, worked closely with him.

Whenever Stanton perceived that CBS or the broadcast industry was under attack, he would leap into the battle with both fists flying, maneuvering with the skill one attaches only to a professional boxer. At that point friendship was placed apart and the battle would be waged impersonally according to what Stanton believed to be the right principles. In my view he was not always right, but he was tough as the going got tougher.

Stanton likes to tell the story about flying to Atlantic City at Lyndon Johnson's request to talk to the President prior to his appearance before the Democratic National Convention in 1964. When the CBS news came on, Stanton, then president of the network, turned on the television set to show the coverage to the President of the United States, only to find that a technician had pulled the plug, blocking the news from the Atlantic City area.

When during the Nixon administration, CBS produced a documentary, "The Selling of the Pentagon," I was critical of it because I thought it represented a biased attempt to slur the military public information program in Vietnam in 1971. CBS frequently took advantage of the services of the very information assistance program it was condemning. I looked at this as a double standard.

Critical congressmen went a big step beyond criticism of the CBS program and tried to subpoena outtakes, film made but not used in the documentary. In the reverse situation I strongly opposed this as a violation of a newsman's rights of editing and of reporting. I supported CBS because this was the TV equivalent of subpoenaing a reporter's notes. When Harley Staggers, a Democratic subcommittee chairman, sought to have Stanton cited for contempt of Congress, I persuaded the President to side with the network president publicly as a matter of principle. Staggers lost and Stanton was not cited for contempt.

When Vice-President Agnew made his searing attack on the networks in 1969 Stanton was first and foremost in the broadcast response. The network president approved the live broadcast of the Agnew address from Des Moines, but within hours afterward he was ready with strong counterattack and was widely quoted.

How the White House saw events and how the network executive viewed them was clearly illustrated in a speech Stanton made on November 25, 1970, before the International Radio and Television Society, a group I had addressed a week before. Stanton felt so strongly about the speech, which came three weeks after the Agnew fireworks, that even two years later he featured its text in a deposition given on behalf of CBS in answer to Justice Department charges of antitrust.

In his speech, Stanton countered Agnew point by point and then reached a preliminary conclusion:

"The ominous character of the Vice President's attack derives directly from the fact that it is made upon the journalism of a medium licensed by the government of which he is a high-ranking officer. This is a new relationship in government-press relations. From George Washington on, every administration has had disputes with the press but the First Amendment assured the press that such disputes were between equals, with the press beyond reach of the government. This all-important fact of the licensing power of life and death over the broadcast press brings an implicit threat to a government official's attack on it, whether or not the official says he is speaking only as an individual."

Stanton was claiming that the rough-and-tumble Agnew Des Moines speech, and another by Agnew which followed on November 20, had brought a new dimension to the warfare between government and press. Within the White House I was strongly critical of the first Agnew speech. And at one time I almost succeeded in stopping the Vice-President from making a second address on the subject, but publicly I was able to defend parts of the speeches within some narrow grounds because I, unlike Stanton, did not and do not believe this brought a "new era" to government-press relations, although it heightened the already existing conflict considerably. There was no indication that the speech represented a threat to station licenses. The networks, incidentally, are not licensed, but their stations are.

One could argue the point against Agnew on a little less stringent grounds than Stanton, but the very fact that the veteran CBS president would speak out so strongly illustrated clearly that he was not intimidated, nor would he be intimidated, nor should he have been.

To my surprise reading the Stanton speech, I found myself viewed as apparently part of an orchestrated conspiracy. The hope for intimidation of newsmen was often on the minds of the President and some of his staff such as Colson and Haldeman, and perhaps Buchanan, but my feelings ran entirely to the contrary. The accusations Stanton made against me illustrate how suspicion and misinterpretation evolve under stress.

Stanton cited the fact that calls had gone from my office to TV stations across the country checking whether they planned editorials. My staff instructions had been only to find out if an editorial was planned and to invite the station to send us a copy if there was to be an editorial. We made such calls frequently, not just on this occasion. We did this also with newspapers regularly. How else could broadcasters inform the executive branch what their broadcast public opinions were? Frequently the stations asked if we wanted to reply. We refrained. Oddly, Stanton and I had followed each other earlier on the platform of a meeting of the broadcast editorial writers association in Park City, Utah, and both had encouraged more editorials. Regardless, Stanton and a growing number of others chose to interpret the telephone calls as an effort to intimidate the stations with the idea we were watching them. Big Brother was watching, they concluded.

I could see his interpretation, but factually it was wrong, and I think that Stanton knew that.

In his speech Stanton then quoted me accurately on an answer I had given on the CBS program "Face the Nation" a week earlier. I had said: "I think that any time any industry—and I include newspapers very thoroughly in this, as well as the networks—if you look at the problems you have had today and fail to continue to examine them, you do invite the government to come in."

After the telecast, Stanton called me personally and congratulated me on my performance under tough circumstances created by Agnew's speech. But the one quote on self-criticism stuck with him, and he interpreted it in a way entirely contrary to my meaning. He talked of the "grave implications" of this, and after stating that television "is the most criticized medium in the history of communications," he went back to say: "But such open criticism is a far cry from sharp reminders from high official quarters that we are licensed or that if we don't examine ourselves, we in common with other media 'invite' the government to move in."

The statement by me did not represent a new philosophy in the news media. I could have been quoting Norman Isaacs, former president of the American Society of Newspaper Editors, or a speech John Chancellor had made in a Colorado Springs panel discussion we participated in, or in other discussions by thoughtful newsmen. I had used the thought as an editor and heard the viewpoint expressed even more strongly by other editors who like myself fear the possibility of opening the door to demagogues who, through the halls of Congress or through strong regulatory commissions with radical appointees, could seize upon the weaknesses of the news industry and regulate the free press out of business with no public outcry. We feared that the public would lose faith in an industry which refused to examine and improve itself on a regular basis, admitting error when error existed.

I made no threat. I was on Stanton's side, the media's side.

In the deposition Stanton gave for the later antitrust suit, it is easy to see how suspicions of conspiracy voiced in his speech before the television society could be enlarged upon greatly by subsequent events which were magnified as the war between the Nixon White House and the networks escalated. Some of the suspicions were justified. But others were not. Stanton and his colleagues chose to link them all together, right or wrong.

Looking back, it is hard to blame them.

In the middle of Colson's 1970 effort to force CBS to give equal time to the Republican National Committee for a reply to a Democratic national chairman's answer to a presidential speech, Colson met secretly with Stanton and urged that the network refrain from giving time to the "loyal opposition," indicating that the administration might seek reprisal by regulation or legislation, if the practice continued.

In 1972, Colson again went directly to Stanton to protest CBS coverage of the growing Watergate story. CBS covered Watergate in the early stages more extensively than did NBC and ABC. In his deposition, Stanton characterized Colson's comments: "Unless CBS substantially changes its news treatment of the Nixon administration things will get much worse for CBS." He also said Colson told him in substance, "You didn't play ball during the campaign . . . we'll bring you to your knees in Wall Street and on Madison Avenue."

Stanton was not in any way alone in his observation that there was a growing White House conspiracy aimed at curtailing the press. The strong feeling was shared by NBC executives and newsmen and, to only a slightly lesser degree, by ABC executives.

There was no organized conspiracy in the White House, but mistrust of the press was strong and ever present.

I had lunch at Washington's Sans Souci Restaurant with my longtime friend Walter Cronkite and discussed some speeches he had made which were strongly critical of White House news policies and of Press Secretary Ron Ziegler. I agreed that some of his criticisms were valid, but even where I could prove that some of his statements regarding the administration and Ziegler, in particular, were wrong, I found it difficult, if not impossible, to convince him. Cronkite is mild-mannered and fair-minded, but it was apparent the negative impressions were deeply imbedded.

For reasons I do not understand, the controversies with CBS always seemed greater than with the other networks even when the chorus of White House critics felt that NBC or ABC had been guilty of badly biased reporting. The White House hatred of CBS was more intense than for the other broadcasters just as the Washington *Post* and the New York *Times* were favorite newspaper targets.

During one of our earliest days in the White House, I listened unbelievingly as the President, in the presence of Henry Kissinger and me, engaged in a tirade during which he accused Marvin Kalb of once having worked in secret for an Eastern European Communist country. The story may have been leaked to the President by J. Edgar Hoover, but we found it had no substance in fact and therefore it was utterly slanderous gossip. Kalb himself confronted me with the rumor a year or so later and, with much embarrassment, I told him that I had heard it and never believed it. I tried to avoid mentioning Nixon but Kalb, a good reporter, was suspicious. Who else had heard the story and leaked it I never found out, but it was part of the controversy with CBS. I do not believe Kissinger was involved in the leak.

Dan Rather, with his controversial style, was a constant irritant to the White House. His tendency to sensationalize the news often was unfair and was carried too far, I think, but on the other side, I believe that the best network interview with President Nixon was conducted by Rather. The spirit of interview combat between the two men added life to the answers of the President. Still, at a breakfast at the Plaza Hotel in New York, John Ehrlichman foolishly asked a CBS executive to move Rather from the White House. Ehrlichman said he was taken too seriously, but I doubted it.

The Daniel Schorr investigation was the most embarrassing. Haldeman and Colson were a key part of this blunder. They were charging forward to satisfy a presidential whim. After some controversial reporting by CBS correspondent Schorr at the Department of Health, Education, and Welfare, an FBI check was ordered on him by the White House. It was the same kind of check given someone considered for high office in the administration. When friends of the reporter, who were part of the FBI inquiry interviews, asked CBS and Schorr what this was about, the matter became a public scandal. The White House cover story was that Schorr was being considered for a high position in one of the environmental protection offices. One of the senior officials in the environmental control framework was so convinced this was correct that he stated it to me as a fact.

This, of course, was a pressure tactic. It was not an effort to recruit Schorr, who would have been one of the last persons to whom a staff job would be offered.

In September of 1971, in the midst of this atmosphere of controversy, I received a call from Dick Moore, who worked first for Attorney General John Mitchell and then joined the White House staff. Moore brought into my office the lengthy text of an antitrust suit he said the Justice Department planned to file against NBC, CBS, ABC, and the Viacom International Corporation, a CBS subsidiary for syndication and distribution of certain programming.

He said that the suits had been developed by the antitrust department, had been "signed off" by Attorney General John Mitchell, but they had not yet been filed because Mitchell, presumably after informing the President of the pending action, was told to hold off until I could meet with the presidents of each of the networks and inform them of the legal action about to be taken. The apparent purpose of my unusual inclusion in this series of legal actions was for me to carry out a promise made earlier in the year when the President had met with executives from each network and, after frank discussions of issues, assured them that we would keep close communication. (Colson and I disagreed about whether this communication meant through him or through me, but the networks preferred me as their point of contact.) I was to inform the broadcast executives that this was a suit not in control of the White House, because it had been developed by the bureaucracy of the antitrust division of Justice, and that the suits were not politically motivated nor did they in any way involve network production of its own news. All of this was true, I believe. But it did not appear that way.

I looked at the suits, and I was horrified. They seemed to me to be out of date and based on sloppy understanding of network production, and, no matter what I would say to the networks, the suit was bound to make us subject to the charge of administration harassment of the broadcast media.

I have no legal background, but I could see the political repercussions of such a suit in 1971, on the eve of an election year.

The civil suits against the four broadcast organizations charged that they had "used their control of access of air time to monopolize prime time television entertainment programming and to obtain valuable interests in such program."

The suits alleged that "the viewing public, independent program suppliers, and advertisers have been deprived of the benefits of free competition in television programming."

Basically, the Justice Department allegation was that the networks, through their own productions, through pressures on advertisers or through financial interests in outside production, provided unfair competition for outside producers who were seeking to develop their own programs and have them accepted by the networks and advertisers. The suits were general but they also aimed at curtailment of the production of feature films by the networks or by producers under their direct control. They asserted that this was unfair to writers, actors, directors, producers, and related talent in addition to the companies involved.

As I looked at the material I was startled by the fact that it had no up-to-date figures. It cited 1957 as a year when, during prime time hours, Justice claimed CBS had interests in 49 percent of its programming, NBC 43 percent, and ABC 31 percent. The suits then skipped to 1967, when it was claimed that the figures were CBS 73 percent, NBC 68 percent, and ABC 86 percent. I asked what was happening in 1971 and 1970 but got no answers. I checked privately and found that for a variety of reasons, including economic, self-production by the networks had decreased drastically. The material was out of date.

I pointed out the discrepancies to Moore and to Mitchell, but my feeling was that the Attorney General felt locked in on the suit because it had been developed by the antitrust division and because he had adopted a policy of giving great freedom to Richard W. McLaren, who had been brought in to head that department with the pledge that he would not be hindered by any of the administration's friendships with the business community.

It appeared to me that attorneys in the antitrust division had begun the plans to sue the networks in 1960 and perhaps even before that. Finally, after all these years, persistency by the bureaucracy was paying off. For many years the subject had been pursued by one of the senior attorneys in the division, Bernard Hollander, who survived changes in both Democratic and Republican administrations. The network question was brought to the attention of McLaren early in his tenure as assistant attorney general of the antitrust division and about the same time, he apparently became aware of the fact that the Federal Communications Commission was considering a rule which would prohibit the networks from acquiring any rights in television programs produced independently. Under consideration also was a ban on domestic program syndication by the networks, syndication of series that had been earlier shown on a first-run basis.

On April 22, 1969, at a time there still was somewhat of a honeymoon between the White House and the press, McLaren sent to the FCC an official letter supporting arguments for such a rule. The letter included a statement which said this action was not intended to "preclude the Department of Justice from taking any action consistent with its responsibilities for enforcement of the antitrust laws."

The proposed rule was not adopted by the Federal Communications Commission, and on the last working day of 1969, McLaren's staff again recommended that Justice institute action against the networks.

I was aware of what had happened in the FCC case, but I had no idea that the matter still was alive in the Justice Department. To a layman "alive" might seem too strong a word because again, the antitrust division took more than a year to "review" the matter before bringing it to the attention of the Attorney General in February 1971. Because even McLaren recognized that the suits might be construed as politically motivated, the assistant attorney general discussed the pending case several times in 1971 with Moore, who was still with the Justice Department as an assistant to Mitchell and who McLaren knew had extensive experience in dealing with the networks while managing television station KTTV. As manager of an independent station in a major market, Moore had been well known for battling network station power successfully.

It was not until October 1971, that Moore, acting upon the request of Mitchell and McLaren, presented the suits to me as a fait accompli. Moore pressed me to contact the networks, but throughout this and other discussions I had the feeling that Moore was pushing me with a great sense of reluctance. The suits obviously were not his idea and he recognized the potential political problems involved.

As I read and reread the material given to me, I wondered why the suits had not been brought up to date if they were so important to the Justice Department at this moment. I found no answer. It probably was my imagination, but the very paper they were mimeographed on seemed old and musty.

I tried to anticipate what the reaction would be to the announcement of the suits, and my first and foremost thought was that this was only a little more than a year before the presidential election. There was no question that, given the atmosphere of press suspicion and controversy between the President and the media, the immediate outcry would be that this was a politically motivated suit, that it represented revenge or intimidation tactics aimed at the broadcast industry. It would appear to be the kind of tactic considered by Jeb Magruder in his "shotgun and rifle shot" memo, where he suggested attacking the news media through the Internal Revenue Service and through other horrifying tactics. But not even Magruder had thought of this.

My talks with Moore and later Mitchell and eventually Hollander convinced me that, despite the appearance of politics, the emergence of the suit at this vulnerable time for the administration was a triumph for the bureaucracy not connected to the White House war with the press.

But who would believe that? Perhaps only me and I could be wrong in this, but not likely. If the atmosphere were different, that would be another case. But at this point the tendency would be to believe the worst.

I reviewed possible extraneous pressures and could find no evidence of outsiders having a role in this matter.

The Hollywood producers and motion picture executives felt that they deserved more support than they were receiving from the administration. Their industry was hurting economically. I later learned that between 1969 and 1971 McLaren had heard complaints against network practices from motion picture attorneys Louis Nizer and Whitney North Seymour and from Jack Valenti, president of the Motion Picture Association of America, but that was legitimate communication and to be expected in the appropriate course of their duties. I knew these men did not influence the Nixon White House and probably did not try to.

At one point Bryce Harlow and I had met with Congressman Barry Goldwater, Jr., and his assistant Jack Cox to discuss their complaint that government public information departments were competing unfairly with the motion picture industry by producing their own films instead of contracting out for them. Goldwater claimed that the practice cost the government money and that it put it in unfair competition with private industry. Secretaries and other workers often were used as actors, costing the real actors jobs. Interestingly, he had statistics showing the Department of Agriculture was the major producer of government films and that its volume amounted to the equivalent of a large producing company.

Goldwater was acting upon the request of his constituents in the movie-oriented San Fernando Valley of California, and I instituted cost studies which I found proved him right in some cases. We made some changes. His was a legitimate concern, I felt, and there was no great pressure involved. If there was any implication of unfair practices, it was against the government.

The motion picture industry had leaders, such as the late Jack Warner and Taft Schreiber (Universal), who were close to the President and to many others of us. It is possible that they may have voiced complaints against the network practices in conversations with the President, but I had heard of none, and certainly I at no time heard of anything indicating White House interest in antitrust action.

Years later, in 1974, when the networks in their fight against the suits requested access to Nixon tapes they believed would provide information of presidential intervention on behalf of the Hollywood industry and against the networks, Henry S. Ruth, Jr., then Special Watergate Prosecutor, told U.S. District Judge Robert J. Kelleher that his staff investigation "has not produced any evidence of criminal activity in connection with the filing of these suits."

Throughout my personal protests with Mitchell and others against the suits I did not try to argue points of law or to suggest that if Justice felt the suits were necessary they should not be filed eventually. I was not qualified to make that judgment, and I made certain that I did not become involved in such a legal discussion, although privately I continued to believe there was no justification for the suits.

I did question why the suits had assumed a priority at this late date and, if there was such an immediacy, why the facts stated were so obsolete. I heard no logical answers to these questions and yet here we were in a politically explosive situation involving millions of dollars. I decided to stall the matter and to hope that someone would see the logic against timing such an action in a way that it would come to the fore in a presidential election year. The Justice Department, through Moore, kept asking, however, when I was going to carry out my assignment so the suits could be filed. I set up appointments with the network executives in October and found a reason to cancel them. I did the same thing in November.

In a confidential memorandum I sent on October 5 to John Ehrlichman, I summarized some of the arguments I had verbalized to John Mitchell:

"I believe the networks will use this to indicate that we are attacking all of broadcasting by getting at a vital economic area, particularly at a time when network income is down because of business conditions. . . . ABC is likely to be hurt the most, and its economic position is not good. Overall, this can be very damaging for us politically and with station and newspaper owners who are our friends. The networks will say to the stations, you're next!"

Looking at the fact that the FCC had cut network prime time in an effort to encourage more local or independent programming, I added that there had not been enough time to determine accurately how even this concept would work out.

When I was pressured again in November I wrote a memo on November 8 to the President detailing the pressures which were being developed against the television industry—none of which reflected actions by the White House but all of which were bound to help create a negative attitude toward the administration, particularly if coupled with a suit which had potential emotional implications.

The memorandum to the President said:

"I think you should know that because of various general Departmental actions in the Government in recent months, there is confusion, and there probably will be injury to our friends at the local level in the broadcast and newspaper industries. This is damaging our relationships. Many or most of these things are contrary to your own philosophy, I believe.

"Following are examples:

"1) The FCC gives strong indications of ruling that newspapers may not own TV stations in their own cities;

"2) Newspapers and magazines are badly hit by the increase in postal rates;

"3) Recent court action upgrades the challenge procedure against local stations, and there is now growing instability among station owners in terms of their license renewals with the FCC. Nuisance challenges are becoming the rule. This will probably require legislation or new FCC action or it could mean disaster to the local stations in terms of investing in new equipment or local news development;

"4) The Federal Trade Commission is moving on many fronts against advertising, even testing why people buy things they don't need;

"5) The antitrust department of Justice is now sending new questionnaires to those newspapers exempted by the Failing Newspaper Act and has promulgated a new set of regulations for applicants for exemption. Among the regulations are those requiring newspapers, on an annual basis, to give the Government all of the financial details of their operation and to publish on the front page of each edition for a two week period the statement of their application for exemption. This is interpreted as antitrust department action contrary to the spirit of the Congress and to the position of the Administration expressed by the Commerce Department and the Failing Newspaper Act.

"6) As you know, I have been asked to announce to the networks Presidents the fact that Justice, after eleven years delay, plans to take antitrust action against their program production procedures. I plan to meet with the broadcasters in this regard tomorrow in New York City. I think the election year timing on this is bad, particularly when added to the other points mentioned above."

On several occasions I asked Haldeman for an appointment to discuss the matter personally with the President. He refused the time.

The tough in the Justice Department got tougher and finally I scheduled a trip to New York City, where I would meet with the heads of the networks after speaking on December 15 to a press group in upstate New York.

The day before leaving I conferred with Ehrlichman following a general early-morning senior White House staff meeting. He seemed to take a new interest in my arguments and asked that I write an additional memo to him. I pointed out that I was still trying to reopen the case with John Mitchell, and I thought the matter was further complicated by the clumsy, unethical investigation of Daniel Schorr. I said that the events I had set forth in my memo to the President, now added to by the Schorr case, "make it appear that such action [filing suit] lends a credence to the charge of a conspiracy against the networks." In this time period I said the action would be "politically disastrous . . . we have too much to lose and nothing to gain." I concluded: "I am making one final plea for a review of this case, which I think can be gravely harmful to the President in an election year. If it has waited 10 years, why not one more?"

Driving to the airport the next day, I received an urgent, coded call from Ehrlichman requesting a telephone call from a booth at National Airport. (My code name was Witness. His was Wisdom.) I reached Ehrlichman and was told that my argument had prevailed and that no action against the networks would be taken at this time. The idea of a suit was not being dropped, but it would be reviewed again and nothing would happen without further consultation with me. Whom Ehrlichman had talked to, I do not know. I decided that I had to keep my network appointments this time, and Ehrlichman and I determined that it would be fair to at least warn the networks that some of the attorneys within the antitrust division had raised questions regarding network production practices. I was to go no further, and I did not. I decided instead to use the meetings to review the progress or lack of it concerning the problems which had been raised a year before in the discussions at the White House between the President and the executives from ABC, NBC, and CBS. I followed this guideline in separate meetings with Julian Goodman, president of NBC, and with Stanton, and at a luncheon meeting with Leonard Goldenson, chairman of ABC, and his top aides, Jim Hagerty and Ev Erlich.

As revealed to me later in affidavits given in answer to the suit, each of the network chiefs thought my visit unusual, although we had met informally many times over the years before. I was serious this time. Goodman sensed that I had purposely dropped the idea that something "was bubbling under the surface at the Justice Department in the way of an antitrust suit." Goodman said he inferred "that there were forces in the administration who wanted to bring an antitrust suit for punitive reasons related to news coverage, and that there also were forces in the administration represented by Mr. Klein, who felt this would be unfair treatment and who had been able to prevent it but were not sure how long that result would hold.

"Although not explicitly stated to me by Mr. Klein, the implication that I drew from, and my understanding of, his statements was that our news coverage could result in an antitrust suit against us."

Goodman said that NBC no longer was involved in more than minimum production of prime-time programming. The Justice suit, I knew, did not reflect this change at that time.

Stanton, who told me that CBS too had dropped back in its productions, also indicated suspicion at the reasons behind any possible antitrust action. He wrote a brief letter the next day which I thought helped prove my contention that Justice did not have up-to-date figures. He said that currently CBS was producing only one show, "Gunsmoke."

It was obvious that in the atmosphere in which we were operating even longtime personal friends such as Goodman and Stanton felt that they had to look immediately at an implication of a suit with suspicion that it was aimed not at production but at news content. Goldenson appeared less suspicious and in his affidavit he said: "To the best of my recollection, Mr. Klein did not discuss at this meeting or on any other occasion whether the lawsuit was or was not politically motivated or did or did not involve the network news function."

Even so, the die was cast. The tough would get tougher and the tough would get going.

The Attorney General did not learn of the results of my network meetings until January 10, and even then, he later told me, he was not sure that when I told Moore I regarded the matter as "closed" he understood this to mean Justice could now proceed normally or whether I considered the entire matter as dead. I hoped the latter was true but could not gain full assurance of this from Ehrlichman, and I did not have access to the President on the matter. I again refrained from discussing the legal position but stayed with the timing and passed along the fact that all three networks assured me they no longer were involved in massive self-production for prime time.

Mitchell took no action before resigning as Attorney General to take full-time responsibility as the manager of the Nixon presidential campaign. I heard no more about it from him. And I considered this a victory over McLaren and the bureaucracy. The matter was dead.

Unknown to me, Hollander and his staff persisted in pushing the matter, bringing it to the attention of the newly appointed acting Attorney General, Richard Kleindienst.

On April 10, 1972, midway in the season of primary elections, I made a brief appearance before the National Association of Broadcasters, meeting again in Chicago. I conducted a press conference and we discussed the normal issues—Agnew, regulation, the possibility of presidential election debates, and administration attitudes toward the broadcast industry. No mention was made of the potential suit. There had been no leaks regarding my December network visits or regarding the battle which had been waged within the executive branch.

During the late afternoon, I was an honored guest at a small cocktail reception given by the networks. Within minutes of my arrival, I was called aside by Erlich of ABC, who informed me that he and others who served as counsel to the networks had been called by Justice Department attorneys to inform them that an antitrust suit was about to be filed unless they agreed within seven days to accept the government's "relief demands." I found this hard to believe. I had no prior notification, and even if I had, why would Justice feel it had to announce the suit on the day I was meeting with the network leaders and other broadcasters? I regarded this as a classic example of bureaucratic stupidity which was certain to undermine my credibility and that of the administration.

I stepped into a bedroom of the suite where the cocktail party was being held and called Moore. He was unaware of the timing and understood my embarrassment. I then called Kleindienst, who professed to be unaware of the history of the case or my role in it. He said he was simply working with his divisions, such as antitrust, and that the matter had been presented to him by the acting head of that department, Walker Comegys, as something which had been long pending. I read Kleindienst off, but it was too late.

As I had predicted, the media interpreted this as an overt and politically inspired attack against the networks. The broadcasters answered by claiming the suits were filed as part of a pattern of harassment. I found myself in the position of believing personally that the suit, which stemmed originally from investigations when Herbert Brownell and William Rogers were President Eisenhower's attorney generals, did not fit current network practices and thus was unnecessary. Simultaneously, I strongly felt that the network defense of political harassment was also unfounded if judged by the facts, not the natural suspicions.

Late in 1974, after Nixon had left office, a federal district court dismissed the suits "without prejudice." In December, the ever persistent Justice Department reinstated the suits and, as this is written, they are still pending.

Suspicions linger on and both sides pursue the cases with toughness which could be expected.

Almost unnoticed, actions which more accurately fit a pattern of administration efforts to dominate broadcast were going on simultaneously with the debate over filing the network suit. These White House actions were aimed at changing the growing pattern of public broadcasting which was emerging more and more in the arena of covering politics.

Peter Flanigan, a major figure in his own right in the field of international banking, was a senior presidential assistant who specialized in problems of trade but also delved into other governmental areas he found of interest. He long had been interested in public broadcasting as a forum for more cultural enrichment and for locally controlled broadcast programming. He found that the trend was the opposite, more centralized programming of a network nature and more emphasis on national news than on culture. At the time the Nixon administration arrived in Washington, the public broadcasters depended more on funds from the Rockefeller and Ford Foundations than from government. Annually, government contributions to public broadcasting were increased sharply, and these funds, provided by Congress, were looked upon by PBS as providing more independence than those from the foundations or from corporations.

Flanigan originally raised the question in 1971 whether the funding was worthwhile and whether it might not be better to withdraw and virtually kill off the new developments or, as an alternative, to seek the way to have more control over it. I think Flanigan was seeking simultaneously more culture and less liberal politics on PBS. He did not seek personal power, but from the outside it would appear so.

In the midst of this internal discussion it was announced that Public Broadcasting was preparing for the presidential election year by hiring Sander Vanocur at an annual salary of $85,000, and Robert McNeil at $65,000.

With this announcement, the casual Flanigan discussions took on heated White House overtones led by the President and encouraged by Colson. Clay T. Whitehead, director of the Office of Tele-Communications, became Colson's chosen weapon to write fiery White House memos and to criticize publicly the actions of the Corporation for Public Broadcasting.

Vanocur was a red flag to the President and to most in the White House. Over the years, his political coverage for NBC had been looked upon by many close to Nixon as a prime example of biased reporting.

There were disjointed plans outlined to gain control of the management of public broadcasting, and Henry Loomis, deputy director of the USIA, eventually was appointed to head the organization. In office he proved less pliable to White House demands than had been anticipated by the President. Other efforts were made to fill vacancies on the board with nationally known figures such as Al Cole of *Reader's Digest* and Jack Wrather of the motion picture industry, who were considered closer to the Nixon line of thinking. Part of the idea was to gain control through them. There were too few appointments open to gain Nixon dominance over the board at any early date.

There was a case to be made for developing public broadcasting in a manner which differed from that of the commercial networks. In my opinion, this has been accomplished. How much the cultural impact of public broadcasting was helped or hindered by the 1971–72 struggle, it is difficult to judge. Regardless of the political aspects, PBS received a major boost which changed the availability of funds to it because of the pioneer effort by the Nixon administration to vastly increase public funding, which was allocated by the Congress with basically no political strings. But without question, there was White House interference—ineffective as it was. PBS struggled and maintained its independence, despite harassment and many wild schemes.

Whatever the efforts by some in the administration to gain control, this never happened, and a complete plan to develop this control logically was never in evidence to me.

But it was a threat.

The going just never got that tough at that time.

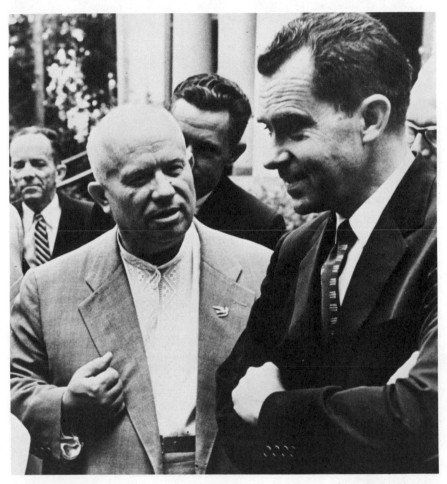

A Russian photographer caught a glimpse of me over Nikita Khrushchev's shoulder at his dacha outside Moscow in 1959.

I could not believe what I heard as Nixon told the press it would not have him to kick around anymore on the morning after the 1962 election. It was my press conference he interrupted. (Courtesy of the Los Angeles *Times*).

Pierre Salinger pauses while examining a diagram of TV studios set up for the first 1960 debate in Chicago.

Cartoonist Basset depicts the Klein dilemma in 1968.

To Herb Klein
With my hope the end will be as pleasant
as the beginning
Lyndon B Johnson

On the day before Lyndon Johnson left office, we met to receive his advice
to his successor, including instructions to ignore the New York *Times*.
(Courtesy of the Lyndon B. Johnson Library).

Every expression, every thought, was different as Chief Justice Warren swore
in Richard Nixon as President.

In the Vice-President's office in 1959, Bob Finch and Rose Woods take notes from Nixon.

Agnew faces reporters after being introduced by me as "Spyro" T. Agnew, Nixon's 1968 choice for Vice-President.

My desk was cluttered but I knew where everthing was; grandson Tommy Howell wasn't sure.

By chance I looked in the sky over Hanoi and saw the American C-135 as it left North Vietnam taking home the first American prisoners of war who were released. It was almost as if I could hear them shouting for joy. I aimed my camera and preserved a little bit of history.

While the press pool records the scene, Bob Finch and I report to the President and Henry Kissinger on our tour of six Latin-American countries in 1971.

The President asked me to sit in his chair as my wife and I prepared to leave the White House in June 1973.

11

Case Studies:
ITT and the "New Nixon"

WHEN MOST PEOPLE think of investigative reporting or the analysis of issues by the media today, Watergate comes to mind first.

It is clear that even in the politics of the day, Watergate cover-up charges would have been bypassed after a few congressional skirmishes had it not been for the persistence of the Washington *Post* in particular, and occasionally some forays by the New York *Times,* the Los Angeles *Times,* and CBS. Like the Congress, most news people found the story too incredible to pursue it hard in 1972, the year of the election.

Until cracks started to appear in the administration's dam early in 1973, there were few heroes in the press or the Congress. And I must confess that while I sensed trouble and sought hard to have the White House rectify it, I did not realize the depth of involvement of the President and some of his senior associates. To me the answer always was obvious: fire those involved and get rid of the issue.

Once the evidence began to mount more seriously with the grand jury revelations of John Dean, Jeb Magruder, and others, the press herd started to move en masse on the case.

And finally it did a thorough and effective job, although it still was inaccurate too often. It allowed its emotions to exceed professional bounds in too many cases, particularly in the long reportorial rhetoric and speeches at briefings by the press secretary, Ron Ziegler.

Ziegler's naïve comment that Watergate was a "third-rate burglary" obviously was the misstatement of the decade.

But it did not justify the shrill unprofessional emotions expressed by newsmen at the daily press briefings. And there was no justification for some stories damaging reputations with rumor, not fact.

Two less emotional happenings which illustrate the danger of the press moving as a herd are the celebrated ITT case revolving around the ill-fated San Diego bid for the Republican Convention and, in a different way, the press discovery, repeated every few years, that there was a "new Nixon" or, finally, a "new, new Nixon" in 1968.

The recommendation of any city for the national convention of a political party normally is made by the National Committee after research and recommendations have been published by a site committee.

The first consideration is the number of hotel rooms, and even in this time of massive travel, few cities have sufficient rooms to house a Republican or a Democratic convention. The committee usually seeks a commitment of about 25,000 first-class rooms. Other requirements, of course, include a convention hall or arena which will seat at least 15,000 persons while allowing room for a massive platform and for delegate seats on the floor of the facility. Space for temporary working areas outside the hall for the thousands of reporters who converge on the scene is another must, as are caucus rooms, where key decisions often are made.

Beyond these things the site committee thoroughly considers political advantages and disadvantages of different locations. In a contested nomination fight, the committee tends to avoid the home state of any leading candidate. It also looks on the strategy of the general election, considering the advantages of extra publicity in the West, Middle West, South, etc.

Beyond that is a major financial consideration. How much will the local community contribute toward expenses? The cost of constructing press areas and caucus rooms, paying expenses of entertainers, promotion, and hundreds of other factors mounts into millions. Television is a strong medium. A convention in the West must convene earlier to reach prime-time Eastern audiences. And the networks inevitably pressure both parties to agree on one city to save the millions involved in their logistics if they can build their facilities for both conventions in only one city.

In recent years, security and the potential of rioting or other troubles have had to be considered.

All of these things were on the minds of the Republicans as they started in 1970 to recommend a convention city for 1972. Houston, Chicago, San Francisco, Miami, New York, and Kansas City were among the many cities surveyed personally by the committee.

Early in 1971, after the losses in the 1970 elections and after the site committee was well into its deliberations, President Nixon began to take an interest in the proceedings. The site committee appeared to be leaning toward Miami Beach as the location, although Houston also was in the running. The networks favored both conventions in Miami Beach.

Nixon decided that California would suit him best politically and personally. San Francisco was ruled out because it was a center of activity for anti-Vietnam demonstrators. Facilities in Los Angeles appeared to be scattered so far apart that logistics and costs would be complicated and expensive.

San Diego seemed ideal to him. He had long called it his "lucky city" because it was from there he had launched his 1968 bid for the presidency and because it was an area he had always carried overwhelmingly. It provided the margin of victory for him over Kennedy in California in 1960—a matter of some personal satisfaction. After his nomination in 1968, he and Vice-President Agnew had flown to the Bahia Hotel in Mission Bay for two weeks of strategy sessions and for a small, private dinner at the home of James S. Copley, owner of newspapers in San Diego, Southern California, and Illinois. It probably was the only small dinner party they ever attended jointly, and it was a festive occasion, with Mrs. Helen Copley, who succeeded her husband as publisher after his death, acting as hostess.

Word was passed to Bob Finch and me to encourage San Diego to make a formal bid for the 1972 convention. This was a late entry, and it required the skills of two Republican congressmen, Bob Wilson and Clair Burgener, plus the work of several in our inner circle such as Leon Parma, a close friend of Jerry Ford, Al Harutunian, a noncontroversial civic leader with boundless energy, the local Republican chairman, Admiral Les Gehres, and Mayor Pete Wilson, aided by the Copley Newspapers. They convinced San Diegans they had a chance for the convention if they would make a serious bid. San Diego at first found this hard to believe although it is one of the major convention centers in the country.

I worked with the City Council and the county supervisors and we finally had a majority in each body, uncertain though it was.

The problem was finances. How much money could the city offer?

Thus began the ITT case.

The Sheraton subsidiary of ITT had moved into San Diego heavily and was building two major hotels to add to a small resort unit, the Half Moon Inn. As a sign of recognition of the community the ITT board met in San Diego.

When the meetings were completed, Congressman Bob Wilson had dinner informally with Harold Geneen, chairman of ITT. During the dinner, Geneen committed to assisting the San Diego civic effort as part of the promotion for his hotel.

Wilson and Geneen worked out an agreement whereby ITT-Sheraton would pledge $100,000 to the San Diego Convention Bureau if the Republican convention was obtained. There was an additional commitment of $100,000 more if San Diego raised $200,000 from other "non-public sources." Thus the matching funds, plus the ITT pledge, made this a $400,000 package.

The text of the agreement was spelled out in the following telegram to Bob Wilson from Howard James, president of the Sheraton Corporation.

"As you know Sheraton Corporation of America will have with the completion of the Sheraton Harbor Island Hotel, a 700 room hotel being located on land owned and created by the San Diego Port Authority, three hotels in San Diego. (All three now are in operation.) In consideration of naming the Sheraton Harbor Island Hotel as Presidential headquarters hotel in conjunction with its opening at the time of the Convention, and as part of the general community effort to establish San Diego as a convention center by bringing the 1972 Republican National Convention to the city, Sheraton is prepared to commit a total of DLS 200 thousand to the bureau for its promotional activities, if San Diego is designated as the convention site, on the following basis: DLS 100 thousand in cash to be available to the bureau on August 1, 1971 and the balance to be paid as a matching contribution when the bureau has raised an additional DLS 200 thousand in cash from other non-public sources." The amount of $200,000 was less than Sheraton had spent in opening a hotel in Honolulu a year before, and it promised great national publicity. ITT also contributed to the Democratic Convention in Miami Beach.

Despite what was to be implied later, there was no secret about the agreement. It was announced by Wilson in San Diego and by me in Washington and at other press conferences. ITT never talked about $400,000 as reported, except in the above terms.

When Wilson and Geneen talked, the congressman had no authority to commit one hotel or another as the one where the President and his staff would stay. But Wilson was a veteran campaigner who had long been a Nixon supporter and had sacrificed his campaign time in 1960, 1966, and 1968 to give extra time helping the presidential candidate.

Certainly, Wilson was not in touch with anyone in the Justice Department regarding pending antitrust action against ITT.

The other interesting fact was that Nixon planned to spend a minimum of time in San Diego, mainly commuting to the convention by helicopter from his home in San Clemente, fifty miles north.

San Diego raised the money, made its bid to the site selection committee and, after some active lobbying by Finch, myself, and others, it was recommended as the convention city.

It was about then that other factors came into play to build the transaction into a national political scandal.

Mrs. Dita Beard, a longtime political operator, was working in the Washington office of ITT as a registered lobbyist. A close personal friend of Wilson's executive secretary, Maggie Young, she also was having dinner at the Half Moon Inn after the meetings and was told of the Geneen-Wilson convention agreement.

Mrs. Beard, eager to impress her Washington bureau chief, Bill Merriam, quickly transmitted the information to him.

What she did after that remains a matter of some mystery.

A few months later, however, the Justice Department reached a settlement in long-pending antitrust suits involving ITT mergers with the Grinnel and Canteen Corporations and Hartford Fire. ITT won early skirmishes in the lower courts and the matter finally was brought before the Supreme Court.

Richard W. McLaren, then chief of the Antitrust Division of Justice and later appointed and confirmed as a federal judge, determined that, looking at the odds in the case, the government would do best to reach a tough out-of-court settlement. He later swore under oath that he was pressured by no one. The United States Solicitor General, Erwin Griswold, a Johnson appointee who would have had to try the case, agreed with McLaren, again before Congress, under oath.

Basically, the settlement called for ITT to divest itself of Canteen Corporation and the fire protection of Grinnel within two years. There were other, smaller divisions to be disposed of but ITT was allowed to keep Hartford Fire and in return it was forced to dispose of three other companies which were among the leaders in their industries. There also were restrictions of further ITT acquisitions.

Even before the case became tainted politically, it created a furor. McLaren, an antitrust-law specialist for twenty-five years, had been brought into the Justice Department with considerable publicity given to a surprise Nixon policy to fight the growth of conglomerates of business.

Businessmen such as Geneen and his public relations vice-president, Ned Gerrity, had called upon me, Peter Flanigan, and others numerous times to protest what they considered antibusiness policy on the part of Nixon and McLaren. The discussions with me were always on a policy level, never seeking any consideration for ITT specifically.

McLaren deliberately made ITT a case upon which he hoped to test Section 7 of the Clayton Anti-Trust Act and its application to breaking up conglomerates.

His decision for a settlement appeared to be a reversal of policy.

However, testifying before the Senate Judiciary Committee, Griswold described the settlement in these terms:

"This was in fact a very substantial victory for the government, and the first one in the whole conglomerate field, probably setting a great precedent in the area, and it seems to be misleading to keep telling the public that the government dropped three suits in the anti-trust field. It didn't . . . the settlement was an extremely favorable one, a very large divestiture of one of the principal conglomerates, and the first case, at least the first case of any size where by any means at all a conglomerate did divest itself of substantial acquisitions. . . .

"Not merely a good settlement, Senator, but a very good settlement."

McLaren described his logic this way:

"I went into this settlement on the basis that I thought there was a good chance of winning. I also knew there was a chance of losing: right? Say it is 60-40. All right, as a lawyer, I analyzed it.

"A 60 percent chance I win, and then I think later when I get all this information, can I really afford to win, and then have these disastrous consequences [involving stockholders and balance of payments] or is there another way around?

"On the other hand, we have got a 40 percent chance that we will lose. All right, if I lose, my whole program is down the drain, so I look for some sort of solution where we purge their violation and where we would still get—have a program and we still have a deterrent."

While the gigantic decision was receiving mixed reviews from liberals and conservatives, several other things broke to make the matter complicated.

Richard Kleindienst, then acting Attorney General—John Mitchell having moved from the Justice Department to direct the Nixon presidential campaign—admitted that he had arranged a discussion between McLaren and ITT officials. He was grilled upon the point in his confirmation hearings. And his handling of the questions was at best clumsy.

Brit Hume, legman for columnist Jack Anderson, came forth with a memo on ITT stationery and signed with the letter "d," which Anderson in his syndicated column a few days later claimed was written by Dita Beard.

Mrs. Beard apparently took a quick glance at the memo when shown it by Hume and admitted it was hers. She then read it more thoroughly and denied authorship. She again denied writing it when under oath before the Senate committee. Even expert typewriter tests, made later, were inconclusive.

The memo addressed to Merriam tied the San Diego contribution to a Justice Department settlement of the ITT case.

I had known Dita casually since the 1960 presidential campaign when she had worked as a secretary for Ted Rogers, our television director. She was known mainly for her hard work and her outspoken rough language. She could outswear most men, but she was a savvy lady. With the Anderson column and all its implications she suddenly was a national figure.

Gerrity called me to tell me he had problems with the whole situation and that it had been handled badly by the ITT Washington office. He denied any tie between the San Diego convention and the Justice Department action and assured me that regardless of Dita, there was no case.

"I don't know now whether she wrote the memo or not, but if she did, it was to brag and it represents nothing factual," he said.

The news herd now was dashing everywhere. Senator Marlow Cook of Kentucky correctly charged the media with a campaign of "innuendo and hearsay" augmented by politically minded Nixon opponents.

It was a strange case stirred by a lobbyist's memo or a forgery of a memo and heated up with the emotions of liberals, who felt that McLaren had backed down to the colossus ITT.

There were other weird developments.

California's lieutenant governor, Ed Reinicke, briefly discussed the San Diego convention with John Mitchell, apparently seeking political credit for gaining the bid for the city. He later testified incorrectly on the conversation and eventually was convicted for perjury. His effort to gain recognition ended a bright, blossoming political career which might have made him governor instead of Jerry Brown, and yet he had little to do with the convention and nothing to do with ITT. He was an "innocent abroad."

Dita Beard disappeared just before she was to testify. She claimed a heart attack while aboard a plane flying to Bozeman, Montana, for a brief vacation, and she was hospitalized in Denver.

It was revealed also that ITT had gone through its Washington files and shredded papers after the Hume confrontation with Dita Beard but before the appearance of the Anderson column. ITT claimed that it was a security measure after its files had been burglarized, but at best it also was a clumsy move for anyone, let alone a sophisticated conglomerate.

The cap on the matter came with a bizarre move by Howard Hunt which should have been a tip-off to someone in the White House of potential troubles ahead. Hunt, directed by Chuck Colson, borrowed a red wig as a disguise from his old employer, the CIA, and paid a secret visit to Dita Beard in her hospital room. Colson and Hunt thought it was a way to find what Dita really knew—all of which reflected a lack of confidence in the truth of the situation. Hunt and Colson found out nothing new.

All these events were fully covered by the press.

But the emphasis on what Senator Cook of Kentucky called "innuendo and hearsay" left a false impression in the public mind. Competition among reporters was such after the Anderson column broke and rumors were so intermixed with facts, that the public was misled. There were exceptions with balanced coverage by some newsmen, but they were a minority.

The facts gained less news attention than the apparent scandals. The truth was that the Senate Judiciary Committee after full public hearings did not seek to counter the reputable judgments of McLaren or Griswold in the case. No one seriously challenged Bob Wilson on his deal for San Diego. Kleindienst was confirmed as Attorney General. And the only real mystery was whether or not the allegations in the memo were correct.

The most ironic part of the entire story is the fact that the President later sought to back away from a convention in San Diego, and eventually it was moved to Miami Beach.

When the President reversed himself on the San Diego site, I again had a delicate problem. How do you tell your hometown the President has changed his mind about it?

Fortunately, the Canadian owner of the San Diego Sports Arena, Peter Graham, had created a serious problem for the convention committee. Graham and the committee were locked into battle on costs and improvements of the arena to handle the special requirements of a national convention. The need for more air conditioning was one of the disputes.

Graham provided a very real reason for changing the convention, because hundreds of thousands of dollars were involved. He was holding out for permanent improvements paid for by the Republicans and retained by him for the future. The Sports Arena battle was our public way out.

But beyond that, the convention did not go to San Diego for two substantial reasons.

There was concern that the ITT story had so colored the picture that there would be constant references to it on television and in the newspapers during the convention. Even now, the Sheraton Hotel, which is built on a beautiful bend on Harbor Island in San Diego Bay, often is referred to in terms of being a part of the convention scandal of 1972.

In addition, the number one factor in reversing the decision was security, and this was later reported in part in the press. The San Diego police and other intelligence forces available to the White House had learned that there were massive plans for demonstrations in San Diego. Violence was threatened.

San Diego's astute mayor, Pete Wilson, had worked with the police and they had a variety of strategies to contain the demonstrators in a way to allow the convention to go forth without violence while allowing the demonstrators to express themselves from a distance.

At best the situation posed problems. But the problems would multiply if the White House were to acknowledge that it had changed the site of a nominating convention because of the pressure of the protesters. San Diego, too, had similar concerns, and leaders there were happy to have the matter end as a dispute with the arena.

The discovery of a "new Nixon" did not figure in the ITT case or the San Diego convention, but the new and the old Nixon were a matter of conjecture in the news media from 1952 through 1970—almost twenty years. When one was working with a man who more often than not was unpopular with the press, the idea of a "new Nixon," a Nixon more acceptable to the newsmen, might be appealing.

Truthfully, I did nothing to kill the stories. But I also never encouraged them, because I do not believe a "new Nixon" ever existed except as a figment in the minds of reporters. My stock answer was that anyone changes with time, but I saw no major difference in the basic Nixon.

In 1952 there were a few stories early in the campaign about the "new Nixon" who was treading a higher road than the gut fighter who had defeated Helen Gahagan Douglas in the senatorial election of 1950.

In 1954, when communism was an issue again and Joe McCarthy was part of many congressional campaigns, the press looked again at Nixon as the "old", prodded on in the background by what they perceived as the rough and tough street fighter, Murray Chotiner.

In 1956, Jim Bassett, veteran Los Angeles *Times* news executive and Nixon press secretary in 1952, directed the traveling campaign staff, and I was his principal assistant. Our titles were press secretary and assistant press secretary.

Together we convinced the Vice-President that he should have numerous press conferences, sometimes three or four a week. Nixon briefed the press informally, even worked with me on signals: he would shake hands after a rally speech long enough to allow the newsmen to file quick early leads before rushing off to the airplane and the next city.

Pleased with Nixon's cooperation with the press, a few of the veteran newsmen wrote of a "new Nixon," and soon the press herd was echoing the stories. Within days there were as many stories about the "new Nixon" of 1956 as there were features in later years about a "reborn Colson."

It wasn't a different Nixon, but it was a Nixon who was treating the press with more thoughtful help than the newsmen had grown to expect from him. It was an easier year for Nixon also. Having weathered Harold Stassen's challenge to his renomination, Nixon enjoyed campaigning on the high road with little pressure to carry the tough, hard line. His strategy of avoiding controversy was beneficial to the ticket at a time when Eisenhower's health dictated that his participation be slightly limited.

From a substance point of view, the most critical point in the campaign came in October when Israel, aided by France and Great Britain, made a successful surprise attack on Egypt. Neither Eisenhower nor Nixon had anticipated this, and in the Nixon party I first learned of the attack as we were campaigning by bus in the suburbs of Los Angeles. I quickly notified the Vice-President and he called off his next speech to get to a telephone and discuss the situation with Eisenhower. Both men decided to take a tough stand against the attack regardless of the potential dangers of political controversy because of a stand against three allies, Israel, Britain, and

France. Even in this situation the relaxed "new Nixon" did not shy from the press. The war was short-lived as Eisenhower prevailed on Britain and France to withdraw support. The decision was one Nixon later regretted when the Suez was closed.

I took a leave of absence again in 1958 from my position as an editor of the San Diego *Union* to help the Vice-President as he took the lead position campaigning for Republicans across the country.

My wife was not sure she would forgive me because we had just completed building a new home in La Jolla and part of our plan was for me to complete some of the work we could not afford to have the contractor do. When she finally realized that the future of the presidency was involved in how Nixon campaigned just two years before he would seek the office, she quickly relented.

Again, 1958 was a "new Nixon" year. At the start of the intense campaign which covered the country five or six days a week over a two-month period the Vice-President held frequent press conferences.

Many of the press conferences were scheduled to give local newsmen a chance to ask questions about regional problems that would have an effect on the local congressional races. Between stops in the airplane Nixon would spend his time either working with speech writers on twice-a-day excerpts for newsmen (aimed at giving new leads for afternoon and morning papers) or poring through a thick black looseleaf book which included background for any possible question.

The newsmen liked the attention they received from the candidate during the first six weeks of the eight-week campaign. The 1958 "new Nixon" was hailed by the press.

At one point during a cross-country trip, one of the reporters, Phil Potter of the Baltimore *Sun*, suffered from severe pains in a disc of his back and was forced to lie flat in the aisle of our aircraft. Potter was a cynic and a tough reporter, but Nixon showed great sympathy for him as he lay in pain. Since Potter was anti-Nixon, the press particularly noted the attention given him, although I considered this only natural.

There was one relaxing swing during the campaign, a trip to Alaska, which was having its first election under statehood. The principal races were for U.S. senator (two), congressman (one), and governor. The governor's race appeared most important because the first leader of the state would have great power in the area of political patronage.

We soon found that there was only one sophisticated candidate in Alaska. He was a Democrat, Ernest Gruening, a former governor and one who had represented the territory of Alaska ably in the Senate.

Trying to make news for our candidates in Alaska was at best difficult. When we arrived, ostensibly to dedicate a new plane for the Alaska Airlines, it took me ten minutes to find the Republican candidates so they could be seen in the pictures with the Vice-President. They were in awe of the office and the man and did not want to intrude.

Gruening, on the other hand, was everywhere when a camera was present. He was in the receiving line at the airport. He had arranged for a room on the floor we had reserved in the hotel where he displayed a sign which said "Welcome Dick Nixon, Gruening for Senate."

The Republican candidates were bright, good-looking, and articulate. But they were so shy it was a full-time task to get them before the newsmen. Alaska is small enough that its early elections were more amateur than city council races in cities of 150,000. Yet the state was about to have major impact politically, particularly in the Senate, where it would have two votes.

On a Sunday, I arranged to have the entire party visit an Eskimo village near Anchorage where I thought good pictures were inevitable. As we rode down the elevator to embark on the trip I spotted Gruening waiting before the cameras at the elevator in the lobby.

In an unkind gesture which I have since regretted, I elbowed him in the stomach, and as he bent over to get his breath, he finally missed being in a picture. Gruening eventually won election to the Senate.

We went to Fairbanks the next day and spent most of one night conducting a campaign school for the candidates. We summoned Congressman Bob Wilson to do what he could in the final days of the Alaskan campaign.

The reporters enjoyed the relaxed "new Nixon" on the Alaskan tour.

In Fairbanks he rode on a dogsled with the Republican candidates, and the reporters became so enthusiastic that they joined in the race between one sled with newsmen and another with Pat Nixon, Rose Woods, and me.

The reporters won when I became the only press secretary to run the wife of a Vice-President into a hidden tree stump with a dogsled.

Upon leaving Alaska we changed planes in Seattle, and there was one unidentified handbag. I opened it and found that one reporter had looked ahead to the hardships of Alaska. The bag carried only a bottle of bourbon and red woolen underwear. I had not been so farsighted. To protect me from the cold, I had only a sweater borrowed from the reporter friend, Phil Potter.

The "new Nixon" tag was dropped near the end of the 1958 campaign as the Vice-President, except when he was in Alaska, became increasingly tense and correspondingly aloof from the press. Two things contributed to his change in attitude.

There were efforts by Nelson Rockefeller and his key aides to keep Nixon out of New York. It was felt he might hurt the Rockefeller candidacy for governor, but for Nixon, such a story coming out of the largest state in the nation would be seriously harmful to his prospective candidacy for President in 1960. We went into New York, where Nixon campaigned for Ken Keating for senator and made an effective telecast for the entire ticket. After the telecast Rockefeller called and arranged to fly from Albany and to join Nixon for breakfast. This was a behind-the-scenes Nixon victory.

We received increasingly gloomy reports on Republican prospects in the national election, despite the all-out Nixon effort.

On the Saturday afternoon before the 1958 election, I dropped out of other activities and spent several hours calling state leaders, demanding an honest evaluation. Ed May of Connecticut gave me the most candid report.

"The Democrats may sweep the state with their candidate for Governor, Abraham Ribicoff [now a Senator], leading the way on the voting machines."

The polls predicted the same thing.

Thus another "new Nixon" dropped by the wayside. But in some ways this led to a favorable look at yet another "new Nixon" in 1960—a time when it counted.

The "new Nixon" of 1960 again was one who gained the plaudits of the press as he breezed through the primaries after a basic announcement of Rockefeller's withdrawal at the end of 1959. Rockefeller support reemerged during the primary, but Nixon did not feel pressured, and he was cooperative with the press.

The "old Nixon" appeared within the first three weeks of the general election campaign, however. He felt veteran reporters, including Phil Potter and the late William Lawrence (New York *Times* and ABC), were ganging up on him unfairly with their questions on the U-2 incident in the Soviet Union.

The candidate became even more sensitive after the first Kennedy debate, and he pulled away from the press into a cocoon, much as he did after the first two years of his full term in the White House.

He was right in asserting that the working press favored Kennedy. He was wrong in fighting this by pulling further away from the newsmen, and this tactic was among those which led to his narrow defeat.

Nixon rarely acknowledged the "new Nixon" game of the media. Two of the most candid exceptions were interviews with Walter Cronkite and James J. Kilpatrick. The Cronkite interview was in September of 1960 in Washington.

Cronkite asked whether Nixon resented "talk of there being a 'new Nixon.'"

The Vice-President answered:

"No, not particularly. I think that our people generally like to appraise their public servants and to detect, if they feel it is justified, any changes that indicate growth or change that they might approve. Now, as far as I'm concerned, when people say there is a new Nixon, that must mean that people who did not like the Nixon that they knew before, now like the one that they know. Now, I happen to believe myself that perhaps many of those who discover the new Nixon may not have known the old one; but seriously, may I say this: we all change. . . . I have learned a lot [in eight years as Vice-President] and it is very possible that I certainly do convey a different impression today than I did previously, because if I hadn't learned, I wouldn't amount to too much. So, I will concede that I have changed, and I hope for the better."

In the Kilpatrick interview for *National Review* in 1968, Nixon approached the problem of his old and new images a little differently:

"They still call me Tricky Dick," he said. (I had never heard him use the phrase in all our long association.) "It's a brutal thing to fight," he acknowledged. "If anyone takes the time to check my public record fairly— and it's all there, the votes I cast, the speeches I made, the things I wrote— he'd have to conclude that on the great issues of the past twenty years, my record is clean and consistent. Look at my record on civil rights and then look at Lyndon's. But I've been in this game long enough to know that few voters have the time or inclination to study a record. The carefully cultivated impression is that Nixon is devious. I can overcome this impression one way only: by absolute candor."

In the presidential campaigns of 1960 and 1968 the "new Nixon"—or, as Jules Witcover and others covering the second race said, a "new, new Nixon"—was more a figment of the primaries than of the general election, when it really counted.

In 1959 after the Kitchen Debate in the Soviet Union and on through the primaries of 1960, Nixon worked well with the newsmen. In 1960 and again in 1968, two of his most outstanding performances were open question-and-answer sessions before the prestigious American Society of Newspaper Editors. After both performances, even the editors accepted a "new Nixon" or felt that their better thoughts about him were confirmed. It should be noted that John Kennedy also impressed the editors in 1960 with a speech which took on the religious issue as he approached the West Virginia primary.

In the March issue of *Progressive* magazine in 1968, Witcover, a long-time critical Nixon observer, wrote:

"Nixon, true to his word about being more open, now frequently lets reporters have a peek into the tent of his political mind and what they see is impressive but not always flattering to him. Newsmen traveling with Nixon get a good look at the pragmatics of his politics—one could even say at the amoral nature of his politics; for Nixon, electing Republicans is the name of the game—liberal Republicans, conservative Republicans, tall Republicans, short Republicans. Party loyalty is commendable, but his total concentration on winning can be a bit chilling when the extent is revealed."

The words mix criticism with slight praise, but the interesting fact is that Witcover (author of *The Resurrection of Richard Nixon*), usually a Nixon critic in both books and articles, thought the reporting of a "new, new Nixon" was important enough to warrant an eight-page article in the liberal *Progressive* magazine.

By the time Nixon was running for President again in 1967 and 1968, the "guard" had pretty much changed among reporters.

The newsmen who had reacted with such emotion over the Alger Hiss case and who had covered the Nixon race against Helen Gahagan Douglas and in the early vice-presidential days were seen only rarely in the campaign entourage.

Lawrence of ABC had died, and Potter was a bureau chief. James Reston of the New York *Times* was still looked upon as the senior statesman of the Washington press corps, but the active leaders on the campaign trail were more the likes of David Broder, then of the Washington *Star* (later the *Post*), Walter Mears of Associated Press, Helen Thomas of United Press International, John Osborne of *New Republic*, Dan Rather of CBS, and Herb Kaplow of ABC.

The stories of "Tricky Dick" or of hard-line anticommunism or roughshod campaigning were more likely to be stories they had heard about or read about than ones they knew from first hand experience.

Thus, the "new, new Nixon" image came easy during the primaries. The candidate made a major effort to mingle with the press and erase the picture of a man who had said, "You won't have Dick Nixon to kick around anymore."

He was there if they chose to kick him around, and he did his best to see that they did not.

In the days of the New Hampshire and other primaries, the Nixon staff was small, but effective, and Pat Buchanan, himself a newspaperman from the St. Louis *Globe Democrat*, joined Bill Safire and Leonard Garment in working closely with the newsmen. Later they brought in Arch McKinley from the National Safety Council to assist in the press operation at the New York headquarters.

The "new, new Nixon" fared well with the press all during the period.

In the general election, he again was more restrained with the press, but we were able to keep relations at a more amicable basis than 1960 with a "press aide" system.

I organized a program in which I directed press activities from the New York headquarters as well as from the plane—with Ron Ziegler as my traveling "press aide." We had constant direct communication. Every two weeks we had a different Republican leader (usually a senator or governor) brought aboard the plane to be constantly available to the press to brief and answer questions.

The stories of the "old Nixon" were avoided in that campaign.

My own thoughts on a "new Nixon" have not changed over the years, and I have expressed them consistently in answer to questions by newsmen.

Despite the thousands of words that have been written and broadcast, I do not think there was, is, or will be a "new Nixon."

The implication from the words "new Nixon" is that the man changes with the political season, that he has a new approach to campaigning, to the problems of blacks and other minorities, that he analyzes foreign policy or communism differently—that, most of all, he has a new attitude toward reporters.

Policies change with time and with ongoing events. Thus an attitude regarding the People's Republic of China and the Chinese Nationalists which fitted United States and world interests in the forties and fifties, and even part of the sixties, could be and was changed by shifting circumstances in the world balance of power. The only direct conflict between United States troops and those of a major foreign power was in Korea, where there was ground and air battle between the Chinese and the United States. But in later years both sides sought moderation to avoid a new conflict in Korea.

In 1959, when I accompanied the Vice-President to the Soviet Union, the Chinese were being feted everywhere we turned in Moscow. When we returned to Moscow in 1972, "People's Republic of China" was a harsh and dirty name in the Kremlin.

Basically, there was neither a new nor an old Nixon involved in recognizing the shifts in world power and moving in the direction he perceived to be the best from the viewpoint of United States interests.

Nixon never counted upon many votes from the black community, and in almost every campaign he missed some opportunities to enlarge his minority constituency. Yet he had more human concern than the political record indicates. A failure to protest the jailing of Martin Luther King, Jr., in 1960 was a mistake politically and morally. The Southern Strategy of 1968 is well known, and yet it could have been combined with appeals to blacks in the North and even more so to the growing Spanish-speaking constituency.

The real Nixon had few blacks in his congressional district and was in office as a senator too short a time to build a record one way or the other. As Vice-President, he headed a committee to persuade business to allow breakthroughs of more rights for blacks.

And consistently, his administration integrated more schools than had any previous one, although politically he was reluctant to take credit for it in a major way. Politics made him awkward in the civil rights field, making him reluctant to take credit for gains he made.

The new or old Nixon the newsmen reflected most was the Nixon who was dealing with the press. The yardstick was not a valid one, but it was the measuring device.

Nixon really never changed much in regard to his attitude toward the media. He was always more comfortable with publishers and editors, or even editorial writers, than with reporters. He recognized that the former were more likely to be Republican or at least right of center, and there was no question but that the majority of reporters are somewhat liberal.

The ill-fated "White House Enemies List" included few publishers and editors and many reporters.

Nixon understood the needs of the press for new leads, excerpts issued in time for deadlines, sidebar features, and filing and broadcast time. Our scheduling reflected this. He fully understood the importance of the press, and, as the years went on, he recognized and perhaps overemphasized the importance of television.

With this background, Nixon normally worked well with the press when the pressure was not extreme. His sensitivities showed most when a campaign or an issue became tense.

Most remember that John Kennedy stopped White House subscriptions to the New York *Herald Tribune* when he thought it was unfair. Few remember that Nixon canceled his subscription to the Washington *Post* when its cartoonist Herblock depicted the Vice-President climbing out of a sewer. He said he did not want his daughters seeing things like this in the Washington *Post*.

In the White House, my answer to reporters on the "new Nixon" question usually was that he had grown and learned with age and experience, that he, like most of us, was more sophisticated than in the days of the old congressional or even the vice-presidential campaign, but basically his instincts were unchanged.

What I did not add was that he had become skeptical of reporters since his first days on the House Un-American Activities Committee and since tasting the hatred of many members of the press after the Alger Hiss case. He secretly admired the minds of reporters but he regarded them as the opposition.

Whether as a campaigner or as an officeholder, he had an instinct for the jugular. As President, he held the most powerful position in the world, but he seemed to secretly admire wealth in the hands of sophisticates, and to look down upon it in the hands of those who did not understand the politics of government, business, or the world.

The "new Nixon" usually emerged under circumstances where his judgment excluded his basic emotions which were negative to the working press. Where the press was concerned, emotion too often excluded judgment.

More currently, there will probably be stories again of a "new Nixon" as the former President gradually moves out of the protected seclusion in his self-made prisons in San Clemente and New York.

It won't be an "old Nixon" the public will see. And it also won't be a "new Nixon" despite what may be written.

The emerging Nixon will be a man who realistically recognizes his public problems and relies on his old instincts and understanding to return quietly to a little more normal life. He will gradually become increasingly public, but in guarded fashion.

"A little more normal life" still will fall short of what most would consider normal and it will exclude a position of political power, long ago lost because the wrong instincts were applied at the wrong time.

12

A Part of the Action

THE BEAT OF THE NEWSMEN who cover the President and Vice-President today extends far beyond Washington or the United States. Its scope is the world.

A summit meeting is hailed as an opportunity for world statesmen to gain a firsthand evaluation of each other, and in a few cases some helpful personal rapport is a result. But much of a summit meeting is a media event with lavish signing ceremonies designed for worldwide television and newspaper coverage. In their own way, the newsmen become almost as much a part of the mission as the principal negotiators.

In few, if any, international trips, however, have the newsmen and women become a more central part of the action than the trip of Vice-President Nixon to the Soviet Union in 1959 which became known as the Kitchen Debate. During negotiations before and during this trip, the newsmen often were unknowingly a part of behind-the-scenes debates, which ranged over subjects from censorship to challenges against the personal integrity of a few of those who were covering the vice-presidential trip.

Less than six months after I had formally been promoted by Jim Copley to the position of editor of the San Diego *Union,* having operated the news side of the paper for several years under other titles, he gave me permission to take a leave of absence, with no strings attached, to handle the forthcoming U.S.S.R.-Nixon trip and eventually the Vice-President's press relations in the 1960 presidential campaign.

The decision to ask the newspaper for another campaign leave of ab-

sence was not an easy one, because we were in the process of building a
publication of respected national reputation. But I felt I had built a strong
staff headed by King Durkee, associate editor, and the challenge to start a
new involvement with the Vice-President by helping arrange an unprecedented trip to the Soviet Union was one which could not be denied.

I arrived in Washington with my family in early June, which was a
good time for us to acquaint our two young daughters, Joanne and Patty,
with our new neighborhood in Arlington, Virginia, and to enroll them in
school, while I was preparing for the trip to Russia and eventually for the
presidential campaign. The politically conscious neighborhood we moved
to even had an unofficial mayor, Robert Swain.

Even for one steeped in the news business, the arrangements with the
Soviets for the trip seemed more complex than I imagined possible. With
routine procedure we sent out notices of the visit to the Soviet Union and
processed the applications for the newsmen who wanted to cover the trip.
It was immediately apparent that the number of reporters desiring to cover
the trip would be large, and the question became how many newsmen the
Soviets would accommodate.

With the help of the State Department and one of its experts, Richard
Davis, I opened negotiations on press arrangements with the Russians
through their senior embassy officers in Washington. As we met privately
at dinner and lunch in Washington, it was apparent to me that each tentative decision we reached with them would not be final until it had been
approved by the Foreign Ministry in Moscow. Unlike me, they were not
free to make independent decisions. My two principal goals were to gain
approval to take close to a hundred American newsmen on the trip and to
reach an understanding that there would be no censorship of any of the
copy or photographs they filed. To the surprise of most of the newsmen,
and more so to the State Department, I won both of my objectives. For the
first time since relations had been resumed between the Roosevelt administration and the Soviets, there would be no censorship, and accommodations would be made for about a hundred American newsmen plus
other nationals coming from all parts of the world. We said little about it
publicly, fearing we would tempt the Russians to change their minds, but
for a Vice-President with strong presidential ambitions, this was a rare opportunity for news coverage. It did not occur to me until I was in Moscow
that the Soviets accepted noncensorship for traveling correspondents but
not resident correspondents, a mistake on my part and a trick on theirs.

The Nixon trip involved no plans for serious negotiation between countries. The idea for the trip was conceived by Abbott Washburn, now an
FCC commissioner. Washburn was then developing cultural exchanges
for the USIA. It was an international visit to enhance the personal relationship between American and Soviet leaders and it was timed to mark

the opening of a tremendous American exhibit which was part of a new cultural exchange program between the two countries. The U.S.S.R. earlier had an exhibit in New York and was to follow with a more major display. In addition to the Vice-President and Mrs. Nixon, the goodwill entourage included President Eisenhower's brother, Milton, George Allen, head of the USIA, and, interestingly, Admiral Hyman Rickover, the Navy's top atomic expert. The tough-minded, brilliant Rickover provided some of the most interesting parts of the trip as he challanged the Russians for information on atomic power plants, but I was not sure why he had been included in this particular official party. Still, he was a major asset.

The first of what was to become a long series of maneuvers between the Soviets and me occurred during the flight to Moscow. All of the official party was to take off from Baltimore aboard Air Force Two except me and Dick Bean, a college friend and press and public relations expert I had borrowed from the Lockheed Aircraft Corporation for the trip. We were to leave with the one hundred newsmen from New York aboard a new intercontinental version of the Boeing 707, which had been purchased by Pan American. Others were joining us in Moscow. Both Pan Am and TWA were negotiating for rights to fly into Moscow, and we arranged for the press to fly to Moscow with one and to return with the other. The Pan American flight on the new international 707 was to be the first nonstop jet flight between New York and Moscow, and the older Air Force Two 707 was scheduled to make one stop for refueling. After several hours of delay in New York, caused by the FAA bureaucracy, which was quarreling over approval of a small backup part for the new plane, I finally called the administrator, Najeeb Halaby, and gained clearance for what was to become a record-making flight. The press plane traveled from New York to Moscow in eight hours, fifty-five minutes, and the time would have been shorter except for a Russian effort to delay the landing because of the publicity which would be given to such an American flight for the press. As we approached Moscow, the rules called for the American crew to turn over control of the plane to a Russian crew. As we passed over Moscow, the Soviets claimed they had to make several circles to check out their airport. When it became apparent they were trying to delay our landing and thus add time to the flight, we finally confronted them, and they made the landing, still in time to set a record which held for many years.

The landing of the Nixon party was greeted in a manner which diplomats describe as "polite but cool." Ambassadors from most countries were there, but no top-ranking Soviet officials. We took this as a sign Khrushchev had given out an order for the visit to be treated "coolly but politely."

On the following day, the first official day, the press unwittingly became part of the next negotiations between me and the Soviet Foreign Ministry. The Vice-President was scheduled to go to the Kremlin for protocol calls on Khrushchev and other Soviet leaders and the American exhibit was to be opened with ceremonies late in the afternoon. I went into the Kremlin with the Vice-President and our senior officials, leaving Dick Bean at the Red Square gate along with the traveling newsmen. On the day of our arrival, the Foreign Ministry had sent me word that newsmen from neither side would be allowed within the Kremlin, but as I went into the first official Kremlin offices, those of President Voroshilov, I spotted Soviet reporters and two cameramen. At the first opportunity, I pulled aside the official United States interpreter, Alex Akalovsky, and his Soviet counterpart, Oleg Tyoyanovsky, and told them they were starting off with a violation of a Soviet-dictated agreement on newsmen. To me this was a test of how we would relate during the next eight days in the U.S.S.R. After a few hurried private conversations, the Soviets agreed to take a message from me to Dick Bean at the Kremlin gate. The message was to designate wire-service reporters and photographers who would cover the same events the Soviets were covering within the Kremlin.

Four shocked newsmen found themselves summoned through the Kremlin gates by the KGB officials. They were Ernie Barcella and Frank Cancellere of United Press International and John Scali and Henry Griffin of the Associated Press. They were ushered into the offices to take pictures of each protocol greeting and observe the first two or three minutes of the meetings.

The Soviets had tried to test and trick us, but they had responded to the challenge and had admitted the newsmen. I learned a lesson. To me it was also a test of faith with the American reporters and photographers because I had assured them they would have at least the same rights of access as the Russians.

What neither I nor the reporters knew about was what happened after there had been polite public greetings between Nixon and Premier Nikita Khrushchev, whom Nixon met after routine earlier calls on the three other top U.S.S.R. officials, Voroshilov, Mikoyan, and Kozlov. As we left the rectangular oak-walled office with its long table covered with green felt, Khrushchev immediately went on the offensive and, in the most vulgar language, expressed his anger over the fact that Congress had passed what it thought was a routine Captive Nations Resolution opposing Soviet control over its bloc in Eastern Europe. The angry one-hour meeting, which had been punctuated by Khrushchev's epithets, was followed by a surprise Khrushchev declaration that he would like to join Nixon for a tour of the American exhibit prior to a special lunch he was giving for us in the Kremlin.

The preopening tour of the large American exhibit area took on circus tones as the Vice-President of the United States and the leader of the Communist world strolled through the grounds accompanied by interpreters, intermixed KGB and Secret Service and a group of almost two hundred newsmen. Veteran New York *Times* reporter Harrison Salisbury seemed never to be more than two feet from the lead, with broadcaster Edward Morgan not far behind.

Long before we had flown to Moscow, representatives of Ampex and RCA had called upon me in Washington two or three times to urge that Nixon and Khrushchev pay a visit to their studio, where the relatively new process of videotape was to be demonstrated. The idea was that the two leaders would appear before the cameras briefly and then be shown immediately how their conversation had appeared on videotape. This was not only unique in the United States but unheard of in the U.S.S.R.

It was in this studio, in a central part of the American exhibit, where Khrushchev, to everyone's surprise, started a public denunciation of Nixon, the United States, and the Captive Nations Resolution, before the audience of reporters from all over the world and a few Soviet workmen. All was recorded on Ampex videotape. The exchange was climaxed when Nixon, after listening politely—for too long, I thought—poked his finger in Khrushchev's chest and said, "You must not be afraid of ideas. After all, you don't know everything." As we left the studio I knew instinctively that the story of the first full day in Moscow would be the debate, not the speeches both men would give during the opening ceremonies later in the afternoon.

We wandered through the grounds looking for interesting exhibits, and during a moment of pause, I caught up with Nixon to tell him that I thought he had let Khrushchev get the better of him during the television-studio exchange and to suggest that he forget some of the politeness if there were another such discussion. I could see the headline: "Khrushchev Lectures Nixon."

Unbeknown to me, Bill Safire, whom at that time I had never heard of, was in Moscow to publicize an exhibit of an average fourteen-thousand-dollar American home, which was a key part of the fair. The home had been built in two parts, with one side showing furnished bedrooms and bathrooms and the other side containing the living room, dining area, and kitchen. A corridor about twenty feet wide separated the two sides. Safire ingeniously removed a small fence in between a Pepsi-Cola stand and the house figuring that Nixon might stop at the Pepsi stand because one of his closest personal friends, Don Kendall, headed Pepsi-Cola.

By accident, not design, we wandered into the Pepsi area and then past the fence Safire had removed to the house, where Safire was presiding. As the two leaders and the reporters crowded into the house, Nixon began to explain to Khrushchev the workings of some of the American appliances, although the Vice-President was far from an expert on the operations of a washing machine or an oven or anything domestic. It was at this point that Khrushchev launched into another attack on American policy, and as the two men stood before the American kitchen, they engaged in the most free-swinging policy debate ever heard in public between two major world leaders. They covered everything from missile bases to foreign policy as reporters scrambled and strained to hear the animated conversation. At the start, I stood outside the house unaware of the debate, trying to figure where to move the group next. When it became evident that something was going on within the house, I tried to work my way into the crowd and found the only open area was in the kitchen standing next to a man who turned out to be Bill Safire.

The Kitchen Debate became the story, and it was evident that in this atmosphere, Nixon came across with dignity but with strength and fire which matched or exceeded that of Khrushchev. That was the news story of the opening of the fair, which had been ingeniously assembled by Harold C. "Chad" McClellan. This clearly was a major international and political triumph for the Vice-President, who displayed his debating skills at their best and in a contest where most of the reporters, despite any political feelings, were clearly on his side. It was one of Nixon's finest performances, and it represents an unduplicated moment in history. Among those who later whispered a commendation to the Vice-President was the Soviet minister Mikoyan.

The day included a lavish private lunch in the Kremlin for the senior members of the Nixon party and the top Soviet leaders, the formal opening ceremonies, and later a dinner at Spaso House, the residence of Ambassador Llewellyn Thompson. The elaborate lunch, which immediately followed the debate was the most unusual of the afternoon events. At one point during the "capitalist-style" lunch beneath gold chandeliers in the Kremlin, I was asked outside for a few moments and found myself at the top of a Kremlin staircase kneeling over a chart laid on the longest strand of red-carpeted rug I had ever seen. I joined three KGB agents and Jack Sherwood of the Secret Service going over diagrams of areas we would cover during the afternoon. When I paused briefly to look at the circumstances I had an eerie feeling. Here I was, deep in the Kremlin working on a security plan with KGB agents, and inside the luncheon room designed beautifully for the tsars, Nixon was being entertained by Communist leaders. But the most interesting factor was that after the morning debates within the Kremlin and at the American exhibit, Khrushchev changed his attitude and, with only a few exceptions, seemed to have a new and friendly personal attitude toward Nixon. At the leisurely Kremlin lunch Khrushchev hosted, the Premier was polite and jovial with

Anastas Mikoyan serving as the straight man for Khrushchev's jokes. Later in the afternoon, one last occasion before we left the fairgrounds after the formal opening ceremonies: Khrushchev and Nixon paused at a table with California champagne on it, and speaking in Russian, the Premier slyly proposed a toast to the end of American missile bases. Milton Eisenhower started to sip the drink and thus accept the toast, but Nixon waited for the translation and countered with a toast to peace and friendship.

The story of the Kitchen Debate was reported everywhere outside the Soviet sphere of influence with long stories and major headlines. Thus, the American people read about it and heard about it through newspaper reports long before they saw the videotape of what had taken place in the studio. In a way, this preconditioned the public for what it was soon to see on television, and, while most Americans thought the videotape was the Kitchen Debate, it actually was the preliminary bout, the studio discussion. With the speed of modern television techniques, the situation is unlikely to be duplicated. But there was a delay of several days between when the public read the account of the Kitchen Debate in the newspapers and when it saw the videotape of the studio debate on television. Thus the conditioning from the news stories and editorial comments helped the weaker studio videotape make Nixon look stronger than he actually was. Where he was outstandingly strong was in the kitchen scene, not in the RCA studio.

Following the American exhibit ceremonies and after that evening's dinner in the Spaso House, I met with my Soviet counterparts and we reached an agreement wherein they would show the videotape simultaneously with the release date within the United States. The negotiations were easy and I was elated. While I thought Khrushchev had done better than Nixon in the unscheduled TV program, I felt that it was to the benefit of the United States to show an American leader standing up to the Soviet Premier, even though Nixon's statement mainly said "you don't know everything." In the Soviet citizens' eyes, Nixon would come across strong because the Russians had not seen anything like that before.

The next morning, July 26, the Vice-President's party was escorted to a park where the Soviets had a permanent exhibit. It was at a time when the Soviets and the People's Republic of China were having a great love affair and the nationality group most apparent and most pampered at the exhibit and throughout Moscow was Chinese.

Shortly after we had arrived at the exhibit, I was intercepted by two officers of the Foreign Ministry who said it was imperative that I accompany them to the ministry immediately. Again, leaving Dick Bean in charge, Dick Davis and I left the party to answer the summons. I had no idea what this was about.

At the Foreign Ministry we were ushered into what resembled a courtroom. We sat at a green-felt table five feet beneath what appeared to be a towering judge's bench. One of the foreign ministry officials took his place in the "judge's" seat and the press officers and interpreters sat at tables adjacent to mine.

With Dick Davis interpreting for me, I learned that I had been summoned to "clarify" instructions for the traveling press when we were to leave Moscow for the remainder of the trip through the U.S.S.R.

While I listened and made a few notes the Soviet spokesman outlined a complete set of instructions which in effect negated all of the agreements I had negotiated while in the United States. The scene became so mixed up that Davis and the Soviet interpreter frequently would argue over the translation of the new instructions being given to me. Basically, I concluded the Soviets had decided that after reading the stories from the press entourage, they would allow only twelve newsmen to accompany the Vice-President beyond Moscow. I had been promised that all American newsmen and some foreign press would accompany us. They had come to Moscow with that expectation and pledge. Censorship would be reimposed on both writing and photography. The Soviets said that the traveling party would fly only in Soviet aircraft. That was all right because we had previously agreed to this. Radio broadcast transmission would be limited, and the reporters would not be able to accompany the Vice-President on some parts of his trip.

When the Foreign Ministry official had finished reading his detailed instructions, he said I now could return to the Nixon party. I sat quietly and said that I would reply before I departed. This seemed to surprise them as they expected me to return to consult with Nixon, Thompson, and others.

With Davis interpreting slowly and precisely, I said that I would not accept their terms. "I can only think that a mistake has been made because this is a violation of all the agreements surrounding the trip of the Vice-President," I said. "If your government holds to these terms, I have no choice but to denounce the Soviet Union as a nation which lies, and the principal story of the two hundred newsmen covering this trip will be about a direct violation of an agreement with the United States regarding the press. It will make your word a mockery," I said. Finally, I concluded with a comment which later shocked even me.

"I will give you exactly four hours to correct this mistake. If that is not done, I will recommend that the Vice-President report your activities to Premier Khrushchev, and then that he leave this country immediately as symbolic of a world protest of this violation of the Soviet word to the press."

With that I stood up and grabbed Davis as he finished the interpretation and walked to our car, leaving behind the Soviets, who seemed stunned by my unorthodox behavior.

Once I was in the car I confessed to Davis that now I was scared. I had no training for this sort of thing and perhaps I had committed a major breach in relations. I was prepared to leave the country by myself if that were necessary. What right did I have to commit the Vice-President of the United States? I wondered.

When we caught up with our American party at the exhibit, there was no chance to talk to Nixon. He was surrounded by Soviet officials who were explaining the various exhibits. I pulled the ambassador, Tommy Thompson, aside and whispered to him what I had done. "I may have you in terrible trouble," I said. Thompson flashed a smile I never will forget and said, "God, Herb, that's great. I wish I could tell them off exactly the same way, but I have to stay here."

I was relieved, to say the least.

During a ceremonial lunch which followed on the fairgrounds, I finally was able to pull Nixon aside briefly and repeat the story, including Thompson's comment. Nixon looked surprised but quickly said I had done the right thing. He would stand by me in this confrontation.

A few minutes later, George Allen, the USIA director, found me to casually tell me he had agreed with the Russians on a change in my plan for the release of the Nixon-Khrushchev videotape. He said the USIA would handle the matter and he had told the Soviets they could show it any time they chose, and we would hold off releasing our copy until after they had run it on U.S.S.R. television. My agreement had been that we would run the tape in each country on the same day and that this would be accomplished without delay after we left the country. Then, seemingly without much thought, Allen said that he felt we had too many newsmen and they sometimes were in the way. He had expressed this idea to the Soviets.

I was too angry to say anything. What a disaster, I thought.

I left the lunch early to return to the hotel for the briefing I had scheduled and which corresponded with my deadline of four hours for the Soviets. As we opened the briefing Scotty Reston of the New York *Times* said he had lunched with Soviet Cultural Minister Zhukov and had been told that only twelve correspondents would be allowed to go beyond Moscow.

The Secret Service earlier had informed me that the briefing room, like my own hotel room, was bugged by the Soviets and so I worded my reply with knowledge that they were listening. I told Reston that there had been discussions of a change of the rules, but that I needed the support of the press corps not to discuss the matter in any fashion or to write of it for a few hours until I could give them a clearer answer. Reston and the other veteran newsmen (such as Richard Wilson of Cowles, Alan Otten, *Wall Street Journal*, Peter Lisagor of the Chicago *Daily News*, Hearst's Bob Considine) accepted my plea without dissent and went on to other questions regarding the vice-presidential trip. They understood the bugging. It was a perfect example of full press cooperation at a delicate international moment when unknowingly they were being used as pawns by the Soviets. If Zhukov's story was correct, they would write it big, but they could wait.

The Soviets apparently had heard enough of the tapes and before the briefing was completed two of them marched up to the microphone and said I had to go to the Foreign Ministry immediately. While the reporters watched and wondered, I said I would finish the briefing and then join them. Deliberately I took ten minutes more of questioning before I said, "I'll take one more question."

Davis and I were ushered back to the same "courtroom" in the Foreign Ministry, but this time there was a different, seemingly more senior, official presiding. Even the atmosphere was different.

Quickly the official explained that someone had made a "horrible mistake" and that there had been no intention of limiting the number of newsmen or of censoring the writers. The newsmen would accompany the Vice-President wherever he went. I agreed not to discuss the "mistake" with the reporters and I did not. One thing I did not foresee. The official had mentioned only writers, not photographers, whom I incorrectly assumed were included in the pledge not to censor. That became a later problem at Leningrad.

At my next briefing, I explained to Reston and the other reporters that there had been a misunderstanding which had been cleared up, and it would be in all of our interests if I did not discuss it further. They accepted the explanation as I announced when we would leave Moscow for Leningrad.

At the same time, unbeknown to me, the videotape of the Khrushchev-Nixon debate in the RCA studio was being smuggled out aboard a Russian Aeroflot flight by the representative of the Ampex Corporation.

The first word I received that the tape was about to be broadcast by CBS came from an enterprising reporter who then worked for CBS in Chicago, Sam Jaffe. The FBI, in 1979, accused Jaffe of being an agent of a foreign intelligence. He represented ABC in Moscow in the sixties. Somehow Jaffe, who I know as a tough, capable, and likable reporter, got a line through from Chicago to Spaso House, where I was attending a dinner party with the Russians. He told me by phone that the program would be played on CBS Television that night. He wanted a comment. My first instinct in view of our agreements was to explain to the Soviets what had happened. By this time, they were having after-dinner drinks. I wanted their assurance that they still would show the tape on Soviet TV. By this time they seemed mellow and they agreed to keep our bargain. At my first opportunity, I left the party to find Dick Bean and see if we could round up Paul Niven, the CBS reporter covering the trip. A fun-loving but tough and straight-shooting reporter, Niven had covered most of the world. He was a personal friend for whom I had the greatest respect. We did not find him, but about an hour later, Niven found me as he returned to the hotel after having a few drinks with some of the newsmen. I explained the negotiations and the delicacy of the situation to Paul, saying that I was in no way sure a new agreement I had reached earlier in the evening at the dinner party would hold if there was widespread early comment in the United States on the tape. Early release might give the U.S.S.R. an opportunity to cancel its showing. We went to Paul's room and he called the CBS president, Dr. Frank Stanton, whom I had not met at that time. When we finally reached Stanton in New York he explained that the "debate" was about to go on the air and that it had been heavily promoted. With that, the Soviet operator cut the connection, and I had no opportunity to make my case to Stanton against the showing. As an aside, I wondered why an RCA studio tape had been given first to CBS. The operator reconnected us with Stanton an hour later, after the tape had been shown. The reaction of the American public, conditioned by the earlier news stories, was overwhelmingly enthusiastic. After we left Russia, the Soviets played their copy of the tape on television, our embassy told me, but I was never able to learn from them what hour it played or on how many stations.

After the initial confrontations between Nixon and Khrushchev, the Soviets treated the American Vice-President with thoughtful respect, although he still felt some irritants from coached hecklers in every city we visited. Khrushchev unexpectedly invited the Vice-President to spend a night at his beautiful riverside dacha and then joined the Nixons the next day for a lengthy social lunch and thoughtful substantive conversations in a wooded outdoor setting. I arranged to have one reporter and one photographer taken to the dacha, about an hour from our hotel, for the preliminary social greetings between the Nixon staff and the Soviet hierarchy. By draw the pool reporter was Ernest Barcella of the United Press and the photographer was Henry Griffin of the Associated Press.

When I arrived at the dacha with Barcella and Griffin, we found Nixon and Khrushchev strolling in the morning sun alongside the Moscow River admiring the view. Not far away was a shy Soviet newsman and photographer already waiting.

Throughout the trip, Nixon took pride in introducing Khrushchev to American newsmen. During the day at the fair, he had randomly introduced several, including William Randolph Hearst, Jr., and Westbrook

Pegler. It was like flaunting American anti-Communist press prestige to Khrushchev, who appeared to have no concept of even a relatively free press, although his Foreign Ministry was providing him with a summary of U.S. press comment.

As Khrushchev and Nixon began to walk down a long winding gravel path to greet other Soviet leaders arriving at the dacha, Barcella stood close by taking notes on every part of the conversation. At one point Khrushchev looked at one of his colleagues, Anastas Mikoyan, and with a loud laugh, said, "He beats his wife." Barcella wrote this down with a note that this was a joke. Khrushchev turned to Barcella and said, "You take too many notes." Barcella replied, "I am accurate." When the social greetings were completed, the party assembled for a group picture with me, an amateur, serving as one of the photographers (the picture became a cover for *Life* magazine). I asked Khrushchev and Nixon how they wanted to summarize the informal morning for the press. Khrushchev seemed puzzled at this but agreed to a Nixon suggestion that the notes of the two correspondents would serve as the communiqué, and that I would certify its accuracy. Barcella and I then took aside the Soviet correspondent, who had made almost no notes. He was not there to gather the facts. Slowly we helped fill in his notes to match ours. When we came to the Khrushchev joke with Mikoyan about wife-beating, the Tass man turned white. "Do we have to include that?" he asked through an interpreter. "Mr. Khrushchev and Mr. Nixon said we should be accurate," we replied.

The printed U.S. version included the joke and labeled it as such. The Tass account did not mention the informal moment.

When we left Moscow a few days later and went to Leningrad, we ran into new incidents involving the press but none as serious as we were to encounter later on that trip. In Leningrad, our offensive confrontation with our hosts was led by Admiral Hyman Rickover. We had been invited for our first view of a Soviet nuclear-powered icebreaker. We had a pool arrangement for the press because of the size of the ship. Reporters took turns going between the dock and the icebreaker.

After listening politely to the routine Soviet explanations of the ship, Rickover said he now would like to see the reactor area. The Soviets conferred and then replied that the area was locked and the man with the key was not on board the ship. Rickover countered that their officers' mess was comfortable and we would be happy to wait until they located him. The admiral and the Vice-President outwaited the Soviets and after several champagne toasts, they finally turned up with the key. Rickover, in typical tough fashion, prevailed.

When it was over, I found Rickover anxious to explain his observations to the press. My problem was to limit his briefing time to the half hour reporters wanted, and to get him to explain in popular words terms which were unfamiliar to all of us. But there was no question Rickover had made quite an achievement in seeing the reactor. That was more significant than his public words regarding the atomic icebreaker.

We had one last confrontation with Soviet leadership before leaving beautiful Leningrad. As we arrived at the airfield to fly to Novosibirsk in Siberia, excited American photographers came up to me and said that their pictures were being held up for censorship. I found that Fran Kozlov, former mayor of Leningrad, who had become a top Soviet official with some understanding of the United States, was not going with us beyond his city. I told him I had the personal word of their government that photographs would not be held up or censored and that it was his responsibility to relieve the bottleneck of photo censorship and avoid embarrassment for Khrushchev. As the door was about to close on the airplane, he agreed. The pictures were released.

That was our last bout with censorship during the trip. It was our last major behind-the-scenes problem.

During the trip from Leningrad to Novosibirsk the Nixon staff, Soviet officials, the KGB, and the Secret Service were on a Soviet plane separate from the news corps. On the official plane, the Russians followed their custom of hanging newspapers in front of them; they were held up by clothespins attached to the overhead coat racks. This gave added privacy in each seat. My seatmate, who was a U. S. Air Force officer traveling with the staff on the Soviet aircraft, seized the opportunity to photograph possible missile or antiaircraft sites, military bases, and the landscape during the lengthy flight into Siberia. The officer knew what he was looking for. Aboard the Soviet airplane, within a few feet of the KGB and other high-ranking officials, he took significant pictures from the airplane window, providing information the United States had not had before, in this era prior to satellite photography. I stood nervously in the aisle when he would nudge me, watching the Soviets to be certain they were unaware of the photo intelligence activity taking place during the goodwill mission on their own airplane.

This was one of the very few things the Soviets let slip by. In Novosibirsk, Siberia, Dick Bean took the press corps into town during the evening to join the Vice-President and Mrs. Nixon enjoying a ballet. I was disturbed by the fact that during the afternoon the Soviet police had driven so recklessly they had hit a Russian woman's car and had deliberately blocked out the press corps autos from the vice-presidential motorcade. I skipped the ballet to confer on this with Don Hughes at the government residence where the Nixons were housed.

We were the only Americans present in the spacious U.S.S.R. guesthouse as we sat down in the large dining room for a dinner featuring fish-

head soup. Hughes left me for a moment to go upstairs to the Nixon headquarters and returned down with a mysterious, wide-eyed look on his face.
Knowing we were bugged, we left the table briefly and walked outside,
where he whispered, "Don't ask me why, but when I jump up from the
table, follow me closely and quickly."

We went back to dinner and then a few minutes later he jumped up
from the table and I followed. We ran up the broad staircase only to be
confronted by six Soviet workers with mops and brooms. They blocked us
temporarily while we could hear frantic scrambling in the Nixon bedroom. We broke loose and entered the room to find that the briefcase had
been moved from where Hughes had left it. The Soviets obviously had
been examining the Nixon papers and had detained us long enough to allow those in the bedroom to escape. We did not mention the incident publicly because of the peace mission and because long before, precautions
had been taken to leave nothing of security value out of the eyesight of the
Secret Service. The briefcase contents meant little.

It is the only instance of which I am aware where there was a direct
effort to search the personal property of an American official of this high
rank. In 1972 during the SALT talks when Nixon was quartered within
the Kremlin, no one doubted the presence of bugs. We found them even
in our hotel. But there were no known physical searches.

As we moved across the U.S.S.R. in 1959 we found the local citizenry
increasingly warm both to the Vice-President and to the press. The farther
we were from Moscow the more cordial the reception. But each step of the
way, my Soviet counterparts carried on a campaign of petty harassment
designed to annoy not only Nixon but the press and to undercut me.

The Soviets had strange ways of dealing with us. During one day we
were driven over rough roads outside Sverdlovsk to a small mining village.
En route we crossed the border marking the separation of Europe and
Asia. As we reached the symbolic line, gypsies appeared alongside the highway and stopped the motorcade to serve champagne. Obviously, the ceremony was well planned by the Soviets. In the village two hours later,
Zhukov, our host for the day, took the occasion of a toast at lunch to
denounce the American broadcast networks for unfair treatment to the
U.S.S.R. We had no idea what he was talking about and Nixon responded
with a toast of praise for freedom in the news coverage. It later turned out
that the Soviets were offended by a broadcaster's speech in the United
States. After the lunch, I borrowed an interpreter from the Russians and
engaged some of the workers in simple conversation about families and
homes. The talk started off in a friendly fashion, but soon the Russians
seemed to be getting angry. Dick Davis appeared to assist me and explained that the interpreter was ignoring what I was actually saying and
interpreting me as making provocative remarks to the Soviet mineworkers.

I went by myself to a nearby village general store to buy Russian dolls for my two daughters and there the local people again were extremely friendly, eagerly seeking to help me with the purchases.

By the time we returned to Sverdlovsk, I had decided it was time for me to take the initiative and I quietly announced to the news corps that this was a time for *mir i druzhba,* peace and friendship. But it was not to be.

When we arrived at the Sverdlovsk hotel we arranged a dinner party for the press corps and for our Soviet hosts. It was to be an evening of fun, with some of the newsmen even borrowing instruments from Soviet musicians to make up our own dance band. Columnist Ralph de Toledano was the leader. Pat and Mary Monroe and Austin Kiplinger helped host the party.

I had just made a telephone call routed through London to my wife when I found ABC's John Charles Daly pounding furiously on my door in the hotel. We had made special arrangements through Moscow for radio lines which would allow each of the correspondents to broadcast directly to the United States with high voice quality. When Daly and his colleagues, Paul Niven and Ray Scherer of NBC, had attempted to arrange time for their broadcasts, the Soviets had told them the lines were not available that day. Daly, Niven, Scherer, and I confronted my Soviet counterparts, headed by Minister Vladimir Popov, and demanded that the Russians hold to their broadcast agreement. At one point the argument became so heated that I had to physically restrain Daly from punching Popov. But the Russians held firm. They apparently feared negative broadcasts. The frustrated broadcast correspondents went to their rooms and placed the same type of call I had made to my wife. This was done by calling from your room and ordering the call on a time schedule. When the connection was made, you were summoned to the hotel desk to make an advance payment, and then you rushed upstairs to pick up the phone in your room. On that particular day these regular phone circuits were so clear that each of the correspondents had no trouble making the call and broadcasting from his room. It was a minor triumph over Soviet bureaucracy.

We had barely started our *mir i druzhba* dinner party when Nat Finney, veteran correspondent from the Buffalo *Evening News,* rushed into the ballroom and said that he and Niven had been routed out of their rooms and ordered to appear before the hotel manager to answer charges that they had dropped fruit and pennies from their rooms to attract Soviet children into the patio below and photograph them scrambling for the capitalist gifts. He and Niven had refused to appear without me being present. While our band played and our *mir i druzhba* party began, I accompanied Finney and Niven into a small but theatrically lighted conference room. At the table in front of us was a woman who claimed to be the hotel manager. To me she looked like a character actress. She proceeded as if she were presiding over a trial with the threat being that Niven and Finney would be denied any further press privileges in the Soviet Union because of charges which she said had been brought by parents of the children who had been abused by these "capitalistic acts."

We listened to the charges, and I cautioned Niven and Finney to allow me to handle the situation while they remained silent. I knew that neither man would do such a thing as they were accused of. Niven did not even have a camera with him. Finney had no film. When the woman recited the fake charges, I stood up and with our interpreter said that we knew the charges were false, and that they were intended to discredit the public tour the newsmen would be taking of Sverdlovsk the next day, by providing a story or an important letter to the editor denouncing the U.S. press corps. I said that we knew without question that the charges were fabricated. "I can only tell you," I said, "that if these false charges are made public, I have your name and position, and when the Vice-President of the United States speaks on Soviet radio and television from Moscow, he will personally expose you as a liar and as someone working against the interest Mr. Khrushchev has expressed in friendship between our two countries." With that we left abruptly and rejoined the *mir i druzhba* party. A few minutes later, Popov asked me to join him in his suite where he expressed apologies for the "terrible injustice" by some local functionaries. He then accompanied me to the party just as de Toledano and band were beating out a Dixieland jazz tune. The Soviets printed nothing.

Our press and government battle with the Soviets ended on a frantic but more friendly note in Moscow. By the time we arrived back in Moscow, Nixon had less than twenty-four hours to prepare for an unprecedented (and still unduplicated) one-hour television and radio broadcast to the Soviet people. (Nixon also addressed a Soviet television audience in 1972 but in a shorter speech.) This was a major opportunity which Nixon had negotiated for prior to his departure from Washington. It was an American speaking directly to the Soviet people without any of the severe restrictions imposed through Tass or any Soviet publications or agencies. Nixon spent a night and a day working in Moscow with Ambassador Thompson, Foy Kohler from the State Department, his secretary, Rose Woods, and occasionally with Milton Eisenhower on the content of this address aimed directly at the average Soviet citizen. Nixon placed great trust in the knowledge and judgment of Thompson and Kohler.

During the flight back from Sverdlovsk to Moscow, I convinced my long time friend John Daly to forgo activity as an ABC correspondent for one day and to work with me on the facilities for this historic broadcast. By this time, the press was so involved in the national aspects of the trip that most would have helped me. Daly was ideal because of his experience in all of the technical aspects of broadcasting and because of our long personal friendship, which made working together easy. In Moscow I went to the U.S. embassy early on the morning of the broadcast to find what our officials knew about the technical aspects of the show. We had no advance men or TV specialists. As I walked into the lobby, I was almost run over by Thompson, who had just received a call that Khrushchev had arrived unannounced at the airport and marched aboard the TWA 707 which had been flown to Moscow to take the press aboard for the trip home. Thompson rushed to the airport and I called Dick Bean at the hotel to find a bus and take the press to the plane to record the surprise visit. Khrushchev was interesting himself in the furnishings aboard a U.S. commercial jet.

Daly and I found that the embassy had little knowledge of what would happen in the Nixon telecast and drove to the television station to meet the Soviet manager, whose name struck me curiously as a tsarist throwback. It was Romanov. In the small pioneerlike studio we worked with Romanov on staging. Daly wrote six TV promos to appear on air prior to Nixon's address, and we arranged a crude set mainly with Nixon and his interpreter sitting at a plain table. The studio had only three cameras, and we employed them all. All were old by our standards. Nixon worked so hard and long on the speech that the interpreter, Akalovsky, received it for translation only an hour or so before the broadcast. When Nixon arrived at the studio he went into Romanov's office, where Daly applied another of his skills and covered the Vice-President's beard with basic powder makeup. (Powder makeup also was what Nixon was wearing when he engaged in his first debate with John Kennedy, but in the Soviet Union a dark beard was probably natural to the viewers.)

The broadcast was most successful, although Daly and I almost had nervous breakdowns as first one camera went out and then the second. The third held up for the conclusion of the historic prime-time discussion with the Soviet people. Television sets were rare and so families with sets gathered in hordes to watch with relatives. The program was aired right after a prime-time comedy show. In several cases the viewing Soviet families were joined by American reporters, who recorded Soviet reactions as highly favorable.

When the broadcast was finished, it was the Soviet staff's time for *mir i druzhba*, and they had arranged a lavish buffet for the press and our small staff at one of their leading restaurants. About an hour into the party, Popov invited me to join him for supper in one of the private rooms adjoining the main dining room. By this time I was concerned enough with Soviet tricks to have Bean follow me and pace and patrol outside the window of the room in which we met. The precaution was unnecessary as we drank vodka and supped on cold cuts while for the first time in the trip talking informally with no political points to make.

The trip to the Soviet Union turned out to be a major plus for Nixon in his eventual 1960 quest for the presidency. But it also brought in a new era of more exchanges between the Soviet Union and the United States, both in exhibits and in personal visits such as that by Khrushchev in 1960, and it illustrated the vital role the newsmen play not only in American eyes but in the view of other major countries.

As we left the Soviet Union there was to be one other major visit by the Vice-President, a stop in Poland. The brief stay in Warsaw also was to be symbolic, giving some subtle support to the Polish cardinal and his Catholic church, which was standing up to the Communists. We were expressing American friendship for the Polish people.

We had read of Khrushchev's visit to Warsaw three weeks earlier and knew that the government had been embarrassed because it could turn out only small, unenthusiastic crowds of welcome. Upon our arrival at Babica Airport, there again was a small official reception, "polite and cool" about like that in Moscow. Nearby we could see Polish troops goose-stepping as they prepared for a quick, official review. We had been told that the Poles had not publicized our arrival, and I prepared the press corps to expect no crowds, particularly since it was a Sunday, not a working day. What we did not know was that Radio Free Europe had announced the Nixon arrival and route in numerous broadcasts heard by the Poles.

As we left the airfield, a few of the soldiers broke ranks to wave enthusiastically, and as we approached the suburbs of Warsaw, we suddenly were overwhelmed by thousands of families who had lined the route and brought flowers from their gardens to throw into the Nixon car and even into the press vehicles which followed in the emotioal motorcade. *"Niech zyje American,"* *"Niech zyje Nixon"* and *"Niech zyje Eisenhower"* became cries one could hear from blocks away—Long live America, Nixon, and Eisenhower. It was easily the warmest, most spontaneous, and emotional reception I have encountered at any time in my political life. It was the Polish way of expressing friendship for America and its people and disdain for the Russians.

Working with the Polish officials was at least as difficult as it had been working with the Soviets. Their Communist leader, Wladislaw Gomulka, was unpredictable and tough, and he conceded nothing for the press. But the newsmen already had their story, the gigantic welcome, and each day, whether we were visiting the Tomb of the Unknown Soldier or a cathedral or ghetto, we would hear the highly emotional Polish song, "Sto Lat" ("May You Live 1000 Years"). The problem was to keep the appearances brief so there could be no danger of a riot against the Communists, a riot which inevitably would have meant death to many of the unarmed people.

Admiral Rickover was a hero in his own right in Warsaw, and Nixon took pride in introducing him everywhere as a man born in the Warsaw area who like many other Poles was a major figure in America.

The Polish welcome, written about warmly by the news corps, which too got caught up in pride of country in such a warm scene, again translated at home as a major political asset for Nixon as he approached a 1960 campaign with John Kennedy as the possible opponent.

When I returned with Nixon to Warsaw, he was able to accomplish far more as President than he had as Vice-President. But the warm spontaneous spark of 1959 was never quite duplicated.

Foreign trips were a major part of Nixon's career as a congressman, a senator, Vice-President and eventually President. The friendly mobs in Manila and the unfriendly mobs in Caracas helped shape the public attitude toward the man. In later years some of President Kennedy's most historic successes were his visit to the Berlin Wall and to Mexico City, and his first conspicuous failure was his early summit conference with Khrushchev. The pattern of media-oriented foreign trips was followed by Presidents Johnson, Ford, and Carter.

The press has had a key role in almost every recent major meeting between U.S. and foreign leaders, including the Kissinger shuttle diplomacy, but the role has not been quite so much a part of the action as in the Kitchen Debate journey.

When one is involved in White House press activity, newsmen figure in any major trip one makes whether or not they are present at the moment. Even Kissinger's secret meetings with North Vietnam and the Chinese eventually had to be recounted to reporters.

On a mission in 1970 which was aimed at generating support for the President's decision to send troops into Cambodia, I suddenly found myself in a position where I had to hide from the newsmen for several hours.

Bryce Harlow and I had been designated to take a group of eight congressmen and senators and four governors on an inspection trip to South Vietnam and into the incursion areas of Cambodia. I served as the spokesman for the group—not the easiest task with ten elected officials representing both political parties, Governors John Love, Raymond Shafer, and Robert McNair; Senators Howard Cannon, George Murphy, and John Tower; and Representatives William Bray, O. C. Fisher, Melvin Price, and William Whitehurst—and the activities of the group were thoroughly covered by the news media from the moment we landed in Saigon aboard Air Force Two and including television shots of the group landing by helicopter on a small hilltop occupied by our artillery within the Cambodian battle area. At another point we landed in a small Cambodian village, Konpong Trach, where boys and girls about fifteen years old were being trained in the manual of arms. Some were using broomsticks as weapons and most wore crude sandals or worn tennis shoes.

On the night before we were to depart Saigon, I received a call from General Al Haig in the White House suggesting that I fly to Phnom Penh early the next morning and meet with the Cambodian President, Lon Nol. I told Haig I had to decline because we were leaving Saigon at noon the next day, and we had a meeting scheduled during the morning with Premier Nguyen Van Thieu. Haig said Harlow and the other could meet with Thieu, but that "Searchlight" (the President) wanted me to have a personal meeting with Lon Nol representing the President in the discussion. Using the embassy backwire, Haig sent me instructions on what I was to say to Lon Nol, and he arranged a small Air Force Jetstar to fly me to Phnom Penh and return early the next morning. I decided I wanted one representative of the group of elected officials to accompany me as a witness, so I awakened Governor Raymond Shafer of Pennsylvania, who previously had requested several times that we go to the Cambodian capital. I was to say to any press I might meet I was going at Shafer's request.

With a time-zone change between Saigon and Phnom Penh we arrived in Cambodia about 6 A.M. and were greeted by a puzzled embassy chargé d'affaires, Mike Riyes, and his aide. An ambassador had not yet been appointed to represent the United States in Cambodia with Lon Nol and the embassy limousine was a Checker cab which had been painted black. The chargé was at least as surprised as was I at the suddenness of the mission, and I tried to explain to him the real purpose for the meeting (to encourage Lon Nol) as we circled through the beautiful city in the cool of the early-morning hour. We drove to the embassy, where I was briefed more thoroughly on the Cambodian government as we waited what was considered an appropriate hour to make an appointment for me and Shafer with Lon Nol. The Cambodian President was not an early riser and was testy if called before nine. While Shafer and I waited inside the residence, local newsmen representing U.S. and other news services began checking into the small embassy offices to discuss any new developments in the war with the senior military aide, Colonel Peach, and others. As we hid in the embassy living room we could see the reporters walking down the driveway just a few feet away from us. I wondered how long it would take the newsmen to discover the small U. S. Air Force Jetstar at the airfield, a field which had been hit heavily by enemy artillery only a day or so before our arrival. Enemy patrols were reported ten miles away. Young Air Force policemen were guarding our military jet, but they would be of little help if there was an accurate artillery attack.

Shafer and I managed to escape the newsmen unnoticed and were

driven in the embassy Checker cab to Lon Nol's quarters, where we and
Riyes met with the Cambodian leader for more than an hour. Riyes interpreted Lon Nol's French for us. Shafer joined me for the first thirty
minutes or so and then, privately, I detailed to Lon Nol the President's assurance of full support as had been outlined to me in the radio messages I
had received only hours before. I was searching for a small goodwill gift
and so I gave Lon Nol a presidential fountain pen which I told him was a
gift from Nixon in the hope that he would use it eventually to sign a victory proclamation. Lon Nol appeared to me to be dedicated to his cause.
But he struck me as being unprepared for his role as a new world figure
leading a country engulfed in war.

We returned quickly to the Jetstar and rejoined our party in Saigon in
time to brief the commanding general, Creighton Abrams, and Ambassador Ellsworth Bunker, on the Phnom Penh mission prior to departing on
schedule for Washington. I gave further details to the President and to
the joint leaders of Congress before holding a public news conference in
Chicago all within a span of less than forty-eight hours.

My final visit to Vietnam was on February 14, 1973. William H. Sullivan, then deputy assistant secretary of state, and I had been designated by
the President to join Dr. Henry Kissinger and his staff on a trip which
was to take us to Thailand, Laos, Hanoi, Hongkong, Peking, and Tokyo
to discuss with officials in each area the relations between the United
States and their country in the light of the cease-fire Kissinger and Nixon
had just negotiated with Le Duc Tho, the special representative for the
North Vietnamese. During our four day stay in Hanoi, in which Kissinger
led the negotiations with Premier Pham Van Dong, Vice-Premier Nguyen
Duy Trinh, and Le Duc Tho, Sullivan, Kissinger, and I were guests in a
French palace surrounded by formal gardens, a building which once had
been the residence of Ho Chi Minh. Across the street in a hotel were a
few reporters who were on the scene to cover the release of the first American prisoners of war. To my amazement, none of the newsmen made an
effort to inquire of us what was happening in the postwar negotiations.

We arrived in North Vietnam aboard Air Force Two, landing at a military airfield several miles out of town. It was apparent that the field had
been badly damaged by U.S. bombers but some temporary, freshly painted
buildings had been installed to house our Air Force crewmen, who were
determined not to leave the plane during our stay there. Le Duc Tho
ushered us immediately to a smaller, Soviet-manufactured propjet aircraft
which was to fly to a municipal airfield, closer to Hanoi. Looking out the
windows of the high-winged, low-flying aircraft, it was apparent that we
were flying instead of driving because most of the bridges in the area had
been knocked out. Later when Kissinger dispatched messages by coded
radio to the President, it was necessary for our courier to commute via the

Russian aircraft to reach our plane. The municipal airport was deemed to have too short a runway for the heavy 707, although, despite intensive bomb damage, the field was large enough to receive the U.S. planes which were to be dispatched to take the prisoners of war from Hanoi to the Philippines.

As we drove from the second airfield in Russian-manufactured vehicles across a newly made pontoon bridge and into Hanoi, the roads were crowded with curious Vietnamese, sometimes riding parallel to us on bicycles, seeking a look at the strange party of Caucasians. There had been no announcement of our presence in the Hanoi newspaper.

During the trip into town and on later trips through Hanoi which I made in the company of Vietnamese security and press officers, it became quite apparent that the stories of carpet bombing which had been printed and broadcast in the United States, the so-called Christmas bombing represented a vast distortion of what had really happened to Hanoi in the final days of the war. Few American reporters had ever been allowed in Hanoi and most of the reports reaching the United States came from North Vietnamese radio or foreign reporters, many of whom sympathized with Pham Van Dong's regime. I saw extensive damage to bridges. The main railroad station had been destroyed, but even across the street from it, small stores were operating undamaged as if nothing had happened. As we drove in the area, we could see that the rails were being restored rapidly. I saw an embassy which had been destroyed and a block of homes which had been ripped out by a crashing, bomb-laden American plane. A hospital wing near another military post had been damaged badly. But in the main, Hanoi looked less touched by the war than Saigon, and its beauty far exceeded that of Vientiane, capital of Laos. Fresh food and flowers were apparent in Hanoi's stores and even the municipal streetcars were operating fully. One-man bomb shelters along the downtown streets looked to be long neglected. They smelled musty and dirty.

As we drove each day to the palace where negotiations were conducted, we regularly passed a high-walled open structure, covered with dirty yellow plaster and topped with strands of barbed wire. I asked my hosts what the building was and each time they hurriedly described it as a place to incarcerate "incorrigibles." What our Kissinger party did not realize until later was that this was the "Hanoi Hilton," which housed American prisoners. We learned later that others were housed in a prison which was only about a half mile from the palace where negotiations were conducted.

In the midst of our stay in Hanoi, the Democratic Republic of Vietnam released the first American prisoners of war. We were tempted to drive to the municipal airfield to see the men off to the Philippines on the first leg of their trip home, but we refrained so as to avoid creating any delays or interference with the process.

At about the hour the first men were scheduled to leave, my North Vietnamese escorts drove me and two Navy photographers in our party to a large park built on reclaimed land surrounding a lake. It was a beautiful but almost deserted park. The North Vietnamese explained that this was the Park of Reunification. It was symbolic of their continued determination to reunite one Vietnam, governed by themselves and including Hanoi, Hue, and Saigon. Ornate signs proclaimed the dedication of the Vietnamese to this purpose, which they attained in 1975 by overrunning Hue and Saigon in South Vietnam long after American troops had left the area.

We were walking through this park of political symbolism when I heard the roar of a jet airplane over the city. As we looked across the lake, and I snapped pictures (some of which I have given to a few former POWs). We saw the first American C-54 plane leaving Hanoi with its precious cargo of American prisoners of war on their way home. We watched in silence, but I could picture the freed prisoners shouting and slapping each other on the back as they looked down at Hanoi for the last time. The North Vietnamese ignored the scene.

The four days of meetings with Pham Van Dong and his assistants ended with a communiqué which said in part:

"The Democratic Republic of Viet Nam and the United States declared that the full and scrupulous implementation of the Paris Agreement on Viet Nam would positively contribute to the cause of peace in Indochina and Southeast Asia on the basis of strict respect for the independence and neutrality of the countries in this region.

"The two sides reaffirmed that the problems existing between the Indochinese countries should be settled by the Indochinese parties on the basis of respect for each other's independence, sovereignty, and territorial integrity, and non-interference in each other's internal affairs. They welcomed the negotiations between the parties in Laos, which are intended to produce a peaceful settlement in that country.

"The two sides exchanged views on the manner in which the United States will contribute to healing the wounds of war and to post-war economic reconstruction in North Viet Nam. They agreed to establish a D.R.V.N.–U.S. Joint Economic Commission. This Commission, which will be composed of an equal number of representatives from each side, will be charged with the task of developing the economic relations between the Democratic Republic of Viet Nam and the United States."

One of the most difficult tasks Kissinger faced was in negotiating the paragraph where both sides reaffirmed a pledge to respect the "independence, sovereignty, and territorial integrity" of all Vietnamese parties. The North Vietnamese made a sham of this when they moved across the South Vietnamese border in force in 1975, two years later.

The reference to a United States contribution "to healing the wounds of war and to post-war economic reconstruction in North Viet Nam" covered a pledge by Kissinger and Nixon that they would seek from Congress several millions of dollars in economic assistance if Pham Van Dong would lead his country in a new direction of peaceful economic development. No reparations were to be paid. Kissinger believed, correctly, that the transition by Pham Van Dong and his colleagues from operating a government at war to one at peace would be difficult. The money was to be a carrot. These were men who were proud that they had fought most of their lives, first against the French, against the Japanese, and against the Americans and South Vietnamese. Many had endured long terms in prison at the hands of the French. They were proud of that and mentioned it constantly. Peaceful government was a stranger among them—and continues to be.

The funds for the Democratic Republic of Vietnam were never sought from Congress by the administration because the signs of economic reconstruction and trade in Hanoi were few, if any. The Vietnamese much later claimed a promise had been broken to them as they asked for the funds as part of a move to normalize relations with the United States, but all of the administrations from Nixon's forward took the position that the earlier 1973 pledge was null and void because of treaty violations.

We left Hanoi via Hong Kong and the atmosphere was entirely different when we arrived in Canton and then flew on to Peking a few days later. Kissinger was greeted by Chou En-lai and other senior Chinese almost as a brother, and during our five days in the People's Republic of China it was apparent that the formal relations developed a year earlier by Nixon and Kissinger now would move ahead even more rapidly with the guns silent in Vietnam. A particular favorite of Kissinger was "Nancy" Tang Weng-sheng, a supreme interpreter who was a niece of Mao Tse-tung and was born in Brooklyn.

I recalled that it was less than three years earlier when I had been in Cambodia, examining Chinese war materiel supplied to the North Vietnamese and captured by Americans. Now the only talk of war came when the Chinese discussed the Soviet Union. The contrast was vivid.

My escorts were Chu Mo-chih, director of Hsinhua News Agency, and Peng Hua, director of the Information Department of the Foreign Ministry. I had met both in the United States earlier when, under the auspices of the American Society of Newspaper Editors and other groups, they had visited Washington. Chu Mo-chih, who was hated by the so-called Gang of Four in China, later was deposed from his position to go to a work camp, but he was reinstated with the rise of Premier Hua and Vice-Chairman Tung. We became friends and during a later visit to the PRC in 1978, he hosted an elaborate lunch for Bob Wood, former CBS president,

me, and my wife, Marge, so we could discuss journalistic problems informally with his staff leaders and the editors of Chinese newspapers.

In China we were never without escorts, who were unaware of our personal desire to shop. When Chou found that the official meetings pre-
cluded our going to the Friendship Store during regular hours, he
reopened the cluster of stores at 11 P.M. to take care of our shopping lists.

I soon learned that the Chinese daily newspaper was a barometer of
how the Chinese regarded the progress in our discussions. When we arrived, there was a two-column story on page one. (There had never been
any mention in the Hanoi press of our visit there.) As meetings
progressed, coverage enlarged until finally a midnight visit between Kissinger and Mao was heralded with coverage which eliminated practically
everything else on page one. On the final evening of our visit to Peking,
Chou insisted that I watch the television news. Television was only in a
beginning stage in China, and even now it is improving but is primitive. I
resisted the invitation, but my host insisted. I went into the room where
the television was situated and found the Chinese had set up a special seat
for me, complete with a glass of cherry wine to sip. I soon learned why.
For the first time PRC television was covering our trip to Peking. Finally
it was a top story. In China in 1973, Nixon and Kissinger were major foreign heroes. I found the same feeling applied when I returned with
Wood, president John Hubbard, vice-president Tom Nickell, and other
officials from the University of Southern California in 1978. Both governments had changed, but in China the personal feeling regarding Nixon
and Kissinger had not.

Since the 1971 arrival of the Chinese ping-pong group in the United
States, American news agencies had been seeking accreditation to have
permanent correspondents stationed in Peking. Other countries that recognized the PRC already had correspondents there, but Americans, except on
rare occasions were confined to reporting from Tokyo and Hong Kong.
One of my prime hopes was to gain an agreement from the Chinese information officials, Chu and Peng, for at least the Associated Press and
United Press to have correspondents in Peking. I spent a long afternoon's
discussion with Chu and Peng talking about journalism, the difference between journalism in our two countries, and the mutual desirability of having newsmen on the scene. I found my first task was to explain why the
United States found it advantageous to have two competitive private news
agencies, AP and UPI, operating outside government control. Would not
a single Hsinhua News Agency system be more efficient, they asked? I explained the importance of competition and eventually we moved from that
to an explanation of the various American journalism organizations, the
American Society of Newspaper Editors, the American Newspaper Publishers Association, the National Association of Broadcasters, AP and UPI

managing editors' groups, and, most difficult of all, Sigma Delta Chi, the Society of Journalists. When the discussion was completed, I felt that Chu would work on behalf of admission of AP and UPI. But, despite hopeful signs at that time and later, the Chinese stood by their principle that there were to be no permanent American journalists in Peking until, in 1979, normalization of relations was completed between the two countries.

In another part of the world a five-nation trip to Europe in September 1971, began uneventfully for me as I made speeches in London, Paris, Brussels, and Rome under the auspices of the Republican Party of Europe, an organization which was growing rapidly and was looked upon as a source of both monetary support and absentee votes. Part of our concern in the campaign of 1968 and during the White House years also was over the influence the foreign press eventually had upon American opinion. There was no way of measuring it, but I believe it has subtle and important impact.

Shortly after the convention which led to Nixon's nomination in 1968, I had met Pier and Tania Talenti. Pier Talenti is an American citizen, educated at Davis in the University of California system. He had large agricultural property holdings near the Appian Way in Rome, where he and his wife lived principally. Between the two of them they spoke eleven languages, and Tania's son, Nickolai, also fluent in several languages, later lived at our home and worked as a volunteer in the Nixon youth campaign of 1972 before returning to his native France to work in the campaign of French President Valéry Giscard d'Estaing. Shortly after I met Talenti in San Diego in 1968, he and his wife volunteered to work with the foreign press in our headquarters in New York, a very successful volunteer venture. During the 1971 trip to Europe, Talenti, by then the honorary Republican chairman for Europe, escorted my wife and me on a city-a-day tour which consisted of speeches, contracts with foreign leaders and Republican business leaders, and a press conference in each country. I considered that part of the job of reaching world opinion leaders. We were to arrive in Rome two days prior to the arrival of President Nixon, whom I was to join in meetings in Italy and Yugoslavia.

As we moved rapidly across Europe, two crises began to build for the President and the nation. In Rome the Communists made plans for massive demonstrations designed to tie up the city in traffic when Nixon arrived, and, more seriously, in the Middle East there were new tensions between the Palestinians and the government of Jordan. What were to have been casual political press conferences for me turned into delicate international briefings where my comments in Europe could be of assistance to the President but where a misspoken word from a senior White House aide in Europe could be seriously detrimental. I chose not to avoid any of the touchy subjects and was encouraged in this by Kissinger's deputy,

General Alexander Haig. Before each press conference, I conferred by phone with Haig, who was skillful at quickly delineating three areas of extreme importance for such media sessions: what things I might say that would be damaging to U.S. policy, what would help U.S. policy, and what were the facts of the situation at the moment. Knowing all of the basic facts and understanding the other two areas of policy sensitivities, I could answer the press with confidence.

In Rome, for example, as a spokesman, I played down United States concern over the potential riots there and said the President would not be deterred in his meetings with Italy's new President, Colombo, and the Prime Minister, Saragat. He does not "believe policy should be made in the streets," I said. Regarding Jordan, I confirmed that ships had been added to the Sixth Fleet in the Mediterranean to "prepare for contingencies." I declined as "bad strategy" answers to questions as to what I meant by "contingencies." We stress our policy of "live and let live" for all in the Middle East, I added. The comments were made to the press, but they were aimed at leaders of all elements in the Middle East crisis.

The Nixon European trip was a major success (his second visit to Italy as President) and, as he left meetings with the Pope, part of which included a lengthy audience with the senior staff and cabinet members present, crowds which were predicted to be potentially unruly mobs turned out more often to be groups of cheering Italians. Secretary of Transportation John Volpe, of Italian descent, probably enjoyed the motorcade most: at every slowdown he leaped from the car in which we were riding to shake hands and to exchange a few words in Italian with the amazed citizenry.

In Yugoslavia, where the President went after leaving Italy, I was greeted by President Tito's press officers, some of whom I had met earlier in Washington. After our late-afternoon arrival in Belgrade, there was an informal evening program of native Yugoslavian dancing. While the program was proceeding, the Minister of Information invited me to join him and his staff for supper after the formalities. Since our excursion in the U.S.S.R. in 1959, I had made it a rule never to accept an invitation in a Communist country without having another American with me. I invited Ziegler, but he declined because of other staff duties. Across the room I spotted J. Kingsbury Smith, the veteran of the Hearst foreign staff who at that point was stationed in Rome. I invited him to join me. I had known Smith for many years, but I had read his by-line from foreign countries much longer—since I was first a youth taking an interest in news stories outside the sports pages of the newspaper. He, in contrast to the more modern Marvin Kalb of CBS, was the old breed of diplomatic reporter, the newsman who grew up seemingly always wearing a trenchcoat, a veteran of wars and peace conferences in every part of the globe.

Smith and I joined eight members of the Yugoslav Information Ministry at a long rectangular table in the midst of a popular Belgrade supper club. In one corner a singer clung to and swayed with a tall thin microphone stand, reminiscent of the twenties and thirties in the United States. As we nibbled on cold cuts and sipped wine, most of the questions from the Yugoslavs first came to me. In the middle of the evening, I noticed that about half of the staff was suddenly engaged in a tense conversation with Smith. The noise was so great from the band and singer that I could not figure out the subject of the separate conversation. Much later, when Smith and I were in my car en route to our quarters, I asked him what had happened. He said he had questioned his hosts about a rumor he had heard in Rome regarding a new turn in Italian policy toward Yugoslavia. The two nations had a tense relationship. The Yugoslavs had not given him an answer, and he had no news story, but they had questioned him closely on the rumor. Suddenly, Smith the newsman had inadvertently become a part of the diplomatic action. The hosts presumed that he must have a close relationship with me and with Nixon because I had invited him to join us. Perhaps he worked, in part, for me, they mused. They suspected we were informally planting information important to them. They never guessed at the casual manner in which the invitation had been extended to Smith by me or at Smith's total lack of information about and participation in U.S. government policy.

Three months later, the Yugoslav Minister of Information again came to my White House office. He asked the origin of the Smith story. The Yugoslavs believed that I had asked Smith to try the idea of an Italian compromise on their government, and they had spent three months trying to trace down any basis for what proved to be only a rumor, not a fact or even a story. Within their ideology it was difficult for them to separate independent newsmen from government officials.

One other matter of a unique nature happened during our stay in Yugoslavia. We were scheduled to fly with Tito to Zagreb to meet with officials in a different part of the country and then to go by helicopter to a small Croatian village in the mountains where Tito had been born, the son of a rural blacksmith. Tito said that out of modesty he would not join us. We landed in Zagreb in the midst of heavy rain but on the streets were thousands of dripping-wet Yugoslavs waving tiny American flags which had been given to them by the government. The weather was so bad that a motorcade to his birthplace had to be substituted for the helicopters, and Tito found himself enjoying the Zagreb visit so much that he changed his mind and volunteered to join us for the trip up into the mountains.

In the small village amid the mountains, we drove to the well-preserved small hut in which Josip Broz Tito had been born. Reporters and photographers surrounded Nixon and Tito as he conducted the tour through the few rooms in the thick-walled adobe house. Finally Nixon and Tito were in the one bedroom, the room in which Josip Broz had been born. Tito pulled out a sideboard from the lumpy bed and the two leaders sat down to talk for the final time in Yugoslavia. By this time Ziegler and I had ushered the newsmen from the house, but as I looked at the windows (which could be closed only by wood shutters, not glass), newsmen were leaning in listening to the unprecedented informal discussion. Hugh Sidey, the astute columnist and Washington bureau chief for Time-Life, was most apparent during the talks, which covered world topics, centering on future peace in the Middle East where Tito also was a major figure. In some ways, this was a Kitchen Debate range of subjects, but the two leaders were polite and friendly and agreed on most topics. As I listened, I thought that here on a crude bedstand in the heart of the Yugoslavian mountains were leaders of opposites talking peace with reporters from around the world listening. I reminisced also on the fact that Tito's aggressiveness in Turkey and Greece after World War II eventually was a factor in his break with Stalin, who thought he went too far in arousing American counteraction. And one of the international scenes which first made a young congressman, Richard Nixon, interested in world affairs was the Greco-Turkey encounter with Tito forces. Nixon had returned from Europe with the Herter committee to support President Truman strongly on Greco-Turkey aid and the Marshall Plan. Tito, who now was talking peace in the Middle East with Nixon, had been the trigger for part of Nixon's early anti-Communist reactions and his foreign-policy interest. Most of the newsmen shared my sense of drama at this uncalled news conference in the birth room of Marshall Tito.

Later, in 1972, when we went to Moscow for the final negotiations on a Nixon-Kissinger dream, SALT I, we found the atmosphere far different from the first trip to the U.S.S.R. in 1959. Besides the fact that Nixon and Kissinger were housed in Kremlin apartments and given office space there, the remainder of us in the party were treated as guests, not adversaries, as we had been in 1959. Bargaining was tough and tricky as always, but personal relations and freedom of movement for members of the party were as different as night from day. The Secret Service had checked and told us that our rooms were bugged, but the Soviets had gone out of their way to provide us with a special dining room and spacious suites, and we found it easier to talk with the Soviet people, even in Red Square. At one point, Bill Safire and I spent a half day exploring areas both inside and outside the Kremlin with no interference.

In 1959, Rose Woods and Don Hughes had great difficulty finding a Catholic or Orthodox church where they could worship. This was not a problem in 1972, and symbolically I helped arrange for the President and

Mrs. Nixon to attend a brief service in a Baptist church in a suburban area of Moscow. An hour before the services, I met with the pastor and arranged it so his Russian parishioners could take turns attending the service for a few minutes each. The overflow crowd of worshipers almost filled the narrow street outside, waiting to get in. The 1972 presidential delegation was so large that even communication was difficult. Nixon, Kissinger, and a few National Security Council staffers were at the Kremlin. Most of the senior staff, headed by Secretary of State Bill Rogers and me, were at the gigantic Rosedin Hotel. Ziegler and his staff and the press were at an entirely different hotel, a mile or more away. Briefings were conducted regularly both by the Russians and by Ziegler, but with the separation of principal people, it was difficult for the reporters to know all of the poker-like sidelights which were taking place.

There were some offbeat things of lesser importance. One of the newsmen I was most happy to have with us was Sol Taishof, publisher of *Broadcasting* magazine, who had been born as a Jew in Russia and whose family had moved him to America at a young age. He had a lifelong ambition to visit Minsk, his birthplace, but had been unwilling to do so because of the danger that the Soviets would seize a Jew in a city outside the tourist orbit. As a newsman, a member of the U.S. party, not a tourist, he could take a day off and find long-lost relatives in his birthplace without any danger.

At one point during the talks in the Kremlin, Nixon asked me to meet with him in his suite following ceremonies accompanying the signing of commercial agreements which were recorded before television cameras. Inadvertently I left my pad of notes beneath a television camera. When I returned a few minutes later, the notes were gone. It took the Secret Service three days to recover them. Meanwhile, I figured the KGB was trying to decipher my bad handwriting. And when it did, it found nothing of a nonpublic nature.

The struggle during the latter days of May 1972, to agree upon what eventually was called SALT I was more difficult than the press realized and the outcome was highly doubtful until the Politburo after a lengthy meeting finally accepted the Nixon terms, which called for an Interim Offensive Agreement temporarily limiting the numbers of intercontinental ballistic missiles and submarine-launched missiles and limited antiballistic-missile sites. Nixon won a tough victory there. Many of the negotiations for this were carried on between Kissinger and Andrei Gromyko during early-morning hours after the perfunctory formalities such as the ballet *Swan Lake* and official dinners. The Politburo acceptance of the agreement on the day before Nixon was scheduled to visit Leningrad came as a surprise to Kissinger and Nixon, who were worried that they were in a hopeless deadlock. The original SALT negotiation teams from both the

U.S.S.R. and the United States had been standing by in Helsinki. Neither side realized that each had a special airplane waiting to bring their negotiators to the ceremonies if an agreement was reached. Nixon learned of the Politburo acceptance of terms only hours before a formal dinner had been planned for Soviet and American leaders at the embassy's Spaso House. The signing ceremony then was scheduled for near midnight. The Spaso House dinner was followed by an emotional, beautiful Van Cliburn piano concert, but gradually some of the officials of both sides, who had special duties, slipped quietly from the room to make preparations. Van Cliburn ended with an international standing ovation, but his audience had diminished. Just prior to the dinner, Kissinger had extensively briefed the American press on the details, so it was ready for the midnight signing story.

During the dinner, Nixon asked me if I would mind missing the Leningrad trip the next day since I had been with him there before. He asked me to stay in Moscow and spend the day telephoning editors to find their initial reaction to the SALT agreement.

Calling through Army Signal Corps lines, which were part of a special switchboard that accompanies the President wherever he goes, I started to find editor friends, most of whom were enjoying weekend recreational activities. Clayton Kirkpatrick of the Chicago *Tribune* and Emmett Dedman of the Field Newspapers of Chicago were startled, for example, to find themselves called off the golf course to the pro shop at their clubs to answer a page from the White House which was being relayed from Moscow. In my check from Moscow, I found the reaction of the press to the SALT agreement to be heavily supportive.

Even on a serious trip of this nature, the humor still shines through in respect to the press.

As we were about to leave Moscow, I changed my mind and decided to fly to Kiev aboard the press plane instead of Air Force One. I was delayed in reaching the press plane because I found a veteran reporter detained by Soviet airport officials. The reporter was scheduled to board a third U.S. plane carrying a party headed by Secretary of State Rogers. The reporter was to accompany Rogers to Europe for a series of briefings in Western capitals on the Moscow summit. Just before Rogers was to take off, I bulldozed my way through the Soviet officials and got the reporter on board. I then walked to the press charter plane, and found my way up to the airplane ladder blocked by a Soviet general, who could not find my name on the manifest. My name was on the Air Force One manifest, not the list for the press plane. Aided by an efficient Russian-speaking U.S. embassy official, I argued with the general, showing him all my credentials ranging from a San Diego *Union* press card to an official White House pass, to my pass to enter the Kremlin. He stood firm as I tried to assess my best bet, whether to run across the Moscow airfield to Air Force One or to charge through the soldiers up the ladder. I wondered about Russian reaction to a sprint by me across the field, but Air Force One's ladder was pulled up as I watched, finally getting nervous. That answered the question. My reporterlike dash up the steps was blocked by two burly U.S.S.R. sergeants. At the door of the press plane, Jerry Warren was shouting that he could not hold the airplane much longer. I was frantic, fearing I would be left in Moscow with my clothes and credentials aboard Air Force One. Finally I convinced the general to accompany my embassy associate to the airport and check my Kremlin pass and clear me while I was boarding. I sternly told the embassy man, "Don't give up the Kremlin pass, I want it as a souvenir."

He later returned it by mail.

We went from Moscow to Kiev to Tehran for meetings with the Shah of Iran. The meetings were formal, mainly centered on defense issues. On the morning after our arrival Nixon was to ride with the Shah into the suburbs to place a symbolic American wreath on an Iranian monument. About an hour before the ceremony, it was unexpectedly called off. The Shah's secret police had uncovered a plot to explode a bomb in the area, apparently in an attempt to assassinate the Shah or President Nixon or both. We could not get details from the Iranians except for the fact that they had apprehended several men allegedly involved in the death plot.

In a lighter way, one of the most widely printed stories from the visit involved Kissinger. The Shah gave a white-tie dinner which was as beautiful as any state dinner I have attended. At the conclusion, I drove to a hotel nearby where the Iranian press office was entertaining our traveling press corps. They had made arrangements for relaxation with the newsmen sitting on cushions around low tables and with entertainment at both ends of the large room. As I was chatting with newsmen, I suddenly noticed Kissinger arriving in white tie with the Iranian foreign minister. We introduced the minister to various reporters and eventually sat with some of the newsmen on cushions not far from one of the stages. A belly dancer was performing on the stage and getting no attention because of the unexpected presence of Kissinger and the minister. She soon left the stage and stepped into the Kissinger circle to perform. Encouraged by applause and shouts, she moved ahead and sat on Kissinger's lap. He was surprised but, once over the shock, he seemed to enjoy the fun, but I was wary of the publicity this would attract. None of the Americans had cameras with them. Their cameras had been forbidden by their Iranian hosts for the evening, but Iranian news photographers were not so inhibited, and they began shooting. I did not want to interfere personally, but I strongly encouraged the U.S. information officers and Iranian officials to act by jumping in front of cameras. I worried about the reaction of hilarity after

SALT. But the pictures were sneaked out by the Iranians despite my efforts. And the result tickled humor about Kissinger "the swinger." It was in no way detrimental.

One other episode in November 1971, illustrates the importance of news reporting where it affects U.S. officials in foreign countries. The President had asked Bob and Carol Finch to arrange a trip to Latin America in lieu of Nixon, who was unable to schedule such a trip with the other major international events taking place. He invited me and my wife and assistant secretary of state for Latin America Charles A. Meyer and his wife, Suzanne, to form the senior group for the trip, which was to include meetings in Ecuador, Peru, Argentina, Brazil, Honduras, and Mexico. Latins have great respect for relatives and close personal friends of the President, and Finch and I represented that. Additionally, we long had a close interest in Mexico and had worked with Mexican officials on mutual problems for ten years or more. Meyer was there because of his great technical knowledge of the area. On the trip, we had various missions ranging from turning over a controversial island to Honduras to discussing tuna fishing problems in Ecuador, to inspecting the results of American aid given to Peru after a beautiful Shangri-La-like valley in the Andes had been shattered by a killer earthquake. The quake had been so violent that half a mountain had slid into the valley, burying hundreds.

In Peru, our first stop, we landed after the dictator-President had seized control of radio and television in his country. He justified this to me by saying Peruvian children were creating wants they could not afford by watching and listening to broadcast advertising, an argument heard in the United States today. We held press conferences in each country, aided by Ignacio Lozano, Spanish-speaking personal friend of Finch's and mine and the publisher of *La Opinion,* a Mexican-American newspaper in Los Angeles. (He later became a U.S. ambassador in Central America.) We encountered only positive results with accurate stories covering our activities in most Latin American and United States newspapers.

Upon our return home, I agreed to meet with the "Sperling Group," reporters from various newspapers who regularly assembled for breakfast with reporters. Godfrey Sperling was the organizer. The news figure at the breakfast has the choice of being on or off the record. I agreed to speak for the record.

Before we got into the main subjects of the Latin-American trip and the usual domestic political discussions, one of the newsmen asked if I had gained any impressions of the stability of the Allende administration in Chile. While we had been in other Latin countries, Fidel Castro had been spending several days in Chile conferring with Allende and denouncing, as usual, the United States.

I carefully told the reporters I had no firsthand knowledge. I was not briefed on Chile, and I had not been there. I then went on to say that diplomats and some reporters in the area had said that Allende was facing severe economic problems in his country. It was their consensus that under such conditions, Allende "won't last long."

I thought little more about the discussion because I was careful to point out that I had no firsthand knowledge and for the newsmen's background I was merely passing on third-hand information from knowledgeable sources. I had no knowledge that the CIA and ITT actively were stirring trouble against Allende. Had I known I would have been even more cautious, but we had no briefing on Chile.

To my surprise, Tad Szulc of the New York *Times* jumped on the story and the lead, played prominently in his newspaper, was based on the prediction by me that Allende would be out of office soon. Deeper in the story Szulc carried my qualification that neither Finch nor I had "direct knowledge of the Chilean situation," but added that our impressions would be part of a report to the President. That was true.

I was as dismayed by the *Times* news play and the emphasis in the lead as I have been by anything I have ever said publicly. I felt the emphasis used my words but vastly distorted the meaning and qualification—all to get a story.

The *Times* story was played in newspapers worldwide.

The result was that Allende shot a protest to the State Department demanding that I be fired from the White House and insisting on an apology from the United States Government for interfering in Chilean domestic affairs. Castro delivered a lengthy address denouncing me personally.

It was an international incident of minor proportion, but Allende used it to the maximum.

Castro and Allende were ignored by the State Department and by the President.

But the whole incident provided a lesson in international news coverage to me which I was not soon to forget.

History will show that my observations were accurate, but that was not the result of personal expertise—just reporting on information the experts had sent back to the President. I take no personal credit for my prediction the *Times* distorted.

13

Hardball

POLITICS, like sports, music, or theater, has its own terminology. The political terms and definitions have changed over the years and some, such as "political bossism," have become pretty much obsolete with changes in times and the political system. But other terms, such as "power broker," are much a part of the process today. The latter refers to those we once would have called kingmakers or to those who wield power by playing one side against the other. To be successful the "power broker" must have political clout and guts.

The words and phrases of today's politics are so numerous and complex that they form the complete subject for an eight-hundred-page dictionary written by columnist and lexicographer William Safire.

Two sports words which have become a part of modern political terminology are softball and hardball.

A softball, in political terms, usually refers to a situation in a press conference where a reporter throws out a question which the candidate or his spokesman finds easy to answer—a question which the speaker can "knock out of the ball park."

Sometimes the question is one that has been planted with the reporter, and thus the candidate is expecting it and hopes it will make a news lead. More often the softball comes from a reporter who is inept or who simply wants to see how the spokesman will react to a soft question.

An occasional softball allows the candidate to hit hard on a subject of importance, and the answer can have major impact. I often have seen the situation, however, where too many softballs can lull the candidate into boredom so that he becomes vulnerable to a sudden tough question or, at best, he simply performs poorly.

A few of the softballs come from reporters who are simply probing the candidate's mind.

Reporters, for example, are inevitably interested in a candidate's assessment of his potential opponent, and in this case, most candidates give an answer flavored with enough fact to be believable, but frequently the answer also is aimed at creating confusion in the opposition camp.

In early July of 1968, for example, Nixon met with Governor James A. Rhodes of Ohio, who was running as a "favorite son" in hopes of becoming a major power broker at the convention. Nixon assured Rhodes he would not attempt to raid the Ohio delegation, and he listened to the governor give him a strong recommendation of New York's Mayor John Lindsay for Vice-President. Rhodes leaked to the press his belief that Lindsay would be a winner.

In a press conference that followed, Nixon was asked:

"You say that you have the advantage over Vice-President Humphrey in November because McCarthy is the most popular Democrat. What if it happens to be a McCarthy-Humphrey ticket: will you still feel that you have the advantage?"

Nixon answered:

"If Vice-President Humphrey is able to circumvent the constitutional problem that I would be confronted with in selecting Mayor Lindsay as a Vice-Presidental candidate [two nominees from the same state], and if you have a Humphrey-McCarthy ticket, that would tend to unify the Democratic Party. The only problem that it would present is how Vice-President Humphrey can reconcile his very basic differences with Senator McCarthy, differences that Senator McCarthy has been speaking to eloquently over the primary campaign. Sometimes that can be done in a convention. I am not sure that gulf can be bridged even by the very shrewd political maneuvering that takes place in national conventions, but you would really have to ask those two men."

Nixon thus dodged the Lindsay question and in the process planted a query which he hoped would be asked of his two potential opponents. Would they run together? In truth, he did not really believe there was the slightest chance of such an amalgamation, even if the constitutional question over the legality of two men from the same state on the same presidential ticket could be resolved. Vietnam represented too much of an emotional difference between the two men to allow a merger of interests.

Despite these facts, we were interested in just how Humphrey and McCarthy would deny the possibility. We recalled that in 1960 most did not believe it was possible to bring on one ticket two such strong-minded men as Lyndon Johnson and John Kennedy. The difference between 1960 and 1968 was that there was not an emotional issue such as Vietnam involved in 1960. There was no such emotion included in differences between Kennedy and Johnson, and Kennedy, a Catholic, badly needed Johnson's assistance in the South. We in the Nixon office were not surprised when Johnson accepted Kennedy's invitation to join the ticket, because three days before the decision we had been tipped by a Johnson confidant that Lady Bird was urging her husband to accept such an offer if it were made. She thought that the physical strain on a Vice-President would be far less than that on a Senate majority leader—or a President.

Hardball, another political term inherited from sports lexicon, has nothing to do with questions from the press.

Safire defines hardball as "rough political tactics; stronger than 'practical politics' or 'pranks,' milder than dirty tricks."

In his earlier book, *Before the Fall*, Safire interrupted a description of Charles Colson to define hardball as "tough-minded operations; use of pressure rather than less subtle means of persuasion; the roughshod ride rather than the more publicly accepted methods of compromise; the velvet fist in the iron glove."

"Hardball" is a word newer to politics than "softball," and even before Watergate, in our inner circles, it was a word applied to many of the Nixon tactics emanating from the Colson office.

Looking back, it is clearly apparent that John Kennedy and Lyndon Johnson also were experts in hardball, but the times were different, and so were their tactics.

For me, however, hardball is synonymous with the name Chuck Colson.

When he issued a staff memo during the 1972 Republican National Convention saying he would gladly walk over the body of his grandmother to assure the election of Richard Nixon, I took him to mean that literally.

Colson was tough and, as he said, frequently, when the going got tough, he got going tougher and rougher.

Colson was loyal to the President. He had a strong feeling of national patriotism. But he was fanatical. He was unscrupulous. He was overly ambitious, a man who loved power and would knock down anyone but the President to achieve it. In his mind, the ends justified the means. Always. In twenty years of campaigns, I met many tough operators, particularly in the big cities of the East and Midwest. I learned how to handle them, how to face them down. Colson was different. He was unmoving.

Within the many facets of the Nixon personality, there is a sadistic side, one which provides satisfaction from thoughts of vengeance. It is part of the Nixon macho pride. Most of us who knew the President well understood these fantasies of vengeance. We rarely reacted to them and a day or two later he would seem relieved that we had not. Haldeman was expert in this technique.

Colson, however, became an extension of this strongly negative part of Nixon. He seemed to me to take the offhand macho comments of the President and to revel in going beyond them. If the President was tough, Colson wanted to prove he was tougher.

If the President wanted an Enemies List, Colson would produce it, enjoying every moment of the exercise. If the President was unhappy with a senator or a broadcaster, it was Colson who would seek some measure of counterattack.

Hardball was his game.

I made the mistake of underestimating Colson during his early months on the White House staff. I suspect that Bob Haldeman did the same thing, but to a lesser extent.

Colson was recommended for the White House staff by Bryce Harlow, the most gentlemanly of all the senior presidential staff. Colson had not come up through the fires of Nixon campaigning as had most of us, but he had learned his politics in the tough wards of Massachusetts. He had served as a senior assistant to Republican Senator Leverett Saltonstall, prior to the latter's retirement.

He was regarded as a successful attorney and one with political experience working with a variety of constituencies. He was recruited to build an office which would engage in special liaison with organized groups ranging from labor to management, from ethnic groups to veterans.

Colson was skillful and successful in all of these assigned areas, bringing into the White House groups which I had thought would never mention the name Nixon without an accompanying swearword.

Early in the administration when there was a very real threat of a postal strike, he stepped in a "side door" and used his labor contacts to help mediate the problem just as hope for settlement seemed to be disintegrating. Still, it was the Postmaster General, Winton "Red" Blount, who did most of the spadework, but Colson ignored this and the President gave him, not Blount, private credit for solving the critical problem.

Colson had nothing to do with the origin of the term "Silent Majority," which first received widespread attention after it was written by Nixon into an impassioned speech he delivered on November 3, 1969, discussing Vietnam. But Colson was quick and efficient in carrying out his part of the follow-up on the speech, organizing supposedly spontaneous support from thousands of veterans across the nation.

Bryce Harlow humorously described Colson as "a tiger on our hands" during the early weeks of Chuck's tenure on the staff. I looked upon him at that time as another less seasoned assistant who would fill a role of more plastic importance than substance. At that point he was a tiger without the tiger stripes Harlow had predicted. I made every effort to cooperate with him.

Early on he called me while I was on a trip to Connecticut to ask if I would break my schedule for a day to help him arrange a meeting with Henry Cabot Lodge so we could convince him to accept a special assignment from the President.

I agreed and Colson secured from the White House a special plane to fly us to Beverly, Massachusetts, where we could meet with Lodge at his beautiful, traditional country estate.

I should have been impressed at that time by Colson's ability to quickly commandeer a plane from the White House fleet. Without the plane, I could not have scheduled in the Lodge meeting; still I would not have requested the aircraft on my own for this rather routine assignment. It was a sign of Colson acting big-time.

The second sign I should have heeded was that here was Colson, a Massachusetts politician, asking me to help with another Republican veteran from the Commonwealth, someone with whom Colson supposedly should have had major influence.

We met Lodge at his home, and after discussing our business Lodge called me aside privately to ask if I would vouch for Colson. I was puzzled but said yes.

I should have observed then that Lodge knew more about Colson than I realized, and that Colson had recognized this weakness in Massachusetts before he asked me to join him on the mission. We on the White House staff had assumed he was strongest in his home base.

But then, at that time, Colson did not seem important enough for me to worry about extensively. He concealed his power-hungry aggressiveness.

Lodge and I discussed the incident several years later. The occurrence was peculiar enough that it had stuck in both of our minds. At the time of the meeting in Beverly, the administration was in the middle of the battle to gain congressional approval for a new antiballistic-missile program. We called this "Safeguard." Some of the major opposition came from Massachusetts, which would have been planned as one of the ABM sites. Colson wanted Lodge to co-author an article for the *Reader's Digest* with Charles J. V. Murphy, a veteran writer for the magazine. The article concerned the disarmament negotiations we were conducting with the Soviet Union and the important relationship of the antiballistic-missile program to the proposed treaty with the Soviets. Lodge wrote the piece with Murphy's assistance and it appeared on June 30 under the title "A Citizen Looks at the ABM."

What neither I nor Colson knew before the meeting was that the President had indirectly sounded Lodge out about becoming a part-time ambassador to the Vatican. When I talked privately with Lodge, he also asked me to be certain that the article he would write would not interfere with his appointment to this post. I said nothing to Colson, but I checked with the President later and both projects went forward. Early in 1970, prior to the appearance of the *Reader's Digest* piece, Lodge was appointed and made his first call upon the Vatican. He was only the second American to hold that post, the first having been Myron Taylor, a former chairman of U.S. Steel, who was appointed by President Franklin D. Roosevelt. President Truman ran into opposition from Congress when he attempted to appoint General Mark Clark to the post and he withdrew his name. There was no U.S. ambassador between the time of Myron Taylor and Lodge, although Clare Booth Luce, Eisenhower's ambassador to Italy, had a close relationship to the Vatican.

In 1970 Colson came to me and told me that he and an associate who was an attorney had developed important information which showed that Senator Joseph Tydings of Maryland was involved in influence peddling. I disagreed with Tydings politically but had only heard honorable things about him as a senator. Colson convinced me that he had enough evidence that there should be some sort of investigation.

Life magazine was in its death struggle and was seeking to save itself with investigative reporting. I agreed that if Colson would put his summary on one page, I would pass it along to a *Life* magazine executive for consideration. I did it exactly that way, with the warning that I could not vouch for the authenticity of the material.

I also regret being even that much a part of the Colson "dirty trick."

Life assigned a reporter, who later was in touch with Colson and others he suggested. The reporter, William Lambert, investigated further and was satisfied he had an authentic story which eventually was published by Time-Life at a critically late time in the Tydings campaign. (After the election, the story was disproved, but it was too late for Tydings. He had lost.)

Colson had the killer instinct. He was not satisfied with just the *Life* article. He organized a "paper" committee, which included names of at least a few Republicans, such as Mark Evans Austad, who were not aware their names were being used. He raised money for the "committee" and came up with his own hardball theme for the ad: "What kind of man is Joe Tydings?" Needless to say, the Joe Tydings depicted by Chuck Colson was not of senatorial stature unless you favored the violent Vietnam demonstrators and leniency for criminals.

Jeb Magruder was the White House contact between my office and our advertising agency, and I was able to get a few changes made in the ad while arguing successfully for less money for its display. Nonetheless, the very damaging ad appeared on the eve of the election, allowing Tydings virtually no time for reply.

Republican J. Glenn Beall, Jr., was elected and I do not believe he knew of Colson's role.

The technique was a throwback to the fifties, when professionals in both parties would, in last-minute ads, smear the opposition.

After the 1970 election, when Colson began telling everyone how successful he had been in defeating Tydings, I realized he was someone to consider seriously, and that he had the potential of danger to the White House with his brand of hardball.

After the elections of 1970, Colson's power grew and his abuse of the power increased. His name was not well known publicly, but behind the scenes his political manipulations were so forceful that no one could mistake his presence. There seemed no way to contain this strong-willed force.

While I was writing this chapter, I saw on television the coach of the Ohio State football team, Woody Hayes, act out of emotion and frustration and strike a player of the opposing Clemson team. Symbolically, it seemed to me that Nixon, who admired Hayes as a coach and a patriot, sometimes would strike figuratively at the opposition in moments of bitter emotional frustration. Later he frequently was unhappy with the thought and hoped nothing had happened. Colson would strike at someone with a feeling of power or vengeance and enjoy the episode, savoring it for months.

My first major confrontation with Colson came at a time when I attempted to protect Magruder from him. Colson had ridden roughshod over Magruder in an attempt to seize control over the direct-mail operation my office had developed. This was a sophisticated program for selective mailings.

Naïvely, I thought I would just call Colson, my junior on the staff, into the office and end the dispute by simply pointing out that the operation had been developed under my initial instructions from the President as I formed the Office of Communication.

With Magruder present, but rarely speaking out, Colson and I argued for almost an hour with no results. He stonewalled me and claimed the President supported him. I thought the argument was too trivial for Presidential involvement.

Magruder and I decided we would invite Colson to lunch at the nearby Sans Souci Restaurant and there, under pleasant circumstances, explain the facts of life. He could not be as unmoving as it appeared, I thought. I also invited Bart Porter, who was working on my staff coordinating national scheduling for cabinet officers.

Colson was the most stubborn person I had met in politics. He simply refused to shift his position an inch or to even discuss a compromise giving him equal use of the mail operation, which I believed important but which did not intrigue me in detail. We were debating principle.

From that point forward, Magruder was in a perpetual state of intimidation by Colson, a situation which became most important when Colson pressured Magruder to increase the campaign intelligence we now refer to as Watergate.

To Colson, everyone was either a friend or a foe. There was no in between. In August of 1970 he received a suggestion from Don Larrabee, who capably ran an independent news service for about thirty smaller news dailies, urging that the President meet with small-town editors. Colson described Larrabee as "one of our true loyalists in the Washington Press Corps . . . a staunch Nixon Republican." Larrabee would have been surprised at the description.

On the other side, in December of 1970, Colson wrote a memo to the staff secretary describing Ernest Furgurson of the Baltimore *Sun* as "a dedicated enemy . . . a guy who despises this administration and is very strongly anti-Nixon—he always has been."

I did not know Furgurson's personal politics then or now, but I did know him to be a capable reporter.

Colson's tirade was directed at Furgurson's coverage of a Nicholas Johnson, an eccentric outgoing Federal Communications commissioner who attacked both the networks and Nixon. From the standpoint of the normally flamboyant Johnson, it was a mild attack, and Furgurson so noted. Colson described Johnson as "a mental case . . . his conduct has been disgraceful . . . the man who deliberately tried to use obscene language simply to test whether they would censor it; WTOP [a local Washington TV station] obliged." Colson's memo illustrated his paranoiac side—"them or us."

Colson was often egged on in his tirades, not only by the President but by Haldeman.

In January of 1971, for example, Haldeman wrote Colson:

"We need to get a project executed to blast the networks and in particular NBC by name—for their attempt to undermine the confidence of the people in the American economy.

"We should compare the current situation to the early 1960s and make the point that one network, NBC, has given more time in the last few months, or the last year, to all the negative comments on the economy than was given on all three networks combined in the 1960s.

"We need a strong spokesman for this, perhaps the Vice President, to blast the networks for their distorted negative comments on the economy."

There were facts to back up Haldeman's irritation. The time-allotment studies we had showed that the networks, particularly NBC, regularly played up negative news on the economy, including unemployment, and positive news went almost unnoticed. My objection to the memo was not to the revealing and damaging documentation of network bias or imbalance but to the instant reaction—"blast the networks."

There were other reasonable and effective ways to work on the problem logically. Increasingly, we seemed dedicated to playing only hardball.

Unemployment figures are issued early each month. Early in the administration, Haldeman and Ehrlichman tried to get the Labor Department to play up total employment and downplay unemployment. The effort met with opposition from the bureaucracy, and it was impossible anyway to disguise any of the figures from the media, good or bad.

In 1971, prior to the decision to "blast the networks" for economic bias, a study showed that when figures were released in January showing unemployment up by .3 percent (up to 6.2 percent) all three networks made this the lead in the evening news, NBC giving it 1:15 minutes' air time, CBS 2:45, and ABC 3:15. The next month unemployment dropped by .2 (to 6.0 percent) and none of the networks used it in the lead. NBC noted the decline in 20 seconds, CBS in two minutes, and ABC gave it 2:20.

The March figures again showed an encouraging unemployment decline of .2 (to an encouraging 5.8 percent). NBC did lead with this, giving it 1:35 minutes. Neither CBS nor ABC recognized this in the lead but both gave the decline over two minutes.

Between April and June unemployment inched up again, going from the 5.8 percent mark to 6.2 percent in June. With the exception of CBS, which gave scant attention to a .2 climb in April, all three networks led with the bad news in April, May, and June. The June announcement was greeted with each network commenting on it for well over three minutes.

July figures related to sharp decline in unemployment, a decrease of .6, dropping the figure to 5.6 percent, a low for the year. None of the networks led with this and NBC gave it 1:15 minutes' air time, CBS only 35 seconds, and ABC a flat two minutes.

When the figures are isolated in this fashion, they appear to document a clear case of network bias or collusion, or both.

There were, of course, other factors to be considered. Other news such as that from Vietnam also was competing for network lead time. The logical White House procedure should have been to weight each factor and then discuss this problem factually with the network leaders. I had built relationships with the networks which would have allowed for this approach. On a national-policy level, what we were most anxious about was the possibility that a continuous drumbeat of doom-and-gloom stories might build negative public psychology leading to unnecessary recession— a recession induced by psychology created by the media. With such a serious danger, the logical approach was not hardball. But Colson was running rampant. The war with the networks was escalated.

Earlier in 1970, Colson produced research showing that during August, the networks had featured in their evening news 35 appearances by eight senators (Republican and Democrat) making negative comments on the conduct of the war in Vietnam. During the same month, 12 senators from both parties had appeared on the air supporting the war policies of the President. But the 12 senators had been seen only once each, meaning the dominance of anti-Vietnam views from the Senate had been 35 TV appearances to 12. A majority in the Senate favored the President's policies at that time, a point the networks ignored.

There was an even better case to be made for an emotional lack of objectivity among newsmen on Vietnam than on the economy. Colson wrote to Rogers Morton of the Republican National Committee, in September of 1970, "the networks are biased," and then he went on to his own kind of solution, urging Morton to organize an effort to "really destroy their credibility . . . put the nail in their coffin."

This was another example of Colson hardball, but the easygoing Morton reacted to the Colson demands by calling me and then deciding to act positively by generating more pro-Nixon public statements rather than take off in a futile fight with the broadcasters.

Vietnam provided the toughest of the problems in seeking favorable, or at least balanced, coverage from the media. Emotions ran as high within the news corps as they did with the public. The only time I have seen a reporter break into tears during a news conference or briefing came during a session in the East Ballroom of the White House, where Henry Kissinger was briefing 150 newsmen on a presidential decision to hit harder in Vietnam. A veteran reporter from the Chicago *Daily News* became so choked up he could hardly complete a question he was asking Kissinger.

An effort to discredit the networks was not going to change bias in reporting on Vietnam. We were better off to develop a stronger case for the President's side of the issue and to use our best spokesmen frequently.

During that summer of 1970 there was a feeling at the White House that we were under siege—from demonstrators, from newsmen, and even from the Senate.

Colson's answer was to organize a Tell-It-to-Hanoi Committee and to raise outside money which would enable him to use the committee for newspaper or television ads, speeches and press conferences. He gained the approval for Senator Robert Dole (Kansas) to lead an attack group from the Senate including Senators Peter Dominick, Barry Goldwater, and Robert Packwood.

Senators George McGovern and Mark Hatfield introduced a bill pledging the United States to withdraw all forces from Vietnam within eleven months. This provided a new focus for attacks engineered by Colson, McCarthy-like attacks on the patriotism of the two senators. Colson had full Nixon support for this.

He developed a game plan which suggested that the McGovern-Hatfield effort be termed a "declaration of defeat." The amendment was to be referred to as the "surrender amendment" and its sponsors labeled as "sore winners." Associates of Senators McGovern and Hatfield raised money for television spots which the Colson game plan called "surrender spots."

"On a positive theme," Colson wrote, "our people can take the line that we are seeking 'peace, not appeasement' and that McGovern-Hatfield sponsors are really trying to steal a political issue away from the President. . . .

"Another major line of attack will be on the tactics employed by McGovern-Hatfield. There is a striking parallel with the tactics employed with the 'America First' movement immediately preceding World War II." Ridiculous!

The Colson approach included a plan for statements by veterans' organizations that McGovern-Hatfield supporters were attempting to "stab the boys in the backs. . . . This would be the first defeat in American Army history—defeated not by an enemy in the field but by irresponsible demigod politicians at home."

The hardball attack on the two senators was developed and secretly directed by Colson and his staff in the White House. But by hiring an outside director for the project, Gene Bradley, and working through the so-called Tell-It-to-Hanoi Committee and through veterans' groups, as well as some supporters in Congress, the President and White House staff were kept clear of any public involvement in the tactics.

To me one of the cruelest falsehoods perpetuated by Colson, with the full encouragement of the President, was a story he planted against Arthur Burns, who by then had left the White House and was chairman of the Federal Reserve Board.

The President was irritated because Burns, who had been his longest and closest friend among any of the national economists, was moving the Fed in a direction more conservative than Nixon and some of his more liberal noneconomic advisers in the White House thought was politically sound. In a discussion in the Oval Office, either Nixon or Colson came up with the idea of planting a story that Arthur Burns was talking against inflation while he was secretly pressing the President for a major raise in his personal salary. I, unfortunately, was out of Washington when Colson devised a plan to have Devan Shumway from my staff plant a story indicating that all of the monetary furor of Burns was aimed secretly at gaining a personal leverage for a pay raise. Shumway is highly capable and ethical and as an ex-UPI executive, he had excellent relations with the press. Colson convinced him that the Burns ploy was a true story. The result was embarrassment first to Arthur Burns and then to Shumway and me. Colson was shielded from the situation, as was the President.

When the story broke, Arthur Burns called me in anguish. I truthfully told him I was unaware of it. As far as I am concerned, he was one of the people in or out of government I admired most. The story was damaging because people believe the negative regardless of the denials. Burns held to principle and Nixon, in a press conference, later defended him strongly and thus backed away from the slander publicly. But the fact was, he had been part of it.

Some time after I had left the White House and Colson had left prison, Burns told me that Colson had come by his office to apologize. "I respect his reborn feeling," Burns told me, "but somehow I cannot find in my heart the will to forgive him." Colson and I have not had a conversation since he left the White House. But I have to share the feelings of the very sensitive Arthur Burns.

At one point, the dispute between Colson and me over the communications operation reached a point where he boycotted meetings I would call. On Saturdays I invited him to my "think tank" operation, where a group of about eight of us would discuss the philosophy of the White House and how best to implement recognition of it.

Colson kept grabbing for power in my communications operation. Haldeman finally tried to settle the dispute by appointing his new personnel chief, Fred Malek, as a labor arbitrator between Colson and me. Malek's decisions, I thought, favored my office more than Colson but again, Colson stalled and the lengthy negotiations ended up in a secret standoff within the White House.

Colson was thorough and effective in organizing various groups for whatever support he thought would be most helpful to the President and his programs. But his strength and, I think, weakness was as a "gut fighter," one who would approach any project with a toughness which knew few ethical bounds. He thoroughly enjoyed his positive work with labor unions and other specialized groups, but I became convinced that in the long run his most intense and dangerous desire was to be in a position of background power where he could dominate the television networks from the White House. I doubt if Colson admitted that to himself, and he justified all of his approaches in the television field with the statement that he was operating in areas where his legal background was important and that he was simply seeking fair play. "This is best for the President."

Both in the desire to intimidate and dominate television news and in the justification of seeking "fair play," Colson echoed the inner and often the outwardly expressed feelings of President Nixon. The tougher the approach Colson took toward the networks, the tougher was my problem in keeping things within the bounds of sanity, logic, and morality.

In 1970 when the White House was in battle with CBS over a problem of equal time for an address by the President regarding Vietnam, I pointed out that we were inconsistent in our view when with Republicans out of office, we had pioneered the idea of televised reply to the party in power.

I recalled that in 1961, the television industry had decided to award gold medals to President Kennedy and to Mr. Nixon for their contribution to TV in 1960 by participating in the four televised campaign debates. Leonard Reinsch, then president of the Cox Broadcasting Company and an extremely able TV adviser to Kennedy and the Democratic Party was to accept for the President. I was designated to accept for Nixon.

As we appeared on the platform of the Waldorf ballroom in New York, Reinsch tastefully accepted with brief and gracious remarks of thanks for the President. He was mindful not only of the political effect of the debates but of the very positive effect the President was having on the country with his then unique televised press conferences from the State Department Auditorium. No need to make waves.

On my own, with no consultation with Nixon, I had decided that television coverage of major speeches, such as the State of the Union, and of the press conferences, was giving the President (then Kennedy) overwhelming advantage in a TV age over the "loyal opposition." As a matter of principle I could not and would not object to television coverage of presidential events such as these. But I felt a need for balance if we were to hear also the voice of the party out of office.

In my Waldorf speech I called for "fair time," not "equal time." My point was that the President was the nation's major newsmaker and there was no legitimate reason for television to provide a time for reply to everything he said. Yet I thought fairness and balance demanded that there be some occasions for reply by the party out of power at times, determined by the networks—not by government decree.

Time now is provided traditionally by each network for a reply to the President's State of the Union speech each year. Nixon had advocated this. And when President Johnson was in the White House there were other equalizing devices such as extensive coverage of the "Ev and Charlie Show," a series of joint press conferences by Senator Everett Dirksen and Representative Charles Halleck, the minority leaders.

Nixon profited more by the "fair time" theory than any other politician when he was given the opportunity to reply on television to disparaging remarks against him and the Republicans by President Johnson in the heat of the 1966 congressional campaign. Nixon's statesmanlike "fair time" reply and his role in the 1966 elections, which saw Republicans make major gains, gave him a major boost he needed toward winning nomination in 1968.

The 1970 summer battle with CBS over "equal time" brought Colson full force into the conflict between the network and the White House.

After a televised presidential address on the situation in Vietnam, CBS had acceded to a demand by the Democratic National Committee for time for a reply. The reply was delivered on July 7 by the Democratic national chairman, Larry O'Brien.

The President was indignant—angry. He would have objected to any TV reply politically arguing against him as the commander in chief. But he would have been less vehement if the spokesman for the opposition had come from the ranks of Congress, not from the Democratic Party chairman. In my view, he had a point: he was the President of the United States bringing the public up to date on the situation in Vietnam. Others might differ with his strategy in Vietnam but he honestly felt he was speaking as President, not as a partisan. The networks must have agreed originally or they would not have granted air time.

Nonetheless, the speech was controversial and a reply could be justified by CBS. Their mistake was to accede to O'Brien, the Democratic Party's political spokesman, instead of inviting an opposition leader in Congress. Again, CBS was launched into a new White House storm center.

Colson leaped eagerly to the defense of the President's position and called upon his legal background to mastermind an appeal to the Federal Communications Commission for equal time for the Republican National Committee to answer the Democratic National Committee's reply to the President. The Federal Communications Commission agreed with the Republican protest and ruled that the GOP committee was entitled to time for reply to the Democrats. CBS appealed the ruling to the courts. With this action, CBS inadvertently helped strengthen the hand of Colson within the White House. He was their constant enemy. He was given the whip hand in this battle.

As the battle ran on and on, consuming the time of the White House, the national committees and the FCC, Haldeman finally handed the full project over to Colson officially with a September 21 memo which said:

"You should assume the lead and take full-time responsibility for working with the networks, advertisers, executives, etc., and really put it to them on this equal time matter. Of course, you will want to work with Herb and Jeb [Magruder], but you are the lead man in this regard."

From that moment forward, Colson assumed he was the lead man in all network matters—a point he and I were destined to dispute constantly.

The Washington *Post* summed up the immediate CBS matter in an editorial which opened by saying:

"The question of fairness on television has been twisted out of focus by the Federal Communications Commission's ruling that CBS must provide 'some reasonable period of time' for a Republican spokesman to reply to the Democratic National Committee's reply to the President. CBS has reasonably asked for reconsideration of that ruling. Whether or not that petition is granted, further clarification of the 'fairness doctrine' seems imperative.

"In our view, CBS was not well advised to turn to the Democratic National Committee for a reply to the President's speech on the war. The network has an unquestioned obligation, under the fairness doctrine, to provide opportunity for expression of an opposing view. But its presentation of the opposition party chairman gave rise to a plausible demand for comparable time from the Republican National Committee, and the FCC sustained that demand in the name of fairness. The issue would not have arisen if the reply to the President had come from an eminent public official representing the Democratic Party, say the majority leader of the Senate, the chairman of the Senate Foreign Relations Committee or a Democratic leader of the House. . . ."

The editorial ended inconclusively by calling for everyone to make a new start and by disputing the idea that the party in power should in effect have twice the time given to the Democrats on the air.

Colson's reply was in a memo to me:

"We've just got to turn around the negative publicity that we seem to be getting in the FCC matter. The decisions went our way and yet we continue to get kicked around in the press. Worst of all, CBS readily complied with one portion of the FCC order, i.e., granting time for the 'Doves', but refused to comply with the other portion of the same order granting time to the RNC. They are using every delay and stall, legally available to them. It seems to me we've got to find some way to continue to discredit them. If they looked bad before, they look worse now. Isn't there anything we can do with Morton, with you, or maybe even consider the Vice President?"

Colson, as always, dealt with a hardball approach. But the matter actually deserved little of all our time except that there was principle involved. We did not want a precedent set where each presidential address would be subject to equal-time demands by the Democratic Party. The principle, as far as CBS was concerned, was that it did not want to set a precedent where the party in power would have first the President speaking and then would have a reply to each Democratic reply, thus gaining a double shot at the subject.

CBS appealed the FCC decision in the courts and it appeared the matter might be stalled until well after the November elections. This possibility increased the frenzy within the White House. There was a counterproposal by Rogers Morton, on behalf of the Republican National Committee. He suggested that CBS provide the requested time to the Republican National Committee with the proviso that the time would be free if the court ruled against CBS and thus supported the FCC ruling. The committee would pay for the time if CBS won the case.

CBS refused the Morton proposal, and, after the elections, the court ruled against the FCC and thus against the Republican National Committee and Colson. It supported CBS.

The decision proved Colson wrong on his legal contentions, and, in fact, it provided no great precedents for either side. Perhaps it slowed down CBS in moving to grant other equal-time opportunities to the Democrats, but it appears unlikely that this was the intention of the network in the first place.

Ironically, out of defeat, Colson the gut fighter built personal power.

Late in 1970, former Eisenhower press secretary James Hagerty urged me to set up meetings between the President and executives from each of the networks. Hagerty then was vice-president for corporate relations at ABC.

After much White House discussion, the concept was accepted and we began to schedule meetings, first with ABC in January, then with CBS in February, and a short time later with NBC.

Again, Colson saw an opportunity to move into a place of influence or pressure with the network executives.

As was customary, I wrote a briefing paper for the President advising him regarding the persons attending the first ABC meeting and suggesting topics they were most interested in, from both the broadcast point of view and from that of the President. Colson immediately moved to get the last word with an "addendum to the briefing paper" which added to his demands to be included in the meeting along with me and Ron Ziegler. Colson's approach was shown with the opening statement in the "addendum."

"ABC executives will raise the political broadcast/equal time question and may ask whether you favor repeal of Section 315 [repeal would permit presidential debates]. Privately we do not favor repeal; publicly, however, you should take no position and indicate that this is principally a Congressional issue; repeal of 315 would, however, raise very serious new FCC regulatory problems. If you want me to, I can expand on this."

Here was Colson urging the President to say something he could not justify personally. We really want a debate but Congress will block it, Colson was saying. The truth was that Nixon did not want to debate and did not need to hedge or lie. A debate puts a President on the spot in questions of national security and that provides reason to say he does not favor the televised discussion. President Ford later debated President Carter on TV in 1976 and the result was detrimental to Ford, particularly on the question of independence within Eastern European nations. One can debate whether or not the President should be confronted by his opponent on television, but one should not urge the President to speak contrary to his own views. Colson, in his addendum, did exactly this.

Once Colson moved in on the ABC meeting to "provide legal advice" he became a regular part of each meeting with broadcast executives and thus enlarged the impression that he spoke for the President when he talked to the broadcasters.

Part of my original franchise within the White House was that I would be the liaison with the networks and other major broadcasters whether with newsmen or executives. Colson gradually enlarged his efforts to broaden his scope in the same field, always dealing secretly with a heavy hand. On one or two occasions he made what I told him were "sneak attacks" by secretly scheduling meetings with his newfound television contacts and then proceeding to threaten them because of what he termed biased reporting. What Agnew did publicly, Colson did privately in spades.

He did not intimidate the networks. He and the President just thought he did. The broadcasters discussed each meeting with me personally, and each meeting led to further confrontations within the White House involving Colson, Klein, and Haldeman. None ended decisively and Colson seemed to feel this gave him further license in his campaign to gain network domination.

When the formal Oval Office meetings with the networks were completed, I told the President we should follow up with a session with the chief executive officers of television companies owning groups of stations, such as Westinghouse, RCA, Metromedia, and Taft. Each of the sessions with network executives had given the President the type of outside knowledge I felt he needed, including an explanation of the problems of network broadcasters in regard to FCC regulations, FTC restrictions, programming, equal time, and similar dialogue, and their private opinions were important politically.

The meeting with TV executives who ran groups of stations was held in the Cabinet Room and to me it seemed a great success. I encouraged the broadcasters to tell the President of their particular problems in the communications industry. At one point, with the encouragement of Colson, one of the Carolina broadcasters made an impassioned address urging each of the broadcast executives to support the President in his 1972 campaign. I thought the comments were not in the tone of the meeting and cut off the broadcaster to avoid embarrassment for the other executives, who were not invited there to pledge political endorsements. They had come to meet the President and to discuss issues with him personally. Most of them privately favored Nixon's reelection, but they were not politicians or union leaders brought in to provide endorsements.

I could feel the negative reaction around the table and could envision the future headline about politics in *Broadcasting* magazine, as the Nixon advocate spoke, seeking endorsements.

I was sure that the outspoken, partisan broadcaster was acting under instructions from Colson, because he and Colson had been in frequent contact during the previous six months. When I cut off the speech, I knew the President was not happy with my move. He would have preferred hearing the words of praise instead of listening to the other executives express their complaints regarding government restrictions. On occasions like this, I could detect the President's boredom, but I strongly believed that—bored or not—he needed to hear about the problems outsiders had with government.

Even more now, I believe he would have been better off during those critical years if he had heard more uninhibited comment—if he were less protected from criticism.

When the meeting ended I went to the White House's West Lobby to catch any last comments our guests might have. Colson went directly into the Oval Office with the President, telling Nixon that I had frustrated his plan to gain the pledges of support from each of those present in the cabinet room. Neither Nixon nor Colson realized a point of journalistic ethics: such pledges are not and should not be made by broadcasters at meetings such as this one.

The effect of Colson's comments against me showed up directly when the White House released the so-called smoking-gun tapes of three conversations Nixon had with Haldeman on June 23, 1972.

A late-morning conversation between Nixon and Haldeman on June 23 covered a range of subjects. Most importantly, they included damning conversation regarding use of the CIA to get the FBI out of an investigation of money which had been "washed" in Mexico before reaching the Cubans who performed the Watergate break-in. Not a word was spoken regarding swift punitive action against all involved in the crime. For Nixon, fatal signs of Watergate cover-up. The conversation of that morning included the problems Pat Nixon and her daughters had with their hair when leaving a helicopter. In the midst of all this fatal but rambling discussion, Nixon jumped from talk of a possible press conference to these sometimes unintelligible taped remarks:

"I spend an hour—whatever it was—45 minutes or so with television executives [unintelligible] all ins and outs [unintelligible]. Look, we have no right to ask the President anything [unintelligible] biased. [unintelligible] says I'm going to raise hell with the networks. And look, you've just not got to let Klein ever set up a meeting again. He just doesn't have his head screwed on. You know what I mean. He just opens it up and sits there with eggs on his face. He's just not our guy at all, is he?"

Haldeman answered Nixon with "No." The President added, "Absolutely, totally, unorganized."

Haldeman: "He's a very nice guy."

The President: "People love him, but damn is he unorganized."

Haldeman: "That's right, he's not."

Later, during the hour-and-a-half conversation with Haldeman, Nixon jumped from a discussion of telephone calls to contributors, editors, and religious leaders to return again to the television meeting I had set up.

"You gotta be careful some ass over in [unintelligible] checked on [unintelligible] that's why you can't have Klein [unintelligible]. He just doesn't really have his head screwed on, Bob. I could see it in that meeting yesterday. He does not."

The tape covered Haldeman replying, "That's right."

The President came back again:

"He just doesn't know. He just sort of blubbers around. I don't know how he does TV so well."

Haldeman replied: "Well, he's a sensation on that—that goes to the [unintelligible] meaning of the thing, you know. What's his drawback is really an asset."

Between the time of that June conversation and July of the next year when I left the White House, I subsequently organized many other presidential meetings and I now suspect the taped conversation between Haldeman and the President was forgotten by both men, particularly as Watergate troubles developed more deeply and there was a growing need for my assistance in dealing with the press and the cabinet. So many delicate projects were assigned to my office in 1973 that on occasion I augmented my staff with volunteer outside top professionals such as Billie Brown, a highly capable New York public relations vice-president.

As I reflect back on the taped conversation, however, I believe it was typical of the lack of appreciation for many of our all-out effective efforts in the 1972 campaign, and the attitude reflected made it easier for Haldeman, Colson, and Ehrlichman to undermine those of us not in the hardball circuit in later months while things in the Oval Office seemed to be moving forward triumphantly.

The critics of the press were the White House stars while their ball was bouncing high. The comment about being "careful some ass over in [unintelligible] checked on" also leaves major questions. Were Nixon and Haldeman just talking or worrying about Watergate? My first hint that there had once been such a demeaning conversation came two years later, on August 5, 1974, when the pressures of Congress forced the release of these tapes. My first information on the release of the tape came not from the White House, although at the press briefing the next day, deputy press secretary Jerry Warren said, "The President numbers Herb Klein as one of his closest friends and will always number Herb Klein as one of his closest friends. . . . Herb Klein understands the events that surrounded that conversation. Herb Klein has the type of mind, I believe, to put that into perspective and to know the President well enough not to blow that out of proportion."

I learned of the tape earlier when two top reporters, Peter Kumpa and Muriel Dobbin of the Baltimore *Sun*, called me in Los Angeles to tell me of it and ask for my response. Oddly, the day the story broke was a Monday when I had taken a rare day off to play golf with my wife and our two closest friends, Tom and Marilyn Pownall, who were visiting from Washington. As we completed the first nine holes there was an urgent note posted to call Maria Searson, my secretary, but uncharacteristically, I chose to wait until we had completed play. I then called and received from my secretary a terse summary of the story with the plea that I get to the office as quickly as possible to answer inquiries. She sensed trouble or controversy.

Pownall accompanied me to the office, and I called the Baltimore *Sun* to find out firsthand what had happened. My first reaction to the story was to say nothing and to believe that the story would be ignored because of the pressures developed from the major revelations of the Nixon and Haldeman cover-up which dominated the tape.

Tom Pownall and my secretary, Maria Searson, were angry. And it turned out that most of my friends were more angry and more upset than was I. Pownall and I talked the issue out. Should I answer? What should be my tone? I decided the issue was not one which would be ignored so I would be best served if I made one brief, calm comment and stayed with it. I banged out a few sentences on my typewriter and called Kumpa and Dobbin back. Basically, I said that I did not take the Nixon taped comments as an evaluation of our relationship. At that point I instinctively felt that the comments referred to the broadcasters' meeting, but I had no immediate means of checking that unless I called the White House. I did not want to do that. I pointed out to Kumpa that I, too, had on occasion made derogatory remarks about friends. Such talk is common in a golf club locker room and at cocktail parties where one may often make a statement he does not really mean.

Truthfully, I was hurt. No one likes to read derogatory comments about himself. No one wants his children or wife to read them, or his friends and professional peers. But I understood Nixon's frequent vent to speak out in casual anger. I felt he had been overprotected so long he did not understand the true meaning of the broadcast meeting he criticized and, incited by Colson, it was easy for him to sound off in this way while meaning little in a serious way. Yet I was seriously disappointed and disillusioned.

The revelation of the "head screwed on" comment became public during the final days and hours before the President resigned from office, but to my surprise, the incident received wide national attention at that time of crisis. Whatever press support Nixon still had was further eroded by the comments. I suddenly found myself a part of editorials and columns and letters, all supportive of me and strongly negative to Nixon. Figuratively, they questioned who "had his head screwed on" at the time of the June 23 tape.

Before the week was over the President had resigned.

I refused to duck the media and accepted invitations from television discussion shows on all three networks on the night of resignation to express my opinions—regretful and supportive, but not bitter.

It was not a time to run away and hide.

Colson and his hardball were by then a part of the process of justice. The attack he had incited against the press and the White House press offices had increased the public negativism toward the President he served with fervor.

On his first Monday morning out of White House office, I was surprised to receive a telephone call directly from Nixon. He was home in San Clemente, now an ex-President. He called to thank me for what I had said on television resignation night and to express regrets for what had been revealed in the June 23 tape. Even then he could not find it in himself to apologize directly. But considering the timing this was a thoughtful and gracious act by the former President.

There was no question in my mind he apologized in his awkward way, and I was grateful to have the incident behind us.

Still the hurt lingered.

14

The Cabinet

WE DON'T THINK OF IT OFTEN, but once the voters have selected the President and Vice-President of the United States, they have had their most direct say as to who will serve as operating heads of varied and gigantic executive branches of the government. The Senate must confirm cabinet appointees, but usually that is routine.

During the campaign there is inevitable speculation within the press corps regarding potential cabinet officers. Inevitably there are rumors that a deal has been made with one politician or the other. But in today's world, the deals are few. The newsmen feel obligated to ask the candidate who will be in his cabinet, but the candidate who answers the question is either naïve or desperate. The candidate realizes that for every person named to the cabinet there are dozens more working in the campaign who aspire to the office.

The selection of the cabinet is easier than that of a strong White House staff because job standards have been established over the years making clear the general parameters of each cabinet responsibility. Cabinets tend to resemble each other, and most officers are expected to be advocates for their department constituency. The White House staff is what the President makes it, and there have not been two which were alike.

A President-elect may find the selection of the right man to become Secretary of State or Secretary of Defense both difficult and delicate. And for Republicans, the selection of a Secretary of Labor has particular difficulties. But for most of the offices there is a well-defined job description, and the difficulty centers in finding someone with an impeccable reputation in

his community, with a political philosophy close to that of the President—
at least as it applies to the cabinet department—and with experience and a
reputation as a leader.

During the selection process, there are outside pressures to find for the
cabinet a woman, a black, a moderate or conservative, a Catholic, a Jew, a
leader who adds geographic distribution to the cabinet makeup—and then
there are some inevitable political payoffs. The President-elect can struggle
with all these elements and more, but he cannot satisfy every pressure.

President Kennedy spent most of the time in his home in Georgetown
as he wrestled through the names and recommendations for his cabinet in
1960. The press waited in the winter cold on the street, chronicling each
arrival at the Kennedy door and speculating on its meaning. Nixon chose
the Pierre Hotel, two blocks from his apartment on New York's Fifth Avenue, for the hideout where he and advisers would confer to form the new
government.

Nixon worked sporadically on the selection of his cabinet. And when
the last post was filled, he assembled the new cast on December 11 in
Washington, where, acting as master of ceremonies before national television, he introduced personally each member of the group, which he described as the strongest the nation had seen. As happens often in such a
circumstance, Nixon faltered only in announcing the name of one of the
men he had known the longest, Maurice Stans.

Nixon did not spend the time I expected he would in selecting the cabinet, and at times he was annoyed because the press said his pace of selection was behind that of Kennedy. Even then, unfavorable comparisons
with Kennedy rankled him. He probably would have struggled longer
with the selection of names had he not worked out with Frank Shakespeare, who was advising him on TV, a publicized date for the dramatic
December television presentation. Thus, an artificial television commitment dictated the deadline for the selection of the President's cabinet.

Long before he was elected President, Nixon had made it clear that he
thought that foreign policy should be the dominant interest of any President serving in the sixties or the seventies. He at one time seriously considered advocating the selection of a formal assistant President who would
make the day-by-day decisions on domestic policy, leaving the Chief Executive more free to concentrate on foreign affairs.

Nixon had two major priorities as he started the cabinet-selection process. One was to find a strong Secretary of Defense, one who would stand
up to and could relate to Congress, and the second was to find a prominent Democrat who could give some sense of bipartisanship to the new administration.

His choice in both categories was Senator Henry "Scoop" Jackson of
Washington, whose views on defense policy generally paralleled Nixon's.

Jackson was more pro-Israel than was Nixon, but he was a respected Democratic leader, an advocate of strong national security forces, and an early candidate for President in 1968. Representative Melvin Laird, Nixon's longtime congressional friend from Wisconsin became a principal adviser in this field of defense, and it was Laird who pushed strongest for Jackson. Jackson had other political attributes helpful to Nixon. He was liberal on domestic policy and he was a staunch ally of the nation's top labor leaders. But as Secretary of Defense he would not affect domestic policy. He would bring friends, but not affect labor policy. On defense he was tough; so was Nixon.

After much discussion, Jackson gave Nixon a tentative yes on accepting the post and word of the probable appointment leaked out to the press. Angry Democratic senators, led by Senator Edward M. Kennedy, besieged Jackson and persuaded him that to accept a Nixon post would be traitorous to his party. Thus Jackson was lost, as was the bipartisan cabinet effort.

With Jackson out of the picture, there was need to move quickly in filling the key position. Laird, who had not sought the post, was convinced by Nixon that he should resign from his senior position in Congress and accept the position of Secretary of Defense. It later would become apparent that Laird was the most independent of all of the cabinet officers and the one most detested by Kissinger and Haldeman. But once he accepted the position, he also set up the most thorough transition office in the new cabinet. Assisted voluntarily by the late Representative Glen Lipscomb, he personally screened hundreds of applicants for positions in Defense while operating from a secret hideaway in the Sheraton-Carlton, a hotel which was headquarters for local Democrats.

One of the last men selected for the cabinet was its strongest member, George Shultz, who left his position as dean of the University of Chicago Graduate School of Business to become Secretary of Labor. I had never heard of Shultz, and I was not sure if Nixon had even met him at the time of the appointment. When the decision on Shultz was made, I was in Detroit to speak at the annual meetings between newspaper publishers and the leaders of General Motors and Ford. When I got the word that Shultz would head Labor, I sounded out Tony De Lorenzo, a GM senior vice-president. We conferred with his president and his chairman, and they knew Shultz very favorably as an astute labor negotiator and an able economist.

After the cabinet had been announced on TV from Washington, Nixon assembled it for its first meeting the next day, a time set aside for indoctrination. Everyone was bubbling with enthusiasm, but it was quickly apparent that out of the senior body, only four knew really what to expect in the executive branch in Washington: Laird, Secretary of State William

Rogers, HEW Secretary Robert Finch, and Stans. The cabinet-ranked counselors to the President, Arthur Burns and Daniel Patrick Moynihan, also knew their way around. The first cabinet assemblage was a day of lectures, not one of discussion.

The President made it clear that their personal public relations activities and those of their departments would be coordinated by me. I tried to guide the new cabinet to some understanding of its press responsibilities. While the cabinet meeting was intended for indoctrination, it set the pattern for the years to follow. Most cabinet sessions in the White House were instructional rather than discussional. It also was made apparent that White House aides would be sending many instructions to the departments. The pattern of White House domination was set that early.

The twenty-four-hour period when the Nixon cabinet was announced and first met and, later, the day of the inaugural, January 20, 1969, probably were the best days the cabinet enjoyed. Nixon had thought that because his choices represented leadership ranging from academic ranks to successful governorship of a large state, he had a team which would be responsive to him but also one which would be strong enough to accomplish his long-held ambition to conquer the federal bureaucracy. When it became apparent later that the new cabinet members were not going to be any more successful in managing the bureaucracy than had their predecessors, Nixon lost faith in most of the men and transferred more power to Haldeman and Ehrlichman, who would tell him that more could be done to manage the bureaucracy except that these cabinet secretaries were too weak. Thus the power of the presidency became more centralized year by year and the cabinet had less opportunity to express itself with the President or to govern its own departments. A potentially strong cabinet became weak.

The cabinet conference table we found in the White House had been given to President Franklin Roosevelt by Jesse Jones of Houston. It was not an antique, and it showed the signs of wear one might expect with a table built in the Depression and used for meetings over the years. It had a nondescript appearance and it was replaced by a more stylized table from Williamsburg, Virginia, during a time when Nixon was seeking to add physical and formal ornateness to the working area. The government provides the chairs around the table, with each assigned to an individual cabinet member. When a cabinet officer leaves, one of his privileges is to buy from the government the chair he occupied, complete with a brass plate identifying his office. Early on I had no idea how many times those chairs and cabinet officers would disappear, as Nixon shook off his official family more often than he originally anticipated. Lyndon Johnson added a gimmick to the cabinet table. Normally the President has buttons by which he can summon a secretary or a messman into the meeting to serve coffee or tea. Johnson added a few choices so he could signal for his favorite orange soft drink or a variety of other light beverages.

Regardless of furniture style, the senior seat in the cabinet room to the President's immediate right is occupied by the most senior cabinet office, the Treasury.

David Kennedy, Nixon's first Treasury Secretary, was among those who early fell from favor with the President and the senior White House staff. Kennedy had headed the Continental Illinois National Bank and Trust Company of Chicago and was widely respected in financial circles. One of his prime advocates was George Champion of Chase Manhattan Bank in New York. But while Kennedy understood every facet of banking, he was a lamb in the wolfland of politics and the press. He selected top personnel for his key staff, but he lacked the dynamism to do the two things the President wanted most from him:

1. Shake up the bureaucracy.
2. Take a leadership role in economic matters which would inspire public confidence in an administration soon confronted with growing inflation, high deficit spending, and unemployment. The "nice guy" eventually was given ambassadorial rank and assigned to trade missions. His successors included George Shultz and John Connally. His key assistants included such financial leaders as Paul Volcker, later Fed chairman, and Charls Walker. No one could doubt Kennedy's integrity or his understanding of the financial world. He simply was not a strong charismatic public figure.

The public seldom remembers a cabinet officer after he has been in office, but the one who will be remembered longest among the original Nixon cabinet was the first man out of it: Walter Hickel.

The inclusion of Hickel in the cabinet was hotly criticized by the environmentalists because they perceived him as a builder and a developer in Alaska rather than a conservationist. His political experience had been limited to the fiftieth state, where national political sophistication was generally an unknown factor, but more than the President realized, Hickel was a rugged individualist with the instincts of a true "diamond in the rough."

In transition-time press conferences I arranged to keep the newly announced cabinet officers from being isolated by individual members of the media before they took office. Kennedy had displayed his political naïveté and, incidentally, shaken the financial world by casually discussing during his press conference a change in the gold standard. Hickel made bigger headlines and started a controversy which lasted through his delayed Senate confirmation hearings when he criticized "conservation for conservation's sake." He allowed the press to entangle him in a discussion of industrial lands versus park lands and capped that with the comment, "A tree looking at a tree really doesn't do anything, but a person looking at a tree means something." That sent conservationists up the wall. After the conference, we assigned a top-level tutoring team headed by Bryce Harlow to work with Hickel before he appeared on Capitol Hill for confirmation hearings.

Still, despite the press conference words, Hickel was a conservationist at heart, and his record as governor of Alaska had been good in the environmental field.

Wally Hickel was a self-made man. He had arrived in Alaska with a few cents in his pocket, and he parlayed his instincts to become a multimillionaire builder and developer and governor of the state.

During the transition period after the 1968 elections, the President had debated between Representative Rogers Morton of Maryland and Hickel as he selected the Secretary of Interior. The latter because of the need for Western geographic balance, particularly in the Interior Department. Morton eventually became the Secretary—and also was a good one. From the start, Hickel was a unique figure in the cabinet. His direct comments at cabinet meetings on everything from economics to young people were viewed by the President as out of line, but I found them stimulating. Still, Hickel's lack of experience in handling the federal bureaucracy handicapped him, and he made the mistake of leaning too heavily on equally inexperienced Alaska friends on his staff. They in turn were dominated by the cause-oriented veterans of the federal establishment. Several times I joined Hickel for lunch at his desk in the Interior Department to discuss the handling of some of his confusing problems. On occasion we were joined by Robert Hitt, from California, his one senior aide with some political background. Hickel seemed to feel he could communicate with me and he did, but try as he would he found himself shut off more and more from other White House senior assistants. He plowed ahead unstoppable and direct. The President never was ready for this unsophisticated approach. Nor were most White House staffers.

Hickel learned moderation from his first Washington press conference and from the confirmation hearings. He and his staff put together early in 1969 the beginnings of major environmental legislation which gradually erased his image as a roughshod developer. In correcting this impression, however, Hickel moved in substance regarding the environment faster than the President and his domestic assistants wanted. He was far more concerned with environment than was the White House. John Whitaker, an experienced presidential aide with some background in matters involving Interior, was assigned as special liaison with Hickel as Ehrlichman sought to gain some control over the department.

By nature and experience, Hickel knew only how to be his own man, a person who could act with due deliberation if he chose but was more likely to "shoot from the hip" if he felt that was best. He was unpredictable. He rarely was indirect, and his pattern did not fit in with the growing Nixon-Haldeman concept of smooth, tight control over all of the executive branch.

Despite his rough exterior, Hickel felt great compassion for people; as the national sentiment surrounding the Vietnam War became more emotional, the feeling also affected the Interior Secretary. I was not aware of that side of him nor of the long conversations he had had with his son regarding Vietnam. I was, therefore, surprised when an assistant rushed into my office on a May morning in 1970 to show me a story in the *Evening Star* quoting extensively from a letter Hickel had written to the President asking him to communicate more directly with young people and to halt the verbal attacks which he felt were dividing the country. It was a letter critical of the President and his posture on Vietnam, and it ended with a comment on Hickel's personal difficulty in meeting privately with the President.

Moments after I saw the story, Hickel called me and said he had written a "private letter" to the President, and he thought I should see a copy of it right away. I asked for the copy by messenger, but told Hickel that the story quoting his letter already was in the press. He professed not to know it had been leaked. He probably was honest with me. My brief investigation indicated that the leak had come from a member of his staff who had worked on the letter and felt he wanted this view to become public. The President found out about the letter first through a call from me to Haldeman. His mail arrived later.

The letter came out at a time of crisis. Students had been killed tragically at Kent State. American troops were in Cambodia. Thousands of demonstrators were surrounding the White House. Hidden inside the White House, even outside my office, we had hundreds of troops at the ready. They were part of the secretly mobilized National Guard.

Hickel's letter made many valid points and should have been studied by the President. But a letter which was leaked before it ever reached the White House took on the appearance of mutiny.

In the midst of the uproar Hickel came to my office to confer and found he had to enter and leave through a side door because all of the main entrances had been closed to keep out the demonstrators. We talked about the problem as the antiwar chants from outside on Pennsylvania Avenue rang in our ears. I cautioned him against enlarging on the issue with the press and said there was little he could say in clarification which would help. He had jumped from the team and the press loved it. Hickel did not want to resign regardless of the turmoil. He differed on a policy but he felt loyal, and believed strongly in the programs he was working on in the Interior Department.

The President was furious, and only the other problems he faced simultaneously forced him to look at the matter reasonably. He had long ago turned against Hickel because he felt he did not understand policy and he was not a team player. He wanted to fire Hickel immediately but decided rationally that to do so after this letter would make the Secretary an even greater popular youth hero than he already was, and that it could be damaging in the coming congressional elections. Strangely, Hickel's publicity thus had made him immune from firing—for the moment.

There were harassments perpetrated against Hickel, however. Pettiness was the word. On a Saturday night I arrived in Williamsburg anticipating a day's respite, and waiting for me was an urgent message to call Haldeman. "Hickel has reservations for tomorrow morning's White House church services," Haldeman said. "The President absolutely does not want him there. You have to tell him not to come to church here." I argued but Haldeman told me that the President had ordered me to make the call to Hickel. In such a tense situation, I did not want to enlarge the issue with Wally so I told the Secretary I thought it best if he skipped the next day's services since the press would be there and would attempt to question him and the President regarding the now famous Hickel letter. Hickel pleaded that his wife was counting on the service and had invited two close friends from Alaska to join them. I felt as if I were bleeding inside. But I was firm. The Hickels did not attend church in the White House.

Even if the letter had not been made public by Hickel's office, I doubt that he would have survived the antagonism which had been built up against him by the combination of Nixon, Haldeman, and Ehrlichman. They did not respect him and made no attempt to understand him.

Hickel was left untouched through the midterm elections. And then after the elections of 1970, on the eve of Thanksgiving, he was fired abruptly.

The Hickel affair dramatized the barriers which were being built between the President and the cabinet. They were barriers which stemmed from an egotism of eliteness within the White House, barriers which were increasingly applied to every department of the executive branch with the exception of Labor, where Shultz and his capable undersecretary, Jim Hodgson, seemed to have built in intellectual exemption.

The egotism of eliteness seemed to stem from a growing feeling that those in the White House were superior intellectually to those in the cabinet. The perception was inaccurate. As the first months turned into the first years of the Nixon presidency, the White House staff developed a growing instinct to direct rather than assist the cabinet officers. Initially, the staff and the President acted more as referees in matters of dispute and jurisdiction among cabinet officers. There was a tremendous overlap of duties in matters such as land management, and there was a need for coordination between departments. But as the White House power grew, the cabinet officers never knew whether the Domestic Council aide who gave them orders spoke for the President or for himself. And because there was a barrier which decreased personal contact between cabinet officers and the President, the widely known cabinet members had little way to check on the orders they received from the almost faceless White House aides.

Shultz was the major exception. His academic credentials could not be faulted. But he coupled them with strong political and administrative instincts which won the grudging admiration of both Haldeman and Ehrlichman. Nixon found some chemical kinship with Shultz, and he consulted him increasingly on matters of broad domestic policy from business and economics to labor as his sphere of influence grew while others decreased. Shultz gave frank advice which was seldom found faulty.

Not all the feelings about relationships between the cabinet and the White House were negative. John Whitaker, who at first had served as cabinet secretary, directed a memo to me and Alex Butterfield on May 29, 1970, containing ideas which if implemented would have greatly relieved the tension. Bob Haldeman was given a copy of the Whitaker memorandum and wrote at the top of it "good ideas. Need to follow up." Unfortunately, he directed his assistant Larry Higby to follow up only with me and with Butterfield, and I was not able to determine how much discussion of the plan there had been with the President, who was the key to its success.

Whitaker was concerned about news stories indicating that there was a "divided cabinet." Among his suggestions were these:

"As I have recommended before, I think the President should schedule one dinner a month for three to four cabinet officers—a variation of this would be something the President seems to want to do, i.e., have five or six people in for dinner who are experts on a subject with the Cabinet officers—for example, Secretary Hardin and four or five experts on rural development.

"When you come right down to it we sacrifice a great deal in human relations in pursuit of efficiency and this is where we make a mistake." (Whitaker was exactly right.) "There is no real substitute for (1) an individual meeting between the President and a Cabinet Officer, (2) a cabinet meeting where the cabinet feels a sense of participation in decision making. Both waste the President's time—I'm convinced the 'option paper way' of decision making is the right way to make decisions, but let's 'waste a little time' to pep up a team spirit." The "option paper way" Whitaker referred to meant that the cabinet secretary submitted to the President several choices and the arguments for each so Nixon could study these and study backup papers before making a decision. The method saved time, but eliminated direct discussion and personal contact.

Whitaker concluded:

"Hard as I tried when Cabinet Secretary to pull off a Cabinet meeting that had a tone of meaningful discussion somehow the agenda came out as terribly dull or the image of the Cabinet being preached at or being told what the decision was rather than participating in it. I had moderate success with one meeting with an open agenda where anybody brought up anything they wanted, but that is chaos if done too frequently. So when you come right down to it, I think the small dinner idea is the best solution plus a new push to make sure telephone call suggestions to the Cabinet members by the President are constantly pushed by the staff. The easiest device is for Herb Klein to watch the news and Bill Timmons the hill, so that the President is constantly supplied with talking points in the form of 'pat on the back' telephone calls lauding a speech, TV appearance or testimony on the hill, etc."

It was an idea that died before it was born. I, like Haldeman, agreed with its merit but dropped working on it after providing two or three "talking points" which brought no response from the President. I should have pursued harder.

Whitaker was right: cabinet meetings had become lectures more regularly than discussions. The Nixon cabinet was not alone in this fault. Eventually it seems to happen to most cabinets in government today.

Typical of those suffering from exclusion was George Romney, who prior to the New Hampshire primary in 1968 had loomed as the odds-on favorite to capture the Republican nomination for President.

Romney was an amateur politician who came successfully out of the automotive business to catapult an interest in constitutional reform in Michigan into the governorship of the state. He was a colorful, clean-cut political figure who seemed for a while to bring a new look to the Republican Party. An individualist, Romney would sometimes get up early to play golf by himself, shooting several balls on each hole and jogging between each shot. At one time, when he was living in a Washington hotel, one of his newly appointed assistant secretaries living in the same hotel found himself awakened at five each morning by the pounding of someone jogging around the roof of the building. After ten days of this, he determined to confront the source of his annoyance. He went to the roof and found his new boss, Romney, jogging. There was no confrontation, the assistant secretary changed rooms, and the new Secretary of Housing and Urban Development continued to exercise with no idea he bothered anyone.

Romney is tough-minded and yet an idealist. As an individualist he was used to acting with little consultation or by confronting easily the man in charge—in this case the President. His wife, Lenore, also a strong individualist, became an outstanding spokesperson for volunteer programs.

From the White House point of view, Romney was seen by the new elite of the Domestic Council as ineffective, a man who did not understand national politics and one who needed to be directed by younger presidential staff assistants. The result was an impasse between Romney and the White House and the White House was the loser.

Another former governor, John Volpe, was more persistent than most in the cabinet. He worried little about protocol and sought out the President wherever he could find him whether his purpose was simply to seek an opportunity for a priest friend to preside at White House religious services or to sell the President on the need to support the supersonic transport so as to protect American dominance in the commercial aviation industry. Volpe became an annoyance to the President and to Haldeman. They did not consider him or his department worthy of major presidential time, and even in the final battle with Congress over support for the ill-fated supersonic project, the control point became the White House and a team headed by Bill Magruder, an engineer and a scientist, not the Department of Transportation.

This was all part of a picture not fully perceived by the news corps.

In the fight for approval of the supersonic transport, the press again became part of the "enemy corps." Dick Cavett, who was then struggling with his late-night interview show on ABC, earned the particular ire of the White House with personal comments judged as one-sided against the project. He also brought on the show guests to support his anti-SST views.

It mattered little that few congressmen were awake late enough to see Cavett or be influenced by him. Cavett became a target of pressure from the White House, which sought to force ABC to allow an administration spokesman on the program to discuss the issue and thus provide some balance. ABC sided with the administration and was attacked publicly by Cavett. Magruder was invited to appear on the show and handled himself well. But the outcome of the battle with Cavett had no bearing on the issue. Congress voted against funds for the SST.

Maurice Stans made a determined effort to upgrade the status of the Commerce Department. He went into office feeling he headed a department which long before had lost its effectiveness, and yet he believed that it could serve a growing role in the area of international trade. Commerce is the smallest cabinet department. Being thorough, Stans asked an aide to give him a copy of the publications produced by Commerce each month. To the amazement of Stans, the assistant said, "Where would you like a truck to deliver the hundreds of magazines and books?" Even a small department like Commerce had become a victim of the bureaucracy and was wasting money in every area, including the field of publications. Stans made gains, but he never really got on top of the bureaucracy despite many innovative steps such as regular luncheon meetings with his top management appointees. Stans, like the others, found it difficult to gain a voice either in his department or in the White House. In his department he was a better communicator than most cabinet officers before or since, but he still faced opposition from the ever-present bureaucracy. He tried.

William Rogers went into the State Department with credentials that should have won him acclaim as an outstanding leader in the foreign-policy arena. He never had a fair chance and was hurt by his unwillingness to fight the White House system. Rogers and Nixon had been close personal friends since early in the Nixon career in Congress. In the critical hours before Nixon made his Checkers Speech, his principal advice had come from Rogers, Chotiner, and Jim Bassett. There was a personal rapport between Nixon and Rogers which went deeper than any others in the early campaigns. They enjoyed similar interests from golf to politics. He was one of the few people Nixon would relax with.

Rogers was never a campaign organizer, but he was a trusted and wise consultant in each Nixon campaign. His record as Attorney General under Eisenhower was excellent. Most of his advice was good, although in 1960 he was one of the advisers who thought Nixon needed to treat Kennedy softly in the debates so as not to rekindle the picture of "Tricky Dick" or an overaggressive Nixon. Nixon carried the niceness too far. That contributed to his loss in public opinion after the first debate. It is easy to second-guess anyone, including this author, who also erred with some advice, but I believe that Rogers also was a major influence in convincing Nixon to ignore the jailing of Martin Luther King at the time Jack Kennedy was telephoning sympathy to him. Nixon's mishandling of the King jailing was considered by political pundits to have helped Kennedy in winning the close 1960 election.

The first time I observed a major difference in feelings between Nixon and Rogers came when both were out of office and competing for business in the field of law. Competition for one client soured them on each other for a period of months in the mid-1960s. This in itself surprised me, because I saw two men who had been through the pressures of political campaigns and the pressures of political issues, and who had found rare pleasure in going to football games and vacationing together. I would never have predicted that commercialism would at one time split them.

That was short-lived. But they were never quite so close again.

Rogers advised but played no major role in the 1968 campaign, yet, despite the differences in competition for law business, Nixon turned to Rogers when he sought a man to head State, one of the departments he felt most important to his success as President. Because of his experience as deputy attorney general and Attorney General under Eisenhower and because of his long personal relationship with the President-elect, Rogers had the opportunity to become the most powerful man in government, outside of the President.

That never happened. Early in the administration, Henry Kissinger, whom the President knew only slightly until he was appointed director of the National Security Council, asserted himself on a daily basis until he soon became the man closest to the President on foreign policy. There probably were three major reasons for this change in favoritism from Rogers to Kissinger: The President was vulnerable to being dazzled by bright, charismatic newcomers, often to the disadvantage of those who had been on the scene longer. John Connally and Peter Peterson, for example, captured the President's imagination when they first appeared on the scene. Two, Kissinger came into the administration with government experience, with a knowledgeable and impressive intellectual background in foreign affairs, particularly as they applied to Soviet relations, and he was aggressive. Three, Rogers was more a family friend than an aggressor seeking his place in the sun, and he soon found himself bogged down in the internal problems of the bureaucracy of the State Department.

Rogers had the prestige and the position which Kissinger envied to a point where he threatened more than once to quit his post unless Rogers was removed and he was appointed Secretary of State. Rogers become so lost in the detailed affairs of his department that he was supplanted quickly as the principal adviser and negotiator on foreign policy in critical matters such as the China breakthrough, the negotiations on Vietnam and the SALT treaty. The President clearly assumed personal leadership on major foreign policy. This was the part of his job he enjoyed most. But when SALT was in the final stages of negotiation, Kissinger had a room in the Kremlin near the President. Rogers was in a suite in the Rosedin Hotel and his meetings more often than not were with Kosygin rather than Brezhnev. And, of course, Kissinger was the negotiator with China and Vietnam.

Despite all his power, Kissinger was jealous of the Rogers position. On an afternoon late in 1972 after the election victory over George McGovern when I was in Haldeman's office discussing domestic-affairs policy, Kissinger broke into our meeting to complain that Rogers had upstaged him on a minor matter and to point out that he had been assured that he would become Secretary of State shortly. When would Rogers be moved out? he demanded. Haldeman did not answer directly but countered by examining in detail a Kissinger press briefing. In this one-hour briefing you referred to the President only once, Haldeman told Kissinger. Kissinger countered with the assertion that he felt he had referred to him more, but when confronted with the text he said that the implication of presidential support was there. Kissinger was right, the implication was there. Haldeman and the President presumably wanted words, not implications.

This incident was typical of infighting between the powerful egos involved in White House policy-making.

Rogers eventually was forced out in August of 1973, but on his own terms. Prior to his departure, when the President needed a friend most, on the day in April when he painfully summoned John Ehrlichman and Bob Haldeman to Camp David to ask for their resignations, it was Rogers he called to his side to help him in the task which was perhaps the most painful he performed aside from his own resignation. Rogers was a very able Secretary of State, but his great talents were not utilized fully.

From the moment that he was appointed Secretary of Defense until the moment that he left office, Melvin Laird remained his own man. He was a key part of the National Security Council, and he was willing to listen to the advice of the generals and the admirals, although he made his own decisions. He followed presidential orders, but not until he had had his say and had exerted his considerable impact on presidential decisions. He often was a voice of restraint in Vietnam. He had a stronger backup than any other member of the cabinet: David Packard, deputy secretary of defense, a man with industrial credentials unequaled by anyone else in government.

Laird, like Rogers, was part of an early coterie of Nixon political friends. Laird and his friend Representative John Byrnes of Wisconsin were two of the men in Congress closest to Nixon when he served as Vice-President. They were close politically, but they also had other mutual outside interests such as football and golf. In November of 1960, after the Kennedy victory, Laird and Rogers were two of the men Nixon wanted with him when on short notice he asked me to gather with us a half dozen friends to go to the Army-Navy game in Philadelphia.

Nixon was more relaxed for the spur-of-the-moment football party than I had seen him in years. It was as if he had finally gotten past the shock of losing the presidency. As we rode to Philadelphia in a compartment in a chartered congressional train, Nixon recounted some of the experiences he savored from his years in public office. At the stadium we met Red Blake, who had retired after serving for years as the coach of the Military Academy. On two days' notice he had collected six tickets for us and a few for the Secret Service, seating us adjacent to the Cadet Corps. Nixon startled the cadets and the other spectators, who found it hard to believe that the

Vice-President of the United States was sitting in the crowd instead of joining the military hierarchy in fieldside boxes for the game.

In the fall of 1959 we went to Wisconsin, where the Vice-President was to be the featured speaker at a local fund-raising dinner for Laird. The long scheduled dinner came at a time when Arthur Flemming, then Secretary of Health, Education, and Welfare, had issued a warning that many cranberries in Wisconsin and elsewhere had been sprayed with a pesticide which could induce cancer. The warning, issued in the Thanksgiving season, became an immediate political issue because of its effect on the cranberry industry at a critical sales time.

At the Laird dinner the first course was a bowl of cranberry relish. The press photographers with us immediately became interested in the key issue of the evening. Would the Vice-President eat the cranberries? Laird and I told Nixon that everyone was watching to see whether he would eat the berries. Nixon, in a rare moment of spontaneous humor, said, "I'll watch you, Herb. When you have eaten your bowlful, I will." I ate the cranberries. Nixon ate the cranberries, as did Laird. The photographers had a field day.

On the same evening, Jack Kennedy faced a similar cranberry crisis in Wisconsin. At this dinner cranberry juice was served. Kennedy downed his juice—and again the news cameras clicked.

As Secretary of Defense, Laird was one of the most interesting and capable men in government. On policy matters, he was probing and decisive. He leaned heavily on his background as a congressman and had excellent relations with the Congress. He knew how to play the news media, and his instincts were sound in this regard. His closest friends in the news business were Rowland Evans and Robert Novak, the columnist team. Anytime they ran a column or an item concerning the Defense Department or Laird, it was presumed that the source of the information was the Secretary of Defense. Usually, the presumption was correct.

The relationship between Laird and Evans and Novak was particularly galling to Kissinger. A paragraph in their column which was shaded to Laird's point of view over Kissinger's inevitably would bring an outraged tirade from Henry. "Laird is a liar. He refuses to accept the truth or to speak it," was a comment Kissinger repeated privately again and again under these circumstances.

Kissinger, I think, felt he could control Rogers. To him, Laird was more like a loose football, he did not know where he would stop on an issue.

The organization of the staged withdrawal of American troops from Vietnam involved many key people, but principal credit for the plan went to Laird. Nixon announced the plan and reported on its progress in a series of short television speeches. But the credit given Laird by the media bothered the President, and, more, it irritated Kissinger.

Partly through his own family, Laird had an understanding for young people and their traumas over Vietnam. Some in the administration looked at him as a dove in the clothing of the Secretary of Defense. And at times, he would have made concessions Nixon did not condone. But he was basically tough and realistic. He left Defense by his own choice in 1973.

The administration's earliest attempt at bureaucratic reform, one which Congress approved, was in the Post Office Department, not in programs of social welfare.

Winton "Red" Blount, who long had been active in Alabama and Southern politics, was brought into the cabinet to operate and to reform the politically moribund Post Office Department. Blount was the most direct person in the cabinet. He had grown up in the heavy construction business, where one did not mince words politically. He and his wife, Mary Kay, had the Southern charm, but he in no way had the slow softness often associated with the South. "Red" knew how to fan fire, and he more than anyone in the chosen team, set out to change the bureaucracy.

The effort of the Postmaster General to remove the Post Office Department from politics went entirely opposite from recent political history. James Farley was both the chief political operative and the Postmaster General for Franklin Roosevelt. The Postmaster General's office is perhaps the most ornate in Washington. Besides an elaborate kitchen and dining room and the gigantic office for the "general," there is a waiting room which resembles a hotel lobby. It was there that Farley met with his political henchmen and dealt out orders and favors.

The phrase "post-office Republican" long had been part of the earlier meager Republican politics of the South. The "post-office Republicans" were appointees from Republican administrations who usually had little qualification for government but were counted on to organize whatever effort could be generated for token Republicanism in the South. The status of the Republican Party in the South began to change with the Eisenhower elections, and it was accentuated by the Nixon efforts in 1960 and 1968 and the Goldwater campaign of 1964. Blount was a product and a leader of the change with no relationship to the old post-office Republicans.

In relatively short order, he and his new department formulated a bill to free the Post Office Department from the political pressures of Congress. He had high hopes that modern mechanization and computerization plus better employee morale would rebuild the old department into one which could carry its own load economically and would improve service. Blount was a battler, and he convinced Congress to give up some of its political prerogatives to "remove the Post Office from politics." I worked with his assistant, James Holland, in developing a program which would have senior assistants from the department in key cities on the day the reform program was announced. The impact from this mass media information blitz helped in dealing with public opinion and eventually with the Congress.

Blount brought more business attitudes and methods into the department. But strong as he was, he never really conquered the bureaucracy and post-office service dwindled rather than increased in the days and years following "reform."

Blount was an outsider in the cabinet who retained his independence but who never had the opportunity to use his full ability beyond the narrow scope of the Post Office Department. When he resigned it was because of job frustration. He was well liked by the President but rarely called upon for the management advice the President needed.

John Mitchell became involved in national politics because of a genuine desire to manage the campaign of a man he thought should be the next President. He was independent by nature and he had made a reputation in law which Nixon envied and admired. He knew the politics of water bond issues, but he was not a politician. To the public and most of the press, Mitchell comes through as hard and abrasive. I found him neither. There was no doubt that he was tough and he was intelligent, but at times he would startle me with his patience and his compassion. He was never comfortable with the press, and he did not understand it. Yet he wrote an Attorney General's guideline on the subpoena of news pictures or information which generally was accepted by the press as fair and protective of its First Amendment rights.

Each step down the political road which eventually led to Mitchell's humiliation and conviction after Watergate seemed to be one he took reluctantly. Initially he had to be convinced by Nixon that he was the man he wanted most to manage his 1968 campaign. He entered the postelection process of cabinet officer selection willingly, but he argued long and often against his appointment as Attorney General. He did not want to manage the 1972 campaign, and even in the early stages of it he took only casual interest as he lingered too long in the Justice Department, allowing Jeb Magruder to handle the original organization of the Committee to Re-elect the President. He did so even though he knew that Magruder was ambitious but weak and inexperienced in politics of this scope —a puppet appointee for Bob Haldeman. Still there was no question that Mitchell loved politics. Even in the Justice Department those closest to him from his deputy attorney general, Richard Kleindienst, and two assistants, Robert Mardian and Dick Moore, who were political allies with a legal background.

Mitchell fought his battles with some of those closest to the President— Haldeman, Ehrlichman, and Bob Finch—and more than held his own.

One of Mitchell's quirks was his dislike of Finch. Why he had this feeling was a puzzle but clearly it was there. After a couple of drinks he sometimes would speak of "Bob Fink" and then smile slightly. He claimed he was quoting Lyndon Johnson, but the meaning was deeper. The Johnson reference came from a telephone conversation between Nixon and the then President on the Sunday before the 1968 election. Johnson had read news reports from a session with reporters in Los Angeles which I had set up for Finch on the Saturday before the election. The subject was the Johnson bombing halt, and Finch had spoken of Johnson's move as one of political desperation to help Humphrey against Nixon. After a few polite preliminary remarks Johnson almost jumped across the phone at Nixon, sounding off furiously about the press conference by "Fink" wherein Finch had challenged the motives of the President. Johnson was angry and made it clear to Nixon that he would respond with a counterattack if there were other criticisms of him. Mitchell and Finch were sitting in the room with Nixon and indirectly heard the conversation. It was one which Mitchell never allowed Finch to forget.

Mitchell's quarrels with Ehrlichman were basically polite, but they centered on substance. Who was the President's lawyer? They disagreed on policy matters, with Mitchell taking a more direct conservative stand than did Ehrlichman. Both worked diligently on school desegregation in the South, and one of the generally forgotten things is that they made major gains in this area for the President, but behind the scenes was the constant conflict between Mitchell's political instincts and Ehrlichman's lack of understanding of politics, PERIOD—according to Mitchell. John Dean was Mitchell's man in the White House, but Ehrlichman tolerated his presence as White House counsel because he did not have the clout to dispute Ehrlichman's legal views. Until Watergate, Dean was handling mainly routine questions.

The Mitchell conflict with Haldeman was more subtle. They respected each other, but in this case there was a power conflict which was central to their relationship. This was fueled by the President, who played one against the other on questions of political judgment. When Mitchell was appointed to head the President's 1972 campaign, Haldeman, who supported the selection, protected himself by bringing his own people into the organization and by moving Gordon Strachan from a junior place on my staff to a key position on his where he could monitor everything that was happening daily with the Committee to Re-elect the President (CREEP) and report it in capsule fashion to Haldeman. One of the questions at the Watergate trials was whether Strachan provided Haldeman with a summary of the "Gemstone" notes which were taken from the wiretaps placed in the Democratic National Committee offices. Magruder to this day strongly believes that Strachan kept Haldeman fully informed. Haldeman denies it.

Mitchell is a complex personality. He has a dry sense of humor which few see. At the height of the demonstrations against Vietnam, Mitchell was in control over the actions of the Justice Department and the police. During critical moments such as these, he remained in his quarters in the Justice Department to call the shots from there. Kleindienst on several occasions was posted along with me in the city police command headquarters, where the mayor and the police chief received all detailed reports of violence. On more than one occasion, when I felt patience was growing too thin in the command headquarters and unnecessary violence might result, I called Mitchell and urged him to act through Kleindienst to bring more reason into our side of the conflict. His response on each occasion was positive.

Given the factors I have mentioned, there is no way for me to explain why Mitchell approved the intelligence budget for Gordon Liddy which provided for the financing of the Watergate entry. When Magruder and Mitchell met in Florida to go over a long agenda of campaign items, I always wondered if Magruder fully explained to Mitchell what he was getting into with the authorization of funds for Liddy. Magruder says he did. What effect did the pressure from Martha Mitchell have on his rationality? Whatever the answer, Mitchell alone had the intelligence, the strength and experience to have stopped the whole bizarre plot. And Mitchell did not. He approved it.

Mitchell's chosen cabinet rival, Bob Finch, had a close political relationship to the President which dated to Nixon's congressional days. Finch, seemingly, was born for politics and Nixon had an affection for him and a respect for his political judgment which was different from the President's feeling for anyone else.

I first met Finch and his wife, Carol, at a campaign bus stop in the South Bay part of the Los Angeles area, where he was running for Congress against a long-entrenched Democrat, Cecil King. Finch recently had returned from military service in Korea, and as we approached the area where our motorcade was to pick up the Finches for joint appearances to help their congressional campaign and the Eisenhower-Nixon campaign, the normally solemn Nixon suddenly called me to his side to describe his enthusiasm for Finch. The rallies were a success, but the Finch campaign was not. He won more votes than expected but still lost to the Democratic incumbent.

When Nixon ran for President in 1960, it was Finch he turned to first to direct his campaign from early 1959 to its completion. And in June 1960, Nixon asked me to come back to Washington to join Finch in or-

ganizing the campaign and in organizing his press operation, focusing almost immediately on a trip to the Soviet Union. When the election was
over, Nixon cited several reasons for his narrow loss to Kennedy, none of
which faulted Finch or me. There were others outside who were more
critical.

Finch came into the 1968 campaign on a part-time basis. Less than two
years earlier, he had been elected lieutenant governor of California, attracting 100,000 more votes than had his running mate, Ronald Reagan.
Finch felt that Reagan never forgave him for winning by a larger margin
and for news stories and columns indicating that Finch was more popular
with the national press than was the governor. This, coupled with the
frustration of Reagan's own presidential ambitions in 1968 and Nixon's
pressure convinced Finch that he should drop out of elective politics in
California, at least temporarily, and accept one of the posts urged on him
in the Nixon cabinet. The closeness between Nixon and Finch was best
illustrated when Nixon asked him to become his vice-presidential nominee
in 1968 and Finch turned it down because he felt that some would interpret this as cronyism or nepotism and thus it would hurt the Nixon
presidential bid against Humphrey.

During the transition period, Finch had a choice of virtually any cabinet post he wanted. He sought none. Nixon urged him to become the Secretary of Housing and Urban Development because he thought the job
was an easy one which would allow him the extra time to spend coun-
seling the President.

Finch, in typical fashion, chose perhaps the most difficult job in the cabinet, Secretary of Health, Education, and Welfare. The HEW bureaucracy had won out over everyone else who had held the job, and he
thought he was the man to conquer it. Finch might have done this had he
been a stronger administrator, but he chose to fight issues and to change
the department rather than to worry about all the bureaucratic details.

The philosophic differences between Finch and Mitchell rarely surfaced during the campaign. Each had his own duties and little time for
conflict. In the administration, however, the clashes became frequent.
Mitchell was pushing for a slow approach to desegregation, "Southern
Strategy." Finch believed that the future of the President and the Republican Party depended on widening the constituency to include more youths
and more minorities. At the start of the administration, Finch could do no
wrong and obtained presidential approval for most of his appointments
even though many came from the ranks of liberals and moderates who he
believed would fit into the running of HEW.

He selected Dr. James Allen, state commissioner of education in New
York, to head education—a publicized advocate of busing. James Farmer,
who had brought CORE to its peak with his activist leadership, became

an assistant secretary. Allen was an open sore from the time of his appointment, but Farmer, whom I had first known when he led a demonstration to oppose the opening of the New York World's Fair, turned out to be more moderate than most anticipated and he was a major asset.

These appointments rankled Mitchell and Haldeman, but the public opposition to them was small until Finch made it known that he was about to appoint Dr. John Knowles assistant secretary for health. Knowles, who had brought mass-medicine techniques to Massachusetts General Hospital in Boston, was immediately opposed by the political wing of the American Medical Association, which felt that he would be a supporter of some form of national health insurance. Knowles became the focal point of a battle between Finch and Senator Everett Dirksen and other conservative Republicans, and he gave ammunition to Mitchell in his battle to decrease the influence of "Fink." Finch aided the case against him by trying too hard and too long to placate Dirksen.

In the long run, Finch was forced to withdraw support for Knowles and, in the process, the President, who had not pressured Finch on the controversy, received the blame from the press for bowing to the pressures of the AMA. Mitchell's case against Finch was strengthened. Finch quickly named another liberal, Dr. Roger Egberg, dean of the University of Southern California medical school. The move was too late.

HEW never lacked issues for a secretary who was determined to face controversy. Once, Finch issued a ruling which would have eliminated the use of cyclamates in soft drinks. This brought the anger of Donald Kendall, the President's close friend, who headed Pepsi-Cola, and other bottlers.

The pressure increased against Finch. He organized a major effort during the 1970 student demonstrations to meet with students. When American troops were ordered into Cambodia, the controversial Allen spoke out publicly against the President's policy. Finch found himself in exhaustion, near a state of a nervous breakdown, and he was hospitalized within hours of the time he was to meet with the rebellious factors within HEW.

Finch recovered physically, but not politically.

A short time later I was in Vietnam and Cambodia to inspect battle areas of the new United States offensive and report to the President. At midnight, Saigon time, I received a telephone call from Haldeman. It was noon in Washington.

"The President wanted me to call you to tell you he has asked Bob Finch to leave HEW and become a counselor to the President," he said. "We will announce it this afternoon."

Finch's true ambition was to become a United States senator from California. In 1964, he had forsaken his own ambitions and managed the successful campaign to elect George Murphy senator. As Murphy came close to the end of his term of office in 1970, he was badly handicapped by a serious throat ailment which made it difficult for him to talk much above a whisper. He looked younger than his age but sounded older and feeble.

Finch and others hoped that Murphy would drop plans for re-election and move into another post in government where he could be helpful. He had an intense interest in international culture exchanges, for example. As the deadline approached when a candidate could file for Senate in California, Murphy showed no signs of dropping out of the race. Finch felt that because of his close personal relationship with Murphy and his own desire for the office he could not discuss this with the senator. It was arranged for Nixon to call Murphy and suggest that perhaps his voice would be such a handicap that he should drop out of the race and support Finch.

Nixon called Murphy, but failed to get to the point. Instead, he asked Murphy how he felt and then listened in silence as the senator reacted with a five-minute oration about his physical fitness. By then the President could find no way to suggest that he retire from office.

Murphy ran and lost to a relatively unknown and weak Democratic candidate, John Tunney. Most political observers agreed that had Finch been the candidate, he could have won easily and thus earned his way to long service in the Senate. He finally ran for the office in 1976, but by then the timing was wrong. S. I. Hayakawa won the primary and went on to defeat Tunney.

In the cabinet and later in the White House as counselor to the President, Finch was one of those who argued for reason and moderation, and I believe that had he retained his position of strength with Nixon, he would have been effective in avoiding a Watergate, or at the least, a cover-up.

Basically, Nixon brought into the government a cabinet mainly made up of men who had strong national reputations. He aimed early to give them independence and thought they could handle the domestic affairs of government while he concentrated on foreign policy. He lost faith too soon to know if they could do this, and he came to believe that other than Shultz, Finch, and Mitchell, they were not equal or close to that ability. And as the cabinet clashed with the White House staff, he grew more distant from his appointees. The cabinet lost power as an isolated Nixon moved more toward centralized power. He became a President too often isolated from public reality.

15

Siege Mentality

WHITE HOUSE STAFFS differ in types of personnel, background, and organization, but they also have many things in common.

The President inevitably starts out saying he wants a small staff, smaller than that of his predecessor. One of the tricks for keeping the staff theoretically small is to place many of the members on the payroll of another executive department, "on leave" from those departments to assist the White House. This frequently brings rumors that the staffer on leave is a spy for the department or for the White House. That occasionally is true, but rarely. Midway in Nixon's first term, Haldeman honestly tried to call a halt to the false reporting on staff members by sending some people back to the departments and recognizing others as being on the White House payroll. During the Johnson administration, the staff not only grew large but developed such intensive competition regarding who would be housed in the working West Wing of the White House that it was almost impossible to walk down the halls cluttered with desks. Nixon was able to change that by establishing his own working office in the Executive Office Building, so the separation of rank between the White House and the Executive Office Building diminished. Nixon's "small staff" was larger than Johnson's at one point, but its offices were more spread out.

There are other similarities of staffs. Most selected for these jobs as Presidents come into office have worked in presidential campaigns, but few have seen government service. The Kennedy staff, for example, was dominated by the Massachusetts "Irish Mafia." Lyndon Johnson had his Texans and Nixon his Californians, and by accident his Germans. Carter surrounded himself with Georgians. Ford and Eisenhower were exceptions because both had been away from their home states long before becoming President. Of those mentioned, Ford had more staff with government experience because he brought with him part of his congressional staff—but most lacked broad national experience.

White House staffs live in a constant state of siege. They never lack a crisis. A calm day becomes unnerving. In the early Nixon years, there was the daily crisis over Vietnam and negotiations for peace. But coupled with this were the battles with Congress over the antiballistic missile and the ill-fated nominations of Clement F. Haynsworth and then G. Harrold Carswell for the United States Supreme Court, student demonstrations and growing national unrest, and new domestic programs such as welfare reform, inflation, and unemployment.

Two weeks after the inaugural, I first felt the result of the siege mentality, which regularly develops pressure, causing staff members to strike out wildly to let off steam. In early February I met for breakfast with a traditionally organized group of reporters headed by Godfrey Sperling of the *Christian Science Monitor*. The group of about fifteen breakfasts with news figures once a week or more. During a general discussion which took a broad view of the administration's early reactions and plans, I was asked if the President had any plans for a trip out of the country. I replied that some possible trips, such as one to Europe, had been discussed but no conclusions had been reached or dates set. Three hours later the Washington *Evening Star* came out with a story headlined "Klein Says Nixon Plans Trip to Europe." The paper was barely off the presses when I received a hurried call from Ehrlichman.

I arrived in his office to find him in a rage. What business did I have to announce a trip by the President? That was up to the President or his press secretary, he shouted. I pointed out that despite the headline, the story did not say I announced anything. I could not have had I wanted to, because I did not know what final plans the President had made. The angry Ehrlichman forbade me to have any White House attachment to either my job title or the White House address on my stationery. I told him that the day I did that would be the day I ceased being effective, and any such orders would have to come from the President, not him. Whether Ehrlichman was put up to this by an overzealous and insecure Ron Ziegler or whether it was solely a reflection of his own siege mentality, I never knew. I ignored the outburst. We never again discussed the subject. But I did not forget it.

The President's trip to Western Europe was announced by Ziegler a few days later, and I was assigned the task of seeing that the cabinet and the White House seniors, such as Arthur Burns, put together major releases each day on domestic issues so the American public would not gain the impression that all work in the executive branch stopped while the President conferred with other heads of state abroad.

It is difficult to convince a skeptical public that there is one other major point of commonality with White House staffs: few if any who have served in this capacity in modern times have used it for advantage monetarily while in office. There was a vicuña coat for Sherman Adams and a refrigerator for Truman's General Harry Vaughan. But that was petty. Many have lost money while serving in government. Some have done well financially later, but many of them would have done so anyway. There are incentives other than money which attract men and women to a job which often runs fifteen or more hours a day, seven days a week. Some of these factors include loyalty to the President, a genuine belief in him and his philosophy, a touch of glamour which exudes from the words White House, the lust for power which too often grows to be dominant, patriotism, and job satisfaction, which stems from major accomplishment. There is no typical pattern. No one sets out to train for the White House. It just happens.

Most of the senior members of the Nixon staff were campaign veterans who had known each other for years, and thus one would have expected the working arrangements to run more smoothly than they did. The only newcomers were Dr. Henry Kissinger, his deputy, Colonel Al Haig, and Daniel Patrick Moynihan. Nixon sought to avoid a strong, all-powerful chief of staff, and he succeeded only to the extent that Haldeman tried to stay away from matters of substance and to concentrate in the field of operations. Even so, Haldeman's power was unchallenged. President Ford went even further and tried to avoid an operational chief of staff with the strength of Haldeman. He described himself as the "hub of the wheel" with the senior staff members serving as spokes feeding in assistance and advice to the hub. But he needed a chief of staff, Robert Hartmann, to at least direct some of the traffic. President Carter made a major effort to shun Nixon-era titles and thus originally had no chief of staff nor even a director of communications. As confusion grew on his staff he eventually found a need for at least some semblance of both jobs.

Despite the newsmen's characterization of the Nixon staff as a "German wall" or an "iron curtain" because of the predominance of German names—Haldeman, Ehrlichman, Klein, Kissinger, and Ziegler—our ancestry had no personal ethnic bonds. I sometimes wondered about the religious ties. Christian Scientists such as Haldeman and Ehrlichman seemed to attract others from their church, and at the next senior rank there were many Mormons, who brought in others.

In organizing the staff, Haldeman had the assistance and counsel of a veteran of the Washington scene, Bryce Harlow, once a member of the Eisenhower staff. But the responsibility was Haldeman's and the task, as it always is in this situation, was greater than he could have imagined. Some of the boundaries were easy. He needed a man to head congressional relations. And Harlow was a natural. Kissinger had been selected to direct the National Security Council, and Moynihan had been recruited as the chief domestic policy planner. But there were immediate and open differences between the conservative Arthur Burns, counselor to the President, and the more liberal Moynihan. Haldeman had a potential problem between the White House press secretary's office and my dominion as director of communications. He left the definition of that to Ziegler and me, and that provided areas of conflict. Ehrlichman originally had the title of chief counsel, but it was apparent that his interests and ambitions went far beyond legal definitions. Leonard Garment was given more free-roving responsibilities in the civil rights arena, but he often found himself at odds with Moynihan or with Mitchell. Haldeman selected a talented former *Time* magazine editor, James Keogh, to organize and mediate between the words and philosophies of an imaginative group of speech writers who varied in views from the more liberal Ray Price and Bill Safire to the more conservative Pat Buchanan and Tom Huston. The President wanted a daily news summary and somewhere Haldeman found Mort Allen, who proved to be an untouchable independent.

The easiest selection was Rose Woods, the President's personal secretary, who was senior to all in years of service. But the clashes between a spunky and outspoken Rose Woods and Haldeman, the disciplinarian, never ended.

Haldeman's major mistake in forming this early staff was in bringing in too many young people in their twenties and giving them responsibility beyond their years. Had he mixed that intelligent but naïve group with greater numbers of staffers in their late thirties and up, he would have achieved a balance that could have decreased the danger of unjustified and overinflated staff ego, which severely damaged relations between the White House staff and the cabinet. The young staffers would claim to be speaking for the President when in truth they barely knew him.

One major exception was Dwight Chapin, who had worked as a young assistant, first to Haldeman and then to Nixon, and who had a coolness of judgment which caught even the interest of Chou En-lai as Chapin met and dined with the Chinese leader while advancing the Nixon trip to Peking. Chou later told me that he moved in his government to upgrade more young people after watching Chapin in action.

The Chapin case, however, illustrates the problem I would not have predicted as I saw this group assembled. Power can be corrupting, and eventually Chapin was convicted on a perjury charge in connection with campaign "dirty tricks" by Donald Segretti. He directed Segretti, at least in part. It was the one time I found Chapin's judgment faulty. Chapin should never have been put into a position of dealing in political intelligence. His conviction and loss was a blow to White House operations and to most of us personally. He was that good.

When I look even now at the original Nixon staff, there was little to indicate to me that any of these people would become involved in crime, much less in what was to become the Watergate cover-up, and only a small but important part of the staff was involved, chiefly Ehrlichman, Haldeman, and Colson (who joined later in 1969). A few others at a more junior rank, who also came in later, such as Magruder, Dean, and Egil Krogh of the "Plumbers" were convicted.

The siege mentality, which led to a Watergate cover-up mentality, grew unobtrusively, stemming from an attitude, encouraged by the President and eventually Haldeman and Ehrlichman and compounded by Colson. The attitude was that the White House was above reproach, it could do no wrong. The attitude did not involve encouragement of wrongdoing.

During the President's first trip to Europe, he was impressed by the dignity of the official reception he received in the old, classical European countries. I often felt that inwardly the President looked at himself almost as an early U.S. immigrant or as a poor boy and a street fighter, and he secretly wanted to be considered an English lord, someone who, like Jack Kennedy, would be praised for upgrading the social dignity to the White House, a social status missing since the era of Franklin Roosevelt, except for the brief Kennedy years. Nixon was proud of his Quaker heritage, but he longed for this elite social distinction. Thus he assigned Ehrlichman to change the uniforms of the White House security force that would greet visiting heads of state. The resultant early-European costume, designed with tall hats and braid, immediately became the laughingstock of the nation and was quickly abandoned, but in a small way it was an effort to emulate Kennedy—to bring European dignity to the White House. Later, Nixon laughed at himself over this episode.

The Nixon staff resembled Kennedy's—but only in part. In some ways Robert Kennedy and Haldeman resembled each other; both were tough and seasoned disciplinarians who knew how to run the show. The President's speech-writing staff was creative and imaginative, but somehow he felt no one there could quite turn out the words of a Ted Sorensen. John Kennedy, like Nixon, enjoyed working on ideas and drafts for his major addresses, but Nixon always was searching for help such as he felt Sorensen had given with the Kennedy inaugural statement ". . . ask not what your country can do for you, ask what you can do for your country."

Nixon frequently asked why his staff could not come up with descriptive terms for his domestic programs, such as Franklin Roosevelt's "New Deal" or Lyndon Johnson's "War on Poverty." We struggled unsuccessfully with "New Federalism." He longed somehow for a Charlie Michel-

son, to whom the press strategy that led to the discrediting of Herbert
Hoover was attributed. At times he looked at Colson as a Michelson. He
seemed to forget that the times had changed. In 1970, one could not get
away with what he could in the 1930s.

With all these factors in mind, Haldeman set about efficiently organizing a business-oriented staff which would be centralized through his office.

Haldeman was a superb but overorganized organizer. I frequently complained in person and in memorandums that his paper-work demands
were so heavy that I was inhibited in carrying out my duties. Some of the
requests relayed to us by assistants in Haldeman's office were so absurd,
in my view, that I finally resorted to locking them in my briefcase lest one
of my aides, such as Magruder, make a commitment in writing to a Haldeman aide which would violate my own press concepts or principles.

Haldeman learned political organization from the ground up, first as a
Nixon advance man in the 1958 elections, then as the chief advance man
in 1960, and finally as the gubernatorial campaign manager in 1962. In
the 1968 campaign, he was the chief of the traveling staff, working with
the candidate on the road while Mitchell pondered state-by-state strategy
from the New York headquarters. Once in office, Haldeman was dedicated to his responsibility in the toughest job in the White House. His
hours knew no bounds and the President's schedule was his.

During the ten years I knew Haldeman prior to the 1958 campaign, I
enjoyed him as an individual as well as someone who shared my interest
in politics and communications. He had moved quickly ahead in the advertising business after graduating from the University of California at
Los Angeles. In the sixties we would enjoy an occasional family social afternoon at the Haldeman or the Finch home in Los Angeles. As I saw
him then, he was relaxed and we would enjoy discussing various aspects of
communications, the collegiate athletic rivalry between UCLA and my
alma mater, USC, and a variety of topics of heavier national interest. Politics was a constant part of the discussion. He seemed open and uninhibited. He delighted in kidding me by calling me "Hoibee." We are friends
who disagree on some issues and methodology.

In the White House, I witnessed two more contrasting sides of Haldeman. There were a few evenings at the Haldemans' where we would
relax and enjoy edited home movies he had made during presidential trips.
He and Ehrlichman were never without movie cameras. His wife, Jo,
seemed to stay clear of the Washington pressures and was a warm, genuinely charming hostess. Occasionally we would meet at a Georgetown social and cultural function, such as dinner at the home of Roger Stevens of
the Kennedy Center. Haldeman was critical of liberal Georgetown functions but he attended some himself. It was a side of Haldeman few of the
staff ever saw. Just as Nixon increasingly functioned through Haldeman,

the chief of staff used as his buffer Larry Higby, a bright but cocky young UCLA graduate who tried to serve as his boss's alter ego. Eventually staffing got so complex that the staff joke was that Higby had a Higby, a totally responsive assistant to the assistant. He worked unceasingly.

Haldeman went into the White House with a dislike and a distrust of the press corps. He trusted and talked only to a few reporters. One of these was Jane Brumley, an accurate and sharp-tongued reporter from *Newsweek* whose husband, Cal, I had recruited from Dow-Jones to work in the Treasury. Jane was the one reporter who could be personally critical of Haldeman without raising his ire—perhaps because of her Irish humor. He also knew she would be honest with him in her stories. He would praise Bill Anderson and Robert Wiedrich, Chicago *Tribune* writers, and Irv Kupcinet, Chicago *Sun-Times* columnist and a TV impresario on his own. He hardly knew the three but he knew the President and I both respected them greatly. They were among his "good guys," although they never knew it and perhaps would have shunned the category.

On occasion, Haldeman would walk into the early-morning senior staff meeting and order all White House personnel to stop conversations with the Washington *Post* or the New York *Times*—or perhaps all reporters. Usually he was carrying out presidential orders. Ziegler and I made it clear that we automatically considered ourselves exempt from such instructions.

Haldeman knew enough about his own instincts with the press that he avoided most interviews and stayed off television except for one or two occasions, including a tape for "The Today Show" in which he referred to demonstrators as giving "aid and comfort" to the enemy, part of the constitutional description of treason. I encouraged his abstinence from the media. The chief of staff and the President laid down the same rule for Kissinger, fearing that his German accent would remind too many of the Nazi war machine at a time when we were in the midst of the Vietnam emotions. I encouraged the use of Kissinger as a briefer for newsmen or for Congress, but concurred with Haldeman when it came to television. He was superb at an off-record briefing. Kissinger since has appeared several times on national television and handled it extremely well. But his position is different now, as is the nation's mood.

Haldeman could be reasonable and understanding of delicate situations. He could be outrageous. I never knew if the mood he reflected came from the President or whether it reflected himself or another staff member bringing pressure on him. To his credit, I knew he sometimes ignored presidential demands he considered extreme.

When the 1972 campaign had been completed, I felt I understood the mood of the country better than anyone else in the White House. I had campaigned back and forth across the country, covering about sixty thousand miles in three months, answering questions, talking to newsmen, students, community leaders, and politicians. I decided to summarize my opinions of the after effects of the election to provide some guidance for the President as he went into the next four years. I debated whether I should press for a meeting with the President or for one with Haldeman on this. Because of the uncertainty of the entire staff (all had been asked to submit resignations) and the resulting White House turmoil in the first weeks after the election, I decided to discuss it first with Haldeman. We met for more than an hour in late November 1972.

My postelection analysis at that time was that the American public, in general, believed that Nixon was doing everything possible to solve the principal problems centering around the economy, unemployment, and Vietnam. I felt we could weather the storms surrounding these still serious problems. The one mystery that may become more explosive, I told Haldeman, is Watergate and the allegations of dirty tricks.

"The President should have acted decisively when these things first surfaced," I said. "He did not, but he now has a second opportunity on the wave of an overwhelming political victory. Clean house now, even though it hurts, and you will end the threat of a bombshell which will linger on and become more damaging as long as the newsmen and the public think that there are unanswered questions."

Haldeman said he agreed with me.

He said that Chapin would be leaving the staff and that there would be other changes which would clean the situation up.

With that reassurance, I made the mistake of stopping there.

We mentioned no names, but I thought we were discussing the exposure of Magruder, perhaps Mitchell and Colson and a few others of lesser position who served on the Committee to Re-elect the President. I had no idea that the man I was talking to was involved in the cover-up along with Ehrlichman and the President.

To my dismay, Magruder was soon elevated to the position of deputy chairman on the inaugural staff as if nothing had occurred. It was not until I read the transcript of the June 23 tape, in which Haldeman, the ultimately efficient staff leader, inexplicably brought the President the news of CREEP involvement in the Watergate bugging and suggested only two alternatives—both cover-ups, one involving the CIA and another the FBI—that I realized Haldeman had been involved since he made this first staff mistake right after the break-in, although I honestly doubt that Haldeman understood that involvement at that moment. He should have presented an alternative to total public exposure of staff members involved, which would have cleaned the sore quickly and prevented the involvement of growing numbers of people, including the President of the United States. One could make the point strongly that the President had this prerogative and responsibility even more. The buck stops with him. The tapes would indicate it never entered his mind. He and Haldeman felt secure in the belief that other Presidents had endured mistakes of a serious nature, but they ended up immune. And Nixon and Haldeman must have thought they also would be immune as they casually underestimated the importance of the situation or the furor which the press and Congress could generate.

In my opinion, Haldeman would not have made that mistake two years earlier. But supported by four years of unchallenged experience in the White House and buoyed by the prospect of an overwhelming election victory, his perspective had changed. He was more jaded, too sure of his powers. That has happened often in the White House.

Haldeman and Ehrlichman had been close friends since college. Ehrlichman had gone from UCLA to Stanford law school and eventually returned to his hometown of Seattle to practice law. He was highly successful. But in 1960 Haldeman urged Ehrlichman to take time out from his law practice and become one of the key advance men. In 1962 John flew down from Seattle for frequent strategy sessions on the California governor's campaign. He was a natural for Haldeman to bring in as his key assistant when he formed the traveling staff for the 1968 presidential race. Ehrlichman had a strong interest in domestic problems and, while there were others with more expertise in particular fields, he was a logical choice for Haldeman to have succeed Moynihan and head the newly organized Domestic Council. Ehrlichman was highly intelligent and willing to move quickly on issues. The structure of the Domestic Council was modeled generally after the National Security Council. Ehrlichman also was an empire builder, and he soon built his staff from a group of a few to a bureaucracy of its own, complete with a set of inexperienced deputy assistants to the President and in turn young assistants to the deputies.

Ehrlichman, like Haldeman, was not predictable. He had an arrogance which made him look down scornfully at many of his colleagues in the cabinet and on the staff as having lesser intellect than himself. On the other side, he had genuine concern for the human element involved, for the feelings of people within government and without. He could be conniving, but he sometimes showed a sensitivity to people which neither Colson nor Haldeman felt. When he left the White House, his successor found that he had completely wired his office so that he could tape any conversation he chose—and he taped many. Colson also taped, but not as extensively. Kissinger had secretaries listen to calls and transcribe them. Haldeman did none of these things. Interestingly, Ehrlichman apparently was not aware of the tapes being made of his conversations with the President. That was a contrivance which was installed by Haldeman and kept secret from all but three or four persons—including Alexander Butterfield, who eventually revealed the existence of such material.

As the 1972 elections approached, Ehrlichman was anxious to be more involved in the campaign than he was, but he found himself limited by Mitchell and Haldeman. He discussed in depth with me the need for both of us to be more involved.

Ehrlichman took a deep interest in everything that went on at the White House, ranging from the state dinner entertainment to newsmen's opinions. It was never possible to know where his scope of inquiry stopped.

At the time of the Kennedy incident at Chappaquiddick, it was Ehrlichman who directed the efforts of Jack Caulfield, a former New York policeman, who conducted a private Nixon investigation into the whole matter. Caulfield later worked for John Dean.

On September 24, 1971, I had arranged in Portland, Oregon, a briefing where Western editors and broadcasters met with several members of the cabinet and the President. The day was more hectic than usual because as the newsmen met in the Benson Hotel ballroom, the President was conferring upstairs in the hotel with George Shultz, James Hodgson, negotiator Curt Counts, and labor leaders in an attempt to avoid a mariners' strike. Others on the staff were making final preparations for the President to have an historic meeting in Alaska the next evening with the Emperor of Japan on his first visit to American soil.

Midway in the briefing, I called a coffee break and Hank Greenspun, publisher of the Las Vegas *Sun*, mysteriously called me aside. He said he had confidential information in his safe linking Howard Hughes with a $100,000 campaign fund contribution given to Bebe Rebozo. He said he suspected the money had been used in the development or furnishing of the Nixon home in San Clemente. He had enough doubts that he had not run a story. I told Greenspun I did not believe there was any possibility that it was true, but I would look into the matter or I would arrange for someone else of major responsibility to talk with him. I knew Greenspun as a free-swinging publisher who had access to a lot of Las Vegas information, some of which had in the past proved right but some had turned out wrong. I felt this had to be wrong. On the other hand, Greenspun once had been close to Howard Hughes and his key associates, and Hughes was a name which seemed to pop up each time Nixon campaigned. There had been a break between Greenspun and Hughes, but the publisher remained a close friend of Robert Maheu, a top Hughes aide who now was involved in bitter and extensive litigation against his former boss. Most of us had known Maheu personally at one time or another when he was most active on the Washington scene.

I had just a few minutes with Greenspun and, while I doubted whether he had substantial information regarding Rebozo or Nixon, I made a note of the conversation, and a short time later I decided to tell Ehrlichman of the incident. He seemed the logical person because of his legal background. Regardless of the merit of the information, I wanted to show Greenspun the deserved respect of having his information considered more fully. I had been anxiously courting the President's endorsement by his newspaper. Greenspun disagreed with Nixon on many Vietnam policies, but admired his working approach with Israel. Greenspun was a known political maverick whose support would be very worthwhile.

Ehrlichman decided that Herbert Kalmbach was the logical person to make the short trip from Los Angeles to Las Vegas and meet with the publisher. Kalmbach spent four hours with him and later reported in full detail to Ehrlichman. I spoke to Kalmbach only briefly about the trip, and he volunteered a desire to assist in other similar important interviews I might recommend. He told me he had gone over all the San Clemente legal papers and assured Greenspun that no money could have been diverted for this purpose. He said he thought that closed the matter.

What, if anything, Ehrlichman later did with the information is unknown to me. Jeb Magruder wrote that in one of the discussions of campaign intelligence, Mitchell had said in front of Howard Hunt and Gordon Liddy that he understood Greenspun had information which would be damaging to Senator Edmund Muskie. Greenspun later said that all he knew damaging to Muskie was his alleged involvement in a minor incident over illegal duck hunting. Greenspun says that Kalmbach seemed more interested in what he knew about a working relationship between Hughes and Larry O'Brien, the Democratic national chairman.

It remains a mystery as to whether the brief coffee-break conversation in Portland had led to later conversations through Ehrlichman to someone else in the campaign or the Plumbers who tied this to activities of Hunt and Liddy. The information also could have come through Robert Bennett, associate of Hunt and Liddy who had both CIA and Howard Hughes connections.

It is a fact that Hunt and Liddy conferred with Ralph Winte, security chief for Summa Corporation and, according to Hunt, they received a sketch of the Greenspun newspaper office from Winte. Greenspun has records showing that when he returned to his office after a few weeks' absence, his door had been forced and his safe damaged in an unsuccessful attempt to open it.

In the view of Greenspun, the idea that he had regular conversations with O'Brien, and perhaps had information embarrassing to the Democratic Party leader, led Hunt and Liddy to breaking into Watergate, where O'Brien had his office, and into the Greenspun newspaper office.

It is a theory that has not been proved. Greenspun's notes from conversation with me at Portland show that he wrote that the breakup of the Hughes empire would "sink Nixon." That was 1971.

Rebozo later was questioned about the $100,000 contribution from Hughes, but again there was no evidence brought out by Watergate investigators that it had been for anything other than a routine campaign contribution. He was cleared.

A siege mentality was not universally present. People on the White House staff reacted differently to crisis. The person who always seemed most calm was Bryce Harlow.

Harlow was a veteran of government service who became a part of the administration. He had served on the White House staff of President Eisenhower, he had worked on Capitol Hill, and he had been the Washington representative and vice-president of Procter and Gamble.

When nerves were tense during a crisis, Harlow could be counted upon to lean on his dry Oklahoma humor and relieve the situation. He liked to pretend to be a country boy from a small town in Oklahoma, but his sophisticated knowledge of the workings of the Congress and of the executive branch of the government provided the glue which held the White House together during both winning and losing fights with the Congress. He was superb on picking assistants, and one of his staff became a Republican governor of Tennessee, Lamar Alexander. Two others, Bill Timmons and Tom Koreolopis, later became two of the most respected lobbyists in Washington. When Harlow needed help from what he called a "sane but tough" guy to write excerpts for congressmen, he joined me in recruiting Lyn Nofziger, a longtime newsman with deep experience in politics, working for Reagan.

Harlow left foreign-policy concerns mainly to Kissinger, but he was the final authority on strategy for dealing with Congress on domestic programs.

Harlow would sometimes be dismayed by the seeming desire of Republicans to be critical, even of a GOP President. "The Republicans have been out of power so long that they act by instinct," he used to say. "If they see a political critter moving, they instinctively snap at it."

The man whose face reflected most clearly, in private moments, how he thought foreign policy was going was Henry Kissinger.

Early in 1969, Kissinger would return periodically from one of his mysterious negotiating trips on which he met with the North Vietnamese in Paris and would come into an early-morning staff meeting bubbling with confidence and cheer. He thought he had progressed to a point where the end of the war was but a few weeks off. A month later he would return and seem to feel so low that one did not have to ask the latest report on the negotiations to end the war.

Twice in the summer of 1971, Kissinger came stalking into the staff meeting in the Roosevelt Room almost incoherent because of his anger over stories he had found a few minutes before in the New York *Times.* One by Tad Szulc in August appeared to have been leaked by the CIA regarding Soviet pressures on India not to recognize East Pakistan. Kissinger feared that the story had compromised our intelligence system and perhaps had endangered a CIA agent in India. It was similar to his outrage over a story later on the so-called Pakistan tilt, a column by Jack Anderson which reflected accurately the direction Kissinger was taking in a secret meeting at the White House with Pentagon officials.

In July of 1971, there was a story in the New York *Times* by Bill Beecher which outlined a secret position the United States had worked out for a meeting with the Soviet Union SALT negotiators. The story went so far as to even state a United States backup position if initial negotiations were stalled. All of us were upset over the violation, but Kissinger and later the President were so angry that they wanted lie-detector tests for everyone remotely connected with SALT in the White House, Pentagon, or State. With good reason, we felt that news leaks were undermining the negotiating policy of the United States.

Haldeman ordered everyone on the staff to break off all contact with the New York *Times* at that time, but there was more effort made to find the leaks than to retaliate with an investigation of the press.

It was press incidents like these, however, which triggered many of the unsuccessful activities of Egil Krogh and David Young of the so-called Plumbers—a security force organized by Ehrlichman under presidential directive to plug the leaks—using whatever means necessary. And it was only a short time later, in September 1971, that Krogh was approving a Hunt-and-Liddy scheme to break into the office of Dr. Lewis Fielding, Jr., Daniel Ellsberg's psychiatrist.

Siege mentality, which affected the President as well as his staff, also led to orders to provide one type of list or another for presidential action. I regarded the lists as useless and a waste of time, but I reluctantly had my staff provide them only to avoid the constant pressure of the staff secretary, who was more interested in completing the paper work and closing the file than he was in the content or the quality of content.

Typical of the requests to my office would be "provide the President with a list of 20 friendly publishers whom he can telephone at a rate of three or more a day."

The President rarely made the calls, and I discovered that he saw the lists even more rarely. It was a "make-work detail" emanating from Colson's office. The battle over providing a list would become more severe when Colson would say that the President wants a list of those writers who are most unfriendly to him or a list assessing the political beliefs and fairness of a group of broadcasters or writers. This was the type of infor-

mation I shunned putting on paper, despite the personal assessments I
formed of each of the men and women I worked with. What the reporter's
party affiliation, if any, was of little importance to me and I rarely knew
what it was. I was more interested in the quality of work and the balance
of a reporter's judgment than in any superficial labels. When the constant
inquiries wore me down, or when I suspected Jeb Magruder was about to
answer them, I provided some perfunctory information, frequently rating
the reporters more neutral than I might have judged them either way in
my own mind.

The ultimate in the list-gathering in the Colson office was the so-called
Enemies List, which later became public. Colson took great pride in the
project and made it a priority matter for George Bell, a very bland older
assistant who probably did not know personally any of the persons he
listed and rated in his book. When I read the Enemies List much later in
the newspapers, I could understand how it fitted the siege mentality, but I
could not understand the selection of names. Some of those listed were
close friends of mine, many had known the President for years, others
were there simply because they differed with the administration on philosophy and policy.

Joseph Kraft was on the list. Joe is an independent columnist who
earned the delight of the Nixon camp during the 1968 campaign because
of many favorable columns; this was looked upon as an important and unexpected windfall because Kraft was generally considered a liberal. I recommended his column to several newspapers. But the "honeymoon" with
Kraft lasted only briefly as the new administration took hold. In June of
1969, Nixon addressed the Air Force Academy with a strong speech on
national defense policy. He labeled some of those he perceived as desiring
to weaken the military as being "new isolationists," a phrase, incidentally,
conceived by Bill Safire. Kraft struck hard against the speech, including
this phrase in his column, "For my money, the President has been showing his worst side—the side that earned him the name 'Tricky Dick'."
From the view of the hard-liners on the White House staff, Kraft was an
enemy thenceforward. When it was known he had interviewed the North
Vietnamese in Paris, Kraft was looked upon as bordering disloyal. Even
Kissinger, who met frequently with Kraft and respected him, privately
raged against him on occasion. There is dispute on the actual procedure
for wiretapping Kraft, but the fact is that he was one of the first on the
wiretap list developed early in the administration.

Personally, I liked and respected Kraft.

There were others on the Enemies List who came as more of a surprise,
for example, Julian Goodman, president of NBC. Goodman had known
the President since his early days in Washington when the now-NBC
leader had been a journalist heading the Washington bureau. Goodman

was someone I respected and always felt comfortable talking with whether we agreed or disagreed.

James Reston was on the list. Reston, long one of the nation's most respected columnists, had known Nixon since he was in Congress and he had been a personal friend of mine since the fifties. He, assisted by his wife, Sally, was a highly quoted reporter in the accurate coverage given the then Vice-President when he visited the Soviet Union in 1959 and later in China. A frequent opponent, yes. But hardly an enemy, unless one looked at anyone who disagreed as an enemy.

A similar example of an oddity on the list was Rowland Evans. Evans had been a personal friend of Jack Kennedy long before he became President.

Among newsmen, Evans was generally considered more Democratic and Novak more Republican, but both had the independence to make it difficult to tell which was which. Both columnists wrote toughly and with a flair for going for the gut. Both worked hard to be sure of the accuracy of information they received. Even so, they were sometimes wrong, like most competitive columnists.

Evans could be outraged by Democrats as well as Republicans if he thought they were doing wrong. Early in the Kennedy administration, when he was Washington bureau chief for *Newsweek,* I received an early-morning call at my home in La Jolla from Evans, who simply wanted to talk over his criticism of what he thought were bad appointments by President Kennedy. The particular occasion was a judicial appointment from Massachusetts which Evans and other newsmen criticized to the degree that Kennedy, under congressional pressure, eventually withdrew his nomination.

Part of the style of Evans and Novak is to analyze politics and part of it is to look for the unusual, the sensational. During the Nixon administration, they ran more stories negative to the administration than favorable to it. But they were eager for information from the White House staff as well as from its opponents. They thrive on so-called inside background information, as Mel Laird knew so well.

Evans was added to the Enemies List probably in part because he had been a friend of Kennedy and had many friends in the liberal Georgetown circle and in part because he was looked upon as a severe critic by those in the White House who remembered him when he was most negative.

That was part of the absurdness of having such a list.

But while the list made headlines—typical of such staff documents—nothing systematic was done about it. Fortunately, the list provided more ego satisfaction than action for the siege mentality.

16

The View from Within

AFTER THE FIRST MONTHS in the White House, when there were open discussions, the Nixon administration fell victim to a psychological atmosphere which seems to infect most presidencies. Debate becomes less and less acceptable, particularly in the presence of the President. The procedure was to listen politely to the President, say what he wants, and above all don't argue with him. Wally Hickel dramatized this point with his letter of protest.

Franklin Roosevelt fell out with some of his wisest supporters, such as Raymond Moley, as the mantle of the presidency became more dominant and the time for differences with the President became an obscure factor. This also happened with Lyndon Johnson and Richard Nixon.

It is difficult to pinpoint how this atmosphere develops in the White House. But anyone who looks at the presidency today or in the past can only conclude that inevitably most Presidents and their staffs change as time in government shapes attitudes. The President may be one like Lyndon Johnson, who delighted in mingling with opinion makers, or Nixon, who detested it, but we have seen in the presidency, regardless of style, a growing inclination for the holder of the office to isolate himself from contrary thought. This saps the strength of his staff advice and the ability of a senior assistant to stand up and speak out to the President when he thinks the President is wrong.

The very atmosphere of the White House and the Oval Office tends to place a restraint on any visitor whether it be a powerful national business or labor leader, a veteran congressman, or a key presidential adviser. Thus it was easy for Nixon (or previously Johnson) to develop a staff more and more unwilling to speak its mind. This was encouraged by Nixon, who, in some moods, would decide to shut off access to himself from someone who argued with him at the wrong time. And too often it was the wrong time.

Haldeman isolated the President by controlling his schedule, but he did so with the full concurrence and encouragement of the President. Haldeman had the ability to sit for hours listening to the President as he seemingly debated an issue by himself, arguing both sides out loud and expecting little meaningful reaction from his chief of staff. Even in the presence of Haldeman, Nixon was a loner. In the midst of this Nixon would let off some pressure by issuing an order, perhaps to cut off funds for a department or to fire an individual. Haldeman rarely disagreed at the moment, but he also had intelligence and the ability to delay until a time when the President, now involved in other problems, would ask whatever happened to his order. He often would seem to expect it had not been carried out and would seem relieved to have this confirmed. Kissinger and Ehrlichman also understood this technique well, as did some of us who saw the President less frequently. Colson, to the contrary, would seem to delight in stirring up the black side of the President and in following through on orders which were troublesome, such as flying to New York to congratulate printers who had organized a wildcat strike against the New York *Times* to protest the printing of an antiadministration ad on Vietnam policy. This anti-*Times* action antagonized even the strongest Nixon friends in the news corps.

During the days just before the 1970 congressional elections, staff unwillingness to speak out contributed to Republican defeats and eventually helped build Senator Ed Muskie as a possible Democratic nominee in 1972.

This was an off-election year in which Vice-President Agnew had been cast as the "heavy," a role Nixon had taken in congressional election years while he was Vice-President. Joined by White House speech writers such as Bill Safire and Pat Buchanan and advisers such as Bryce Harlow, Agnew was the cutting edge in the campaign to gain more congressional and senatorial seats for Republicans. Typically the party in the White House loses seats in off-year elections, but this was a time when the Vice-President was riding high with his attacks on the press and on his opponents with such eye-catching phrases as "nattering nabobs of negativism," "vicars of vacillation" and "pusillanimous pussyfooters," all terms aimed at making news and putting down administration policy foes. Not all the foes were Democrats. Charles Goodell of New York, for example, was a target and he eventually lost to Jim Buckley, a conservative.

The other side of the strategy was that while Agnew was the slugger,

Nixon would campaign with a style presidential in attitude, taking the high road.

During the final week before the election, Nixon himself entered the fray with a short cross-country speaking tour. At San Jose State College, he spoke to a large evening crowd and then emerged to find an unwieldy mob of demonstrators menacing the presidential motorcade and the press bus. The scene was intermixed with supporters and young opponents. Nixon made the foolish move of standing on his limousine to speak a few words and wave to the crowd. The demonstrators became more angry and as the President scrambled into his car, rocks and bottles were thrown, denting the vehicle and even hitting the press bus. Cynics in the press accused Nixon of provoking the incident deliberately. That was cynicism, not fact. Nixon was not about to provoke an attack on himself to help other candidates. The eventual scene was in some ways like that which Nixon had faced as Vice-President when he was at Caracas in 1958, but the danger was in no way similar. At Caracas he barely escaped with his life. At San Jose there was police protection along with the normal Secret Service activities.

The incident upset Nixon personally. He regarded it as an affront not just to him but to the presidency, and in that highly emotional state of mind he decided that the attack could be turned politically to sway voters toward candidates who were stronger on the law-and-order issue or on presidential Vietnam policy than their opponents. The presidential limousine was made available for press inspection in an effort to hype up the event, but the newsmen, swayed in part by sympathy toward Vietnam opponents and yet opposing violence which had endangered even the press bus, tended to look at the event coolly. Their question was, Had Nixon provoked the crowd by standing on his limousine? Inadvertently, perhaps so; deliberately, as some newsmen said, no.

The strategy that evolved from the incident, however, dictated that the next Nixon speech, which was scheduled to be delivered at an air base in Phoenix, would be a tough one. The high-road strategy would be left aside for a tough law-and-order speech reflecting on the nation's unruly demonstrators, as illustrated by those who had resorted to violence in San Jose. The San Jose incident probably would have received even more public attention had demonstrations against the President not become so commonplace, but in the emotional context of Vietnam demonstrations, it did not excite the American people.

As we flew on Air Force One to Phoenix, Nixon said he felt the Phoenix speech would be so good that he could avoid the traditional election-eve speech from a studio, an address which provides the political party's last appeal to the voters, and instead we could use a tape of his Phoenix law-and-order appeal. This was a late decision, and no special preparation had been made for the videotaping of the speech in color or even for obtaining copies of the tape from the Phoenix television station, where time had been bought for a live presentation.

As the President mounted the platform for the rally, I took Haldeman to a nearby officers' club where we would be away from the noise and could watch the program on live television. Haldeman and I found the technical aspects of the broadcast poor. Some passages of the speech were difficult to hear. The picture was in black and white and there were electronic-interference blips in the picture. Still we watched shots of the audience and listened to the speech and decided that the technical problems we were experiencing were from an out-of-adjustment television set on a military base with much electronic equipment and not part of the transmission to other areas of Phoenix. To the President's delight, the decision was made by the traveling staff to recommend that he would not have to prepare another speech and helicopter to Los Angeles on election eve. This would be it.

It was a classic case of bad staffing.

Most of us were inwardly bone-tired from the campaign, and unspokenly welcomed the respite from one more chore. We did not raise doubts, as we should have.

More important, it was clear that the President felt he had hit upon just the right note at Phoenix and that he did not want to be bothered with one more speech or argument from us. These factors were enough to make the staff feel it should not challenge a President who "deserved a little rest." No one raised the point that Nixon, as long ago as 1960, had decreed that he would not use a rally speech for any major national television political program, but would insist upon quiet studio or office discussions keyed to the quiet of a family living room.

We bought tapes from the Phoenix television station and Jeb Magruder was dispatched to buy time from each network and make arrangements for replaying the program as the final Republican appeal on election eve. At each network, Magruder found the technical experts confounded by the poor quality of the tape. Magruder urged that we drop the Phoenix idea and arrange for the President to speak live from Los Angeles on election night, but his pleas fell on deaf ears. Magruder was right!

No one in a senior position could believe that the tape could be that bad. Only Bill Safire and one or two other staffers bothered to drive to Los Angeles and view it with Bill Carruthers, the technician, and even they were intimidated against trying on an all-out basis to change election eve plans. Basically, none of us wanted to speak up to the President on the issue and few or none of us felt that the program was that poor. Mainly, it was clear that the President did not want to be bothered with one more television program, and no one challenged him directly. Our fear of running contrary to the President's desire allowed him unknowingly to drift into a major political error, because none of us spoke out.

Election eve was a disaster, and the President recognized it immediately. Muskie appeared with a thoughtful, quiet appeal for Democratic support. Muskie immediately became a strong potential as a Nixon opponent in 1972. The President appeared with the wrong speech at the wrong time and with technical faults which should have been associated with the pioneer days of television in perhaps 1946 or 1948. In effect, he had helped boost Muskie as Johnson had boosted Nixon with his outburst against him in 1966.

Isolation created other problems from the start of the administration in 1969. It was difficult for those inside the White House walls to get a full understanding of all the emotion attached to the era of demonstrations.

I had a sense of the depth of feeling within the minds of the demonstrators because I remembered the late thirties, when there were lesser campus demonstrations against war. Many of them were Communist-inspired, but nonetheless these were demonstrations against war, and there were doubts in many of our collegiate minds in those days as to whether the United States should be involved in a war that was spreading in Europe. If there was any doubt left in my own mind, it was absolved quickly by Pearl Harbor.

I had friends who strongly opposed the Vietnam War. As I went into the White House, my background included both World War II experience and knowledge as one who had talked during the sixties to the young and the not-so-young across the country, those who urgently wanted to get the country out of Vietnam regardless. I did not agree with them, but I had gained a sensitivity and respect for their ideas and emotions.

Among the few of us in the White House who were frequently out in public, it seemed increasingly that the demonstrators would turn up anywhere for a variety of causes, not just Vietnam. Demonstrations were a part of the time of unrest. Often emotion exceeded logic.

At the invitation of the University of California at Los Angeles, I spoke to a student audience at the time when the President had followed up his ill-fated nomination of Clement F. Haynsworth to the Supreme Court with the nomination of G. Harrold Carswell, a far weaker candidate than Haynsworth (who was victimized and defeated in Senate debate more because he was a Southerner than because of his judicial qualifications). As I looked over the UCLA audience I noticed that a group of about forty organized demonstrators was moving into the first three rows of the large hall.

Even during the introduction, it was apparent that I was in for a difficult hour. The tactic adopted by the demonstrators was not to boo or to disagree openly, but to cheer every clause of my informal address. I said, "I appreciate the opportunity to address the UCLA student body," and the band of forty stood up and cheered. So about every fourth sentence, on the signal of the leader, the crowd would drown out anything I was saying. They hated Vietnam, but on that day Carswell and Klein were their targets.

Some of my ancestral Germanic instincts set in and I was determined not to be routed from the hall by forty out of five hundred students. A friend, Ed Barner (who had been a volunteer in my office but who professionally manages top golfers and other athletes), moved forward to protect me in case there was a fight. My answer to the students was that I had been invited to speak and I intended to do so. I also planned to take many more questions after the speech and if they would give me the courtesy of free speech, I would answer their questions afterward.

With that, there was a signal and those in the front row stood up and threw marshmallows at me. The scene of flying marshmallows was certainly unique. I stood still and all missed. The audience then quieted down to the point where we had an open discussion on Carswell and Vietnam; the demonstrators were quieted.

On other, more peaceful evenings, with the Yale Political Union and students at other universities, I gained more insight into the sincerity and the intensity of feeling of the time among many responsible students. There were also, of course, many caught up in a mood of irresponsibility.

It was difficult to transmit that dual sensitivity to others in the White House, where we also had intensity of feeling. With few exceptions, we on the staff felt the President was pursuing the best course possible on Vietnam. We had a few individual doubts on the Haynsworth nomination and many more on Carswell. But our duty was to defend them. And we did. I would defend Haynsworth again. Carswell was a bad choice.

There was little temptation on the White House staff to argue with the President regarding foreign policy and, more particularly, Vietnam. We never doubted that he and Henry Kissinger wanted peace as much as or more than anyone. Here was an area where one could argue the pro and con of the bombing policies or other tactical decisions, but we did not have the expertise in this field. We could and did argue for better understanding of public reaction, which was our field.

On the night Nixon announced that we were moving into Cambodia, I felt genuine fear in the bottom of my stomach.

Most of the staff was as surprised and fearful as I was. After being in Cambodia personally and later meeting in Hanoi with the North Vietnamese, I think the decision probably was right, but I knew instinctively at the time that no matter how logical the President seemed in announcing his decision, he was leading to further demonstrations and destructive protest within the United States. I had gone into the streets and unobtrusively mingled with demonstrators with their red Hanoi flags, and I wondered if we were going to see violence leading to revolt. Here we were facing a public sentiment to limit the war or get out of it, and our policy was to decrease American involvement—yet suddenly we were enlarging the theater of action. The President felt this was the way to end the war more quickly, and I think he was right; but if I was scared, what about the public? What we were lacking on the presidential staff, and what is lacking on most, was the ability to coordinate major strategic decision with an evaluation of how this affected a very disturbed American citizenry. A President cannot act by studying public opinion polls, but he should consider how the public will react and how best to deal with the reaction when making any major decision. The President incorrectly felt he could go to the public via TV and that would suffice.

During Vietnam both the Johnson and the Nixon staffs were under pressure to promote the views they felt were right, but in the process, they had too few opportunities to understand what the outside reaction was or would be. As in many political situations, it is a simple matter of "them against us."

I believe that a President must act on his best instincts regardless of the vocal opposition. But one must also recognize that there will be opposition, and that it is important to deal with it fully by understanding it.

The President's later characterization of the demonstrators as "bums" during an offhand statement at the Pentagon was stupid, but it was treated unfairly. Nixon had in mind intruders who had burned the life-long work of a scholar at Stanford. He had known the terror of rough motorcycle gangs with chains parading within three blocks of the White House, but the word "bums" made headlines and only antagonized the situation. It was a poorly selected word uttered at a time of mental and emotional exhaustion. The President's visit to students in the early-morning hours at Lincoln Memorial also was viewed as superficial, and yet he was, he told me, seriously trying to understand the students and to have at least a handful understand him. His was a very human reaction which was, typically, misunderstood.

Two of Nixon's unplanned, instinctive public acts proved to be disastrous in their effect. One was the sudden "last press conference" of 1962. I later told a friend that people had said they wanted to see a human, genuinely emotional side of Nixon; however, when they saw it, it was personally disastrous. The Lincoln Memorial meeting with the students was equally spontaneous. He suddenly was struck with an idea and an emotional challenge, and without conferring with anyone, he ventured out when he knew everyone around him would have advised him to stay away from outside contact with the demonstrators. The dilemma was a serious one. Had Nixon called Ziegler to tell even a few in the press corps that he was about to venture out with the students, the press would have suspected this was a "media event," a "photo opportunity." When he related the story to one reporter, Garnett Horner of the Washington *Star,* the other newsmen resented that and were more than willing to accept the negative from any student's interpretation of the dawn discussion or from the reaction to the later use of the word "bums" in the halls of the Pentagon. When the demonstrations were at their height, the President should have seen some of the students who were in my or Bob Finch's office instead of claiming to be watching a football game on television. That was contemptuous. Had he chosen to see the leaders of the demonstration, he would have been in a no-win position where they would have denounced him regardless of how patiently he listened unless he announced to them that he had called a halt to the Vietnam War, but a spontaneous drop-in on groups Bob Finch had invited to his office would have provided him and student leaders a little new insight.

The confrontation between the students and the National Guard at Kent State has had a lasting impact upon the American psyche, and yet at the time the tragedy occurred, the White House staff underestimated its importance. Again, in parallel, it was like the failure to recognize the political impact in 1960 of the jailing of Martin Luther King. The Kent State tragedy was destined to be an emotional rallying point for the dissidents, but in the isolation of the White House, we did not fully recognize it as being separate from the series of traumas we had been subject to at the time. We mourned Kent State but took little action.

In many ways the continuous pressures of the demonstrators made the administration less sensitive to them. We did not expect any new philosophic declarations to emerge from the demonstrators' speeches on the steps of the Lincoln Memorial and the Capitol. However, the announcement that the youthful anti-Vietnam troops were being marshaled again, in effect, turned the White House operation away from the business-at-hand and focused it on planning strategies to minimize violence and maintain absolute control of the situation. Effective government leadership came to a virtual halt as all efforts were directed at containment of trouble. There were some voices "within" seeking to drown out the voices of the "enemies," but basically, the problem was one of control. There were methods for counting the potential number of demonstrators who would descend on Washington. We checked with bus companies across the country, and particularly in the Northeast, to see how many charters had been arranged. Experience gave some idea as to how many students one could expect would drive cars versus how many would arrive by bus, and thus it was possible to estimate in advance the probable number of demonstrators who would move on Washington.

Buses were the key to many things. The south wall of the White House grounds was protected by buses parked bumper to bumper around the open areas. If a mob got out of hand, it would be difficult for it to scale a wall of buses and march intact toward the diplomatic entrance to the White House. If some made it over the bus wall in numbers they would be met by National Guardsmen who had been brought into the White House and bivouacked in our halls and offices.

I am not sure how the reporters who covered the events felt, but for me it was eerie to find angry dissenters surrounding me as I tried to work in the buildings which housed the most powerful governing center in the world.

There was no doubt of some Communist infiltration in the many violent activities against the government. That was minor, I think, but remembering that Nixon had grown to fame on often contested claims of Communist activity, I and others, such as Garment and Safire and Keogh, made certain that this did not become a point of major contention. Most of those protesting were helping the Vietnamese enemy, we felt, but they did so out of a genuine feeling that they, as American citizens, were taking the right side for the United States. Right or wrong, we did not feel the same about leaders such as Jane Fonda, Tom Hayden, and Shirley MacLaine. We did not think they were Communists, but we did feel they were enemies. They encouraged the Vietnamese to think that American public opinion eventually would force us to accept the terms of Premier Pham Van Dong. I believe they slowed the effort to end the war, while they were seeking in their own way to end it.

One night there was an endless candlelight vigil of marchers who came up Seventeenth Street, turned on Pennsylvania Avenue, and marched silently by the White House. On a Saturday afternoon I walked outside the White House gates and moved into the mobs who turned at the intersection where Pennsylvania Avenue bumps into a temporary end against the White House grounds with the majestic Treasury building overlooking the scene. I saw hundreds and hundreds of protesters marching from the Capitol, many carrying the Communist and North Vietnamese flags. I wondered how many countries in the world could withstand this type of adversary action. Were we going downhill, and could we survive at all? After an hour of watching, I had to move when I was recognized and threatened. I went back to my own office, which was surrounded by National Guardsmen who had been hidden and bivouacked in the building. There were so many on the scene that I could hardly walk through them to my door. They had been brought in through an underground passage from the Treasury building.

The tension on me was great first in my own office and later as I moved my location to the central control area and tried occasionally to cool reactions to reports coming into the headquarters on Pennsylvania Avenue.

The President feigned nonchalance but the tension on him had to be at least as great as any President has felt since the veterans marched on Washington after World War I. And this was more massive.

A few weeks later we had a more violent demonstration which resulted in the arrest of hundreds. The handling of the arrests was declared illegal by the courts but, wrong as it was, it may have prevented more violence than we had seen. On this occasion, as I drove to my office at 7 A.M., I listened to radio reports of vandalism. When we got closer to the White House we found roving young bands kicking over trashcans, threatening vehicles, waiting at traffic signals to threaten government workers, and generally moving to a point of terrorism in the city. The effort was directed at shutting down government offices for the day or longer.

Weeks and months such as these made one sadly less sensitive to tragedies such as Kent State.

We countered the demonstrations with Honor America Day, led by one of the unsung heroes of the time, Willard Marriott, and organized more technically by Jeb Magruder and his game plans. This was Magruder in an area of personal strength. Marriott's vice-president, Tom Burke, kept a balance between patriotism and realism. Billy Graham was the principal speaker for the gigantic rally near the Lincoln Memorial, and with good judgment he was the right voice and the right conscience for the time. At many times, Graham was even more of a spiritual force within the White House than he has been credited with being.

A Kent State investigative commission was appointed by the President, but the time was too late. Anti-Vietnam demonstrations might have cooled off much earlier had we listened more to the outside and reacted fully and immediately to the Kent State shootings instead of taking this as just one more event in the series of public problems surrounding the war. The White House could not have prevented Kent State, but it could have reacted with far better understanding than acting through a commission.

Personally, I learned much from long, quiet talks with two sons-in-law who returned home for short visits to Washington from Vietnam. One son-in-law, Tom Howell, returned on leave from carrier duty off Vietnam, where he had been an enlisted plane captain. One of my thrills just before entering the White House had been to challenge, partly in fun at a reception, Mel Laird, the designated Secretary of Defense, to prove he could communicate with the Navy in Vietnam by sending word to the carrier that our daughter, Patty, had given birth to Henry Thomas Howell II. The message was delivered by the Secretary-designate of Defense via a puzzled admiral to a joyous enlisted man. I also learned in greater depth of the mixed views of many young people from Bob Mayne, my older son-in-law, who I knew opposed the war but accepted his duty willingly and served well with the Army as a lieutenant in Vietnam. I learned of the pro-and-con feeling of his enlisted men and peers and of their sensitive feeling for and relationship with the suffering, battle-torn natives outside Saigon and other bases in the besieged delta area. In the White House the general feeling was that everyone in Vietnam felt he was fighting for a just cause and paid little attention to the opponents at home. Talks with Bob Mayne, in particular, and also with Tom Howell and others I met in Vietnam and Cambodia made it clear that we did not have the full perspective, and the bigger problem as the war progressed was how to convey this thought within the White House.

In a similar way, the release of the Pentagon Papers brought forth a problem not generally understood, first by us and, secondly but equally importantly, by those outside, including many of my friends in the media.

We had no warning that the New York *Times* suddenly would break the first release of the so-called Pentagon Papers. The existence of such a document was a mystery to us. It was not the political case of knowing something was breaking and having an assistant outside the circulation docks of the newspaper to grab a copy of the first edition and report from a pay telephone what has been written. The reaction in the White House was slow. By a coincidence Tricia Nixon Cox's wedding was reported in the same edition of the *Times* as the Pentagon Papers, and the President was not even aware of the story until Sunday morning. But from there on, the action was furious. On Saturday afternoon, June 12, all of us had been concerned more over the weather for Tricia's Rose Garden wedding to Eddie Cox than anything else. Seemingly half the local Air Force was patrolling showers in the sky to allow the ceremony to be timed to thirty minutes when it was not raining.

Immediate checks on Sunday morning made it apparent to us that the Pentagon report related only to previous administrations and had no direct bearing on Nixon or his conduct of the war. There was a temptation to say nothing and let the fallout do whatever damage it would to Lyndon Johnson and possibly Jack Kennedy or even Dwight Eisenhower, who had sent the first few advisers to Saigon. There was a danger for Nixon, however, that the reports would give more ammunition to the anti-Vietnam critics.

Henry Kissinger clarified his view on the issue almost immediately. He was concerned with the effect this report would have on his negotiations with the North Vietnamese, and on his and the President's relations with the South Vietnamese government.

During the next thirty-six hours there was more confusion within the White House than at any other time I was there. There were hurried meetings in my office, where some of the speech writers, John Mitchell, and I pondered what was coming next and how we should handle it.

The Pentagon Papers included mostly nonclassified material, but there was some information which still had military and intelligence classifications. Included in the reports, for example, were the names of active secret agents of the United States. If the *Times* printed any of their names it could have meant their death. It also would make it more difficult to recruit others for intelligence work and to deal with foreign governments. We immediately had word that both Communist and non-Communist foreign leaders were questioning how much they could say to us in confidence without the danger of public exposure. It also appeared that there had been more than one draft of the Pentagon Papers, so we could not be quite sure just what was included in those pages that had been leaked to the *Times* and possibly other newspapers and television. Around the White House, Kissinger seemed to be in meetings everywhere. The President studied the matter. John Ehrlichman conferred with Mitchell and others on legal recourse. Haldeman and Ziegler were concerned about the question of whether the press was about to steamroller us while we dropped back silently. That bothered me too.

Throughout the White House the "them versus us," "press versus government" psychology was rampant. The feeling was that we were in a new war, this one with a rampant press. We heard rumors that other Pentagon chapters were being offered to newspapers and some were accepting them, others were not. The rumors were correct. The news media themselves were puzzled as to how they should handle the situation. How much, if any, should they print? What were the implications regarding secrecy and national security? I was relieved that there was no directly anti-Nixon material, not only because I did not want the President and his policies attacked, but because I was not sure how I could have reasonably controlled reaction within the White House had its present occupants been the subject of the attack under these circumstances.

I had no question about the patriotism and sense of duty of the editors and publisher of the New York *Times* or other newspapers handling the story, but I seriously questioned their ability to judge what involved sensitive military and intelligence security and what did not in such a case. I reasoned that, as an editor, I would not have full confidence I could differentiate in every case. I had been confronted with a few less important but nonetheless authentic cases where material was given to me regarding the United States' missile effort and the principal weapon, the Atlas, which was being produced in San Diego. I had checked the stories out with proper authorities and then made my decision.

Two of the questions projected then—questions which remain today—are how much power of judgment, in such a matter involving security, an editor should assume on the thesis of a public right to know and how far the government should go to protect itself, and presumably the American public, on a matter of national security. The official title of the document leaked by Daniel Ellsberg was "The History of U.S. Decision-Making Process on Vietnam," and among the material was a description of the role of President Kennedy in the South Vietnamese coup which led to the death of President Diem. The disclosure was not necessarily shocking to sophisticated Americans since it had been rumored and believed over previous years. At one time Colson and Howard Hunt had tried to leak such material with a fake telegram. Even the disclosure of contrary statements made by President Johnson, at a time when he was pledging to cut back on the war even while escalating it, generally involved matters of knowledge to foreign governments, and they did not add now to the already present general public lack of confidence in Johnson's credibility during the war or the credibility of the presidency. The security problem from the government's point of view was more technical, stemming from questions whether certain codes had been broken or what matters disclosed by Ellsberg involving strategy and people could endanger future intelligence and military efforts. From the administration's standpoint there was also a major problem of increased public cynicism, which seemed an almost certain result of these disclosures. Regardless of who had deceived the public, such documents seemed likely to add to the already growing public distrust in government and its leaders and its Vietnam policies. This, of course, seemed to us to be the major reason behind the Ellsberg decision to leak the papers, but it did not justify the legal action of the magnitude undertaken by the government. On the other hand, we did not feel we could ignore the Ellsberg security breach, and I believe that was right.

Years before the Ellsberg leaks, the New York *Times* made a judgment that it had been badly mistaken when it failed to print a story about the training of troops for what turned out to be the Bay of Pigs. President Kennedy was reported to have told the *Times* later that in retrospect, he might never have allowed the CIA to carry out the misdirected action had the *Times* printed the story, which it withheld because of security implications. In the midst of our internal White House debates over the Pentagon publication, a veteran New York *Times* reporter told me privately that the memory of this earlier decision had been a factor in prompting the publisher, Arthur Ochs "Punch" Sulzberger, to approve publication of the papers.

There was another factor in our White House discussions. Why had the *Times* decided not to try to use the Freedom of Information Act to gain legitimate release of the documents it held? The *Times* had been a prime advocate of the act, and yet the timing of the release of the documents was not such that the weeks or even months necessary to seek such clearance would have changed their meaning. Of course, more delay might have caused Ellsberg to leak his documents elsewhere. We presumed the *Times* felt it would have been refused full clearance under the Freedom of Information Act, but I felt that had this route been taken the editors would have benefited from some expert opinions on what was considered classified among the material it was publishing.

Among the mixed opinions which were part of the eventual Supreme Court decision on the case, Chief Justice Burger wrote that the *Times* had analyzed the Pentagon Papers for three or four months before beginning its series, yet he asked:

"Would it have been unreasonable since the newspaper could anticipate the government's objections to release of secret material, to give the government an opportunity to review the entire collection and determine whether agreement could be reached on publication? Stolen or not, if security was not in fact jeopardized, much of the material could no doubt have been declassified since it spans a period ending in 1968.

"With such an approach—one that great newspapers have in the past practiced and stated editorially to be the duty of honorable press—the newspapers and government might well have narrowed the area of disagreement as to what was and was not publishable leaving the remainder to be resolved in orderly litigation if necessary. To me it is hardly believable that a newspaper long regarded as a great institution in American life would fail to perform one of the basic and simple duties of every citizen with respect to the discovery or possession of stolen property or secret documents. . . ."

The *Times* printed on June 13, 14, and 15 lengthy articles refined from its search through the forty-seven volumes of Pentagon Papers turned over to it by Ellsberg. As might be expected, it rightfully refused to reveal the source of its information, but Ellsberg's identity was quickly traceable through the Rand Corporation, which had custody of the papers and for which he had worked.

The decision of the White House and the Justice Department to take unprecedented legal action of prior restraint against further publication of material in the Ellsberg documents came basically from a decision by the Justice Department and John Mitchell with the concurrence of John Ehrlichman and the President. Most of us who had worked on the problem were not aware of the decision until after Mitchell had ordered the U.S. attorney in New York to seek restraint of publication. The public and press reaction to this action was not discussed with those of us concerned with such sensitive matters. It should have been.

Shortly thereafter, portions of the papers began appearing in the Washington *Post*, the St. Louis *Globe Democrat*, the Boston *Globe*, and elsewhere. It was like fighting a wild brushfire with the flames leaping from place to place regardless of the administration arguments. Newspaper and broadcast organizations were strongly united in testimony before the Congress against the government's use of prior restraint. The principle of stopping publication far superseded the contents of the papers in the minds of newsmen. They argued, as did some Justices in the Supreme Court decision, that the government had no right to prior restraint, an act they considered a First Amendment violation, although some agreed that it could sue after the fact on a variety of grounds from receiving stolen papers to violating government secrets. Even when the Supreme Court agreed to hear the case on June 27, it gave the *Times* the right to print material not cited specifically by Justice as objectionable. The *Times* responded that it would delay publication rather than submit even to this type of censorship.

The case moved from the Federal Court in New York to the Second Appeals Court to the Supreme Court, all in rapid manner. The Washington *Post*, which also had printed articles, became another central part of the case and thereby the District Court of Washington and the Ninth Court of Appeals were a part of the Supreme Court review.

With a final vote of six to three the Court, in a brief ruling read by Justice Burger, said, "Any system of prior restraints of expression comes to this court bearing a heavy presumption against its constitutional validity. . . . The government thus carries a heavy burden of showing justification for the enforcement of such a restraint." In effect the court ruled that the government had not shown sufficient justification for its case, for its effort seeking this unprecedented prior restraint.

The New York *Times*, the Washington *Post*, and other involved newspapers thus were cleared to publish whatever additional material they deemed newsworthy and proper. The victory was theirs.

The unusual variety of views expressed by the Justices in their opinions of both concurrence and dissent, however, still leave open many questions on the future effects of the Pentagon Papers case on Supreme Court decisions regarding prior restraint and other matters involving press freedom. Here was a case where a pressure of time on government, newspapers, and the court resulted in a monumental decision but not one necessarily decisive on the restraints or freedoms regarding the news media of the future. A case presented under less time pressure might have resulted in clearer ground rules established or rejected by the Court, although it seems unlikely that prior restraint would have been accepted in any case.

The decision of the administration to seek prior restraint was born out of pressure, haste, lack of understanding, and a great desire not to buckle under. The decision was wrong and other procedures, such as prosecution for other violations or even negotiation with the newspapers to be certain of security, would have been preferable. Some government action was essential, I believe. The newspapers hailed the case as a tremendous victory, and it was for the moment. But the mingled opinions of the judges leave more long-range implications dangerous to the press than was immediately realized.

Joint opinions by Justices Byron White and Potter Stewart, for example, commended the *Post* and *Times* on printing material which might "prevent any part of the government from deceiving the people and sending them off to distant lands to die of foreign fevers and foreign shot and shell. . . ."

In a variety of opinions, however, the point was made that the protection of the First Amendment is not an absolute. Some of the Justices also indicated that Congress could enact further statutes against such publication or that the government could sue.

White and Stewart, for example, said, "In the First Amendment the Founding Fathers gave the free press the protections it must have to fulfill its essential role in our democracy. The press was to serve the governed, not the governors. The government's power to censor the press was abolished so that the press would remain forever free to censure the government. The press was protected so that it could bare the secrets of government and inform the people. Only a free and unrestrained press can effectively expose deception in government. . . ." Later they said they concurred in the judgments, "but only because of the concededly extraordinary protection against prior restraints enjoyed by the press under our constitutional system. I do not say that in no circumstances would the First Amendment permit an injunction against publishing information about government plans or operations. . . ."

Their argument was that the "United States has not satisfied the very heavy burden which it must meet to warrant an injunction against publication in these cases, at least in the absence of express and appropriately limited congressional authorization for prior restraints in circumstances such as these."

The two concurring Justices went on to say, however, that the "material poses substantial dangers to national interests" and the papers must face the "consequences of what they publish. I would have no difficulty in sustaining convictions under these sections on facts that would not justify the interventions of equity and the impositions of prior restraint."

In the White House we interpreted this to mean that the newspapers were free to publish, but that if they violated the statutes regarding secrecy they would be subject to prosecution.

This was a view the White House would have been better to follow in the first place.

Justices Hugo Black and William O. Douglas, in their concurrence, said: "Prior restraints require an unusually heavy justification under the First Amendment, but failure by the government to justify prior restraints does not measure its constitutional entitlement to a conviction for criminal publication. That the government mistakenly chose to proceed by injunction does not mean that it could not successfully proceed in another way."

In retrospect, nothing the newspapers published would have justified criminal proceedings. They edited out most of the sensitive security material which would have compromised United States agents or important government secrets or codes. But in my opinion the entire matter could have been handled to the greater benefit of both sides had either the *Times* checked some of its facts prior to publication or the government sought to warn the *Times* and others against the minefields they were treading through. It was a case of neither side trusting the other.

In the end result, there remain in court records opinions encouraging further congressional action and threatening the news media with criminal prosecution for certain acts the justices say are not covered by the First Amendment. Since the time of the Pentagon Papers there have been more and more court decisions which can be considered to infringe on prior established rights of a free press. The news media are losing the battle with the courts. From the administration's point of view, it lost in many ways in the Pentagon battle. The prior-restraint action united both friends and foes of the administration and the President in one common cause to protect press rights and fight administration efforts. It widened the press-government gap. Eventually the losing battle led to the attempt to further discredit Ellsberg and to the break-in of the office of his psychiatrist and, as a result, the conviction of several in the administration, including Egil Krogh and John Ehrlichman. The process undermined the President at every step of the way. Anger influenced judgments which should have been made unemotionally.

Looking at the inside from another perspective, the White House senior staff members constantly studied not only the issues but the individuals who influenced the President's ideas.

When Nixon moved into the White House he had portraits of Woodrow Wilson and Theodore Roosevelt moved into prominent positions in the Cabinet Room. He suggested that Haldeman redecorate the "Fish Room," a staff conference room just off the Oval Office that displayed prominently a large fish caught by Franklin Roosevelt. The redesignated room became the Roosevelt Room, leaving some doubt between the significance of Franklin or Teddy; but with the furniture changed to basic Colonial Williamsburg design and the President's known admiration for Teddy, there was no doubt in our minds where the influence came from. At historic moments, such as when he was preparing a State of the Union address, Nixon read the speeches of both Theodore Roosevelt and Woodrow Wilson extensively.

In real life on a daily basis, the people who seemed to have influenced

Nixon the most were Dwight Eisenhower, Jack Kennedy, Lyndon Johnson, and—later—John Connally. Each, we could see, had an influence on
Nixon's ideas and his approach to problems.

Of the past Presidents, the Eisenhower influence pervaded on the
broadest scale. Early on, Nixon tried to avoid giving any one staff member
the power of a Jim Hagerty or a Sherman Adams, but, like Eisenhower,
he placed major emphasis on the National Security Council structure and
lesser emphasis on the formal meetings of the cabinet. For special problems, Eisenhower organized committee studies. Nixon did likewise.
Unlike Eisenhower, Nixon took a deep interest in politics and the future
of the Republican Party, but even this was a natural but studied contrast.
Here he learned from what he considered to be an Eisenhower weakness.
Like Eisenhower, Nixon relied on his own personal political organization
for the major campaigns, depending little on the Republican National
Committee. Thus CREEP was born for the 1972 campaign, designed to
keep the campaign away from the RNC.

In 1968, the Republican national chairman, Ray Bliss, could have provided major help after the Nixon nomination because of his knowledge of
political structure, particularly in the Midwest, but Bliss's role was limited
to once-a-week consultations with our campaign committee during meetings in New York, and after the election his removal became a priority
item. The veteran of the National Committee, Ab Herman, outlasted all
and in his way contributed to each campaign because he was an independent operator with vast experience.

Nixon adopted the staff paper system followed by Eisenhower, and thus
most of us found ourselves bound more by written presentations summarizing the pros and cons of an issue or outlining talking points for a meeting rather than participating in discussions.

Eisenhower deeply impressed Nixon at the time of Ike's decision to
send troops to Lebanon to stabilize the situation there. Nixon liked to
repeat the story in which Eisenhower heard all the favorable recommendations for the troop landing and then startled the military by asking
what would happen in the worst of circumstances. He thus started action
which proved successful but with knowledge of all possible consequences
if there was failure. The lesson is well taken for any President.

The Kennedy influence on Nixon was not one of organization but of
style. He never admitted it publicly, but even in matters such as working
with Pat Nixon to redecorate the White House, the image of the Kennedys was on his mind. Nixon admired Kennedy's dramatic way with
words, but he never understood the Kennedy relationship with the press. I
have no doubt but that when he was confronted with some of the crucial
decisions as to Watergate and the cover-up and the tapes, he was influ-

enced by thinking that both Kennedy and Johnson had wended their way through troublesome personal spots by just hanging tough.

It is doubtful if Nixon ever gave deeply serious thought to burning his tapes as trouble began to develop early regarding Watergate. He felt secure in the protection of executive privilege, and he did not believe that the existence of the tapes would become known. Alex Butterfield, who revealed to the Senate investigating committee the existence of the tapes, apparently did not realize the seriousness of the information he was volunteering. Two days before he testified in the Senate, I had a chance meeting with him on a flight between Los Angeles and Washington and asked if he had anything new or important which would come out when he met with the committee.

His answer was "No, I have no important information."

It would be interesting, but probably impossible, to know what influence Nixon's image of Kennedy and Johnson in tough moments had upon his thinking when he rejected his final opportunity to destroy the tapes. This came after the Butterfield testimony, when Nixon was in the hospital recovering from phlebitis. Alexander Haig, by then chief of staff, found himself confronted by two of the top Nixon attorneys, Len Garment and Fred Buzhardt, each with a different view on what should happen to the tapes.

Buzhardt argued that they had not been subpoenaed and therefore were not yet legal evidence and thus they could be lawfully destroyed. Garment argued that tó destroy them would be to destroy legal evidence. Haig decided that this was a matter only the President could resolve, and he took both men to the Nixon hospital bed to present their case. Nixon listened, discussed the case, and said he would let them know his decision in the morning.

His fatal hospital-bed decision was not to burn the tapes. There was no second chance after that.

Nixon studied Johnson carefully during his years out of office and made at least two decisions which were to have great bearing on his style within the White House.

He decided that Johnson was far too available to the press and the result was that "familiarity bred contempt." Seemingly, he did not care to consider the fact that Kennedy also had been extremely close to the press, particularly early in his administration, and had been accorded a longer than usual honeymoon as a result. In moments of anger, Nixon often would write me or Ziegler or both of us and instruct us to make the point that he had never called an editor or a publisher to protest a reporter's action—as did Kennedy and Johnson. With Nixon it did not seem to count that he had urged us and others on his staff to make such calls.

More importantly, Nixon decided that Johnson reserved too little time for himself and failed to delegate properly. When he had been Vice-President, Nixon hardly knew what it was to delegate. He was a poor administrator. But after watching Johnson mistakes, sometimes coming from a lack of delegation and too much attention to detail, he made greater isolation and more delegation—particularly on domestic issues—a key point of policy. The point had merit but he and Haldeman carried it too far.

Connally burst upon the scene in a different manner.

During the early years of the administration, there had been some who suddenly caught the President's attention and became temporary superstars. The most emotional departure of any of the White House staff was made by Pat Moynihan, an early superstar who was returning to the Harvard faculty. When the President learned what Moynihan planned to say upon his departure, he arranged a meeting in the East Ballroom of the White House, where most of the cabinet and the assistant secretaries of the department were summoned along with the White House staff to hear Moynihan deliver an emotional and eloquent farewell address admonishing all to work harder and give the President the recognition and support he deserved.

Peter Peterson arrived to handle trade and soon became Secretary of Commerce. His logical presentation of ideas excited the President to a degree where he instructed me to set up special meetings with political and business leaders as well as with newsmen to hear him discuss problems of trade and the economy, but, sadly, he was a superstar for a limited time.

With John Connally, the President seemed for the first time to see a man who was his political equal and yet who he felt he could trust with, as he said, "any job in government." When the economic crisis was at its peak, he selected Connally as the voice of the administration, the spokesman singled out to lead all the varied economic leaders within the administration ranging from George Shultz to Herb Stein to Arthur Burns and Peter Peterson.

Early on, Connally convinced the President that his public relations effort did not do him credit. The enthusiasm which Connally could inspire by his dynamic personality was unequalled by anyone else. He was right, there was only one John Connally. With his knowledge of government at all levels and his ability to inspire, Connally worked on all of us and for a time the President seemed satisfied that the PR pace had changed.

My impression from the inside was that the influence Connally wielded with the President was excellent because it was based on practical knowledge and it was positive, in contrast to the many others we had who too often put the President in his dark and mean moods, which sometimes were destructive. Nixon would have liked to see Connally as President.

Connally was gone from the cabinet long before May 1, 1973, which was one of the most emotional days any of us inside the White House ever went through.

The President had just announced that he had accepted the resignations of Bob Haldeman and John Ehrlichman, and he gathered the cabinet to explain his new plan of organization.

The President was applauded as he entered the Cabinet Room, and then he proceeded routinely to announce that Ken Cole would assume responsibilities for domestic policy. "He has my total confidence." National Security is unchanged, he said, and scheduling would be handled by Steve Bull and David Parker with the Office of Management and Budget in charge of all budget activities. The cabinet now would meet every two weeks and the new Domestic Council would get under way that afternoon.

Then came the more emotional part.

"Bob Haldeman and John Ehrlichman are two of the finest men I've ever met," he said. "But we have made a change. I've been around this track before. When Sherman Adams resigned it was like losing a combination of Haldeman, Ehrlichman, and Henry Kissinger. When it happened the cabinet took less responsibility. But we won't panic on decisions. Time will be the test of change without allowing differences to develop, without adding burdens on the President."

The President began to ramble and repeat himself, then caught himself by saying, "We must move forward on our great goals."

Thinking of Watergate, the President turned and said, "The conduct of the investigation will be under Richardson. He is in charge. I expect full cooperation." (Richardson would remember that later.)

"If there is any member of your staff you feel may be involved, let him [Richardson] know. I have no information of any legal liability. If you have some information you may not be sure of, give them a leave of absence."

Then he wandered again and it was hard to tell if he was talking about Haldeman and Ehrlichman or others as he said, "They will in the end survive and be vindicated."

After a few sentences, the President went back to the subject: "There must be no question of people being totally free of involvement. I have the greatest faith and confidence in you. Tell your people that."

Just prior to the cabinet meeting the President had found an FBI agent in front of Haldeman's office door, guarding against the removal of any material. In anger he had shoved him.

Recalling that incident, he said, "We will not allow them to be treated as criminals. This is the most arrogant and despicable action I have seen. They are honest men."

His old friend Secretary of State Bill Rogers came to his rescue and said, "We have a heavy responsibility to treat them as well as possible in our personal conduct.

"This isn't the end of the world.

"It is important how we act. Everyone is listening for some comment. As responsible officials, we will avoid that."

When there was a crisis or the President was in a down mood, the staff frequently urged the cabinet to greet him warmly and usually the cabinet secretaries went out of their way to be elaborately supportive.

Dick Kleindienst had announced the day before that he was resigning because "persons with whom I had close personal and professional associations could be involved in conduct violative of the laws of the United States," and "fair and impartial enforcement of the law requires that a person who has not had such intimate relationships be Attorney General of the United States." Earlier he had withdrawn personal participation from the Watergate investigation as more and more stories appeared concerning his predecessor John Mitchell and his friend, Fred LaRue.

But on this, his last day, Kleindienst was the first to join Rogers:

"I would like to say what a great honor you have served on me," he said. "What an honor and privilege." Before the meeting was over, Kleindienst left to make a Law Day speech, and as the cabinet applauded him, Nixon said, "We love you."

Richardson followed Kleindienst's comment quickly with:

"You have told me of the way you want this carried out. I will do it right to the best of my responsibility, and I will do it right knowing the way you want it done. I give great credit to dedicated people and to my predecessor. He has done a great public service."

Nixon could not get his mind off the FBI agent and Haldeman.

"Who ever ordered FBI agents to stand in front of the door will pay. This is cosmetics like New York. I want it done but no cosmetics. You don't do it as if these men are criminals. I have defended every one of my men. . . . That rubs me the wrong way. I don't like it. . . . I came in the hall and they were there. I am not going to have public embarrassment to two honest decent men. We are going to have every effort to get at the task. We will get the facts." He still clung to the belief Haldeman and Ehrlichman would be vindicated.

Cap Weinberger changed the subject:

"You made the point, and we will get at the facts. We must move ahead with our programs."

That returned the meeting to other subjects, and after the President welcomed Rogers Morton back from a hospital bout, he called on George Bush, in his usual astute fashion, for a political assessment. Bush told of Republican victories in Oakland, California; Columbus, Georgia; and Orlando, Florida, and then commented, "Teapot Dome was followed by GOP gains." Bush, at that point, was GOP national chairman.

The President's response was, "It is so easy to be trapped by the press. Can we govern? We can fire all of you or some people, but they will target us. Their target wasn't Roy Ash or John Ehrlichman or Bob Haldeman. There will be partisan comment, including some from Percy. His target is running for President, which he will never be if I'm around."

The Percy comment came from out of the blue.

But it was not the first time the President had verbally attacked Percy, the Republican senator from Illinois.

17

The Tentacles of Superpower

GOVERNMENT REORGANIZATION, which was ordered in 1973 by President Nixon in a genuine effort to gain some control over the unresponsive and vast federal bureaucracy, appears to me in retrospect to have been the most dangerous move of all he made.

Watergate revelations have shown the tremendous power concentrated in the hands of a few on the White House staff. The power, which was so immorally abused in the Watergate cover-up, pertained to the dealings between the White House and a few leaders of the executive branch of the government and the Re-election Committee. The public felt the sting of the deception and abuse but the excessive power of the few did not reach into the bureaucracy. Or affect substantive government policy.

The administrative reorganization announced by the President early in 1973, just a few weeks after his landslide election victory of 1972, delegated managerial control over the entire executive branch of the government into the hands of just eight men and the President. Four were appointed members of a supercabinet, a rank designated to control the bulk of the executive branch of government. The four, in turn, worked with four White House assistants designated by the President as his operations chieftains.

The plan, designed in the main by John Ehrlichman, represented an attempt by the President to overcome his frustrations that stemmed from an inability to budge the Congress or the bureaucracy in making the federal departments responsive to the will, the policies, and the orders of the President of the United States, the chief executive officer.

Watergate tapes revealed, in part, what those of us on the senior staff had known since the earliest days of the presidency. Nothing brought the President to anger more quickly than what he saw as a battle in which he rarely won even a small skirmish. The battle centered around his strong effort to attune the protected civil servants to the policies he felt had been part of his election mandate.

Haldeman, Ehrlichman, Finch, Harlow, and Moynihan probably spent the most hours listening to the President vent his anger with the immovable federal giant. But all of us heard it considerably. I recall long discussions of this on the presidential yacht which were interrupted only briefly when Nixon waved occasionally to surprised yachtsmen or to passengers on the Potomac tourist boat. One time we sat with drinks in the yellow Oval Room of the White House living quarters listening to the President discuss the need to renew our efforts to get the cabinet secretaries to stand up more to the bureaucrats. "Get the cabinet to kick their damn bureaucratic asses," was the conclusion.

Frustration with the bureaucracy was not a presidential quality unique with Nixon. Government was but a tiny fraction of the size it is today when, in 1883, Congress approved the Pendleton Act, which gave the United States Government what we know as the civil service system to replace the spoils system, which had been fought by political reformers for thirty years or more.

Few today would advocate a return to the spoils system, which bred inefficiency and dishonesty, but it was responsive to elected officials. All of the modern Presidents since Franklin Roosevelt have sought unsuccessfully to do battle with the bureaucracy. Popular Republican theory is that the bureaucracy is dominated by Democrats, and the voting patterns in Washington and nearby sections of Virginia and Maryland would seem to prove that. The many years of Democratic tenure in the White House as government grew larger and larger also lend credence to the theory. Democrats attracted activist Democrats into government, and they stayed.

In 1936, Roosevelt asked Louis Brownlow of the University of Chicago to head a committee on administrative management designed to examine the restructuring of the executive branch. It urged stronger powers for the President. The Hoover Commission, appointed in 1947 to study the organization of the executive branch of government, represented in many ways the efforts of President Truman to find a better method to manage. Many of the highly impressive recommendations of the Hoover report did become law.

Other Presidents have sought outside help in curtailing the bureaucracy. President Johnson had a task force headed by Ben W. Heineman which said in part, "Some criticism arises because of alleged organizational and managerial weaknesses. After several months of study, we believe the organizational criticism is merited." Heineman recommended more White House policy power, but, again, little changed. Nixon's counter to this was the Ash Commission, which in its first report urged the formation of a Domestic Council similar to the National Security Council. This recommendation was followed. Ash's second report urged the reorganization of the cabinet. Congress balked.

Decentralization of government has been a theme in most recent presidential campaigns. Barry Goldwater emphasized this. George Wallace made the bureaucracy his principal target with reference to "pointy-headed liberals" and to "briefcase-toting bureaucrats." Nixon strongly criticized big government in his 1968 campaign. Carter did in 1976.

Following up on the second Ash Commission report, Nixon sent a message to Congress on March 25, 1971, which in some parts had language foreshadowing that of the Jimmy Carter speeches made during the 1976 campaign.

"When I suggested in my State of the Union message that 'most Americans today are simply fed up with government at all levels,' there was some surprise that such a sweeping indictment of government would come from within the government itself. Yet it is precisely there, within the government itself, that frustration with government is often most deeply experienced. . . .

"The problem with government is not, by and large, the people in government. It is a popular thing, to be sure, for the public to blame elected officials and for elected officials to blame appointed officials when government fails to perform. There are times when such criticism is clearly justified. But after a quarter century of observing government from a variety of vantage points, I have concluded that the people who work in government are more often the victims than the villains when government breaks down. Their spirit has usually been willing. It is the structure that has been weak."

(The point about the nobility of government workers was exactly the opposite of how Nixon expressed himself privately, but in this message he was seeking a change in structure, not people.)

Nixon continued:

"Good people cannot do good things with bad mechanisms. But bad mechanisms can frustrate even the noblest aims. That is why so many public servants—of both political parties, of high rank and low, in both the legislative and executive branches—are often disenchanted with government these days. That is also why so many voters feel that the results of elections make remarkably little difference in their lives. . . .

"At this moment in our history, most Americans have concluded that government is not performing well. It promises much, but it does not deliver what it promises. The great danger, in my judgment, is that this momentary disillusionment with government will turn into a more profound and lasting loss of faith."

Nixon's frustration with the bureaucracy sometimes centered on internal opposition to his approach to major problems such as desegregation, cutbacks in failing social programs, and reforms of the welfare system. All found effective opposition within a federal bureaucracy which sometimes resisted all change and, on other occasions, felt the President was moving too slowly.

A minor case involving one individual struck me as one of the best illustrations of bureaucratic resistance.

In 1970, I was asked to join the President and William Rogers in the Oval Office to meet Mr. and Mrs. Harold Bell. The President had received a long, handwritten letter from Bell referring to the times he had met Nixon and Rogers while he was a caddy at Burning Tree Country Club and then going on to express strong admiration for the President's conduct regarding the Vietnam War.

During the course of a warm reunion in the Oval Office, Bell recounted how he felt he had learned much in the late fifties from Rogers, then deputy attorney general and later Attorney General, and from Vice-President Nixon. He said that he sometimes would hide from the starter at Burning Tree if he had heard that Nixon and Rogers would be golfing so he would have an opportunity to caddy for them. On several occasions after golf, he would wait on the service road adjacent to Burning Tree and hitch a ride into town with the two Eisenhower leaders. In these conversations in the car, they strongly encouraged him to go into college.

Neither Nixon nor Rogers had seen or heard of Bell, their black caddy, since the Eisenhower administration had left office in 1961.

Bell, in the meanwhile, had gone to college in Indiana and met his wife, another college graduate, who was teaching school. Bell explained that he was working for the District of Columbia specializing in youth athletic projects.

Nixon explained to the Bells his views on Vietnam and expressed his obvious gratitude for the letter and for its supportive statement. He was relaxed and enjoying the reunion. As the Bells were leaving the office, Nixon followed his usual custom and presented Mrs. Bell with a presidential pin and gave the former caddy a souvenir golf ball and a presidential fountain pen.

"If you would ever like to change jobs and come into the full federal government, why don't you give Herb a call and let him work with you on finding the best place for you," Nixon said. "Don't let him talk you into working in a bureaucratic office. With your talent you should work with recreation and athletics. You can be a great influence on young people," he concluded.

Bell was flattered, he said, but he added that he liked his present job. I gave Bell my White House telephone extension without expecting to hear much more about the conversation. But a few days later, Bell called and said he had been thinking over the President's encouragement and would like to talk to me about finding the right opportunity for him in the executive branch.

I mistakenly thought civil service would not be that tough to handle in this case, and, after all, this was the one and only time the President of the United States had asked me to find a job opening for an individual and at a level far from the top.

I asked Rob Odle and Ron Baukol, two of my young assistants, to check with the executive departments and see where there might be a job fitting Bell's experience and falling within the outdoor-activity guidelines set by the President. They located such a position in the Defense Department, where Bell would work within a program assisting athletes who were in the military service and who might be contenders for the United States Olympic team. The middle-level job also included an opportunity to work with youth groups, particularly those in the black community.

Then came the struggle in seeking to carry out the job offer of the President. We put a minimum of comment in writing but verbally informed Mel Laird, the Secretary of Defense, of the proposal. He asked my staff to work with one of his senior personnel officers, who in turn identified the job more formally and made preparations to hire Bell. With this kind of job assurance, Bell quit his position with the District of Columbia and reported shortly to his particular area in the Defense Department. What neither Bell nor I realized was that a military colonel and a senior civilian in the department felt we were imposing on their realm and so, while they assigned work to Bell, they failed to fully qualify him and to place him on the payroll. They resented being imposed upon by the President.

Several weeks later, a few days before Christmas, Bell called me to say he had not yet been paid and that he was afraid to tell this to his wife with Christmas rapidly approaching. Only then did I find he had not been employed officially.

I could envision one of two negative stories suddenly appearing in Jack Anderson's column. After all, some of Anderson's best sources were in the Pentagon. One possibility would be a story about either Herb Klein or the President trying to bypass normal civil service procedures and force patronage on the Pentagon, appointing a man who had publicly supported the President on Vietnam. (With Bell's permission, I had told the press of the meeting between the former caddy and Nixon and Rogers.)

A second version of the story might imply we had tricked a black man into resigning his job and then left him in economic plight on the eve of Christmas.

I decided that whatever had happened, it would be a mistake to go through the bureaucracy and try to get well-deserved back pay for Bell. That might only enlarge the story and encourage a leak.

Unknown to Bell, I called the Republican National Committee and persuaded its people to find someone to pay Bell for what he would have made had he remained at work for the District of Columbia.

The unbelievable maze of work to get one qualified man a job in the bureaucracy took additional time even after that. There were meetings of Bell and the personnel officer in my office and again we had to involve the time of the Secretary of Defense. Even after Bell was formally placed in his job, he frequently came by to see me and to complain that he was being harassed by old-timers in the Defense bureaucracy.

Following Ash Commission recommendations, what Nixon sought in his 1971 message to Congress seeking executive reorganization would not have solved Harold Bell's problem with the system, but the President believed a consolidation of some executive departments would decrease overlap, increase federal efficiency, and in the process make the bureaucracy more manageable.

The basic Nixon proposal was to retain Departments of State, Treasury, Defense, and Justice in their traditional form but to consolidate several independent agencies and the cabinet departments of Labor, Commerce, Agriculture, Transportation, Health, Education, and Welfare, and Housing and Urban Development into four new departments, thus cutting the cabinet to eight. The new departments would be Human Resources, Community Development, Natural Resources, and Economic Resources. The old departments would not have been moved bodily into one or another of these new executive branches but would have been divided by functional topics and programs.

Human Resources, for example, would have included a variety of education, health, food stamp, migration, and other activities then scattered among Agriculture, HEW, the Office of Economic Opportunity, and others. Other interests of Agriculture, Labor, and Commerce, including migrant labor and varied statistical resources, would have been consolidated in the Department of Economic Resources.

The plan was supported by considerable logic. It had been apparent to us from the start of the administration that there was constant overlap between cabinet departments. Early on I had a briefing in Des Moines for farm editors, and, when we were asked a question concerning sewers, I looked at the seven cabinet officers on the platform and asked which covered this in his department. Five men raised their hand. Looking around further we found there were four agencies and two departments running the management of federal lands and three departments and six agencies dealing with recreation areas. Early in the nation's history, departments such as Labor, Agriculture, and Commerce were formed to provide a voice for their constituencies in Washington. They were advocates. Even in the more modern cabinet structure, the secretaries of these departments are looked at principally as advocates rather than as national problem solvers. Consolidation might have made the departments less unwieldy.

The plan was widely heralded by the President, with Roy Ash leading many of the briefings both within and outside of top government circles. Dynamic John Connally addressed the cabinet and subcabinet on the plan and moved from there to television appearances, where he was a convincing salesman for the plan. The President felt he finally was doing something about the bureaucracy. He had a winner.

His miscalculation came in underestimating the bureaucrats who preferred the status quo. Vast change such as that planned here left them uncertain where they would stand, and this affected individuals and their perception of their job status. They cranked up massive resistance.

The Congress was even more negative. The elected representatives and senators have built a network of committees framed around the structure of the existing executive branch. Less departments would mean fewer congressional committees, fewer chairmen, less of a role, particularly for the more junior members of the legislative branch. If there were no Department of Agriculture, what role would the chairman of the House Agriculture Committee have in the new structure, or the chairman of the House Commerce Committee? Would he find himself chairing a subcommittee instead of a committee? How many subcommittee chairmen would be displaced?

Some of the opposition to the plan was on a philosophic basis from those who suspected that this was a massive Nixon effort to eliminate or curtail domestic programs and departments within the structure. But for most others, the opposition was just a matter of practical politics. They valued their committee roles.

And thus the plan never had a chance. The Congress and the bureaucracy had triumphed impressively over the President. Later in the Carter administration, Congress even added a cabinet office—Education—and provided more status for congressional chairmen in that area.

Throughout the first four years of the administration, Nixon had turned increasingly from dependence on the cabinet to originate or carry out his policies and to more dependence on the ever-growing White House staff to delve into every detail of the domestic departments of government. While the President was constantly disgusted with the performance of the departments, he concentrated little of his personal time on domestic matters, preferring to devote his major attention to the ever-widening problems and areas of opportunity for progress in foreign policy. Not only were there White House assistants and junior assistants piled upon junior assistants seeking to direct the domestic cabinet departments, but under Ehrlichman a system of task-force teams was implemented to include many of those of middle rank in the executive branches for studies which were made on a working-project basis. The concept was that the top man knew less than his underlings in the cabinet department and thus the White House would govern the bureaucracy by tapping it for technical information which the senior official was presumed not to have. Frequently, however, plans affecting a department were developed which were contrary to the views of the department secretary.

The system was cumbersome. It did not work well. Ill conceived!

With all these elements in the wind, it was not surprising that Nixon would be interested in a new battle plan for the war against the bureaucracy which he could place in effect as he entered his second term. Had the President been out campaigning he would have had less time for tinkering with a structure he really knew little about—not unlike most Presidents.

Ehrlichman was the principal author of the new plan for a supercabinet and a super-White House corps which in many ways would mean the appointment of eight assistant presidents. In his book *The Plot That Failed*, Richard P. Nathan has aptly described this as a program for an "administrative presidency."

The supercabinet was a plan by which Nixon hoped to effect the consolidation of power he had envisioned in his ill-fated executive-reform proposal, but it had the major advantage for him that he could execute it upon his own orders without consultation with the Congress and therefore with no possibility of a congressional veto. He simply designated four cabinet secretaries who, while at the same pay level, would rank above the other department heads and would guide all policy. Where the executive reform had involved eight cabinet positions, this would cut that in half and give superpower to four—superpower granted by the President, not Congress.

Nixon proceeded methodically immediately after his election in 1972 to move to execute his new plan. His first action was to follow election-night victory parties with early-morning White House executive meetings, where he gave a brief word of thanks for support and then a firm word of demand for the resignations of all senior appointees in government. While he did not accept all of them, he made it clear he wanted a drastic change in personnel.

After being with Nixon on mornings after the election in almost every race since 1946, I found this postelection act the most disheartening, most surprising, and most cruel of all. Only his postelection statements at the press conference of 1962 might exceed this in coldness, but they were delivered to outsiders—the press—not to loyal assistants who had worked unceasingly for him as President and for his election. The 1972 action might be looked at as efficient, but it was ungrateful and it was bitterly cold.

The President dropped his resignation bomb, then left Washington for rest at Key Biscayne, and, as it turned out, for a review of the plan to reorganize the new government along the lines set forth by Ehrlichman. Then followed a long stint at Camp David, where the President and Haldeman discussed with most of the senior officials their personal futures. Watching the daily helicopter ferry operations for the officials was like watching men being marched to and from a court-martial. Each met Nixon and either Ehrlichman or Haldeman and learned his fate. He was to stay or to leave. There was little chance for debate.

Hints of what might be coming went unnoticed in rare presidential meetings with the press. The first was a long interview with Garnett Horner, veteran Washington *Star* reporter, in whom the President had confided earlier when he met Vietnam demonstrators as the dawn broke over the Lincoln Memorial. The Horner election interview was granted even before the campaign was completed. The President also met with reporters near Camp David to alert them to major changes forthcoming in the cabinet and subcabinet. Like almost everyone else, the press did not fully comprehend the significance of what the President was saying.

The President's new cabinet, which he rushed to announce in December, no longer carried the look of the original 1968 model, a collection of some of the top names the President could find in the country. This new cabinet had its strong men, such as Caspar Weinberger, who was shifted from the Office of Management and Budget to HEW, where his frugal approach to budget earned him the description in the press of "Cap the Knife." He was tough but fair. George Shultz continued to add great strength as did Elliot Richardson, who was shifted surprisingly from HEW to the Department of Defense (later to Attorney General). Bill Rogers was to stay on for a short time at State, but many of the others in the new noncharismatic cabinet were men with far lesser names than a George Romney or a Melvin Laird or a Bob Finch of the first cabinet.

In an informal discussion, Ehrlichman once described the new cabinet to me as one "which will jump when the President says 'jump.'" Nixon had a no-name lineup. It included capable but unknown figures. Even with these changes, the structural shift the President was about to take eluded me. I was more concerned about the growing effect of daily stories on Watergate.

On January 5, 1973, Nixon announced his supercabinet, four men who would be designated "counselors to the President" and would have offices and staff in the White House in addition to their headquarters in their own cabinet departments.

In turn, they were to interface with four "super seniors" from the White House, Haldeman, Ehrlichman, Kissinger, and the newly appointed director of the Office of Management and Budget, Roy Ash, chairman of the earlier Ash reorganization plans.

The new "counselors" (a title previously given to Finch, Pat Moynihan, and Arthur Burns to provide cabinet rank) included Agriculture Secretary Earl Butz, head of Natural Resources; Weinberger, Human Resources; the new Secretary of HUD, James T. Lynn, Community Development; and Shultz, who directed Economic Affairs.

When looked at as individuals, all of the supercabinet designees were highly respected and capable men who knew the operation of the executive branch. The newest and youngest star in the group was Lynn, who had won White House attention particularly when he served as undersecretary of the Commerce Department, working under Peter Peterson, who left his cabinet post during the postelection change of the guard. Lynn, like Frank Carlucci, who was appointed undersecretary of HEW during the shake-up, was looked upon as a strong comer on the scene.

A second key part of this major reorganization was designed by the White House's hard-nosed personnel man, Fred Malek. It set out to place several of the White House deputy assistants to the President in key positions in the cabinet department where they could use their ties to Ehrlichman to guide the change in policy while operating from a rank below Secretary, but clearly in a role which, with easy access to and from the White House, made them untouchable as far as many of the new cabinet secretaries were concerned. The cabinet officer would become more of a figurehead to be manipulated by the supercabinet and the White House network of undersecretaries. Egil "Bud" Krogh, for example, became undersecretary of Transportation, and John Whitaker was given a similar title in the Interior Department. Some of those so designated, such as Krogh, Edward Morgan, who was sent to Treasury, and Alex Butterfield, who was named chief of the Federal Aviation Authority, later became, for different reasons, names known through one phase or another of the varied Senate Watergate investigations.

The 1971 executive-reform proposal had the merit of realigning the cabinet and many independent commissions which had started as small organizations and grown to be gigantic in nature. It probably would have knocked out considerable duplication and eliminated many of the rivalries between departments competing for the same money and attention. The hope was that it would have made it easier for the average citizen to deal with government. The unknown factor was whether it would have provided the protection to broad segments of the population—such as labor, agriculture, and business—which had been envisioned as needing strong advocates when the departments were formed. The toughest job would have been handling the ever-resourceful and liberal bureaucracy in the Department of Health, Education, and Welfare.

The supercabinet and super-White House staff plan of 1973 did nothing to consolidate departments except in cases where one of the chosen four would determine to overrule the advocates in a particular department and thus by executive or administrative procedure avoid duplication. The 1973 plan did not eliminate departments of congressional committees, it merely placed a new level of appointees over them, and in doing so it decreased the diversity of views that I believe is so important to a President if he is to be attuned to the citizenry.

From the White House standpoint, George Shultz already had brought the Office of Management and Budget into a place of preeminence where his organization examined every major program not only from a budgetary point of view but for policy and legality. Weinberger had carried this dominance forward and the new appointee, Roy Ash, had the credentials in business and as the chairman of the reorganization committee to ensure that the office would remain strong regardless of the supercabinet position.

Kissinger's status was not changed by the new orders. He had dominated Defense and State through his National Security Council, and he knew that eventually he would become Secretary of State.

Haldeman and Ehrlichman already had been unquestioned as the strong men of the White House. They dominated everyone with the exception of Kissinger and possibly Colson.

Thus the only apparent reason for giving the four staff members special recognition at the time of the supercabinet announcement was to make it clear that, while the President was saying he would open his doors to the new "counselors," the fact was that they still would have to clear through Haldeman and sometimes Ehrlichman to gain the ear of Nixon.

The danger I saw in the program was not in the hands of the men selected for the supercabinet. Few, if any, would question the integrity and "guts" of Shultz, Weinberger, Butz, and Lynn. Nothing in their records would indicate that they were men grasping for power or men who would abuse the power given to them. Each man was strong and capable in his own right.

But when one looks at Watergate and other incidents in the White House, and sees how power can be abused, it is apparent that a structure which concentrates power with a limited few can be dangerous—it poses great danger. If one presumes that Shultz, Weinberger, Butz, and Lynn would have been scrupulous in avoiding the abuse of the great power thrust upon them, one still should not assume that the system was a good one. If Watergate had not occurred they inevitably would have been faced more and more with the problems of limited access to the President and of domination by Haldeman and Ehrlichman, whose control they were strengthening because of the very nature of this more limited system of operating the executive branch of government. Given the independent nature of each member of the supercabinet, it is highly likely that one or more would have resigned if faced long enough with these policy conditions. Looking at the appointments to the cabinet of 1973, it is apparent that their replacements would have been more likely to jump when the President says "jump," or when the "supergroup" said "jump."

I believe that the system of a supercabinet had dangers of concentrated power far exceeding those of Watergate. The Watergate cover-up spelled great disaster to the nation. It caused the resignation of a President and it undercut public confidence in the fairness of the American system of government. Still, its immediate effect on general policy or legislation was minute or at least indirect until the final days of the Nixon presidency. The supercabinet was designed to affect every domestic policy of government and thus the potential abuse of power or even this supreme concentration of power posed a danger far greater than Watergate.

The plan was not designed and executed to grab the tentacles of superpower for the benefit of a few; it was a frustrated President's last effort to gain hold of the bureaucracy. I believe he honestly felt that other efforts had failed and that he needed an "administrative presidency" to govern under modern conditions. The plan gave him the opportunity to control through administrators what he could not control through executive order.

The supercabinet concept died soon after it was born in 1973, and thus there was little chance for political scientists to judge its merits in action. With a President under seige because of Watergate and with the resignations of Haldeman and Ehrlichman, the super-eight became six and the "counselors" returned to their departmental activities almost as if vanishing from a night in the White House.

President Carter later attacked the problem of the bureaucracy through a plan to reform the civil service, but important as these ideas are—and they are—they fall short of an overall plan to reorganize the gigantic executive branch of the government without overconcentrating power in the hands of a loyal few.

Presidents come and Presidents go, but the bureaucracy still reigns supreme.

18

Near the End, Lows and Highs

IT IS DIFFICULT to find two people close to the Washington scene who view Richard Nixon's presidency or public life in the same way. But no one lacks an opinion.

Veteran newsmen who perhaps would be best able to evaluate the Nixon public career often find their views clouded by the controversy which over the years surrounded most of Nixon's contact with the press, controversy which finally developed fully into a highly emotional running warfare between the media, the President, and his press secretary during his last two years in office.

When astute observers try to judge the Nixon presidency on the basis of national and international issues, the former President usually gets high marks on foreign policy and, at best, medium marks on domestic accomplishment. Beyond that, many overlook the political fact that for many years he single-handedly made major contributions to keeping the Republican Party alive and, at times, growing, even though he personally had little respect for the official party organization, the Republican National Committee. As Vice-President and as President, he gave the party dynamism, and when he resigned in disgrace, he gave the party an almost fatal setback, a setback which changed the rules of the political game.

On the domestic scene, Nixon's most frustrating experience was his failure to make a real dent in the bureaucracy, a failure common to all American Presidents in the past half century or more. After leaving the White House he put the blame for the Watergate debacle on many things, including the failures of himself and his key staff, but he felt deeply that somehow his two primary institutional enemies, the bureaucracy and the press, finally held the sword which struck him fatally.

Nixon's first interest was foreign policy, and he felt that this was the most important area to concentrate on during the time he served as President, but he also went into office with high hopes that he could leave a legacy of accomplishment in domestic policy. Revenue sharing was one of his controversial landmark programs which fitted his concept of turning more control back to the local community and away from Washington government—a concept embraced by Jimmy Carter in his antiestablishment campaign of 1976. Revenue sharing and peaceful Southern school desegregation are among the programs Nixon is most proud of today. Observers vary greatly in their evaluation of the Nixon efforts regarding the economy, desegregation, government reorganization, environmental controls, education programs, welfare reform, postal depoliticization, or the efforts cutting back or eliminating Johnson and Kennedy programs ranging from the Peace Corps to the Job Corps. He returned thousands of acres of federal land to states and local communities with his parks programs headed by Darrell Trent. His concept of making more parks available to those who cannot afford trips to National Parks looks better each day. The entire Nixon family was part of this legacy dedication program.

In matters of foreign policy, I have never doubted Richard Nixon's zeal to develop relationships which could lead to lasting world peace. Controversy still surrounds his policies on Vietnam, but he achieved peace, peace which might have lasted if it had not been for Watergate. Watergate weakened the United States' ability to act in any area of foreign policy, and, importantly, it negated the weapon of uncertainty on how strongly Nixon might react to an aggression. Ford was not in the same political position regardless of how he felt personally, and eventually the Nixon peace was erased by Communist victory in Vietnam, Cambodia, and Laos. Nixon received able and untiring assistance from Henry Kissinger in achieving the historic breakthrough in China and the completion of the SALT talks and in Vietnam. Deputy secretary of state Joe Sisco added much to the patient policies and negotiation which eventually lessened the Soviet military presence in Egypt and other areas of the Middle East.

Foreign policy successes clearly are the high point of the Nixon presidential career. Watergate is invariably the low mark.

From a career or personal satisfaction point of view, it is difficult to categorize the high and low points of Nixon. Each point I would mention, however, involves the press in one way or the other.

Nixon's closest bout with death came in 1958 in Caracas, when the cars in which he and his wife were riding in were attacked by angry students and almost destroyed before, with the help of Jack Sherwood, Rex Scouten, and a few other Secret Service men, along with interpreter General

Vernon Walters and military aides Bob Cushman and Don Hughes, the Nixons, by some miracle, escaped the determined, mad mob. It was a close escape which the small corps of reporters and photographers, including Herb Kaplow, then of NBC, and Bob Hartmann, then of the Los Angeles *Times,* recorded thoroughly as they too battled for their lives from the back of an open press truck.

The former President's moments of greatest personal exhilaration are hard to record. I do not recall a moment when I saw him completely lost in happiness—although he may have felt it and contained it within.

The moments most important to his political career were all thoroughly recorded by the press. The events that had the greatest positive effect on his successful public life were, in my view, the Alger Hiss case, Nixon's selection from a group of ten as the Eisenhower candidate for Vice-President, the Kitchen Debate in Moscow, the 1966 campaign successes, his first comeback victory in New Hampshire (in 1968), and the break-through in China. New Hampshire and California, at opposite ends of the nation, were the states which were most important for him politically. Of those positive, highlighting events in his public career, he later told me that the arrival in Peking and the end of the war in Vietnam were the most satisfying to him personally. China meant a complete reversal in his publicly stated personal views of yesteryear, and it meant he would have a unique place in history, a place he greatly coveted. It made Nixon a head-line figure in history. Of all these events, the Hiss case was covered most controversially by the media, but all of those events, which had a great effect, had widespread news coverage.

Nixon today believes that the investigation of the Hiss case gave him knowledge of Communist post-World War II efforts in the United States that he could not have learned of otherwise, and he credits his basic education in international communism to his trip in 1947 to Europe as a freshman congressman as part of the Herter committee to study plans that eventually became part of the Marshall Plan. Nixon had been in the South Pacific with the Navy during the war, but he had not been to Europe before.

During a talk with Nixon at San Clemente long after he had returned into so-called self-imposed exile, he said that the most important speech he had made early in his career was the "fund" speech in 1952, when he gained overwhelming Republican and public support that developed into his own national constituency, which was strong and supportive during later disputes with President Eisenhower and others in that adminis-tration.

The days and hours between when the Nixon fund controversy broke in 1952 in a syndicated column by Peter Edson and when the vice-presidential candidate went on television to defend himself were times of great despair and had long-range personal effects on both Pat and Dick Nixon. During that time the press reported every rumor it could find, as well as the facts. At one moment a Western Union official, who was part of the traveling party, sat down in a bar in the Ambassador Hotel in Los Angeles and told a personal friend that he thought Nixon would quit within the next twenty-four hours. The meaningless conversation was overheard by a UPI reporter and within minutes it became a bulletin on the United Press wire.

But during that battle, Nixon, while disappointed by a lack of Eisenhower support, was able to think through strategy to save himself. He was mobile and alert. The incident proved Nixon's ability to think coolly during crisis.

The three lowest moments in the Nixon political career were ones in which there was no hope in sight.

The last and greatest of these low periods came with his resignation from the White House and his emotional departure for San Clemente. I was not there at that moment, but I believe that he retained his sanity by reviewing his life and its many high points and by restudying in the past tense some of the individuals who had worked with him for so many years. This was apparent from some of the telephone calls he made to me and to others the week following his arrival in San Clemente as the ex-President.

The press was the butt of his public animosity when he learned in 1962 that his own Californians had turned him down on his bid to be governor of his native state. It was an emotional, bearded and exhausted former Vice-President who stumbled through the attack of his "last press conference." Later in the afternoon of the postelection day, he disappeared from home, wandering off unannounced to drive along the ocean and wearily try to confront a new future. Desperately we alerted friends to call if he turned up at their office or home. He finally wandered back.

When I first heard he had disappeared, I was reminded that on the night of the Kennedy inaugural he learned that his car and his loyal driver, John, would remain with him until midnight, at which point control of the limousine would change hands. He spent the last two lonely hours driving and walking, meandering through the Lincoln Memorial and other monuments in Washington, lost in his own thoughts and seeking solace from great leaders of the past.

The press was not immediately aware of the third major low point in the public life of Richard Nixon. It became most apparent on the fourth day after the 1960 election, on a Saturday. And it was a day when I believe John Kennedy also felt the full impact of his contested razor-thin margin of victory.

On the afternoon after the election, the campaign party had flown back from Los Angeles to Washington, to begin the tortuous task of dismantling the Vice-President's office. Later in the week, Rose Mary Woods invited the Kleins, the Finches, and Don Hughes to join the Nixons at Key Biscayne to sort out thoughts and to participate in his deliberations whether he would contest the election, particularly in the light of the revelations of vote fraud being unveiled by the Chicago *Tribune* and others. The necessity of making such a decision kept the Vice-President from facing the full realities of the loss of the presidency. Finch and I conferred with him, but he made the personal decision that he would not contest the election because he felt that the prolonged debate over the vote count not only in Illinois but in states such as Texas, Missouri, and New Mexico would further divide the nation and make it vulnerable to power moves by the Soviet Union at a point of national indecision.

The decision not to contest the election was courageous and patriotic, and it flew contrary to the advice of Murray Chotiner, Len Hall, and many of the astute Nixon political advisers who had examined the evidence of fraud. Finch and I sided with the view that a contest would be no win for Nixon or the country. The Vice-President's decision was one which historically sets a precedent of stability in American elections.

When Nixon made and announced his decision, there was little press at Key Biscayne, outside of the coverage of the powerful Miami *Herald*. But both the decision and the divided Republican views concerning it were well covered by the media.

With that key decision made, Nixon suddenly was struck by the consequences of the loss of the presidency.

The small staff group was to meet with the Nixons at their hotel villa for cocktails and dinner. As we arrived, it was apparent that Nixon was at a low point of depression. While Pat Nixon tried to keep the conversation sociable, Nixon found it difficult to even speak. I wanted to ask him about breaking away for a week on St. Croix, where some of our closest personal friends, Tom Pownall and Representative Bob Wilson and their wives, had joined us in renting a house where we could get away from the campaign for a few days of skin diving. The Wilsons and Pownalls already were there awaiting our arrival.

But in the tense atmosphere of the evening, I knew this was not time for a topic like that.

Joined by Bebe Rebozo, we went to dinner nearby at the Jamaica Inn, and as we arrived, Hughes and I were told that there was an urgent message from our hotel operator.

I waited a few minutes and then called the hotel, where I found that Herbert Hoover was trying to call the Vice-President. I went into a small telephone booth in the lobby and called the former President, who told me that he had just had a call from the future President's father, Joe Kennedy. Kennedy had asked Hoover to find out if Nixon would be amenable to a meeting between the two presidential contestants to discuss the political divisiveness in the country which had split its vote almost evenly, and what might best be done about it. It was a unifying gesture.

I told President Hoover I would call back.

At the table over cocktails, I reported to Nixon on the Hoover conversation. Immediately he became a different, animated person. He had a major decision to make. We discussed the question, and he decided he should meet with Kennedy. I then returned, with my dime and credit card, to the telephone booth and asked Hoover to find out how we could best make such arrangements at Key Biscayne. He called Joe Kennedy.

About this time, the newly revived Nixon decided he should call President Eisenhower at Augusta, Georgia, and inform him of his decision and seek any advice he had. We went back to the Jamaica Inn's phone booth, where Don Hughes this time used the dime and the credit card and put the Vice-President on the telephone with the President.

As I waited for the outcome, the telephone rang at the maître d's desk, and I was told this also was a call for Mr. Nixon. I took the telephone and the voice on the other end of the call was that of President-elect John Kennedy. I followed our regular procedure and told him the Vice-President would be with me shortly, and I would have him call immediately.

Kennedy was chatty, however. He gave me his personal number at Palm Beach and then proceeded to talk about the election. He generously discussed my personal role as press secretary and praised me for my post-election TV appearance, which he said he waited to see before making his own victory announcement. As we talked informally I gained the impression that this too was the day when the full impact of his narrow victory had hit him. It was as if at this same hour he and Nixon had finally felt the emotional meaning of the closely split election and both were climbing back on top of the scene by the stimulation of this meeting being arranged.

I thanked the President-elect, and after Nixon had finished talking with Eisenhower we returned to the dinner table to discuss the latest turn of events.

It was at this point that Nixon again went back to the much-used telephone booth, where the same dime and credit card placed him in his first postelection direct conversation with Jack Kennedy. Between them they arranged for a meeting in Key Biscayne at midday two days later.

At the Key Biscayne discussion that followed, Kennedy and Nixon conferred inside the small hotel villa while Salinger and I sat under the sun and discussed our own relationship—which was to be cooperative. The President-elect asked the Vice-President to take a cabinet post in his new administration, and Nixon declined, saying he felt a great responsibility not to be divisive in our politically torn country, but adding that he believed there was an important role to be filled responsibly as "the voice of the loyal opposition."

The state of depression had departed, at least temporarily, for both men, and the first policy decisions had been made for the postelection era.

And the telephone booth at the Jamaica Inn went on serving the public with few knowing that briefly it had served as a focal point for a moment in history involving a former President, an ambassador, a Vice-President, a President, and a President-elect, plus Hughes and Klein.

Personal relationships, such as these between leaders, often have a bearing on national and international policies. Personal staff relationships also have far more impact on the President than the nation usually recognizes. Kennedy had a closely knit staff with great built-in loyalties, and he related well to it. The Nixon staffs also had great loyalty, which was forged over the fires of battle, but somehow Nixon at important times had difficulty understanding this personally.

Nixon had great appreciation for loyalty, but he had difficulty with these personal relationships. It is doubtful, however, if this problem damaged his efficiency—until it came to Watergate and the post-1972 election thinking, a time when a lack of understanding became a major factor leading to downfall.

Interestingly, Bob Haldeman, who spent far more personal time with President Nixon than any other individual on the staff, treated the subject briefly in his book *The Ends of Power*. Talking about his deep personal relationship with Nixon, Haldeman said:

"Nixon viewed Klein and Finch in human terms, as people, which meant he would have trouble dealing with them on an official basis. He didn't see me as a person or even, I believe, as a human being. I was a machine. A robot . . . he was considerate of those who worked for him, even though rarely close to them on a personal basis. (To this day he doesn't know how many children I have or anything else about my personal life; he never asked—and I was his closest professional associate.)"

The Haldeman book, ghostwritten by Joseph DiMona, probably exaggerated Haldeman's feelings on his personal relationships. I had never heard a Haldeman complaint of that nature before. Nixon had, for example, shown an interest in both the Haldeman and the Ehrlichman children, who were in college, and in Hank Haldeman's participation in the 1972 youth campaign for Nixon's election. On more than one occasion, he kidded about Hank's streaming long hair, which was in distinct contrast to the crew cut of Bob Haldeman.

Nixon, even during critical presidential moments, would take the time to ask Finch and me about our children. He was interested in Kevin

Finch's athletic career in track and football. When Maureen Finch became an international debutante in ceremonies in New York, Nixon called her personally and, reflecting upon the fact that he had been through such ceremonies with his daughters, told Maureen how "tough" the presentation was on fathers. When Maureen was to be married in La Canada, a suburb of Los Angeles, to John Shaw, Nixon made a point of being in San Clemente so that he and Mrs. Nixon could attend the ceremonies. He had hoped to stay even for a reception at the nearby home of the close Nixon friends Mr. and Mrs. James Reynolds, but the Secret Service convinced him this would only increase their problems and might inhibit the party.

Throughout the twenty years of campaigns in which I became involved almost every two years, my daughter Joanne's November 4 birthday inevitably would arrive a day or two before election. We have joked that she has the greatest collection of birthday telegrams of anyone, all from Richard Nixon, wishing her well and apologizing for her father's absence on her special day.

Nixon feels that other than his governmental experience his greatest educational process in preparation for the presidency came between 1963 and 1967, when, as a private citizen, he visited countries in four continents, meeting informally with foreign leaders while ostensibly conducting some private business. His four separate tours included Europe and its NATO nations, Africa and the Mideast, Asia from Japan to Iran, and South America. He believes these private trips gave him understanding he needed later as President.

Two of the speeches Nixon recalls as being most meaningful vary entirely in content and in circumstance. One address was given at the Lakeside in the prestigious Bohemian Grove in July of 1967, a podium graced by many world leaders, but a podium where the rule is that the speech is never covered by the media. This was a critical point in Nixon's comeback effort toward the presidency, and his detailed survey of world events, all given without a note, is remembered by the two thousand business leaders of the nation who gather in the redwood Grove north of San Francisco as one rating in the annals of the club alongside with a Herbert Hoover farewell address to his campmates. The Nixon speech gave the future candidate the stature he needed to garner opinion-leader support at the highest levels.

The second speech Nixon relates most to his presidency was made on May 8, 1972, when he made the decision to mine Haiphong Harbor at a time when he was preparing for the SALT talks with the Soviets. Most critics predicted that the Russians would break off the forthcoming summit. But Nixon feels that the speech enabled him to retain public support in such a way that the Soviets felt they had little to gain by breaking off the forthcoming meeting in Moscow.

The day which to me showed the greatest misunderstanding of human relations by Nixon, abetted by Haldeman and Ehrlichman, was the day after the election in 1972—the most shocking day of my political career.

Nixon's landslide victory in 1972 came as no surprise to anyone, but the overwhelming victory provided exhilaration for all of us—veterans or the younger people in their first campaign. Election provides a night of tears, some nights of joy, and others of disappointment and sorrow. I have experienced all, and even in the sports world, there is no moment quite like this.

For the first time since 1956, I had found election night to be relaxing. During election day, Bob Finch and I had flown back from California after spending the last day before election campaigning the length of the state, with press conferences and meetings beginning with breakfast in San Francisco and extending through Chico, to the north, Salinas, Sacramento, Fresno, Los Angeles, and finally, in the evening, San Diego on the Mexican border. For the first time on an election night, we were not asked to set up our elaborate forecast system, and from the moment the polls closed, it was apparent that Nixon would be a landslide victor over his Democratic opponent, Senator George McGovern. I spent the evening appearing on various television shows, analyzing the campaign and forecasting events of the next four years of the presidency. Watergate cover-up was not among them.

Before the 1972 campaign started, I had decided that this, my fifth presidential campaign, would be my last, and despite the polls, I would campaign as if we were behind so that if the "impossible loss" occurred I would not have a guilty feeling of failing to do my utmost. I had done my best in some small states and in every large state in the country for both the President and a number of candidates for senate, governor, and Congress, traveling about sixty thousand miles in three months.

Two White House meetings were scheduled for the day after the election, one for the cabinet and one for the senior staff. I, like most everyone else, expected these to be routine pep sessions with the President thanking us for our successful efforts in his behalf and perhaps outlining briefly his goals for the next four years.

The staff gathered in the Roosevelt Room and the cabinet in the Cabinet Room.

As the President began to speak to us at the senior staff meeting, I noted that he did not have the enthusiasm I anticipated. I knew that in the middle of his preparations for appearing on television the night before, he had lost a cap on a tooth and had to have emergency dental repairs. Momentarily, I thought that was the problem. He did not appear exhausted, as on other mornings after elections, but it was obvious to me that he was struggling over a problem.

The President started in natural form, "I have been very proud of this staff." He went on to praise the efficiency of the organization, which he said had been criticized as overefficient, and he briefly discussed the election results which foreshadowed a tough opposition Congress.

As I made notes on a yellow pad, his next few comments made me wonder what he was getting at:

"Everybody here as he examines his office should go at it with the feeling that there are no sacred cows. We will tear up the pea patch in the cabinet, not in terms of individuals but in terms of the cabinet as an institution." (I had no idea that in the back of his mind was the supercabinet.) "Now is the chance to clear out the dead wood without having to pander to bureaucrats who say we had a razor-thin margin"—referring to 1968.

My notes of the next few sentences show the words, "Change is necessary."

"Disraeli," Nixon said, "at the age of sixty-eight, became Prime Minister for the second time, defeating Gladstone after Gladstone's enormous success in reforming the British government. Disraeli's description of Gladstone was 'an exhausted volcano.' That's true in life, in sports, in politics. After a burst of creative activity we become exhausted volcanoes." By this time I anxiously wondered where he was going in his comments. The President thrived on reading history, but I was not a student of Gladstone and Disraeli, and I wondered if this was just a show of intellect or if he had some other meaning to the "exhausted volcano" theory. The President went on to say it was his responsibility as a leader, "despite our victories, to see that we not climb to the top and look over the embers that once shot their sparks up into the sky." This sounds absurd.

"Whatever you decide, we will always regard the people in this room as members of the first team. You made possible what was recorded last night, but it happened long before." With that he departed with the ring of applause from the staff in his ears.

We were stunned.

It was Haldeman's role then to amplify the "exhausted volcano" theory with a direct request for the resignations of all in the room and a request for similar letters of resignation from our senior assistants. He was not clear how far down in the ranks he wanted to go in requesting the resignation letters, and he was entirely vague as to how many of the resignations would be accepted. The implication, however, was that many of the letters would be accepted. As we puzzled over the events during the next few days most of us thought, "He must mean some of the others on the staff, not me." Whatever the thoughts, the President's speech and the Haldeman follow-up left the staff in demoralized disarray. Haldeman graciously praised the staff for dedication, but few heard him. Only a handful, including Haldeman, Ehrlichman, and possibly Ziegler, knew what was to be forthcoming. Most work at the White House came to a halt.

There was no opportunity to savor the flow of victory. There was only demoralized confusion.

I went back to my office to determine how I would break the news to my own staff. Haldeman's tone indicated to me that the senior professionals would be among those expected to write letters. On my staff, this included Ken Clawson, Margita White, Paul Costello, Devan Shumway, and Al Snyder. I decided to exclude some of the others, such as Wanda Phelan, Jeni Brown, Donna Kingwell, and Mary Ann Snow, who were highly capable deputies but not ranked as senior assistants.

With my five senior assistants, I took an optimistic note and referred to the resignation letters in less serious tones than I felt. I wondered in particular about the one woman in the senior group, Margita White, because at one point a year or so before Haldeman had denied my request that she be given an official presidential commission and a pay raise which befitted her ability and her position. I felt this was clearly a case of prejudice against high-ranking women.

For several weeks before the election, I had analyzed the value of redefining the structure and operations of the office of director of communications to improve capability in the light of our experience during the first four years of the administration. After several meetings with the staff, each of the senior members had been assigned a role in our voluntary reorganization of the office. We had actually been through several drafts of this plan before the postelection announcements by the President and Haldeman, and I decided to speed up work on this to have the program ready for presentation to Haldeman and Ehrlichman after a personal vacation I planned to take a few days after the election. The President, accompanied by Haldeman and Ehrlichman, flew to Key Biscayne for what also appeared to be a period of rest. Actually the time was used to fine-tune the plan for accepting staff and cabinet resignations and for the eventual formation of the supercabinet proposal the President had hinted at during his "exhausted volcano" talk. Much later Nixon told me that while Haldeman helped execute the plan, it was Ehrlichman who made most recommendations on structure, and he wielded the ax on personnel.

In Puerto Vallarta, where my wife and I joined Leon Parma and friends at Quinta Laura, a large rented home President Nixon had occupied at a time he met with the President of Mexico, I kept a nervous eye on what was happening with the President by reading the English-language Mexico City *News*, and by telephone calls to my office. We moved ahead and completed our plan for office reorganization, which did not call for resignations but rather accepted even a heavier workload. The President soon

flew from Key Biscayne to Camp David, where the daily accounts indicated he planned a series of meetings with each of the cabinet officers,
with chiefs of key agencies, and with senior White House staffers. Newspaper reports talked of a helicopter shuttle that was flying the key people
to and from the mountaintop presidential retreat, and almost daily there
were reports of some resignations being accepted and others rejected.

I knew the time was coming for a decision regarding me when I received a telephone call from Larry Higby, Haldeman's young assistant, re-
laying a request from the President for a meeting at Camp David. I explained the distance factor from Puerto Vallarta and gained a three-day
delay of the meeting so as to enjoy at least a few more hours of rest and re-
cuperation from the ardors of the campaign for the President.

Once in Washington, I conferred again with my staff regarding our
plan for reorganization of the White House approach to communications
and I was then driven to the Pentagon, where I was to pick up a helicopter for the shuttle to Camp David. As we sat in the craft flying low over
the Maryland woods, I noticed the beautiful fall colors, but my thoughts
were centered on selling this new program to the President and to Haldeman. I did not know Ehrlichman's tough role. Herb Stein, who headed
the President's economic council, sat next to me, but he also seemed lost in
his own thoughts. Neither of us was certain what would happen once we
landed in the grassy field adjacent to Camp David's living and working
quarters.

Camp David, which originally was President Roosevelt's Shangri-La,
and was later renamed by President Eisenhower in honor of his grandson,
David, had its cabins scattered in the woods. Activity centers were in two
multiroom lodges, Aspen and Laurel. During these series of meetings, one
lodge was being used as a holding area and the other was occupied by the
President. Ron Ziegler greeted me and took me into one of the holding
rooms, where I started to explain the papers I carried outlining our proposals for restructuring the communications apparatus. The plans retained
the feature of two separate offices, mine and Ziegler's, reporting to the
President, but they envisioned more revitalization and modernization of
the cabinet communications offices. I noticed that Ziegler seemed unusually nervous as we talked and was distracted to a point where he paid
little attention to the new plan.

Finally, I asked Ziegler what was the plan of action for the morning.
Was I to meet Haldeman first, or Haldeman and the President jointly?
He said he did not know but that Ehrlichman was conferring with Stein
and would not be a part of the meeting.

"I'm not sure what is going to happen, Herb," Ron said, "but I want
you to know I have nothing to do with it. You may not like the meeting or

the President's ideas today, but whatever, I want you to know that I am not a part of the plan."

Ziegler today contends that this was true. And I believe him. But I have in the past had doubts.

Eventually Ziegler took me to the President's lodge, where I met Haldeman, who was waiting to take me in directly to meet with Nixon. As Haldeman, the President, and I exchanged brief pleasantries and discussed the campaign, I saw the White House photographer, Ollie Atkins, outside shooting pictures of us through a window.

I started to tell the President that I had with me a plan for the reorganization of the office of director of communications but he quickly changed the subject and talked of the need to cut the size of the White House staff and to reorganize all of the cabinet departments to make them more effective as he started his second term of office.

Haldeman then interjected that a smaller White House staff would mean, among other things, that my office would be cut in size and that in the new plan it would report to the press secretary, Ron Ziegler.

That meant I had lost the power struggle in which I wanted to strengthen the scope of my office. I was out.

"We know that you have said that you plan to leave the government sometime in the next year or so," the President said, "but I thought you might like a position which would involve international relations. What would you think of being the director of the U. S. Information Service, or perhaps you would like me to appoint you as our ambassador to Mexico. I know you have a lot of interest in Mexico."

I was not totally surprised at the plan to cut back my office. I had long wondered what would happen because of the power struggle we had been through. I considered such a blow a possibility as Haldeman moved, impersonally, to consolidate his power as chief of staff by eliminating some of us he could not control completely. I did not realize Ehrlichman's part in planning this centralization of power. I was surprised by the two jobs the President was offering me. He was making a change in White House structure, but he was deferential to me; still, I resented the situation.

I had never made a secret of my intent not to serve on the White House staff for a full second term. In various forums before television and news industry audiences, I had announced as early as in 1970 that I would leave the White House sometime early in the second term, even if the President was reelected. (These early announcements were recalled by many reporters as they started looking at those who were leaving more unexpectedly, some under Watergate pressure.)

I told the President that I wanted some time to consider the USIA directorship and the ambassadorship, and that because of my total absorption in the combination of running my office and of campaigning, I had not yet made up my mind exactly when I planned to return to private enterprise. I told him I would give him my decision in a few days.

The President seemed to detect by my manner that I was surprised at the direction our meeting had taken. It was as if he believed I had had discussions of this earlier with Haldeman or someone else. Suddenly he seemed awkward and turned the conversation to the days we had spent together in Alhambra when he was a congressman. With that he stood and thanked me again for all I had done. The meeting was over.

I did not seriously consider either of the jobs offered me, but I wanted time to decide what course I wanted to take. The United States Information Agency provided interesting opportunities to improve communications internationally, but it was outside the White House and seemed secondary to what I had been engaged in, directing communications for the executive branch. Frank Shakespeare, a former CBS executive, had done an excellent job with the agency, but he was returning to the broadcast field.

Ambassadorship to Mexico is most coveted and I was interested in the country and the post, but I felt an ambassadorship was a move toward retirement and probably required spending rather than earning money. I, too, coveted the job, but the timing was not right for me. When I left the White House, I needed to get back in the newspaper and television fields, my career areas.

While I was holding off my answer, I suddenly heard that Jim Keogh, who had headed the White House speech writers, had been given the USIA appointment. The choice could not have been better. Keogh was intelligent and tough, and had a background of experience not only in the White House but as an editor of *Time* and as an author. Nonetheless, I felt I should have had the opportunity to formally say no.

I did say no to the appointment as ambassador, and I was asked promptly by Haldeman not to announce I was leaving or to rush out of office. His explanation was that he wanted to be fair to me, and that he felt timing would be important to the press acceptance of my departure. I thought he also feared a negative press reaction. From that point on, I again set my own timetable, although it was clear between us that I was leaving and my office would be downgraded after I left.

In later years, many in the press have said that they believe the situation should have been reversed, with the President urging me to stay longer than I planned—particularly in light of problems that were to develop for the press secretary's office, as the press and congressional furor over Watergate answers from the administration increased month by month during the next year and a half.

Finally concurring with Haldeman, I decided that it would be in the best interest of the President and in my own best interest if we moved forward with the activities of my office as if nothing had happened. Ziegler and Haldeman assured me that was the personal intent of the President. I did not want to discuss it with him directly.

I did, however, make it increasingly public that I would be leaving sometime soon and the gratifying result was that I was overwhelmed with inquiries as to whether I was now ready to consider outside business opportunities, particularly, but not exclusively, in the media field.

After the blow of Camp David, it was exciting and reassuring for me to find this type of professional recognition in the private business world. But in the White House there was an eerie feeling. Younger staff members were coming to ask for advice. And the President, who was puzzling the government and the public with wholesale changes in staff and cabinet, was under pressure, particularly during the stepped-up December bombing in North Vietnam. Many in the media looked at the bombing as vengeful.

Most of us had thought that the climax of the first four years of the Nixon administration was to have been on election day. As things turned out, the postelection days were more traumatic. Many of us were altering our personal lives as we prepared to leave the White House. Watergate hung over everything like a black cloud, and emotions again were on the rise over a Vietnamese War which the administration had led the public to believe was all but over.

As this transition from the old term to the new term came on the scene, the inaugural became more and more the focal point for the timing of all activity.

More than half of the staff members had not been in Washington when the 1969 inaugural was staged, and so they were torn between the excitement of looking forward to participating in this event highlighting their careers, and the anxiety and uncertainty many felt as they were leaving the White House.

In a situation which now appears incongruous, most of us on the White House staff had to rely on Jeb Magruder, by then the operating director of the inaugural committee headed ceremonially by J. Willard Marriott, for the coveted tickets to the actual swearing-in ceremonies and the inaugural balls. I was surprised that the auto license plate number issued me for the inaugural was 8, while my number for the car in 1969 had been 12—a small point of ego or protocol.

For most of us who had trudged the campaign trails for so many years, the inaugural itself lacked the personal drama of 1969. The victory had been overwhelming. We still believed that the next four years would be years of greatness for the President and for the nation. We were nervous about Vietnam, although we felt that the end was near. It was nearer than we knew. We were apprehensive about Watergate, still not knowing anything of the details of the cover-up other than what we read in the papers. We did not believe all we read, and even these stories were fewer for the moment. I suspect that the President, Ehrlichman, and Haldeman were confident that the crisis was past, and on that inaugural day their thoughts were to the future. They were confident. Mitchell, Magruder, and Colson may have been more worried personally, but that was not apparent as we chatted at the Capitol and in the White House inaugural review stand.

I thought again of the inscription on the picture given to me by Lyndon Johnson at the time of the inaugural of 1969. "To Herb Klein: May the end be as pleasant as the beginning." For me the impending end was not as pleasant because of the abrupt circumstances of the Camp David dismissal, not because of what I saw in my future. For the President, I was confident the end would be far more pleasant than the beginning. Vietnam was still a fact but the atmosphere of riots, dissent, burnings, and violence seemed quieted. The "Christmas bombings" had brought anguish, but I thought the end of Vietnam was near because of the international strength the overwhelming election victory had given to the President.

Even the inaugural balls lacked luster for me and for most of the veterans of the staff. Cabinet officers and those of us who were well known publicly were divided to attend different balls, with some in major hotels and others at public buildings. We and our guests were at the Smithsonian. The crowds were such that dancing was nearly impossible, and glimpses of the President and the Vice-President were brief. It was a mob scene with everyone then clamoring to be on the bandwagon.

But the fun had gone.

In the presidential box at the inaugural parade review, Julie Eisenhower had whispered to me that she needed to talk to me sometime in the near future. I asked her to call the office at her convenience.

I always have considered the Nixon daughters as very special people. Their ages are similar to those of my own daughters, Joanne and Patty, but the four daughters had been more acquaintances than friends. Ours had lived in Washington but grown up in Southern California. Julie and her sister Tricia were Californians who had spent most of their lives in Washington. The four girls had been together on rare occasions, usually public, such as a Disneyland dedication, but I personally felt close to both Tricia and Julie, and I admired them.

During the campaign, the husbands of Julie and Tricia had met with me several times concerning their own political roles. For many months, even after the election, David Eisenhower considered running for Congress, but he felt that he did not want to take the time of the President for such discussions until he was closer to making up his own mind. David had an affinity for politics which I first noticed in the 1968 campaign, when he would be among the last to leave a campaign party, listening to the stories of the veterans of the fun and the heartaches of past campaigns. He was bright and incisive, and unless you knew, you would not be aware of the fact that here was a young man with both Eisenhower and Nixon family relationships. He was shy.

Tricia's young New York lawyer husband, Eddie Cox, lacked campaign background. But 1972 was a year when all of the family eagerly participated, and no one was more eager to contribute than Eddie. He would consult with me and others on how to project himself publicly, and it was apparent that he was charming and quick to learn.

In the earlier years through the 1960 presidential campaign, the Nixons kept their young daughters sheltered from the political wars, even to the point of banishing the Washington *Post* from the house because of Herblock cartoons.

By 1968, however, the daughters were eager to campaign, as was Julie's fiancé, David Eisenhower. At times when the girls were exhausted, I found that David was my best means of help to get Julie and Tricia to pose for "one more picture" or to talk to "one more reporter."

The White House brought the family fully into the political world, and with the addition of Eddie Cox to the trio, they were among the most effective spokesmen the President had on his side. The combination of the Eisenhower family and the Cox family was unique in presidential campaigns and the press covered them well. All were loyal to their father (or father-in-law) and his programs, but each had his or her own independent political philosophy. Tricia was the most conservative, Julie the most outgoing and pragmatic. All were effective.

Pat Nixon had entered the White House reluctantly, but by the time of the 1973 inaugural she had developed her own style and had dropped some of her dislike for public speaking. I helped her find her first press secretary, Gerry van der Heuvel (Donovan), a charming and well-respected reporter for the New York *Daily News*. In my view, Gerry, who like Mrs. Nixon was low-key, carried out her duties in a style suitable for the First Lady. After the first year, it became apparent that the fashion did not fit Haldeman or perhaps even Nixon. Mrs. Nixon's viewpoint I was not able to ascertain.

In some ways the case against Gerry van der Heuvel paralleled the frenzy within the White House for better public relations. This started with the fact that the President took great pride in his wife's achievements. Mrs. Nixon contributed superbly to causes in which she believed, such as better education and voluntarism and the "legacy of park lands," but she had no intention of being a major headline maker. More like other First Ladies than like Rosalyn Carter, she was never hesitant to discuss issues with her husband, but she was not one to help shape broad political opinions on key national problems.

Gerry van der Heuvel was among the victims of the post-1970 squeeze for a new look in the White House, and she was replaced by a more flamboyant but capable woman who came from the industrial public relations area, Connie Stewart.

Despite all of the first-term combat between the White House and the press, Gerry was the only senior press aide to become a casualty. More should have been. Mrs. Nixon made certain that she had a respectable place in the State Department and later she was moved to the embassy in Italy by the diplomatic corps bureaucracy, which was suspicious of her intimate White House ties.

During the van der Heuvel time, there was much controversy between the White House and women reporters, mainly because of pressures from the President's staff, which read the so-called women's pages as avidly as the political columns. But with Connie Stewart, who was capable but more pliable to staff demands, the controversy only increased. There was no way she could win. It was all part of the battle between press and White House, a battle which knew no bounds or sex. On a few occasions individual women reporters were banned by Nixon from covering White House social events.

Despite the press secretary problem, Pat Nixon on her own continued to gain respect and admiration from the American public, respect which holds today even through the agonies of Watergate.

As I went into my final months at the White House, I thought of Pat Nixon often, knowing she must be puzzled by the growing scandal around her husband and the White House. I have seen her reluctant to enter publicly many of the frays or even the more pleasant events, but I have never seen her unable to handle well the most quiet delicate situation or the most public situation in the international political arena. Inwardly she might be ruffled or angry, but outwardly I have never seen her lose her calm or get emotional in public.

Lady Bird Johnson went through many political crises, but no First Lady in modern times has undergone all of the turmoil that has confronted Pat Nixon even before Watergate. And few have ever found her falling short.

In the campaigns of the fifties, it took me months to convince her she should meet with the press on her own. In 1956 I finally convinced her to have tea with the reporters. Even then one of her ground rules was "no tape recorders." She never lacked confidence; it was a matter of being certain she did not in any way contradict the candidate, her husband.

In the informality after a campaign day, when most of us might gather for a drink or just to talk, she was never hesitant to critique the efforts of the day, ranging from small details to the effect of the candidate's view on the issues. When she spoke out everyone from the President down listened.

Foreign countries brought a new aspect to her role as she would work on an independent schedule, regardless of the country we were in, playing the role of an ambassador to the people while her husband negotiated the more serious details with the leaders.

With this background with the Nixon family, my last months in the White House had added delicacy. They could not understand why I was leaving at that time of crisis. The President had not told them he was eliminating my job, and I did not feel I should.

Julie came to my office shortly after the inaugural to discuss the rumors, which again were growing in number, regarding Watergate and people both in the White House and those who had served on the Committee to Re-elect the President. She found the stories hard to believe and wanted to know why the press would carry them. None of the questions concerned any possible involvement of her father; that was unacceptable to her and basically it was to me also at that time. Julie wanted to be a part of any effort to counter the rumors, and again she was puzzled by the fact that I was leaving the White House at a time like this. I could only assure her that my departure would not be immediate, and meanwhile all of us were working hard on calling public attention to the positive aspects of the President's second-term program. I somehow could not tell her the facts surrounding the timing of my departure.

There was growing doubt in the mind of the public as to whether it had been told all it should know about Watergate, and there was no way to stop investigative reporters from digging further into the case. Criticism of the press was the answer from the White House, but it was the wrong answer. Instead of reacting to the press, the President should have been moving to fire those involved, and he should have been moving to close ranks by involving those of us with experience in handling delicate problems surrounding such firings.

The President still was savoring the heady flavor of his landslide election victory, and I felt one of the problems was to be sure neither Julie nor anyone else in his loyal family goaded him into a new major attack on critics of our Vietnam policy or of Watergate involvement. This was the time for the positive, but not all the staff or the President believed that.

Immediately after the inaugural, at the time of the January 23 presidential announcement that Henry Kissinger had initialed an agreement with the North Vietnamese for the end of the long war, there was a quiet but strained battle within the White House over the value of attacking our critics on a wide front, in the press, the Congress, and the public sector.

The staff differences on what strategy should be adopted regarding critics of the administration covered a range of subjects including Watergate, Vietnam, and the economy.

With the self-confidence generated by the landslide vote for Nixon over McGovern, some felt the time was right to drive the critics to their knees, to humiliate them publicly. Pat Buchanan and Chuck Colson were two of the proponents of this strategy. Others, led most vocally by Bill Safire, but including me, Bryce Harlow, and John Scali, felt we had a chance for more reconciliation if we approached our opponents with more olive branches and fewer hammers.

Within a few hours of the time Kissinger had reached the final agreement with the North Vietnamese, the President asked Ron Ziegler to request from the networks time at 10 P.M. for him to address the nation "on a matter of vital importance" regarding Vietnam. As was the custom, when there was a major, dramatic announcement such as the decision to send troops into Cambodia, the President asked Bob Haldeman to arrange separate briefings for the senior staff, the cabinet, and the bipartisan congressional leaders.

Haldeman presided over the staff meeting and asked Kissinger, who usually arrived at such meetings only a few minutes later than I did, to give us a sketchy briefing on what had happened, saving the details for the President's actual address and for a background press conference Kissinger was to conduct the next morning.

This was a moment of the greatest satisfaction for all, but particularly for the President and Kissinger, who had suffered most among us as they listened to the taunts of critics and while they saw the country sometimes seeming close to being destroyed as it tormented itself over the conduct of the war. As we awaited Kissinger in the staff meeting, many of us were thinking about the days much earlier when he thought the war was about to be over and when he seemed to drop to the depths emotionally as an agreement to end the war turned into another North Vietnamese offensive in the battlefield. But this time it was for real. The war was within days of being over. There was an opportunity to "bring us together," as Nixon had said on the morning after his election triumph of 1968.

Nixon always has been sentimental about his birthday on January 9 and traditional staff and friends have made special note of the day. His greatest birthday present came in 1973, because it was on this day that Henry Kissinger told him he finally was sure the war in Vietnam was over. Excited as Nixon was over the news, he and Kissinger had to contain themselves, and even in his inaugural address of 1973, Nixon had to refrain from any premature discussion prior to the final announcement three days later on January 23. Nixon showed it little, but unquestionably, after the criticism of his conduct of the war, including that most recently in the McGovern campaign and the "Christmas bombing," this was an emotional high for him.

Kissinger was exhausted, but obviously happy. Still he was cautious. He warned us to do nothing to antagonize the North Vietnamese—in effect to be certain we did not attack their manhood before the final agreement was fully signed.

Kissinger cautioned that he did not want to give any reason for the North Vietnamese "to leave Paris without signing the agreement next Saturday. If Le Duc Tho claims a victory, so can we," he said, "but let's wait until after the twenty-seventh"—when the formal agreement was to be signed fully. Kissinger went on to warn against claiming military victory prematurely. "That will cause Hanoi to claim it and Saigon to claim it," he said. He predicted accurately that the next few days still would see fierce fighting as both sides jockeyed for position at the time of the ceasefire.

It was in the midst of this discussion that the staff again got into a debate over the attitude to be taken toward critics. Haldeman raised the question about how the opponents of the President, those who had followed Senator McGovern, would greet the announcement. Would they question publicly why we had not accepted terms like these earlier? Was this the peace with honor the President had constantly reiterated as his goal?

Kissinger took no stand on what our domestic strategy should be, but he outlined the potential attacks in this way:

"As I see it, there are three lines of attack against us: One, we could have had this settlement four years ago. Two, what we had last October"—when agreement appeared certain but the North Vietnamese changed views at the last, apparently thinking election pressures in the United States would serve them well—"was good enough. Three, only the pressure of the doves made us do it."

After that there was little discussion of the probable attacks but considerable opinion expressed as to how we would approach the critics.

Haldeman obviously had talked to Buchanan prior to the meeting and asked him to prepare a position paper for the staff directing a hard-line attack against the Vietnam doves. I believed it foreshadowed an overall head-on battle with our opponents on all subjects, including Watergate and the economy.

The general Buchanan approach was that this was a victory for the Silent Majority, which had stood strong with the President against "relentless, harsh, and vitriolic attack from the left." Buchanan went on to read a line which indicated that had the doves in Congress prevailed against the President, we would "be witnessing a bloodbath on an unprecedented scale, the victims of which would be those Vietnamese who placed their confidence in the word of the United States." He then went on to an indication that the opponents represented "American surrender."

I believed it was true that the Silent Majority had provided the President with much-needed support and that he had been subject to unfair, vitriolic attack from the doves of the left and the press, but I disagreed strongly with the last lines of the position paper calling for personal attack on our leading opponents, including those in Congress and the media.

As the debate went on, it became apparent that Haldeman wanted only one result, an agreement to attack our "enemies." At one point the chief of staff referred to "Herb Klein's past experiences with the President," and said the President himself would be generous to his opponents only "if he has the luxury to do so." I saw his point that the President was referring to some of our past experiences where he had been markedly heavy-handed, and Haldeman felt that he would follow the tough line again unless he was assured that his cohorts would carry on a vengeful attack in his behalf. There had been times when I had refused the attack role and he had taken up the cudgels—always finishing the worse for it.

We were seeing that the President, at this moment of victory, wanted to be sure his opponents did not get on the offensive and his thought was that someone had to attack them—to put them on the defensive. He wanted to taste the blood of revenge.

As the meeting broke hurriedly to allow time for some of us to attend the cabinet meeting and then the briefing for congressional leaders, it was clear that for the moment the staff debate had been resolved: we would attack. Haldeman, I knew, did not expect anything momentous, but he wanted to be able to assure the President that if he kept above the fray, others would strike the body blows. It was a tough position for Haldeman, who did not necessarily believe in the attack theory, but he was making the best of two options: someone else attack, or the President will.

In his comments to the cabinet the President seemed impatient to get through with the meeting, but he was more candid and more generous than usual to his aides and supporters. He gave indirect praise to Mel Laird for the plan of Vietnamization, which had provided for the orderly withdrawal of American troops as Vietnamese strength grew. He cited union hardhats as supporters and the wives of prisoners of war as those who had lent stability to his efforts for "peace with honor." But he could not restrain criticism of the Congress, which he described as "totally irresponsible" in some of its actions, such as the Mansfield resolution, which called for unilateral American withdrawal.

The depth of the President's feeling about his opponents was reflected publicly in his press conference after the announcement. He said: "As far as this administration is concerned, we have done the very best that we can against very great obstacles, and we finally have achieved a peace with honor. I know it gags some of you to write that phrase, but it is true, and most Americans realize it is true, because it would be peace with dishonor had we—what some have used in the vernacular—'bugged out' and allowed what the North Vietnamese wanted: the imposition of a Communist government in South Vietnam. That goal they have failed to achieve. Consequently, we can speak of peace with honor and with some pride that it has been achieved."

I was pleased to hear him repeat his "peace with honor" phrase, but I blanched when I heard him say to the reporters, "I know it gags some of you." He was right, it did "gag" some of the reporters and columnists to be wrong, but why say it? Many of the newsmen were unprofessionally emotional but this was a moment of national joy and the word "gag" rang too loudly in the tone of the bitter "last press conference." Somehow, whether others attacked for him or not, he had to get in at least a lick. And it should be said that despite the debate and the Haldeman order, the staff attack was so miserable as to have been lost in the events of the day.

It was clearly apparent that Haldeman had been right, and the press had goaded the President over the months to a point where, had he not been reassured that others would "carry the ball," this too might have been another moment for more major confrontation between Nixon and the press. Neither Julie nor any of the Nixon family, nor any of us on the staff, could have stopped the President from finally speaking out at least briefly to express his strong feeling that this event proved he had been right and his opponents in the media had been wrong. He was challenging them to concede the magnitude of his victory. Many did not.

There was one other thing bothering the President personally. He had kept Lyndon Johnson informed of the progress of the talks with Hanoi, but the former President died hours before he could hear and share the final announcement that the war was over, and that there was neither a Communist government nor a coalition government in Saigon. The South Vietnamese (at least for a time) would control their destiny in what Nixon expected to be an era of peace.

A few days later, Nixon told me that he wanted me to go to Hanoi and to China with Henry Kissinger. We were to visit Thailand, Laos, Hong Kong, and Japan, but our major mission was to negotiate a plan for future peacetime relations between the North Vietnamese and the United States and to translate this into improved future relations with the Chinese, who we were also to meet.

With Watergate starting to develop more in the public domain, and with my own plans for departure, I was not certain why I was making this particular trip. The President said he wanted to be sure that at this critical moment all of the credit for the end of the Vietnam War did not settle on Kissinger. I was to watch for this. Moreover, he also wanted me to give my

Making It Perfectly Clear

observations from the trip to newsmen and to the public on television. I wondered if this trip was a reward for service and an apology for the Camp David episode. Or, realistically, if it was to be certain we communicated factually what happened as we opened what we believed to be a new Vietnam era. But after I went on "The Today Show," on my return I saw the President's point more clearly. My role was to present an authentic news report since there could be no press coverage of the various negotiations. All through the trip I perceived that Kissinger looked at me with dual feelings: he wondered, first, whether I had been planted to report on his press handling, if any, and, second, in what areas I could be of most help to him during these delicate negotiations. The trip worked out in such a way that I could be of help in some of the negotiations, although Kissinger clearly was the dominant policy leader, assisted by Ambassador Bill Sullivan. I admired Kissinger's style as he handled the difficult circumstances of postwar Vietnam. He was tough, and he was understanding and knowledgeable on every major issue. On the other hand, I was able to communicate what had happened to the press and the public, and my praise of the Kissinger abilities was strong. He was great.

I returned from Vietnam and China expecting my final few months in the White House to be calm and easy. That was not to be the case.

The year 1973, which started out as a time of triumph for Nixon with his inaugural and the end of the war, turned more and more into a time of nightmare. Watergate revelations soon were a matter of daily headlines. Jeb Magruder was being questioned by the federal grand jury. John Dean, about whom I—and most of the staff—knew little, soon was in the headlines, and he was talking to the prosecutors. In April, the President found himself faced with the involvement of Haldeman and Ehrlichman in the scandals, and had to ask for their resignations.

By that time I had decided to leave the White House in April and to accept an offer to become a vice-president for corporate relations with Metromedia. But hours before I was going to announce this, Ziegler called me and warned that he could not tell me all that was developing regarding Haldeman and Ehrlichman, but it was important that I delay my plans for an announcement and for leaving.

Today, I am frequently told, "You are lucky, you left before everything started breaking in Watergate." But the fact is I left some time after the Haldeman-Ehrlichman dam had broken, and my last few months were devoted to working with Alexander Haig, the new chief of staff, and the President, and Ziegler, trying even then to restore some sanity to the relationship between Nixon and the press and the public. I was pressured by Haig to stay "a little longer," which I did, but the President at that time did not ask me to change my decision to leave eventually. Had he done so, I might have stayed one more year. Fortunately, I did not.

In early May, with Haldeman and Ehrlichman gone, I went to the President and told him that the best way to regain public confidence was to remove anyone else on the White House staff remotely connected with the cover-up, and to start a new campaign of openness with the public and the press. He agreed in a general way but was not specific. Yet on May 9, when he met with the staff and its new chief, Al Haig, he outlined a plan of more openness. The plan was good, but he never executed it. When the President left the meeting, Haig gave a staff pep talk in which he stressed a new policy of more access to the President and more openness with the media and the public. Haig was a breath of fresh air, and I never found a moment in the White House or in our later relationships when he was not very direct and candid with me. I do not know anyone who could have handled the growing problem better.

Following the President's talk my office developed a program to combat the swelling anti-Nixon tide. Ziegler and I signed the memo introducing our plan. We said that in carrying it out "some of the suggestions we make may be difficult to swallow and would not be offered in ordinary circumstances, but could be used to the President's advantage and to put the press in a spot to be more conciliatory." This was a plan of desperation to get back on the right track.

We outlined an eight-point program, which had as its linchpin a conversation between the President and network anchormen to be followed within a day or two with a quickly called news conference for the White House press corps.

Had the President accepted this program and thus dramatized new openness, we would have insisted on follow-up meetings with columnists, television commentators, and even Chinese journalists who were touring the country under the auspices of the American Society of Newspaper Editors. We also felt we should have a series of dinners with media, mixing broadcast and print and including, probably in the second dinner, "Punch" Sulzberger, publisher of the New York *Times* and Katherine Graham, publisher of the Washington *Post*. A few days before we wrote the memo I had, by chance, met Mrs. Graham at the *Newsweek* offices and she had asked me into a private office to express a hope that we in the White House realized that she took all of the allegations seriously and felt a great responsibility to be fair and accurate. It was difficult to convince anyone in the White House that she had said that, but I felt that she was worried and meant every word.

Ziegler and I concluded the memo with a recommendation that similar programs be launched to reach Congress and the business community. We likened the plan to a World War II general boldly entering the center of battle to give new inspiration to the troops, "in this case the American people."

The plan was never followed.

Once Watergate began to roll with the constant drumbeat of the televised Senate hearings and news stories breaking in the press daily as the reporters scrambled to catch up on the story, it was apparent that we inside the White House were feeling the effect of a growing snowball gaining speed as it raced down the hill.

Near the end of July, days before I was to leave the White House, Haig and Ziegler asked me to undertake one more major assignment. They wanted for the President a summary of what cabinet officers, public-opinion makers, and my own professional public relations friends thought of the President's situation. There were many questions we wanted the best answers to from major opinion leaders. How was the public now perceiving the President, particularly in view of growing stories regarding the White House tapes and the pressure by Congress, Judge Sirica, and the Special Prosecutor, Archibald Cox, to obtain copies of the tapes. Had the President undercut his position on retaining the tapes by allowing Haldeman to listen to them? What was the reaction to the testimony by John Dean? What suggestions were there as to how the President should approach the growing demand for more answers from him?

With the delicate nature of this priority project, I had some of my national survey conducted by the remaining senior members of my staff, but I needed outside help both to collect the opinions and to give the project an objective outlook, which was no longer possible in the heavily bombarded White House. I asked for, and gained, help from Billie Brown, a highly respected professional from a major New York advertising agency. She proved to be a skilled, ideal volunteer, who could draw from government and business leaders answers they had not given publicly. Most of them were pessimistic, but they also offered to "help the team."

In the discussions with leaders I respected, ranging from author James Michener to Robert Gray of Hill and Knowlton, to Tony De Lorenzo of General Motors and Jim Shea of Southern Pacific, and with all of the cabinet officers, it was apparent that the consensus was that time was running out for the President and the public badly needed an explanation of what was happening. Some we surveyed said the President could last only six months. Others suggested a shorter time span. Even in the Western states, the situation was deteriorating almost as rapidly as in the East, contrary to the belief of many in the White House, where much of the staff regarded the entire situation as affecting primarily the press and leaders in Washington and New York.

Hobe Lewis of the conservative *Reader's Digest*, said that the President's job was riding on how he handled this now. "If he is arrogant, the people will turn away from him. He needs to be prudent and tough-minded." That was typical.

The feeling we gained overall at that date was that the public would still forgive the President, despite the clamor against him, if he went on the air and admitted error and gave a full explanation of what had happened. Some suggested that the tapes be given to Senators Erwin and Baker or to Cox or even Sirica to do some selective screening, which would protect in part the doctrine of executive privilege. The content of the tapes and the extent of presidential involvement was unknown to all of us.

In my report to the President I pointed out that public doubt was growing and that his failure to provide answers to the questions being raised by testimony before the Senate was reviving the "Tricky Dick" image. "The feeling is that the President is not showing leadership," I said. "He must be forthright, and we cannot minimize the catastrophic nature of the situation."

I recognized that the anti-Nixon bias of the press and broadcast reporters was becoming more apparent daily. In their frantic effort to be first or to catch up with the story, many of the newsmen were printing accusations they had not checked out thoroughly, and they were unfairly damaging the reputations of some of the more innocent members of the administration. This is not a time the media can be proud of. Each day Nixon delayed meeting the press added to the emotional bias. The newsmen were turning the daily press briefings of Ziegler and Warren into an amateur circus.

My suggestion, relayed to the President in August 1973, was that he take what further steps were needed to clean out wrongdoers, that he go on national television and give a full exposition of Watergate to the public, based on the best facts he could muster. With that I felt that he could urge an end to the Senate hearings and the forthcoming House hearings, which obviously were disrupting the nation more and more. I strongly recommended a meeting with the media, whether it be with three network correspondents, a large or a small press conference. I thought a precalled large press conference was the least desirable of the alternatives.

These suggestions, which were similar to those in May, also went unheeded, at a time when candor still might have saved him, but the President knew he would have undercut some of those he thought most highly of, such as Mitchell, Haldeman, and Ehrlichman.

In an exchange of letters on June 5, 1973, I resigned from the White House, effective July 1. In my "Dear Mr. President" letter I pointed out that over almost twenty-seven years of friendship we had been "together at some moments of triumph." I expressed confidence that his leadership "will leave an indelible stamp on history, both internationally and domestically."

The President's "Dear Herb" letter expressed "deepest personal regret" for my resignation to continue a career in the media. "You can look back on your term in office as one which achieved the vital goal of effectively informing the American people about their government. These accomplishments comprise a distinguished record of service to our Nation," he wrote.

In the press briefing releasing the letters, Jerry Warren explained the probable change in communications office structure by answering a question with: "It is very difficult to replace Herb Klein. Herb had created a unique position in government, unique to himself. I don't think—and Ron agrees with me—that there is another man in the country who could, in effect, succeed Herb Klein. With his leaving, there will naturally be adjustment. . . ."

What I had thought would be my last month turned into two because of special projects urged on me by the President during the latter part of June, and thus I went off the government payroll at the end of June, but did not actually leave my office until the end of July.

As we drove back to California in early August, I had my first chance in almost five years to think in relaxed fashion of the highs and lows of the Nixon presidency, its accomplishments and its failures. My mind was not clouded by Watergate and the cover-up because, like most of my colleagues, I could not accept the possibility of the President's involvement. It seemed that it would have been unbelievably stupid of him to have become a part of it, particularly with the wall which had surrounded him during his time in office. Loyalty clouded the view of too many of us.

My thoughts of that time, reinforced by what I have seen since, make me believe there will be the equivalent of two Nixons as history records his presidency.

The Nixon who resigned his office as Congress moved to impeach him cannot escape historic notice covering his departure from the White House. The public animosity which accompanied the final revelations of deceptions on his part in the cover-up, and his departure from Washington, long will be an embarrassing part of the American scene. In foreign countries, particularly China and the Soviet Union, where bugging and deceit are routine, the United States reaction to Watergate and its phenomenon of disgrace remains incomprehensible. Even in the Western world, puzzlement over the American reaction is widespread. But not in the United States. There is more public sympathy for Nixon today than six years ago, but the percentages are against him heavily. He is forever out of the political scene as an effective leader.

The other side of history will, I believe, look at the Nixon record in office, the record the President wanted to preserve so desperately that he allowed his conversations to be taped secretly.

My personal view in 1973 and now, stepping momentarily aside from Watergate and looking at the rest of the picture, is that Nixon served the country better in 1969 through 1972, his only full term, than he would have in a similar four-year period had he been elected President in the 1960 race against John Kennedy.

The comparison of a 1961 Nixon presidency, had he won, against a 1969 presidency, when he did win, is difficult because of the change in circumstances during that brief eight-year span. Had Nixon become President in 1961, he, like Kennedy, would have been confronted with the question of whether to push forward with a CIA-planned invasion of Cuba. I think he would have done so, but I doubt if he would have left the matter in the hands of the CIA. He would have supported the landing forces with full Navy bombardment, if necessary.

More certain, although foreign policy intrigued Nixon even as Vice-President, he would have concentrated more heavily on domestic policy than he did when he eventually became President. In 1969 he delegated domestic policy to others. He would not have done so in 1961. He would have been less inclined toward new social-welfare programs like those of Kennedy and Lyndon Johnson, and more toward decontrol and fiscal conservatism. That might have meant he was running against the times but the nation would have been less plagued with inflation than it later became.

History seems to remember Presidents, however, more for what they accomplish in foreign policy, and that was the area where Nixon eventually concentrated most of his energies. Nixon took office at a time of tragic national turmoil, at a time when the country was boiling with emotions ranging from civil rights shortcomings to our continued involvement in Vietnam. He made mistakes, but in a time when foreign policy provided the openings for world progress, he basically served the country well by assessing the big international issues and making the necessary decisions.

Nixon learned much from Eisenhower during his eight years as Vice-President, but he probably learned as much or more during the less political years in Los Angeles and New York law offices leading to the time he was elected President in 1968.

Henry Kissinger was a major factor in Nixon's accomplishments. His remarkable academic and political life had fitted him as a foreign-policy adviser and negotiator at a time when bold new steps were possible in foreign policy, and the two men, of entirely different backgrounds, teamed up well.

Nixon had the time, when out of office, to travel to foreign countries in four continents without being pressured to make political statements, and the time to learn from business associates more about the arts of negotiating, of planning, and of delegating lesser responsibilities. Skilled as he was in foreign policy in 1960, he was so tied into Republican political policy and campaigns that he might have missed many of the signals coming from a changing Communist world had he become President when he first sought the office in 1960.

When Nixon took office in 1969, he went almost immediately to Europe when he strengthened lagging United States relations with NATO nations. He was at home with the Western leaders, whether they were the incomprehensible Charles de Gaulle, whom he admired greatly, or the newer leaders of Germany and Great Britain. During his term in office, the European alliance remained generally strong despite major Communist gains in France and Italy. Nixon gained probably his greatest personal pleasure in office during a European trip when he went from Italy, Yugoslavia, and Spain to Ireland and became the guest of a personal friend and major campaign contributor, John Mulcahy. In Ireland, Nixon found part of his roots, the areas where many of his Irish ancestors had been born.

Nixon went into office with strong plans to revitalize United States relations with Latin America and Africa, but these were areas which suffered from neglect and which had low priority compared to the crises of other regions of the world. Among the lows had to be the American failures on these two continents, where Nixon had major personal experience and where communism has made gains in recent years. In the presidency, policy often gets to a matter of priorities, and obviously China, the U.S.S.R., and the Middle East were higher priorities.

The most unusual country we dealt with in this relationship was Mexico, where Nixon felt a very personal relationship, as did Bob Finch and I. Mexico varies between more conservative and liberal presidents, and midway in 1972 Luís Echeverría was to visit the United States. It happened that I had a number of friends who were leaders in Echeverría's campaign, and in the period between his election and inaugural I had flown to Mexico, upon his invitation, to meet informally with his campaign managers and advise them regarding our transition experiences and the program for press operations. Over a period of time, Echeverría and his staff met several times with me and Finch, not on matters of major international substance but on ownership of property by Americans, and the problems of dealing with the press on both sides of the border.

The Echeverría visit to the United States was among the most unusual by a foreign leader. He and Nixon varied vastly on some issues, particularly foreign policy regarding uncommitted nations and Cuba. But they agreed strongly on the necessity of building a closer relationship between the two countries. Nixon had visited Mexico often, including on his honeymoon, and felt a personal bond toward the Mexican people. Echeverría went before a joint session of Congress and was strongly critical of United States policy toward Mexico, and yet privately he was extremely cordial toward Nixon and toward Finch and me. With some encouragement through his staff, he had arranged to speak in cities where there was a large Mexican-American population which could be helpful in building Nixon support in the forthcoming election. He was both friendly and critical, and beyond the understanding of most American politicians, out of the public criticism, we built a stronger international relationship than was generally apparent.

One of Nixon's basic theories of international relationships was that a strong opponent, such as the U.S.S.R., must recognize that the United States acting in self-interest was likely to respond to any test of its strength. And yet one of the assets he coveted was that the international opposition was never quite certain how he would react. They only knew he would not back away from confrontation.

All of this was part of his dramatic development of foreign policy, which led to the new relationship still revered by China. The Chinese did not at that time expect the United States to drop its concern for self-interest, and yet their radical turn toward a relationship with the United States also represented what Chou En-lai regarded as China's self-interest. The time had come when new understanding was in the self-interest of both sides.

The SALT I agreement with the U.S.S.R. represented another major turn in United States foreign policy and that of Richard Nixon, who had been an outspoken cold war enemy of the Soviets during his earlier years. He had the strength and knowledge to bring about a new policy everyone recognized as based on strength, not weakness.

The solution to the Vietnam War, I believe, was a major achievement, although this is the most controversial of the historic evaluations of Nixon foreign policy.

President Carter made great strides forward toward peace in the Middle East, but it was Nixon, aided by Kissinger and Joe Sisco, who had the confidence of the Israelis and gained the confidence of the Arab nations, causing them to withdraw from under the Soviet curtain. In the Nixon time, the United States had a major influence on not only Israel (and Israel had major influence on the United States), but the United States' impact was undenied in Egypt, Jordan, Iran, and Saudi Arabia.

All of these factors in the foreign-policy arena mark great achievements for President Nixon in the arena of peace.

Interestingly, despite the running warfare between the Nixon administration and the media, all of these feats, with the exception of Vietnam, were widely hailed publicly with full credit given to Nixon and Kissinger.

In Vietnam and in the domestic area, the press was far more critical of Nixon—often unfairly, in my opinion.

Looking at the policy highs and lows, one would have to say that one of the major Nixon mistakes domestically was the acceptance of wage and price controls, even temporarily. Controls violated all of Nixon's long-seated beliefs, and it was strange during this economic phase to hear him describe himself as a Keynesian. This was a failure on his part, built on a desperate effort to right the economy as he saw federal deficits climbing during his administration. He could blame inflation, probably rightly, on the Johnson decision to have butter and guns during the earlier phases of Vietnam, but he still was unable to cope adequately with the phenomenon he inherited. He now admits controls represented a major mistake.

At one of the more notable cabinet meetings, Dixie Lee Ray, then chairwoman of the Atomic Energy Commission, made the case for an all-out effort to move quickly into the next generation of atomic energy. The decision was to support a program for development of the breeder reactor as the successor to the present water-cooled reactors. This is still a subject of major controversy, and the breeder and fission reactors, which were looked at then as far away, still remain on the drawing boards. Had Nixon remained in office it is likely that more progress would have been made with both modern nuclear techniques, and the protesters, perhaps, would have been larger in number than even the crowds assembled after the 1979 Three Mile Island disaster, but he would have carried the program forward. Nuclear power was destined to be an area of emotional controversy. Nixon, even after leaving office, felt his energy program was right, and he resented congressional energy roadblocks, as did Presidents Ford and Carter.

A similar crash program was adopted by the cabinet to plow more money into cancer research. It was found that money alone would not solve the immense medical problem. There was only so much qualified research which could be funded, because there were limits on numbers of qualified researchers and research. But this was and is a major stride.

During Nixon's last week in San Clemente before moving to New York in February 1980, we had two long personal conversations regarding his own assessment of his presidential career. He said that despite all of the larger, more publicized projects, three programs were most personal to him. Most important was the cancer project, which he announced in his State of the Union speech of 1971. This raised funds for cancer research to $100 million. Nixon has since made personal contributions to the American Cancer Institute, including a check of $100,000 upon the death of John Wayne. Nixon said he felt his life had been touched deeply by those who had died of cancer. When Pat Nixon was twelve, her mother, Kate Ryan, died a victim of cancer. Close Nixon friends who died of the disease included Senators Robert Taft and Ken Wherry of Nebraska; General Hoyt Vanderberg; John Foster Dulles; Elmer Bobst, an early Nixon supporter; and two newspapermen, Kyle Palmer and Stuart Alsop. After the federal research program had been funded two other men who had influence on Nixon died of cancer: Rogers Morton and Chou En-lai.

Nixon named the two other programs he felt closely personal about as being the effort to combat drug abuse and a program for catastrophic health insurance.

Art Linkletter, whose daughter was a victim of LSD, was a major motivating factor with the President and the White House in the efforts to curb drug abuse and drug importation. The programs varied from public-education efforts through my office in cooperation with television leaders such as David Hartman to stepped-up efforts to gain cooperation from Turkey, Thailand, and other countries to curb the flow of drugs. In his conversation, Nixon also recalled that his ninety-year-old aunt, Edith Milhous Timberlake, had a grandson who shot himself to death while under the influence of LSD.

Nixon's personal attachment to the need for voluntary insurance against catastrophic illness stemmed from his childhood when his older brother, Harold, was stricken with tuberculosis. Mother Nixon's frequent stays in Prescott, Arizona, where Dick Nixon also attended school at one time, almost wiped the family out financially before Harold died, a youthful victim of TB. As a freshman congressman, Nixon joined Representative Russell Davenport in sponsoring a bill for voluntary catastrophic health insurance. The bill failed, as did the Nixon program organized and pushed by Elliot Richardson, then Secretary of Health, Education, and Welfare. Nixon is critical of Richardson on Watergate but praises him for that 1972 effort.

Nixon deserves credit, in my opinion, for cutting back or eliminating many of the notable failing programs in social research, such as the Job Corps, which sounded more effective than it was per dollar. Still, in a more major field, Nixon failed, despite his strong desire, to reform welfare effectively.

One could enumerate more successes and failures in the domestic field. But basically, when history looks at the non-Watergate aspects of the presidency it will find Nixon short but not weak on domestic accomplishment, and strong in the international field. Looking at the times in which he lived as President from 1969 through his first term, I believe he will rate as a man who led his country strongly in the areas most important to future generations. Watergate so clouded the second term that it is difficult to discern accomplishments with balanced perception.

Some of the battles between Nixon and the press, battles which left a negative impression on the public regarding the President, were fought on major issues, but all too many were skirmishes over issues that had little import.

During the last months of his second term, the inaccurate reporting which bothered the President most (other than Watergate) was that inspired by Hanoi propaganda, which turned the so-called Christmas bombing from what it was—a purely military exercise—into what the public was led to believe was a civilian massacre. When we met the North Vietnamese in Hanoi, they admitted privately to us that the bombing had been a key factor in their decision to accept a peace agreement. This was not the impression given by the press and thus, even today, it remains unfairly as a negative factor in the minds of those judging Nixon.

Interestingly, Nixon now refers to his resignation from office as his "aborted flight into the second term."

Had Nixon left office after one term, he would have been regarded as a great President because he accomplished great things in foreign policy at a time when this was the most important part of the President's agenda. The only question mark would have been whether Vietnam would have been ended by a lame-duck President before he finished one four-year term.

Had the United States adopted the proposal for one six-year term for a President, there would have been no Watergate, and no Committee to Re-elect the President. At the pace with which Nixon was moving forward in the foreign policy field, his record probably would have been brilliant.

But Nixon, like most of his predecessors, sought a second four-year term, and a six-year presidency is an idea, not a law.

Strong as Nixon was in evaluating foreign leaders, he underestimated the ability of the press and the Congress, and eventually the public, to probe into his Achilles' heel—political chicanery at a level which should not have been dignified by the presidency.

19

Tension at the Top

ANY DETAILED LOOK at the history of the American presidency and the press will establish that there inevitably will be a conflict between these two basic United States institutions unless intervention by the courts or the Congress should sometime change the interpretation of the law in a way which would alter the balance of power. That possibility of serious hostile action by the courts or even the Congress must be recognized as a major growing danger which (and most newsmen believe this) would be highly detrimental to the nation.

Whoever the President may be, history shows that he always starts with at least a short honeymoon with the media, but that the relationship wears thin over a period of time and usually ends in hostility on both sides. From the President's viewpoint the most destructive weapons of the press are the reporting of facts which are negative, and disparagement, and criticism, too often tainted by bias. The effort of every President is somehow to find the way to manage the press, to deliver his message and the image he sees for himself in a way which will be popular with the American public. The press often provides a far different perspective.

Whether the press secretary be Jim Hagerty, Pierre Salinger, George Reedy, Bill Moyers, George Christian, Tom Johnson, Ron Ziegler, Jerry terHorst, Ron Nessen, or Jody Powell, he will be caught inevitably in the struggle between the media and the President. He feels responsible to the President and the President alone, but if he is performing skillfully, he also will be an advocate for the media on occasions when the President is wrong.

A press secretary could dream he was in heaven if he worked for a President who never was offended by false, unfavorable, or inaccurate stories, who was willing to meet with the reporters as often when things were going badly as when they were going well, who at all times projected a warm and friendly attitude to the public and the newsmen. That is an unattainable dream.

And the dream of a President who pictures sympathetic newsmen transmitting all of his ideas and programs to the public in supportive fashion also is absurd—and such a situation would be dangerous to the welfare of the nation.

To achieve the nation's highest office, the President must be a politician, whether or not he calls himself one, and as a politician he is an advocate. A journalist can sometimes (or often) be an advocate himself, but in dealing with the White House or other branches of government in today's world, he is skeptical of advocacy and of politicians, and more likely than not he will regard himself as a dedicated adversary.

The press secretary is, of course, the principal point of contact between the President and the press, and he soon becomes one of the best-known and most quoted members of the administration as he serves as the President's spokesman. He appears to be in a glamorous position of great responsibility who has access to the powers of the world. But most of his time is spent as almost a hostage of both the President and the press. His life is dependent upon the President's during every moment he serves. He has no real schedule of his own. He counsels and serves the nation's highest officer, but he also works for the press, meeting deadlines, arranging facilities and transportation, handling a compendium of duties vital to the orderly reporting of a major news story. A staff handles the details but the responsibility is his.

The press secretary must have public relations expertise as he seeks to present the President in the best posture possible, but, unlike most in public relations, he has no problem gaining news attention for his client. The President's every move gains news attention.

The prying eye of newsmen usually bothers even the President who may seek publicity. All want some time for privacy. President Eisenhower had privacy on golf courses such as Burning Tree near Washington and Augusta National in Georgia, where newsmen had an agreement to watch him tee off and then allow him the solitude of fun with his foursome (in addition to the Secret Service), until he returned on the eighteenth hole. Nixon found a beach on the Camp Pendleton, California, military compound where he could get away quietly, and Jimmy Carter even used a helicopter to reach an occasional remote fishing spot. Herbert Hoover built his own retreat alongside two fishing streams in the Shenandoah Mountains of Virginia and turned the property over to the government when he left office. For Franklin Roosevelt and his successors (except for Harry Truman, who used the Florida Keys), the retreat was Shangri-La in the western mountains of Maryland, later named Camp David.

The lack of privacy, however, has bothered all of the Presidents the nation has seen. The President who seemed most unexpectedly annoyed and surprised to find that his every move was of public and press interest was Grover Cleveland. The bachelor President married Frances Folsom and left the capital for a honeymoon in Maryland. Newsmen, many of whom were surprised at the wedding, were not about to let the honeymoon story disappear, and to Cleveland's great annoyance they followed him to his retreat and stood watch a short distance from the bride and groom's cottage, reporting, in detail, even the food served the couple each day.

Cleveland's phrase for what he considered harassment was the "pestilence of newspaper correspondents."

Like Harry Truman, who bitterly wrote the music critic of the Washington *Post* for his criticism of the singing performance of his daughter, Margaret, Woodrow Wilson's greatest annoyance was aroused by speculation in the press concerning his daughter's marriage. He threatened to "thrash the man" who repeated the stories.

Truman also did not shun even a physical confrontation with newsmen when his family was involved. The President, who was deeply offended by Nixon's use of the word "traitor" in 1954, used the word himself in an interview published in *The New Yorker* in 1951 after he felt Margaret had been unfairly victimized. In the interview he said that he thought that any newspaperman "who doesn't have a sense of responsibility, prints a lot of lies and goes around slandering without any basis in fact—I think that sort of fellow can be called traitor." He then jumped to columnists, particularly those who attacked his family, and concluded, "I'm saving up four or five good, hard punches on the nose, and when I'm out of this job, I'm going to run around and deliver them personally."

The interview was vintage Truman.

In more recent times, Presidents Johnson and Nixon encouraged coverage of their daughters' weddings, although they too were upset by what they considered petty sniping at the family. A Washington *Post* description of Tricia Nixon's clothes as resembling an "ice cream cone" resulted in White House sanctions against the social section reporter. Amy Carter's every whim was chronicled in detail, although less attention is given her brothers. Jacqueline Kennedy did everything possible to preserve the privacy of her two young children, but Lyndon Johnson's daughters were older and their lives were more public.

The battle between the press and the President has taken different forms over the years. Even George Washington was suspicious of the press and he deeply resented the printed criticism of his conduct in office. In those earliest of years, the press was dominated by outright party newspapers. The *National Gazette*, probably egged on by Thomas Jefferson, launched some of the heaviest attacks against Washington. On the other side, the *Gazette of the United States* was the Federalist organ, supporting Washington. The first American President had his farewell address published in the *Pennsylvania Packet and Daily Advertiser* instead of delivering it personally, but he left office bitter toward the press.

Newspaper speeches frequently include a quote from Jefferson, where he said:

"Were it left to me to decide whether we should have a government without newspapers or newspapers without a government, I should not hesitate a moment to prefer the latter. But I should mean that every man should receive those papers and be capable of reading them."

Yet, on more occasions than not, Jefferson also was strongly critical of the newspapers of his time—except for the *National Intelligencer*, which was his subsidized constant supporter.

The early days even had what might be called a Washington and New York axis, with men such as James Gordon Bennett, who eventually became publisher of the New York *Herald*, and Horace Greeley of New York's *Tribune* wielding strong influence competing for power with the various Washington newspapers; there was also some impact outside the "axis," mainly from Philadelphia and Boston.

Greeley was particularly influential with Abraham Lincoln whose other favorite was John W. Forney, publisher of the *Chronicle* in Washington. Abolition also brought Henry J. Raymond, New York *Times* editor close to Lincoln. A formal discussion of press relations with Lincoln probably would have left the President puzzled, and he too was the subject of attack over the conduct of the war and over censorship. An advance text on something like the Gettysburg Address was not in the President's scope of understanding or that of the *Times*.

Theodore Roosevelt, on the other hand, had a better understanding of the press and even had the equivalent of a press secretary in William Loeb, Jr. But Roosevelt also was known to take major offense at an unfavorable story, sometimes reacting by refusing to talk to the reporter or by giving an exclusive to a rival newsman. Lyndon Johnson had a bout with the press over pulling the ears of a dog, and Franklin Roosevelt exploded over a story claiming his children had tortured a turkey on the White House grounds.

John Kennedy had almost unbelievably good relations with the media during his first months in the White House, but probably no President has exerted stronger influence on the press than Franklin Roosevelt. Things he was able to do with the press during his time would be unthinkable today.

As a President meeting with reporters for the first time, Roosevelt said: "My hope is that these conferences are going to be merely enlarged editions of the kind of very delightful family conferences I have been holding in Albany for the last four years." And in many ways his hope was fulfilled. During Roosevelt's first four years he held 340 news conferences, mainly in his own office. He had conducted 998 conferences before he died in 1945.

But Roosevelt's manner was such that he could get away with suggesting how a lead should be written for an important story. Who could do that today? When a New York *Times* reporter queried him on a third term, Roosevelt answered, "Go off in a corner and put on a dunce cap." What an uproar that would cause today! During World War II Roosevelt decided to take a trip across the country to inspect the military and to cruise briefly with the Navy near San Diego. His press secretary invited three correspondents to make the trip on the understanding that they would write nothing until they returned safely to Washington. The reporters, all of whom later became Washington news legends over many years of covering Presidents, were Douglas Cornell, Associated Press, the late Merriman Smith, United Press, and Bill Theis, then representing the old International News Service. Coast to coast, thousands of Americans (including me), saw Roosevelt in aircraft and munitions plants, and on military bases, but the pledge of silence was kept.

Even with this favored treatment from the reporters, Roosevelt personally felt sharply the barbs from the editorial pages, where the more conservative publishers dominated the columns. He also believed, with some justification, that he was waging war with newspaper opponents such as Colonel Robert McCormick of the Chicago *Tribune,* Cissy Patterson of the Washington *Times-Herald,* William Randolph Hearst (who broke with him during his first term), columnist Westbrook Pegler, who took particular aim at Eleanor Roosevelt, and Time-Life chief Henry R. Luce.

Teddy Roosevelt gave reporters their first full access to the White House when he allowed them to work from the reception area of the West Wing, an area thenceforth used by the newsmen until Nixon and Ziegler had a new newsroom built on the site of the old swimming pool. Many Presidents also had assistants who specialized in working with the press, but it was Woodrow Wilson who came closest to inaugurating the modern version of the news office with the appointment of a well-liked Irish politician, Joseph Patrick Tumulty, as his secretary. Wilson also held news conferences regularly, and the skillful Tumulty began the practice of daily briefings in which he spoke for the President.

In my view, however, the three men who have served most ably as press secretaries were Steve Early with Roosevelt, Jim Hagerty with Eisenhower, and George Christian with Johnson. Charlie Ross with Truman would be a probable fourth. Pierre Salinger became one of the best-known personalities, and he was effective, as was Bill Moyers. Hagerty rates highest as an all-around effective press secretary, in my opinion.

All of these men but Moyers had a news background, and each faced different problems. A capable press secretary must fit the personality of the President and have his complete confidence. The personalities of Roosevelt, Eisenhower, Johnson, and Truman all were vastly different, as were those of the news secretaries.

Hagerty, my top choice, had to go beyond the scope of his normal duties at times and act as an assistant president. He was strong, respected, occasionally volatile, and always articulate, and, above all, he knew what was going on and how to assess it from the standpoints of the President and of the media.

The small press corps which covered Roosevelt grew to triple its original size during Truman's term of service, and it first became gigantic during the Eisenhower term, when television joined print and radio reporters as a major part of the White House news constituency.

No press secretary has been subjected to the abuse and harassment that Ron Ziegler underwent during the last year or year and a half of the Nixon term. Normal briefings sometimes ran an hour and a half as frustrated reporters, who felt Ziegler was not leveling with them, played games the equivalent of sticking needles in a doll. It was understandable frustration, but it was unprofessional, and on the point of courage alone, Ziegler deserves more credit than has been given him.

Still the attitude of the veteran White House correspondents toward the President and his press secretary was expressed most candidly during a survey conducted by Dom Bonafede for the June 16, 1973, issue of *National Journal*. They thought the press secretary merely represented the general White House attitude. The survey followed my June 6 announcement that I would be leaving the White House and that Ziegler's responsibilities would be expanded to make him an assistant to the President. At about the same time there had been some statements calling for Ziegler's resignation from the White House. The critics of the beleaguered press secretary included James Reston of the New York *Times*, Wayne Sargent, the influential Nashville *Banner* publisher, and a variety of Republican political leaders. Ziegler was given sympathetic support, incidentally, from three former press secretaries, Reedy, Hagerty, and Moyers, but that was to be expected.

Of the newsmen queried, fewer than half favored Ziegler's removal, and even among them many did not blame the problem on the press secretary directly. Typical was the comment of Robert S. Boyd, Knight-Ridder newspaper bureau chief, who said, "It would be very wise to replace him.

I don't particularly blame Ziegler, but he has been a spokesman for misinformation."

Dean Reed, who headed the Newhouse News Service, opposed the firing "based on the assumption he's a capable press secretary passing on the best information he can get."

The attitude of Jerry Greene of the New York *Daily News* was, "It's the President's business. I don't have a positive feeling that Ziegler should or shouldn't leave and if he did, it wouldn't make a particle of difference." The same view was held by Ward Sinclair of the Louisville *Courier-Journal*: "Ron Ziegler's presence doesn't make one iota of difference. He is a reflection of an attitude and if he were gone, there would be another individual doing the same thing."

Dan Rather of CBS took a more philosophic view of the outcry and the new responsibilities given Ziegler: "It was pretty obvious—although he always denied it—that Ziegler had to deal through the filter of Haldeman and Ehrlichman, particularly Haldeman. In his new position, Ron will have more direct access and more talking time with the President and not have to get his marching orders from Haldeman. As a result, we should be able to get better information out of the press office."

Basically, the newsmen, who are always deeply and vocally concerned over who will be the press secretary when a new President enters office, took the attitude four years later that a new face might add credibility to the news office temporarily, but that the man holding the job reflects the President and his attitudes. A change in personnel would not be likely to reflect a change in the relationship between the President and the media.

Woodrow Wilson and Joe Tumulty laid the foundation for the modern White House press operation, but the advent and expansion of broadcasting plus the phenomenal growth of Washington coverage by newsmen— not only from all over the United States but from all over the world, including the Soviet Union and now the People's Republic of China—has complicated immensely the job of the news secretary.

President Truman inaugurated the use of the beautiful old Indian Treaty Room in the Executive Office Building for his stand-up news conferences, and television first became a factor when the cameras were allowed in the room to film the opening minute or so of the conference. A sound booth was built into the area and thus radio could pick up the voice of the President for delayed, sometimes edited, broadcast. But it still was an era when the news service reporters would run up the aisle into booths with open telephone lines to dictate their bulletin leads seconds after the "thank you Mr. President" had been delivered.

The informality of the time was reflected in Truman's poker games with some of the correspondents or his bourbon and branch water with them. Once, while he was crisscrossing the nation by train during his

1948 campaign, the President offended two veteran AP and UP photographers, Henry Griffin and Frank Cancellare, who then retreated to their photo compartment on the train, refusing to shoot any more pictures of the President until he apologized. Truman stopped by the photographers' car and made his peace.

Griffin and Cancellare were unlike any photographers Washington had known. They were a breed of their own. Once during a Nixon campaign, they complained that the car with the photographers' darkroom and compartment was too far ahead of the back platform of the train. I sympathized, but explained there was little I could do about it. Later they stayed aboard the train as we pulled into Pittsburgh, assigning local wire-service photographers to cover the candidate. When we returned from the rally, I found that the undaunted photographers had located a railroad supervisor and told him I had asked them to have the cars rearranged. A switch engine was pulled up and cars were switched to place Griffin and Cancellare closer to the rear platform. When we returned there was nothing we could do about it—except laugh.

Television came fully into its own at Jack Kennedy's first presidential news conference in 1961. Pioneering, I had experimented with a live televised news conference for the candidate during the 1960 campaign, with Peoria, Illinois, as the spot for the tryout. Nixon arrived late and I ad-libbed the first three minutes on the air, but the format worked well for him. It was Kennedy and Pierre Salinger who observed the innovative technique and recognized the full impact of the medium and moved the presidential press conference to the State Department building to allow full use of live television coverage. The format put Kennedy in the most delicate position any President faced because there could be no editing of this live program and the public could not only listen to the words, it could watch them being delivered. The advent of televised debates in 1960, and the superb live press conferences by Kennedy, gave TV news its biggest boost, and each President and press secretary since has had the many added implications of television as part of his agenda.

The breakthroughs of broadcasting and the enlarged coverage by newspapers illustrate part of the major difference between the battles Presidents since George Washington have had with the press in years long past and the new scope of the press battles facing our present-day leaders. The likes and dislikes, the criticisms and the praise, heaped upon Presidents of the past may have affected them mentally and emotionally as much in the 1800s as they do Presidents today, but the added element is that the public now is much more a part of the conflict than it was in the distant past and, to a President, favorable media coverage is more a measure of success or failure than before. The rapidity of communication, even with satellite coverage, makes the world which the President and the press survey more complicated, more immediate, and more important than it ever was before.

Every query the press office has from a responsible journalist has the immediate possibility of being important. Something which turns out to be "no story" is as important to check as something which turns into a headline.

During the latter part of President Johnson's term, for example, Merriman Smith, UPI's senior White House correspondent, received a report from a Midwestern radio station regarding a rumor that Lyndon Johnson was dead or had suffered another heart attack. Smith placed no credence in the report, but dutifully asked George Christian about the President's health. Christian said he had seen the President earlier in the afternoon and he had looked in good health, but as a precaution he would check. A phone call to the White House residential area verified the falsity of the radio station's rumor, and Smith routinely reported this to his client. There was no story.

A few hours later, Smith was at home, where he and his wife were hosting a small dinner party. The UPI correspondent received a telephone call during cocktails and the voice on the phone was that of the President, who told Smith, "I understand you think I may be dead." The veteran correspondent protested that he had no such idea but was merely checking out a query. Johnson, however, insisted that Smith come to the White House immediately and see for himself the status of the President. The correspondent declined and said he was hosting a small dinner, but the President insisted that he bring the group with him to the White House. The dinner was delayed as Smith and his wife and guests followed instructions and drove to the White House, where Johnson awaited them. The group shook hands with the President, who personally confirmed that he was alive. Before Smith could depart, the President insisted that he and his guests join him in the White House Theater with some Mexican-American guests to view a film of his daughter's wedding at the ranch in Texas.

Smith, who later recounted the story to me, said there was no way to deter the President. "I want you to sit right behind my ass so you can watch and hear everything," he said the President told him.

An hour and a half later, the party was excused from the White House to return to a slightly burned dinner. All because of a routine query from a UPI client.

In 1972, the nation was startled to read and hear news stories which first were reporting rumors and then confirmed the fact that Senator George McGovern's first choice as a vice-presidential nominee, Senator Thomas F. Eagleton, had previously undergone psychiatric treatment in a hospital. What little chance McGovern had in the race was further diminished as the newsmen swarmed on the story, giving rise to the subsequent debate over whether Eagleton would stay on the ticket. With modern communication, the story had instant impact and brought the already faltering campaign to a halt.

There was a similar situation affecting Nixon directly in 1968. Had this story been printed on the eve of the close election with Hubert Humphrey, it probably would have changed the results of the election, even though the story turned out to be inaccurate. The press is that powerful today.

Between 1950 and 1955, Nixon, first as a senator and then as Vice-President, paid an occasional visit to the Park Avenue office of Dr. Arnold A. Hutschnecker, an internist. There was no secrecy about the calls, particularly when Nixon, as Vice-President, would park in front of the doctor's office with a limousine and with Secret Service agents accompanying him. Dr. Hutschnecker, as it turned out, also was studying psychiatry, and in the latter part of the fifties he began to move his specialty into this field. Even before the doctor began changing his practice, it was agreed that for appearance' sake it would be better if Nixon discontinued the medical relationship, although he and Hutschnecker remained personal friends, and even while Nixon was President, the doctor communicated to him his ideas on such subjects as Vietnam and on violent crime and drug abuse.

A few days before the 1968 election, on October 29 or October 31, depending on whose calendar you check, syndicated columnist Drew Pearson called Hutschnecker and said he had received a tip that the physician-psychiatrist had treated Nixon while he was Vice-President. The implication was that Nixon had required some psychiatric treatment and had turned to Dr. Hutschnecker. The physician says that he talked with Pearson only briefly during a morning call and had confirmed that Nixon once had been a patient, but he in no way implied that the routine examinations and treatment had any relationship to mental health. He had a patient with him when the call came in, and he asked Pearson to call back at 4 P.M., when he would be more free to speak. During the afternoon call, the doctor denied more clearly that any psychiatry was involved and pointed out that he was at that time licensed as an internist, not as a psychiatrist.

I first met Dr. Hutschnecker a few days after his call from Pearson when Rose Woods relayed the story to me and to Murray Chotiner. Hutschnecker has written both articles and books, but he is meticulously ethical about discussing doctor-patient relationships. With the approval of Nixon, relayed to the doctor by Rose Woods, he agreed that he would discuss the case with Chotiner and me as the designated representatives and friends of the candidate. We each met with Hutschnecker separately.

I felt the doctor was candid with me as he opened his Nixon medical records and said they showed that mainly he had given him routine physical examinations and that one of his complaints was that he sometimes suffered from severe headaches. This, the doctor diagnosed, was the pressure of Nixon's public offices and his campaigns. He advised more relaxation.

We prepared for an election-eve Pearson column, and I sought and obtained a partial list of subscribers to his widely circulated, well-read column. We felt we had to be ready to react immediately if an inaccurate column appeared and, given the history of the Nixon-Pearson relationship, we expected such a thing just before the election. We had friends on a few newspapers ready to alert us if they received advance copies of such a column. Our position was that any public statement by us in advance would increase interest in a Pearson column and perhaps offer authenticity to it; but if it were to appear, we wanted to be ready to deny the story in a way that editors would be cautious on the use of the material. The problem is that people remember the negative, even if denied, and even a little doubt can sway a swing voter to vote against a candidate.

Our alert was premature. Pearson, who had tangled with Nixon in almost every campaign since 1946, finally decided that it was too close to the election and did not run the column at that time. Had he done so, it is likely that many newspapers would not have run the column, but many others would have, and thus one damaging column could have tipped the close election.

Shortly after the election on November 14, Pearson was honored by the National Press Club and in the course of answering questions regarding criteria for what he printed, the columnist cited his untold decision to withhold the Nixon-Hutschnecker story as an example of his efforts to check out each item he printed. He went on to say, however, that he subsequently had heard that Hutschnecker had been called by the Nixon office during the day of the Pearson inquiries and advised to deny that Nixon had ever received psychiatric treatment. Pearson added that Hutschnecker "had expressed some worry privately that Nixon had problems—or did have a problem—of not standing up under great pressure."

The story from the National Press Club carried by the news services included denials by Dr. Hutschnecker. Years later the physician again verified the denials when he gave the same testimony under oath before both Senate and House committees which were holding confirmation hearings for Jerry Ford to succeed Spiro T. Agnew as Vice-President. He was asked to testify because he had met with Ford once in his Park Avenue office and once in Washington, both times discussing Southeast Asia and neither time discussing Ford's personal health. Hutschnecker is not an expert on international relations, but he has studied the subject intently and applied his knowledge of the mind to what he believes can be useful diplomatic innovations.

Hutschnecker later told me that he believed the source of the rumor Pearson picked up regarding his treatment of Nixon was a former patient he described as a "paranoiac schizophrenic who hated Nixon with the same passion he hated his own father." He speculated on what values a reporter had who would even repeat such a statement of a mentally ill man.

A few days after Pearson's appearance before the press club, we received word that he had written a column on the subject and that it would appear on November 20. Pearson led off by saying "several of my editors have been complaining that I should have written the account of Mr. Nixon's psychotherapeutic treatments in the column before the election instead of talking about the matter at the National Press Club after the election.

"Under the circumstances, I owe them and my readers an explanation. It is true, as some have pointed out, that if this had been published before the election the outcome might have been different. The problem of a news confirmation and its timing is exactly what I was trying to illustrate at the luncheon which the press club had set up in my honor."

Pearson then went on to retell the story in detail and question why Nixon "should go all the way to New York and to consult a well-known Park Avenue psychotherapy specialist concerning his internal medical problems, when some of the best internists in the U.S. are located at Walter Reed Hospital and Bethesda Naval Hospital, where the Vice President could have had their services on the cuff." The fact is that over the years Nixon has conferred with private physicians, such as Dr. John Lungren, of Long Beach, even while under the constant attention of his friend Dr. Walter Tkach, his White House physician.

Pearson concluded the column by urging that all candidates disclose facts regarding their health. He included this paragraph:

"Some of this information, I admit, was learned during the closing days of the campaign, and I could have published it at the last minute. But, as I explained at the press club luncheon, I decided it was unfair to use it so late. It was one of those difficult decisions a newspaperman has to make."

Pearson mentioned in his column that in the course of his investigation of the story, he had asked Jack Anderson, his deputy and coauthor, to check on it with me and that I had "flatly denied that Nixon had ever consulted a psychiatrist." This was true, and I believe the denial had a part in Pearson's delay in the story. Anderson, who now writes the syndicated column, and I have had a long and unbroken relationship with each other although we disagree frequently on issues and people.

When, at the campaign headquarters in New York, we heard the Pearson column was to appear, we sent telegrams to editors and many held back on it or printed a note containing our denial.

But the impact of the column not printed before the election and the column printed after the election raises several points of importance. How far should a newspaper go in printing a rumor, particularly when the editor has no idea of the source of the story—in this case, according to Dr. Hutschnecker, a mental patient?

Pearson and probably Anderson deserve credit for refraining from the last-minute entry into the campaign.

But when one looks at the column printed on November 20, the danger of this kind of reporting is illustrated in the first paragraph when Pearson refers without qualification to "Mr. Nixon's psychotherapeutic treatments," assuming wrongly that there was such treatment. He simply stated this as fact. To back this up, he later refers to Dr. Hutschnecker as a "psychotherapy specialist," which he was at the time of the Pearson telephone call, but importantly, not at the time of the Nixon treatments—another wrong premise which the reporter writes without the smallest qualification.

This is the type of writing which turns Presidents and others against newsmen—with justification. Nixon and his staff assumed that Pearson had volunteered the rumor story before the press club and printed the later column as a vitriolic punch at the President-elect he had openly expressed dislike for on many public occasions over a twenty-year span.

One also could ask whether we apply a double standard: although many Americans find help in psychiatric treatment, they look with doubt at a high public official who has had such past experience. But that is another subject.

Interestingly, Jack Anderson printed some of the first major stories regarding Senator Eagleton's psychiatric treatment. The evidence for such a story was much stronger than in the Hutschnecker-Nixon case or in stories which could have been sensationalized unfairly regarding Jerry Ford when he was up for confirmation as Vice-President. It puzzles me that the eminent Dr. Hutschnecker popped into the national political scene often.

One of the most difficult decisions in a campaign centers around what to do about rumors that a last-minute "bomb" is about to be dropped just prior to the election. In Nixon campaigns in 1960 and 1962, the "Hughes loan" to Don Nixon was always one of the subjects of worry. In 1960, it appeared that Drew Pearson or the Ritter newspapers were about to unload some kind of "blockbuster" regarding the loan on the eve of the convention. (Ritter broke such a story in the Long Beach *Press-Telegram* on the eve of the 1962 elections.) In this case, Len Hall, Bob Finch, and Nixon decided that the best way to defuse such a story was to outline frankly to Peter Edson the Nixon side of the case, which was basically that this was a business deal with Don Nixon and involved nothing illegal, such as any kind of political promise from Richard Nixon. The Vice-President was not aware of the loan negotiations. Edson was the columnist who had broken the first information on the 1952 "Nixon fund," and it was felt this increased his credibility as we chose to discuss a negative story rather than sit back and wait for a column to put us on the defensive. This was a gamble. The election was close and no one actually knew what Pearson might write, if anything. We put out a story knowing it was negative, but feeling that we could better protect our side of the story. Bob Finch scooped Pearson with Edson, but to this day we have no way of knowing whether the tactic was correct. It does reflect the difficulty of decisions regarding last-minute smears which can alter the results of an election—often wrongfully.

The changing communications world has brought innumerable shifts in the power of the media and the President.

Franklin Roosevelt's Fireside Chats are long remembered as the first full use of radio broadcast to convey a message to the American people. The eight Fireside Chats he made during his first term in office did much to restore American confidence and to gain support for the Roosevelt domestic programs. His own voice soon became unmistakenly recognized by most Americans. The presidential "chats" during the war helped move the nation into action, and they kept calm at times of turmoil and defeat.

Presidents Nixon and Carter, in more recent times, found radio to be a powerful instrument for low-key messages of national importance, but since the fifties, television has easily outdistanced its rivals as the most powerful means of direct communication between the President and the citizenry. Reporters have complained that Presidents such as Nixon have overused television and have gone on the air to deliberately bypass the newsmen in communicating with the public. Both charges have merit, and the fact is that live radio and television broadcasts give the President an edge in the battle with the sometimes prejudiced media, an edge denied to earlier occupants of the Oval Office. Television adds another dimension to the presidency. Communication on the air has its own way of revealing the weakness in a presidential personality as well as the strength in it. Some people can come off well in speaking on television, others simply cannot, reflecting something in the way of unexplained personal chemistry. The result has been great emphasis on television-acceptable personalities for candidates at all levels.

Both Franklin Roosevelt and Harry Truman's favorite whipping boys in the media were the publishers. Although there was a dramatic contrast in the personalities and style of each of these two Presidents, both felt they could relate to reporters and neither made a major effort to cultivate publishers. They observed that the reporters were much more likely to be liberal in their political philosophy and the publishers more likely to be conservative. Roosevelt and Truman played to strength, concentrating on the reporters, and while they often were angry over publisher-inspired editorials and columns, they believed the tone of the news stories would be more important in reaching voters, particularly at a time when most newspapers were clearly identified by political philosophy which they held to predictably.

It is still true that the publisher or the broadcast owner or network executive is more likely to be conservative, and that reporters tend more toward political liberalism of various degrees. However, in today's world, most publishers and broadcast executives have far less influence on the content of the news than they have had in the past. In Manchester, New Hampshire, the unpredictable, irascible William Loeb still dominates his influential *Union-Leader* with a strong hand, but one of the marks of the growing number of group newspapers, such as Gannett or Knight-Ridder, is that they allow editorial independence in each city where they own the newspaper as larger and larger local autonomy becomes more and more important to the company fearful of antitrust action and to the public. More often than not, the publisher learns of most stands taken in his newspaper when he reads the first edition, although it would be rare if the owner did not have a strong voice in priority editorial endorsements, such as those for presidential candidates. The power of the editorial voice of a smaller newspaper is stronger on a per-reader basis than that of the impersonal larger publication. Editorial boards have become the decisive element in most major editorial decisions, although many publishers, such as Otis Chandler of the Los Angeles *Times,* sit as part of these boards. The *Times* editorial board of past generations included only Otis Chandler's father, Norman, and his valued political editor, Kyle Palmer. Some newspapers, such as the L.A. *Times* and *Newsday,* now refrain from presidential endorsements—a mistake in my opinion. If they express opinions freely on everything else, why not the presidency?

In the newsroom the separation of power between management and editors, news directors, producers, and reporters is much more closely defined than in the past. Newspaper publishers occasionally have a voice in news coverage today, but in most broadcast facilities, the general manager selects his news director and/or producer and it is there that his influence stops. Even the network news president does not try to edit the evening news, although he will change personnel if his ratings drop.

These changes in the balance of newsroom power are also reflected in the greater free hand given to the reporter covering the Washington scene.

In fits of anger, Presidents Kennedy, Johnson, and Nixon have directly or indirectly tried to influence the selection of the reporters covering the White House, but usually with little success.

Throughout American history, Presidents have found it impossible to ignore what the press was saying, although few were avid readers of many newspapers. Of the modern Presidents, John Kennedy had the most intimate relationship with newsmen. Washington *Post* editor Ben Bradlee and columnists Charles Bartlett and Rowland Evans were, for example, close personal friends of the President. Lyndon Johnson followed the news so closely it was almost as if he were keeping an hourly box score on how he fared with the media. In his office were three television sets, printers from Associated Press and United Press International, and a variety of newspapers and magazines. Nixon rarely watched television and read relatively few newspapers and magazines, but his interest in what was reported was as intense as that of anyone who has occupied that office. He thoroughly read through twenty to forty typed pages of a news summary prepared by Mort Allen and his staff each day, frequently making notations of comment or instruction for action by the staff regarding the stories. The summaries included newspapers, wire services, television, and magazines, but they had the fault of being selectively edited for him in the same way he complained of the editing of television news for a wider audience. My office collected editorials and editorial cartoons to give him a cross section of views on any one issue. These summaries and procedures of collection for outside articles and cartoons were followed also by Presidents Ford and Carter.

The President, the government, and the media do not have a balanced overview of how their statements or their reporting is affecting the American public. Newspapers and magazines can judge readership overall by circulation, television and radio by ratings, and the President by polls, although in-depth polls by a few major newspapers have been refined to a point giving them previously unobtainable insight; but none of these measurements provide a sensitive, reliable examination of the important inner thoughts of the public they all try to reach. Most of the letters to the editor in newspapers outside Washington and New York express views on subjects the readers feel comfortable with. They are limited. Many have a strong view on negotiations with the Soviet Union or inflation, but few will express themselves publicly on Social Security reform or the change in governments in Great Britain or the price of gold. Most, however, have strong feelings as to whether they like or dislike even the newspaper they subscribe to or the television they watch most. And more often than the public expresses it, the feeling of distrust extends to both the media and the government and leaders it covers in the news. Confidence, however, is another key factor, and here the public currently places far more trust in what it hears and reads in the news than in those who make the news.

It is here the newsmen outpoint the White House, particularly since the Woodward and Bernstein outbreak. But confidence in the press and the government is subject to continual change.

In a national poll taken by the Los Angeles *Times* in September 1979, 80 percent of the 1,453 people surveyed telephonically expressed "some" or a "great deal" of confidence in the people running the press. That compared with 76 percent for the military, 69 percent for major companies, 68 percent for the executive branch of government, 68 percent for Congress, and 57 percent for labor. All of the ratings are high compared with two or three years earlier, but all this is subject to change.

And yet, if the Spiro Agnew attacks on the press in speeches in Des Moines and Birmingham and elsewhere proved anything, they showed widespread resentment for what the public perceived as bias in the news they were getting from the networks and from newspapers.

Conversely, the same Los Angeles *Times* survey which registered confidence in those running the press came up with figures which expressed the belief that reporters are "biased for or against people they cover." This puzzled even *Times* editor Bill Thomas. The two polled attitudes don't fit. The report said that 13 percent of the respondents felt the media made President Carter look better than he was, and 36 percent felt the newsmen made him look worse. Only 44 percent felt he was treated fairly. In contrast, 34 percent believed Senator Edward Kennedy was being made to "look better," only 12 percent to "look worse," and 46 percent felt the treatment was fair. That probably changed later. The percentages for Governor Jerry Brown of California were 14 percent "treated fairly" and 15 percent "look worse." The overwhelming opinion of 56 percent said Governor Ronald Reagan was being "treated fairly" in 1979 with 16 percent opining he was made by the media to "look better" and 12 percent to "look worse." Jane Fonda was tested in the same measurement and 30 percent said she was being made to "look worse."

The poll also reflected the fact that people had opinions on news bias. Only 7 to 8 percent of those polled had no opinions regarding the treatment of Carter and Kennedy and 16 percent regarding bias on Reagan. The more unknown Jerry Brown registered 27 percent no opinion.

Newspapermen and broadcasters recently have taken long-needed constructive steps to place greater emphasis on accuracy and to gain closer insight into public opinion of the product. The Washington *Post* installed an ombudsman in the early 1970s, and while several persons have filled that post, each has had freedom and support in criticizing reporters in internal memos and in publicly correcting errors of fact in the newspapers. But this unfortunately does not touch on the bias problem, with some exceptions, nor even staffwise privately on cases of apparent bias. The biased reporter exists with the tolerance of his editor or news director/producer.

The Los Angeles *Times* editor Bill Thomas made a breakthrough when he in giving one of his reporters, Gaylord Shaw, a free hand to rove the nation writing in-depth articles on trends and problems of the communications industry. The public and the newsmen join in insatiable interest in reporting. The San Diego *Union* found that its ombudsman, Alfred JaCoby, was writing his criticism of the newspaper and its editing, and reporting it in such entertaining fashion, that it gave him a weekly column to express his critical views of the *Union* to the readers.

Other newspapers have invited opinion leaders of their community to sit on boards which meet regularly to criticize the publication constructively. Most major newspapers now run daily correction columns, but these are obscure and do little more than clear the conscience of the editor.

No one has devised a systematic method of periodic review to examine the case where accusations made against an individual have been investigated later to determine whether the charges were false. Few, if any, make as major an effort to clear the name of the damaged individual as they did to get the story containing the original charges. Pride applies even here.

In all these fields, broadcast has trailed the print publications badly. The Federal Communications Commission requires cumbersome "ascertainment" reports at the time of station license renewal, wherein, at considerable expense, the broadcasters are compelled to go into the community and ascertain its opinions regarding their stations' programs and their contribution to public service. These surveys have been ineffective, costly, and cumbersome. More, they do not apply nationally to the networks.

Rarely does a local or a network broadcaster come on the air and admit outright error, and even more rare is a broadcast effort to clear an individual or a corporation who is a victim of a past injustice. The most open free forum on the air comes in talk shows and in replies to broadcast editorials.

One of the most serious problems separating the public from the media is that of statements taken out of context.

Particularly with an inexperienced public official, he may include one sentence or paragraph among many which sounds nonsensical, harsh, or sensational when separated from the remainder of his comments. Even Presidents make such mistakes, uttering the one wrong sentence which is repeated over and over. The paragraph makes news because by itself it sounds controversial. But often, when one reads the entire context rather than the most quoted paragraph, the sense of what is said is entirely different.

This creates an important problem for the public official or, in many other cases, the publicly minded businessman and the press. What the news quotes is what the speaker said, but the impression from a statement out of context may be 180 degrees different from what the true views of the speaker reflect in full context. The news media, including those at

White House briefings, too often amuse themselves by trying to draw from the spokesman a controversial statement instead of seeking the full scope of his thoughts.

Earl Butz, a brilliant Secretary of Agriculture, was unfairly made to appear like a bigot and forced to resign, because of a nonchalant joke on an airplane overheard by John Dean, then a reporter for *The Village Voice*. Butz appeared to be a racist, which was not the fact. Dean was unethical.

Network news selection means that a few sentences out of many a public figure utters before a camera will appear on the air. The selection of which sentences are used and the combination of sentences selected can have tremendous impact on public opinion. There is no way the process can be changed, but it puts prime responsibility on balanced selection. Many public figures shy away from anything but a live television appearance to avoid the danger of editing on a taped interview. Practically the idea is bad, but it is understandable.

The public figure least likely to communicate the fact that he has made an error is the President of the United States. And his cabinet officers and the bureaucracy pretty much follow the pattern. Every President says things to the press in error. But error becomes more commonplace in a rapid-fire style such as President Truman's, or in President Johnson's absurd sessions with the press while he walked in hurried fashion around the White House grounds with panting reporters running behind him trying to take notes or record his voice. Equally dangerous gimmickry was exemplified by President Carter's early habit of staying on the platform after a press conference to answer catch-as-catch-can questions informally with the newsmen surrounding him. Somehow the presidency has inherited the idea that the chief executive who does not answer every question thrown at him, regardless of how petty it may be, exhibits weakness in knowledge of government. No one can know about everything in government, and with the time pressures on the President he should not attempt to be an expert on every small detail.

Another factor in the changing relationship between the government and the press is the growth of the theory of advocacy among reporters. Journalism schools, which were fighting to keep alive in the early sixties, now are overcrowded with activist students who perceive the news arena as the place where the action is. For too many, their interest in journalism is deeply intertwined with an interest in advocating causes and in swaying public opinion. For these self-indoctrinated young journalists, the report of the event is less important than their opinion of the event, and given the greater freedom from editing accorded to the reporter today, this is another reason for change in the relationship between the media and the government.

Advocacy today is curbed frequently by more tradition-minded editors, producers, and news directors, but given the dedicated motives of the advocate in journalism, this element of reporting-commentary may become an even greater factor in examining how the public perceives its elected officials in the future. Today's reporters will be tomorrow's editors.

The trend is a curious one because the early American journalists were strong advocates and that style eventually was rejected by journalists and the public. Later, the advocates were followed by the sensationalists of the prime Hearst era. Eventually journalism moved toward more staid straight reporting coupled with interpretation and commentary, and newspapers gained higher professional respect.

The Watergate investigations by the youthful Woodward and Bernstein, and a few other investigative reporters, had tremendous impact on all American political institutions. Earlier, Clark Mollenhoff, prize-winning reporter from the Cowles newspapers, probably was before his time, because his bombastic, ardent personal investigatory work stood out alone in a sea of journalism complacence. But his work did not appear in New York and Washington, and while it had impact, it never received all the recognition it deserved.

The Woodward and Bernstein phenomenon, however, had overbearing impact, not just on the news coverage of the Nixon presidency, but on many other press-government relationships. Two reporters changed journalistic outlook—for a time, at least.

The reporters who cover Washington today are the best educated the capital has seen. But education is not necessarily the equivalent of judgment, ethics, or experience. Many of the newsmen and women have doctorates and master's degrees, and a few have been able to practice their reporting profession in areas of their own expertise, such as law. But in the field of politics experience counts heavily. Sensitive judgment and perception are involved. Some of the best reporters of the past never attended college, and one wonders what they might have accomplished with a stronger educational background.

Two trends that have set in with the newer journalists have been an eagerness to focus on the personal lives of holders of public office and a growing practice in broadcasting to place equal weight on entertainment and reporting. The latter is more prevalent among local stations than among networks. The personalization too often makes the reporter feel he is a consumer activist rather than someone assigned to cover a story factually.

Both political parties have found it more difficult to attract strong candidates for office because of the heavy focus on personal journalism, where any mistake the candidate may have made in the past is subject to wide public exposure. Everyone, including newsmen, makes mistakes, but few mistakes become matters of public interest until one seeks office. The resentment of this personal intrusion also has been reflected in the growing number of congressmen who have retired from office prematurely.

Yet with all of this, scandals such as those of payments by South Korea are allowed by the Congress and the media to drag on until they are of lesser news value and thus lesser public impact when they finally reach a climax. Bill Safire of the New York *Times* probably did more than anyone in keeping attention focused on the seamy "Koreagate" misdeeds of elected officials. But the broad coverage did not reflect the intensity of pursuit one might have expected from news professionals in this age. There was none of the furor of Watergate, or even of the Bobby Baker issue.

The Wilbur Mills public fall into the waters near the Jefferson Monument and the arrangement of convenience between Representative Wayne Hays and a so-called secretary deserved public exposure, but the personal lives of most others in Congress do not fit into these extreme categories. One who has spoken out most strongly against this personalized journalism is Ted Knapp, a Scripps-Howard veteran, who was one of Ziegler's most vitriolic briefing room opponents during Watergate.

Double standards among newsmen are all too common, but one of the classic cases occurred shortly after Martha Mitchell began commanding national attention with her comments and telephone calls.

Martha and John Mitchell called me early in 1970 to ask assistance in finding a press secretary for Mrs. Mitchell. I was relieved to have an opportunity to arrange for some outside guidance for the unpredictable comments by Martha, and I recalled that Bill and Kay Woestendick, two longtime newspaper friends, had recently moved to Washington, where Woestendick, a veteran editor from the Houston *Post* and *Newsday*, had become news director for the growing educational TV outlet.

Kay Woestendick had been the women's editor of the Houston *Post* and had a deep interest in politics. She seemed a natural to go to work for Martha, and after some persuasion on my part, she accepted the position. The choice turned out to be excellent, and she was liked and respected by the Mitchells as well as by me and the news corps.

At the education station, the reaction was different. The WETA reporters seemingly resented the favorable publicity being gained by Martha Mitchell, and they filed a politically inspired protest that Bill Woestendick had a conflict of interest because of his wife's job. To my amazement, the reporters were backed by the station's management and Woestendick was left with the choice of resigning or getting his wife to leave her job with Martha Mitchell. No one on the broadcast staff raised the point that many of the same protesting newspersons had spouses who worked for other politicians in the House and Senate—seemingly a parallel case, if one were to believe the absurd theory that this was a conflict of influence.

Plain and simple, this was a clear case of double standard. Woestendick stood by his principles, and resigned rather than force his wife unfairly from her new role on the Martha Mitchell staff. The Woestendicks later left Washington and returned to newspapering in Colorado Springs and eventually in Tucson.

The newsmen who face the most complex problems today in covering Washington are those assigned to the White House and to the State Department. Comparatively, those who cover Congress, or departments such as Defense, Agriculture, and the Treasury generally have a more predictable span of news they will be called upon to report than do their White House cohorts.

Today's State Department reporter finds himself called upon to concentrate his knowledge not just on the traditional major powers of the East and West, but also upon nations, trends, and leaders in areas which would have been ignored just a few years ago. For the State Department correspondent, travel with mobile Secretaries of State is a constant and sometimes irritating factor.

The focus of the White House press corps is basically political, no matter what the reporters might say to the contrary. There are a few philosophers in the ranks, such as John Osborne of *New Republic*, and veterans of a variety of Washington wars, such as Bob Pierpoint of CBS. The assigned leaders, Helen Thomas and Frank Cormier, of UPI and AP respectively, have covered the scene for so long that little will surprise them. They are true professionals, but they, unlike others, have managed to avoid being jaded and overly cynical, despite years on the beat. They add an atmosphere of responsible calm and confidence to the often excitable White House briefing room. One of the problems of White House coverage is that reporters are left on the beat too long. Seniority builds contacts, but it also builds bias, techniques in which the reportorial "herd" loses independence, and a feeling of class arrogance among reporters.

When a reporter shows up for the late-morning or midday briefing of the press secretary, he may have a specific subject he wants to dig into, sometimes to the discomfort of the White House, but he also may be called upon unexpectedly to write or broadcast on subjects with which he is totally unfamiliar, ranging from the economy to a presidential warning on a Soviet troop movement in Cuba or South Yemen or Afghanistan. Regardless of the subject, he is expected to be the instant eyes and ears and reporting instrument for the 220 million people of the nation—and perhaps for the world.

Like the press secretary, the White House reporter's schedule is subject to that of the President. And thus if the President plans Christmas at Plains, Georgia, or San Clemente, California, the reporter or his substitute must be there—with or without family.

The President must be covered constantly. During such holiday trips the White House usually arranges special air fares for family aboard the chartered planes. But the President's staff can usually transport its families free on a space-available basis.

The press office frequently puts a lid on when there is a promise that no more news will be announced during the day, barring an emergency, but the White House reporter finds himself spending considerable idle time talking to other reporters and thus stories frequently follow the thoughts of one of the leaders of the news herd such as John Osborne, who as a respected magazine commentator has more time for deep thinking than the reporter, who has to meet deadlines each day. The inbreeding of thought among reporters in the herd results in sudden spates of stories on one personality, one issue, or a line of political speculation—all built along the same theme during a period of perhaps a week. The herd phenomenon defeats some of the individuality one would expect from reporters of this caliber, and it can result in a sudden national upturn or downturn in the press view of a presidential program or political issue or candidate. The demands on the White House news corps are such that rarely can the reporter break away from his beat to gain firsthand impressions from those of impact outside the Washington inner circle. The practice of using a team of reporters to cover a campaign also would be healthy if extended to the White House, and even could be useful with smaller newspapers, which could interchange local reporters. It would be expensive but useful, and with larger news bureaus it would provide challenge at no extra expense.

On another side of the equation, the President, whose office is not far from the newsroom podium, finds himself in a position different from that of any other chief business executive in the nation. Compared to Washington, Jefferson, Hoover, or even Roosevelt (Teddy or Franklin), the President's policies and administrative responsibilities now encompass the world. The President operates from a constantly growing federal budget in excess of half a trillion dollars. He is expected to be an expert in finance, military and diplomatic strategy, domestic problems—and all the while he postures as "one of the people." The public's most urgent yearning is that he be a leader who inspires its confidence and limits its worry.

No matter what other demands may require, the President must take the time to deal successfully with the intricate worlds of politics and the press. Earlier Presidents of the nation could deal with these areas on a relatively small personal basis, and they could afford to take or leave any contact with the press. That day is long past.

The chief executives of America's largest firms can pay as little or as much attention to the media as they choose, even though a lack of attention has been proven unhealthy. Advertising will affect the corporate bottom line, but press relations will have less immediate visible impact. The executive can concentrate only on the financial press, which does have more measurable influence on employee reaction and on market prices of stock, but to ignore overall public relations is a mistake at a time of increased interest in economics and business. More and more leading businessmen are recognizing the importance of growing and improved community and media relations, but, unlike the President of the United States, they still have the choice. A President of the United States cannot hide. Obscurity may be detrimental to a businessman, but he has that option.

The business leader's participation in politics is by choice, although, again, more are recognizing the rapidly growing influence government has on the very life of their companies.

For the President of the United States, politics and the media are deeply interrelated and a major part of everyday life. A President who loses the ability to communicate effectively with the American people loses the political strength to govern effectively.

Other than in matters of war and peace, there are no stakes higher for the President than communicating effectively in both the political and media worlds.

The politics of the presidency today are far more difficult than even in the time of Eisenhower. Presidents traditionally have had to work with Congresses which have varied in their balance among Republicans and Democrats, liberals and conservatives, but usually they have dealt with strong leadership within the House and Senate. Congress in recent years has been governed more by committees, and the domination of a Lyndon Johnson or a Sam Rayburn is a thing of the past. Dealing with Congress and its long-entrenched committee bureaucracy requires special political skill and understanding not given to most Presidents.

The arena of national campaign politics is a ball game unduplicated anywhere else in the political spectrum. A candidate highly qualified in congressional politics, or even state politics, can easily find himself unable to grasp the complexities of campaigning on a national scale. Four prime examples of the inability to convert expertise in the workings of Congress into the politics of the nationwide electorate were Johnson, Henry "Scoop" Jackson, Stuart Symington, and Edmund Muskie, all of whom failed in efforts to move from the Capitol to the nomination for President. Lyndon Johnson did win the nomination and the presidency in a landslide in 1964, but it was because of the circumstances of his presidency and the vulnerability of his opponent, Barry Goldwater, not because of his comprehension of national presidential politics.

A campaign revolves around the candidate, his opponents, the issues, the organization, the strategy and timing—and the press.

Politics and the press are as big a problem for the President once he wins office as when he seeks it. If the President is to be effective with the Congress and with the people who will probably have to vote on his reelection, he must be able to communicate in convincing fashion with the American public.

Relatively few successful politicians are willing to be openly critical of the press. But privately, most of the candidates and their followers believe they are treated unfairly by the media. They accuse the newsmen of writing and editing to suit their own purposes, and while they usually are wrong, they are right too many times. News management is a phrase frowned on by media practitioners. But in a literal sense an editor or news director must manage the news to fit a format.

The press is absolutely right when it says the candidates and the President seek to manage the news, often but not always, to a reporter's delight. In a local sense, "media events" are staged today to accommodate television and thus gain more exposure for the candidate or officeholder. The politician is much more likely to draw TV coverage if he denounces the lack of street repairs while standing before the cameras knee-deep in a hole in the highway than he is if he makes the same announcement before a microphone in a sterile city hall.

Public relations and news management was brought to a new level of intensity during the Nixon administration. The concentration of effort to interest the media and the public through various gimmicks and media events has not decreased since then; probably it has increased. President Carter invited more outside Washington newsmen into the White House than any of his predecessors, and the effort resulted in increased coverage both in Washington and in local communities involved. But it showed no effect of influencing political opinion polls.

Any news event with the President as a participant does involve an inordinate amount of his personal time.

Reasonable, logical news management often works to the public's advantage. A televised press conference during prime time gives the President wide exposure, but it also allows the public to join the newsmen in examining the President firsthand. The landing of a presidential aircraft in prime viewing time on a historic mission gives more of the public a chance to indirectly experience the event, whether it is in Moscow or Peking, than would be the case if the timing were midnight or early morning.

Part of the problem for the President is to keep the press interested in an event or in what he has to say. The President can always make news; the question is, What kind of news? A bored reporter is more likely to be negative and to center his story on some minor fact that suddenly interests him: the President has stumbled on the steps of his airplane or bumped his head, or the President has lost zip in the delivery of his speeches. And one negative story or one negative reporter begets another.

Like entertainment stars, Presidents also worry about overexposure, particularly on television. Nixon would occasionally tape a presidential statement or speech for radio, so as to save his television impact for more dramatic foreign-policy considerations. Each President debates the question of what time he should appear before a joint session of Congress for his State of the Union address. The attention given to timing can rival the time given to substance. Usually the decision is to appear during prime evening hours on television, but on some occasions the President resorts to just sending a written message.

Television is a major governing influence on the President, studied by the White House almost as intensely as by the networks. The need for exposure and the fear of overexposure often govern whether the President will hold a television news conference in midday hours with less of an audience or before the full-size evening audience.

President Carter is more accessible to newsmen than any of his predecessors. Just as Nixon was hurt by being far too inaccessible, Carter may have injured himself by being far too available to a major array of editors and broadcasters from across the country as well as from Washington. The system of regional briefings and meetings between the President and out-of-town press was designed by my Office of Communications and put into effect by Nixon, but Carter has implemented it to its fullest extent, inviting regional groups to the White House regularly.

In the years of the earlier Presidents, the American public was more likely to accept incomplete reports or bias in the press as part of life. During that time there were more newspapers, and avid readers could gain a cross section by reading a variety of publications.

In most cities today, competition comes more from competing media than from a variety of newspaper views. The number of two-newspaper cities is comparatively small, and even in those communities the number of people reading more than one publication has decreased considerably. In cities where one company publishes both the morning and the evening newspaper, the increased cost of newsprint has led to a situation where the newspapers do little, at best, to encourage duplicate circulation.

Television, with its vast impact, and radio offer the strongest local competition for the powerful newspapers. And while viewers switch favorites among news programs, on any given night they are more likely to watch the news on only one TV channel, not several. Thus the broadcast commentary or news slant the TV viewer receives is more likely to come from one broadcast source, although there will be differences between the local and the network evening presentations.

Among magazines, the growth has been in the specialty fields, such as sports or hobbies or local city magazines, but among major news magazines, most Americans who read the publications have a favorite, whether it is *Time, Newsweek,* or *U.S. News & World Report,* and each consolidates the news according to its own philosophy, with *U.S. News* being the most conservative. Thus the public is likely to be subject to one view in magazine reading. *Time* and *Newsweek* are far more likely to display the political bias of a regional editor than is *U.S. News,* but all three wield tremendous power with their widespread, well-edited news coverage. Magazines of commentary such as *Harpers, Atlantic, New Republic,* and *National Review* have strong impact because they reach opinion leaders, even though they have comparatively low mass circulation. In this field, strong editors, such as William F. Buckley, Jr., of *National Review* and Lewis H. Lapham of *Harpers,* have become more and more widely quoted, and they definitely are opinion-oriented.

One of the debates in the journalism profession for years has been over the use of unattributed sources in news stories, particularly those emanating from Washington. Meetings between journalists and their news sources (mostly in government) are handled under a variety of rules: on the record, off the record, background, deep background, the Lindley rule, and a few other specialized procedures. In the stories resulting from these sessions, the news figures can be referred to as "news sources," "sources close to the President," etc. The Lindley rule, named for veteran correspondent Ernest Lindley, means no attribution at all. The speculation is ostensibly only that of the reporter. For years, Henry Kissinger conducted background sessions for the correspondents traveling with him on Middle-East shuttles, but the stories referred to "a source close to the Secretary" or "closest to the Secretary," and in each case newsmen and diplomats knew that this was code for the fact that it was Secretary of State Henry Kissinger speaking.

The variety of ruses used to avoid direct quotation is subject to criticism, but they serve the useful purpose of allowing a public figure to say things which the ground rules of diplomacy or politics do not allow him to say directly on the record. One of the minuses is that the tactic allows the speaker to launch trial balloons or to make statements which he can easily back away from if criticized. Among the critics of "off the record" are editors and many readers interested in politics.

Overall, I believe the background quotations benefit the public and that the arguments for unattributed sources outweigh those against it. The reporter can judge his sources, and he gains more information this way than would otherwise be possible.

In 1970, Ben Bradlee of the Washington *Post* and I participated in a forum at Yale University, in which Bradlee launched his own trial balloon when he said that he was considering withdrawing Washington *Post* reporters from all background sessions not originated by the newsmen. He reasoned that if the public official called such a background session or set those rules for an interview, he was using the reporter for his own purposes. If the reporter volunteered such ground rules, he was in control of the situation and thus there was no danger of a news manipulation in the process. As one would expect, Bradlee stated his case eloquently.

Bradlee's plan became a reality a few weeks later and Washington *Post* reporters began using other newsmen as their sources of information when there was a backgrounder. If the meeting with the official was to be off the record, it was boycotted by the *Post*, but the *Post* reporter felt free to question other newsmen who had attended the session and use their notes to quote the official directly by name. They could do this because they had not agreed to ground rules. The application of the rule became open to public debate when the respected veteran *Post* reporter Carroll Kilpatrick, on Bradlee's orders, refused to join a pool on Air Force One to avoid the off-the-record rule. On the press plane he followed his editor's orders and took the notes from the Air Force One reporters' pool and quoted the sources of the information by name.

The Bradlee rule caused much concern in the White House, and it probably cut down background sessions by 50 percent, with more and more of the staff members and cabinet officers speaking on the record but withholding information they would have given out on a background basis. It did not affect President Nixon personally because he was not speaking to reporters at that time. In moderation, it was a healthy stimulus to avoid unnecessary backgrounders, but I did not hesitate to go off the record when it was important to do so. I felt Bradlee was wrong and arbitrary.

When the Washington *Post* began to dig into the Watergate story, almost all of the sources quoted were on nonattributable, off-the-record basis. The most famous unnamed source was "Deep Throat," who I believe was a fictitious character developed by Woodward and Bernstein representing a combination of two or three of their sources of information. How often the *Post* reporters went to the sources of the story and offered immunity from quotation, and how often the nonattribution was at the insistence of the source, is a question only a few on the *Post* could answer.

I have consistently disagreed with Bradlee on most interpretation of rules regarding background sessions. Perhaps the strongest case for nonattribution was contained in the authoritative Theodore White books on *The Making of the President*. White was taken into the confidence of opposing candidates and their staffs on the understanding that much of what they told him would be for nonattribution, and although he initiated most sessions, sometimes he was invited in by the candidate or his staff.

When one looks realistically at the process of communication between the government, the candidates, and the press, there are widespread grounds for criticism on all sides.

One can concede readily that reporting today is the best it ever has been and that the quality of the media in the United States is unequaled anywhere else in the world. Our government has its idiosyncrasies of unnecessary secrecy, but particularly with the Freedom of Information Act, it, too, is unequaled in its openness. In fact, the Freedom of Information Act goes so far in revealing intimate details of government that it has grown to be inhibiting to some internal communication.

The human element in reporting also leads to faults in presenting the news.

An interview, for example, is conducted to elicit newsworthy information for the public. Its number one purpose should be to gain all the information possible from the interview subject and to report accurately the information received. Too often, however, the interview turns into a battle of words between the reporter and the news source. Television programs such as "Meet the Press" and "Sixty Minutes," in which the effort of the reporter to go for the jugular adds drama to the presentation on the air, often sensationalize the interview to a point where the viewers' impression or the news headline which emerges pertains to a minor—and probably negative—part of the interview. This can be less of a problem—in fact, sometimes it can be turned into a plus—if the person interviewed is a skilled communicator, but most of those interviewed do not have this background of experience and the result is a distortion of his or her views on the subject of the interview. If the person being interviewed wanders afield and exposes a weakness, almost by instinct even the most mild-mannered reporter is likely to attack. I have even found myself doing this on occasion.

Larry Spivak, who originated "Meet the Press," was a master of the short tough question, and more often than not the television viewer gained the impression he was negative by nature. I recall being nervous during my first postelection appearance on "Meet the Press" in 1968, and the program opened with Spivak hammering at me with four quick, tough verbal jabs. When I had finished my answers there was a commercial break in the program and Spivak gave me a large grin and a sign that I had handled his questions well.

With that I lost whatever nervousness I had. Dan Rather and Mike Wallace provide a similar technique: they can be murderous when performing before the cameras but mild-mannered and pleasant when the lights on the set go off.

The competition to get the story on the news wire first used to mean spirited foot races between reporters from United Press International and Associated Press to see who would get to a telephone first with a bulletin.

Periodically the wire services would chronicle how many times they had beaten the opposition.

There is still competition over who gets the first-time break on a moving story, as was illustrated most dramatically on all aspects of the John Kennedy asassination, but a new focal point of the competition between all of the media centers on who can break the story first on an event about to happen. Lyndon Johnson so greatly resented the leaks on appointments he was about to make to a high office that on a few occasions he changed his decision just to retaliate against those who leaked the information and against the newsmen who reported the story in advance of the event.

Like the wire service reporters of another generation, the media are in a rush to have the news first, and that is admirable. But in the process, they too often accept unsubstantiated information which proves to be wrong, and when they err they rarely admit the mistake.

No one faults a sports writer when he picks the wrong team or speculates in advance on strategy upon which the coach has no intention of relying, but the matter is more serious when it relates to public policy or public figures. The rush to be first with minor but wrong news leads only to increasing public distrust of the accuracy of reporting in general. Most of the advance leads, which give personal satisfaction to journalists, do not thrill the reader or the listener, who would much rather have accurate reporting than gain a one-day jump on the news.

Strong investigative reporting has returned to journalism, but, particularly on local television, the investigations that interest the viewer are shallow and often wrong, because the demand for constant on-camera appearances by the reporter diminishes the thoroughness of the investigation. Once a reporter has accepted an assignment to investigate, too often he feels he must come up with some kind of story even if it does not represent all of the facts. He rationalizes that clarification will come later. But the truth is that a half story damages the media reputation and it often infringes unfairly on the rights of an individual, who has no equal chance to defend himself.

A wrong story is difficult to remedy. Maurice Stans pleaded in his book *The Terrors of Justice* for the restoration of his "good name." He had been tried sensationally in the press for dozens of crimes, including the Vesco scandal, where a jury eventually found him and John Mitchell innocent. He finally pleaded guilty to five misdemeanors based on faulty campaign reporting, but the negative speculation from untrue stories all but destroyed his "good name." And no one in the media has set out to remedy that.

The terror of shallow investigative reporting or reporting on city hall prevails despite recent efforts to correct errors in newspapers and magazines. Broadcast has yet to evolve a satisfactory way to admit that an error was made. As a result, the viewer or listener is left with the wrong impression.

Objectivity is almost a passé word in the news profession, particularly in the coverage of controversy. No matter how hard an individual tries to maintain his or her objectivity, we all form our own opinions on most matters. The newsman should be different and discipline himself against his own prejudices. The goal of objectivity should loom ahead of him like the Holy Grail. But unquestionably bias naturally creeps into the news. This raises an even bigger question: How balanced is the coverage? Newsmen too often fall short here also. Editing is a problem for the President or his colleagues, as they determine what to say and how it will be reported. A newspaper has to edit, but in the process of selection of the news and of paragraphs of a story, it comes down to the varied impressions of newsman versus politician on what really is important and makes news. The problem becomes more acute when it relates to television or radio. A leader may have a thirty-minute press conference, and eventually a network team will work this into a news segment which might run from thirty seconds to five minutes. What the reporter or editor thinks is news may be far different from what the politician thinks is news; thus a key comment on farm prices or unemployment may be lost in the selection of news which centers its coverage on the President's welcome of a foreign visitor or his press secretary's statement on health insurance. Broadcast editing makes it possible to take a person regularly out of context, and although the show's producer may honestly want to highlight the key topics of the candidate, he often is most intrigued by a negative attack by the speaker—or upon the speaker by outside disturbances. This routinely reaches a degree where the viewer gains a far more limited view of the candidate and what he stands for than he realizes he has received.

One wonders if a reporter, particularly a television reporter, thoroughly understands how immense his power is. It is easy to say, "I only report what the candidate says," but the selection of material included in a broadcast news report has far greater impact than most reporters are willing to admit. Most are careful to try to bring forth a balanced presentation of the news, but all have some personal opinions as they report on news and it is the highly vocal and opinionated figures who usually make the news reports. Advocacy reporting only hypes the influence of subjectivity in individual news reports.

Self-righteousness also is a common fault among Washington reporters, many of whom feel that they are so close to the news that few are qualified to second-guess them. The standards of truth or even morality that they set for those they cover in the news do not necessarily apply to the reporter personally. This process of anointing oneself to stand above the populace leads to bias in the news.

Ray Price, in his book *With Nixon,* stated the case the news sources of any administration might make with a comment that the reporters "have acquired a power out of proportion to their accountability, and out of proportion to the ability—or inclination—they have yet shown to use that power responsibly."

Editors and broadcast producers, generally speaking, take their responsibility for fairness and balance far more seriously today than even a few years ago. Discussions within and without the industry have pinpointed the gravity of the news responsibility. There is a serious question, however, whether many of the reporters, or even news industry leaders, fully realize how powerful they have become in an age when communication has a vital role in determining public attitudes on a variety of complex governmental-political issues. Confronted with ever-present deadlines, it is difficult for the newsperson to take the time to think through fully the political and international consequences of decisions made daily on the reporting and play of a story. Many would argue that a study of the consequences is not the newsperson's job, and that generally is true—but not always. Many editors and broadcasters do sweat out their communications responsibilities daily, but obsession with a story leads to irresponsible decisions on too many occasions. Photo editors pick the oddities, and they too can give an unfair impression.

As Senator Edward Kennedy inched forward before finally jumping into the 1980 presidential picture, even his vaguest comments on higher office commanded attention. This high news interest gave him the power to move into or out of the presidential scene with a control over the headlines that few, if any, previous politicians have had. Even before he announced a decision, NBC ran a five-part series on him, pro and con. What other unannounced candidate could command this? Yet he was peculiarly newsworthy.

Simultaneously, a President on a losing streak finds it difficult to make the news which would bring him back out of the slump. In a crisis he commands attention. President Ford found this to be the case when news stories depicted him as a clown or a bumbler, as various minor physical mishaps were chronicled. A fall while skiing, a head bump, or a missed golf shot became news, and yet Ford probably was the most accomplished athlete to occupy the White House. The picture of him given to the public was distorted that badly. President Carter ran into similar difficulties in trying to overcome problems of a lack of leadership and of the personal life of staff members such as Hamilton Jordan. It is fair to ask if Carter and his staff were as bad in 1979 as the news depicted them then, or as good as they were portrayed in 1977 or early 1980.

The other side of the picture is that government officials and candidates too often fail to communicate effectively with an understanding of the public they seek to reach or of the modern media they must deal with.

As recently as in the early 1970s, newsmen and politicians agreed that the campaigns for President ran far too long and that both the public and the newsmen became bored with the physically draining primary-election process. There was serious consideration given to setting the dates for the national nominating conventions closer to the date of the general election. Three factors changed all of this: Jimmy Carter rose from Georgia obscurity to the presidency with one of the longest campaigns on record; the federal election laws provided an advantage to candidates who started their campaign by raising money for so-called committees to explore the presidency; and the very process of running for the presidency became more expensive and more complicated as more and more states began changing their laws to accommodate primaries, caucuses, and even meaningless straw ballots. States sparred with New Hampshire, seeking to preempt the privilege of holding the first primary election. And all of the events, including straw votes, attracted media and thus candidate attention —or vice versa.

For both a candidate and the President, the media become oversensitive to early primaries and often react irresponsibly. It is the candidate or the President who loses more often than the media in this situation.

Nixon's decision to begin wiretapping came because of serious concern, frustration, and anger over leaks of sensitive government material. Those we know of who were tapped included Bill Safire, a few reporters, such as Joe Kraft, and some members of the National Security Council staff. Leaks provide a great harvest of information for newsmen, and for reporters such as Jack Anderson or Evans and Novak they have become a part of their stock in trade.

As a President reads the stories of leaks provided the media or pried out by the media, he is inclined to believe he can trust almost no one, and usually he finds himself helpless in combating the process. Pierre Salinger tells the story of tracing a leak after being requested to do so by an angry President Kennedy. He found that Kennedy himself was the source for the leak Salinger was investigating. That has happened more than once.

No one, not even President Nixon, knows how much time and effort was put into trying to locate "Deep Throat," the source of the leaks to Woodward and Bernstein, but the effort was major.

Government sources leak information for a variety of reasons, but they do so successfully to an amazing degree. In the past some of the sources of such information were those who sought favor from reporters or who liked being sought after by them. In a few cases, insiders have been paid for information. A good reporter can pick up one small clue from one source and more information from others and piece together an authentic story. Politicians and White House staffs often leak information to gain some political advantage, either positive or negative; the practice is common. Nixon's National Security Council, from Kissinger on down, was a constant source of news leaks. Probably the most dangerous leakers, as far as public policy is concerned, are those who secretly disseminate leaks to influence a policy or a program within the government. During the Nixon administration this process was illustrated by one of the important leaks that infuriated both the President and Kissinger, the so-called Pakistan tilt. In 1971, after a special task-force meeting in the White House's West Wing situation room, which included only senior military officials cleared for "top secret" and their aides, a story about the meeting was leaked to Jack Anderson saying that the United States, while publicly proclaiming neutrality, was "tilting toward Pakistan" in a period of critical hostility between Pakistan and India.

The column was essentially correct, but the policy reflected an effort to avoid further fighting between the two nations by "tilting" toward the apparently weaker country, Pakistan. It was not a long-range commitment. The leak appeared to come from someone in a trusted inner circle who disagreed with the policy Kissinger had enunciated to the group. It was also possible that in the bureaucratic process of Xeroxing everything, including secret notes, a copy had slipped out to someone outside the ranks.

Regardless of the culprit, the leak caused both congressional and international tremors of major magnitude.

A leak given to a newsman should require responsibility on his part in checking its authenticity and the purposes behind it, determining, for example, if the information is only partial. Anderson did check his sources carefully, and the "tilt" story won him a Pulitzer Prize. But the primary responsibility is that of the government, the point of origin for the information. And administrations are invariably weak in dealing realistically with the problem. Leaks from within the White House, for example, were one of the reasons why President Carter's position was undermined early in his tenure in office.

With the power inherent in the Oval Office, it is common to confuse substance with public posture. When a President finds himself in difficulty with the American public he usually blames the media first. He then may react by withdrawing further from the newsmen, as did President Nixon, or by overdoing press relations, as did Presidents Johnson and Carter. History illustrates, however, that public relations and media events are no substitute for substance. A good program or policy requires consistent effective selling by the President and his colleagues if it is to gain acceptance, but eventually a weak program or inconsistency will be shown to be such regardless of the superiority of the effort to sell it through a variety of media events.

Public attention focuses first on the President, but his supporting cast—the cabinet and the staff—plays a major role in conveying vital information to the public through the media. This also reveals a weakness in government. A cabinet officer is never picked because of his ability to communicate, and even the consideration of his ability to operate a multibillion-dollar part of the government frequently is lost in political considerations of selection for the office. A cabinet with well-known names is more likely to assist the President with the public and the press than is one with publicly unknown character. The President needs "stars." Still, outside of Washington, only a few names in the cabinet stick in the public memory or command major attention. One of President Nixon's mistakes in shifting cabinet officers after the 1972 election was failure to realize that in building a new no-name cabinet he may have gained better administration, but he lost the people who could have rallied needed public support for him if he had chosen the route of moving earlier to admit mistakes regarding Watergate.

James Lynn, who became Secretary of Housing and Urban Development and was named to the supercabinet in 1973, was an able administrator, but compared to his predecessor, George Romney, his name was obscure, and what he had to say gained less attention.

Regardless of who the cabinet secretary may appoint to operate his public information department, the bureaucracy tends to dominate. Because of the various titles given information specialists, no one in the Office of Management and Budget knows how many millions are spent in various forms of government communication. The bureaucracy tends to equate ability with how many employees one supervises, with little regard for standards of efficiency or proved bottom-line results. Even in the selection of information officers, it is difficult to attract the professionals one would seek because of the pay and the inherently short-term nature of the job. One of my personal disappointments was in failing to recruit some of the top professionals I hoped to attract for these cabinet assistant jobs.

Even with the government, like business, the information departments communicate with each other too little, and the result is contradictory stories within the same administration. Only since 1969 have these departments started to catch up with the electronic world, but they still lag.

The result of all of this is substandard communication between government and the media and thus between the administration and the public.

The government relationship with the media would be enhanced if public officials had a better understanding of the press and the confidence to deal more openly with the media. Mel Laird was an exceptional cabinet officer with a long history of good press relations while he served in the

House of Representatives, and he was an effective communicator even though the Department of Defense was one of the most sensitive areas of government. He had able press assistants in Dan Henkin and Jerry Friedheim, and Dick Capen on the congressional side. But Laird was an exception in an arena where officials, Republican or Democrat, tend to look at press relations as a necessary evil, and they are prone to keep back information the public is justified in knowing. The result is that reporters are forced to seek bureaucratic sources of information within the departments, and this does not necessarily result in a balanced set of facts, positive or negative.

The pressure of television, now increased by newspaper reporters, who no longer feel TV newsmen are their prime enemies, has made the cry for the debate a part of most campaigns, local or national.

The running debates between Lincoln and Douglas are looked upon with romantic fantasy as the model for such confrontations, but none of the major TV debates the public has witnessed nationally have any resemblance to the classic Lincoln-Douglas encounters. In the old style, the two men operated under accepted ground rules, as do political debaters today, but that is where the similarity ends.

The debates of the television era have been sponsored by the League of Women Voters, by Des Moines newspapers, and by television stations and networks. But invariably the candidates are questioned by newsmen more than by each other. These are media events, which attract tremendous audiences because of media buildup, and they seldom result in any enunciations of new policy.

In effect, we have been converted to watching and examining personalities rather than studying in depth the intelligence of answers given by the candidates. Makeup, voice, personal chemistry, mannerisms, proneness to error, and audience charm become the important factors of today's debates. Who keeps count of debaters' points of substance in answers? The phenomenon will continue to be a major part of the election scene, but it is questionable whether the debates of today are as enlightening as the media would have the public believe.

The candidate for the presidency also creates a problem for himself and the media when he resorts to the inevitable practice of giving the "standard speech" at most of his appearances. The speech has been perfected in numerous appearances and the theme is one he judges will have most appeal for a rally audience wherever he may be. He recognizes that everything he says in standard fashion has been covered by the traveling newsmen many times, and he compensates for this with "excerpts" which he fits into "the speech." The excerpts represent his selection of information he wants for a new news lead that day. If the excerpts are weak, the reporter may turn to his own devices and ignore the speech to speculate on other political trends. Those who hear the candidate speak are confused frequently because the lines in the speech that stimulated them most are missing from the news report they read or heard. The lines are no longer new to the reporter. The newspaper or broadcast report of the local appearance of the candidate thus may be at strong variance to the way the local observer at the rally would have seen the speech. The result is frequent protest that the coverage was unfair because it ignored the tough, "cheer" lines.

One solution is for the local newsmen to report the speech as if it had never been made before, augmenting that coverage with the new excerpts. But this is more difficult in the short context of a broadcast report than in a newspaper, and it does not fit network television, which the local observer also sees.

Clearly, the American public would be the major beneficiary of less warfare and better communication between the government, the candidates, and the press.

In the field of campaign coverage, the contemporary newsperson uses more modern techniques than his predecessors, but generally the elections are still covered in about the same fashion as a baseball game, with key elements being hits, successes or runs, strikeouts, and crowd attendance.

Other states have infringed upon New Hampshire's influence on the eventual selection of a nominee for President, but headlines out of that tiny New England state still are larger by far than deserved. New Hampshire has powerful influence because of the media coverage, not because it represents even a small cross section of the United States. And more recently, Iowa caucuses fit in the same category. They are significant only because of media coverage.

The media have improved their election coverage in a few ways in recent years. In the 1960s and before, one reporter generally would be expected to cover the entire campaign of a given candidate, regardless of his feeling toward that candidate, pro or con. The use of one reporter failed to take into account the transition from trains and prop planes to jets and the sheer monotony a reporter faces in listening to the same basic campaign speech hour after hour, day after day. The mental exhaustion of the newsman was reflected in his stories or reports. Newsmen today generally work with spacing, which gives them time off from the campaign trail and finds them switching candidates they cover so as to break up the deadly routine. The break in routine also adds perspective, which makes it less likely that they will be enchanted by one particular candidate. As I mentioned earlier, more switches in White House coverage would be equally advantageous.

There have been other improvements in coverage: The networks and some major newspapers and magazines have begun to interview voters after they have cast their votes to get more feeling in depth, not only on whom they voted for, but why. This provides an invaluable postelection tool. The *Wall Street Journal* has developed its own special brand of features and interviews covering key parts of the election. The growth of powerful supplemental news services, led by the New York *Times* and the combination Washington *Post*–Los Angeles *Times* service and including other enlarged coverage by such organizations as Knight-Ridder, the Chicago *Tribune,* and Gannett, has provided the manpower for preelection analysis of what is happening in key states for both primary and general elections. Newspapers find it easier to cover this type of in-depth survey because they have more space than television has time. Television's use of skilled special commentators during an election year provides more depth than formerly was the case, and while time is still a limiting factor, all this adds up to improved coverage.

In the White House we had all types of polls available for our analysis. Some of these were commissioned by the campaign committees and a few by the White House, but they tended to be routine telephonic or interview surveys and none pretended to represent interviewing on a broad scale to learn more than just the routine answers from those persons being asked the questions. I found it helpful to exchange polling information with Jimmy "the Greek" Snyder, who has a proven track record in politics as well as sports. Jimmy had his own unorthodox methods of mass polling, and they provided input not available through the political scientists. At one point, "the Greek" was asked by a client to come up on four days' notice with information predicting the winner of hotly contested Senate and gubernatorial campaigns in Kentucky. Jimmy abandoned his normal mass polling techniques and paid several bartenders to ask each of their customers whom they would vote for. The theory was that no one lies to his bartender. Whether the theory is true or not, the fact is that the bartender poll provided the winners. Another pollster with a record of success is Charles Kerch of San Diego, who interviews people leaving supermarkets on Saturday afternoon. His theory is that this represents a fair cross section, and his polls are accurate. He is rarely wrong.

But none of these interesting, unscientific polls or the newspaper stories of interviews with local leaders in a given state provide all the information that could be available. There are still surprises—such as the George Bush triumph in the 1980 Iowa caucus and Ronald Reagan's New Hampshire comeback.

One thing that would add to the coverage of a key state is a full study of the organizations being developed by the candidates. Early in a primary election in an important state, the organization counts more than the headlines made by the candidate. More often than not the candidate's appearances serve more to bolster organizational support than to sway voters. The news surveys fall short in this category.

The nation's editors, broadcast producers, and editorial writers are too remote from the scene to judge accurately the quality of the coverage they are getting from their staffs. The pressures to stay in one's office are great, but there is no substitute for getting out in the field occasionally to get a direct evaluation of the political scene. Remoteness offers protection, but it can also be a fault.

There are other areas for improvement. The demands on the time (and sometimes the laziness) of a reporter covering the White House are such that he finds it difficult to break away from the newsroom as often as he should to be fully informed. Some of the same sources the White House press secretary uses can be made available to the newsman if he cultivates the source sufficiently, and thus it is possible for him to get information firsthand instead of through the briefing-room transmission belt. The reporters and columnists who develop a well-known name as they cover the White House have an advantage they sometimes overlook if they try to contact high-ranking cabinet or government officials. They sometimes forget that they, too, are celebrities in the eyes of even a sophisticated official. Often there is a lack of communication between a correspondent covering the Capitol and one covering the White House for the same company, and an exchange of information would improve reporting for both.

On almost any afternoon when the President is in town, the senior White House newspersons who represent broadcast can be seen on the White House front lawn summarizing the events of the day or of a particular story. They have been informed how much time probably will be allocated and what action film will be shown, but too often they do not see or hear the final editing in the context of other coverage besides their own. In an area as sensitive as the White House this can be a handicap in the presentation of the news.

Personality conflicts figure into the news coverage more than they should. A reporter doesn't have to like the press secretary, the President, or his news source, but his feelings of like and dislike, human as they are, should not figure in the coverage. Yet they do.

In my opinion, there is a place for more columns like that written by Hugh Sidey for *Time* magazine, or John Osborne of *New Republic*, where the newsman has an opportunity to put the big picture in perspective. Barbara Walters offers special, penetrating perspective with her TV interviews.

On a newspaper the reporter who reaches the maturity where he can look at the picture with perspective often is offered administrative responsibilities as an editor or a bureau chief as a reward for growth. It would frequently be better to pay him more and develop him as a news superstar, unless his personal ambitions lie more in administration. Television handles this problem far better than the printed medium.

Radio and television stations are required by the Federal Communications Commission to interview people from all elements of their community in ascertainment studies to determine attitudes and opinions regarding their broadcasts. It would be healthy for broadcast producers and reporters and for print editors and reporters occasionally to spend a week or two at the grass-roots level to learn the public's opinion; there would be far less bias expressed if they did. In the same way, editorial writers need to spend more time in the seat of government and in the city hall instead of relying on opinion they conjured up in the ivory towers of their publications. With a few newspapers it is the practice to get the writers outside, but not with enough of them.

Economics play a growing role in most major stories whether they are domestic or foreign. Yet this is an area of weakness for most newsmen. All too few have had more than preliminary exposure to economic principles in their studies and even fewer understand how to apply this information to the complicated energy or foreign-policy questions. Journalism schools traditionally have kept themselves "pure" by avoiding contact with the business schools. It is true that the business side of the media should not inhibit the reporter or editor, but business and economics of the nation and world are a part of the news today and the change in the importance of this part of the news report finds the profession generally unprepared.

Television has speculated more and more in recent years over the possibility of increasing daily network news coverage from a half hour to an hour. In many large cities, local news even now covers a two-hour span. The popularity enjoyed by the "Sixty Minutes" news magazine would seem to indicate that the public is hungry for more news in the right format.

One-hour network television news seems inevitable in the future, and if it is used properly, it can do much to provide more balanced and detailed coverage of the news and more credibility for TV reports.

There are many commercial problems local stations and the networks must adjust to if the news time is to be extended, but when it is doubled to one hour it will open a new world of opportunity for needed full coverage of events of importance. The impact and responsibility of TV news coverage will be greater than ever.

In another area, more and more one hears informed members of the public debating whether any President can withstand the continual onslaught of press criticism, which seems to grow in tempo each four years. The impact of unfair criticism is debasing to the presidency, but in an increasing way, it is also undercutting media credibility. Without question there are serious governmental problems for the media.

During the Nixon administration, most of the journalistic speeches decrying government encroachment against the free press were directed at Spiro Agnew, the President, and their White House colleagues. At times the Congress has been a subject for journalistic suspicion as some legislators have proposed regulations ranging from licensing journalists to various curtailments of free speech.

Today the danger clearly comes from the courts, where there are more and more restrictive rulings against the traditional procedures of reporting. The court rulings pose far greater danger than an antagonistic administration or a hard-nosed Congress because elections can change attitudes or rulings by those two American bodies. But elections do not change precedent-setting court rulings.

Two of the things that have handicapped the newsmen in their battle with judicial rulings have been (1) the fact that many of the cases they have brought before the courts have been weak and therefore invited a decision against them and (2) the fact that the court is moving aggressively at a time when the public is not aroused to join newsmen in concern for freedom of reporting.

On the side of government, there is much need for improvement in communication. Freedom of information within the cabinet departments and agencies should be handled by the information offices, not the legal offices.

There is a need in government for more high-caliber professionals with considerable experience in communicating outside of government. Newspapermen and broadcasters participate in various seminars, such as those sponsored by the American Press Institute in Reston, Virginia.

The military also have programs like these, and government information would benefit greatly from such educational seminars, sometimes just for federal employees but at other times intermixing the private and the public sectors, perhaps even under private sponsorship, like the Press Institute. A little thoughtful training like this also would be of major assistance to improvement for administration staffs.

The battle between Presidents and their colleagues and the news media frequently degenerates into immaturity, with neither side benefiting from the "them versus us" attitude. The temptation to retaliate because of an apparent slight, unfortunately, can be detected within the news corps as well as the government.

Television has had a major role in covering government for almost thirty years now, but most government news operations are still run with a print mentality. In the White House one or two persons are usually brought in as television experts, but even when one of them is from the

TV news field, such as Ron Nessen, President Ford's press secretary, there is neither the accommodation nor the understanding within the government to make maximum use of this effective means of communication.

If I were a new President appointing government officials, the qualification of strong communications aptitude would get top priority. A cabinet officer may be a genius in his own field, but he must communicate leadership to the bureaucracy and to the public and press if he is to be fully effective.

Loyalty is inherent in this premise so that the signals coming from the cabinet officer will not undercut agreed-upon presidential policy. Cabinet meetings that are marked by a spirit of openness, and smaller committee-like meetings between the cabinet officers and the President, would encourage active understanding of policy and loyalty. No modern cabinet has operated in this fashion.

A President should refrain from being "one of the boys" and mixing with the press or friends in Congress, but he should cultivate enough private interchange so as to avoid isolation from the undercurrents which influence the media and the politics of Washington. A President must not be isolated, but he also needs time to concentrate on the big issues he and the nation face. Balance here is a key ingredient for success.

Long before the election, I believe the President should seek out two men or women who have stamina and experience, a reputation among their colleagues, an understanding of government, and, even more, an understanding of the President. Two such people to head up the news organizations of the White House and the government are needed as well. Some would say this idea is only cosmetic, but the importance of communications makes the idea substantive. The President should want the two top communicators to have the independence to speak their mind within the White House and particularly in the Oval Office.

Government today has grown so large that it needs more than just the traditional press secretary's office. The news secretary finds himself torn between the needs of a hungry and inquiring press corps and his role as a senior White House adviser. To be informed he must attend countless meetings, ranging from the National Security Council to the various domestic and political committees. He must be on hand at presidential meetings to understand and later repeat the views of the President. Accuracy is his life's blood, so he cannot afford to learn only half the facts. For many years there has been a briefing by the press secretary twice each day. On a normal day, however, the time of the news secretary would be better utilized if he briefed at the main midday session and turned shorter afternoon meetings over to his trained assistant, unless a major story is breaking, or if he eliminated most second sessions. This practice is being followed more and more.

The news secretary should be dealing mainly with those who cover the President. They are his clientele, and that relationship represents more than a full-time operation.

The second strong communicator selected should be assigned to coordinate with a strong hand the news operations of all parts of government other than the White House. He would attend, on a need-to-know basis, some of the meetings the news secretary also must audit, and he would work closely with the television, radio, newspaper, and magazine reporters and leaders, in effect acting as a cabinet representative for the vital communications field. To deal fully with the media at all levels he would need a professional background that would command full respect. His purpose would be to serve as a national listening post for the President as well as a focal point for stronger communications with the media world, both local and national. This was my director of communications concept.

With this type of White House information program, the President would need to accord each of the two men he selected equal rank, and he would have the right to insist that they worked in coordinated fashion, almost as one. But both would need full access to the President.

History would indicate that intense tension between the media and the President is inevitable. The newsman has goals he must serve with integrity, and he must have an ever-inquiring mind. The President has different goals he must serve with integrity and creativity and perseverance, if he is to succeed as an inspiring leader.

If both sides accept the fact that while the professional goals differ, both are dependent upon public understanding, and war between the President and the press need not follow history and thus be inevitable.

As Lyndon Johnson wrote to me at the time of the 1969 inaugural, "With my hope that the end will be as pleasant as the beginning."

An intelligent President who fully understands the need for substance and for sensitive communication with the American people, giving full weight to both, could reverse the history of running warfare between the media and the White House. The newsmen need not be less aggressive, but they must assume greater responsibility for accuracy; and for his part, the President cannot allow himself to be intimidated or bothered by petty media criticism. A middle ground of substantive communication leadership and understanding of the American people is still possible, and it is all-important.

Tell it like it is.

This is essential if the end is to be "as pleasant as the beginning."

Index